W9-BBE-405

The Making of Byzantium, 600–1025

The Making of
Byzantium, 600–1025

MARK WHITTOW

University of California Press
Berkeley   Los Angeles

University of California Press
Berkeley and Los Angeles, California

Published by arrangement with Macmillan Press

Published in Great Britain in 1996 under the title
The Making of Orthodox Byzantium, 600–1025

Library of Congress Cataloging-in-Publication Data
Whittow, Mark, 1957–
     The making of Byzantium, 600–1025 / Mark Whittow.
         p.   cm.
     Includes bibliographical references and index.
     ISBN 0–520–20496–4 (alk. paper). — ISBN 0–520–20497–2 (pbk.:
alk. paper)
        1. Byzantine Empire—History—527–1081.   2. Byzantine Empire–
–Church history.   3. Orthodox Eastern Church—Byzantine Empire–
–History.   I. Title.
DF556.W45   1996
949.5—dc20   95–44924
                                                                              CIP

Printed in Malaysia

9   8   7   6   5   4   3   2   1

Contents

List of Maps

Transliteration and References

Greek names and place names are transliterated with *k*s and *o*s, save where a Latinate or Anglicised version is so familiar that it would be pedantic to use anything else: therefore *Nikephoros, Herakleios, Kaisareia*, but *Nicaea, Thessalonica, Cappadocia. Ankara* appears rather than *Ankyra* on an analogous principle. Modern place names in Turkey follow current Turkish useage; Arabic names and place names follow a simplified version of that in the *Encyclopaedia of Islam*, New Edition (Leiden, 1960–). In particular the Arabic *kāf* is transliterated as *k* rather than *q* and *djīm* as *dj* rather than *j* or *ǧ*. Hence *Kālikāla* rather than *Qāliqāla*, and *Djabala* rather than *Jabala* or *Ǧabala*. The *'ain* has generally been omitted, but a diacritical line (-) indicating a long vowel seems useful as a guide to pronunciation.

The endnotes give specific references to texts, and to secondary literature of immediate relevance. Primary and secondary works that underpin a chapter in a more general way are found in the chapter bibliographies at the back of the book, together with a guide to further reading.

List of Abbreviations

AASS	*Acta Sanctorum* (Brussels, 1643–)
AB	*Analecta Bollandiana*
ACO	*Acta Conciliorum Oecumenicorum,* ed. E. Schwartz, 5 vols in 32 parts (Berlin and Leipzig, 1922–)
BAR, Int. Ser.	British Archaeological Reports, International Series
BASOR	*Bulletin of the American Schools of Oriental Research*
BBTT	Belfast Byzantine Texts and Translations
BMGS	*Byzantine and Modern Greek Studies*
Byz	*Byzantion*
BZ	*Byzantinische Zeitschrift*
CFHB	Corpus Fontium Historiae Byzantinae
CSHB	Corpus Scriptorum Historiae Byzantinae
Chron. 1234	*Anonymi auctoris chronicon ad annum Christi 1234 pertinens,* 2 vols (CSCO CIX, CCCLIV, Scriptores Syri LVI, CLIV, Louvain, 1937–74)
Chronikon Paschale	*Chronicon Paschale,* ed. L. Dindorf (Bonn, 1832); tr. M. Whitby and M. Whitby, *Chronicon Paschale 284–628 AD* (Translated Texts for Historians VII, Liverpool, 1989)
CSCO	Corpus scriptorum christianorum orientalium
DAI	Constantine Porphyrogenitus, *De Administrando Imperio,* ed. Gy. Moravcsik, tr. R. J. H. Jenkins (CFHB I, Washington, D.C., 1967)
De Cer.	Constantinus Porphyrogenitus, *De cerimoniis aulae Byzantinae libri duo,* ed. J. J. Reiske (Bonn, 1829–30).
De Cer., ed. Vogt	Constantin VII Porphyrogénète, *Le Livre des Cérémonies,* 2 vols, ed. A. Vogt (Paris, 1935–40)

ix

De re militari	*Three Byzantine Military Treatises,* ed. and tr. G. T. Dennis (CFHB XXV, Washington, D.C., 1985), pp. 246–335
DOP	*Dumbarton Oaks Papers*
EI/2	*The Encyclopaedia of Islam,* New Edition (Leiden, 1960–)
Genesios	Josephus Genesius, *Iosephi Genesii regum libri quattuor,* ed. A. Lesmueller-Werner and H. Thurn (CFHB xiv, Berlin, 1978)
GM cont.	Georgius Monarchus, *Vitae imperatorum recentiorum,* in Theophanes Continuatus, ed. I. Bekker (CSHB, Bonn, 1838), pp. 763–924
HUS	*Harvard Ukrainian Studies*
JGR	*Jus Graecoromanum,* ed. J. Zepos and P. Zepos, 8 vols (Athens, 1931)
JÖB	*Jahrbuch der Österreichischen Byzantinistik*
Laurent/Canard	J. Laurent, *L'Armenie entre Byzance et l'Islam depuis la conquête arabe jusqu'en 886,* rev. M. Canard (Lisbon, 1980)
Lemerle, *Les plus anciens recueils*	P. Lemerle, *Les plus anciens recueils des miracles de saint Démétrius,* 2 vols (Paris, 1979–81)
Leo Gram.	Leo Grammaticus, *Chronographia,* ed. I. Bekker (CSHB, Bonn, 1842)
Liber pontificalis	*Le Liber pontificalis,* ed. L. Duchesne, 2 vols (Paris, 1886–92); 1 vol., additions, corrections and indices, ed. C. Vogel (Paris, 1957)
Liber pontificalis tr. Davis I	*The Book of the Pontiffs (Liber Pontificalis),* tr. R. Davis (Translated Texts for Historians v, Liverpool, 1989)

Liber pontificalis tr. Davis II	*The Lives of the Eighth Century Popes (Liber Pontificalis)*, tr. R. Davis (Translated Texts for Historians XIII, 1992)
Mansi	*Sacrorum conciliorum nova et amplissima collectio*, ed. J. Mansi, 31 vols (Florence and Vienna, 1759–98)
MGH	Monumenta Germaniae Historiae
MGH SRLI	Monumenta Germaniae Historiae: *Scriptores rerum Langobardicarum et italicorum saec. VI–IX* (Hannover, 1878)
Michel le Syrien	J.-B. Chabot, *Chronique de Michel le Syrien*, 4 vols (Paris, 1899–1924)
Nik.	Nikephoros, Patriarch of Constantinople, *Short History*, ed. and trans. C. Mango (CFHB, XIII, Washington, D.C., 1990)
ODB	*Oxford Dictionary of Byzantium*, ed. A. Kazhdan *et al.*, 3 vols (Oxford, 1991)
Oikonomidès, *Les listes*	N. Oikonomidès, *Les listes de préséance byzantines des ixe et xe siècles* (Paris, 1972)
PG	*Patrologiae cursus completus, Series graeca*, ed. J.-P. Migne, 161 vols (Paris, 1857–66)
PLRE, I–III	*Prosopography of the Later Roman Empire*, 3 vols, ed. A. H. M. Jones and J. Martindale (Cambridge, 1971–92)
PO	*Patrologia Orientalis*
Praecepta Militaria	'Strategika imperatora Nikifora', ed. J. A. Kulakovskij, *Mémoires de l'Académie Imperiale des sciences de St.-Petersbourg*, 8th series, hist. phil. class, VIII. 9 (1908), pp. 1–58
Procopius, *Wars*	Procopius, *Wars*, ed. and tr. H. B. Dewing, 5 vols (Cambridge, Mass., 1914–28)

Pseudo-Sym.	Symeon Magister, *Annales* in Theophanes Continuatus, ed. I. Bekker (CSHB, Bonn, 1838), pp. 601–760
PVL	*Povest' vremennych let*, tr. S. H. Cross and O. P. Sherbowitz-Wetzor (Cambridge, Mass., 1953)
REArm	*Revue des études arméniennes*, New Series
REB	*Revue des études byzantines*
Sebeos, tr. Macler	Sebeos, *Histoire de Héraclius*, tr. F. Macler (Paris, 1904)
Sebeos, tr. Bedrosian	*Sebēos' History*, tr. R. Bedrosian (Sources of the Armenian Tradition, New York, 1985)
'Skirmishing Warfare'	*Three Byzantine Military Treatises*, ed. and tr. G. T. Dennis (CFHB XXV, Washington, D.C., 1985), pp. 144–39
Skylitzes	Ioannes Skylitzes, *Synopsis historiarum*, ed. H. Thurn (CFHB V, Berlin, 1973)
Stephen of Taron i	Étienne Açogh'ig de Daron, *Histoire universelle*, tr. E. Dulaurier (Paris, 1883)
Stephen of Taron ii	Étienne Asolik de Tarôn, *Histoire universelle* tr. F. Macler (Paris, 1917)
al-Tabarī	*The History of al-Tabarī*, ed. I. Abbas et al., 38 vols (SUNY Series in Near Eastern Studies, Albany, New York, 1985–). [References are given to the volume and page of the Arabic text, ed. M. J. De Goeje, 15 vols (Leiden, 1879–1901) which is quoted in the SUNY English translation.]
Theo.	Theophanes, *Chronographia*, ed. C. de Boor, 2 vols (Leipzig, 1883). [All references are to the text in vol. I.]

Theo. Cont.	*Chronographia*, in Theophanes Continuatus, ed. I. Bekker (CSHB, Bonn, 1838), pp. 3–481
TIB	Tabula imperii Byzantini
TM	*Travaux et Mémoires*
Vasiliev, *Byzance et les Arabes*	A. A. Vasiliev, *Byzance et les Arabes* I, *La dynastie d'Amorium (820–867)*, French edn, H. Grégoire, M. Canard (Brussels, 1935); II, *La dynastie Macédonienne (867–959)*, part 1: *Les relations politiques de Byzance et des Arabes à l'époque de la dynastie Macédonienne (première période 867–959)*, French edn, M. Canard (Brussels, 1968); part 2: *Extraits des sources Arabes*, French edn, H. Grégoire, M. Canard (Brussels, 1950)
'Vaticanus Gr. 163'	A. Markopoulos, 'Le témoinage du Vaticanus Gr. 163 pour la période entre 945–963', *Symmeikta* III (1979), pp. 83–119 (text, pp. 91–100)
West-Syrian Chronicles	A. Palmer, *The Seventh Century in West-Syrian Chronicles* (Translated Texts for Historians XV, Liverpool, 1993)
ZRVI	*Zbornik radova Vizantološkog Instituta*

Chronological List

Note: Given the evidence available, dates for the Islamic conquest of Syria, Iraq and Egypt can only be probable, but the error is not more than a few years.

Date	EMPERORS/*Patriarchs* (from 595)	Events
527–65	JUSTINIAN I	
541–2		Appearance of bubonic plague in Mediterranean.
565–78	JUSTIN II	
568		Lombard invasion of Italy.
578–82	TIBERIOS I	
580–3		Break up of Ghassānid confederation.
582–602	MAURICE	
591		Peace with Persia.
595–606	*Kyriakos*	
602		Mutiny of army in Balkans; murder of Maurice.
602–10	PHOKAS	
603		Persian war begins.
607–10	*Thomas I*	
610–41	HERAKLEIOS	
610–38	*Sergios I*	
614		Jerusalem falls to Persians.
616		Persian invasion of Egypt.
624		Beginning of Herakleios' Transcaucasian campaigns; final loss of southern Spain.
626		Avar–Persian siege of Constantinople.
628		*Chronikon Paschale* stops;

741–3		Revolt of Artabasdos.
744–7		Third Muslim civil war.
749–50		Overthrow of Ummayad caliphate; establishment of Abbāsid caliphate.
751		Lombards conquer Ravenna.
753		Pope Stephen crosses Alps to appeal to Peppin III, king of the Franks, for military support; Iconoclast Council of Hieria.
754–66	*Constantine II*	
759–75		Constantine V's Bulgar campaigns.
766–80	*Niketas I*	
774		Charlemagne conquers Lombard kingdom in Italy.
775		Battle of Bagrevand; Arabs crush Armenian revolt.
775–80	LEO IV	
780–4	*Paul I*	
780–97	CONSTANTINE VI (IRENE, REGENT 780–90)	
782		Major Arab invasion of Asia Minor reaches Bosphoros.
784–806	*Tarasios*	
787		Council of Nicaea II; first restoration of icons.
796		Frankish armies destroy Avar qaghanate.
797–802	IRENE	
800		Charlemagne crowned emperor in Rome.
802–11	NIKEPHOROS I	
*c.*802–14		Krum, Bulgar qaghan.
806–15	*Nikephoros I*	

806–7		Caliph Hārūn al-Rashīd leads major raids into Asia Minor.
809–33		Abbāsid civil war.
811		Nikephoros I's Bulgar campaign.
811	STAURAKIOS	
811–13	MICHAEL I	`
812		Byzantine recognition of western imperial title.
813–20	LEO V	
813		Theophanes' *Chronographia* stops.
815–21	*Theodotos I Kassiteras*	
815		Council of Constantinople; iconoclasm restored as official dogma.
816		Peace with Bulgars.
819–37		Revolt of Babek in Azerbaidjan.
820–9	MICHAEL II	
821–37?	*Antony I Kassymatas*	
c. 826		Arab invasions of Crete and Sicily.
829–42	THEOPHILOS	
c.835–9		Magyars driven into western Ukrainian steppes.
837?–43	*John VII Grammatikos*	
838		Sack of Amorion.
839		Byzantine embassy plus Rus envoys to Louis the Pious at Ingelheim.
842–67	MICHAEL III (THEODORA, REGENT, 842–56)	
843–7	*Methodios*	
843		Restoration of Orthodoxy.
846		Arabs sack St Peter's, Rome.

847–58	*Ignatios (first patriarchate)*	
851–5		Bugha the elder crushes Armenian revolt.
858–67	*Photios (first patriarchate)*	
860		First Rus attack on Constantinople.
861–70		Turkish assassination of caliph al-Mutawakkil followed by nine-year 'anarchy'.
862		Ašot I Bagratuni appointed prince of princes by caliph.
863		Destruction of raiding army of Melitene; Cyril and Methodios sent to Moravia.
864–5		Conversion of Bulgaria.
866		Caesar Bardas murdered by Basil.
867–86	**BASIL I**	
867–77	*Ignatios (second patriarchate)*	
869–83		Zandj revolt in Iraq.
869–70		Council of Constantinople
871		Emperor Louis II captures Bari from Arabs.
876		Byzantines occupy Bari.
877–86	*Photios (second patriarchate)*	
878		Byzantine capture of Tephrike; Arab capture of Syracuse.
879–80		Council of Constantinople.
884		Ašot I crowned king of Armenia by caliph.
885		Moravian mission expelled and takes refuge in Bulgaria.

885–6		Byzantine expeditionary force under Nikephoros Phokas the elder campaigns in Southern Italy.
886–912	LEO VI	
886–93	*Stephen I*	
891		Creation of theme of Longobardia.
893–901	*Antony II Kauleas*	
893–927		Symeon, emperor of the Romans and Bulgars.
894–6		Magyars invade Bulgaria; Pečenegs drive Magyars on to Hungarian plain.
901–7	*Nicholas I Mystikos (first patriarchate)*	
902		Fall of Taormina in Sicily to Arabs.
904		Arab sack of Thessalonica.
907–12	*Euthymios*	
909		Fātimid caliphate established in Ifrīkiya (North Africa).
911		Byzantine failure to reconquer Crete.
912–25	*Nicholas I Mystikos (second patriarchate)*	
912–13	ALEXANDER	
913		Murder of Smbat Bagratuni, king of Armenia by the emir Yūsuf.
913–59	CONSTANTINE VII PORPHYROGENITOS	
913–14	REGENCY COUNCIL	
914–19	ZOE, REGENT	
915		Byzantine intervention in Armenia; allied Byzantine and Italian forces destroy Arab base at Garigliano (Southern Italy).

970–3	*Basil I Skamandrenos*	
971		Svyatoslav surrenders to the emperor at Silistra on the Danube; Bulgaria annexed.
972		Otto II marries Theophano.
973–8	*Anthony III Stoudites*	
975		John Tzimiskes' campaign in Syria, Lebanon and Palestine.
976–1025	BASIL II (active reign)	
976–9		Revolt of Bardas Skleros.
978–80	*Vacancy*	
980–92	*Nicholas II Chrysoberges*	
981–2		Būyid embassy in Constantinople; Otto II's invasion of Southern Italy defeated by Arabs in Calabria.
986		Basil defeated in Bulgaria.
987–9		Revolt of Bardas Phokas.
992–6	*Vacancy*	
995		Basil relieves Fātimid siege of Aleppo; arrest of Eustathios Maleïnos.
996–8	*Sisinnios II*	
997		Battle of Sperchios (Greece); Nikephoros Ouranos defeats Bulgars.
998–1001	*Vacancy*	
1000		Byzantine occupation of lands of David of Tao (Western Transcaucasus).
1001–19	*Sergios II*	
1001		Basil agrees ten-year truce with Fātimids.
1009		Caliph al-Hākim orders destruction of church of

Preface

THE NEED for a new introduction and survey of Byzantine history between 600 and 1025 hardly requires to be justified, but two points may strike the reader as unexpected.

Firstly, I have set the Byzantine world in a very broad perspective. The geographical introduction ranges from Iran to Italy, and a large portion of the book deals with the empire's neighbours in the Transcaucasus, the steppes and the Balkans. I have done so partly because I do not believe that events inside the empire can be understood without a basic appreciation of this wider world, and partly because there is very little else published in English that fills this gap.

Secondly, this book is not a 'textbook synthesis', but a personal interpretation that some may regard as controversial. Although I hope that the reader will find here a clear and reliable coverage of events, institutions, and social, economic and cultural change, historical research thrives at all levels when there is something to argue about, and if some of the interpretations in this book are greeted by specialists – and even more by their students – with a chorus of disagreement then it will have served one of its purposes.

Among the chief pleasures of writing a book is thanking people. I owe an enormous debt to James Howard-Johnston and Cyril Mango, for their help, advice and encouragement. Sue Barnes prepared the maps for publication; I am very grateful for her skill and care. My thanks to Hugh Barnes, Robert Beddard, Jeremy Catto, Clive Foss, John France, Simon Franklin, Peter Heather, Stephen Humphreys, Jeremy Johns, Christopher Lightfoot, Michael Maas, Alison McQuitty, Mark Nesbitt, Alan Walmsley and Bryan Ward-Perkins, who have all generously given information, listened as ideas took shape, and saved me from some of my errors. I am also happy to acknowledge the kindness and support I have received from the Provost and Fellows of Oriel College, Oxford, and the early encouragement in things Byzantine given by Michael Maclagan – with whom I shall always associate the pleasures of drinking madeira. The book, however, is dedicated to my wife, Helen, and to her father, Dugald Malcolm, without either of whom it would not have been written.

Wapping   MARK WHITTOW

1. Sources for Early Medieval Byzantium

As ONE would expect, this book is written on the basis of a body of Byzantine sources, written mostly in Greek between the seventh and the eleventh centuries, that includes chronicles, saints' lives, law codes, property documents, inscriptions, the acts of church councils, works of theology, sermons, homilies, letters, panegyrics and handbooks to diplomacy, warfare, court ceremony and protocol. More evidence comes from archaeology, numismatics and art history; and the whole has been interpreted in the light of how regional geography shaped the historical development of the empire, and of how comparable societies developed elsewhere. But in fact this list is rather misleading. Even compared with other early medieval societies Byzantium is an obscure and ill-recorded world, and it is worth making clear at the outset of a book on Byzantium that it is based on significantly less evidence than is available for any of the other important Christian states of the early medieval world.

The biggest gap is in documentary material. Byzantium was a literate society which produced a great number of documents of all sorts. The best proof of this lies in the lead seals which the Byzantines used to close confidential communications and to authenticate documents. A piece of string was inserted through a hole in the document, and the two ends were then passed through the channel in a lead blank. The lead blanks used in this process vary in size but they can be imagined as roughly equivalent to that of a coin. The blanks were cast in a mould and so made that they had a hollow channel from top to bottom. The string was passed through this channel and then knotted. The lead blank was then placed between the jaws of a *boulloterion*, a device which resembled a pair of iron pincers with disc-shaped jaws, a little smaller than the lead blank itself. The face of the jaws was engraved with an inscription, or an image, or a combination of the two. The boulloterion had a projection above the jaws so that when it was struck with a hammer the lead blank would be compressed, sealing shut the channel and locking in the two ends of the string attached to the document. At the same time the design engraved on the boulloterion was stamped on the lead blank.

1

The emperor, the patriarch, all imperial and ecclesiastical office holders, institutions and a great number of individuals had boulloteria, usually engraved with their name and title. As an individual changed office over his career, or was promoted in rank, so a new boulloterion was engraved with the new title. These stamped inscriptions are a vital source for Byzantine history, but the seals themselves are also the ghosts of vanished archives. Over 40,000 lead seals are preserved in public and private collections. Of these perhaps a quarter pre-date 1025. Each was once attached to a document, but the number 10,000 is only the tip of an iceberg. Apart from the comparatively rare cases where the seal was authenticating a document of special importance, most seals had served their purpose when the document was opened. Lead was not expensive, but it was not without cost, and most lead seals would almost certainly have been recast as new blanks. What the proportion of surviving lead seals is to the number of documents once issued in the Byzantine period cannot even be guessed at, but quite clearly we are talking about a society which produced a very great number of documents indeed.

As the inscriptions on the lead seals and occasional mentions elsewhere show, imperial officials and administrators, monasteries, cathedrals and many lay households sent out documents, and kept archives. It many cases these would have amounted to no more than a chest full, but for major institutions in state and church one must envisage something more substantial. The excavations of the headquarters of the Byzantine military governor at Preslav in Bulgaria found over 350 seals from the period 971 to 986. Given what has just been said about the reuse of lead seals, this presumably is the ghost of an archive which had amassed several thousand documents in under fifteen years.[1]

The greatest archives of all were those of the departments of state in Constantinople. In the mid-sixth century John Lydos tells us that the Praetorian Prefecture of the East, the office that up to the seventh century ran the civil administration of Thrace, Asia Minor, Syria and Palestine, kept its legal records dating back to the 360s in the vaults which supported the raised banks of seating in the hippodrome in Constantinople. When John Lydos was writing, this archive stretched some 250–300 metres along the east side of the hippodrome from the imperial box to the curve of the race track at the southern end, and it was arranged so that any case could be retrieved on request.[2] The empire after the seventh century did not rule such extensive territories, and its archives were probably not quite on this scale, but they certainly existed. The fact that a great many of the thousands of seals now known were collected from the shores of Constantinople next to the site of the imperial palace is proof that in the early middle ages tax records, military lists, and reports from all over the empire, financial documents, diplomatic papers – all the materials in fact that a historian of Byzantium could desire – were once preserved here in quantities.

Nearly all of this, however, has disappeared. Important collections have survived in southern Italy, but – as shown in the last section of Chapter 8 – this is hardly representative of the heartlands of the empire in Asia Minor, the Balkans or Constantinople itself where virtually everything has been destroyed. The largest surviving collection of Byzantine documents drawn up before 1025, containing about 75 items, is preserved in the monasteries on Mount Athos (near Thessalonica in northern Greece) which exceptionally have had a continuous history from the tenth century to the present day. Only one of these texts dates to before 900.[3]

There is therefore nothing to match the thousands of ninth- and tenth-century documents preserved either in their originals or in later copies from Catalonia, northern and central Italy, France or Germany. Anglo-Saxon England has left a richer documentary inheritance than Byzantium. When one remembers that some of the most striking advances in the historical study of these societies have come from the masses of information preserved in monastic and episcopal archives, it does become clear what the lack of this resource has done for our knowledge of the Byzantine world. A number of the most innovative and exciting studies, for example, on the social and political structures of the early medieval west would be impossible to write on Byzantium.[4]

What survives are principally fragments which have found their way into literary works, the acts of church councils or into various handbooks. The most remarkable examples of the latter are perhaps those associated with the emperor Constantine VII Porphyrogenitos (913–59). The emperor wrote or rather sponsored the production of a number of literary works, among which are included two traditionally know to scholars as the *De Administrando Imperio* and the *De Ceremoniis* – titles coined by their first editors in the seventeenth and eighteenth centuries respectively. Neither of these works is really a homogeneous work of literature; rather they are tenth-century manuscript collections of documents from the imperial archives. They have undergone a certain amount of minimal literary reshaping, and received prefaces setting out Constantine's overt aims in producing them, but they remain very much manuscript 'scrapbooks'. The *De Administrando Imperio*, for example, contains amongst other things a detailed official report on a Byzantine attempt to seize by subterfuge the strategic Georgian stronghold of Ardanoutzin, an eyewitness description of a journey down the Dnieper river, as well as a list of military service owed by officials and property holders in the Peloponnese.[5] The *De Ceremoniis* not only includes the descriptions of court ceremonies its title would imply, but also such items as a list of salary rates for various classes of official, and a remarkable collection of documents associated with the failed expeditions to retake Crete from the Arabs in the tenth century. Among these is an attempt in the immediate aftermath of the 949 expedition to draw up accounts and to assign responsibility to various departments to cover the costs. The document reveals officials unsure of who went on the expedition, and uncertain as to who had the responsibility for paying them, trying to pass the problem off on to another department.[6] Both the *De Administrando Imperio* and the *De Ceremoniis* are texts of great importance which give a tantalising glimpse of what the imperial archives must once have contained, but the fact that they are used so often – in this book as elsewhere – serves to underline how much has been lost and how much of our picture of early medieval Byzantium rests on only a very few pieces of evidence.

A type of evidence which can go some way to fill the gap are Byzantine letters. About 1700 written before 1025 have survived, and they are an essential historical source – but at the same time their value is also limited. No archival collection of Byzantine letters has survived. In Egypt the peculiar climatic conditions have preserved a huge body of papyrus fragments from the Roman and Islamic periods which include great numbers of letters saying all the kinds of things of passing interest one would expect: children asking their fathers to bring them a present back from town, traders reporting on prices, families sending news of relations, husbands telling wives they miss them, all written in a very unremarkable standard of Greek, Coptic, Hebrew and Arabic. Using this extraordinary material one can construct a detailed picture of medieval Egypt that is quite impossible for Byzantium.[7] Without any doubt the Byzantines did write letters like this, but none survive. The ones which have been preserved instead belong to a distinct and elevated literary genre somewhat distant from the reality of contemporary life.

Letter writing of the type preserved in Byzantine manuscripts was a branch of rhetoric and had a long classical ancestry. They were not composed in the language of contemporary spoken Greek, or even in the standard written language of official reports, but instead in a deliberately elevated style modelled on the Attic Greek of the fourth and third centuries BC, and their authors embellished them with references to classical and biblical texts. An ordinarily literate Byzantine would almost certainly have found many of these letters difficult to understand – and modern readers have shared the same problem. Those in search of historical information have tended to find them very frustrating: some Byzantine letter collections give the impression of saying very little, at length, very elegantly. In some cases this has been exaggerated by the means of their preservation. The major incentive behind publishing a letter collection in a manuscript was not a desire to record documentary information, but admiration of the letters' literary qualities. If a copyist were short of space what he was most likely to cut was the (from this perspective) non-essential references to specific events, leaving more room for the rhetorical flourishes which made the letters attractive. The result in that case would tend to be an elegant but timeless literary text.

Recent research, sympathetic to the literary values these texts embody, has done a great deal to show how much information they can provide. Of the 1700 letters the great majority were written after the late eighth century. Among these are large collections of such important political figures as Theodore, the abbot of the Stoudios monastery in Constantinople in the late eighth and early ninth century, Photios, patriarch from 858 to 867 and again from 877 to 886, and Nicholas Mystikos, patriarch from 912 to 925. By comparison with some, such as for example the small late tenth-century collection of Nikephoros Ouranos,[8] who either by personal choice or later editing reveals comparatively little about his key role in the politics of Basil II's court, these letters show their authors as closely concerned with the real events of the world around them. All three had tempestuous careers, including periods of exile, and each used the circle of letter writing to maintain and reinforce the ties of friendship and political loyalty. In addition the two patriarchs carried on diplomacy by letter. The recipients of Photios' correspondence include successive popes, the ruler of Bulgaria, the prince of princes and the katholikos of Armenia, and the patriarchs of Antioch, Jerusalem and Alexandria. Nicholas was even more involved in foreign policy, first as regent for the infant Constantine VII Porphyrogenitos in 913–14, and then later from 917 to 925 as the only Byzantine authority that Symeon of Bulgaria was prepared to recognise. As a result Nicholas' letters to Symeon are of crucial importance for the history of Byzantine–Bulgar relations (see the fourth section in Chapter 8), and together with his letters to the caliph al-Muktadir, the emir of Crete, the prince of Abasgia, and various Italian leaders go a small way to make up for the lack of a foreign office archive, at least for these few years.[9]

Yet this should not disguise their limitations. An author chose this manner of communication in an elegant, polished and often deliberately obscure style, because as well as the message itself the letter carried a cultural statement. Between friends such letters gave the pleasure of a shared membership of an élite literary coterie (similar to that enjoyed by early twentieth-century Englishmen sending Horatian odes to one another); rivals and enemies could be patronised by a demonstration of literary superiority; letters asking for a favour were more likely to be successful if the potential patron had first been given a suitable literary gift; diplomatic letters in this form demonstrated the sender's cultural status and preserved face. In each case, however, the purpose of the letter was to present a carefully polished image according to a literary ideal. In such letters,

Theodore, Photios, Nicholas and others do reveal a considerable amount about their actions and ideas, but it is always in a manner shaped and transformed by the demands of the genre. The reality behind it is hard to assess.

With so meagre a documentary base more attention is inevitably focused on the Byzantine chronicles and histories which have to provide the basic narrative account of the years between 600 and 1025. Unfortunately their coverage is patchy, they are often written long after the event, and they are frequently distorted by a propagandist bias. The same could be said of great deal of early medieval history writing. The Italian chronicles are little better and the Spanish considerably worse, but in both cases their deficiencies can be off-set by other material. In the Frankish world – at least from the last quarter of the eighth century onwards – there are more documentary sources and the chronicles are better, not just in themselves but there are more chronicles and histories giving alternative and independent accounts.

At the beginning of the seventh century the late Roman tradition of chronicle and history writing was still active. One of its later products was the extremely valuable *Chronikon Paschale* which stops in 628. After this there is a break in the surviving texts until the appearance of Nikephoros' *Historia Syntomos* in the 780s and Theophanes' *Chronographia* in the early ninth century. These two are closely related and were obviously using the same sources. For the period between 629 and the end of the *Chronographia* in 813 we are essentially dependent on the information they contain. Neither is a very impressive work of history. Their coverage of the seventh century is poor (Nikephoros in fact misses out the years 641–68; Theophanes only covers them by repeating a Syriac chronicle which he knew in a Greek translation). For the eighth century the value of their brief account is limited by the politically correct desire to abuse the iconoclast emperors – Leo III (717–41), Constantine V (741–75) and Leo IV (775–80) – and to admit as little as possible in their favour.

After Nikephoros and Theophanes there survive from the ninth century little more than two short fragments of a work conventionally known as the *Scriptor Incertus* ('The Unknown Writer') and possibly to be identified with the *Ecclesiastical History* of Sergios the Confessor,[10] and the Chronicle of George the

Monk. The latter was written apparently during the reign of Basil I (867–86). Its author had available a no longer surviving mid-ninth century reworking of Theophanes known as the *Epitome* which continued the *Chronographia* up to 829. From 813 to 829 he reproduced that (although with much left out), but from 829 to where it finishes in 842 the text is hardly more than an anti-iconoclast rant.[11] Apart from these two the history of the ninth century is only recorded in texts compiled in the second half of the tenth century: the Logothete's chronicle;[12] the History of Genesios; Theophanes Continuatus; and Pseudo-Symeon *magistros.*

The Logothete's Chronicle also copies the *Epitome* but in greater detail than George the Monk, and its author had a longer version of the text which extended to 842. The tone throughout is moderately hostile to the reigning emperors. From 842 to 913 the Logothete gives an extremely critical account of the rise and reign of Basil I and his successor Leo VI, the first two emperors of the Macedonian dynasty. Possibly he was copying another ninth-century text like the *Epitome* but nothing can be said with certainty.

Genesios (who stops in 886) and Theophanes Continuatus are closely related and like the Logothete begin approximately where Theophanes stops. They give a different account of the first half of the ninth century to the Logothete, but one equally hostile to the iconoclast emperors of the Amorion dynasty. After 867 and the rise to power of the Macedonian dynasty the tone changes dramatically to one of loyalist flattery. Theophanes Continuatus, book five, is a panegyrical biography of Basil I commissioned by his grandson, Constantine Porphyrogenitos, but otherwise their sources are unknown.

Pseudo-Symeon *magistros* is a late tenth-century compilation based on the Logothete's Chronicle but with chaotic interpolations from a variety of sources that include Theophanes Continuatus and a pamphlet written in the ninth century to vilify the patriarch Photios.[13]

None of this is very impressive and the historical quality of these texts hardly improves when they reach the century in which they were compiled. The first version of the Logothete carries on up to 948. It is usually said that the Chronicle is written from the standpoint of the Lekapenos family who seized power in 919. If so, its account of the reign of Romanos I

Lekapenos is strikingly ill-informed. Theophanes Continuatus repeats the Logothete's inadequate history of Romanos with a few details added from a lost eight-volume biography of the emperor's leading general, John Kourkuas.[14] From 944 to where it stops in 961 Theophanes Continuatus returns to praising the ruling Macedonian dynasty. For this, its anonymous author used a panegyric of the emperor Constantine VII, which dwelt on his building activities, and a chronicle favourable to the emperor's leading generals, the Phokas family. Neither of these survive, but the chronicle is independently repeated in a more or less abbreviated form by Pseudo-Symeon *magistros*, and in a second version of the Logothete's Chronicle which has been continued to 963.[15]

The late eleventh-century historian John Skylitzes copies Theophanes Continuatus up to 944, but from 944 to 963 he reproduces a near contemporary anti-Macedonian account of the reigns of Constantine Porphyrogenitos and his son, Romanos II. For the thirty years after 959 Skylitzes is supplemented by the History of Leo the Deacon who gives a flattering account of the reigns of Nikephoros II Phokas (963–9) and John Tzimiskes (969–76), and some stories set in the early part of the reign of Basil II, but after 989 Skylitzes is the only Greek narrative source to survive. The account it gives is disjointed and ill-informed, and were it not for the Arabic chronicle of Yahyā b. Sa'īd, an Egyptian Christian who moved to Antioch in the early eleventh century, the latter part of Basil II's reign from 989 to 1025 would be virtually unintelligible.[16]

Apart from the uneven coverage, the main problem with all these texts – even the better ones such as Leo the Deacon – is their obvious unreliability. This is a problem that is as applicable to Nikephoros and Theophanes as it is to the later writers, and it is one that some modern Byzantinists still ignore. For much of the period between 600 and 1025 only one account of events has been preserved – or at least only one with minor variations. This does not mean that it can be regarded as basically correct. The Byzantines had inherited from the traditions of late Roman literature the view that all historical writing should serve a didactic end. The Byzantine author set about recording the past for a purpose, whether to praise his patrons, abuse his enemies, attract reward, or generally to present a version of the past which fitted contemporary political and religous dogma and served current ends. For example, all the authors whose works survive believed, or thought it politic to be seen to believe, that the eighth-century iconoclasts were dreadful heretics and thus they regarded the principal purpose of recording the history of these heretics as to show how these God-detested people came to an appropriate end. The ninth-century iconoclasts were treated in much the same way in the tenth-century sources, but the historiography, is further complicated by the fact that the then ruling Macedonian dynasty had its dubious origins in the mid-ninth century. Consequently all the tenth-century accounts are written either to blacken or to whitewash the current regime. The Logothete's chronicle presents a uniformly critical account of the Macedonian emperors. Does it represent the attitude of the great military families who may well have wished to present all their civilian rivals as knaves and fools? Does it come close to the truth? Even where we have an alternative version it is very difficult to judge. In Theophanes Continuatus the emperor Constantine VII Porphyrogenitos is presented as a wise and learned statesman; Skylitzes preserves an account which presents him as a hen-pecked drunk with unholy designs against the patriarch Polyeuktos. Theophanes Continuatus may represent the official version during the reign of his son, Romanus II; the origins of Skylitzes' account can only be guessed at.[17] The key point, however, is that in the absence of other evidence there is no good reason to believe one rather than the other, and a combination of the two is just as likely to be a combination of two totally misleading versions.

The problem of reliability and truth can be highlighted by comparing Byzantine history writing with the production of Byzantine saints' lives. While there are comparatively few Byzantine histories and chronicles, Byzantine saints' lives survive in huge numbers, and what is known of Byzantine reading habits shows that they were a much more esteemed and appreciated genre.

Consider the following passage from the Life of St Ioannikios:

> The wife of Stephen who was then *magistros*, because of the jealousy of the devil was hated by her servants, and took poison from them, which, by God's permission, she unwit-

tingly drank and lost her mind. Having expended a great deal of money on doctors to no advantage, she finally went to the holy father, and throwing herself at his feet she begged him to obtain mercy. The saint knowing that this had come about by magic, said: 'O woman, if you wish to obtain healing and agree not to punish those who planned to kill you, the Lord will swiftly cure you.' Having agreed this by oath, the saint prayed over her and sealed her three times with the sign of the life-giving cross, restoring her mind to sanity so that she departed in health praising God.[18]

This is a typical story from a saint's life, perhaps only remarkable for its comparative lack of miraculous content. At first sight there is no need to take it as any more than a pious legend. All the component parts of the story are hagiographical clichés. The poisoning inspired by the devil, the failure of doctors, the promise not to punish the guilty, the successful cure after which the woman goes on her way praising God, all have hundreds of precedents in saints' lives. Anyone familiar with the genre will know that the greater part of it is made up in this way out of ready-made component parts.

Consider now this passage from a work of history, Theophanes' *Chronographia*:

[811] Having gathered troops not only from Thrace, but also from the Asiatic themes, [the Emperor Nikephoros] invaded Bulgaria. With the soldiers went many poor men armed with their own hunting slings and clubs, and many blasphemers too. When they reached Markellai, [the Bulgarian *qaghan*] Krum, fearing their numbers, asked for peace. [Nikephoros] however was prevented from doing so by his own bad counsel and the counsel of his advisors who were of the same opinion .... Three days after the first engagements he ascribed his glorious success not to God, who had made him victorious, but rather he praised the good fortune and wise counsel of Staurakios alone, and he threatened those officers who had opposed the advance. Without mercy he ordered animals, and children and people of all ages to be slaughtered; he allowed the dead bodies of his own troops to remain unburied, thinking only of collecting the spoils; and shutting up Krum's

treasury with bars and seals he ensured that in future they would be his own.[19] [The passage then goes on to describe how Nikephoros tried to return to imperial territory by crossing the Haimos mountains, but was ambushed, defeated and killed.]

Theophanes wrote this within four years of the event and the natural response is to take this as a basically reliable account. But in fact Theophanes detested Nikephoros, and it seems just as likely that the story of the expedition which led to the emperor's disastrous defeat and shameful death in Bulgaria gave him an ideal opportunity to denigrate the dead man. What at first sight seems a straightforward narrative, on close examination – just as the story from the life of St Ioannikios – breaks apart into a series of clichés. The poorly equipped army, the ill-advised rejection of peace, the hubris of failing to attribute success to God alone, the merciless slaughter, the impiety and the premature greed are all the ready-made components of a military disaster story. Clearly there is a truth behind Theophanes' words. Nikephoros was defeated and killed in Bulgaria; but how much of this account is owing to literary precedent and a desire to abuse a fallen enemy, and how much actually occurred is very difficult to say.

Part of the difficulty is that the clichés of historians and chroniclers are harder to spot than those of the authors of saints' lives. The latter was a literary form created out of a combination of the pattern of the life of Christ decked out in the rhetorical structure of classical panegyric biographies. The model allowed a wide degree of creative variation, but at its most basic a saint enjoyed an exemplary childhood, attended by suitable prodigies, after which came a period of withdrawal from the world and isolated ascetic endurance, corresponding to Christ's forty days in the wilderness. Following this the saint would return having subdued all earthly passions and bodily desires, and henceforth he would be able to act as a channel for God's power to be exercised in this world. The saint would then demonstrate this by a series of miracles, which usually included healing the sick, casting out demons, foretelling the future and cursing the ungodly. In due course he would foresee his own death, and die in a literal odour of sanctity. The sweet-smelling and miraculously preserved corpse would subsequently act as the focus for a series of posthumous miracles.

As well as the overall framework, the hagiographer could draw on the existing literature for a huge body of hagiographic commonplaces, of which the failure of the doctors in the passage quoted above is an example. In saints' lives no one appeals to a saint for a cure but they have already tried and failed with secular doctors. Such commonplaces provided an enormous repertoire for the hagiographer, and it was quite possible to stitch these together within the standard framework of a saints' life to compose a life of St X with virtually no concrete evidence at all. (Indeed this was a problem often faced and surmounted.)

However, hagiography could also be used to tell the truth. The life of a real saint – and the Byzantine world produced many whose lives conformed in varying degrees to this model – well known to his hagiographer, and written within a few years of his death for an audience who themselves had known him, is inherently bound not to stray far from the truth. That truth will have been filtered through the demands of the genre, but nonetheless must still have been generally recognisable. For the modern historian the signs of reality are when the life does not quite conform to the model, and includes stories and details firmly rooted in a particular time and place. Even works of pure fiction can be far from complete fantasy. The Life of St Andrew, the holy fool of Constantinople, who certainly never existed, gives a vivid picture of early eighth-century Constantinople, as well as a remarkable insight into its author's beliefs concerning heaven and the end of the world.[20]

In the case of the passage from the Life of St Ioannikios, even in this predictable story, hagiographic cliché has not entirely swallowed historical reality. The Life was written by a monk called Peter very shortly after Ioannikios' death in 847. Peter had known Ioannikios himself, had spoken to others who had known him too, and was writing for a similarly well-informed audience. The story of the cure is a commonplace. Ioannikios was a great saint, and this was how great saints were expected to perform cures. The woman, however, is not just any woman, such as one would find in so many saints' lives, but the wife of the *magistros* Stephen. Stephen was quite a common name, but the title *magistros* at this date was not, and as a result he can be identified as one of the major iconophile figures at the imperial court in the early ninth century.[21] The appearance of his wife in the story is the only piece of evidence which links Stephen with Ioannikios, and hence it is a valuable clue in building up a picture of this political and religious world.

A similar approach is needed to get the best out of histories and chronicles. They repay detailed reading, with a careful watch kept for commonplaces and clichés, and for the incidental detail – valuable in itself – that might lend credence to the main story. But in the end the limitations of this material must not be over-looked. The fact remains that it is not possible to write an intel-lectually convincing detailed narrative political history of Byzantium. Neither the documentary evidence, nor the literary sources exist.

Drawing attention to the problems is not intended to close down discussion; rather the reverse. Although the Byzantine world is comparatively ill-documented, a substantial and varied body of material has survived. The difficulties close some doors that have been opened to good effect by historians working on the early middle ages in the west, but they also pose an inter-esting challenge. Historians of Byzantium need to ask new questions of their texts, and to explore alternative types of evidence. Numismatics has already made an important contri-bution to the understanding of the Byzantine economy, and more can be expected. The inscribed lead seals are a vital source – unique to the Byzantine world – and, in the absence of the documents once attached to them, much can be learnt from the names, titles and dedications they contain. Again much has been done and more can be expected. The future, how-ever, lies with archaeology. Medieval Byzantine archaeology hardly exists. What is available has largely been obtained as a spin-off from the excavations of classical cities. Much of the basic work has yet to be done, especially in the countryside, where funda-mental questions including, 'How large was the Byzantine popula-tion?', 'How wealthy?', 'Where did they live and how were they employed?', cannot really be answered. Turkey in particular rep-resents a huge untapped field for medieval archaeology. But there are hopeful signs. The recent publication of the Byzantine pot-tery from the Saraçhane excavations in Istanbul,[22] the work at the important Byzantine city of Amorion in central Anatolia, the on-going survey of castles in western Turkey, all give hope that we are on the edge of a very exciting period in Byzantine studies which will transform our understanding of the Byzantine world.

2. The Strategic Geography of the Near East

TAKING ANY modern map of the Near East and its neighbours large enough to show the whole region from the steppes of the Ukraine and southern Russia in the north to the deserts of Arabia in the south, and from the Balkans and Egypt in the west to the borders of Afghanistan in the east, six major geographical blocs will stand out: the Balkan peninsula, the steppes, the Fertile Crescent, the desert, and the plateaux of Anatolia and Iran. To understand the history of the Byzantine state and its place in the Near East it is essential to have a basic knowledge of the geography of these blocs and how they relate to each other. With so few written sources available geography becomes even more important than usual in setting the parameters to a convincing interpretation of the past.

The Balkans

Starting in the north-west is the Balkan peninsula, a term usually applied to the lands south of the Danube and Sava rivers. In the north-western corner lies the way to Italy, in the south is Greece, to the east is the Black Sea, and at almost its easternmost point is Constantinople, modern Istanbul. The dominant feature of the Balkan landscape is the mountain ranges. On the west side of the peninsula the mountains run via the Dinaric Alps in the north, through the Črna Gora, or Montenegro, the Albanian mountains and the Pindos range to the Gulf of Corinth and the Peloponnese in the south. In the east of the peninsula the Haimos mountains, otherwise called the Stara Planina, form the southern section of an inverted 'S', of which the Carpathians are the northern bend. The range runs from the 'Iron Gates' where the 'S' is cut by the Danube in an arc towards the Black Sea. South again are the Rhodope mountains, cutting a similar arc along the northern shore of the Aegean Sea. The centre of the peninsula is filled by the mountains and high plateaux of central Macedonia.

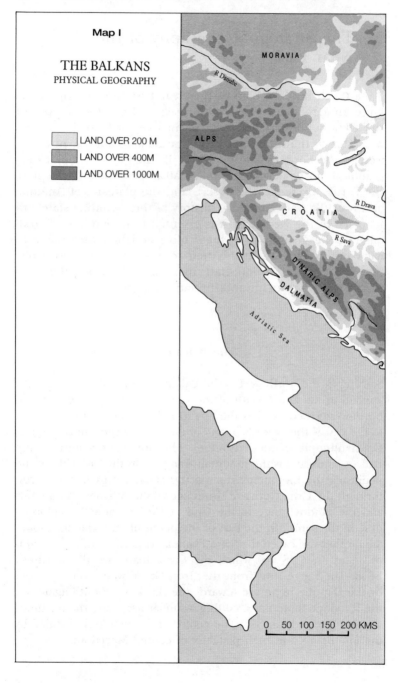

Map I

THE BALKANS
PHYSICAL GEOGRAPHY

LAND OVER 200 M
LAND OVER 400M
LAND OVER 1000M

MORAVIA

R Danube

ALPS

CROATIA

R Drava

R Sava

DINARIC ALPS

DALMATIA

Adriatic Sea

0   50   100 150 200 KMS

This knot of mountains is cut by several major rivers. Since many of the Balkan ranges are only crossed by a very limited number of practicable passes these rivers, and the roads they allow, constrain travellers, traders and armies to a tight route system which has governed the peninsula throughout its history. Above all, four major roads stand out. The first is the *Via Egnatia* which runs east–west across the peninsula from Dyrrachion on the Adriatic shore via Thessalonica to Constantinople. The second is the main military highway which leads from Constantinople across Thrace via Adrianople and Serdika, Modern Sofia, to Naissos, modern Niš, and thence to Singidunum, modern Belgrade, on the middle Danube. From here the traveller can either continue to follow the valley of the Danube towards southern Germany and Gaul, or he can turn to the west and follow the valley of the Sava river leading over the mountains into northern Italy. The other two routes are essentially branches of these. The third leaves the main military highway at Adrianople and heads north, passing over the Haimos mountains at their lowest point close to the Black Sea coast. It then turns west passing through the plains south of the Danube, crosses the mountains south of the Iron Gates and rejoins the military highway near Belgrade. The fourth route is the major north–south route across the central Balkans, running from Niš to Thessalonica. Each of these routes carried an important Roman road, but they remained at least potentially difficult. In winter they are liable to be blocked by snow and their high narrow passes are ideal for ambushes and resolute defence. Given that these are the best routes in the Balkans it should be clear that the peninsula is not a natural political unit.[1]

Divided by the mountains and linked by the routes, the Balkan peninsula also contains a number of fertile plains. The most important by far are the eastern plains looking toward the Black Sea. In the north are the plains of the Lower Danube between the Carpathians and the Haimos, and to the south are those of Thrace, lying between the Haimos and the Rhodope. Smaller and in general less productive are the Serbian plains, above the 'Iron Gates' and around the rivers Sava and Morava, and the Mediterranean coastal plains, of which the most significant are the small isolated patches of Dalmatia and the larger plain of Albania along the Adriatic coast, and the Aegean plains of

Boeotia, Thessaly, and Lower Macedonia. High in Central Macedonia there are a number of generally small basins of fertile alluvium surrounded by mountains.

The Balkan peninsula is not by nature a wealthy agricultural region. There are too many mountains, and the plains are too small. The climate and water supply also present problems: the high inland parts of the peninsula suffer from long cold winters and southern coastal districts face regular droughts. Some of the plains are very fertile, but their small size and isolation limits their importance in terms of the Near East as a whole. Such plains are perhaps more suited to be the support for small independent or autonomous states than great kingdoms or empires. For long periods of the peninsula's history city states, such as Athens and Sparta in ancient Greece, or Dubrovnik in medieval Dalmatia, have been characteristic of Balkan political structures. Larger units have tended to be short lived or imposed from outside.

Only the Black Sea plains form something of an exception. Both those of Thrace and the Lower Danube have the potential to be major agricultural zones. Under the Ottomans they were extensively farmed, producing a great part of the grain which fed Constantinople. Since the late nineteenth century they have formed the major part of the agricultural base of Bulgaria and Romania, south and north of the Danube respectively. As much in the ancient world and the early middle ages as since the Turkish conquests in the fourteenth century, these plains rather than those of Greece have had the greatest potential to provide agricultural wealth and the basis of political power.

The Steppes

North of the Balkans lies the Hungarian plain, surrounded by the Alps to the west, and by the arc of the Carpathians to the north and east. These plains are the largest area of steppe grassland in Europe and as such they have been of considerable strategic importance. They supported Attila's Huns in the fifth century, the Avar qaghanate in the sixth, seventh and eighth century, and the Magyars who raided throughout eastern and

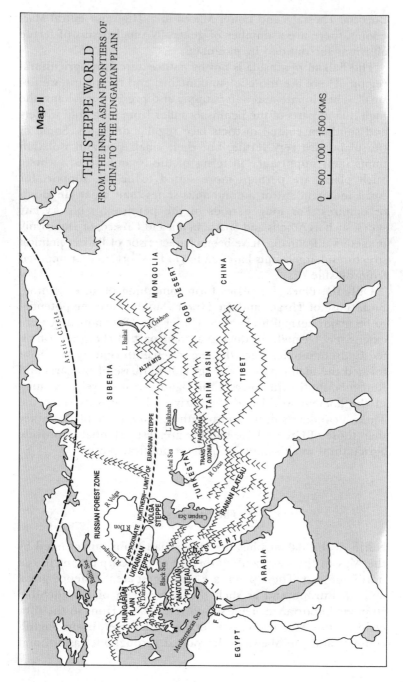

Map II

THE STEPPE WORLD
FROM THE INNER ASIAN FRONTIERS OF
CHINA TO THE HUNGARIAN PLAIN

0   500 1000 1500 KMS

Arctic Circle

MONGOLIA

GOBI DESERT

CHINA

L. Baikal

R. Orkhon

ALTAI MTS

SIBERIA

TARIM BASIN

TIBET

L. Balkhash

EURASIAN STEPPE

NORTHERN LIMIT OF

FARGHANA

TRANS OXONIA

Aral Sea

R. Oxus

RUSSIAN FOREST ZONE

R. Volga

VOLGA STEPPE

TURKESTAN

IRANIAN PLATEAU

Caspian Sea

R. Don

APPROXIMATE

UKRAINIAN STEPPE

R. Dnieper

FERTILE CRESCENT

Baltic Sea

Black Sea

ANATOLIAN PLATEAU

ARABIA

HUNGARIAN PLAIN

R. Danube

Mediterranean Sea

EGYPT

western Europe in the tenth century. However, large though they are in comparison to other European grasslands, the Hungarian plains are in fact no more than an isolated outlier of the vast expanse of the Eurasian steppe to the east. Beyond the Carpathians lie the Ukrainian steppes which in turn form the western end of a belt of steppe grasslands stretching across Central Asia, via the steppes of the Volga and Turkestan to Mongolia and the Inner Asian frontier of China. The steppes embrace a variety of climate and landform, but the dominant feature of this zone of Eurasia is the millions of hectares of steppe grassland.

With variations that reflect altitude and distance from the sea, the Eurasian steppes share a common climate of hot dry summers, bitterly cold winters, green springs and bleak autumns. As the experience of the German army which successively sweated and froze at Stalingrad on the Volga in 1942 and 1943 can illustrate, this is a harsh environment with great contrasts between the seasons. In the spring of 1934, an English traveller, Robert Byron, could describe the steppe as, 'a dazzling open sea of green [in which] bearings, landmarks, disappeared, as they would from a skiff in mid-Atlantic'.[2] The same view in winter would move Fred Burnaby, another Englishman travelling in 1875–6, to write: 'A large dining room table covered with naught but its white cloth is not a cheery sight. To describe the next one hundred miles ... indeed only extend the table cover. ... A picture of desolation which wearied by its utter loneliness, and at the same time appalled by its immensity'.[3] At one season in the Ukrainian and Volga steppes the grass will grow shoulder high, at another the temperatures can drop to below - 10°c.

Up until the twentieth century this environment was exploited by nomad pastoralists, whose economy depended on sheep and horses which they moved according to the season to find pasture and water, and to avoid the worst effects of the climate. As travellers from the sedentary world were frequently warned, they would only survive on the steppes in winter if they exchanged the animals they had brought with them for the hardy steppe horses bred for these conditions, and found someone with steppe nomad skills to guide them.

At its fundamental level the key units of nomad society are the household centred on a single tent, and most important,

the camping group made up of a few families and their animals banded together for cooperation. The size of the camping group is governed by the number of sheep and other animals
the available pasture can support. Steppe nomads are not poor.
Indeed a poor nomad is something of a contradiction in terms,
because without a certain number of animals pastoral life is
impossible. Each household on the steppes will therefore possess
a minimum of about 100 sheep, and in many cases 200 or
more. The exact figures obviously vary depending upon the
quality of the grass, but even in the relatively fertile steppe of
the southern Ukraine flocks of many more than 1000 sheep
would have led to overgrazing where the sheep coming behind
cannot find enough to eat. Thus, although the number of tents
in a camping groups varies among different nomad societies
and can also change with the seasons, there are often only two
or three tents, and rarely more than half a dozen. Hence in
April 1934, Robert Byron, quoted above, was also struck by the
'multiplicity of . . . nomadic encampments, cropping up wherever
the eye rested, yet invariably separate by a mile or two from
their neighbours. There are hundreds of them, and the sight
therefore, seemed to embrace hundreds of miles.'[4]

These are the fundamentals of nomad life, and in consequence
nomad society is inherently fragmentary, stateless and egalitarian.
Larger political groupings are not essential to nomadic pastoral
production.[5] Yet in the early middle ages far from this scene
of peaceful pastoralism, the steppes were dominated by a series
of powerful militaristic nomad states which played an essential
part in the strategy of the age.

The first factor behind this is the inherent military ability of
the nomads. The same skills of horsemanship, archery and endurance which they had developed to cope with the demands
of life on the steppe, made nomads highly effective warriors.
Separated into camping groups these martial skills were dissipated
in small-scale raiding on other nomads and their settled neighbours; united into great polities which could muster tens of
thousands of nomad horsemen, they were the most powerful
military force of the pre-gunpowder age.

Unity at a level larger than the camping group offered some
advantages within nomadic society regarding the practical arrangement of the annual cycle of pastoral life. Migration routes,

for example, between winter and summer pastures could be better arranged at this level. Much more significant, however, unity offered security in the face of enemies, whether sedentary or nomadic, and it offered the prospect of wealth.

The demand for security acted as a domino effect on steppe society. As in an arms race, if one group of nomads united into a force capable of seizing the pastures of their neighbours, the latter had little choice but to do the same or submit. Beginning in the east, where steppe nomads faced the aggressive power of imperial China, the unity of one nomad state had provoked unity in its neighbours.

The prospect of wealth further encouraged the process. Another fundamental feature of the nomad economy is that it is not self-sufficient. It needs access to the sedentary world. Camping groups could not support artisans and manufacturers; and whatever the proportion of animal products in an individual nomad's diet, he still needed grain and vegetables. In this relationship with the sedentary world the nomad was always at a disadvantage. Whereas the nomad needed what the sedentary world could provide, what the nomad could offer in return by way of animals and animal products was not essential to the sedentary economy. Since nomad stocks of animals could fluctuate wildly from year to year as they faced summer droughts, an exceptionally cold winter or disease in their flocks and herds, and since the worse their pastoral position became the more they needed agricultural products, nomads often found themselves at the receiving end of a very hard bargain. Much better for the nomad to be united, for then he could dictate terms, either by direct conquest, or by tribute, or by plunder and booty.[6]

The potential of steppe nomad states was enormous. In the fourth and fifth century, a relatively minor and short-lived nomad empire, that of the Huns, had set in motion the migrations which had led to the fall of the Roman empire in the west, and had terrorised the imperial government in Constantinople. In the thirteenth century the Mongols had conquered China, Persia and Russia, and raided as far west as Germany. Events in the steppes were bound to be of concern to any neighbouring sedentary power, and the Byzantine empire of the early middle ages was no exception.

Two factors, however, did limit the impact of the steppe nomads upon the settled powers. One was the inherent tendency of steppe society to fragment. The closer to its nomadic roots a particular society was the more likely it was to be politically unstable. A major setback or crisis and the nomad empire could dissolve into its fragmentary, stateless past. The history of the steppes is of a succession of nomad empires. If the states of the settled world could surmount the initial crisis of a nomad attack, their institutions were much more likely to endure in the long term. On the other hand, if a nomad state developed away from this structure, and became closer in form to a sedentary state, it might well become more stable but only at the price of losing the particular characteristics that made it militarily formidable in the first place. Both these tendencies can be seen operating among the Byzantine empire's steppe neighbours in the early middle ages.

The second limiting factor derives again from features of nomadic life inherent in pastoral nomadism. Nomad military strength depended upon large and very mobile cavalry armies. The size of these is open to debate, but the armies with which the Mongols conquered the Middle East in the thirteenth century were certainly well over 100,000 strong, and some historians would wish to make them bigger still. The mobility of such a force was ensured by each warrior having numerous remounts. Like the Pony Express of nineteenth-century America, when one horse was tired the rider moved to the next. Marco Polo observed thirteenth-century Mongol warriors with as many as 18 remounts. This may be exceptional, but ten was quite typical. If a horse is to be kept on grazing alone, it has been calculated that it will require slightly more than 10 hectares of pasture a year. If one multiples 10 hectares by ten remounts by 100,000 warriors it soon becomes plain that nowhere in Europe or in the Near East south of the steppe grasslands was there sufficient pasture to support such a huge number of horses. The Ukrainian steppe was the end of the central Asian grasslands. Further progress west is barred by the Carpathian mountains. Once over this barrier, nomads find themselves again in the familiar steppe landscape of the great Hungarian plain. Yet this, the largest area of natural pasture in Europe, is a pocket handkerchief compared with the huge expanses to the east. At most the Hungarian plain contains 42,400 square kilometres of pasture;

and in reality only about half of that would have been available to pasture horses reducing the number of potential nomad warriors to about 20,000. Thus the mathematics of pasture determine that the odds are strongly against any nomad power from the steppes establishing itself south of the steppe zone without eventually having to transform the patterns of nomad life which had brought it to power in the first place.[7]

Anatolia and Iran

The same constraints apply if a nomad power wishes to move south instead of west, into the next geographical bloc: the plateaux and mountains of Anatolia and Iran. The basic configuration of this bloc is perhaps best understood if one starts from Armenia, the high region of volcanic mountains and small alluvial basins which forms a hub for the mountain systems of the Near East. Armenia is separated from the steppes of the Ukraine and the Volga by the Caucasus mountains, much steeper on the south than the north side, but heavily wooded country, difficult to subdue and crossed by only a limited number of defensible passes. From Armenia great ranges of mountains extend to surround the plateaux of Anatolia in the west and Iran in the east.

Starting south of Lake Van and moving west, are first the Hakkâri mountains, then the Anti-Taurus and next the Taurus mountains which lie along the south coast of Turkey facing the Mediterranean. To the north, facing the Black Sea, are the Pontic mountains which are continued west by lesser ranges in Paphlagonia and beyond. The mountains of Anatolia are with few exceptions higher in the east than the west, but the overall pattern is to create in the peninsula of Asia Minor of central plateau – that is Anatolia – surrounded by ranges of mountains which facilitate east–west rather than north–south movement. Above all the mountains on the south-eastern side of the plateau, especially the Anti-Taurus and the Hakkâri mountains, form a formidable barrier to communication between Anatolia and Syria and Mesopotamia beyond.

East of Armenia the same configuration is broadly repeated,

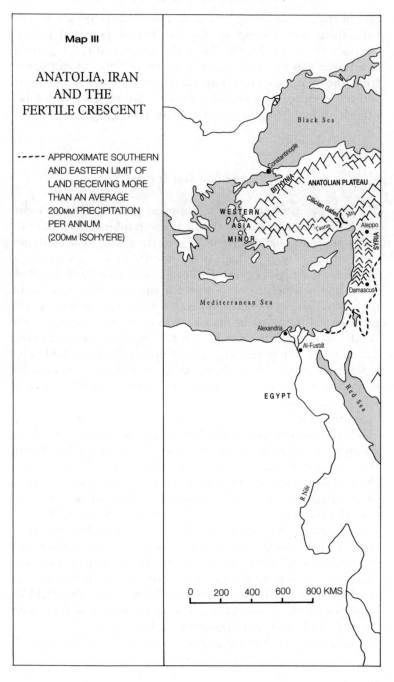

Map III

ANATOLIA, IRAN AND THE FERTILE CRESCENT

- - - - APPROXIMATE SOUTHERN
AND EASTERN LIMIT OF
LAND RECEIVING MORE
THAN AN AVERAGE
200MM PRECIPITATION
PER ANNUM
(200MM ISOHYERE)

Black Sea

Constantinople

BITHYNIA

ANATOLIAN PLATEAU

Cilician Gates

WESTERN
ASIA
MINOR

Taurus Mts

Aleppo

SYRIA

Damascus

Mediterranean Sea

Alexandria

Al-Fustât

EGYPT

Red Sea

R. Nile

0   200   400   600   800 KMS

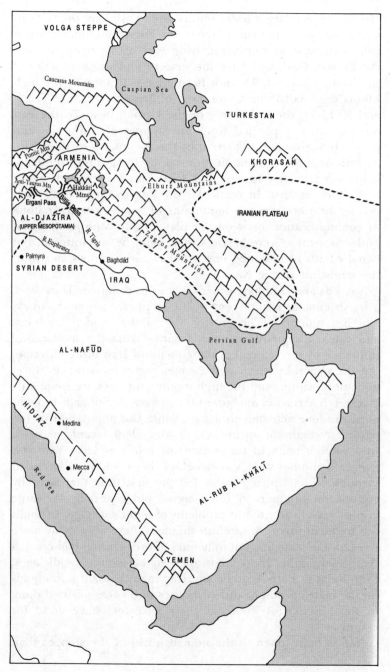

save on a much larger scale. South-east of Lake Van, the Hakkâri mountains join the main range of the Zagros mountains which run north-west to south-east, lying east of Mesopotamia and the Persian Gulf, and form the western and southern sides of the Iranian plateau. The northern edge is formed by the high Elburz mountains which join those of Armenia north of Tabriz and lie along the south side of the Caspian Sea. To the east the plateau is separated from the steppes of Turkestan and from Afghanistan and Pakistan by the mountains of Khorasan. As with Anatolia, communications along the grain of the land-scape – north-west to east and south-east – are much easier than those against. In particular the Zagros range is an even greater barrier than the mountains of south-eastern Anatolia to communication between the plateau and Mesopotamia. In both cases these were barriers that could be surmounted, but equally both represented important factors for division within the landscape of the Near East.

Anatolia and Iran have other features in common. They share a harsh climate reminiscent of the steppes, with cold winters and hot summers. The greater size of the Iranian landmass and the consequently greater distance from the moderating influence of the sea makes the climate of Iran more extreme, but the general pattern is the same. Heavy snow makes travel difficult in winter, and the high mountain passes are frequently blocked. In Armenia the bitter winters have traditionally brought most outdoor activities to a halt, while the population of the mountains wait for spring. On 7 May 1990 I came across a snow-plough team in the mountains south of Lake Van who expected another week's work before they could open the road through to an isolated valley for the first time that year. By contrast in summer, in some areas, and especially for large armies, travel can present problems of water shortage. Drought is a frequent threat. In prehistoric times there were many more trees on the plateaux, but millennia of over-grazing had created the present rather bleak landscape long before the middle ages. Even today in both Anatolia and Iran many peasant households on the plateaux still heat their houses with cakes of dried dung in the absence of wood, as their ancestors have done for centuries.[8]

Iran is more open to the nomad world of the steppes than

Anatolia. Beyond Khorasan to the north-east are the steppes of Turkestan, and there is also a large and important area of grassland in Azerbaidjan, facing the Caspian south of the Caucasus, which stands in relation to Iran and Armenia rather as does the Hungarian plain to the Balkans. Azerbaidjan has formed a base from which various nomad powers have been able to dominate Iranian politics, but attempts to dominate the Near East from here have ended in failure. Nomads have been an important factor in Anatolia from the Turkish invasions in the eleventh century through to the settlement programmes of the last century and a half; in Iran the relationship is older and continues to the present day; but neither plateau can provide the expanses of pasture necessary to maintain a great nomad power.[9]

Travelling through Anatolia or Iran in high summer can easily give the impression that these plateaux are little more than semi-desert. This would be mistaken, or at least a serious exaggeration. Large areas of Iran and a rather smaller part of the centre of Anatolia are extremely arid and bleak, and mile after mile of bare rock and scrub can be a characteristic feature of the landscape. However in spring both plateaux look very different, presenting a scene of bright green grass and luxuriant wild flowers, and it is worth remembering that throughout the early middle ages the majority of the population of Anatolia and Iran made a living as peasant farmers. However, it is equally easy to exaggerate the agricultural resources these plateaux represent. Both contain basins of fertile agricultural land – for example, those around Ikonion (modern Konya), Melitene (modern Eski Malatya or Battalgazi), and Kaisareia (modern Kayseri) in Anatolia, and those of Isfahān, Shiraz, Yazd and Kirman in Iran – but even so neither plateau is one of the key agricultural zones of the Near East. What the modern traveller sees is distorted by the revolution wrought on rural life in the mid-twentieth century by tractors and fertilisers; in the past farming these regions has often amounted to a precarious living. Drought and consequent famine is a persistent theme in the historical sources. Historians have frequently referred to Anatolia and Iran as 'the heartlands' of the Byzantine and Persian empires respectively, yet if that phrase gives an impression of a natural agricultural wealth which underpinned imperial power, then it is misleading. Anatolia and Iran have traditionally been little more than agriculturally self-sufficient; the resources to support an empire had to come from elsewhere.

The Agricultural Plains

In both Asia Minor and Iran the naturally fertile regions lie away from the central plateaux and towards the sea. In the west of Asia Minor facing the Aegean Sea are the great alluvial valleys of the Hermos, the Kayster and the Maeander (or Menderes), proverbial since Croesus in the sixth century BC for wealth. The Hellenistic and Roman ruins in this region are evidence of the prosperity of what was one of the richest provinces in the Roman empire, and any modern tourist visiting these sites can see in the surrounding fields of fruits, vegetables and cereals, the source of the wealth which paid for them. The same applies on only a slightly lesser scale to the plains of eastern Thrace and Bithynia which surround the Sea of Marmara, and to the plains of Pamphylia and Cilicia on Asia Minor's southern shore. To the north, facing the Black Sea, the coastal plain is no more than a thin strip, but it has supported a string of ancient cities, and its eastern part, in Pontos, was the base for the later medieval empire of Trebizond.

The most obvious equivalent for the Iranian plateau are the lowlands facing the Caspian. The peculiar natural conditions created by the low level of the Caspian Sea (28 metres below normal sea level elsewhere), and the high mountains of the Elburz range immediately to the south, produce along much of this coast a hot-house climate of steamy heat very favourable to agriculture. To this day the Caspian lowlands are the most densely populated region of Iran. By contrast, Iran's southern coast between the Zagros and the Persian Gulf is a narrow strip with a harsh climate less favourable to agriculture than the plateau itself. The coast is sparsely populated, and centres have grown to exploit the sea rather than the arid land.

In relation to the Iranian plateau, therefore, the role of the Aegean and Marmara coastlands in Asia Minor is filled not so much by the Caspian lowlands, and certainly not by the strip along the Persian Gulf, but by Iraq – Mesopotamia: the land between the two great rivers of the Tigris and the Euphrates. This in turn takes us out of the zone of plateaux and mountains, and into a different bloc in the geographical structure of the Near East.

South of the plateaux is the zone of the 'Fertile Crescent', beyond which lies the great Syrian and Arabian deserts. The Fertile Crescent stretches up the Nile through Egypt, north via Palestine, the Lebanon and Syria, to the plains of northern Syria (the *Djazīra*) which border the mountains of Anatolia and Armenia, and thence turn south, following the Tigris and Euphrates through Iraq to the Persian Gulf. The concept of the Fertile Crescent is a useful geographical shorthand. Although these lands certainly share a potential for agriculture – in dramatic contrast with the barren wastes of the desert beyond – it is equally important to draw the distinction within the lands of the Fertile Crescent between those areas where there is sufficient rain to make farming possible, and those where agriculture must depend on irrigation. The crucial factor is the course of the 200-millimetre isohyere. Within this notional line more than 200 millimetres of rain or snow falls a year. From 200 to 400 millimetres per annum is a dry climate but agriculture is still quite possible. Below this point irrigation is essential. Amongst the lands of the Fertile Crescent, much of Palestine, Transjordan, Syria and Upper Mesopotamia lie within the 200-millimetre isohyere; indeed substantial parts receive more than 400-millimetres per annum. However, both Egypt and Lower Mesopotamia lie outside the line. Were it not for enormous human effort harnessing the waters of the Nile, and the Tigris and Euphrates to irrigate huge areas of crops, these regions would both be desert. If, as did occur in Lower Mesopotamia after the ninth century, the irrigation system breaks down, then agriculture will collapse; but if the system is maintained then these two major areas of irrigation agriculture are by far the most fertile and productive regions of the Near East. The other parts of the Fertile Crescent where rainfall agriculture is possible constitute a very important agricultural resource, but they are of secondary importance when compared with the potential wealth of Egypt and Iraq.[10]

Any visitor to Egypt is bound to be struck by the proximity

of the narrow green strip of the Nile valley to the desert. A few kilometres walk takes one out of the fields and into barren wastes. In Transjordan and Syria the transition is less abrupt, but within 40 kilometres to the east of both Amman and Damascus the desert begins, and it can easily be raining and misty in the mountains of Lebanon or the hills of Transjordan while so short a distance to the east the desert remains hot and parched.

The Desert

In area the Fertile Crescent is dwarfed by the huge expanses of the desert. It is over 2000 kilometres from the fields of northern Syria to the fertile lands of Yemen in the south-western corner of the Arabian peninsula. With the principal exceptions of the *Nafūd* in north central Arabia, and the vast *Rub'al-Khālī* – 'the Empty Quarter' – in the south-east, the desert is not an undifferentiated sea of sand. The greater part can more accurately be described in strict geographical terms as semi-desert or arid steppe: bleak plains of gravel and rock, patchily covered with drought-resistant shrubs, and when the rain falls grasses and wild flowers. There are also a number of important oases around which it is possible to cultivate limited areas of cereals and dates. Yet the fact remains that the desert is an extremely harsh environment. It is also in terms of the settled world isolated. The northern sections of the desert between Syria and Palestine to the west and Iraq to the east are crossed by routes carrying armies and traders, but to the south the vast Arabian peninsula is easily bypassed by sea. Before the rise of Mecca as the pilgrim centre of the Islamic world brought outsiders into the desert, travellers from the Fertile Crescent would have had little or no reason to go there.[11] Until the discovery of oil transformed its potential, the population of the desert was bound to be few in number and very poor.

Despite this isolation and poverty the desert was a region of considerable strategic importance. Like the Eurasian steppes to the north, what concerned the states of the outside world was not the territory as such, but rather the people who lived there, and in particular the martial qualities which were a factor both in their ability to survive in this hostile environment and in their contacts with their neighbours. The population of the desert was homogeneous in the sense that it was wholly tribal and shared a common culture and language. They were the *bedouin*, the Arab inhabitants of the desert. However, contrary to the popular image, not all bedouin were nomadic camel herders. Survival in the desert required the use of all available resources, and probably as many bedouin were settled oasis dwellers as nomads. Apart from camels, the bedouin also kept sheep and where possible horses, a highly prized animal in this culture. The bedouin characteristially keep a number of options open. Individual bedouin may spend part of their year as nomads, part as farmers and part as warriors – all potentially profitable occupations. At one level this was a self-sufficient society, where the oasis dwellers could provide the agricultural produce and artefacts the nomads could not produce; however at the same time, the poverty of their own environment and the wealth of their neighbours, created fundamental ties which bound the bedouin, however he made his living, into the world of the Fertile Crescent.[12]

One tie was formed by the demands of the bedouin pastoral economy. As with the nomads of the steppe, the bedouin did not simply wander aimlessly, but were rather bound to a strict seasonal calender and a limited range of geographical options. The desert generally receives much less than 200 millimetres of rain a year, which will fall in some areas and not in others, varying from year to year. In the spring when the desert produces its very limited vegetation, the bedouin will move their animals in search of grazing. As summer advances the vegetation will disappear, and the bedouin again have to move. In many parts of the Arabian peninsula the oases provide the water supply necessary to survive, but over the desert as a whole it is an attractive option for the bedouin to take their animals on to the edge of what is in effect the greatest oasis of them all, the Fertile Crescent. This brings them into territories that are also attractive to settled farmers. In theory, and to an extent in practice, the interests of the nomads and the settled are complementary. The bedouin should only move into the Fertile Crescent when the crops have been harvested, and their flocks can graze on the stubble while at the same time manuring the fields for next year's crop. The bedouin need to buy grain, dates, weapons and tools from the settled communities, and in exchange they can provide meat, milk, hides, and the animals themselves. Indeed as from the third/fourth century AD onwards the Arabian camel became increasingly the major means of carriage throughout the Near East (save on the plateaux where the camels could not endure the climate) the camel-herding bedouin became an essential part of the regional economy. However, the successful practice of this relationship had distinct limits. Above all the climate could not be relied upon. Throughout the Near East the lives of both settled farmers and nomads would naturally be effected by a drought, but for the bedouin trying to exploit an area so marginal for human survival as the desert even a year only slightly drier than usual could force them to find grazing elsewhere, and the settled farmers would be faced with the bedouin moving on to their growing crops. Even in the wetter years relations were rarely smooth. The bedouin enjoyed raiding: to take part in a raid was an important rite of passage for a young man, and compared to the precarious struggle for survival in the desert it could offer easy and substantial profits. It was also fun. With the advantage of the developed camel saddle during the Roman period the camel-herding bedouin had a supply of highly effective mounts for desert raiding. A state of permanent peace would have been foreign to the culture and economy of bedouin society.[13]

The importance of this aspect of the relationship was, however, quite limited. Isolated bedouin raiding seems never to have presented a very serious political or economic threat to the settled communities of the Fertile Crescent. Like droughts and locusts, bedouin were another pest of the agricultural year which centuries of medieval peasants have been able to surmount. Moreover, while camels were excellent beasts for raiding, the horse was the key animal in serious warfare. The settled oasis dwellers had as many, if not more, horses than the nomads. The genuine military potential of Arab tribal society should not be confused with the endemic, but strategically relatively insignificant practice of raiding.[14]

Much more fundamental were the ties created by the fact

that, unlike the steppes, the desert did not provide sufficient resources to support the creation of a state. Outside areas such as the Yemen, known as Arabia Felix to the Romans, which receives sufficient rain for agriculture from the monsoon, and was placed to exploit the spice trade between India and the Mediterranean, pre-oil Arabia is a classic example of a stateless society. The tribe – and all desert Arabs were members of a tribe – was a hierarchical organisation headed at each level by a sheikh. However, in the desert such men had in effect only a primacy of honour, and their power to coerce lesser tribesmen was very limited. Consequently so too was the impact such a fragmentary society could make on the powerful and well-organised states of the Fertile Crescent.

The basis for the creation of a state does exist in desert society. Either drawing upon the influence of a charismatic religious leader, or harnessing the economic power of one of the larger oases, it has been possible to create tribal confederations whose leaders have the power to coerce their subordinate tribesmen. Over the last two thousand years northern and central Arabia has been periodically dominated by various such tribal groupings. However, as long as they were confined to the desert such confederations have proved to be transitory. The inherent logic of the desert environment undermines any central authority. The desert does not produce sufficient pasture to support large groups brought together for any length of time. To avoid over-grazing the bedouin are naturally divided into small groups each competing for scarce resources. Mounted on camels they are mobile and difficult to discipline. For the individual tribe feud and dissension is a part of normal life; for the larger confederation this is even more so, and the desert of its own does not provide the surplus which would enable higher authority, even one drawing on the resources of one of the larger oases, to impose its will. The only way out was to find an external source of wealth to reward followers and create a military force bound to its leader by non-tribal ties. That in effect either meant conquering part of the Fertile Crescent for oneself, or persuading one of the settled states to accept the Arab state as a client to be subsidised or granted territory. It is therefore not surprising that many Arab states have not originated in the desert at all, but instead on the margins of the Fertile Crescent. In either case, whether used directly or indirectly, the only asset the world of the desert had to achieve unity and wealth was its military ability.

Like steppe nomads, the bedouin needed the settled world to survive in a way that the self-sufficient settled world did not need them. At some periods the states of the Fertile Crescent have been able to ignore the bedouin, at others their military potential, built upon a culture which highly prized skill at arms and horsemanship, was able to demand attention. One such period was the third century AD when the rulers of the Syrian city of Palmyra built up a state on the northern edge of the desert. The considerable wealth and power of Palmyra was derived from the profits of trade on the route between Syria and Iraq, and oasis agriculture. The prosperity of the state enabled its rulers to form alliances with the desert tribes. Palmyra became a Roman client-kingdom, but in 270, at the height of the empire's third-century crisis, Queen Zenobia turned the Palmyran cavalry against Rome. In 275 she was defeated and Palmyra sacked, but only after a series of Arab triumphs which had for a short period overthrown Roman rule in Syria, Palestine and Egypt itself – the whole episode was a precedent for another such period: the seventh century and the rise of Islam.[15]

Conclusion: a Strategic Geography

Reviewing this sweeping survey of the geography of the Near East two key factors stand out. The first is that up until the discovery of oil – and to a large extent even then – any state of more than merely regional significance had to be based on control of one or more of the principal agricultural zones. Trade might make a useful contribution to a state's revenues, but only agriculture could provide the resources to support a major political power. (For example, figures for the Ottoman empire in the early seventeenth century suggest that between 63 per cent and 94 per cent of total revenue came from the land tax, compared with between 4 per cent and 6 per cent from customs.)[16] Any state with wider pretensions would have to control several of these zones, and any lasting hegemony was probably impossible without the resources of either Egypt or, until the ninth century, Iraq. The significance of the various zones has not remained constant. In particular the collapse of large-scale irrigation agriculture in Lower Mesopotamia after the ninth century, and the retreat of settled agriculture in the Fertile Crescent between the middle ages and the nineteenth century altered important elements in the equation, but the basis of the approach remains valid, and is as applicable to the Ottoman empire as to the empires of the ancient world. It is also applicable to the Near East between 600 and 1025.

The second factor concerns the steppe and the desert. To north and south the settled states of the Near East faced regions that were of little obvious value. Their inhabitants needed the settled world far more than the latter needed them, but even so they presented a potential threat which could overturn the calculations of emperors and caliphs. The settled states could neither ignore nor conquer their neighbours; instead they were forced to a variety of partial solutions. Depending upon the balance of power, relations veered between alliances, the creation of client states, and outright hostility.

The overall strategic picture is therefore one of competition between states for the control of key agricultural zones, carried on at the same time as a constant additional theme of relations between the settled Near Eastern states and the peoples of the desert and the steppe. It is a picture that could be applied to other periods, before and after the early middle ages, but for the Byzantine empire between 600 and 1025 it provides an important context within which the fortunes of the state ruled from Constantinople can be analysed.

3. The Roman World in 600

The Strategic Outlook

IN THE YEAR 600 the Roman empire still included substantial territories in the central and western Mediterranean. In 533 Justinian had sent an expeditionary force to Africa under the command of Belisarios which reconquered the Vandal kingdom with its capital at Carthage. In 535 Belisarios had invaded Sicily and the following year begun the conquest of Italy. The Ostrogothic kingdom of Italy at first looked as if it would collapse as speedily as had its Vandal neighbour, but in fact Roman forces did not subdue the last Gothic stronghold until 561. Roman control of the whole of Italy proved short-lived, because in 568 the Lombards invaded from the Hungarian plain and rapidly occupied much of the Po valley in northern Italy, and the districts around Spoleto and Benevento in the centre and south respectively. By 600 it was probably clear that the Lombards were in Italy to stay, but the greater part of the peninsula was still in Roman hands. The Lombards had been ejected from much of the rich Po valley by a combined Roman–Frankish offensive in 590, and the key fortress city and former capital of the western Roman empire in the fifth century, Ravenna, was still Roman too. Further south, a block of imperial territory linked Ravenna to Rome, and extended south of the city to include Naples, Calabria, much of Apulia and the wealthy island of Sicily. Beyond Italy and Africa, Justinian's armies had occupied the islands of Corsica and Sardinia, and a coastal strip of south-eastern Spain centred on the port city of Cartagena. These were still imperial territory in 600.

It is almost certainly a mistake to see the western territories as simply an expensive handicap for the empire. Sicily and Africa were wealthy provinces which after their initial conquest (including in the case of Africa the suppression of the Moorish revolt) should at least have paid for themselves. In Spain and the western Mediterranean islands the Roman commitment was too small to represent a serious burden. In Italy the damage done by over twenty years' war of conquest, followed by the

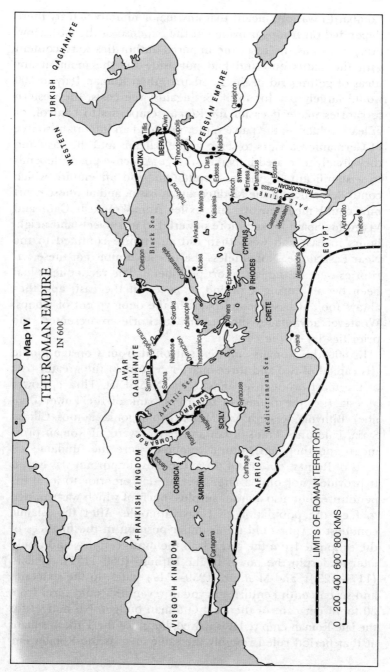

Map IV

THE ROMAN EMPIRE
IN 600

WESTERN TURKISH QAGHANATE

TURKISH QAGHANATE

PERSIAN EMPIRE

Tiflis
Dwin
IBERIA
LAZIKA
Theodosiupolis
Trapezous
Dara
Edessa
Nisibis
Ctesiphon
Melitene
Kaisareia
Antioch
SYRIA
Emesa
Damascus
Bostra
TRANSJORDAN
Gerasa
PALESTINE
Caesarea
Jerusalem
Ankara
Nicaea
Constantinople
Chalcedon
Ephesos
CYPRUS
Athens
RHODES
CRETE
Alexandria
EGYPT
Aphrodito
Thebes
Cyrene

Black Sea

Cherson

Sirmium
Singidunum
Sardika
Naissos
AVAR
QAGHANATE
Salona
Adrianople
Dyrrachion
Thessalonica

Adriatic Sea

FRANKISH KINGDOM

Genoa
LOMBARDS
Rome
LOMBARDS
Naples
SICILY
Syracuse

Mediterranean Sea

CORSICA
SARDINIA

VISIGOTH KINGDOM

Cartagena

Carthage

AFRICA

0 200 400 600 800 KMS

LIMITS OF ROMAN TERRITORY

Lombard invasion, meant that any major military activity there depended on troops provided at the expense of the east. However, if, as was the case, the imperial authorities were content with the status quo and had put aside for the moment any ideas of getting rid of the Lombards, then Roman Italy in 600 would largely pay for itself. Set against the costs, the western territories made it easier for Roman emperors to control, or at least influence, the papacy; they provided an important source of Germanic warriors to serve in the Balkans and the east; and they greatly increased imperial prestige. Effective power depends to a significant degree on reputation, and an empire which controlled much of the Mediterranean basin, and at whose court one could meet envoys and exiles from Frankish Gaul and Visigothic Spain looked more powerful to its subjects and neighbours in east and west, than did an empire confined to the Near East alone. Nonetheless there is no doubt that these territories were in the last resort peripheral. The reconquests had been begun during a period of peace in the east, and they always took at best second place in the deployment of troops. Whatever advantages the western territories represented, the priorities lay to the east.

In 600 the Roman empire controlled from Constantinople (its capital of two and three-quarter centuries) the greater part of the most productive lands in the Near East. Thrace, Lower Moesia (i.e. the plains on the right bank of the Lower Danube), Bithynia, western Asia Minor, Paphlagonia, Pontos, Cilicia, Syria, Palestine, Transjordan and Egypt, were all Roman provinces, and their agricultural resources were the fundamental basis of Roman power. Of these the most important was Egypt. It provided not only a large revenue far superior to local expenditure, but also a grain surplus much of which was shipped to feed the population of Constantinople. After the Islamic conquest Egypt would fill a similar position in the finances of the caliphate from the seventh to the ninth century, and would later underpin the power of the Fātimid (969–1171), Ayyūbid (1171–1250), and Mamlūk (1250–1517) states. In the sixteenth and seventeenth centuries Egyptian revenues would form from 30 to 40 per cent of the total Ottoman budget. No budget for the late Roman empire has survived, but since the Turkish sultans at that period ruled roughly the same area as the Roman em-

perors in the sixth century, one can with some caution suggest
that it was of comparable importance to the Roman empire in
600.[1]

The only rival the Roman empire faced was the Sasanian
empire of Persia, which since the third century AD had ruled
in Iraq the only other region of the Near East with a comparable agricultural output to that of Egypt. In addition the
Sasanians controlled the fertile Caspian coastlands, Khorasan,
and the Iranian plateau.

The superpower rivalry between Rome and Persia is one of
the major themes in the history of the pre-Islamic Near East.
In the first three centuries AD the relationship had been shaped
by Roman aggression, and the growing impotence of the later
Parthian empire in the face of Roman attacks was an important factor in its replacement by the Sasanian dynasty in the
third century. A phase of frequent warfare had come to an
end in 363 when the disastrous defeat of the emperor Julian's
attempt to conquer Iraq, and consequent territorial concessions by the Romans, convinced Roman policymakers that for
the time being at least a Roman conquest was not a realistic
objective. During the fifth century both empires had been preoccupied by other enemies to their west and east respectively.
Both in fact were faced by a more pressing threat posed by
steppe nomads: the Romans were struggling with the direct
and indirect consequences of the Hun invasions; the Persians
waging war with first the Kidarites and then the Hepthalites.
In the sixth century the two returned to confrontation, and a
succession of wars. Rome and Persia fought each other from
502 to 505, from 527 to 532, from 540 to 562, and from 572 to
590, with a short truce in 574 and 575. Outside these major
wars unofficial conflicts were waged by local forces in Armenia
and between the superpowers' Arab clients on the edge of the
Fertile Crescent. Even at moments of apparent peace the diplomatic atmosphere was one of tension, suspicion and mistrust.

In trying to assess the outlook for the Roman empire in 600
it is worth separating the long- and short-term prospects. Taking the hostilities of 502–90 as a whole, the Persians had been
able to inflict some outstanding defeats on the Romans, but
they had notably failed to achieve any significant permanent
gains. The sack of Antioch in 540 and the loss of the great

frontier fortress of Dara in 573 – which contemporaries believed to have sent Justin II mad – accompanied in both years
by widespread Persian ravaging, and the extortion of huge sums
from the threatened cities of Roman Mesopotamia, were serious blows to the Romans, but on each occasion Roman armies
soon managed to re-establish the status quo, and repay the
damage by counter-strokes into Persian territory. On the central front between Syria and Iraq, where the two empires faced
each other across the Mesopotamian plain, dotted with heavily
fortified cities, fortresses and forts, despite various alarms, the
frontier in 590 stood almost where it had done in 502. Events
to the north, in Armenia, similarly favoured the Romans. A
major attempt by the Persians to conquer the Roman client-
kingdom of Lazika, on the Georgian coast of the Black Sea,
came to nothing after early successes; and although one should
not exaggerate the control Roman administrators could effect
on the hill-peoples of Armenia and Georgia, these years saw a
steady and significant consolidation of the Roman position.

Two factors behind Roman success in the long term stand
out. One lies in the military ability of the Roman army. The
evidence is scattered, but careful reading of the accounts of
Roman military operations given by the sixth- and early seventh-century historians – Procopius, Agathias, Menander and
Theophylact Simocatta – together with the *Strategikon* (a late
sixth-century handbook on the Roman army attributed to the
emperor Maurice) combine to give a clear picture of a relatively professional and well-motivated force.[2]

A second was Christianity. Ever since Edward Gibbon in the
eighteenth century it has been usual for historians to stress
the importance of the divisions between Chalcedonian and
Monophysite Christians in creating a fundamental weakness in
the late sixth-century empire. The split concerned differing views
of the relationship between the human and divine in the person of Christ. The argument was carried on in terms derived
from Greek philosophy. Chalcedonians accepted the 'two nature
in one person' creed formulated at the Council of Chalcedon.
Those who rejected this formulation were 'accused of merging
the human and divine in one nature and have come (unfairly
for the most part) to be known as 'Monophysites', from the
Greek *monos*, 'one', and *physis*, 'nature'. Both groups consid-

ered themselves orthodox, and their rivals heretical. Whereas in the west the only patriarchal see was Rome, in the east Alexandria, Antioch, Constantinople and Jerusalem all held this rank, and were potential sources of theological doctrine, and in part the division between Chalcedonians and Monophysites reflects a battle between the major centres of the eastern church to be accepted as the true source of orthodoxy.

The last Monophysite emperor had been Anastasios who had died in 518. Since then all his successors had been Chalcedonians, and Chalcedonian 'two-nature' doctrine had been the official orthodoxy of the empire. The association was such that by the mid-sixth century Chalcedonians were commonly known as Melkites, from a semitic word, *malik*, meaning king or emperor. The Chalcedonians were, not surprisingly, strong in Constantinople, as well as in Asia Minor, southern and western Syria and Palestine. The Council of Chalcedon was also accepted without question by the papacy and its followers in the west. The major centres of Monophysite support were Egypt and northern and eastern Syria. Persian Armenia was also a centre of Monophysite Christianity. In most assessments of the state of the Roman world in 600 it would be usual to draw attention to this geographical and political division as a fundamental flaw.

Historians take this line because of the nature of the sources. Much of what we know about the Monophysite community comes from the contemporary writings of their leaders, especially John of Ephesos, who was evidently trying to present a picture of a righteous community, bearing comparison with the heroic days of the early church, holding fast to the truth while persecuted by its enemies. It would have made neither ideological nor literary sense to portray relations with the Chalcedonians as anything other than unremitting conflict. Otherwise we depend on much later authors, such as Sawīrus (Severus) ibn al-Makaffa in the tenth century, Michael the Syrian in the twelfth century or Bar Hebraeus in the thirteenth. For these authors a major part of what defined their communities in Egypt and Syria after several centuries of Islamic rule, was their consciousness of unwavering orthodoxy as against Chalcedonian heresy. Part of their very purpose in writing history was to give historical depth to their conflict with Chalcedon, and to portray themselves as a worthy martyr's church. Accordingly when they came to describe the distant past of the sixth century they inevitably gave a picture of unremitting hostility between the two creeds.[3]

Yet there is other non-polemic material, and it gives a different picture. Imperial religious policy always took it for granted that the Monophysites were natural members of the orthodox community. To achieve unity the emperors tried a mixture of persuasion, compromise and persecution, but when compared with campaigns against the Jews and Samaritans, imperial persecution of the Monophysites was only half-hearted. That organised by the emperor Maurice was sufficiently unmemorable for him to become the subject of a Monophysite saint's life.[4] The force used was limited, and no legal penalties, such as a ban on receiving inheritances, were imposed. In return the Monophysites appear as loyal subjects of the empire. There are no cases where contemporaries thought that Monophysites had betrayed a Roman city to the Persians. Instead throughout the series of sixth-century wars the Monophysite districts of eastern Syria provided a resolute bulwark to the empire. Indeed the mountainous district of the Tūr Abdīn on this frontier can be said to be famous for two things: its devotion to its Monophysite monks, and its combined loyalty to the Roman empire and hostility to the Persians.[5]

A more representative picture of Chalcedonian–Monophysite relations, and their place in sixth-century Roman culture, is also emerging from Egypt, where the exceptional papyrus documentation allows one a contemporary view of what mattered to sixth-century Egyptians rather than one filtered through much later sectarian polemic. One individual about whom sufficient material has survived to give a picture of his world is Dioskoros, who has been the subject of a recent study. He was a lawyer, poet and a member of the local élite of Aphrodito, a city in the middle Nile valley, 500 kilometres south of the Mediterranean. Three aspects of Dioskoros' world stand out in his writings. Firstly he saw himself as a Roman. He wrote sophisticated Greek poetry in a style typical of the late Roman educated élite anywhere in the Near East. He was aware of events in the imperial capital in Constantinople, which he had visited on the business of his home city and saw its politics as part of his world. In 565 he wrote a Greek panegyric to celebrate Justin II's accession. Secondly Dioskoros was an Egyptian. He wrote legal documents written for the local clergy in Coptic, and his writings in both languages are filled with the details of local life. His Romanitas did not effect the fact that he was one of an Egyptian local élite, deeply rooted in the society and culture of his native land. Thirdly, Dioskoros was a Christian, Sixth-century Egypt was a fundamentally Christian culture and this pervades his writings. Yet nowhere does he make clear whether he was a Monophysite or a Chalcedonian. Given his close identification with local Egyptian society, and the fact that Aphrodito lay in the heartland of Coptic Monophysite Egypt, he was almost certainly a Monophysite, but plainly this meant no more than he was an orthodox Christian by the lights of his community. Certainly Dioskoros gives no sign of a fundamental split between Egyptian Monophysites and imperialist Chalcedonians; much more striking is the way Aphrodito, its culture and its local concerns were bound into the wider Roman empire and linked to the imperial capital over 1500 kilometres to the north.[6]

In fact it can be argued that the ties between Constantinople and Aphrodito were stronger than those between Constantinople and Rome. Despite their shared faith in the Council of Chalcedon a division was opening up between the papacy and the eastern church. It is symptomatic of their relations that the great issue which preoccupied the eastern church, the relationship of the human and divine in Christ, attracted very little interest in the west; whereas the papal battle against the heretic Arians, represented in 600 by the Visigothic kingdom of Spain and the Lombards in Italy, was generally disregarded in the east. Given what has already been said about Roman territories in the west not being an imperial priority in Constantinople, one can see the basis for both a cultural and a political parting of the ways.

Within the Near East, however, Christianity was a powerful unifying factor which transcended the Chalcedonian–Monophysite dispute. Whereas Zoroastrianism, the state religion of Persia, was an exclusive ethnic cult of the Iranian warrior nobility, Christianity was an inclusive cult which provided the Roman provinces of the Near East with an identity which united believers and excluded non-believers. Some of the non-believers were themselves Roman provincials, such as

Jews, Samaritans, and pagans; but increasingly, as the empire became more thoroughly Christian in the fourth, fifth and sixth centuries, the majority of non-believers lay outside the empire. Encouraged by assiduous imperial propaganda, it was hardly suprising that by the sixth century the empire was seen as the quintessential Christian state, and that the identity of Christians and Romans had tended to merge, to the considerable advantage of the Roman state.

The nature of this achievement deserves stressing. The Roman Near East was made up of a wide variety of cultural and ethnic groups. By 600 the sense of being Romans and Christians was well on the way to turning the region into a cultural bloc in its own right coinciding with the political bounds of the empire. As such, the process bears comparison with that which transformed the Chinese empire from a similar empire of military conquest to the China that still exists today.

The association between the Christian church and the Roman state was not of course complete. Conflicts between church and state were perhaps inevitable, but much more important, the extension of Christendom beyond the boundaries of the empire brought considerable diplomatic bonuses. Unlike Zoroastrianism, Christianity was exportable, and the Zoroastrian magi looked with alarm as members even of the Iranian nobility converted to the Roman religion. In the sixth century there was a large and growing Christian community in Persian Iraq and Mesopotamia; the Persians' principal Arab allies were Monophysite Christians and for much of the century south Arabia had been in pro-Roman Christian hands; Persian Armenia was also solidly Monophysite. In Iraq Roman attempts to pose as the natural protector of all Christians were rendered less effective by the fact that the majority of Persian Christians were Nestorians – that is Christians who adhered to a variant of two-nature Christology that had been declared heretical in 431 and was regarded as beyond the pale by both Monophysites and Chalcedonians. The Nestorian church was heavily influenced by Persian culture and was loyal to the Sasanian shahs. Even so the Zoroastrian magi in effect supported Roman pretensions when in time of war they persecuted the Nestorian church. Among the Arabs and Armenians Roman diplomacy could operate to much greater effect. Above all in Armenia, Persian anti-Christian persecution created pro-Roman sentiment and actual rebellion which the Romans could exploit.[7]

Finally Christianity was a useful morale booster. The sense that God and his saints would protect Christians fighting the wicked pagans not only provided a common cause for soldiers serving in the Roman army – reflected in the blessing of banners and in the *trisagion* chanted by Roman troops morning and evening, and before going into action – but also stiffened the resistance of the empire's cities in the face of Persian attack.[8]

If the long-term Roman position in the Near East appeared generally secure, the ten years from 590 to 600 brought about a remarkable further improvement. In 589 the Romans had been at war with the Persians since 572. After a disastrous start, culminating in the loss of Dara, the Romans had recovered, so that in 589, despite the betrayal to the Persians of the important Mesopotamian city of Martyropolis in the spring, their forces appeared to hold the initiative. During the winter the Romans besieged Martyropolis, but events there were overtaken by a dramatic political crisis inside the Persian empire. Vahram, a Persian general fresh from successes against the Turks in the east, and now commanding the Persian army in Armenia and Azerbaidjan, revolted. This provoked a palace coup in the Persian capital, Ctesiphon, in Iraq, and the Shah, Hormizd, was deposed and killed. His son, Khusro II, was put in his place on the throne, but Vahram continued his march on the capital. Khusro tried to confront Vahram outside Ctesiphon, but his support dissolved and in desperation he fled to find refuge in the Roman empire, leaving Vahram to be crowned shah.

The appearance of Khusro in the empire asking for help divided opinion at the Roman court. Many evidently thought that a Persian civil war was a blessing of which they should take advantage, and the longer it continued the better; but in the event the emperor Maurice decided to back Khusro as the legitimate shah and use Roman arms to restore him to the Persian throne. Khusro may have helped his cause by dropping hints that he might convert to Christianity, but there was no question of a written statement to this effect, and no reason to think that he ever meant this seriously. His most public association with Christianity was in January 591 when he appealed to St Sergios at his great Monophysite shrine at Resāfa

(Sergioupolis). Possibly he did want the saint's help, but it also made a useful propaganda point, and encouraged Roman hopes of a Christian shah.

In the summer of 591 Khusro returned to Persia at the head of a Roman army. The decisive battle was fought in Azerbaidjan. Vahram was defeated, and Khusro restored to the Persian throne. The peace treaty which followed, bringing the Roman–Persian war to an end, was Maurice's reward. The Romans not only recovered Dara and Martyropolis, but also Arzanene (which was the section of the upper Mesopotamian plain north of the Tūr Abdīn and east of the Batman river), Iberia (which now makes up the central district of modern Georgia west of Tiflis) and most of Persian Armenia, so that the Araxes valley to within a few miles of Dwin (the Persian capital of Armenia) and the northern and western shores of Lake Van were now in Roman hands.[9]

This was a major territorial advance in itself, but more important the prospect of a lasting peace with Persia offered the opportunity to deploy Roman troops elsewhere. Throughout the sixth century it had been clear that in order to contain Persian attacks it was essential to deploy the bulk of Roman military resources in the east. Justinian's western offensive had only been possible during a period of peace with Persia, and once war restarted the Balkans, Italy and Africa had to make do with the limited forces that were left.

The effect this had on Italy was discussed at the beginning of this chapter, and the situation in the Balkans was comparable. For most of the sixth century Roman policy in the Balkans depended on a combination of diplomacy with the minimum deployment of military force, the major expenditure appearing to have gone on fortifications. This did not stop devastating raids by the Slavs and by two nomad peoples from the Ukrainian steppe, the Kutrigurs and Utigurs, but it made possible a certain level of security while the Roman field army was used elsewhere. Key to this policy was the existence of two Germanic states north of the Danube – the Lombards in Pannonia and the Gepids in the Hungarian plain – whom Roman diplomats could play off against each other.[10] Unfortunately for the Romans this arrangement was destroyed by the arrival of the Avars, who were a well-organised steppe-nomad state, ruled by a qaghan, and with a formidable military reputation. When the Avars first appeared in the Ukrainian steppe in the late 550s the Romans saw them as a useful addition to their northern neighbours. The Avars could be used to control the Kutrigurs and Utigurs, and they could be played off against the Gepids and Lombards. The following years proved this to be a serious miscalculation. The Avars first conquered the Kutrigurs and Utigurs, as well as other groups on the Ukrainian steppe, and then in 567 in alliance with the Lombards they destroyed the Gepids and occupied the Hungarian plain. Since the Lombards themselves were likely to be the Avars' next victims, they migrated into Italy the following year, leaving the Romans to face a single power dominating the whole of the empire's frontier north of the Balkans.

The direct consequences of this were bad enough. Through the 570s, despite the absence of major Roman forces due to the renewal of war with the Persians in 572, the Avar impact was limited by their lack of a bridgehead over the Danube, but it was only a temporary delay. In 581–2 the Avars captured Sirmium on the Sava river, the major Roman fortress in the north-west Balkans, and with it a way across the Danube. For the rest of the decade the Balkan plains, Thrace above all, were open to devastating Avar attack.

Yet arguably the indirect consequences were worse. Since the early sixth century the plains between the Lower Danube and the Carpathians – Oltenia and Wallachia – had been occupied by the Slavs. Unlike their neighbours, the Slavs were not a united people. They generally operated in small groups based on the extended family, although they could unite into larger groups under temporary leaders in time of war. The stateless nature of Slav society was a particular problem for the Romans in that it was impossible to control them by diplomacy or subsidies. Such techniques only work if there is an acknowledged leader with whom one can establish binding agreements. No one in Slav society had that kind of lasting authority. Their material culture was relatively primitive, and they found a particular niche in the forest and marsh regions underexploited by their more sophisticated neighbours. The Slavs had been raiding the Roman Balkans throughout the sixth century, but the establishment of an aggressive Avar hegemony was a serious

threat, and to avoid this new danger from the 570s onwards
they began to migrate in search of permanent homes south of
the Danube. Datable hoards of coins (buried by Romans fleeing
for their lives), as well as the accounts of contemporary historians, reveal a dreadful twenty years for the Roman inhabitants of the Balkans.[11]

One should not exaggerate the strategic significance of this
for the Roman state. As has been said already the Balkans was
not part of the vital interests of the Roman empire. The major
centres, including Thessalonica on the Aegean coast, Dyrrachion
on the Adriatic, and Serdika (now Sofia, the site of the modern Bulgarian capital), were still in Roman hands, as was the
crucial fortified frontier region along the Lower Danube. As
in the fifth century in the face of Attila's Huns, and later in
face of the Goths, it made some sense as a use of resources, to
allow the Balkan peninsula to be a zone of defence-in-depth,
protecting Constantinople from its northern enemies. However,
in the 580s it had clearly gone beyond this. The Romans could
not accept a rival power dominating the Balkans, in part because Constantinople itself was a Balkan city. News from Greece
of the sack of Athens in 582, and worse the ravaging of the
property of Constantinopolitan citizens in nearby Thrace, was
broadcast in the city.[12] Given the imperial ideology of a victorious Christian empire, this very visible failure obviously threatened the stability of the regime.

The situation would have been particularly frustrating because, despite their quality as individual warriors, the Roman
army did not regard the Slavs as very dangerous opponents.[13]
Yet as long as war continued in the east there was little that
could be achieved. The treaty of 591 finally gave the empire
the opportunity to strike back. By 600 both Avars and Slavs
had been forced on to the defensive. In the last years of the
sixth century Roman armies were operating across the Danube
in Avar territory on the Hungarian plain, and against the Slav
settlements among the marshes of Oltenia. Looking to the future
the Avar state was showing signs that, typical of so many nomad polities, it would fragment under the pressure of military
defeat. Further attacks on the Slavs north of the Danube, especially if carried out in winter when they were less able to
escape Roman raids, might be expected to stop Slav migra-

tions from the north, after which the empire could turn to the problem of subduing and assimilating those already settled in the Balkans.[14]

With the apparent waning of Avar power in 600 the outlook on the steppe world was, from a Roman perspective, more favourable than it had been for at least a century and arguably much longer. The great steppe nomad power of the sixth century had been the Gök Türk ('Sky Turk') qaghanate which had overthrown the previous Juan-Juan rulers of Mongolia in 552. The Avars may have been the remnants of the Juan-Juan, and hence of Mongolian origin; their identity is not certain, but the Avars were certainly refugees from the rise of Turkish power which pursued them across Eurasia. By the 570s the Turks were in control of the steppes around the Volga and north of the Caucasus, and as far west as the Crimea and probably beyond. Roman relations with this steppe superpower were slightly difficult. As early as the 560s the Turks were proposing joint action against Persia, but despite an exchange of embassies this came to nothing, and Turkish westward expansion led to attacks on Roman territories in the Crimea and the Caucasus. Thus it was no loss to Roman interests when in 582 the Turkish empire split into an eastern and western Turkish qaganate. In 588 a western Turk attack on Persia was defeated by Vahram, the Persian general who seized power in 590, and the western qaghanate broke up in civil war. In 600 the western qaghan had recently professed friendship with the emperor Maurice; what threat the western Turks still represented was directed at Persia rather than the Romans.[15]

The outlook on Rome's desert frontier in 600 was equally satisfactory, and as elsewhere Maurice's reign had seen important changes to the Roman advantage. Since the third-century crisis in the face of Zenobia and Palmyra, Roman policy had passed through two phases. The first was characterised by massive expenditure on an extraordinary building programme of fortresses, forts and watchtowers stretching the whole length of the desert frontier from Syria to the northern Hidjāz. Even by the end of the fourth century it was clear that the expense of maintenance and troop deployment was not remotely justified by the threat. As the majority of these fortifications were abandoned or moth-balled, Roman policy on the desert frontier came to depend instead on Arab client confederations.[16] The power of these clients depended upon Roman subsidies and the other advantages of reliable access to the Fertile Crescent which provided the wealth to create a centralised political authority among the bedouin. With this they could dominate the desert. The relationship was obviously extremely attractive and a succession of potential clients fought for this privileged position. The Romans maintained a number of clients at any one time, but for most of the sixth century the dominant client group was the Ghassānid confederation whose leader, al-Hārith ibn Djabala (known to the Romans as Arethas), was recognised as a king and given the important court title of *patrikios* by Justinian. The Ghassānids justified imperial confidence. They served with distinction in Roman campaigns against the Persians, and on their own account shattered the rival power of the Persian Arab clients, the Lakhmids of Hīra in south-western Iraq. Their triumph, however, gave them the potential in Roman eyes for a dangerous independence, and it was surely this rather than their devotion to Monophysite theology, as sectarian sources state, that persuaded first the emperor Tiberios in 580 and then Maurice in 582–3 to break up the Ghassānid confederation. The example of the Avars, who had begun as one among a number of Roman allies on their northern frontier and had then established themselves as the sole regional power, with disastrous consequences, may even have prompted the Roman action.[17]

The end of Ghassānid supremacy allowed the Romans to subsidise a greater number of lesser allies. The most important were probably the Djudhāmids in the very north of the Hidjāz, but several others are known. Roman control over these groups was not total; in about the year 600 some un-named Roman clients went on an unofficial raid into Iraq which led to a short-lived but uncomfortable diplomatic crisis with Persia. Yet, as the evidence, which we shall look at in the second part of this chapter, for economic prosperity in the territories on the edge of the Fertile Crescent shows, the Roman empire in 600 did not have a 'bedouin problem'.[18]

The one region where Roman interests had suffered what seemed to be a lasting reverse was in far distant south Arabia and the Yemen. The area was a focus of great power competition because of its agricultural wealth (comparative to the rest of Arabia), and its trading links with India. In or about 525 the Christian Ethiopians had conquered the Yemen as Roman allies, but by the 570s they had been expelled by a Persian expedition which established a Persian governor and a local puppet king. Given the advantages of peace after 591, it would hardly have served Roman interests to have gone to war over somewhere in the last resort so peripheral.[19]

Taking all these fronts together, the strategic outlook for the Roman empire was more favourable in 600 than at any stage since at least the mid-fourth century. As at any period there were problems, but the Romans could look forward with great confidence to the future. The next major tasks for Roman arms perhaps lay in restoring full imperial control in the Balkans, and beyond that in Italy. Apart from the already alarmed Avars and Slavs, the Lombards and even the Franks and Visigoths might beware imperial intentions.

The Social and Economic Base

By the normal standards of an ancient or medieval pre-industrial state the Roman empire in 600 was wealthy and well able to support its imperial pretensions. Since the rest of this section will be taken up with the evidence for prosperity it is as well to begin by pointing out how harsh those normal standards were.

For the vast majority of the population of the Roman Near East in 600 life was uncertain and uncomfortable. To modern eyes the late Roman world had a limited technology and an even more limited control over its environment. A crucial annual concern to everybody from the emperor to the humblest peasant was the harvest. If the population was to eat and pay its taxes, and not riot in desperation, if the army was to be fed and paid, a reasonable harvest was essential. Yields were low, yet even these were at the mercy of an unpredictable climate which regularly produced winters that were too cold or too long, springs that were too wet or too dry, and summers where the rain failed entirely. A characteristic feature of late Roman society was the Christian holy men to whom all sections of the population turned for advice and help. Regularly in the lives of such saints we hear of droughts, floods and famines. When the climate was not to blame the saint might be asked to deal with locusts, crop disease, or cattle pest.[20]

When the crops failed, disease frequently followed and the population would again turn to the saints in desperation. Life expectancy was short. Infant mortality rates were high, but the study of funerary inscriptions and the few so far excavated cemeteries shows that even among those who survived childhood the majority would not see forty. A seventh-century charnel-house on Crete has revealed a malnourished population, teeth damaged by gritty bread, dying young. Even in normal years most Romans lived in insanitary conditions. Medicine was primitive, and in the face of illness and disease the efforts of doctors were worse than useless.[21]

If the harvest failed in one district while being good in another, the majority of the population could expect relief only if they lived on the coast or next to a navigable river. The rich could always find food at a price, but the poor would be likely to starve. Despite the Roman roads transport remained unsophisticated. Wheeled carts, mule trains, and camel caravans each had their advantages, but the transport of bulk goods, such as grain, by land remained prohibitively expensive and extremely slow. Even shipping was technologically limited. The Mediterranean was an easier sea than the Atlantic, but it was still dangerous. Ships available in 600 were generally not taken to sea in winter, through justifiable fear of shipwreck, and at all seasons sailors found it very difficult to make headway against the wind. The story of the emperor Maurice who was nearly drowned in the 590s making a short journey along the coast of the sea of Marmara is typical of a great number which underline the danger and unpredictability of the sea.[22]

In practice the demands of the market were constantly thwarted. Poor communications and primitive methods of production limited supply. Barring sails on ships, and water-mills for grinding corn, the only source of power was human and animal muscle. Goods were generally produced in small workshops, and their exchange was frequently hampered by shortages of coin, inadequate credit systems, arbitrary confiscations by the state, extortion by social superiors and the ravages of war.

At all levels from the imperial government to the poorest peasant late Roman society was faced by constraints for which there was no human solution. A society which turned to holymen and the 'magical' consolations of religion is often character-ised as superstitious and irrational, but clearly apart from com-plete resignation, there was under most circumstances little alternative. Man's endeavours were so frequently set at naught by forces over which he had no control that appeal to God was the obvious and intelligent positive response.

Yet in saying this, what is being presented is a set of truisms, applicable to every other pre-industrial society in the Near East. Despite attempts to see an 'agricultural revolution' in the early middle ages brought about as a consequence of the Islamic empire of the seventh century onwards bringing together differ-ent and previously isolated traditions of agricultural produc-tion, it seems on the contrary quite clear that there was no fundamental change in what has been called 'the structures of everyday life' before modern times.[23]

As with all later economies of the pre-industrial states of the Near East, the Roman economy in 600 was based upon the agricultural labour of millions of peasant farmers. Despite more than a century of scholarly effort the status of the late Roman rural population is still far from clear. We do not know what proportion were free, what proportion tied to the land by vari-ous forms of serfdom, or the relative importance of slave and wage-labour; but although important these are secondary ques-tions. Whatever the terms of tenure may have been, we can say with some confidence that over most of the Roman Near East the basis of production was peasant households farming the land in relatively small units. There is no reason to believe that large demesne estates or *latifundia* worked by serfs or slaves were a common feature of the landscape.

Legal texts, and contemporary historians, mention great es-tates but they are in a sense distant views which do not reveal the practical reality of rural life. If one looks at the saints' lives, some of which describe the countryside in some detail, or the Egyptian papyri, which include substantial fragments of estate documents and tax registers, then a different picture emerges. The large estates do exist, but they appear as con-glomerations of small rent-paying farms. From Asia Minor to

Syria and Egypt, the true base of the Roman economy was the peasant cultivating his small farm.[24]

This peasant economy did not exist in fragmented isolation, and the basis of Roman wealth lay in the fact that, however imperfectly, it was linked together by a market network of cities. Again evidence from a variety of sources shows peasants bringing their surpluses to sell at market, and in turn using the proceeds to pay taxes and rent, to save for emergencies (such as the death of an essential ploughing ox), to pay for dowries and other expected expenses, and to spend on necessities and luxuries not available in the village.[25]

Leaving aside exceptional and usually isolated areas of steppe, desert and mountain where tribal units could survive, the Roman empire in the Near East was divided into hundreds of individual city territories. The *Synekdemos* of Hierokles, a gazetteer of Roman cities partially revised in the sixth century, lists over 900 in those territories controlled by the empire in 600, and the fact that it was compiled at all expresses the traditional view, still current in the sixth century, of the empire as a conglomeration of cities. Each city had a rural territory usually containing a number of villages. In turn the cities were grouped into provinces with a provincial capital known as a *metropolis*. Above that the provinces were divided between the dioceses of Thrace, Dacia, Macedonia, Asiana, Pontika, Anatolike (known in Latin as *Oriens*, the East), and Egypt, whose capitals included such major cities as Thessalonica, Ephesos, Kaisareia in Cappadocia, Antioch and Alexandria. All these sites were known as cities, but obviously a huge gulf separates a great urban centre such as the imperial capital at Constantinople, with a population estimated at nearly 400,000 in 540, from such a place as Mysotimolos in western Asia Minor – to take one from hundreds of cities at the bottom of the administrative hierarchy – which would come much closer to the modern definition of a village. Indeed some names on Hierokles' list can have had little real existence, but when any section is examined in detail (I have done this for western Asia Minor), the great majority fulfilled at least some of the functions the Romans expected of a city, above all that of a market.[26]

In several important respects the period from the fourth to the seventh century was one of marked change in the history of the Roman city. Up until the fourth century these were to a large degree autonomous, ruled by a hereditary oligarchy of landowners who made up a council, known in Greek as a *boulē*. The *bouleutai* were responsible for collecting taxes and a number of other tasks, such as billeting troops or repairing roads, which the imperial government might from time to time demand. Provided they fulfilled these duties imperial intervention was rare.

The city councillors expressed their status through the part they played in the civic ceremonies of pagan religion, especially the cult of the emperor, and most durably in lavish expenditure on public buildings. As individuals competing with each other, or acting together as a council in rivalry with neighbouring cities, they built public baths, theatres, temples and stadia; they erected statues and they adorned their cities with inscriptions. The remains of this peculiar cultural phenomenon are obvious to every tourist who visits the white marble ruins of the classical Near East.

In the late empire this urban culture was changed in important respects. Firstly, as a response to the crisis which faced the Roman state in the third century, the apparatus of imperial government expanded so that there was much less scope for urban autonomy. Increasingly the imperial capital, which after 324 was at Constantinople, the emperor's court and the departments of state attracted the civilian élite of the empire. John Lydos, a citizen of Philadelphia in western Asia Minor, who in the sixth century followed a successful career in the office of the Praetorian Prefect of the East in Constantinople, can stand as an example of many who might once have spent their lives as active members of the council of their home city, but increasingly looked to the capital instead.[27] Most of course stayed, but the wealthiest tended to combine this with an official post in the growing imperial hierarchy, which exempted them from membership of the council. For those remaining the council involved what could be very expensive duties with lessening prestige, and gradually membership ceased to be a sought-after mark of social status and became instead something to be avoided. The decline of this institution is a marked feature of the life of provincial cities in the late empire. By the mid-sixth century the *boulē* was a thing of the past.

A second major factor is Christianity. Long before 600 the

Roman empire was a fundamentally Christian society. Whatever the continuing importance of classical culture, with its obvious pagan roots, it was seen in a Christian context. As a result the temples, altars and public sacrifices of the pagan city were replaced by churches, monasteries and ecclesiastical processions. The effect upon the appearance of the Roman city was reinforced by a contemporary, but arguably independent development whereby the fashion for large public baths, stadia and gymnasia waned. By 600 the man who might once have paid for a new temple or bath, would wish to build a church, a hospital or an old peoples' home. At the same time the urban environment was also being reshaped by a revolution in transport as the carrying trade of the Near East moved from wheeled vehicles requiring open streets to camels and mules which could pass along narrow alleys. The formal open spaces and grid street plans associated with the classical city were being replaced by the densely built-up townscape, accessible only by an arterial network of lanes and alleys, typical of the Near Eastern city up to modern times. The change was gradual, but in Constantinople itself the striking lack of evidence for a grid street pattern strongly implies that even the imperial capital would not have seemed a very 'classical' city in 600.[28]

The Christianisation of the city also speeded the decline of the *boulē*. Since the fourth century clergy had been exempt from service on the city council. Increasingly, as members of wealthy lay families became bishops, priests and deacons, the church became a dominant part of every city's ruling élite. It comes as no surprise that when in the sixth century Persian armies appeared outside the city walls of Roman Mesopotamia, it was their bishops who provided leadership and acted as negotiators.

The changes, both to the institutions of city government and to the physical appearance of Roman cities, have in the past too easily been equated with decline. This is a value judgement to be avoided. It was simply a development from one type of urbanism to another; the change perhaps from the ancient to the medieval city. Leaving the assumptions of classical aesthetics aside, there is no reason to judge either one as superior – they are just different.

In any case these changes disguise a great deal of continuity. Although the city councils had long disappeared by 600, cities of the Roman Near East were still dominated by landowning oligarchies. The principal difference was one of organisation and cultural behaviour. Some of the descendants of those who would have served as *bouleutai* in the third century had by 600 moved to Constantinople, but most remained, controlling the city either as clergy, as the holders of certain lay municipal posts, as members of the imperial civil or military hierarchy, or simply as wealthy property owners who would *de facto* dominate their own community. Still in 600 the Roman world was essentially an urban civilisation where cities were the centres of local power, the seats of administration, justice and religion, and above all, as the site of workshops and craftsmen, and as markets, the economic centres for the surrounding countryside.

The evidence for the wealth of the Roman empire in 600 comes from all over the Roman Near East, with the partial exception of the Balkans. Even there, in cities such as Thessalonica or those along the Lower Danube, there is evidence for the remarkable durability of Roman city life, but it has to be seen against a background of decay and sometimes abandonment. The Roman counter-attack against the Avars and Slavs in the 590s had not come too soon for the cities of the Roman Balkans and the region's economic prosperity. Yet the Balkans was not part of the empire's economic heartland, and it is in Constantinople and its hinterland, in western Asia Minor, in Pamphylia and Cilicia, in Syria and Palestine, and in Egypt that one would look for, and find, evidence of the empire's continuing prosperity in 600.[29]

In a fuller study evidence could be taken from a wide variety of sources, but there are four types of material which deserve special attention: coinage, pottery, buildings and silver.

The Roman empire in 600 was a monetary economy, in that although there was a major role for barter, labour services, payments in kind and other types of non-monetary exchange, economic life was still fundamentally tied to payments and reckonings in coin. Official salaries, the wages of labourers, alms to beggars were all paid in coin; and one would have expected to use coin to buy property, to purchase food and goods on the city market, and above all to pay taxes. However limited a role coinage might play in some individuals' lives in 600, it would have been very difficult to escape its use completely.

All coinage was minted by the empire at a small number of mints, of which the most important were at Constantinople, Thessalonica, Kyzikos, Nikomedia, Antioch and Alexandria. Coin was minted in gold and copper. The basic gold coin was called in Latin a *solidus*, or in Greek a *nomisma* (plural *nomismata*). Great fortunes were measured in hundreds and even thousands of pounds of gold (72 *nomismata* to the pound); others would use gold coins for a substantial purchase, such as a horse; but for most people in their normal daily lives in the late Roman period a *nomisma* represented quite a large sum. At the beginning of the seventh century 40 nomismata would feed the household of a frugal bishop for a year, while a labourer might earn about one twentieth of a *nomisma* per day. A single *nomisma* would feed 57 families their vegetable allowance, buy 100 loaves of bread, four blankets or a second-hand cloak; three or four *nomismata* would buy a donkey.[30] The ability of the Roman state to raise large sums in gold to pay its soldiers and officials and to subsidise or subvert its neighbours impressed contemporaries, and should also impress modern historians, but more significant perhaps for the picture it gives of the Roman economy is the copper coinage.

Copper coins, or *folleis* (singular *follis*), were the basic monetary tools of daily exchange. Their rate to the nomisma varied, but under the emperor Maurice each gold coin was worth 480 copper folleis.[31] Whereas a nomisma was too valuable to lose without careful search, copper coins are regularly found littering any late Roman site. As a result the scatter of stray copper coins dropped by ancient shoppers is a useful guide to the scale of daily exchanges and hence to the economic vitality of the Roman economy.

The gradual disappearance of copper coins on Roman sites in western Europe, beginning in Britain and Gaul in the fifth century, and extending to most of Italy and then to the Balkans in the sixth century is strong evidence for a growing economic recession. The reverse however, the continued appearance of copper coins in quantities on Roman sites in the eastern heartlands right through the sixth century up to 600 and beyond, is equally strong evidence for the prosperity of that economy and its continued avoidance of recession. Wherever the copper coins of the late Roman period have been collected, whether on city sites such as Ephesos, Sardis and Aphrodisias in western Asia Minor, Gerasa (modern Jerash) and Pella in Transjordan, or at Constantinople itself, or at villages such as Déhès in the limestone massif of northern Syria, there is no important break in the copper coin finds in the sixth century. At Sardis in western Asia Minor, where a row of shops has been particularly well excavated, the scatter of copper coins dropped over the years by generations of late Roman shoppers right through to the seventh century, can serve as an illustration valid for the whole Roman east.[32]

The study of late Roman pottery helps to confirm this picture. In the Roman world the dining tables of the rich were covered with silver vessels and plates. In addition to these, or instead for those who could not afford them, the population of the Roman empire used high quality pottery, generically known as 'fine ware'. Pottery of this type was not made by the local potter, but was manufactured at a number of centres. For other purposes – cooking or storage – and again for those who could not afford fine wares, there was much simpler, more robust pottery known as 'coarse ware'. There were particular centres of coarse ware manufacture but in general this was the type of pottery produced in thousands of potteries all over the empire.

Fine ware pottery is one of the characteristic artefacts of Roman material culture. To the archaeologist it has several advantages. Building upon the results of generations of research it is generally possible to identify and date most fragments of fine ware pottery. Since fine wares were used by an extremely large section of the population this has the practical effect of making it relatively straightforward to identify and date Roman settlements. The principal types of fine ware in use in the late Roman Near East were all so-called 'Red Slip' wares. One of the biggest centres of manufacture was in North Africa, others have been identified in Cyprus, western Asia Minor and Egypt. The wide distribution of these types throughout the Roman Near East in 600 is good evidence of the continued vitality of an economy which could sustain demand for such a manufacture and had the trading network to distribute its wares.[33]

Working on the assumption that fine ware pottery would only have formed part of the cargo or load with which a ship or caravan reached its final destination, the patterns of pottery distribution can also be seen as a reflection of trade in other goods of which all trace has disappeared. Most coarse wares are too little researched to help in this way, with the important exception of *amphorae* which provide even more direct evidence for late Roman trade. *Amphorae* are the large two-handled storage jars, with a pointed rather than a flat base, which were the basic containers of ancient seaborne trade in such bulk commodities as wine, oil and fish sauce (*garum*). Over a hundred years of research has identified the major types of Roman *amphorae*, and in many cases it is possible not only to date an *amphora* but also to state its place of manufacture. With this knowledge it has been possible to reveal through the excavation of types of *amphorae* current in the years around 600, the continued existence of a widespread seaborne trade crossing the Mediterranean carrying bulk goods between Egypt, Palestine, Syria, Cilicia, western Asia Minor, Constantinople, and, to some extent, further west to North Africa and Italy.[34]

Buildings are further evidence of the prosperity of the Roman Near East in 600. One obvious preliminary point is that one must be sure to be looking at the types of buildings which were important to contemporaries. The ruins of temples, public baths, gymnasia and stadia which appear to have littered the Near East at the end of the sixth century are excellent evidence for the cultural changes which were transforming Roman cities; however, they do not reflect on that society's wealth. Individuals and communities in the Christian empire of the sixth century wanted to build monasteries, hospitals, old peoples' homes, orphanages, and, above all, churches, and it is the list of buildings of these types which can act as an index of their wealth.

Building evidence for the late sixth century is particularly good in Syria, Palestine and Transjordan, where lack of economic development until recently preserved the monuments and there has been a comparatively active tradition of interest in late Roman archaeology. At Gerasa, for example, (modern Jerash in Jordan), four new churches were erected between 559 and 611, a major restoration of one of the city's baths was undertaken in 584 and work on the cathedral was completed in 629. Further south in Madaba a new cathedral was built in 595–6, and work on the decoration was only completed in 607–8. The evidence does not only come from cities. In the countryside of the Hawrān in southern Syria 19 village churches can be dated to between 550 and 634. This pattern of new building can be matched by examples from southern and western Asia Minor, from Constantinople and even from Thessalonica in the Balkans. However, our knowledge of the dates depends upon the survival of building inscriptions, and continuity in the fashion for putting them up, and it has to be acknowledged that there certainly are substantially fewer inscriptions for the late empire when compared with the centuries before AD 250. It is easy to jump to the conclusion that this is evidence of economic decline rather than seeing it as another aspect of late Roman cultural change. However, this is almost certainly wrong. More excavations aimed specifically at the problems of the late Roman economy are required, but from what has been done so far, at sites such as Ephesos in western Asia Minor or Pella in Transjordan, the evidence points strongly to continuing prosperity. Perhaps the most striking results have come from the cities of the Negev desert in southern Palestine. Using highly specialised techniques of desert agriculture this region was exploited to support a number of small cities that were thriving in the years around 600.[35]

Nonetheless problems remain. In northern Syria between Antioch and Aleppo lies a region of limestone hills, which have been particularly well known to historians and archaeologists since Tchalenko published his survey of their remarkable late Roman remains in 1953. His work was only based on surface survey, rather than excavation, and his dating of the stone churches and houses is dependent on stylistic assessments and the survival of dated building inscriptions. Tchalenko himself was inclined to see the prosperity of the limestone massif continuing through to the seventh century, but a recent re-examination of his material points out that the building boom which had reached its zenith at the end of the fifth century and during the first half of the sixth century, tailed off after about 550. The obvious conclusion seemed to be that this was evidence of economic decline.[36]

An alternative interpretation, however, has been introduced by the work of Marlia Mango on late Roman silver. Until very recently archeologists and art historians were so convinced of the terminal decline of the Roman world by the second half of the sixth century that any particularly fine objects with a markedly classical decoration would be dated to the first half of the century at the latest. This applied to objects of all types, and led for example to serious mis-dating of the sixth-century mosaics found at Antioch and Apameia. A number of important Roman silver treasures are known from the Near East, including such magnificent and highly classicising pieces as the series of silver plates found on Cyprus, decorated with scenes from the life of David. Conventional art-historical wisdom would have dated them no later than the mid-sixth century, but in fact they are marked with official date stamps, and hence they can be correctly dated to between 613 and 629–30.[37] The system of official stamping of silver was introduced under the emperor Anastasius at the beginning of the sixth century and lasted into the reign of Constans II in the second half of the seventh. Not all silver was stamped, but there was also a contemporary fashion for marking vessels with dated inscriptions. Taken as a whole there is a considerable body of silver objects produced in the decades around 600.

The evidence of the objects themselves is supported by contemporary written sources. As already mentioned the tables of the late Roman élite were covered with silver vessels; so too were late Roman churches storehouses of silver. Almost every church seems to have had silver liturgical objects, and in some even their interior was coated with revetments of solid silver. This wealth was an important factor behind Persian attacks on Roman Mesopotamia, which sometimes seem to have had little more strategic purpose than to extort silver from these opulent cities. The churches of Edessa alone produced 112,000 pounds of silver.[38] Even more significant this was clearly a renewable asset. The same cities were forced to pay several times. Plainly, just as the eleventh-century kingdom of England's ability to raise millions of silver pennies in repeated payments of Danegeld demonstrates the wealth of the late Anglo-Saxon economy, so the silver payments of late Roman Mesopotamia are excellent evidence for the empire's prosperity.

To return to the limestone massif, one of the major treasures of this period was found in the region early in the twentieth century at the village of Kaper Koraon. The treasure belonged to the village church of St Sergios. It consisted of up to 56 silver liturgical objects (some are in pieces), including seven patens, nine chalices, six crosses, two candlesticks, two liturgical fans and a large number of other smaller items. The greater part can only be dated to between 540 and 640, but 16 items, including many of the best pieces, are securely dated by stamps to the years after 577. Many have inscriptions and about 50 donors are named. Four have titles. One is an archbishop of an unknown see; another, who gave some of the finest pieces, came from a local landowning family but went on to follow a successful career at the imperial court during the 580s; the third may have worked in a state-run silver factory; the fourth held a middle-ranking post in the provincial administration. Otherwise all the donors were moderately prosperous lesser landowners, merchants and artisans. Most appear to have been members of four or five prominent families who would have dominated village life. Clearly what seems to have happened at Kaper Koraon is that the church as a building already existed as a result of the earlier building boom. In the second half of the century the community's patronage of their church moved to the next phase, that of providing appropriate liturgical silver. The treasure is thus important evidence to show the continuing prosperity of the region right through to 600 and beyond.[39]

This pattern can be confirmed from the evidence of the only excavation so far carried out in the limestone hill country. Surface examination alone of the ruined village of Déhès, 30 kilometres north-west of Kaper Koraon, would have suggested that the village declined after about 550. In fact the excavation has proved that Déhès was occupied and prosperous right through the sixth century and seems to have declined only several centuries later. There was certainly much less building after the mid-sixth century, but the evidence for people living and farming at Déhès, and dropping a continuous scatter of copper coins, carries on without a break.[40] The excavation here was a very small undertaking, and it would be wrong to claim too much for it, but it is striking that throughout the Near East research is pointing more and more firmly in the direction of a Roman world whose heartlands continued to prosper at the beginning of the seventh century.

So far there has been no mention of the sixth-century plague. A conventional account would have placed this at the centre of this section. It would have described how the plague appeared in 541–2 and spread from Ethiopia to Egypt and thence throughout the Roman world and beyond. Contemporary descriptions show it to have been bubonic plague of the same or similar type to that which afflicted Europe and Asia from the outbreak of the Black Death in the fourteenth century up to the late eighteenth century. In spring 542 it reached Constantinople and raged for four months. According to a presumed eyewitness the death toll reached 10,000 a day.[41] After 542 the plague returned at regular intervals until the middle of the eighth century. Apart from the devastating immediate impact, the plague is conventionally seen as undermining the Roman empire and its economy, creating conditions ripe for disaster. It is argued that the massive mortality of the initial outbreak and its regular reappearances reduced the population by over a half, leading to social and economic ruin. Cities, it is claimed, were worse hit than the countryside, and the settled population in general far worse hit than the nomadic population of the desert. Since urban life was so crucial a part of late Roman civilisation and the settled population was the basis of the Empire's fiscal resources, it is in turn argued that the plague created a structural imbalance in favour of the desert Arabs. Thus to follow this argument, in 600 the Empire's resources were depleted and its power fatally weakened.

The major problem with this view is that apart from the literary sources, which by their very nature give vague and unquantifiable accounts of the disease, there is no evidence for this devastating impact. In fact, as already discussed, the economy of the Roman Near East in the years after the plague seems to indicate business as usual. The only area where there is evidence of difficulties is the Balkans and that is due to other causes. In particular it is striking that the Egyptian papyri give no indication either of an economic crisis or even of population decline. It is also troubling that despite stories in the literary sources of bodies overflowing graveyards, nowhere has any archaeologist working in the Near East discovered a plague pit. A further peculiarity concerns the continued prosperity of marginal areas in the Near East such as the limestone massif of northern Syria and the Negev desert. Tchalenko thought that the economy of the limestone region was based on a near monoculture of olives for an export trade in olive oil. It now seems that in fact the region's agriculture was based on the typical mixture of wheat, vines and olives one found throughout the Roman Near East, and that the numbers of olive-presses Tchalenko discovered were not exceptional.[42] At a period after the ninth century the population of the massif fell dramatically, so that when European travellers first visited the Roman ruins in the nineteenth century the region was virtually deserted. Even in the twentieth century the scattered population reflects the marginal nature of farming in these hills. This in turn implies a remarkable demand for land from the fifth century onwards. The same applies even more so to the Negev, where farming has only begun again this century because of the acute demand for agricultural land in the modern Israeli state.[43] In medieval England almost the first consequence of the Black Death was the abandonment of agriculture in marginal areas like the fells and the moors. If the population of the Roman Near East fell between a half and a third, why did the rural economy of these marginal areas carry on as usual?

This is not to deny the existence of the plague, but simply to doubt whether it had the catastrophic effects that most modern historians – with a few exceptions – believe. Comparison with later plagues, especially the pandemic which began in the fourteenth century and carried on with regular later outbreaks up to the eighteenth century, may suggest an alternative approach. Unfortunately in the Near East, our current understanding of the social and economic consequences of this later plague is almost as vague as for the sixth century – with one interesting exception. Contrary to the hypothesis that the plague would have ruined the settled population while sparing the nomads, recent archaeological work in Jordan suggests that settled agriculture actually enjoyed a period of expansion beginning about a hundred years before the Black Death and continuing for at least a century afterwards, and in some areas considerably longer.[44] It may well be that cities and villages suffered more than nomads, but in the fourteenth- to sixteenth-century Near East this did not lead to economic collapse; and there is no need to presume very different results in the sixth century. Much more is known about the plague in western Europe, where the surviving documentary evidence fully confirms the literary accounts of high mortality. Historians are agreed that somewhere between a third and a half of the population of Europe in 1346 perished before 1352, and the death toll of later outbreaks remained high. Yet in spite of this catastrophe fourteenth-century Europe surmounted the crisis. In some areas the loss of population and falling food prices encouraged recession, but over the continent as a whole there is no evidence of social and economic collapse. Indeed the Black Death has been described as having a 'purgative rather than toxic' effect on what had previously been an over-populated society facing Malthusian checks.[45] After the first outbreak fourteenth-century Europeans returned as soon as possible to farming, trading, building, manufacturing, and fighting wars as usual. They adapted to a smaller population and the regular threat of new bouts of the plague. Taking Europe in the late fourteenth and fifteenth centuries as a whole, the age of the Italian Renaissance can hardly be characterised as one of decline. Many questions still need answering but on the face of it there seems no reason to think that the sixth-century Roman experience would have been very different. The existence of the plague should not divert attention from the fact that the Roman empire in 600 was a powerful state, facing favourable political conditions, and supported by a prosperous economy.

4. The Fall of the Old Order

The Last Roman–Persian War

ON 4 DECEMBER 1691 the Secretary of State for Scotland, the Master of Stair, wrote to Lieutenant-Colonel James Hamilton, warning him to prepare for a punitive campaign against the MacDonalds of Glencoe, 'for the winter time is the only season in which we are sure the Highlanders cannot escape us, nor carry their wives, bairns, and cattle into the mountains'.[1]

A similar strategy was being planned in Constantinople in 602 against the Slavs living north of the Danube. 'It is preferable', wrote the author of the *Strategikon*, a contemporary military handbook associated with the emperor Maurice, and reflecting military thinking at the imperial court, 'to launch our attacks against them in the winter when they cannot easily hide among bare trees, when the tracks of fugitives can be discerned in the snow, when their household is miserable from exposure, and when it is easy to cross over the rivers on the ice'.[2] The Roman field army, however, was less amenable to the emperor's plans than was the Earl of Argyll's regiment to the Secretary of State's instructions. Soldiers of the Roman field armies had a relatively high status in society; it was an advantage to be able to succeed to a father's place in the ranks. They were comparatively well paid in cash, and they enjoyed two to three months leave every winter. They could also expect to take booty from a wealthy opponent. The orders to winter north of the Danube were received with dismay. The army was already suspicious of Maurice's intentions to reform their conditions of service. They had just spent a long campaigning season fighting the Slavs with great success, and a winter campaign would be bitterly uncomfortable; it would offer little or no prospects of worthwhile plunder, and they wanted to go home. As a result the army mutinied, and so set in motion a train of events that in less than half a century had brought down the entire old order of the Near East.

Maurice's fall was rapid. Under one of their number, called Phokas, the army marched on Constantinople. The city's political

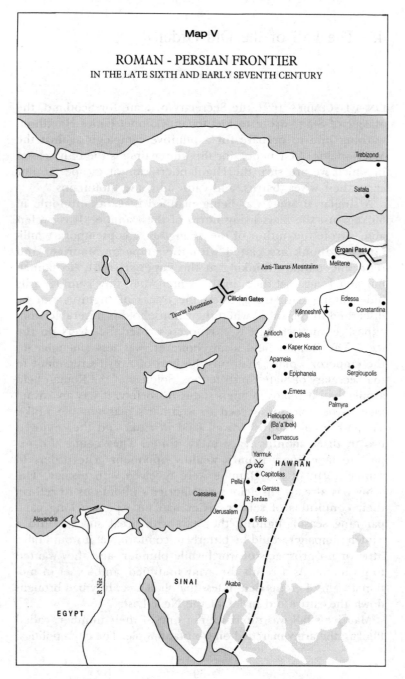

Map V

ROMAN - PERSIAN FRONTIER
IN THE LATE SIXTH AND EARLY SEVENTH CENTURY

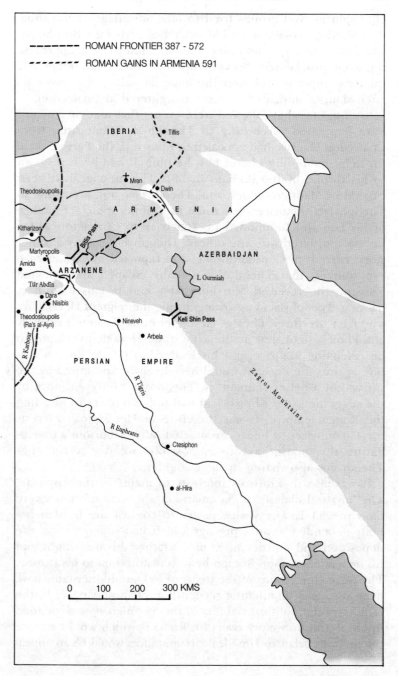

- - - - - - - ROMAN FRONTIER 387 - 572
- - - - - - - ROMAN GAINS IN ARMENIA 591

élite split as rival groups tried to take advantage of the situation. Rioting broke out, and Maurice fled across the Bosphorus. The following day, as no other credible candidate had appeared, the army proclaimed Phokas emperor. On 25 November 602 the new emperor took over the imperial palace, and two days later Maurice and his sons were slaughtered at Chalcedon.

Essential to what followed were events that may or may not have happened. According to Theophylact Simocatta, from Chalcedon Maurice had appealed to Khusro II, the Persian shah, for help, reminding him of how he himself had been restored to his throne by the Romans in 591. The message had been carried by Maurice's eldest son, Theodosios, but, according to Theophylact, Maurice soon came to a philosophic acceptance of his fate and summoned his son back to Chalcedon where he was murdered with the others. Theophylact knows another story, current in Constantinople, and reported by various eastern sources, that Theodosios actually escaped and reached Khusro, who received him hospitably and promised military backing. Theophylact was writing during the reign of Herakleios, who later overthrew Phokas. He therefore represents a strongly anti-Phokas slant, but at the same time Herakleios' claims to be revenging Maurice and his leadership of the Roman empire against the Persians would have been compromised by the survival of a better claimant in Theodosios and even more by the suggestion that Khusro had had noble motives in invading the Roman empire. It was therefore in Herakleios' interests for Theophylact to be so certain that 'after laboriously investigating this matter as far as possible, we discovered that Theodosios also shared in the slaughter'.[3]

It was also in Khusro's interests to maintain the opposite. The 'mystical majesty' of Sasanian kingship had taken a severe blow in 590–1. The shah's power to control the Iranian nobility depended upon a prestige which had suffered from the deposition and murder of Khusro's father, his own flight and his dependence upon Roman help to restore him to his throne. The huge concessions of the treaty of 591 would inevitably have been seen as a humiliating recognition of subservience. In the long term the political stability of the Sasanian state depended upon a military victory over the Romans which would restore the previous balance. The ideal circumstances would be an appeal from Maurice which would pay back the aid given in 591. If Theodosios did not arrive at Khusro's court, it would have made sense to have invented him.

The Persian attack began in 603, making initially rapid progress, but after the capture of the famous Roman frontier fortress of Dara in 604 resistance stiffened.[4] The Persians, however, continued the pressure and slowly fought their way through the key defences of Roman Mesopotamia. The breakthrough came between 608 and 610 with the fall of Amida, Theodosioupolis (that is Ra's al-Ayn on the modern border between Turkey and Syria, rather than modern Erzerum which had the same Roman name), Konstantina and Edessa. The Persians also captured Mardin, whose loss signalled the Persian conquest of the Tūr Abdīn, the staunchly Monophysite hill-country which had for so long been a loyal bastion on the Roman frontier. All these cities were powerful fortresses where the Romans had spent large sums on updating the defences in the sixth century, and their loss opened the way for the Persians to overrun Syria and Palestine.

An important factor in Persian success was clearly political disunity on the Roman side. Whatever Theophylact says, many Romans in Syria thought that the man with the Persian armies was Maurice's eldest son, Theodosios, and believed they could recognise him. As soon as he heard of Phokas' coup, the chief Roman general in Mesopotamia, Narses, who had had a distinguished career fighting the Persians under Maurice, including the command of the expedition which restored Khusro in 591, rebelled. He seized Edessa and let in Theodosios, Khusro and the Persian troops, and it was here in 603 that Theodosios – whether really Maurice's son or a pretender – was formally proclaimed emperor.[5] Forces loyal to Phokas recaptured Edessa the following year, but the Roman war effort in the east continued to be dogged by political dissension. At least in its early stages, the war had more of the characteristics of a Roman civil war than our partisan sources like to admit.

The Romans also faced difficulties in Armenia. As in Syria many thought that recognised Theodosios. The new territory brought into the empire by the treaty of 591 was unfamiliar country for Roman armies, and relations with the independent-minded Armenian nobility were strained. When they had been ruled by the Persians their common Christianity had seemed a close tie with their Roman neighbours; now they were part of the Roman empire, they had the opportunity to discover the differences of culture and theology which divided them. Relations had also been upset by Maurice's attempts to conscript the Armenian nobility to serve in the Balkans, and by two attempts to settle Armenian families in Thrace.[6] In 605 a Roman defeat in the upper Araxes valley was blamed on Armenian treachery. By 609 the major Roman fortresses, blocking the road west, Kitharizon, Satala, Nikopolis and Theodosioupolis (this time the Armenian city, now modern Erzerum) were in Persian hands. In the case of Theodosioupolis, a decisive factor in the decision to surrender was a meeting with the man claiming to be Maurice's son. These Roman commanders were apparantly convinced.[7]

A further cause of Roman difficulties is more hypothetical. One clear lesson of sixth-century wars against Persia was the need to deploy the full weight of Roman resources on the eastern frontier. If that were done then repeated experience showed that the Romans had the military edge. One of Phokas' first decisions on learning of Khusro's invasion had been to increase the payments made to the Avar qaghan, so that he could transfer Roman troops to the east.[8] However, it is striking that at least until 610 imperial control seems to have continued unaffected in the Balkans. It is known that after that Roman troops were removed from the region and the Balkans was largely overrun. The implication appears to be that Phokas, who after all had served in the Balkan campaigns and may not have wished to see the efforts of the 590s go for nothing, kept reduced but still substantial sections of the Roman field army in the Balkans throughout his reign. If so this may have been a vital strategic factor in the fall of Roman Mesopotamia.

· None of the surviving accounts presents Phokas' side of events, but the lists of high-ranking officials, army officers and relatives of the late emperor put to death after accusations of plotting, which are given in the generally accurate and near-contemporary *Chronikon Paschale*, point to an insecure regime.[9] Given the background of military defeat this was hardly surprising, and for several years bloody repression kept Phokas in power. In 608, however, Herakleios, the military governor of Carthage rebelled. At that distance, and with no spare troops to form an expeditionary force to restore the province to obedience, there was little Phokas could immediately do. In 609 Herakleios' nephew, Niketas, marched into Egypt and in a few months had established control. Constantinople was now isolated from its wealthiest province, and critically for Phokas' support in the city, the rebels had stopped the supply of Egyptian grain. On Saturday, 3 October 610 Herakleios' son, also called Herakleios (and the one Herakleios being referred to from now on), arrived at the head of a fleet in the Bosphorus. Phokas' support crumbled rapidly; in less than forty-eight hours his naked body was being dragged through the streets and on the same day the Romans had a new emperor.

With a new leader, and some sense of renewed political unity, events promptly turned to the worse. One of Herakleios' first decisions was to withdraw Roman troops from the Balkans. Left to depend on local resources, imperial control collapsed in an ill-documented process of Avar and Slav invasions, sacked cities and fleeing refugees. The new troops made no difference to the tide of defeat in the east. In 611 the Persians capitalised on their decisive victories in Mesopotamia by seizing western Syria. By the end of the year Antioch, one of the greatest cities in the Roman east, Apameia and Emesa (Homs) were in Persian hands. The Roman counter-attack was delayed by a two-year campaign to get the Persians out of Cappadocia where they had advanced from Armenia to seize Kaisareia. The campaign achieved no more than forcing the Persians into a strategic withdrawal, and the counter-attack when it came was a disaster. The Roman army was defeated in front of Antioch and Herakleios was forced back on to the Anatolian plateau, abandoning the wealthy plain of Cilicia in his retreat.

In command of western Syria the Persians had effectively broken the Roman empire in two. Herakleios was forced to defend Anatolia from secondary thrusts, while the main Persian attack concentrated on Palestine and Egypt. In 613 Damascus fell, and in 614 Jerusalem was stormed. The bloody sack of Jerusalem, the slaughter of priests and monks, the destruction of so many relics and churches, including the loss of the fragment of the True Cross found by Constantine's mother and hence closely associated with the very idea of Constantine's

Christian Roman empire, and finally the handing over of this city to be governed by the outcast Jews, was a symbol of Roman defeat. As the news reached Constantinople few if any had a realistic hope of future victory.[10] In the following year a Persian army invaded Asia Minor and pushed on to capture Chalcedon, immediately opposite Constantinople. Watching from the walls the empire's rulers were effectively beaten, and an embassy was sent to Khusro to beg for terms.

Whatever the shah's initial war-aims, they had now been surpassed and there opened up the possibility of recreating the Achaemenid empire of Cyrus, Xerxes and Darius which in the fifth century BC had included Asia Minor, Thrace and Egypt. The Romans were defeated and it was simply a matter of imposing his will. The Armenian historian, Sebeos, later records a letter which Herakleios had read out to his troops to prove there was no possibility of a negotiated peace: 'From Khusro, beloved of the Gods, master and king of all the earth, son of the great Ahuramazda, to our slave, imbecile and lowly, Herakleios. . . .'[11] The Roman emperor, no more than a rebellious slave to the shah, was lost; his God could not save him; if he surrendered now Khusro would generously give him some land to farm. The letter might have been a piece of Roman propaganda, but the fact that the ambassadors from the Romans were left to die in a Persian prison suggests Khusro was committed to the utter destruction of the Roman state.[12]

In 616 the Persians invaded Egypt. In 619 Alexandria, the city which had rivalled Rome as the citadel of Christian orthodoxy, fell, and by 620 the country was in Persian hands. Various fragmentary papyri surviving from these years demonstrate the consequences of this victory. The taxation machinery can be seen continuing to operate, but now in the service of a Persian governor.[13] From now on, not only was Constantinople again cut off from its grain supply, leading to famine in the capital, but the fiscal wealth of Egypt was available to support the Persian war effort, whereas the Romans faced financial crisis.

By 621 the empire was clearly doomed. Not only were the wealthiest provinces of the east lost, Asia Minor open to invasion, and the state bankrupt, but Herakleios' policy in the Balkans had turned to disaster. The justification for allowing the Avars a free hand was the hope that the troops made available by such a passive policy would halt the Persian advances in the east. By 621 not only had that failed, but the Avars had spent the last decade mastering the Slav tribes and overrunning the Balkans. The local success at Thessalonica in about 618 when the Avars were narrowly prevented from capturing the city meant little in Constantinople. Its rulers were well aware that the Avars were now looking toward the imperial city and a final replacement of the Roman emperor by the Avar qaghan. The only practical hope for the moment was persuading the qaghan that the Romans were less defenceless than they seemed, and that the Avars should concentrate their efforts for the next few years on campaigns in the west against the Franks and Lombards. To this end in 623 Herakleios arranged a conference with the qaghan at Herakleia in Thrace. The meeting was set up with chariot-racing and all the paraphernalia of imperial court ceremony. In the event Herakleios was lucky to escape with his life. The qaghan had sent forces to cut the emperor off from Constantinople. Herakleios learnt this at the last moment and clutching little more than the imperial crown he fled back to the city. The Avars ravaged the suburbs of Constantinople, taking large numbers of prisoners, but they were eventually persuaded to retire by the promise of an annual payment, recorded as 200,000 *nomismata,* and the handing over of members of the imperial family as hostages. Whether or not the figure is correct, this humiliating payment was only made possible by stripping the churches of Constantinople of their accumulated wealth, and in any case it was quite obvious that the Avars would be back, and that the city could expect a major siege.[14] The only mitigating feature of the outlook in the early 620s was that the Persian refusal to negotiate in effect meant that the Roman ruling classes in Constantinople had little choice but to remain relatively united behind Herakleios and keep fighting. Few Roman emperors had remained on the throne with such a record of constant defeat.

By this date Herakleios seems to have reached the conclusion that only in the lands of Armenia, Azerbaidjan and the Caucasus was there the possibility of Roman victory. First of all Armenia and the Caucasus offered Christian allies with considerable military potential. Although the Armenian nobility had been unreliable at the beginning of the war, over ten years of

Persian rule was likely to have restored their natural pro-Christian and pro-Roman sentiment. In addition, the eastern mountains provided the kind of terrain where luck and local support could play an important part in the outcome. In Armenia in the past small armies had often surprised contemporaries by defeating larger opponents, and a series of campaigns here could provide an opportunity to give a demoralised Roman army that was full of new recruits the chance to gain confidence and experience. More important, victory in this region would open up a route over the Zagros mountains into the heartlands of Persian Iraq. A blow to the Persian capital, Ctesiphon, might persuade the shah to negotiate. Finally, and this was almost certainly the predominant factor, beyond the Caucasus mountains in the Volga steppes lay the only power which might have the military resources to defeat the Persians, that was the western Turks.

The first moves to assemble and train an army, and put this policy into action, began in 622; but they were stopped by the news of the Avar advance into Thrace. Herakleios hurried back to Constantinople, and there followed in 623 the near-disastrous attempt to negotiate with the qaghan at Herakleia. However, with the Avars bought off for the moment, Herakleios left Constantinople for the east on 25 March 624; he would not return for over four years. The first two years were spent in inconclusive but quite successful campaigns in Armenia, the Caucasus and Azerbaidjan (where the Romans destroyed the greatest of the Zoroastrian fire temples in revenge for the sack of Jerusalem), and in negotiations with the Turks.

While these events posed little immediate threat to Persian domination of the Near East, there was obviously a need to put a final end to Roman resistance, and in 626 the Persians launched their great assault on Constantinople. At the same time the Avar qaghan had massed his people and their Slav subjects, and attacked the city from the west. Constantinople was surrounded and under siege on both sides; the climactic crisis of the war had arrived.

It is possible that the presence of both armies in front of Constantinople at the same time was coincidence, but it is more likely that this was a deliberate plan. The Persian generals had seen Constantinople before from Chalcedon, and would have been aware that, lacking a suitable navy, they needed to attack the city from the European side if they were to have a chance of success. The Avars had also considered the problems of a siege of Constantinople over the previous years. They were not lacking in siege engines, but they did not have a very good record against well-defended and fortified sites. Most recently they had failed to capture Thessalonica,[15] and it may have been that which persuaded the qaghan that he needed Persian expertise to break his way through the most powerful city defences of the ancient world. The plan depended upon the qaghan providing boats to transport the Persians across the Bosphorus.

In contrast to 623, Herakleios did not rush back to the imperial city. He sent reinforcements from his army, but otherwise he trusted to the lay and ecclesiastical leadership inside the city, the forces already there and the imperial fleet. He seems to have remained in western Anatolia, with his army threatening the Persians at Chalcedon from a distance. In the event the siege was a triumph for the Romans and an unexpected catastrophe for the Avars. The qaghan launched two assaults on the city using Avar and Slav warriors, presumably trying to take the city wholly for himself, and it was only when these had failed that he tried to transport the Persians across. The attempt using Slav canoes in the face of Roman naval galleys armed with Greek fire was a disaster; a further land and sea assault failed four days later, and in the wake of this the Avar siege broke up in confusion, with the Slavs rebelling against the qaghan's leadership. Avar power never recovered from this humiliating setback. The Persian army had little choice but to retreat from Chalcedon too.[16]

With Roman morale and Herakleios' political standing strengthened by this victory, the Roman army reopened the campaign in the east, acting together with a powerful force of Turkish steppe nomad cavalry. The spring and summer were spent overrunning Iberia and Albania (the latter being the great plain ideal for steppe nomads lying south of the Caucasus facing the Caspian Sea, approximately equivalent to the modern republic of Azerbaidjan), and in the siege of the Iberian capital of Tiflis. At the end of the campaigning season the main Turkish force retired to the north, but Herakleios with the Roman field army, and an important contingent of Turkish cavalry, pushed on into Azerbaidjan. Even then the Persians might have expected him to move into winter quarters, but instead he turned south, and crossing the Zagros mountains Herakleios led the Roman army and its allies into Persian Iraq. At Nineveh (near Mosul) they were confronted by a Persian army, but the ensuing battle on 12 December was a decisive Roman victory. Herakleios followed this up by pursuing Khusro across northern Iraq, and devastating the countryside.

Faced by this crisis which Khusro showed himself unable to control, the Persian nobility broke into competing factions. At the end of February 628 Khusro's eldest son, Kavadh Shiroe, deposed his father, and a few days later Khusro was put to death. The new regime began negotiations with Herakleios, encouraged by continuing Roman and Turkish devastation of Persian territory, but little had been decided, and Syria, Palestine and Egypt were still occupied by Persian troops six months later when Kavadh Shiroe died. Herakleios now decided on a bold policy to use the divisions within the Persian nobility to regain the eastern provinces, get rid of the Sasanian dynasty altogether and replace them with a Christian shah upon the Persian throne. Earlier in 626 he had made contact with one of the Persian generals, Shahrbarāz, when he had been commander of the Persian army in front of Constantinople, and now in 629 Herakleios arranged a second meeting at which he promised Roman military support for a coup to place Shahrbarāz on the Persian throne. In return Shahrbarāz was willing to evacuate the occupied territories, restore the True Cross and accept the baptism of his eldest son with the Christian name Niketas, who would succeed him as shah.[17] This was the most extraordinary triumph of Roman arms and diplomacy only a few years after the Roman cause seemed utterly lost. The ideology of Christian victory which characterised Herakleios' court during these years is well caught by the image of the triumphant David depicted on the great silver plate from Cyprus stamped with the mark of the imperial mint and the date 629.[18] When Herakleios made his ceremonial entrance into Jerusalem in March 630 to restore the True Cross to the church of the Holy Sepulchre, the Christian Roman empire must have seemed on the brink of a golden age of uncontested hegemony in the Near East.

Against this triumphant background a statement found in the Syriac chronicle usually but misleadingly known as the 'Chronicle to AD 724' which suggests that the treaty between Shahrbarāz and the emperor marked the frontier between the two states as the Euphrates may seem extraordinary. By such an agreement Herakleios would have ceded the very fortresses whose loss had led to the collapse of the Roman east after 611, and the fact that other texts mention Herakleios' presence in Edessa (one of the most important of these trans-Euphrates fortresses) in 629 would make it easy to dismiss this story as a mistake. However, the Chronicle can be dated to c.640 and its author, the priest Thomas, had close ties to the monastery of Kēnneshrē which lies on the left bank of the Euphrates in what would have been ceded territory. Thomas was in a position to know, and the sense that he is telling the truth is reinforced by an earlier passage where he notes people emigrating from the east to the west bank of the river.[19]

In the event, although the Persians did evacuate the eastern provinces, the conversion of Persia came to nothing. Shahrbarāz was assassinated after reigning less than three months, and the Romans held on to Edessa and the east bank territories. But what the episode reveals is the high price Herakleios had been willing to pay for his treaty with Persia. Although the Roman empire had been victorious, it had been at an enormous cost. The war had lasted over twenty-five years, and for nearly two decades the eastern provinces had been under Persian rule. The battle to recover them had demanded every resource the empire could find – witness the melting down of church treasures and public monuments in Constantinople – and had left the state considerably poorer than it had been in 600. Even then, Herakleios' victory had depended upon Turkish help and upon a political crisis in the Persian empire. In the end the eastern provinces had been recovered by negotiation, not reconquest. If the Persians had refused to evacuate it would have been very difficult and slow to force them to leave.

Looking to the future, the Romans had a long task ahead to rebuild their power in the Near East. A whole generation had grown up in Syria, Palestine and Egypt which had no experience of being part of the Roman empire. The government in Constantinople needed to re-establish the whole complicated structure of administrative and personal ties which bound the provinces to the capital. The defeat of Persia was a triumphant vindication of the Christian empire, but it would require time to recover from the strains of war and set about realising the opportunities of the post-war world.

The Islamic Conquests

The Roman empire, of course, was not to have time to recover and rebuild from the great war with Persia. Within a few years of Herakleios' victory the armies of Islam had overrun the east, and when he died in 641, the Roman empire was facing as deep a crisis as any in the worst years of the Persian war.

The Islamic conquests present enormous historical problems with which modern historians are only slowly coming to grips, and which in most secondary works and general accounts continue to receive unsatisfactory treatment. The previous section of this chapter has given, relative to the space available, a reasonably full narrative of the Roman–Persian war from 602 to 629. It provides a base from which to understand later developments, it is a good story, and the sources are available to reconstruct an account of events. In absolute terms the evidence for this war is very slight, but among what survives are a combination of contemporary or near-contemporary record, as well as copies of Herakleios' victory despatches by which he kept Constantinople informed of his campaigns in the east. Keeping in mind the strategic factors discussed in Chapter 2, it is possible to construct a basic narrative. The details are bound to be debatable, and much remains obscure, but one can state confidently that the account given above broadly approximates to what happened.

With the Islamic conquests begins a period in which the Greek, Armenian and Syriac sources are either very brief or confused or ill-informed or all three. To be set beside these are the works of Islamic historians, which purport to draw on contemporary and eyewitness accounts, and which provide a record of events in immense detail. Not surprisingly the standard approach to writing the history of these years has been to create a narrative framework out of the Islamic tradition, and then fit in materials from Greek, Armenian and Syriac sources where appropriate and not too contradictory.

This approach, however, overlooks the fact that the Islamic sources for the seventh century are of a fundamentally different nature to those produced in the Roman world. The greater part of the basic narrative framework is provided by the works of al-Balādhurī, al-Ya'kūbī and al-Tabarī, all composed in the later ninth and early tenth centuries, but recording earlier sources, written down in the later eighth and ninth centuries – that is between one hundred fifty and two hundred years after the event. No earlier Arabic written historical sources have survived. Before this the transmission of historical information apparently depended upon an oral tradition of Muslim scholars, the *ulamā* and the story-tellers of the bedouin tribes.

Since at least the 1950s anthropologists have demonstrated how fluid and adaptable oral history can be. To simplify for present purposes, this work has shown how the oral history of a tribe was primarily concerned to explain the present, and to this end would adapt and shape its view of the past, rapidly omitting details which were no longer relevant, and creating stories with supporting details to explain and justify present circumstances. Even under settled conditions an accurate memory of the past effectively lasted no more than two generations; in times of migration or other social upheaval change is quicker and more profound.[20] Arab society in the seventh century is a classic example of such oral history-making at work. Indeed to some extent it still is. In 1988 I was with Jeremy Johns and Alison McQuitty who were directing the first season of an excavation of the site of a medieval village at Fāris, near al-Kerak in Jordan.[21] Members of the locally dominant tribe in whose territory the site lay were concerned to stake their individual claims to what our activities suggested might be valuable property. A sunny afternoon would bring a succession of visitors to the site, each with a vivid and contradictory account of how they, or their father or grandfather had been brought up in the house we were excavating. They would point to features they remembered as they came to light, and tell stories to associate themselves and their ancestors with the site. All this in spite of the fact that the house we were excavating at that moment had not been occupied since the middle ages, and their stories of deeds fighting the Turks in the First World War were easily contradicted by contemporary written materials. The appearance of foreign archaeologists was prompting the creation and adaptation of the oral history of the tribe to serve present purposes.

The oral tradition of events in the Arab world in the seventh century is further complicated by the fact that the rise of Islam was not simply a tribal conquest of the Fertile Crescent; it was the creation and establishment of a new religion. What Islam was to mean in practice was only slowly established over the course of the seventh and eighth centuries. One force shaping the new religion was the *khulafā*, the caliphs (singular *khalīfa*), whose title in this period, *khalīfa Allāh*, means 'deputy of God', with all the implications for making decisions on religious matters that exalted title implies. These were the successors of the Prophet as the acknowledged leaders of the new community. However, they were successfully rivalled in this role by the *ulamā*, the religious scholars, who by the ninth century had established themselves as the only legitimate source of religious authority for orthodox *sunnī* muslims, leaving the caliphs with only political power. The *ulamā* based their claim to religious authority on their role as transmitters of the teaching of the Prophet. That teaching and subsequent events crucial to the formation of the Islamic community and its conquest of the Near East had occurred within a historical context, but the *ulamā* did not memorise it as a coherent narrative. Instead they transmitted isolated sayings, short accounts of particular incidents and references to historical events. Cut off from a real context these fragments of oral tradition were progressively shaped by the evolving demands of the new religion. Under the classic pressures of oral transmission in a time of far-reaching change the real past of the seventh century was transformed to serve the purposes of what was by the eighth century the dominant religion of a political superpower. By the later eighth century the historical traditions of the conquest years had been written down. From now on it would be more difficult to change the orthodox account. Even so one can see in later texts a strong tendency to subject earlier versions to arbitary reworkings that would serve contemporary interests. If this has happened since the eighth century, how much more must it have occurred in the flux years of the creation of the Islamic world?[22]

The result of these processes is that we receive our historical accounts of early Islamic history once they have been through a double mill of tribal tradition trying to come to terms with a era of shattering change, and of the *ulamā* battling to control and create the development of a new religion. Only then was it set down and frozen in an orthodox written form that was accepted in the ninth century. Some of this tradition as it has reached us obviously reflects reality, some is later creation or misinterpretation. Until recently there has been a tendency to disregard the obviously miraculous or improbable and analyse the rest following the same kind of strategic and political assumptions that are used to interpret the late Roman and Byzantine sources in this book. An authoritative example of this approach is F. M. Donner's *The Early Islamic Conquests*, which since its publication in 1981 has been widely used by Byzantinists looking for a reliable guide. However, despite the undoubted qualities of Donner's book, this type of analysis is clearly at the end of an intellectual road. Given the forces which shaped the Islamic historical tradition as we have received it, a story which sounds probable and is full of convincing detail is no more likely to be true than one full of evident impossibilities. The *ulamā* and the bedouin story-tellers both knew their world better than we do, and just as the visitors to the medieval village site in Jordan, their stories will sound convincing.

For the historian this poses formidable difficulties. The way forward seems to be through a painstaking re-analysis of all these texts – Arabic, Syriac, Greek and Armenian – to discover what seventh-century realities can be discerned behind them, and rather than accept Donner's seductive certainties, historians of Byzantium should be watching with attention to see where this new work will lead.

One area where already the problems are much clearer is the Syrian Christian tradition, of which Theophanes in effect forms a part since his account of eastern events is copied from a Greek translation of a Syriac chronicle. Like the Islamic tradition, the most detailed narratives appear in eighth- and ninth-century compilations, by which date, as recent work has shown, they are no longer independent of the Islamic accounts. Thus unfortunately the appearance of an event known from al-Tabarī, for example, in Theophanes, Agapios or the Syriac texts which reproduce the lost chronicle of Dionysios of Tel-Mahrē, does not amount to independent confirmation. However, unlike the Islamic sources a number of seventh-century Syriac chronicles and other texts have survived. They are short, and for the most part obscure and fragmentary, but they are contemporary, and as such of enormous value. A detailed narrative (which some historians still yearn for) is out of the question, but the Syriac material does allow one to identify a meagre but secure core of fact.[23]

Thus in spite of apparently prolific sources, the current working consensus of what happened during this key period in Near Eastern history can amount to little more than a bald summary. (Even this goes beyond what can strictly be proved, especially as regards the dates which should be treated with caution.) By the late 620s it seems that the tribes of Arabia were united under the Prophet Muhammad, and had probably begun raids into Palestine. The conquest of the eastern provinces began in about 633. Progress was rapid as a succession of cities in Transjordan, Palestine and Syria surrendered to the Muslims. In 635 Damascus fell. In 636 a large Roman army brought the Arabs to battle near the Yarmūk river in the north of modern Jordan. The result was a decisive Muslim victory, and there seems to have been no further effective attempt to drive the Arabs out of Syria and Palestine. Jerusalem, so recently recovered from the Persians, surrendered in 638. With his earlier victories reversed and the high hopes of 629–30 in ruins, Herakleios died in March 641, possibly in time to avoid hearing of the fall of the city of Caesarea on the Palestinian coast after a lengthy siege, and of a decisive Roman defeat in Egypt. Dara (the fortress whose loss was said to have sent Justin II mad), Edessa (the city whose fall had led to the Persian breakthrough after 611), and Antioch (the capital of Roman Syria) had been lost already. In 645 a counter-attack recaptured Alexandria, but the Roman forces were soon ejected and by the summer of 646 Egypt was wholly in Muslim hands. The Arabs pressed on in the 640s to raid Africa, and to launch attacks over the Taurus mountains on to the Anatolian plateau, and over the Hakkâri mountains and through Azerbaidjan into Armenia. In 653–4 the citizens of Constantinople for the first time saw a Muslim army on the shores of the Bosphorus.[24]

The only slight encouragement may have been that the Persian position was far worse. Before Herakleios' death the Arabs had defeated the Persian armies at the decisive battle of al-Kādisiyya (a re-creation of which regularly appeared on Iraqi television throughout the 1980s during the Iran–Iraq war), the Persian capital, Ctesiphon, had fallen, and the shah and his nobility were refugees on the Iranian plateau. By the mid-650s the Sasanian state had effectively ceased to exist. The old political order had come to a rapid and unexpected end.

Given the nature of the sources it will always remain difficult to explain the collapse of the Roman east in the 630s and 640s, but certain factors do suggest themselves. Firstly, like the steppe nomads to the north, the Arabs were excellent warriors within a culture that prized personal valour. Isolated bedouin raiders were no particular threat, but united Arab groups such as the confederate allies of the Romans were a much more formidable proposition. The Ghassānids had been as effective in pitched battle against the Persians as any other Roman troops.

Mention of the confederates helps to emphasise the point that this was not an invasion of alien nomadic barbarians overthrowing the civilised settled world of the Near East. It was not even an obvious enemy invasion like a Persian attack. The appearance of the Muslim armies had more of the characteristics of an internal struggle for power. The Roman eastern provinces were full of Arabs, nomadic and settled, who had been in a close relationship with the empire for centuries. In particular, as seen in Chapter 3, from the fourth century onwards a succession of Arab political confederations had developed on the edge of the Fertile Crescent, whose leaders depended on Roman subsidy and political recognition, and whom the Roman authorities used for various military purposes, including the suppression of internal revolts. New Arab confederations had tended to advertise their presence by attacking the empire's existing Arab clients whom they hoped to replace. Cities in this region, like Bostra, many of whose citizens were in any case ethnic Arabs, were quite prepared to come to terms with such confederations, knowing that in a few years they would have become part of the Roman provincial hierarchy. After a

nineteen-year absence of imperial authority from the region
an inter-Arab struggle to become the next favoured clients on
the return of Roman administration was to be expected. Later
sources, both Islamic and Syrian Christian, emphasise the numbers of Arabs fighting on both sides.[25] Neither the provincials
nor the imperial government would have had good reason to
think this was the beginning of an exceptional crisis that would
transform the Near East. Cities sensibly came to terms to avoid
damage to their surrounding fields and gardens, and like the
imperial government waited to see who would come out on
top; both parties imagining that the victors would in due course
be integrated into the Roman world.

Yet the situation in the 630s was of course rather different.
Nearly two decades of Persian rule had accustomed the provincial population of the east to the absence of Roman authority. In fact a generation had grown up without ever knowing
Roman rule. Imperial control was still slowly being reconstructed
when the Muslim invasions began, and much of Palestine, Syria
and Transjordan was effectively self-governing under their bishops
and local notables. The Muslim Arabs must have appeared, at
least to start with, as a desirable continuation of this state of
affairs.

Much more significant, unlike the past, the Arabs in the 630s
were united under the leadership of Muhammad and his successors, and provided with an ideology which did not look to
Constantinople. Previous Arab confederates had all been Christians. The only immediate outside influence on the Muslims
seems to have been the Jews, but again this would have been a
force for change. A phase of messianic anti-Roman fervour is
well-documented among the Jewish population in the Near East
in the early seventh century, and they were certainly a group
excluded from the empire's Christian–Roman identity with every
wish to see the old order fall.[26]

Finally the empire had only a limited ability to strike back.
The Romans had achieved victory against Persia through a Turkish alliance, and by making a supreme effort to raise an army
despite the loss of the empire's most productive regions. If
Herakleios' eastern campaign had failed in 627–8, then there
were no further stocks of church treasure to melt down, and it
would have been some time before the attempt could have

been repeated. Even in 629 the eastern provinces had not been reconquered. Herakleios had gained his ends by causing a political crisis in the Persian heartland, and using these divisions to negotiate the return of the eastern provinces. As the history of Roman–Persian warfare in Mesopotamia shows, if your opponent held on to the major fortress cities, it was very difficult to make any significant advances. Once the Muslims had taken the cities of the east, won a decisive battle at Yarmūk and forced the Roman army to regroup in Anatolia it was always going to be very difficult to reverse the situation. A decisive victory in the field was the best hope, but without the eastern provinces, the war-weary empire lacked the resources and the allies for such an endeavour.

The End of the Ancient Economy, c. 650–750

MILITARY defeat brought with it the end of the old economic order. By the second half of the seventh century the Muslims controlled the richest parts of the Near East – Iraq and Egypt, Syria, Palestine, the Caspian coastlands and Khorasan – and in these areas the underlying prosperity of the Near East at the beginning of the century continued. Indeed there is a case that it was gradually enhanced by the new opportunities for commercial activity within the huge bounds of the Muslim empire, and the spread of the cultivation of different crops from their previously more limited ranges.

Looking at those areas which had been part of the Roman world in 600, the best evidence for continued economic prosperity comes from Jordan, and above all the site of Pella in the Jordan valley where an Australian team is currently revealing impressive evidence of urban wealth in the seventh, eighth and now ninth centuries. Finds of public and private buildings, coins and pottery show a city that was different from a Roman city of, for example, the second century AD, but very much in line with the developments in urban culture already well under way at the end of the sixth century. Similar evidence has come from other sites in Jordan, from the cities of Jerash (Gerasa), Beit Rās (Capitolias) and Akaba, from villages such as Fāris near Kerak, and from the so-called desert palaces (perhaps constructed by the Ummayad caliphs and their associates to keep in touch with the bedouin tribes who had brought them to power). Further north in Syria one can point to the continuing prosperity of the villages of the basalt Hawrān district and of Tchalenko's limestone massif, in the south and north of the country respectively. Damascus with its agricultural hinterland, the *Ghūta*, was also thriving. In Egypt the papyri show the region's agricultural wealth being turned to the benefit of its new rulers, whose new capital, al-Fustāt, was booming in these years. Historians and archaeologists no longer believe the Ummayad Near East to have been the victim of bedouin devastation. Instead its economy can be seen as the continuation and natural development of the prosperous world of 600 which had supported Roman imperial power.[27]

In what remained of the Roman world ruled from Constantinople the position was very different. The detailed picture will remain uncertain as long as medieval archaeology remains so underdeveloped in Turkey and Greece, but there is no doubt that devastated by continuing Arab invasions and raids by sea and land, and cut off from the main trade routes of the Near East which now focused on Syria, Egypt and Iraq, the empire's economy rapidly fell away from the levels of 600. In Chapter 3 coinage, pottery and buildings were used as a gauge of the empire's economic health at the end of the sixth century. Turning again to these materials, the economic life of the empire a century later has clearly undergone a remarkable collapse. The best evidence comes from copper coins, which are a good guide to the level of basic monetary transactions. While they continue to be common in Muslim territory, they virtually disappear inside the empire. In excavations at Ephesos, Sardis, Priene, Miletos, Pergamon, Didyma and Aphrodisias – all cities in the western Asia Minor coastal plains, which was one of the few major agricultural areas left in Roman hands – very few copper coins of this period have been found. The same applies to Corinth and Athens in Greece, and seems to be true of every so-far excavated Roman provincial city site.[28]

The study of pottery shows the same picture. The 'red-slip' fine wares, imported from North Africa or produced in Phokaia in western Asia Minor, are no longer found. A long tradition of manufacture and distribution had come to an end. After the mid-seventh century late Roman forms of amphorae (previously used as cargo containers) disappear. The same occurs in the Islamic world, but there they are replaced by large quantities of new pottery types. With the partial exception of Constantinople where John Hayes's work on the material from Saraçhane has marked a major advance in our knowledge, it is very obscure what the emperor's subjects used for pottery from the mid-seventh century onwards. It would certainly be wrong to conclude that pottery was no longer made or used in the provinces, but the fact that archaeologists have been able to ignore its existence points to low-quality locally-produced coarse wares, with all that that implies for the disappearance of centres of production and the end of long-distance trading networks.[29]

Buildings too show an economy in severe decline. Romans in 700 still wanted to build churches. Indeed in Armenia, where a lightly-taxed nobility could still afford to do so, a number of very fine buildings date to these years. In Roman territory the list of churches built before the tenth century is very short, and for the seventh and eighth centuries there is almost a total blank. Unlike the limestone massif where it was argued that expenditure on church silver had become an alternative focus of patronage, there is no sign from this period in Roman Asia Minor of compensating activity in another medium.[30]

However, there is an important distinction to make – the economy had suffered severe recession not complete collapse. The level of prosperity indicated by the physical remains of Roman provincial cities during these years can give an extremely gloomy impression. Indeed when the archaeological evidence was first studied, material for the two centuries after 650 seemed to be so scant that it was easy to believe that most sites had been abandoned. Urban life it was argued had come to a virtual end over most of Asia Minor, and the population now lived in dispersed villages, looking to refuge castles in time of Arab attack. This was a reasonable interpretation on the basis of the evidence available, but the evidence was not a proper reflection of the early medieval world. It was provided only as a by-product of the researches of classical archaeologists, who were principally interested in recognisable fine-wares and structures

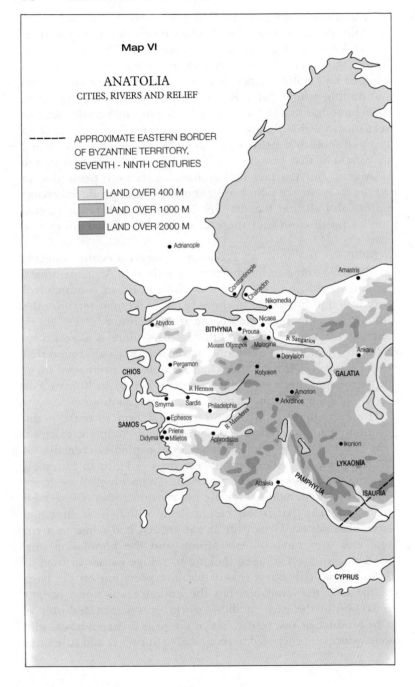

Map VI

ANATOLIA
CITIES, RIVERS AND RELIEF

---- APPROXIMATE EASTERN BORDER
OF BYZANTINE TERRITORY,
SEVENTH - NINTH CENTURIES

LAND OVER 400 M
LAND OVER 1000 M
LAND OVER 2000 M

Adrianople

Amastris

Constantinople
Chalcedon
Nikomedia

Nicaea
Abydos
BITHYNIA Prousa
Mount Olympos Malagina   R Sangarios
Dorylaion   Ankara
Pergamon   Kotyaion   GALATIA
R Hermos   Amorion
Smyrna Sardis   Arkrolnos
Philadelphia
Ephesos
SAMOS   Priene   R Menderes
Didyma Miletos   Aphrodsias   Ikonion

LYKAONIA

Attaleia   PAMPHYLIA
ISAURIA

CHIOS

CYPRUS

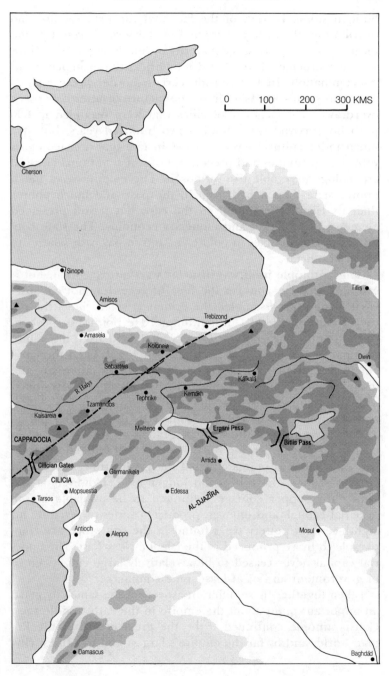

0   100   200   300 KMS

Cherson

Sinope

Amisos

Amaseia

Trebizond

Koloneia

Sebasteia

R. Halys

Tephrike

Kemakh

Kalikala

Tzamandos

Kaisareia

Melitene

Ergani Pass

CAPPADOCIA

Cilician Gates

CILICIA

Germanikeia

Amida

Bitlis Pass

Mopsuestia

Edessa

AL-DJAZĪRA

Tarsos

Antioch

Aleppo

Mosul

Damascus

Tiflis

Dwin

Baghdād

built in stone. In view of the fact that the manufacture and distribution of fine-wares stopped in the seventh century, and up until recently the large majority of buildings in Asia Minor were constructed of wood and mud-brick, the evidence needs re-examination. In fact outside certain border areas such as Cilicia in south-east Asia Minor the picture of utter collapse is overdrawn. The majority of cities that were occupied in 600 probably survived the following two hundred years, but at a much lower cultural level – so low in fact that archaeologists with the techniques and preconceptions of traditional classical archeology were able to overlook it. The empire was a much poorer state than it had been in the past, and much poorer than its Islamic neighbour to the east, but it still preserved elements of a market and monetary economy. The state continued to collect taxes in gold coin, and to pay cash salaries to imperial officials.

Constantinople itself was in many ways an exception, but it can also serve to confirm the idea of recession not collapse. Cyril Mango has assembled the evidence which shows the decay of early medieval Constantinople. He points to the contraction of the city's port facilities by about a quarter; the failure to repair the aqueduct of Hadrian (which had been the city's chief water supply) for nearly one hundred and fifty years; the disappearance of ancient public buildings, leaving the city dotted with dangerous ruins, together with a very small list of new constructions, almost entirely limited to the imperial palace and its environs; and the signs that much of the city was given over to farm land, leaving isolated pockets of habitation inside the walls. He also points out that the great fifth-century open cisterns seem to have been no longer used. However, at the same time copper coinage continued to be available in the imperial capital, and one can produce a series of seventh and eighth-century pottery types found in the city which are comparable to those produced in the Islamic Near East. The imperial capital never ceased to be a relatively large city, a centre of government and of at least some commerce.[31]

Taken together these different aspects of the same city make an important point about the empire in the early middle ages. Constantinople continued to be the great centre of the Roman world, and by far the empire's largest and wealthiest city.

Indeed it was now the empire's only such city; and from the seventh century onwards throughout the early middle ages it was relatively more important than it had been in 600 or before. Its preservation was essential to the empire's survival. However, its prosperity was relative to the picture of decay in Asia Minor and the Balkans. In the chapters which follow this fact should not be forgotten.

After the mid-seventh century a gulf opened up between the wealthy Islamic world and the economies of its western neighbours. The prosperous economy of the ancient world had been receding to the east for several centuries. In Britain it had ended in the fifth century, in Gaul and Italy it had ceased to operate effectively by the end of the sixth century; now Constantinople and Asia Minor suffered, perhaps not so severely, but certainly something of the same fate. The world had been divided before the seventh century, but the Roman empire was no longer on the right side. This development is fundamental to an understanding of the early medieval Near East.

5. How the Roman Empire Survived

From Rome to Byzantium

TO BEGIN WITH a question of terminology. In previous chapters I have stressed the power, prosperity and stability of the Roman empire in 600. That empire was very different in a number of ways from the empire of the third century, let alone the first century AD. Mention of the Roman empire can often conjure up images of marching legionaries, pagan temples and the Latin language. None of these characterised the empire in 600. The striking force of its army was now cavalry; it was Christian; and the dominant language was Greek. Yet it was still the same empire which had dominated the Near East continuously since the first century; indeed at the end of the sixth century it seemed more firmly entrenched than ever. The Chinese empire was a very different state in the tenth century than in the first century or the eighteenth. Even so there is an underlying continuity behind its cultural changes, and, despite fluctuations, its imperial ambitions were always focused on the same regions. As a result no one argues about calling this Far Eastern state in different periods, and under different dynasties, the Chinese empire. The same seems to apply to the Roman empire in 600. It had changed, but no more than one would expect in the history of a state over several centuries. It was still the Roman empire, and known as such to its citizens and enemies. Historians, however, need to signal different periods. Lacking the convenient dynastic labels which are available to Chinese historians, something is necessary to refer to the Christian Roman empire of the fourth to seventh centuries, and I find the term 'late Roman empire' accurate and convenient.

After the mid-seventh century a major change occurred. The Romans were still there, but no longer a superpower; instead they were a medium sized regional state based on Constantinople, and fighting a dour battle for survival. Never again would they dominate the Near East. The subjects of this empire still called themselves Romans, and a small number of historians have continued to discuss this period in terms of the 'late Roman empire' or the 'eastern Roman empire'. It is quite correct to point out that the last emperor of the Romans died in 1453 when the Turks stormed Constantinople. However, this has the danger of implying a degree of continuity between the empire of 600 and that of 1000 (let alone that of 1400) which did not exist. Hence I think it more helpful to term the empire after the mid-seventh century the 'Byzantine empire'.

This is primarily no more than a historiographical convenience. The term derives from the fact that Constantinople before Constantine refounded it as the new imperial capital in 324, was a city called Byzantium, in theory named after an eponymous founder called Byzas. Most Byzantines in the early middle ages referred to Constantinople as 'the imperial city', and it is likely that the majority of the inhabitants of the city would not have known what 'Byzantium' meant. However, in literary texts, even ones of fairly limited sophistication, the name appears quite frequently. Its use was a piece of minor pretension, giving an educated gloss. Whenever it appears 'Byzantium' means Constantinople, and the 'Byzantines' are the inhabitants of the imperial city. When it is used in a wider sense – for example a ninth-century saint's life refers to a general arresting a rebel as a 'Byzantine general' – it means no more than someone who is loyal to the government in Constantinople.' As a term to describe the empire it was popularised among scholars in the sixteenth century as a classicising variant of the common medieval French term for the empire, 'l'empire de Constantinople'. As such it describes quite accurately the political and cultural character of the empire after the Islamic conquests.

This use of the terms 'Byzantine' and 'Byzantine empire' has become quite common, but there is certainly no uniform usage among historians and archaeologists. Many use the term for the empire from 324 onwards, which leads to the curious result that archaeologists working in Syria, Israel, Jordan and Egypt talk of the 'Byzantine' period coming to an end before the usage in this book allows it to start. At the time I was writing the section on archaeology in Chapter 1, I happened to meet an archaeologist who was working in Jerusalem, to whom I complained that there was virtually no Byzantine archaeology. Since she had spent a career doing what she termed as just that, there were a few strained moments until we sorted out our respective terminology. This is likely to remain an occupational hazard for the foreseeable future.

How the Empire Survived: the City of Constantine and Theodosios

By the mid-seventh century the Roman empire was clearly facing extinction. The empire's wealthiest provinces were lost to an enemy whose armies were rapidly overrunning the Near East. By the early eighth century the Ummayad caliphs ruled from the borders of India and Tibet to Spain, and from southern Egypt and Arabia to Armenia. The last Sasanian shah, Yazdagird III, was killed in 651, and with his death the Persian empire came to an end.[2] As Arab forces pressed on Constantinople by land and sea, it could reasonably have been expected that the Roman empire would suffer the same fate before the end of the century.

In trying to explain why the Roman empire survived, it is useful to begin by examining why the Persian empire was destroyed. At first sight the Persians would appear to have enjoyed some advantages. Although the economic heartland of the Sasanian empire, Iraq, was divided between a number of religious and ethnic communities among whom Iranian Zoroastrians were a minority, the Iranian homeland was not there but on the plateau. There the population shared to a much greater extent a single cultural identity, and it was protected from Arab attack by the formidable obstacle of the Zagros mountains. Yet in the seventh century neither cultural unity nor natural defences did much to delay the empire's final destruction.

Persian resistance was ineffective because with the loss of Iraq the Persians had lost not only their wealthiest province but their capital, Ctesiphon, and with that the political centre of the empire. The Sasanian state may well have had a less developed sense of unity than its Roman rival. Zoroastrianism was a much more exclusive religion than Christianity, and its adherents were a minority, certainly among the diverse communities of Iraq. However, Ctesiphon and the Sasanian court provided a powerful political and cultural focus that went beyond religious allegiance. As long as that survived the Persian empire could cope with disasters such as the defeat and death of shah Peroz at the hands of the Hepthalites in 484, or the Roman invasion of 627–8 and the fall of Khusro II. Without Ctesiphon and the court, the comparative ethnic unity of the Iranian plateau and the mountainous barrier it offers to an invader coming from the west counted for every little as the Arabs hunted down the last of the shahs.

The Roman empire was able to survive because by contrast its imperial capital was not in the Fertile Crescent. If in the fourth century Constantine had chosen Antioch, Alexandria or Palestinian Caesarea as a capital there can be little doubt that the Roman empire would have gone as swiftly as the Persian.

Constantinople's principal advantage was simply that of its distance from the Fertile Crescent. The journey by land from the Ummayad capital at Damascus to Constantinople was about 1200 kilometres, by sea over 1500. If an army went by land it had to cross the Taurus mountains and then make its way across the Anatolian plateau. Even without opposition this was a long and arduous journey. The journey by sea, open to the usual perils of early medieval navigation, was made more difficult by the pattern of winds and currents in the eastern Mediterranean. These vary according to season, but the basic fact is that it is more difficult to sail anti-clockwise round the sea or from south to north across it, than it is to sail in a clockwise direction or from north to south. Thus it is easier to sail from Constantinople to the Syrian coast, and from there to Egypt, than it is to muster a fleet in either the Egyptian or the Syrian ports and sail it to Constantinople. This factor only applies south of Asia Minor. Once a fleet is based in the Aegean, at Ephesos, or on Crete for example, this particular difficulty is overcome, but as long as Muslim fleets had no permanent base on the north side of the sea they would always be operating against the 'slope'.[3]

Beyond the process of simply getting the necessary force of men and animals to the other side of Asia Minor, was the formidable logistic problem of keeping it fed when it was there, made worse by the recession in the Byzantine economy – all

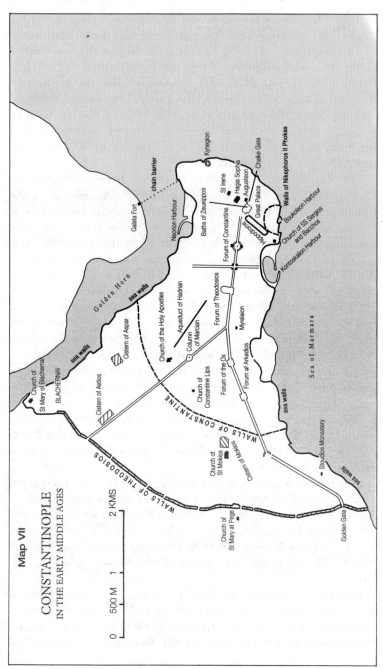

Map VII

CONSTANTINOPLE
IN THE EARLY MIDDLE AGES

Church of St Mary at Pege

Golden Gate

WALLS OF THEODOSIOS

Church of St Mokios
Cistern of Nikolaos

Stoudios Monastery

sea walls

Cistern of Aetios

BLACHERNAI
Church of St Mary of Blachernai

sea walls

Cistern of Aspar

Golden Horn

sea walls

Church of the Holy Apostles

Aqueduct of Hadrian

Column of Marcian

Church of Constantine Lips

Forum of the Ox

Forum of Arkadios

WALLS OF CONSTANTINE

Forum of Theodosios

sea walls

Myrelaion

Sea of Marmara

Galata Fort

chain barrier

Neorion Harbour

Baths of Zeuxippos

Forum of Constantine

Kynegion

St Irene

Hagia Sophia
Augusteon

Hippodrome

Chalke Gate

Great Palace

Walls of Nikephoros II Phokas

Boukoleon Harbour

Church of SS Sergios and Bacchos

Kontoskalion Harbour

0   500 M   1   2 KMS

this being preliminary to the military challenge of capturing the city. To begin with, as the impotent presence of Persian armies at Chalcedon in 616–17 and 626 shows, for an attacker from the east Constantinople was on the wrong side of the Bosphorus. The weakest point in the defences were the sea walls. Ideally an attacker wanted the naval dominance and the technology to launch an attack from the sea. This combination in the hands of the Venetians was to take the city in 1204. But even if that was impracticable, any successful siege demanded a navy capable of safely ferrying an army across to the European side. Once there, however, the real problems were only beginning, because the attacker now had to face what were probably the most powerful city defences of the ancient world.

The triple walls of Constantinople are a key factor in Byzantine history. Their construction had been begun by the emperor Theodosios II before 413, but they were not finally completed until the middle of the century.[4] The inner wall, about 12 metres high and 5 $\frac{1}{2}$ metres thick, was defended by 96 square and polygonal towers, rising some 11 metres above the curtain wall. Beyond this was a second wall about 10 metres high, defended by a further 92 towers. Outside this was a moat between 15 and 20 metres wide, and between 5 and 7 metres deep, beyond which was a third low wall whose principal function was to act as retaining wall for the moat. Ten gates crossed these defences, of which the Golden Gate at the southern end of the walls was the ceremonial entrance to the city. The triple walls, which despite centuries of damage and some rather unfortunate recent restoration are still one of the most impressive ancient monuments in either Europe or the Near East, represent an enormous undertaking. They are over 5 $\frac{1}{2}$ kilometres long, and being built a kilometre and a half beyond the then existing Constantinian walls they almost doubled the area inside the city's fortifications. This huge area between the Constantinian walls and the Theodosian walls was never built up, and never regarded as part of the city proper. In the fifth and sixth centuries, burials, which at that date were still illegal inside the city, were freely allowed here; the system of urban regions into which Constantinople was divided was never extended to include the territory between the walls. Instead this land was used for farming and to provide a secure water-supply, which was contained in huge cisterns also built in the fifth and possibly early sixth century. One of them, the cistern of Aspar, built in 459, was until recently, when it was filled by a shopping-centre, big enough to contain a village and a football pitch. The other two are on the same scale. Whether the cisterns continued in use after the seventh century is not clear. There is no direct evidence, but they are no longer mentioned in the Byzantine period, with the possible exception of a tenth-century saint's life which may be describing the empty cistern of Aspar under the name of the 'dry garden'. If they had still been in use one would have expected some mention of these very large structures, even in the scanty sources for Byzantine Constantinople.[5] In any case it does not alter the important fact that the existence of open land inside the walls was a vital factor in the city's ability to resist siege. Used to grow crops and graze animals it provided Constantinople with a limited but secure source of food. As a result, the imperial city was in the fortunate and very rare position that as long as the population to be fed was not too large, and what could be grown inside the walls was supplemented by stocks brought into the city beforehand, the besieging army in a war of attrition was more likely to starve than the besieged.

Theodosios II and his advisors were frightened into building this enormous belt of fortifications by the threat of the Goths and Huns. Had they not been built the empire would not have survived. Without them, not only would it have been impossible to resist the Arabs, but the Muslim armies would have arrived to find that the last Roman emperor had already been replaced by the Avar qaghan. And had they not been built in the late Roman period, the post-seventh century Byzantines had neither the resources nor probably the technology to have built on anything approaching this scale. Throughout the early middle ages the Byzantines kept the land-walls in repair, which sometimes involved quite major reconstruction; but where it was necessary to build a new stretch of wall, such as the extension to surround the church of the Virgin in the suburb of Blachernai at the north end of the land walls, contructed by Herakleios after 626, or quite probably the greater part of the sea walls, which seem to have been built, or at least extended to include the whole city at about the same period, the result was very inferior.[6]

Because Constantinople survived, the empire survived. However decayed the city became, however much the population may have dwindled, it remained the centre of politics, diplomacy and administration, and the source of the empire's identity. To be a Roman was to be a servant of the emperor in Constantinople and to be a Christian as defined in the imperial city.

The site of the imperial city and its triple land-walls is not only a key factor in its own right, but also emblematic of the general point that the Roman empire survived the seventh-century crisis by drawing on its late Roman inheritance. One aspect of that inheritance was the site of the imperial capital chosen in the fourth century, and the land-walls built in the fifth century. The existence of Constantinople as a secure base of Roman power allowed the Byzantine empire to make use of other aspects of its inheritance. It is worth stressing again that the empire in 600, let alone the empire of the previous two centuries, was by the standards of the pre-industrial world, a powerful, well-organised and wealthy state. It had surmounted the crises of the last war with Persia because of, not in spite of, its political, cultural, administrative and military traditions. Driven from Syria, Palestine and Egypt, the empire could no longer be a great power. It was now battling for its very survival, and to do so it would have to adapt, but equally it could only survive by drawing on its imperial inheritance built up over centuries. Without it the prospects of an independent state in an increasingly decayed Asia Minor would have been absolutely nil.

In practical terms the survival of Constantinople preserved a number of fundamental late Roman institutions: the fiscal system, the imperial court, the army and the orthodox church. In each case these institutions changed so much during the early middle ages that to talk of simple continuity is rather misleading. Nonetheless the Byzantine world was working from a base established in the late Roman period, and comparison with the history of the post-Roman kingdoms in the west shows that without this inheritance none of these institutions would have been likely to develop.

Taxation

IN SOME ways the differences between the Byzantine empire of
the early middle ages and the other post-Roman kingdoms in
the west were small. Certainly in terms of economic wealth,
military power or cultural sophistication the differences were
not very great; but in terms of political structure, what distinguished them was fundamental.

The root of these differences lies in taxation. The late Roman empire in west and east had been based on taxation. In
particular areas, at various times for various purposes taxation
had been collected in kind, but the basis of the fiscal system
was the general payment of taxes in gold coin. The western
kingdoms naturally tried to maintain this valuable privilege,
but nowhere in the west (outside the remaining imperial territories in Italy) did the ability to impose general taxation survive the sixth century. With taxation disappeared centralised
states on the late Roman model, and the power of civilian
administrators who had once collected and dispensed the fiscal
revenues. Power now came to rest on the possession of land,
and the personal support of a warrior retinue. Increasingly an
effective king was a warrior, whose victories provided booty to
reward his supporters, and whose year passed in a constant
itinerary to keep up personal links with a widespread landed
nobility.[7]

In the Byzantine world, however, behind the walls of Constantinople, there was preserved the necessary expertise to
maintain a system of general taxation. For most of this period
the official in charge of administering the land tax – the most
important of the Byzantine taxes – was the logothete of the
genikon based in Constantinople where his subordinates kept
registers recording the tax liabilities of the empire. As well as
these keepers of the central register, his staff included officials
based in the provinces who kept local registers, revised individual
liabilities, and actually collected the tax. Most importantly all aspects of fiscal administration on the ground were independent
of the rest of the provincial administrative system. Tax collectors and other fiscal officials reported directly to the logothete
of the *genikon*, not to the strategos of the military province or
theme (for whom see pp. 171–2 below), and in many cases the

fiscal province, the *dioikēsis*, did not coincide with the theme.[8]

In the sixth century some tax had been paid in kind, but the greater part was paid in gold coin, and this mixture of cash and kind continued from the seventh century onwards. The payment of most taxes in gold is well documented for the period after 800, but for the seventh and eighth centuries this is a controversial issue. Several historians have felt that the poverty stricken empire of these years could not have maintained taxation in gold. This conclusion receives some support from the appearance in Byzantine texts of the term *synone*, which in the late empire had referred to the official requisition of goods in kind. It is not absolutely clear whether the Byzantines used *synone* to mean the land tax itself or only a supplement, but the fact that this is not clear serves to emphasise the point that payments in kind must have played a large part in the early medieval tax system.[9] However, against this one can point to the reference in Theophanes to Leo III's decision in 740 to levy an extra *miliaresion* (a silver coin worth a twelfth of a nomisma) on every gold coin paid in taxation, an act which implies that taxation was normally levied in coin; and to the story told by both Theophanes and Nikephoros that Constantine V taxed people so heavily in 767–8 that farmers were forced to sell their products extremely cheaply to find the necessary sums in cash.[10] More important, throughout the seventh and eighth centuries the imperial government continued to mint fine gold coins, and to make payments to soldiers, civil officials, foreign powers and native artisans in cash. Without a constant inflow of gold in the form of taxation both the minting and the payments would soon have come to a halt – as they did in the Frankish world where, after taxation ended, the gold coinage rapidly became extremely debased and then disappeared.[11] Clearly, even if taxation in kind became more important during these years – in some areas perhaps becoming the predominant form of tax – over the empire as a whole monetary taxation on a substantial scale always survived. How the inhabitants of war-torn Asia Minor managed to make these payments is an interesting problem, but it must confirm the point already made at the end of the last chapter, that however decayed the Byzantine world became, it never wholly ceased to be either a market or a monetary economy.

The survival of a tax system which brought a substantial revenue in gold coin to Constantinople allowed the imperial city to remain the political centre of the empire. The loss of the eastern provinces was bound to make Constantinople relatively more important; but in addition, the existence of a tax revenue flowing into the city ensured that nothing else in the much raided territories left to the empire could match the imperial capital as a source of wealth and hence of political power. The Byzantine political community as members of the army, or as holders of imperial posts and titles, were paid salaries out of tax revenue. No amount of landowning provided a real alternative. If it is possible to characterise developments in the early medieval west as amounting to a privatisation of power, in which individual great landowners could successfully defy the residual powers of the state, in the Byzantine world power remained in state hands, and the individual could only be powerful in such a society in so far as he could share in the running of the state. Byzantine history is full of rebellions and coups, but none represented a major threat to the unity of the empire. The only purpose of a revolt was to take over the centre of power in Constantinople. If it succeeded then there followed a new emperor on the imperial throne; if it failed the rebel's supporters would soon desert in favour of the regime in Constantinople which alone could pay their salaries.

The Imperial Court

The details of how the imperial court was organised changed considerably over the period between the seventh and early eleventh centuries, but its fundamental role remained the same. Backed by the indispensable revenues provided by the land tax, the imperial court in Constantinople acted as the focus of the Byzantine political community. The unity given to the Byzantine world by the imperial court was as essential to the empire's survival as the city walls.

The home of the emperor and the imperial court was the Great Palace which lay in the south-eastern corner of Constantinople, south of the Great Church of Hagia Sophia, east of the hippodrome and bordered on its other sides by the sea. The Great Palace was made up of a number of separate halls, pavilions, courtyards, barracks, kitchens and churches, approached by land through the Chalkē gate in the north-west corner, and by sea through the palace harbour of the Boukoleon on the south side.[12] The dispersed character of the whole complex must have had much more in common with that of the Ottoman Topkapı palace which now covers the hill to the north of Hagia Sophia, overlooking the Golden Horn, than with later western palaces such as Buckingham palace or the Louvre. The Great Palace had slowly evolved since the fourth century, so that even by the seventh century parts of the palace were already an ancient monument, and over the course of the early middle ages sections fell into disuse and ruin and were replaced by others. As a result by the early eleventh century the core of the palace had slowly shifted to the southern end of the site leaving behind derelict buildings that had once been at the heart of imperial life. Opulent the Great Palace certainly was, but it would probably have struck the modern observer as a peculiarly chaotic and rather run-down series of structures.

The palace was the political centre of the empire. Byzantines flocked to the imperial court in search of rank and office. They wanted these because imperial rank was the only recognised mark of status in Byzantine society, and because officially through imperial salaries, and unofficially through opportunities for what we would call corruption, imperial office of any sort brought wealth.

First a piece of essential explanation. Byzantine titles were divided into honours and offices. The titles of *magistros* and *patrikios*, for example, were both senior titles in the court hierarchy, but their holders had no particular office. *Magistroi* and *patrikioi* can be found performing a variety of tasks, but from the title alone one could merely deduce that its holder was an important figure at court. 'Logothete of the *genikon*', or 'domestic of the *scholai*', however, are the titles of a particular office. The logothete of the *genikon* has already been mentioned; the domestic of the *scholai* was the commander of one of the imperial guards regiments. From the eighth century onwards the *scholai* were an élite regiment, and in the ninth and tenth centuries the domestic of the *scholai* was usually the commander-in-chief of the imperial field army on the eastern front. It was usual for office holders to combine their post with an honorific rank. In the case of the domestic of the *scholai* or the logothete of the *genikon*, both important figures, one could expect a fairly senior honorific title. By the tenth century both would probably have been *patrikioi*.[13]

The system was not static. Over the centuries there was a tendency both for the titles of active offices to become mere honours, and for there to be a gradual inflation of honours. For example, the term *spatharios* ('sword-bearer') had once referred to active guardsmen either in the service of the emperor or serving as a general's bodyguard. In 532 Belisarios used his own *spatharioi* when he stormed the hippodrome to suppress the Nika riot, at the same time as imperial *spatharioi* were guarding the emperor. By the end of the seventh century, *spatharios* had simply become a fairly high ranking and purely honorific title. Over the following two centuries, the status of the title gradually declined, and senior officials who as late as 750 might have been *spatharioi* are increasingly found as *protospatharioi*, 'first sword-bearers' – a title that had originally indicated the officers of the imperial *spatharioi*. By the mid-tenth century at the latest, there were large numbers of *protospatharioi*, from a whole range of backgrounds and with no military potential whatsoever. The effect as they lined up for ceremonies must have been akin to the sight of the rows of merchant-bankers, stock-brokers and wine-merchants who at the end of the twentieth century form the Royal Company of Archers, guarding with their bows the sovereign in Scotland.[14]

At any particular period, however, the ranks and offices of the imperial court could be arranged in an ordered hierarchy. Several lists survive from the ninth and tenth centuries which not only give the individual honours and offices in order of precedence, but also set out the precedence of the various possible combinations of the two. The most elaborate of these, the *Kleterologion*, was produced by a certain Philotheos in 899 and is in effect a treatise on the hierarchy, its order of precedence, and the ceremonies which marked the imperial year.[15] Although in practice the hierarchy was much more flexible and dependant on the emperor's will than such lists imply, they still justly reflect the ideal of an ordered stable hierarchy which lay at the heart of the imperial court and hence of the Byzantine political world.

Like all other Near Eastern societies, medieval and modern, about which anything is known, the maintenance and assertion of personal and family honour was a major activity in the life of all Byzantines, other than those such as slaves and beggars who had no claim to 'honour' in the first place. The Byzantines had a concept of being 'well-born' or 'noble', *eugenēs*, and over the course of the early middle ages the Byzantines seem to have become gradually more conscious of the importance of this quality. *Eugeneia*, nobility, was associated with birth and 'blood', but the link was never defined more closely than that it depended on being free-born, rather than a slave, and being recognised by others as *eugenēs*. The result of this lack of definition was, as in other similar societies, a ceaseless competitive status-conscious assertion of personal honour.[16] In the Byzantine world this social behaviour was focused on the imperial court. The easiest and most reliable way to achieve or assert nobility was through imperial office and court rank. The holders of such positions were by definition *eugenēs*: and in imperial ceremonies the holder of an imperial title could display his *eugeneia* to his peers, rivals and inferiors. An ambitious Byzantine could not keep away from court because without imperial rank his honour would always be called into question by those with a title; while once he had title the assertion of his status would demand his presence at court to take part in the ceremonial which would display and confirm it.

The importance of court ceremonies in such a system is perhaps a point which needs stressing. Ceremonies which clearly displayed the imperial hierarchy and the individual's place within it were central to the Byzantine political and social system. Their role and importance can be compared to the line-up of politburo members on the tomb of Lenin for the May day procession in Moscow, which in the Stalin and Brezhnev eras was so crucial a guide to Soviet politics.

As well as status, the Byzantine was looking for wealth. Most imperial titles and offices brought with them a salary paid in gold coin; and increasingly as Arab raids ravaged Asia Minor and the economy decayed, they came to represent a virtually unique source of wealth on this scale. As with so many other aspects of the Byzantine world, the best description of the system in operation – that given by the Italian, Liudprand of Cremona – is no earlier than the tenth century, but the payment of salaries is well attested in the late Roman period, and there are occasional references to show the system still operating during the intervening centuries.[17] Liudprand's account dates from 950 when he was in Constantinople as part of an embassy for the king of Italy, Berengar II:

In the week before the Feast of *Baiophoron*, which we call the Feast of Palms, the Emperor makes a distribution of gold nomismata to the military, and to various officials, each receiving the sum appropriate to his office. Because he wished to interest me the Emperor commanded me to attend the distribution. It took place after this fashion. A table ten cubits long and four wide had been brought in, which table carried nomismata tied up in purses. The recipients then entered at the command of somebody who read out the list of names according to the dignity of the officials involved. The first of these officials is termed the *rector domus . . .*, and his nomismata together with four *skaramangia* [ceremonial tunics] were placed not in his hands but upon his shoulders. Next were the officials termed the domestic of the *scholai* and the droungarios of the *ploimon*, the one of whom commands the military, the other the navy. These, because they were of equal dignity, received an equal number of nomismata and *skaramangia* which, on account of their bulk, they were unable to carry off even upon their shoulders, but dragged off behind them with the aid of others. After these there were admitted the *magistroi*, to the number of twenty-four, who each received the number of pounds of gold equal to to their total of twenty-four, together with two *skaramangia*. Then after these followed the order of *patrikioi*, and they were given twelve pounds of nomismata together with a single *skaramangion*. As I do not know the number of *patrikioi*, but only what each was given, I do not know the total amount involved. After these an immense crowd was summoned: *protospatharioi, spatharioi, spatharokandidatoi, koitonitai, manglabitai, protokaraboi*: of whom some received seven pounds, others six, five, four, three, two, or one pound according to the degree of their dignity. I do not wish you to suppose that this was effected in a single day, for it was begun at 6 o'clock, and continued until 10 o'clock, on the fifth day of the week, and it was completed – as far as the Emperor was concerned – on the sixth and seventh days. For those who received less than a pound are paid by the *parakoimomenos*, over the entire week which precedes Easter.[18]

By the tenth century the system had built in a further link between the Byzantine political community and the imperial court. Titles were for sale, usually at a standard price, but it could easily rise when there were doubts as to the candidate's suitability. When a Byzantine bought a title, he was also buying an annual salary which, according to the figures that have survived, represented a return of about 3 per cent on the original investment. It was also possible at a considerably higher price to purchase an increased salary, amounting to a return of about 10 per cent; or to purchase the right to dine at the emperor's table at ceremonial feasts. There is no evidence for this system in operation before the tenth century, but in view of the lack of materials the silence is no evidence either way. In any case this system of investment by the political community in the finances of the state was a natural development of the ties binding Byzantines to the imperial court.[19]

Outside such official benefits of a title, any imperial office or contact at court brought opportunities for unofficial advantage. Stories in saints' lives and histories, the requests made in letters, the concern expressed in imperial grants to protect beneficiaries from the actions of imperial officials, and by the tenth and eleventh century, the direct evidence of the documents from the monasteries on Mount Athos all show a world of bribery, extortion, illegal violence and corruption of all sorts. It is an enduring theme of Byzantine history wherever the evidence survives to reveal it, that there was law, which in theory governed how people behaved, and influence at the imperial court, which in practice acted as a short-cut for the benefit of the holders of title and office. Again as with the pursuit of honour, political and administrative corruption, and a steady exploitation of contacts at court so that the law only fell with full rigour on the unprotected outsider, was a fundamental reality of Byzantine life that the empire shares in common with almost every other Near Eastern political culture up to modern times.[20]

Politics in this environment was rarely a matter of policy, but instead a battle for status and the spoils of office. Closeness to the emperor was everything, with the result that whatever the formal court hierarchy might indicate, real power and influence was often most effectively wielded by the staff of the imperial bedchamber, grooms of the imperial horses, and officials such as the Keeper of the Imperial Inkstand who looked after the red ink with which the emperor signed imperial grants. Many of the emperor's close attendants were eunuchs, and it is a useful illustration of how their position as trusted allies of the emperor could circumvent the official hierarchy to note that during the reign of Constans II (641–68) one eunuch of the bedchamber is found commanding a fleet sent against an Arab invasion of Cyprus, and another not only went to Damascus to negotiate with the caliph, and organised the arrest and execution of a rebel soldier on his return, but later the same year led a mid-winter night attack on Amorion which had temporarily fallen into Arab hands.[21] Many other examples could illustrate the same point. This potential for power and influence attracted candidates and it could be a useful investment to castrate a young member of the family and send him to serve in the imperial court. In one of the versions of the *Synaxarion* of Constantinople (a collection of abbreviated saints' lives) there is a story of a childless man called Metrios from the countryside of northern Asia Minor, whom God rewards for an act of virtue by blessing him with a son. Metrios promptly castrates the child and sends him to Constantinople where he rises high in the imperial service and becomes *parakoimomenos* ('Keeper of the Imperial Bedchamber') and *patrikios*. Thus does Metrios make his fortune, and so virtue is rewarded.[22]

To a modern observer it is difficult to accept that the snake-pit politics of a corrupt court can be of benefit, but the example of Metrios and his son well illustrates the role of the imperial court in the lives of thousands of Byzantines throughout the remaining lands of the empire. As long as this focus existed it was possible for the state to survive. Without it, it is difficult to believe that the inhabitants of Asia Minor would have shown greater powers of resistance to Islamic conquest than did the nobility of Iran.

The Army and Navy

Both the Byzantine army and the Byzantine navy were institutions inherited from the late Roman empire. Both had to adapt to the shattering consequences of defeat in the seventh century; and as one would expect with any institution over several centuries, both services developed and changed considerably over the early medieval period as a whole. Yet behind the changes there is considerable continuity. Still in the tenth century there were regiments with a continuous history stretching back to at least the fourth century. A major factor in the empire's ability to survive the crisis of the Arab invasions, was the existence of armed forces, composed of volunteers paid in coin from the proceeds of taxation, commanded by officers appointed by Constantinople from among the court hierarchy, and preserving a tradition of military expertise from their late Roman predecessors.

Looking first at the army, the assessment given above runs counter to what is still in some quarters the established orthodoxy that the seventh century saw the rise of a free peasantry, who had been given land by the state in exchange for a hereditary obligation to serve in the army. These peasant soldiers formed the backbone of the theme armies, and their determination to defend their farms and families in Asia Minor, was an essential factor in the empire's survival.

This thesis owes most to a late nineteenth-century intellectual fashion in Russia which looked to a free peasantry as a source of economic strength, moral virtue and military qualities. In contrast great estates and aristocratic landlords were unproductive and corrupt, suppressing the fine independent qualities of the rural population, and leaving them no incentive to defend their masters' lands against invaders. This antithesis, born out of contemporary issues and debates, was applied to the history of Byzantium, which thus became a moral story

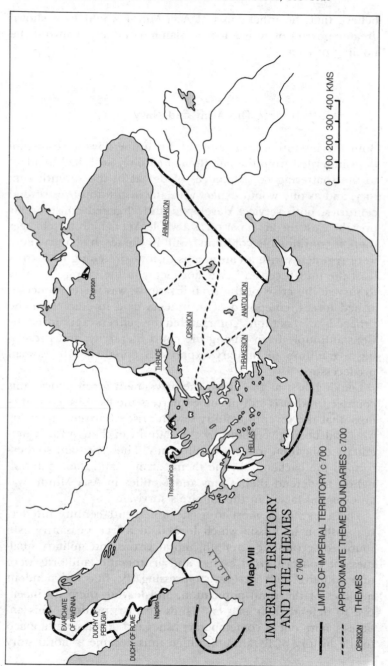

Map VIII

IMPERIAL TERRITORY
AND THE THEMES
c 700

LIMITS OF IMPERIAL TERRITORY c 700

APPROXIMATE THEME BOUNDARIES c 700

OPSIKION THEMES

0 100 200 300 400 KMS

of how the empire was saved in the seventh century by its free peasants, but fell to the Turks at the end of the eleventh century because from the tenth century onwards they had again been reduced to serfdom by the rise of a corrupt aristocracy who had once more divided the land into great estates.[23]

The case for the rise of a free peasantry and a fundamental reform of the system of recruitment and maintenance of the Byzantine army in the seventh century rests in part on evidence for social change in the countryside, and in part on the evidence for the distribution of land to soldiers in exchange for military service. The evidence for social change rests heavily on one document, the *Nomos geōrgikos*, usually known as the 'Farmer's Law' or the 'Rural Code'. This is a collection of 85 articles regulating relations between farmers within a village. Some of the articles concern share-cropping arrangements, but the document is primarily concerned with such matters as property boundaries, straying animals and minor crimes among social and economic equals. The oldest manuscript of the text dates to the eleventh century, or just possibly the end of the tenth. In most of the earlier manuscripts, of the eleventh to thirteenth centuries, the text is included as an appendix to the *Ekloga*, a legal collection attributed to the emperor Leo III (717–41). The exact title given to the Farmer's Law in these manuscripts varies, but in several it appears as 'Chapters of the Farmer's Law extracted from the book of Justinian'.[24] Because of the title it has been argued that the text must be later than the reign of Justinian I (527–65), and the association with the *Ekloga* has been held to imply a date in the seventh or eighth century. Some would go further and argue that the emperor Justinian was Justinian II (685–95; 705–11). So dated, the Farmer's Law has been used to show that a revolution had taken place in the Byzantine rural world; instead of great estates, the countryside of seventh- and eighth-century Byzantium was dominated by the free peasantry whose activities the Law apparently describes.[25]

However, this is not very convincing. First of all, the title proves nothing. The Justinian concerned is likely to be Justinian I, the great law-giver, and creator of the *Corpus iuris civilis*, but the mention is no more than a typical Byzantine case of linking a text to a famous name. It merely proves that medieval

Byzantines associated Justinian with law-making. In any case there is nothing to show that the title is not a later addition. Secondly, although the link with the *Ekloga* suggests that the Farmer's Law was in existence by the eighth century, there is nothing in its content to suggest that it is not considerably older. Recent work comparing the Farmer's Law with other late Roman legal texts would suggest that the Farmer's Law is a fairly typical piece of late Roman vulgar law, similar to the various early law-codes of the western kingdoms, which reflects the application of Roman law as enshrined in the Theodosian Code or the Justinianic Code to the practical problems of the day-to-day administration of justice. As such it fits into a broad context of late Roman law, and there is nothing about the text *per se* which ties it to a specific period.[26]

Since it cannot be fixed in the seventh and eighth century the Farmer's Law loses its value as evidence for a Byzantine rural revolution; but even if the date were solidly attested, this whole approach to the evidence for social change is fundamentally flawed. Legal codes at their most revealing are no more than specific solutions to particular problems. They are not descriptions of the society which produced them. A collection of 85 articles on relations between farmers in a village can be a text that would have been very useful to contemporaries without being a full description of the Byzantine rural world. Even if it had been composed in the eighth century, it would not in any way prove that there were more peasants and fewer great estates than in the past. In fact if one looks at the numerous late Roman saints' lives which describe rural life in the fifth and sixth century, peasant farmers were a dominant characteristic of late Roman rural society long before the Arab invasions. One of the most vivid examples is the Life of St Theodore of Sykeon which is set in the region of Galatia in west-central Asia Minor at the turn of the sixth and seventh century.[27] The Life depicts a world of peasant farmers and villages indistinguishable from that presented in the Farmer's Law, and whatever the date of that text there is clearly no good evidence as yet to suggest that there were more free peasants in 750 than in 550.

If the Farmer's Law is not accepted as decisive evidence, the case for social and military change can be approached from the military side, making various presumptions as to what was likely and what was impossible in the seventh century. One such presumption is that the paid army of the late Roman world could only have been supported out of the revenues of Egypt, Palestine and Syria. With the loss of the eastern provinces, and the devastation of what remained, the empire could not have continued to pay soldiers in cash. The only asset the empire still had available was land, in particular, some would suggest, the imperial estates. Therefore these were distributed to the soldiers in exchange for a hereditary obligation to military service, creating a new class of small independent landowners – in other words the free peasants – who were the basis for the new theme armies. Theophanes is the first to use the word *thema* to mean a military unit, and he does so in the context of Herakleios raising and training a new army against the Persians. On this evidence it has become usual to attribute this reform to Herakleios and date it to the early 620s.[28]

However, this is really no more convincing than the interpretation based on the Farmer's Law. The hereditary obligation on holders of *stratiōtika ktēmata* ('military properties'), to serve in the theme army is well attested by imperial legislation, but none of this dates to before the tenth century. The ninth- and tenth-century evidence seems to suggest that prior to this legislation the obligation to serve was personal rather than tied to the property, but this still takes one back no earlier than the end of the eighth century.[29] The passages from Theophanes are so imprecise that they can be made to mean whatever one wishes, and without them there is nothing to link military service to the land until a much later period and under very different circumstances (see Chapter 7); on the contrary the evidence, although scanty, points firmly in the direction of a paid army on the late Roman model.[30]

The most important piece of evidence comes from a text already mentioned, the *Ekloga*, the law code associated with the emperor Leo III and compiled in the first half of the eighth century in order to bring aspects of Justinian's sixth-century code up to date. If Herakleios, or some other seventh-century emperor, had distributed land to the army in exchange for military service then it would have been essential to ensure that the military service became a hereditary duty associated with an obligation not to dispose of the distributed land. Otherwise the imperial government would soon find itself back in exactly the same position in which it started, except minus the land it had now given away. Chapter sixteen, sections one and two of the *Ekloga* concerns soldiers. Since it is presented as new legislation and has no sixth-century precedents it presumably refers to conditions in the early eighth century. In these sections a soldier is freely permitted to make a will and dispose of his property to whomever he wishes. There is no mention of any constraint, nor of hereditary military obligation, nor of keeping the land intact. In the case where after the death of their parents a soldier and his civilian brother continue to live on the family property, any distribution is to be entirely equal between the brothers, and this is to include the soldier's pay and his arms and horse. It is only if the division takes place more than fourteen years after the parents' death that the soldier is allowed to keep his arms and horse for himself. This legislation is clearly incompatible with any hypothesis of an army supported by military lands. Instead the *Ekloga* takes it for granted that a soldier's major means of support was his pay, which it seems would normally be shared with his family in exchange for his keep outside the campaigning season.[31]

Given the evidence for economic decay, and the apparent disappearance of copper coinage in Byzantine Asia Minor, the argument that the empire could no longer have supported an army to be paid in coin is rather appealing, but there is no doubt that it is contradicted by the evidence. As with the imperial court, the cycle of coin from tax payer to the state, and from the state to its servants, continued to be the basis of imperial power. Seen in the context of economic recession one can easily understand that, just as with titles at the imperial court, a salary paid in gold coin was a powerful attraction to recruits, and the more the Byzantine economy contracted the stronger that attraction became. As long as the state could maintain such payments there would never be a shortage of recruits, or any need to introduce hereditary military obligations. In fact a regular salary paid in gold coin must have had a considerable premium value. Given the scale of the Byzantine monetary economy all over Asia Minor implied by the absence of copper coin, it must have been difficult to raise even small sums in gold to pay taxes or make substantial purchases. A small regular salary in gold would have been an important asset in such circumstances. As a result it is likely that many families would have been keen to have a son or son-in-law in the army whom they would be willing to support in exchange for a share in his income. This seems to be the kind of arrangement presumed by the clauses in the *Ekloga*, and implies that the state could have been paying salaries much lower in real terms than in the buoyant years of the prosperous sixth century and still attracting recruits. As long as the state was virtually the sole source of substantial payments in gold coin, its monopoly would ensure that it had only to pay a low price for services. This would help to explain how, despite the loss of the eastern provinces and the clear evidence for decay and contraction, the empire managed to maintain the system of tax revenues and cash payments.

The evidence for payments in kind forming an important element of seventh- and eighth-century taxation does not undermine this picture. It has been persuasively argued that an obvious use for grain collected as tax would be to feed the army, and that arms and equipment may have been obtained by the same means. It has also been suggested that the *kommerkiarioi*, who appear in the sixth century as officials involved with foreign commerce, had by the second half of the seventh century become responsible for aspects of this system. The evidence comes from a series of lead seals which link the *kommerkiarioi* to the imperial depots (*apothekai*) and to army units in Asia Minor. With their former commercial role hardly applicable here, provisioning or equipping the army seems to be the obvious explanation.[32] This, however, need not imply a reshaping of the fundamental basis of military service. It could just as easily be seen as a simple matter of feeding and equipping soldiers who still served for cash payment. As long as that continued to be so – which is the situation described by the *Ekloga* – the political and fiscal control which characterised the late Roman state's relationship with its armed forces remained in place.

If the case for a radical reform of the Byzantine army in the seventh century is not accepted it becomes possible to see how the army is another example of a late Roman institution continuing into the Byzantine world and enabling the empire to survive. As the empire contracted, the remaining imperial armies in the east and in the Balkans were withdrawn into Asia Minor. They were not posted to the frontiers partly because the Arabs were already, in the 640s, raiding deep into Byzantine territory and therefore they were better placed inside the empire; and partly because it made administrative sense to base them near their supplies of food and future recruits.

From the early seventh century onwards these armies were known as *thema* 'themes'. The derivation of this word is obscure, but the most convincing suggestion is that it comes from the steppe world, from a word meaning a division of 10,000 men or an army. The borrowing would be natural enough given Roman and Byzantine familiarity with the fighting qualities of their Turkish and Avar steppe nomad neighbours; and in any case an army is exactly what it means in the earlier references in Byzantine sources.[33]

The four original seventh-century themes were the Anatolikon, the Armeniakon, the Thrakesion, and the Opsikion. The first two were the armies of the former *magister militum per orientem* and the *magister militum per Armeniam* respectively (*oriens* being the Latin for 'east', and *anatolē* being the Greek). The army of the east was pulled back from Mesopotamia and Syria and based in south-central Asia Minor as the Anatolikon theme, from which the modern term Anatolia is derived. The army of Armenia was withdrawn from Armenia across the upper Euphrates into north-eastern Asia Minor, henceforth known as the Armeniakon. In the west troops could no longer be spared for the Balkans, and consequently the army of the *magister militum per Thraciam* was removed from Thrace and redeployed in the fertile coastal valleys of western Asia Minor as the Thrakesion theme. The final theme, based in north-western Asia Minor close to Constantinople, was the Opsikion, which incorporated a number of imperial guards regiments and the remains of the sixth-century central field army.[34]

Up to the first half of the eighth century when the *Ekloga* was compiled, there was no deliberate far-reaching reform of the late Roman military system. After the mid-eighth century the theme commanders, the *strategoi,* or for the *Opsikion*, a *komes* or 'count', would take over the civilian administration and the themes would become militarised provinces, but in this early period a theme is simply an army, its strategos a general, and the civil administration remained in the hands of civilian governors. The lead seals surviving from their vanished documents show that what was essentially a late Roman civil administration continued to administer the provinces through to the eighth century.[35]

The survival of the late Roman army through the seventh century in the guise of the four themes of Asia Minor was a crucial factor in the survival of the empire itself. The qualities of the late Roman army can easily be obscured by concentrating too much on its failure to defeat the Muslims, and forgetting the army's victories over the Avars, Persians and Slavs. The ninth-century Arab compilers who provide the only detailed accounts of the Arab conquests describe small Arab forces mowing down innumerable Byzantines, and this image has been perpetuated in modern Arabic pulp fiction whose heroes still slaughter treacherous and cowardly Byzantines by the dozen. Yet the available contemporary evidence belies this impression. Even after defeat Byzantine armies stayed in the field, and the Arab commanders and caliphs of the seventh century were sufficiently wary of their ability to strike back to be willing to buy off the Byzantines with tribute during periods of civil war in the Islamic world.[36]

Taking a long view of Near Eastern history it seems clear that the best natural soldiers have always been found among the steppe nomads, the bedouin, and the various mountain peoples of the Balkans, Armenia and the Caucasus, the Lebanon and Anatolia. Men brought up in a culture which puts a high price on individual bravery and skill at arms start with an advantage that the sons of farmers and merchants lack. An army raised from the settled population must compensate by being better organised, better equipped and better drilled. By the mid-seventh century the Byzantine army had lost one of its main recruiting grounds in the Balkan mountains. It still attracted Armenians and Caucasians, and the mountains of Isauria in southern Asia Minor remained in Byzantine hands, but the bulk of the army was recruited from the settled population of Asia Minor and their military ability was above all the consequence of the effectiveness of the army as an institution.

The late Roman tradition provided first of all a sense of

regimental identity, fostered by training and drill, and marked by banners and names. The army was conspicuous in early medieval Byzantium for preserving features of the late Roman past. Many officers still had Latin titles, regiments had names going back to the fourth century.[37] Studies of twentieth-century armies have stressed how important such arcane traditions are in forming the group solidarity which makes for effective fighting units. If a soldier is not already part of a tribal group which can provide the necessary emotional support, the regiment provides an alternative.

Regimental tradition also preserved military skills. A great deal of Byzantine military writing is academic and literary, but some has practical utility and it all reflects a sense of the Byzantine army as the repository of ancient martial knowledge. One should not underestimate the value of inherited experience in all aspects of military life, from operational skills such as how to draw up battle-lines, arrange skirmishers, scouts, fortified camps and so on, to the training of recruits and the organisation of supplies. In any case whether or not the particular tactical systems the Byzantines inherited were exceptionally effective is perhaps less important than the spirit of organisation they brought to Byzantine forces. Again studies of modern armies confirm the importance of soldiers feeling themselves to be part of an organised body carrying out procedures that have worked in the past.

A particular area where inherited technical expertise was an asset was in the building and defence of fortifications. A good illustration of this is the fortress built on the steep acropolis hill above Sardis in western Asia Minor.[38] The fortress was built in the later seventh century to protect the fertile coastal plains from Arab conquest. The acropolis hill at Sardis is one of the outstanding natural defensive sites in the region. Only on one side is the approach simply steep; on the others the hill is surrounded by cliffs and eroded gullies. The defences, largely built from reused blocks which had been carried up in huge quantities from the city below, concentrate on the weaker side and their most striking feature is a massive bastion, constructed from stone blocks with a vaulted brick superstructure. The enemy struggling up the slope towards the fortress is faced by three triangular projections with the characteristic openings for a balista battery, while the defenders remain undercover from counter-fire in the brick fighting gallery. It is a very sophisticated structure reflecting a long tradition of late Roman military fortification, with parallels in Mesopotamia, Africa and the Balkans. It is certainly not a building put up by the local population as an occasional refuge. The only institution with the technology, experience and powers of organisation to build such a fortress was the army, and in this region it must be attributed to the Thrakesion theme. As such it is important not only as direct evidence of the preservation of late Roman skills in fortress building, but also as an indication that the themes would have been able to preserve less tangible traditions of the late Roman army.

As important as those aspects of the late Roman military tradition which contributed to the Byzantine army's effectiveness in action, the seventh-century empire also inherited and maintained a tradition of political control over the army which was equally essential to the empire's survival. In part political control was preserved by the tax-pay cycle, but the example of the dissolution of Byzantine Italy into fragmentary territorial blocs and their piecemeal conquest by the Lombards, despite what was essentially the same system of taxation and a paid army that operated in Asia Minor, shows that political obedience was far from being its inevitable consequence.[39] Important though the preservation of an army dependent on pay was, equally fundamental was the way the military hierarchy was bound into the civilian hierarchy at the imperial court. All the reasons that were adduced in the previous section to explain the attraction the court could exert over the Byzantine population apply as much to soldiers as civilians. In Italy the imperial court was too distant, geographically and socially, from the officers of the Byzantine troops based there. In Asia Minor soldiers went to court to find promotion and reward. Their generals were appointed in Constantinople as a result of court politics, and there was a rapid turn-over to ensure political loyalty. Armies rebelled and protested, but no one was in any doubt that the imperial court was the necessary seat of any decision. As long as this remained so the Byzantine emperor would be a more significant figure in the strategic geography of the early medieval Near East than the resources of his empire might otherwise justify.

On grounds of importance discussion of the Byzantine navy's role in the empire's survival ought not to be limited to the brief remarks here, but in a sense in its very importance the navy is only a further illustration of the general theme that the empire survived by drawing on its late Roman inheritance. This is often overlooked by the exaggerated significance allowed to 'Greek Fire', a highly inflammable substance produced from petroleum, which could either be projected through syphons or thrown in earthenware pots which would shatter on impact in a fashion akin to a Molotov cocktail.[40] It has traditionally been believed, on the basis of the Byzantine accounts alone, that Greek Fire was invented by an engineer from Helioupolis (Ba'albek) in Lebanon, who fled to the empire in 673–4; that the new weapon was a vital factor in the failure of the Arab siege in 717, and that thenceforth the Byzantines kept its manufacture a state secret which guaranteed their naval supremacy.[41]

In fact even if Greek Fire was a new invention in the later seventh century, and only used to begin with by the Byzantines, their monopoly can have lasted only a short time, since Arab texts soon show that Muslim navies were equally familiar with its use. By the tenth century, although the emperor Constantine Porphyogenitus could include the 'secret' of Greek Fire among the concessions never to be granted to barbarian nations, the reality as indicated by Greek and Arabic handbooks on naval warfare is that far from being a 'secret weapon', Greek Fire was a standard part of a warship's armoury.[42] In any case it was never a decisive weapon that gave its user inevitable superiority in battle. Had it been so then it would not have disappeared from the arsenals of later medieval Mediterranean fleets. Like all fire-weapons used in naval warfare against wooden vessels, Greek Fire must have been at its most effective against unprepared enemies in confined waters and with favourable wind and sea conditions; and much more likely to cause serious damage to a small lightly constructed vessel than a heavy-timbered warship. These conditions certainly seem to have applied in 941 when an outnumbered Byzantine force inflicted a decisive defeat on a large Viking–Rus fleet made up of vessels designed to be carried round the rapids on the Dnieper river (see Chapter 8). In 717 the threat of fire seems to have prevented the Arabs moving their ships into the confined waters of the Golden Horn and taking advantage of the city's weak sea walls, but the Byzantines appear to have been using fire-ships – that is, burning boats packed with inflammable material and allowed to drift into the enemy ships – rather than warships armed with Greek Fire. Later in the same year Greek Fire may have been more important in a Byzantine attack against the Arab fleets sheltering in ports in the sea of Marmara.[43] The prominence given to Greek Fire in Byzantine sources reflects contemporary propaganda, and the common desire to believe that your own side has the better weapons. As such Greek Fire appears in Theophanes' account as a technological equivalent to the supernatural protection granted to the city by the Mother of God. The thought of both was good for the city's morale.

While Greek Fire may have been a useful addition to the empire's naval armoury, the real basis of the Byzantine ability to keep the Arabs away from the sea walls was the existence of a fleet which had inherited late Roman naval skills and technology. The sixth-century navy no longer had to face a rival war-fleet in the Mediterranean after the defeat of a Gothic fleet at Senna Gallica in the Adriatic in 551, but Roman naval power continued to be a crucial factor in the western Mediterranean and on the Danube river for the rest of the century. The same superiority in seamanship and naval tactics which defeated the Goths in 551 frequently prevented the Avars from crossing the Danube in the last quarter of the century, and most important, in 626 prevented the Persians joining the Avars in a joint assault on the land walls, and defeated the Slav attempt to attack the city by sea.[44]

Several references in the sources for the seventh century to emperors building new ships for particular expeditions have been interpreted to mean that there was no permanent imperial fleet until the 670s, when we first hear of a naval commander called the strategos of the Karabisianoi.[45] Yet even the scanty sources for the mid-seventh century record substantial naval operations by Byzantine warships in 648–9, 655, 668–9 and 672–3; in addition to which repeated raids by Muslim fleets are recorded in the Arab sources against which the Byzantines cannot have been completely unprepared.[46] Mediterranean naval warfare was complicated, technically demanding and expensive.

Since the building and operation of the Anglo-Greek trireme launched in 1987 at Piraeus, it is now much better appreciated that these complicated vessels require highly skilled shipwrights to build them, experienced crews to row them and port facilities to keep them in operation from year to year. The differences between a seventh-century Byzantine *dromon* and a replica of a fifth-century BC trireme do not detract from the point. Even if it had not been financially ludicrous not to keep these vessels once built in repair, a fleet was only possible at all by maintaining a continuing core of expertise and experience. As Pericles (in words ascribed to him by Thucydides) said in the fifth century BC: 'The fact is that sea power is a matter of skill, like everything else, and it is not possible to get practice in the odd moment when the chance occurs, but it is a full-time occupation, leaving no moment for other things.'[47] Since Constantinople was not defensible without a fleet, the Byzantine navy must have had the same kind of continuous history as the army, the court or the city walls. That the official title of its commander is not mentioned before the first reference to the strategos of the Karabisianoi in *c.* 680 is beside the point. The continuous tradition of the late Roman navy was another factor vital to the empire's survival.

The Church

The fourth late Roman institution essential to the empire's survival was the Christian church, essential not so much as a contributor to military and civilian self-confidence – important though that probably was – but as an organisation which enabled the mass of the emperor's subjects to identify themselves with the fate of Constantinople. In practice most of the emperor's subjects saw themselves less as 'Romans' than as 'orthodox Christians' – and by 'orthodox' they meant Chalcedonians, that is Christians who followed the Constantinopolitan definition of orthodoxy.[48] The survival of Constantinople in the face of Arab attack and their continued membership of an empire ruled from Constantinople was important because their hope of salvation depended upon it.

In Constantinople, as vital as its walls and armies was the sense among its inhabitants that this was a holy city that placed them personally at the heart of sacred history. Byzantine Constantinople was a city filled with churches and the relics of the saints and the passion. When founded in the fourth century the imperial capital had been conspicuously lacking in Christian associations. Its church was not an apostolic foundation. The story that St Andrew ordained the first bishop of the city is no older than the sixth or seventh century. The only local saints were two obscure martyrs, SS. Akakios and Mokios. Yet by the mid-sixth century a massive gathering-in of cults and relics from all over the empire had taken place. Migrants to the new capital had brought with them cults from Asia Minor, Syria, Italy, Sicily, Palestine and Egypt. Constantinople had become unquestionably a holy city, and a microcosm of the Christian world.[49]

At the beginning of the seventh century Constantinople was not only the New Rome, but increasingly too the New Jerusalem, the God-guarded City under the special protection of the Virgin Mary, and the Navel of the Universe which would play a central role in the apocalyptic drama of the Second Coming and the end of the world.[50] These ideas are vividly expressed in a remarkable text known as the Life of St Andrew the Fool. The Life is a fiction and St Andrew never existed but the text gives a striking picture of the world view of the Constantinopolitan élite at the beginning of the eighth century. For most purposes the Christian world has shrunk to Constantinople and its hinterland, stretching to Thessalonica in the west and Asia Minor in the east. The divine plan for the salvation of mankind will be acted out here. Heaven, which St Andrew visits in a vision, is not surprisingly imagined as Constantinople and the imperial court writ large.[51] During the 630s and 640s the Christian cities of the Roman Near East had negotiated and surrendered certainly for military reasons, but also because their identity and hope of divine salvation was not incompatible with some accommodation with their new rulers. The more Constantinople was placed at the heart of the apocalyptic drama the less room there was for anything save resistance to and defiance of Arab attack.

At the head of the church in Constantinople was the patriarch, presiding over several thousand clergy – more than 600 in Hagia Sophia alone – and what amounted to an ecclesiastical theatre which displayed in ceremony and ritual the identity of interest between empire and church.[52] By the time the Life of St Andrew was written this idea was well established inside Constantinople but it was also being spread through the remaining territories of the empire, and this remarkable achievement was the work of the secular church.

Well-documented by saints' lives and the archives of Mount Athos, Byzantine Christianity is more famous for its monasticism, its monks and its ascetic holy men than for its secular clergy. The spiritual values of monks and ascetics pervaded Byzantine culture. Throughout the empire ascetics dispensed advice and counsel to an admiring clientele that ranged in wealth and status from imperial courtiers to farmers and shepherds. During the tenth century, one hermit – St Luke the Stylite – looking for a spot to escape the snares of the world chose the top of a column opposite the imperial palace. His clients, if we are to believe his hagiographer, included the patriarch.[53] In the same century, an emperor – Nikephoros II Phokas – had wanted to become a monk on Mount Athos. Instead he seized the throne and was later assassinated as he passed the night emulating his ascetic heroes, wrapped in a saint's bear-skin mantle, asleep on the palace floor.[54] Monks frequently came from families of the military and civil élite. Theophanes, the author of the *Chronographia*, is an example among many.[55] Others from the same background who did not themselves 'leave the world', gave money and lands to build and endow monasteries. Such a widely shared admiration for holy men and monks was certainly a bond uniting the Byzantine world, but the accessibility of the evidence has arguably led to a comparative neglect of the secular church and a failure to see the importance of its role in the empire's survival.

From the fourth century onwards every city – which means in this context not only the urban settlement itself, but also its surrounding territory – had a bishop. Every bishop had a supporting body of clergy drawn it seems from local families. The bishop was a leading figure in the community. He was a major landowner, a key figure in local administration, and a provider of patronage and authoritative decisions. With the exception of those placed under the emperor or the patriarch, all monasteries in the diocese fell under his authority. The bishop and his clergy played a central part in the rituals of local and personal life. The cycle of the year was punctuated by feasts and processions over which the bishop presided; the cycle of an individual's life was punctuated by rituals to mark birth, marriage and death that from the seventh century onwards became increasingly an ecclesiastical monopoly. To some extent too the day and the week were ordered by the performance of the eucharist and the liturgical hours. Most important of all throughout Asia Minor and what survived of imperial territory in the Balkans local identity was frequently focused on saints' cults, choreographed, performed and presided over by the bishop and his clergy.[56]

The bishop's role is well known for the sixth century, but the evidence for the seventh century onwards is comparatively slight. No episcopal archive has been preserved, and there are very few individual lives of holy bishops, and no series of bishops' lives to match Italian examples such as Agnellus' *Book of the Pontifs of the Church of Ravenna* or the anonymous *Deeds of the Bishops of Naples*.[57] The best evidence for the seventh century comes from Thessalonica where the *Miracles of St Demetrios* show the city led by its bishop and by its martyred saint (who was believed to dwell in his shrine in the great basilica of St Demetrios) resisting Slav and Avar attack.[58] Evidently the status of the bishop was linked to the wealth and vitality of the community over which he presided, and as urban life decayed so drastically after 600 the bishop's position inevitably suffered. But if the bishop of Thessalonica could still lead his community at the end of the seventh century it is difficult to believe that the bishops of Ephesos, Ikonion, Nicaea, Kaisareia or Amorion were any the less influential in the lives of their own cities, however much they had decayed since the sixth century.

Positive evidence for the episcopate in the eighth, ninth and tenth centuries is fragmentary and concentrated at the end of the period, but it is enough to show that the bishop was still one of the leaders of his community. George of Amastris, for example, is described as interceding with high officials and tax collectors, and organising the evacuation of surrounding villages during an Arab raid. Bishops near the monasteries of

Mount Athos were asked in the tenth century to act as judges, to validate documents, arbitrate in disputes and establish boundaries. The bishop of Herakleia near the mouth of the Menderes river in western Turkey was doing the same for the monks of Mount Latros in 987. Leo, bishop of Synada in western Anatolia a few years later, has left in his letters a vivid image of a bishop being greeted with formal ceremonies when he entered his episcopal city, bringing in artists and craftsmen to embellish the episcopal palace, and riding on his horse amidst a throng of suitors, begging for his alms and attention.[59] The physical remains of churches and wall-paintings also contribute to the picture. As important as the evidence of new building and new decoration, are the number of large late Roman cathedrals which were still standing and in use at the beginning of the eleventh century. A good example is Ephesos, where the survival of the huge church of St John through the early middle ages proves the existence of an active and relatively prosperous bishop and clergy to keep the building in repair.[60]

The importance of this network lies in the fact that bishops were closely linked to Constantinople, and they acted as a conduit bringing the ideas of the Constantinopolitan élite into the empire's provinces and spreading the view that Christian salvation and imperial rule were closely bound together. Naturally over an area as vast as Asia Minor, and as traditionally open to rival ecclesiastical influences from Syria, there are signs of regional distinctions, but as a whole what is striking is the apparent uniformity of the secular church. The bishops dispensed doctrine and canon law imported from Constantinople. Their liturgy and the form of their churches increasingly followed Constantinopolitan practice. The icons and wall-paintings of their churches displayed to their congregations St Andrew the Fool's message that heaven was a divine archetype of the imperial palace. All over the empire angels, for example, could be identified in visions because like their painted representations they were dressed as eunuchs of the imperial court.[61]

All bishops were not equal. The secular church was arranged in a hierarchy, and as with the ranks, titles and offices of the imperial court so the ecclesiastical hierarchy was set out in lists (the *notitiai*) whose numerous manuscripts testify to the importance of the idea.[62] At the head was the patriarch in Constantinople. He was a judge and arbiter of canon law and correct doctrine, whose authority was recognised by all orthodox bishops in the ecclesiastical province of Constantinople. The reality of his authority and the extent of the ties involved is well illustrated in the surviving letter collections of patriarch Photios in the ninth century and patriarch Nicholas I Mystikos in the early tenth century. Both show their authors regularly intervening in ecclesiastical affairs throughout the empire, disciplining, ordering, correcting and encouraging.[63]

Beneath the patriarch most bishoprics were arranged in ecclesiastical provinces each presided over by a metropolitan bishop. Bishoprics were ranked in order of precedence within the province, and each province was in turn ranked in the hierarchy. The only exceptions were a number of bishoprics, referred to as autocephalous archbishoprics, which had no suffragan sees and were subordinate only to the patriarch. They ranked below the metropolitans but above all the other sees. A gulf clearly separated the metropolitans and archbishops from the hundreds of ordinary suffragan bishoprics. Letters from the patriarch to a metropolitan, or between metropolitans, usually flatter and charm; letters to a suffragan bishop from either source merely order. The metropolitan sees – including cities such as Kaisareia, Ephesos and Thessalonica – were larger and at least relatively far wealthier than any suffragan bishopric. Their bishops were usually it seems outsiders, typically men who had been educated in Constantinople and promoted to what was seen as a lucrative and prestigious office. (Although obviously rather more lucrative and prestigious at a see such as Ephesos, than at the lowly metropolitanate of Synada.) Suffragan bishoprics were far less glamorous appointments and much more likely to be filled by local candidates.

The scattered evidence, including the letters of Photios and Nicholas Mystikos, shows not surprisingly that the patriarch's closest contacts were with the metropolitans. In part this reflects personal ties. The patriarch and the metropolitans were generally recruited from a similar background and tended to have Constantinopolitan literary culture in common. Both Photios and Nicholas had close friends and loyal political supporters among this group. The close ties also reflect the fact that most metropolitans regularly came to Constantinople. A few held posts in the patriarchal hierarchy which demanded their presence from time to time in the city. In the tenth century it was presumed that there would be at least 12 metropolitans in Constantinople at major feasts to take part in the ceremonies of the imperial court, and while there the metropolitans formed with the patriarch the *endemousa synodos*, the 'standing synod', which acted as a regular ecclesiastical court. The metropolitan bishops were thus readily available to act as conduits for Constantinopolitan influence into the provinces.[64]

Contacts between Constantinople and the hundreds of suffragan bishoprics were for the most part through each bishop's metropolitan. Suffragan bishops who came to Constantinople to pursue cases in front of the patriarch or appeal against their metropolitan's judgements seem to have been exceptional, but without a patriarchal register or an episcopal archive it is hard to be certain. Large numbers of suffragan bishops did, however, come to Constantinople for the great church councils of 680–1, 691–2, 754, 787, 815, 843, 869–70, 879–80 and possibly also that of 920. For these remarkable occasions every bishop subordinate to the patriarch was summoned to the imperial city (or as in 787 to Nicaea). For most of the councils the list recording those who attended has survived, and the number who came, including some from very remote corners of the empire, is impressive testimony to the extent of imperial authority. Councils were obviously events that only took place at most once a generation, but equally they were extraordinary occasions likely to have had an enormous impact on those who attended. Presided over by the emperor (or rather the emperor's representative) and the patriarch, the assembled bishops would have been exposed to the full didactic force of imperial ceremony and sent away with the clear message that salvation lay in orthodoxy alone and that orthodoxy demanded adherence to what was preached in Constantinople. On each occasion the bishops would have returned home to apply the council's doctrinal and sometimes disciplinary canons in their own dioceses, and directly and indirectly to pass on the message of the unity of church and empire.[65]

By whatever means the provincial clergy were kept in contact with Constantinople, their role was crucial. Without their message imperial rule would have been for many in Asia Minor and the Balkans little more than a military hegemony which brought high taxes and limited security. Yet thanks in large part to the operations of the secular church the empire enjoyed a common identity which linked the emperor's subjects to Constantinople, and gave them a sense that present loyalty would ensure salvation in the world to come. In the empire's perhaps rather surprising ability to endure repeated military defeat, economic collapse, and yet still survive and avoid political fragmentation, the secular church and the ideology it preached was no small advantage.

6. The Shock of Defeat

The Byzantine World View

SO FAR the crisis which overwhelmed the late Roman empire at the beginning of the seventh century and the Byzantine empire's ability to survive has been presented in strategic and structural terms. Would this analysis have made sense to contemporary Byzantines?

On one level the answer is clearly yes. Given the information that was available – and one should bear in mind a world without maps, of slow communications and of considerable ignorance regarding all foreign peoples – the Byzantine ruling élite certainly made coherent strategic plans. Rational calculations of strategic and tactical advantage are plain for example in Theophanes' account of the emperor Anastasios II's preparations at Constantinople to face the impending siege of 716–18, or in the changing long-term military and diplomatic response to the Arab threat which will be examined in Chapters 7 and 8. However, it is clear that to the Byzantines these were essentially secondary considerations.

In this the Byzantines differ from the modern western perspective, but it is worth remembering that it is we who are odd, and the majority of human cultures have shared the Byzantine approach. The logic of those who do not share western concepts of causation was first set out by the anthropologists Evans-Pritchard and Gluckman, on the basis of their research in central and southern Africa during the 1920s and 1930s. Take the case of a hut which collapses killing its sleeping occupant. The peoples among whom Evans-Pritchard and Gluckman worked would easily agree with us that the hut had fallen because termites had eaten through its principal supporting beam, but they would regard that as only a rather obvious first step. For them the real question of causation would be why the termites ate through that beam in that particular hut, and why it fell with a particular individual inside. The modern western response that this was only a matter of bad luck or mischance would be seen as a bizarre failure to answer the obviously significant questions.[1]

For most of the peoples that Evans-Pritchard and Gluckman studied the evident answer was witchcraft. Witches do not play the same role in the medieval Near East, but for the Byzantines too to say that the hut fell at that particular moment by accident hardly begins to answer the question. In the same way my strategic and structural analysis is not sufficient. It was a matter of common observation that man's best efforts were regularly set at naught by drought, flood, locusts, disease and storm. Theophanes' *Chronographia* is full of naval expeditions, well-equipped and prepared, yet wrecked by storm. Why was that year chosen for the expedition? Why was that day chosen to set sail? Why was there a storm then? From this perspective, how best to organise and equip a fleet would take an important but nonetheless secondary place.

The Byzantines do not share the African concept of witchcraft, but in their everyday life a similar role was played by demons. Any reader of Byzantine sources is soon struck by the fact that their world was infested by the devil and demons. But at the same time these demons are rather pathetic. Byzantine demons conjure up images of little black figures smelling of blocked drains. The harm they cause is scarcely of cosmic proportions. They turn fresh milk sour, throw stones at travellers, upset business ventures, and the like. At worst they send people mad or make them ill. The principal demonic weapons against the monks and holy men who set themselves up as targets for the devil were usually no worse than the occasional demon disguised as a scorpion, and such tried favourites as boredom and dirty thoughts.[2]

All Byzantine sources make it clear that the devil was fundamentally powerless. Time and again demons turn themselves into dragons or temptingly beautiful women, or take possession of some unfortunate, only to be chased away by a holy man making the sign of the cross. Byzantine enthusiasm for such ascetic individuals suppressing their sexuality with savage mortifications reveals a culture hardly sympathetic to the flesh, but at the same time Byzantine culture was certainly not dualist. The Byzantines were in no doubt that the only power in the universe was God. To think otherwise, as did the Paulicians based in eastern Anatolia between the seventh and ninth centuries, or the Balkan dualists from the tenth century onwards, was a rare and dreadful heresy.

If the only power was God, the Byzantines also believed that the emperor, who received his authority from God, was the only legitimate ruler of the inhabited world. Being the inhabitants of a divinely inspired empire, ruled by a Christ-loving emperor who dwelt in the God-guarded city, it was natural to think of themselves as the new Israelites, a Chosen People.[3]

This self-perception might be expected to have encountered difficulties when it came to the Chosen People's failures and defeats, but in fact this was surmounted by the very deep-rooted belief that God was punishing them for their sins. As obvious as the presence of demons in Byzantine sources is the basic Byzantine tenet that set-backs at all levels were caused, or at least allowed, by God as a punishment for sin, and that repentance and the turning to a more Godly life would allow them to be spared.

Even the disasters of the seventh century did not overturn Byzantine faith in this explanation of human affairs, but nonetheless the loss within fifty years of the most fertile regions of the empire, the repeated defeats of imperial armies, and the devastation and growing poverty of what remained was a profound shock to the Byzantine world. Why should God have allowed the Arabs so to humiliate the Chosen People of the Christian empire? The only answer within their system of beliefs which offered any reassurance for the future was the familiar one of God's punishment of sin, which in turn, given the scale of the disaster which had overwhelmed the empire, implied the need for a fundamental reassessment of their relations with God if he were to restore to them his favour. Much of the history of the Byzantine world from the seventh to the ninth century can be seen as a series of attempts to make the empire pleasing to God so that they would be able to drive back the God-detested Arabs.

Already in the reign of Herakleios this was a prominent line of thought. The clear revelation of God's anger in the loss of Syria, Egypt and Palestine, and above all in the sack of Jerusalem and the removal of the True Cross, demanded an ideological response from Herakleios if he were to have any continued credibility as a war-leader. Inevitably Roman resistance had much of the character of a Holy War. The contemporary *Chronikon Paschale* counterpoints news of disasters in the east with descriptions of liturgical innovation in Constantinople.[4] Sources close to Herakleios reflect a growing biblical triumphalism as the Romans finally experienced success.[5] Yet even with victory they could not be confident. The experience of nearly a quarter of a century of defeat had persuaded the emperor and his advisors that Christian disunity, in particular between the Chalcedonians and the Monophysites, was a scandal in the eyes of God. The years of Persian supremacy had been a warning to which it was now their duty to respond. Already in the 620s Herakleios had been in contact with various Monophysite groups, and in 631 he opened negotiations with Athanasios, the Monophysite patriarch of Antioch. Talks were also held with another Monophysite group in Egypt, and finally, agreeing on the formulation of one energy in Christ – Monoenergism – a document of union was issued in June 633.[6] Vocal Chalcedonian hostility to Monoenergism gave the patriarch Sergios, Herakleios' close ally in this matter, second thoughts which led to a reformulation of the terms of union on the basis of a single will in Christ – Monotheletism. In 638 Herakleios issued an imperial edict, the *Ekthesis*, that from henceforth this was to be orthodox belief.[7]

For a period in the 630s and 640s it could have been argued that Arab success was God's judgement on continued Christian disunity. If the Romans would unite around Monotheletism then God's favour would be restored and the Arabs would be defeated.[8] The failure of the papacy and the western church to accept Monothelete doctrine, and the continued opposition of Chalcedonian monks such as Maximos the Confessor, a Palestinian who had taken refuge first in North Africa and had then moved to Rome, were certainly difficulties, but these could easily have been surmounted had Monotheletism brought victory. In fact Constans II's Monothelete regime suffered a series of set-backs so that his death in 668 marked the effective end of Monotheletism.[9]

By the 670s the loss of Egypt, Syria and Palestine had removed the issue of unity from the immediate agenda, since with the major Monophysite centres all under Arab rule there were very few Monophysites left to negotiate with. Consequently first Constantine IV (668–85) and then his son Justinian II (685–95, 705–11) presided over a return to Chalcedonian doctrine re-established as official orthodoxy at the Sixth Oecumenical Council

of 680–1 and confirmed by the Quinisext Council, called 'in
Trullo' after the domed hall in the imperial palace in which it
was held in 692. The triumphal tone of these councils reflected
the turn of events. The Arab blockade of Constantinople between 674 and 678 had ended in failure, and was followed by
Arab civil war. The position was so bad for the Arabs that the
caliph Mu'āwiya was willing to buy off the Byzantines, a concession the latter gleefully interpreted as tribute. All seemed to
give the seal of God's approval, and the predictions of the Apocalypse of Pseudo-Methodios would appear to voice a general expectation that the reconquest of the east would soon follow.[10]

In fact Justinian II's regime lasted less than three years after
the Quinisext Council, and his fall in 695 inaugurated over
twenty years of political instability. In 696 Carthage fell to the
Arabs. A Byzantine expedition temporarily recaptured it in the
following year, but its second fall in 698 marked the end of
Byzantine Africa. In Asia Minor Arab raids began again, and
by 706 the caliph's armies had resumed their campaign to conquer Constantinople. In 708 a Byzantine army was defeated in
Anatolia and the major fortress of Amorion was sacked. In 711–
12 Amaseia and Sebasteia on the northern side of the plateau
suffered the same fate. More alarming was the progressive Arab
conquest of the fertile coastlands of western Asia Minor giving
their armies a base to attack the imperial capital itself. In 716
the two most important fortresses maintaining a Byzantine military presence in this region, Sardis and Pergamon, fell to the
Arabs, and in the same year the Arab attack on Constantinople began.[11]

The second Arab failure to take Constantinople did something to lift the gloom, and this seems to be reflected in the
relative optimism of the contemporary apocalypses attributed
to St Andrew the Fool and the prophet Daniel, but it was a
very brief respite.[12] In the 720s Arab attacks began again. In
723–4 Ikonion in southern Anatolia was captured, and in 726
God's displeasure was even more plainly displayed in the huge
volcanic eruption which blew apart the Aegean island of Thera.
In 727 the Arabs closed in to besiege Nicaea, the holy city of
the 318 God-inspired Fathers of the First Oecumenical Council, less than 120 kilometres by land from Constantinople.[13]

Icons and Iconoclasm

Leaving Nicaea in suspense for the moment it is necessary to turn aside to consider icons and their role in Byzantine life. Like Islam, Christianity is a monotheist religion of a single virtually unreachable God. In Christianity the gulf between God and man is partly bridged by the concept of God coming down to earth as Christ, and in most forms of the Christian tradition that bridge is further reinforced by the idea of the Virgin Mary and the saints interceding on behalf of men at the court of heaven. In late Roman and Byzantine Christianity of the sixth and seventh centuries the gulf was also crossed by a belief in living saints, holy men marked out by their ascetic lifestyles as having particular access to the court of God and his saints (an image obviously paralleling the earthly court of the emperor and his entourage); and in addition by the very widespread use of icons.

Icons, the images of Christ, the Virgin Mary or the saints, made of mosaic or fresco and covering the walls of churches, or more accessibly painted on wooden panels where they were frequently found in private lay hands, were seen as doors into the spiritual world. Not only were the saints easily recognisable in visions from their images in icons, but the icon itself was regarded as having an intimate relationship with the holy reality it represented. Icons could bleed, sweat and cry. The scrapings of an icon mixed with the water and drunk as a potion would cure illness.

Icons of all sorts were a characteristic and extremely widespread feature of early Byzantine culture. The sense that an icon made God and his saints visibly present meant that they naturally played a key role in the defence of the empire. Icons went into battle with Christian armies: Herakleios' fleet sailed from Africa in 610 with icons of the Virgin Mary at their mast heads; icons were carried round the walls of endangered cities; they were painted on the outside of towers.[14] And yet city after city fell to the Arabs.

Which takes us back to Nicaea in the summer of 727. As the large Arab army tightened its grip upon the city the icons of the 318 fathers – famous enough for a western pilgrim, the Anglo-Saxon bishop Willibald, to make a special point of visiting them on his way to the Holy Land a few years later[15] – were processed round the walls. Despite this the Arabs continued to press their attack and managed to make a breach. At this critical moment a certain Constantine threw a stone at an icon of the Virgin Mary. Writing nearly a century later but using earlier materials, the chronicler Theophanes ascribed the victory which followed to the intercession of the icons, and tells that Constantine, having first seen a vision of an irate Virgin Mary, naturally recognisable from her icon, was killed the day after his impious deed by a catapult stone.[16] Nonetheless it is easy to suspect that Theophanes, or rather the anti-iconoclast source he was following at this point, felt the need to tell this story in order to refute a widespread alternative version that the siege of Nicaea had turned to victory when all seemed lost from the moment when Constantine threw his stone at the icon.

Whatever happened at Nicaea – and neither version is of course likely to be the truth – it is clear from the contemporary letters of the patriarch Germanos that by the 720s there was a growing current of opinion among the clergy of the frontline Anatolian cities and probably too in the army, that the Byzantine attitude to icons amounted to idolatry contrary to the Second Commandment: 'Thou shalt not make unto thee any graven image, or any likeness of anything that is in heaven above, or that it is in the earth beneath, or that is in the water under the earth: Thou shalt not bow down [which translates *proskyneō*, the verb regularly used in Byzantine texts to describe the normal worship of icons] thyself to them: for I the Lord thy God am a jealous God, visiting the iniquity of the fathers upon the children unto the third and fourth generation of them that hate me' (*Exodus* 20:4–5).[17]

At first sight it is curious that the Byzantines chose to identify icons as the source of God's displeasure. Until the mid-seventh century the only religious group of any significance to prohibit sacred figural images were the Jews – a fact anti-iconoclasts were keen to point out. Early Christian theologians had attacked pagan cult statues, but no orthodox group in the late Roman period, whether Nestorian, Chalcedonian or Monophysite, had ever considered that the Second Commandment applied to their own painted images. However, after the rise of Islam two developments brought the issue of images to the fore.[18]

The first was the growing division of the Near East into an Islamic world where sacred figural images were prohibited as idolatrous, and a Byzantine world where Christian and imperial culture became increasingly identified with figural icons. Islam's prohibition of sacred figural art seems quite a natural development given the partially Jewish roots of the new religion, but it was a gradual process as the religion took shape over the course of the seventh century. A key step on both sides occurred in the 690s. In the Byzantine world the Quinisext Council of 692 ordained that from henceforth Christ was not to be portrayed by the symbolic representation of a lamb, but rather by his image in human form. At about the same time Justinian II made a major alteration to the design of Byzantine gold coinage. Since the fourth century gold coins had been struck with an image of the emperor on the face (technically the obverse), and a personification of victory bearing a cross on the reverse. During the critical years of Herakleios' reign the reverse image had been changed to that of a cross on steps. The change is obviously of a piece with the other ideological developments of those years, but it was a change of emphasis rather than a radical redesign. Justinian II, however, transformed the coinage. The emperor now appeared on the reverse holding a cross, and on the obverse appeared an icon of Christ. Given the understanding of icons as doors into the spiritual world with the closest of relationships with what was portrayed, the new coins were an extremely loaded association of the empire with the visual portrayal of Christ.[19]

Up to this point the caliphs and their governors had struck coins resembling Byzantine and Persian types already in circulation. The appearance of Justinian II's icon of Christ forced the Islamic world to a decision. After various attempts to establish an Islamic imperial imagery on an equal footing with the Byzantines, the caliph Abd al-Malik abandoned figural designs completely. From the mid-690s the Islamic world was to be associated with an aniconic imagery. Henceforth Islamic coins would bear Koranic inscriptions on both faces and no other image at all. At about the same time on the Temple Mount in Jerusalem the Dome of the Rock, which whatever its purpose and significance was the greatest sacred building project yet undertaken in Islam, was being decorated under Abd al-Malik's orders with non-figurative mosaics and Koranic inscriptions. A decade later the Great Mosque at the caliphal capital at Damascus was decorated in the same fashion. By the early eighth century the victorious caliphate had come to be identified with the rejection of figural images, while the Byzantine empire was linked to icons and defeat.[20]

Icons, however, were not the only feature closely associated with the empire's ideology which distinguished Byzantium from Islam, and it was a second development which seems to have focused Byzantine attention upon icons in particular. The lands of the caliphate in the wake of the Islamic conquests were a world where the comparative ideological certainties of the previous generation had been shattered. It was an age of migration, of uncertainty, and of opportunity, where a new culture was being formed. Given that Islam was the product of a matrix of Jewish and Christian ideas, these two communities above all had to struggle to maintain their membership, while at the same time hoping to shape the developing religion of their new rulers. A major Jewish charge against Christianity was that of idolatry against the Second Commandment, and in the circumstances of seventh-century defeat and insecurity some Christians seem to have accepted its justice. By the second half of the seventh century there was a body of Christians in Syria and Palestine who had begun to explain God's anger against them in Jewish terms – that icons were an idolatry to be destroyed. Syrians and Palestinians certainly came into imperial territory regularly enough in this period, and some of these are likely to have had iconoclast ideas, but as long as the hopes for God's favour and consequent military success were pinned on Monotheletism or the Chalcedonian reaction, these ideas would have had no particular significance. However, by the 720s as the Byzantines desperately cast around for a means to regain God's favour iconoclasm was a radical and simple idea that met the needs of the hour. The fact that it had no roots in orthodox Christian thinking was a positive advantage, since it consequently did not provoke a standard refutation.[21]

Once the emperor had been persuaded and iconoclasm established as an imperially sanctioned doctrine – a stage marked by the deposition of the patriarch Germanos in January 730 – the best argument in favour of iconoclasm were the evident signs of God's approval. In spite of the hostility of our one major Byzantine source, the anti-iconoclast chronicle which forms the basis of both Theophanes' and Nikephoros' accounts, it is quite apparent that Leo III (717–41) and his son, Constantine V (741–75) had long and successful reigns. The Arabic sources record a number of defeats suffered by Arab forces in Asia Minor between 727 and 732, and even if the rest of the 730s seem to have been a difficult decade for the Byzantines, Leo never lost his grip on power and they ended in 740 with a major Byzantine victory at the battle of Akroïnos in western Anatolia. Constantine V began his reign by winning a civil war against his brother-in-law, Artabasdos, one of his father's leading generals and supporters. By 745, secure on the imperial throne, he was able to take advantage of the fall of the Ummayad caliphs and the resultant civil war to go on the offensive. Between that year and 756 when he agreed to a truce and an exchange of prisoners, Constantine's armies raided deep into northern Syria, Cilicia and western Armenia. In the 760s he launched a series of devastating offensives against the Bulgar state in the Balkans. Even the resumption of Arab raids after 764 achieved no great success in his lifetime.[22]

The events of this period are largely hidden by the lack of evidence. The very few sources we do have are for the most part violently hostile and misleading propaganda. Yet the military successes of Leo and Constantine were recognised even by their enemies, and just discernable behind the silence is an important period of imperial revival which consciously looked back to the late Roman empire of Constantine, the founder of a Christian empire in the fourth century, and the great Justinian in the sixth. Constantine V projected himself as a 'New Constantine': a victorious orthodox emperor. Triumphal processions in Constantinople drawing on traditional Roman imperial imagery, and focusing on the hippodrome – the late Roman arena for chariot-racing, itself an imperial activity *par excellence*, which lay immediately to the west of the imperial palace – acted out in public the association between the emperor and victory. Wall paintings of the emperors hunting, driving four-horse racing chariots, winning victories over the barbarians – again all late Roman symbolic images of imperial power – further reinforced the message.[23] The same years saw Leo and Constantine playing

other traditional late Roman imperial roles: the emperor as
law-giver, the emperor as builder, and the emperor, who as
'equal to the apostles' – an imperial epithet closely associated
with Constantine the Great – summoned and presided over
oecumenical councils which defined orthodoxy for the whole
Christian world. The last years of Leo III saw the issue of the
Ekloga, a law-code which revised and abridged Justinian's codex
for current use; the early years of Constantine V (Leo's choice
of name for his son is of course significant in itself) saw major
rebuilding work on not only the land-walls of Constantinople,
but also on the great Justinianic church of St Irene, the dome
and upper stories of which had collapsed in the earthquake of
740; and in 754 Constantine presided over the Seventh Oecumenical Council held in the palace of Hieria in the imperial
city.[24] Looked at in isolation it is easy to underestimate these
achievements, but in the context of eighth-century Byzantium
– a war-ravaged poverty-stricken rump of the Roman empire of
the year 600 – and compared with the political instability and
defeatism they had inherited, these years marked an important reassertion of imperial power.

Constantine was succeeded by his son Leo IV, who seemed
to enjoy much the same military good fortune as his father.
The Arabs presented a growing threat in these years, but even
so Leo's armies managed to invade northern Syria in 778 and
mitigate the worst effects of an Arab counter-attack in the following year. However, in 780 Leo died, leaving five brothers
and a nine-year old son, Constantine, for whom his mother
the empress Irene acted as regent. Seven years later, after an
abortive first attempt in Constantinople, Irene brought about
an Oecumenical Council at Nicaea, which dismissed its predecessor as a 'counterfeit, full of deadly poison', condemned
iconoclasm and restored icons.[25]

The end of the first phase of iconoclasm was essentially due
to what Theophanes recognised as the 'unexpected miracle'
which brought the iconodule Irene to power. Given the court-
centred structure of politics in the Byzantine world, the beliefs
and wishes of the emperor and his immediate entourage would
always have a paramount role in the shaping of orthodoxy, but as
the failure to impose Monotheletism can demonstrate, any creed
lacking wider support was very unlikely to establish itself.

The sudden end of the first phase of iconoclasm, and probably the knowledge of hindsight that from the ninth century onwards icons were to be placed securely at the heart of orthodox spirituality, has encouraged a number of historians to argue that although many Byzantines were willing to follow any doctrine enjoined by their bishops and emperor, iconoclasm enjoyed very little fundamental support based upon conviction. Iconoclasm, this argument goes, was essentially an imperial heresy. Its most convinced proponent was Constantine V, and after his death the restoration of icons was only a matter of time. From this perspective Leo IV's reign represents merely the half-hearted continuation of the policies of his father.

This is certainly the impression given by the sources, virtually all of which are anti-iconoclast and for the most part written after 787, and it may represent the truth; yet it is worth remembering that such an impression was very much in the interests of all parties at the time. If many Byzantines had been convinced iconoclasts, the victors in 787 would have wished to hide the strength of their opponents, and the vanquished had every incentive to shut up.

Looking at the evidence with this caveat in mind, it still remains true that it is difficult to document enthusiastic support for iconoclasm other than from a small number of leading individuals, and from the *tagmata*, the guards regiments, which became at this period the élite of the Byzantine land-forces (see Chapter 7), and which were closely associated with Constantine V.[26] The bishops who acclaimed iconoclasm at the Council of 754 may have been merely acquiescing to imperial policy, but even so the presence of 338 is an impressive figure compared with the Sixth Oecumenical Council of 680–1, whose numbers never rose above 157.[27] More significant perhaps is the evidence that Constantine V enjoyed popular approval in Constantinople. The accounts of the martyrdom of St Stephen the Younger in November 765, or of Constantine's humiliation of the monks in the hippodrome which took place in the August of the following year, describe the people of Constantinople abusing and assaulting the emperor's enemies.[28] Neither of these episodes can really prove that iconoclasm had a popular following in the city: as will be seen it is not certain that iconoclasm was the issue at stake in these events, and in any case it is not clear who the 'people' in these cases were. It is also true that a few eighth-century sources, such as the Miracles of St Theodore the Recruit and the *Deeds of the Bishops of Naples*, show that it was possible to admire Constantine without endorsing iconoclasm.[29] Nonetheless it does appear to be significant that in 787 Irene moved her planned Council from Constantinople to Nicaea. The first attempt to stage the Council in 786 in Constantinople had been broken up by soldiers from the *tagmata*, but before the end of the year they had been disarmed and dispersed, which implies that other factors made Constantinople unsuitable for a second attempt to hold a Council there.[30] Theophanes, who is the sole source for this episode, only mentions the opposition of the *tagmata* in 786; however, since he also blames the killing of St Stephen the Younger on the *tagmata* alone, omitting the major role played by the populace of Constantinople as described in the Life of St Stephen, it is quite possible that he did the same here, and iconoclasm in fact enjoyed a more widespread and enthusiastic support in the city than we can now demonstrate.

If iconodules looking back over the period from the 720s to 780 had an incentive to disguise the degree of support iconoclasm enjoyed, they also had a strong interest in exaggerating the opposition to iconoclasm, and in portraying any opposition the emperors faced as provoked by their impiety. It is, however, worth remembering that between 695 and 717 seven emperors had been overthrown by coup in twenty-two years. Before that four seventh-century emperors had suffered the same fate, and one could add a substantial list of attempts by unsuccessful rebels. The Byzantine world view discussed at the beginning of this chapter would entail that a successful coup was the judgement of God, but this certainly does not mean that the Byzantine élite lined up in clearly defined religious parties. Between 695 and 717 for example, Philippikos (711–13) was a Monothelete – or at least he reimposed that doctrine after he had seized power – but otherwise the period saw a succession of Chalcedonian emperors depose, slaughter or mutilate each other. The Byzantine court élite could easily find grounds for violent competition which transcended their definitions of orthodoxy. Both Leo III and Constantine V enjoyed long reigns and faced several revolts and coup attempts but there is no *a priori* reason to associate all or any of these with opposition to iconoclasm.

In 741, at the very beginning of his reign, Constantine V had had to face the revolt of Artabasdos, and it was not until 743 that he regained control of Constantinople, Nikephoros and Theophanes are using the same source, but the version in Theophanes does make a greater effort to associate the usurper with icons. Even so it is rather half-hearted. Plainly this was not the main issue at stake, and Artabasdos' inglorious defeat meant there was little gain to be had from pretending otherwise.[31]

Both Nikephoros and Theophanes mention numerous martyrs to iconoclast persecution, but these allegations are only supported by highly unreliable works of partisan hagiography written nearly a century later.[32] Much more important, if their accounts could be relied upon, is the extraordinary episode, dated to 21 August 766, of Constantine V's public humiliation of a number of monks in the hippodrome. The emperor is said to have forced all the monks to take a wife while in the background a loyal crowd howled abuse. Theophanes and Nikephoros go on to describe how four days later 19 leading civil and military officials were paraded in the hippodrome, spat upon and executed, and finally how on 30 August the patriarch Constantine was arrested and exiled. A year later the deposed patriarch was brought back to the imperial city. On 6 October he was publicly interrogated in Hagia Sophia, and then next day taken to the hippodrome where he was humiliated and put to death.[33]

The account given by Theophanes and Nikephoros implies that the basis of this episode was an iconodule plot against the heretical emperor, but in fact the involvement of the patriarch Constantine makes this almost impossible. The patriarch was a leading figure of iconoclasm who had presided over the Council of 754, and he above all others could not simply have said that iconoclasm was an unfortunate mistake and still hoped to keep his freedom, let alone his post as patriarch. His involvement makes it almost certain we are looking at a conventional coup attempt, whose leaders, like Artabasdos before them, had no intention of restoring icons.

Nikephoros may even have been aware that the idea of a plot to restore icons led by the great iconoclast patriarch would carry little conviction because, unlike Theophanes, he omits in his version of their shared source all mention of the crucial fact that the patriarch was an iconoclast. Both accounts, however, do their best to make the emperor appear a dreadful monster by beginning the story with the humiliation of the monks. Constantine they claim was carrying out a uniquely impious attack against monks as such. To a Byzantine audience there can be no defence for an emperor who behaves in such a dreadful fashion and the rest of the account serves only to confirm the impression of Constantine's awfulness. Modern historians have tended to accept the accusation that Constantine was an enemy of monasticism, and it has formed the basis for two important studies of his reign.[34] But other than Theophanes and Nikephoros, and the equally anti-iconoclast Life of St Stephen the Younger, there is no evidence to support this thesis, and at least one major piece against.

The near contemporary Life of St Anthusa only survives in a later summary, but it has fortunately preserved the important information that Constantine V was in fact a generous patron of this very large Anatolian monastery, and actually named one of his daughters after its abbess. If this is true – and Constantine's later reputation would make it a very peculiar story to invent – then Constantine cannot have been an enemy of monks as such.[35] In which case the humiliation of the monks in the hippodrome was not an attack on monks in general but on this group in particular whom Constantine evidently saw in some way as false monks. What their crime was is nowhere stated, but it is useful to remember that many Byzantine monks came from wealthy and powerful families. The monk and chronicler Theophanes was himself the child of a high-ranking naval commander at Constantine V's court who owned large estates along the southern shore of the sea of Marmara, and he is a far from unusual example. The monks in the hippodrome could well have come from the same social background as the 19 lay officials whom the emperor executed four days later. Rather than any ideological issue, the crime which united the false monks, the lay officials and the iconoclast patriarch is most easily explained as a conventional coup attempt.

To suggest that eighth-century iconoclasm may have had more support and created less opposition than is usually believed, is not to deny that principled opposition existed, nor that many of its opponents were to be found in monasteries. The well-organised display of theological expertise at Irene's Council at Nicaea and the existence of an important body of monks who bitterly opposed former iconoclast clergy remaining in their posts is good evidence on both points.[36] However, before Leo IV's death in 780 few martyrs for the cause can be identified, and the most vocal critics of iconoclasm were to be found outside the empire, in Syria (where John of Damascus was writing), and in Rome (where the papacy never accepted the imperial position). Any orthodoxy is the product of acceptance and time. Iconoclasm was a break with the past and with the inherited wisdom of the Christian tradition, but by 780 iconoclasm had been imperial orthodoxy for over fifty years, and confirmed by an Oecumenical Council for twenty-six; the third iconoclast emperor in succession reigned in Constantinople, and he had a healthy male heir to succeed him as a fourth. Just as the Council of Chalcedon in 451 had imposed a definition of orthodoxy that had lasted in the face of bitter opposition, so the Council of Hiereia of 754 looked to be achieving the same end. Against this background it is hardly surprising that Theophanes was to regard the overturning of iconoclasm, not as an inevitable matter of course, but as an 'unexpected miracle'.[37]

The form the miracle took seems to have been principally political. A factor in Irene's decision may have been, as several have suggested, the possibly greater support for icons among women, but one does not have to be unduly cynical to question whether Constantine V had really married his eldest son to a closet iconodule, or if Irene's support for icons was in fact a product of her circumstances in 780.[38]

Whatever the reliability of the sources, the events of her career make it plain that Irene was a determined and ruthless politician. The previous female regent, Herakleios' widow, Martina, had had her tongue cut out after less than a year in power. Her five brothers-in-law were all more likely potential rulers, especially as the threat from the Arabs was worsening year by year, and the élite guards regiments, the *tagmata*, looked to an active male emperor to lead them. The existing hierarchy in the church, the army, the civil offices and the court had been created by her predecessors and owed her nothing. Under these circumstances a return to icons offered the necessary revolution to confirm her in power. The overthrow of iconoclasm provided Irene with the opportunity to create her own supporters out of the iconodules, and to place them in office. Their loyalty to her was guaranteed, for the moment at least, by the fear of an iconoclast backlash. Similarly, the existence of a body of violent iconodules demanding the deposition of past iconoclasts, gave Irene the means to gain the loyalty of those that remained from the previous regime. As long as they were loyal to her, she would confirm them in office and protect them from their iconodule enemies.

However, the return of icons did not win God's favour. The following years were marked by military defeat on all fronts, an earthquake and a series of fires around the imperial palace in Constantinople. As Constantine came of age court politics degenerated into a savage power struggle between mother and son, which culminated in August 797 when Constantine died of the injuries inflicted when he was blinded on his mother's orders.[39] With her son murdered, her grandson dead, and her brothers-in-law blinded or mutilated, her supporters fought amongst themselves for the succession. Finally in 802, one of them, Nikephoros, *patrikios* and logothete of the genikon, carried out a successful coup, and Irene died in exile in the following August.[40] The new emperor maintained iconodule orthodoxy, but it brought him little more divine favour than it had Irene. Theophanes was one of a rival faction among Irene's iconodule supporters, and his violently hostile account of Nikephoros' reign has to be discounted, but there is no doubt that it ended in disaster. In July 811 Nikephoros' army was caught retreating through a pass over the Maimos mountains. The emperor and a major portion of the Byzantine army was slaughtered. Theophanes gleefully reports that the Bulgar qaghan had Nikephoros' skull stripped to the bone, lined with silver and turned into a drinking cup.[41] His only son, Staurakios, survived the battle, but was severely wounded and the next few weeks passed with various factions waiting for his death and competing among themselves for the succession. At the beginning of October Staurakios was deposed by his brother-in-law, Michael, and he finally died of his injuries early in 812. Michael I's reign continued the pattern of military defeat and political instability. In July 813 he fell to a military coup which brought one of the leading Byzantine generals, Leo the Armenian, to the imperial throne. Michael was exiled to a monastery, and his sons castrated.

Even the iconophile Theophanes admits that Leo was not alone in drawing the obvious conclusion from the history of the previous thirty-three years. God plainly disapproved of icons. Whereas the iconoclasts Leo III and Constantine V had had long and successful reigns, and even Leo IV had successfully defended the empire and died in his bed, every emperor since the restoration of icons had been defeated by the Bulgars and Arabs, and had ended their lives in misery.[42] With clear support in Constantinople, in the army and among the clergy, Leo prepared the way for a renewal of iconoclasm. In April 815 a Council was held in Hagia Sophia, presided over by Leo's eleven-year old son, Symbatios, who was significantly renamed Constantine for the occasion. The Council of 754 was recognised as the Seventh Oecumenical Council, that of 787 in Nicaea was repudiated, and iconoclasm was again declared the orthodox creed of the Christian world.[43]

However, unfortunately for Leo V and his two iconoclast successors, Michael II and Theophilos, God had by this stage changed his mind – or rather changed it sufficiently so that the association between iconoclasm, victory and imperial longevity was broken, Leo V's reign was moderately successful against the Bulgars and Arabs, but he was assassinated after a reign of less than seven years on Christmas day 820. The bitter civil war which followed between Michael of Amorion, commander of one of the imperial guards regiments, and Thomas the Slav, who was in charge of one of the principal subdivisions of the theme of the Anatolikon in central Asia Minor, lasted nearly three years until Michael's final victory at the end of 823. In so far as Michael was victorious, his defeat of Thomas was a sign of God's favour, but even the surviving examples of the official account of the war put out by Michael's regime suggest some difficulty in presenting this war of attrition as a glorious triumph.[44] In any case the impact of Michael's victory was within a few years offset by the news of the invasion of Sicily and Crete by the Arabs.

The damage to Byzantine interests caused by the loss of these islands was not simply a matter of territory and revenues, although in the case of the large and fertile island of Sicily this was certainly a factor. More important these islands brought Arab sea-power to the northern side of the Mediterranean. Christian coastal communities in Italy and the Aegean, which had previously been protected by the combination of distance, currents and climate, which made seaborne raids from the Syrian or Egyptian ports a relatively minor threat, now faced persistant Arab attack operating from bases within easy sailing time of their targets. This Arab advance opened a new period of raids, destruction, piracy and chronic insecurity in Mediterranean waters.[45] The Byzantine ruling élite in Constantinople was not ignorant of the change (the Life of St Gregory the Decapolite, for example, contains good evidence of the widespread climate of fear in the Aegean coastlands, reaching even the coasts of Bithynia where several Byzantine magnates had large estates),[46] but more politically damaging was probably the sight of successive naval expeditions, assembled at great expense, officered and commanded by holders of court titles, setting out to disaster in Crete or Sicily.[47] Michael II died in 829 leaving these problems to his sixteen-year-old son, Theophilos.

The accidental death of Theophilos' young son, Constantine, drowned in a palace cistern in 830 or 831 was a poor omen,[48] but despite a major Arab raiding expedition into Asia Minor in 830, and continued bad news from both Sicily and Crete, for most of the 830s Theophilos' military endeavours on the empire's eastern frontier were just sufficiently successful for him to be able to portray his regime as a return to the era of iconoclast successes in the eighth century.[49] In an attempt to extract the full political and ideological benefit, Theophilos held two ceremonial triumphs in Constantinople in 831 and 837, deliberately harking back to Constantine V's triumphs in the eighth century. At the same time he had struck a substantial issue of copper coins to publicise further the association with victory. On the obverse these coins show Theophilos wearing the same headpiece he wore in these processions, a circlet decorated with a plume of feathers, called a *tiara* or *toupha*, which was traditionally associated with imperial victory celebrations; on the reverse reads the legend: 'You conquer, O Theophilos Augustus'.[50] A substantial building programme, in the imperial palace, on the Asian side of the Bosphoros, and along the walls of Constantinople, can also be seen as in large measure reflecting the desire to associate himself and his regime with the traditional image of the successful emperor that had been exploited so successfully by his iconoclast predecessors in the eighth century.[51]

All of this, however, was overshadowed by the events of the summer of 838 when the caliph al-Mu'tasim invaded Asia Minor. The Muslim forces were divided into three armies. One of these managed to rout what was probably a superior Byzantine force commanded by the emperor himself. The Byzantines suffered very heavy casualties, and Theophilos was lucky to escape alive from the carnage. As the Byzantine defences crumbled, the Arab forces united to take the important fortress of Ankyra (modern Ankara), before marching south-west across the Anatolian plateau to the city of Amorion, 165 kilometres away. Amorion was a city of considerable strategic and ideological importance with powerful defences. A ninth-century Arab geographer, Ibn Khuradādhbih, considered it one of the only five genuine cities of Byzantine Asia Minor – the others he dismissed as fortresses. Amorion was the headquarters of the theme of the Anatolikon, it was also the city after which the ruling dynasty was named, and possibly the birthplace of the emperor himself. As the Arab armies approached in 838 the city had just been reinforced by the hasty despatch of three out of the four imperial guards regiments, the *tagmata*, whom Theophilos had sent to join the existing garrison under the command of Aëtios, strategos of the Anatolikon. Yet after only a fortnight's siege, Amorion fell. The various sources give various figures, but the point of their rhetoric is the same: large numbers of citizens, soldiers and refugees were slaughtered, and among the crowds of prisoners taken back to Syria were a substantial roll-call of the empire's military élite.[52]

The long-term military consequences of the sack of Amorion turned out to be insignificant. The Arabs did not follow up their victories of 838, and the walls were eventually rebuilt. At the time, however, there was no doubt that this was a humiliating disaster to match the worst defeats suffered by any iconophile emperor. Stories of a traitor who revealed to the Arabs a weak point in the wall took nothing from the fact that iconoclasm was supposed to be a creed that brought God's favour on his chosen people, and yet here would seem to be the clearest demonstration that it had failed.

Less than three and a half years later, Theophilos, not yet thirty years old, died on 20 January 842, leaving his wife, Theodora, as regent for their one-year old son, who had already been crowned as Michael III. A year later, on 4 March 843, the iconoclast patriarch, John the Grammarian, was deposed and replaced by the Sicilian Methodios. Some sort of ecclesiastical assembly was gathered and on 11 March 843, which was the first Sunday in Lent, icons were restored and iconoclasm condemned as an abominable heresy.[53]

The parallels with the situation in 780 are obvious. The position of an empress-regent was bound to be insecure; indeed the precedent of Irene's disastrous career is very likely to have made it more so. Theodora needed to consolidate her hold on power. The restoration of icons offered, as it had done for Irene in the 780s, ideological justification for her rule and the opportunity to place her own supporters in office.

However, in several ways Theodora's position in 842 was stronger than that of Irene in 780. First of all she had the backing of an influential faction at the imperial court headed by the eunuch Theoktistos, who as Keeper of the Imperial Inkstand had been at the heart of court politics for the last two decades. She also had the backing of an extensive family who in the years since Theodora had married Theophilos in 830 had established themselves in high military and civilian office. Apart from her brothers, Bardas and Petronas, there were a number of sisters, brothers-in-law and other relatives by blood and marriage whose immediate interests depended upon the success of the regency.

A further advantage was the comparative weakness of the opposition. The sources imply that there was effectively none at all, but their silence cannot be taken at face value. We do, for example, hear that shortly before Theophilos' death, Theodora's brother, Petronas, and the eunuch Theoktistos executed a certain Theophobos, a Persian general in Byzantine service; nonetheless apart from this political murder, the true extent of the opposition the empress faced remains completely obscure.[54] However, one can say with some confidence that it did not amount to the same threat that Irene faced from Constantine V's brothers.

There is also no doubt that the iconophile position was much stronger in 842 than in 780. Instead of trying to overturn a doctrine that had been widely recognised as orthodox for several decades, acclaimed at an oecumenical council, and whose acceptability with God had been demonstrated by a series of imperial victories; Theodora was faced by a contentious creed, condemned at an oecumenical council, and against which there had been a substantial and principled opposition. No one in 842 could be unaware that iconoclasm had once been rejected as a heresy and might be so again. Above all iconoclasm was no longer closely linked to victorious and long-lived emperors, but instead, and particularly since 838, it conjured up images of defeat and political instability.[55]

A final factor which may be seen as an advantage was the age of Theodora's son. Whereas Irene had very few years before Constantine came of age, Michael III was not yet two when his father died. Whatever her other difficulties, the reversionary interest would not become a factor in Byzantine politics for a few years yet.[56]

Even so just as in the 780s it is too easy to imagine that iconoclasm had become an irrelevant dogma with very little committed support. Again we are the prisoner of our sources and it is important to be aware of what they may be hiding. The ninth-century phase of iconoclasm is at first sight much better documented than that of the eighth-century, but looked at more closely a great deal of this material consists of hostile anti-iconoclast hagiography, mostly written after the restoration of icons, and forming a mass of self-justifying propaganda. However, two contemporary letter-collections have also survived. The largest and oldest of these is that of Theodore the Stoudite. Its author, born in 759, came from a wealthy and well-connected family of Constantinopolitan civil officials. He became a monk in 780, abbot of the Stoudios monastery in Constantinople in 798, and by half way through the first decade of the ninth century he had become the effective leader of the extreme rigorist faction among Byzantine monks. Theodore's writings reveal him as a brave, proud, usually principled and intolerant figure; he was bitterly opposed not only to iconoclasm but to what he saw as other forms of heresy and error among the orthodox. It is significant that he was exiled three times in his life, once by the iconoclasts, but twice under an iconodule regime. His letters, of which 557 are known, are particularly interesting for the period after the return to iconoclasm in 815. Theodore was exiled by Leo V, and used his correspondence to keep an extensive network of iconophile supporters, friends and relations loyal to the cause. His letters can easily give the superficial impression that virtually the entire civil and ecclesiastical hierarchy was made up of closet-iconophiles, waiting for the opportunity to practice their faith in public.[57]

The second collection is much smaller, only 64 letters, but they have the peculiar interest amidst the overwhelming dominance of the iconophile point of view of being written by an iconoclast. Their author was Ignatios, sometime deacon and *skeuophylax* of the Great Church in Constantinople, metropolitan of Nicaea, and producer of court propaganda for Michael II and Theophilos. Ignatios' high rank among the clergy of the Great Church – the *skeuophylax* or sacristan ranked number three in the patriarchal hierarchy and was appointed by the emperor himself[58] – and his post at Nicaea (well-placed to visit Constantinople and play a prominent part in court life) show his importance during the 820s and 830s. His acknowledged authorship of the official version of the civil war with Thomas the Slav, intended to put Michael II's iconoclast regime in the best possible light, and also the strong case that he wrote the iconoclast epigrams which were inscribed in public on imperial buildings in 815 or very shortly afterwards are further signs that Ignatios was a major figure in the second phase of iconoclasm. Yet his letters do not bear the slightest trace of any enthusiasm for iconoclasm. Ignatios appears as either a man taken up with the routine administration of his see, or one riven by remorse for his temporary fall into iconoclast heresy. With this picture of Ignatios it comes as no surprise to find him writing two violently anti-iconoclast lives of the patriarchs Tarasios and Nikephoros.[59]

At first sight these letters and the lives of the two patriarchs might serve to confirm the impression left by Theodore the Stoudite's correspondence that virtually the entire Byzantine establishment were closet iconophiles waiting the opportunity to let their true opinions show. But this is almost certainly a mistake. Even Theodore's letters, which focus on his iconodule friends and relations, reveal in their anxious concern to keep the iconodule flock united and faithful to the cause that there was a very serious threat to that unity and faith. After Theodore's death in 826 his fears proved justified and overt opposition to iconoclasm seems virtually to have come to an end. Later iconophile propaganda could point to very few victims of iconoclast persecution between 826 and 842, and these were mostly foreigners, a few Palestinian monks and a Khazar painter.[60] More carefully read Ignatios' letters also lend themselves to an alternative view. It is after all hardly possible to believe that such a prominent iconoclast never mentioned iconoclasm in his letters from Nicaea, or indeed that he had such a limited correspondence – of only 64 letters to have been preserved less than 30 date from his period as metropolitan and all of these deal with essentially very trivial matters. Quite plainly these letters have been weeded to hide their author's true past. After the restoration of icons in 843 Ignatios was deposed from his see and effectively imprisoned as a monk in a Thracian monastery. Under these depressing circumstances, with an iconodule regime establishing itself in Constantinople, Ignatios was neither the first nor obviously the last author faced with imprisonment and isolation to rewrite his past in an attempt to fit the new orthodoxy. The silence of the letters and the anti-iconoclast hostility of the lives tell us more about Ignatios' desperation after 843 than his true opinions at any stage of his career. It is certainly quite unrealistic to accept them as an accurate guide to the degree of support enjoyed by iconoclasm among the Byzantine clergy, let alone the populace at large.

There are further signs of a rewriting of history closer to the heart of imperial affairs. The empress Theodora is presented in chronicles and hagiography as a pillar of orthodoxy, who had always remained faithful to the worship of icons, even when married to an iconoclast emperor.[61] (A partial exception to this picture is given by a tenth-century tradition which requires the empress to be convinced of the need to restore icons by a certain Manuel, acting himself under the influence of the monks of the Stoudios monastery, only 'after much conflict and discussion'. However this tradition has no historical value, being simply a reflection of different factions among the iconodules striving to claim the credit for the restoration of icons.)[62] The same picture of long-standing iconodule piety is applied in these sources to Theodora's family and to the eunuch Theoktistos around whom a cult seems to have developed, and whose life was probably written up to make him an iconodule saint.[63] In both cases this is wildly unlikely. Theophilos would hardly have tolerated either his wife and her kinsmen, or one of his closest personal officials carrying on a heretical cult offensive to God at the heart of the imperial palace.

Methodios, the patriarch who restored icons, is also not free from suspicion. A ninth-century life exists which gives the patriarch all the proper credentials of a life-long iconodule and a near martyr to the cause, but this does not accord with the apparently well-attested fact that in about 838 Methodios was summoned from exile to spend the remaining years of the emperor Theophilos' life living in the comfort of the newest section of the imperial palace and discussing the emperor's reading of theology and the scriptures.[64] What Methodios was actually doing and thinking during the iconoclast years cannot now be known, but quite plainly this is a further example of the rewriting of history in the interests of the iconodule regime from 842 onwards.

Behind this widespread rewriting may have been a great deal more genuine support for iconoclasm and less covert enthusiasm for icons than is usually imagined. Even in the ninth century it was by no means impossible that Byzantine Christianity would join the two other monotheist religions to which it was closely related – Judaism and Islam – and reject pictorial religious images for good. In the end Byzantium failed to take this step, not because of any fundamental antipathy to iconoclasm among the population at large, but for short-term political reasons. Theodora and her supporters restored icon worship because they, as the then dominant faction of the ruling élite, no longer believed that iconoclasm was the key to winning God's favour. Their decision may well have been influenced by iconodule argument. Both sides had appealed to the authority of the early church fathers and over the years, as the texts became better known, the real truth that the early church was not iconoclast must have told in favour of the iconodule position. But the key factor was almost certainly their conclusion from the events of the past twenty-seven years that iconoclasm would not assure them personally of long lives and victory over their enemies. Iconoclasm had initially held out that hope, and especially in the eighth century had seemed to achieve it. By 842 the evidence pointed the other way, and icons were restored in the following year.

The end of iconoclasm in 843 proved to be final. The propaganda and rewriting of history which portrayed iconoclasm as a loathsome heresy eventually served to make the doctrine as fundamentally abhorrent to the orthodox Chalcedonian as the heresies of the Arians or the Nestorians. In a sense Byzantine Christian thinking had been innoculated against iconoclasm so that it could not be mentioned by the orthodox save in terms of horrified rejection and abuse. The novelty which had allowed it to be accepted as a part of orthodox belief in the eighth century no longer existed.

The end of iconoclasm also marks the passing of a watershed. For the Byzantine empire the immediate shock of defeat was over. Arab conquest was no longer imminent and after 863 the Byzantines were able slowly to move on to the offensive. A new era was opening in the Near East, leaving behind the ideological issues left by the fall of the old order in the seventh century and by the years of painful readjustment that had followed.

Iconoclasm and the Making of Orthodox Byzantium

The nature of Byzantine iconoclasm and its role in Byzantine culture will always remain obscure because of the very slight and partial material on which all discussion has to be based. Even so there are two important points which need to be emphasised.

The first is that Byzantine iconoclasm was not an autonomous creed generated within Byzantine culture. The Byzantine world began to question its relationship with God because of the Arab conquests. Monotheletism failed because Arab victories continued; Chalcedonian orthodoxy reestablished itself in the 670s and 680s because the Arabs turned to civil war and allowed the Byzantines to recover and achieve some military success. The assertion of effective control by the Marwānid caliphs Abd al-Malik and Walīd I, and their interest in the conquest of the Byzantine world led to political and ideological crisis for the empire and in turn to iconoclasm – itself a creed initially developed by Christians inside the new Islamic world. The first two iconoclast emperors, Leo III and Constantine V, benefited during the 730s and 740s from the greater interest which the later Marwānids had in the Persian as opposed to the Byzantine world, and then from the political crisis which led to the fall of the Ummayad caliphate and its replacement by the Abbāsids. By the 770s the Abbāsids were secure in power and turned their attention to the holy war with Byzantium. This growing military threat was inherited by Irene, and her return to icon worship was blighted by Hārūn al-Rashīd's personal involvement with holy war and his concern for the frontier regions facing Byzantium. His successors in the early ninth century were largely preoccupied by internal political struggles until the end of the 820s. Ironically, however, this gave Nikephoros I the opportunity to pursue an aggressive policy in the Balkans which led him and icons to disaster in Bulgaria in 811. Elsewhere in the Islamic world, Muslims outside the political control of the Abbāsid caliphate, such as the Aghlabid emirs of Ifrīkiya (North Africa) who invaded Sicily in 827, and the exiled Spanish Muslims who came via Alexandria to conquer Crete at about the same time, shook confidence in restored iconoclasm, but its fall coincided with the renewed interest of the Abbāsids in holy war during the 830s which culminated in 838, the year of the sack of Amorion. Restored icons had the fundamental advantage of the growing divisions within the Islamic world from the mid-ninth century onwards and the resulting impotence of the Abbāsid caliphate. The end of the Arab threat set the seal on the restoration of icons.

The Islamic world was the inheritor of the two greatest agricultural regions of the Near East, Egypt and Iraq, in addition to a number of agricultural regions of secondary, but still considerable, importance, such as Syria and Palestine. It also preserved and developed much of the urban and market economy of the ancient world which had largely disappeared in Byzantium. Based on the militaristic values of Arab society, and backed by imported Turkish warriors from the steppes, the caliphate was the sole superpower of the early medieval world, against which Byzantium was a satellite state whose path was dictated by its vast and wealthy neighbour. This applied to politics, and also to ideology. The whole episode of iconoclasm in Byzantium is essentially one of a satellite culture in a satellite state.

The second point concerns a major shift in the empire's culture which took place between the seventh and ninth centuries, and in many ways marks the fundamental division between the Roman and Byzantine worlds. Iconoclasm, as we have seen, preoccupied the Byzantine ruling élite for a century and a half because they were struggling to come to terms with a massive decline in power and influence. The sixth-century Roman state had considered itself to be the greatest power of the inhabited world. Its emperor, appointed by God, was the sole legitimate source of human authority in the universe. Indeed from a contemporary Roman perspective this to a great extent conformed to perceived reality. Sixth-century Romans knew nothing of China, and apart from a few diplomats, underrated not only the size and importance of the steppe powers and (with more justification) the kingdoms of western Europe, but also that of the only acknowledged rival, the Persian empire. Looking to the future, the Romans saw themselves at the heart of an eschatological drama leading to the Second Coming. The Roman empire would last until the end of the world, which was expected sooner rather than later. Before it took place they could expect, on Christ's own authority, to see the conversion of the whole world to the Roman religion, after which, according to some versions, the emperor would travel to Jerusalem to give up his crown to God and usher in the events of the last days. In this context it is easy to see that the years between Herakleios' victory over the Persians in 628 and the onset of the Arabs in the mid-630s, when for a short period it seemed as if a Christian shah might preside over the conversion of Persia, and Herakleios himself travelled to Jerusalem to return the True Cross to the Holy City, opened dizzy perspectives to the Roman élite.

Such fantasies were, of course, very rapidly dashed. At first sight the problem of trying to fit the idea of the emperor as the sole legitimate God-given ruler of the universe with the evident realities of the post-Roman world, dominated by the power of the caliphate, might appear insurmountable, but in fact an answer was found inside the Judao-Christian tradition by the example of the Jews. The Byzantines could see themselves as the New Israel, a Chosen People dwelling in the New Zion: the New Jerusalem beleaguered by enemies because its virtue as a bastion of orthodoxy defended by God made it the last target for the malice and envy of the devil in an otherwise fallen world. The Byzantine emperor still ruled the universe because the orthodox empire was the only universe that counted. The eighth-century Byzantine élite had come to see Roman history almost entirely in relation to Constantinople, and the end of the world as a drama focused on the imperial city to the exclusion of anywhere else.

This ideology gave the Byzantine state a vital sense of self-esteem in the battle for survival in the face of triumphant Islam, but it also involved a serious cost. The sixth-century Roman empire had been a genuinely Near Eastern state. It was pointed out in Chapter 2 that the doctrinal and ethnic divisions of the sixth-century empire did not invalidate the contemporary sense of a Roman identity embracing the whole Christian population of the Roman Near East – Copts, Arabs, Syrians and Latins as well as Greeks; Monophysites as well as Chalcedonians – and reaching out to include populations beyond the empire's borders. As the Islamic world would later embrace the whole Near East, with minor exceptions, in a common Muslim identity, or as in the Far East the Chinese empire would gradually persuade its subjects to think of themselves as Chinese, so the late Roman empire was well on the way to persuading its diverse subjects to think of themselves as Romans.

The centre of this Roman world was certainly the imperial capital at Constantinople. Politics was focused there by the presence of the emperor and the imperial court; an enormous body of appeals from distant provinces made it a legal centre; it was also, after a late start, growing as a religious centre. However, the late Roman empire was not merely the empire of Constantinople. Roman culture was not simply Constantinopolitan culture. Indeed one of the most striking features of the sixth-century capital is the fact that its leading cults, such as those of St Michael the Archangel, SS. Cosmas and Damian and SS. Sergios and Bacchos, were all imports from outside. The empire did not copy Constantinople, but instead the imperial city copied in these cases Anatolia, Syria and again Syria respectively. The imperial city was only one great city among several. At desperate moments in the seventh century Herakleios is said to have considered moving the capital to Carthage and Constans II was accused of planning to keep the capital in Italy.[65] The empire was still a larger and older idea than one particular city on the Bosphorus, and both emperors clearly believed there was no fundamental reason why the empire should not move its capital from Constantinople to a new site, just as it had once moved from Old Rome to the New Rome of Constantinople.

The events of the seventh and eighth centuries destroyed this Near Eastern empire and its culture for good. The siege mentality of Byzantine culture from the seventh century onwards meant in effect that the orthodoxy, whose purity ensured the empire's survival, was equivalent to the practice of Constantinople. Not surprisingly those Christian communities which had rejected the Council of Chalcedon played no part in the Byzantine vision of the orthodox world, but even the Chalcedonian communities in east and west were gradually alienated from Constantinople. The Melkites – the Chalcedonian Christians inside the Islamic world – were virtually ignored from the seventh century until the Byzantine armies returned to Syria in the tenth century.[66] By then they had become a predominantly Arabic-speaking community with little reason to regard Constantinople as a natural leader of the Christian world. In the west too, the papacy was increasingly left to fend for itself so that by the mid-eighth century the pope was forced in the face of Lombard pressure to appeal to the Franks for protection. In 800 the pope crowned the king of the Franks, Charlemagne, as Emperor of the Romans, thus creating a new axis in European politics, culture and ideology.

Iconoclasm was a symptom of this process. The issue of iconoclasm preoccupied the Byzantine élite because of the Chosen People's need to find favour with God who had temporarily deserted them. Secondly it was a factor giving the empire an increasingly inward-looking and introverted culture. Despite its apparent roots in the east, iconoclasm became in practice an almost wholly Byzantine issue. When the empire was officially iconoclast it was not in communion with the other Chalcedonian churches, but even after the restoration of icons there was still a dividing gulf. The experience of iconoclasm had created a set of issues central to Byzantine Christian culture but marginal to the experience of the other Chalcedonian churches.

The creation of a Byzantine ideology focused on Constantinopolitan orthodoxy was also a rejection of the Roman heritage of an inclusive Near Eastern culture. Non-Greeks still played an important part in the Byzantine empire, but when ninth-century Franks described Byzantium as the empire of the 'Greeks' it underlines the fact that to non-Byzantines the universal claims appeared hollow.[67] The Jewish tradition in Christian guise of a Chosen People isolated by their virtue was bound to be an exclusive ideology, and it was not one with which to attempt to reconquer the Near East.

7. The Byzantine Response: On to the Defensive

Adapting the Late Roman Military Tradition

As SEEN in Chapter 5, the Byzantine army was a late Roman institution which survived the crisis of the seventh century, and whose skills, organisation, and sense of tradition were a vital factor in the empire's very existence.

Under Herakleios the major Roman field armies had been pulled out of the Balkans and the eastern provinces and redeployed in the only substantial territory left to the empire, Asia Minor. For the rest of the seventh century there were four such armies, or 'themes': the Anatolikon (the former army of the east), the Armeniakon (the former army of Armenia), the Thrakesion (the former army of Thrace), and the Opsikion (made up of various imperial guard units and the remnants of the sixth-century central army). The provinces of Asia Minor were divided up between them. The north-west went to the Opsikion, the north-east to the Armeniakon, the centre of the Anatolian plateau to the Anatolikon, and the west to the Thrakesion. The areas involved are huge; but at this stage there was no question of the 'strategoi', the generals commanding these armies, having any responsibility for local administration. That was still in the hands of civilian provincial governors whose names regularly appear on seventh- and early eighth-century lead seals. These themes were the empire's major field armies, and as such the areas in which they were based represent no more than regions of recruitment and cantonment. It was generally expected that Arab dominance could only be temporary. Soon God would forgive his Chosen People and victory and reconquest would begin. The field armies were not in Asia Minor to stay.

How long these ideas of an imminent reconquest survived is difficult to say. Certainly they were current in Syria as well as in Byzantine territory in the seventh century, and the author of the Life of St Andrew the Fool shows that the same expectations were still current in Constantinople in the 720s. Optimism

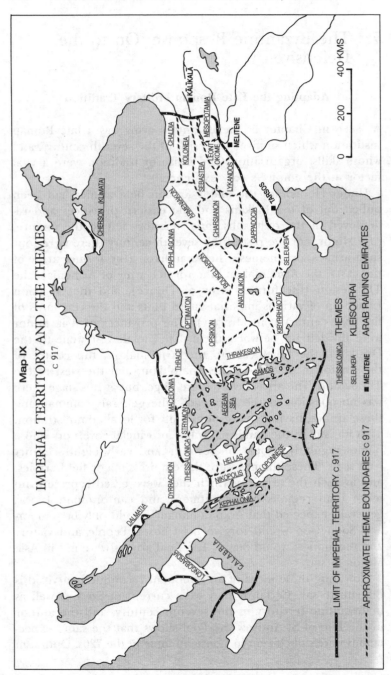

Map IX
IMPERIAL TERRITORY AND THE THEMES
c 917

CHERSON (KLIMATA)

KALIKALA
CHALDIA
KOLONEIA
SEBASTEIA
LEONT OKOME
MESOPOTAMIA
MELITENE
LYKANDOS
TARSOS
ARMENIAKON
CHARSIANON
CAPPADOCIA
PAPHLAGONIA
BOUKELLARION
SELEUKEIA
OPTIMATON
ANATOLIKON
KIBYRRHAIOTA
OPSIKION
THRAKESION
MACEDONIA
THRACE
SAMOS
AEGEAN SEA
THESSALONICA
STRYMON
HELLAS
PELOPONNESE
NIKOPOLIS
KEPHALONIA
DYRRACHION
DALMATIA
CALABRIA
LONGOBARDIA

0   200   400 KMS

THEMES
KLEISOURAI
ARAB RAIDING EMIRATES

THESSALONICA
SELEUKEIA
MELITENE

LIMIT OF IMPERIAL TERRITORY c 917

APPROXIMATE THEME BOUNDARIES c 917

at this late date may reflect the recent failure of the Arab siege of Constantinople in 718, for by the early eighth century the brutal reality was not of imminent reconquest, but of a desperate battle for survival which the Byzantines showed every signs of losing. In addition to the list of sacked cities and ravaged territories already described, two particularly significant developments of these years were the first steps in the colonisation and settlement of Cilicia, and the decisive suppression of the Armenian nobility. The fertile Cilician plain had to this date been a contested no-man's land between the Arabs and Byzantines; from the early eighth century, however, it was gradually converted into secure Muslim territory.[1] The developments in Armenia are discussed in the next chapter, but it is worth noting here how the imposition of an effective Arab hegemony shut out the Byzantines, leaving them yet more isolated in the face of the advancing power of Islam.

The Byzantine reaction to this crisis was in the first place not a military but an ideological reform – iconoclasm – and initially at least the organisation of the Byzantine armies under the iconoclast emperors remained much as before. The only substantial change to take place under Leo III was the division of the former fleet of the Karabisianoi between a naval theme of the Kibyrrhaiotai, covering south-western Asia Minor and the Aegean islands, and a central imperial fleet based in Constantinople. Whether this was a reflection of the unwieldiness of the previous arrangements, or a political reaction to the attempt by units of the Karabisianoi to overthrow his regime in 726, is unclear.[2]

Real change seems only to have come after Leo's death in 741. In the following year Artabasdos, Leo's son-in-law and the count of the Opsikion, seized Constantinople and had himself and one of his sons crowned emperor. The Opsikion had been constituted out of the élite units of the sixth-century army, and it still played an élite role in the eighth century. The theme closest to Constantinople, acting as the emperor's own army when on campaign, its support was generally decisive in any bid for the imperial throne. However, in 743, backed by the themes of the Thrakesion and the Anatolikon, Constantine managed to defeat Artabasdos' forces at the battle of Sardis. This victory was probably something of a surprise to contemporaries, and once in control Constantine naturally set about restructuring the Byzantine military to lessen the chances of a similar threat in future. One step was to break up the over-mighty Opsikion into three smaller units, one of them continuing with the name of the Opsikion, the other two being the new themes of the Boukellarioi and the Optimates. Another step was to replace the Opsikion in its role as an élite field force with a new body of imperial guards, to be based in Constantinople, and who would owe their loyalty to the emperor alone.[3]

The new force was initially made up of two guards regiments (*tagmata*, singular *tagma*), the Scholai and the Exkoubitores. Both units had been active guards regiments in the late Roman period, but like the *spatharioi*, they had long since become purely decorative bodies. Procopios tells the story of how Justinian in the mid-sixth century used to cause panic among the Scholai by including them on lists of units to be sent on foreign campaign, thus forcing them to buy the emperor off.[4] Constantine V transformed these regiments. Henceforth, well-paid, well-equipped and attracting the best recruits, the tagmata would be the élite field force of the Byzantine army.[5]

The Scholai and the Exkoubitores were naturally the partisan military supporters of the iconoclast emperors. Favoured by Constantine and Leo above the soldiers of the theme armies, and led to no doubt profitable victory against the Arabs and Bulgars, they above all other groups in the Byzantine army were bound to find the years of defeat and insecurity which followed the restoration of icons difficult to come to terms with. Indeed, Irene's first attempt in 786 to restore icons at a council held in the church of the Holy Apostles in Constantinople was brought to an abrupt halt when soldiers from the tagmata burst into the building and broke up the proceedings. From Theophanes' account what seems to have happened next is that Irene used the pretext of a pretended Arab invasion later the same year to summon the tagmata to the Bithynian fortress of Malagina. Meanwhile the theme armies who had been campaigning in Thrace were persuaded to back the empress. They marched into Constantinople, and the tagmata reached Malagina to be faced with a demand to hand over their arms. Theophanes' account attributes their passive surrender to their 'being made foolish by God', but the implication of the story appears to be that with their families in Constantinople at the mercy of the pro-Irene theme soldiers, they had little choice.[6]

Theophanes states that Irene sent the tagma soldiers together with their families into exile, but it is clear that she did not disband the tagmata as such. Another near contemporary source, Constantine of Tios' virulently anti-iconoclast account of the fate of the relics of St Euphemia, says that Irene simply carried out a purge, filling their ranks with soldiers loyal to her.[7] She further reinforced her position by creating a new tagma, called variously the *Arithmos* or the *Vigla*. (The latter being a Greek transcription of the Latin for the 'Watch'.) If, as has been argued, this unit was part of the Thrakesion theme brought to Constantinople to act as a loyal balance to the power of the existing tagmata, then the whole episode shows not only Irene trying to undo the effects of the military reforms of the iconoclast emperors, but also demonstrates that by the end of the eighth century such a return to the past was impossible.[8] The tagmata had become militarily and politically indispensable.

Irene's attempts either to purge or offset the power of the Scholai and the Exkoubitores set a pattern which would be a major factor in shaping subsequent Byzantine politics. Her successor, Nikephoros I (802–11), brought in a regiment called the *Phoideratoi* from the Anatolikon theme (recruited from the highlanders of Pisidia and Lykaonia in the south-west of the Anatolian plateau) to act as an alternative tagma. He also raised a new tagma called the *Hikanatoi* to be commanded by his son, Staurakios. Michael I (811–13) purged the tagmata of potential opponents, kept the *Hikanatoi*, but sent the *Phoideratoi* back to the Anatolikon, Leo V (813–20) seems to have limited himself to appointing friends to the key commands, and purging opponents; but his successors, Michael II (820–9) – one of the friends turned murderer – and Michael's son, Theophilos (829–42), combined purges with the raising of new units of loyal supporters.[9] For a while Theophilos made considerable use of a force of Kurdish refugees, and he seems also to have raised an 'Ethiopian' unit, possibly again refugees, in this case perhaps black slaves of whom there were large numbers in Abbāsid Iraq.[10] A lasting innovation of these years was, however, the establishment of the *Hetaireia*, a unit which appeared on the battlefield but whose principal function was the emperor's

personal security inside the palace.[11] The origin of the *Hetaireia*
is obscure, as is the question of whether it was always intended
as a unit of foreign troops, or whether the Khazars and the
Turks from the Farghāna oasis in Central Asia were only attached
to a main body of native Byzantines. In either case the foreigners
were clearly of great importance, and their presence marks a
further fundamental change in the structure of Byzantine politics.
From now on insecure regimes would have more faith in foreigners than natives, and the emperors' imported bodyguards
would be a typical feature of the imperial court. The pattern
of purging and bribing the tagmata continued through the ninth
and tenth centuries, but increasingly, if slowly, emperors began
to see a largely non-Byzantine army as the answer to their problems. A major step in this direction was to be Basil II's recruitment of Russian mercenaries at the end of the tenth century
(see Chapter 10). Even then there was a long way to go before
the position in the twelfth century when it could be regarded
as a commonplace that 'the Greeks are an unwarlike people'.[12]
Yet there is a logical development from Constantine V's creation
of the tagmata in the eight century, via the ninth-century recruitment of exotic palace guards, to the twelfth century when
Byzantine armies were almost entirely composed of imported
western Europeans, Russians, steppe nomads and Turks.

The rise of the tagmata, their establishment as the élite field
force of the Byzantine army and the potential arbiters of Byzantine politics, obviously entailed the decline of the empire's former
field army, the themes. During Constantine's own lifetime there
is no evidence for resentment at this process, but when his
son, Leo IV, at the beginning of his reign took large numbers
of soldiers from the theme armies and transferred them to the
tagmata it sparked off disturbances in 776 which reveal the
tensions within the Byzantine military. According to Theophanes'
typically obscure account, the angry officers of the theme armies
marched on Constantinople and brought their troops into the
city, where they were only with difficulty pacified.[13] Only ten years
later Irene could use the themes to disarm the pro-iconoclast
Scholai and Exkoubitores at Malagina, and it is tempting to
see resentment against the tagmata as a factor behind these
events, and possibly too as a factor in more general anti-iconoclast
support for Irene's regime.

The decline in the status of the theme troops was furthered by a contemporary shift in Byzantine strategy which will be discussed in the next section, but which in effect amounted to the adoption of a policy of 'defence-in-depth'. Instead of trying to prevent Arab armies invading Anatolia they would be allowed to enter the plateau, where they would be shadowed and harrassed by relatively small mobile units. Only when large Arab forces tried to push on to the west of Anatolia into the coastal plains on the Aegean coast and toward Constantinople would they be confronted by Byzantine field armies and brought to battle. The first clear evidence of this strategy in action comes from 778, and for long after that the bulk of any major Byzantine field army was bound to be composed of theme troops, but the implications were plain. The unrewarding role of a defensive force permanently based in Anatolia would fall more and more to the themes.

Associated with the themes' new role as part of the territorial defence of Asia Minor was a growing range of administrative responsibilities. When the word 'theme' first appears in the seventh century it means an army. For the purposes of their deployment in Asia Minor each theme had been assigned the territory of three or more late Roman provinces, but the provinces survived as did the civil authorities who administered them. Each province was under the authority of a governor usually of proconsular rank – an *anthypatos* in Greek – who was subordinate to the Praetorian Prefect in Constantinople. By the tenth century the situation had altered entirely. The emperor Leo VI writing at the beginning of the tenth century states that the strategos is the sole authority responsible for all aspects of the theme, civil and military, and by 'theme' Leo no longer has in mind the army, but the territory in which it was based.[14]

One step in this transformation seems to have occurred by the end of the seventh or the beginning of the eighth century, by which time we find the seals of civil officials who are either governors or tax supervisors of the provinces of a theme. From this it is a relatively easy step to the idea of the theme itself as the principal territorial unit of the empire. However, the final disappearance of the late Roman provincial system takes more than another hundred years, and it is not until about the mid-ninth century that the last is heard of the Praetorian Prefect and the civil governors, and the strategos takes over all responsibility. By this date too the great themes of the seventh century had been further broken up, so that in some cases their territory was roughly equivalent to that of a late Roman province. Cappadocia, Paphlagonia and Chaldia all appear as themes in the first half of the ninth century. From about the same date that the strategoi take over full responsibility for both the civil and military administration of their themes the rank of *anthypatos* becomes part of the usual title of a strategos.[15]

This development has generally been taken as evidence for the growing authority of the strategoi and the importance of the themes. But taken with the creation of the tagmata as the empire's élite field force and the development of a defensive strategy in Asia Minor which required something closer to a territorial militia, one can perhaps see the strategos' new responsibilities in a different light. Left in charge of a landscape ravaged by Arab raiders, the final abolition of the civil administration was simply a further sign that the themes had ceased to be the empire's field armies, based in Asia Minor only until the reconquest began, and had become a second rank defensive force while the prestige and power increasingly lay elsewhere.

Even the writings of the emperor Leo VI, whose *Taktika* is one of the principal sources for the new role of the strategoi, are rather ambivalent as regards their real status and qualities. Leo's ideal strategos is a paragon of military and social virtues, but in those sections of the *Taktika* where he allows himself to comment on the real circumstances of the early tenth century empire, the impression is of inefficient theme armies of dubious military, worth, to be compared unfavourably with the military virtues of their Arab opponents. The same impression is given by other tenth-century writers on military affairs.[16]

The theme armies throughout this period were not all recruited from the same sections of provincial society, and there is a clear distinction in our source between the themes' infantry and cavalry. In fact we know very little about the infantry save the fact that they existed. Presumably they were paid like all other Byzantine soldiers, but paid less. In the tenth century when the Byzantines wanted to operate offensive expeditions deep into Arab territory it was necessary to raise new units of infantry, which rather implies that the older units of theme infantry were not of a very high standard. Parts of Asia Minor – such as Isauria, Lykaonia and Pisidia in south and south-west Anatolia – have been associated with the recruitment of foot-soldiers from the ancient world up to the Ottoman period; and it must always have been an easy matter to hire lightly armed foot-soldiers who were probably disbanded when no longer required.

The rise of the tagmata and the relative decline of the themes had little impact on this group; or at least there is no sign anywhere that the imperial government ever had any difficulties raising foot-soldiers. The case of the theme cavalry was rather different. The themes were essentially cavalry units, and almost all specific references to theme soldiers are to cavalry. Unlike the infantry these mounted troops appear with grooms, spare horses and equipment all provided by themselves, and the theme cavalry on the march is followed by a substantial baggage train of their possessions and servants. Even if it is anachronistic in a Byzantine context the term 'gentry' can usefully imply the sort of moderately wealthy provincial landowners who had traditionally filled the ranks of the theme cavalry.[17]

For these men the rise of the tagmata was a significant factor in undermining their enthusiasm to serve in the themes. The attractions had once been a useful cash salary, the hope of occasional booty, and the status of being a soldier. None of these had completely disappeared, but now a soldier in the tagmata would be better paid, have better hopes of booty and have a higher status in Byzantine society. If the figures from the documents associated with the Cretan expedition of 949 apply to an earlier period, then the pay differential between the themes and the tagmata was considerable.[18] In addition the tagmata could expect to spend much of the year in or near Constantinople, and in any political crisis they could look forward to being bribed. Naturally potential cavalry soldiers wished to join the tagmata.

Recruitment of the 'provincial gentry' to the theme armies seems already to have become a problem by the beginning of the ninth century. The imperial government's response was to make military service compulsory and hereditary. The first evidence both for compulsion, and for difficulties in finding cavalrymen, comes from Theophanes' hostile account of the reign of Nikephoros I (802–11), where under the year 809–10 he lists the emperor's 'evil deeds'. The second deed in the list is an imperial order to the effect that indigent peasants are to be recruited as soldiers and the cost of their equipment is to be shared among the other members of the new soldier's community.[19] Plainly it is not simply a matter of equipping a foot-soldier with a sling or a spear, rather the emperor is trying to spread the cost of cavalry service among a group of people hitherto excluded by their relative poverty. The major change, however, is signalled in a series of ninth- and tenth-century saints' lives which reveal in their anecdotes of provincial life that military service – and again it is quite plain that they mean service in the cavalry – is now a hereditary obligation, and that those liable are now listed in military rolls kept in the themes.[20]

These reforms seem to have been sufficient to fill the ranks of the theme armies for the rest of the century, but there was an obvious difficulty with such a system. Over time the fortunes of individuals and families rise and fall. Whereas under a system of voluntary recruitment the ranks of the theme cavalry would only have been filled from the prosperous, under a compulsory and hereditary system the theme would gradually find many of those bound to serve too poor to do so.[21] Nikephoros I's order that various poor men were to be drafted into the army at their neighbours' expense points to the way this problem was surmounted during the ninth century, but as tenth-century complaints from Leo VI onwards show, such methods could not halt the gradual decline in the wealth, status and it seems efficiency of the cavalry contingents who formed the basis of the themes' military potential.

It is against this background that one can see the significance of the mid-tenth century decision to tie military service to the land. Between 944 and his death in 959 Constantine VII Porphyrogenitos issued a new imperial law (such pieces of legis-lation are known in Greek as *nearai*, in Latin as *novellae*, and in English as 'novels') to the effect that since the position of soldiers in the theme armies had decayed over the generations, from henceforth each individual liable for military service in the theme army should have land to the value of four pounds of gold assigned to his support and that this inalienable property should be registered in the military rolls.[22] This novel has been frequently misunderstood. It does not involve the distribution of any new land; nor does it assume that the soldier will spend part of his time farming the property himself. Either the registered land worth four pounds will be made up of various pieces of property owned by different individuals who, as in Nikephoros' second 'evil deed' will be jointly responsible for one soldier's support, or the soldier will be the property owner himself, in which case since land worth four pounds is a substantial property he would employ farm labourers to do the work for him. Indeed, if the soldier was the property owner himself, there is no reason why he should not have owned considerably more than the land registered in the military roll, and hence his total property would have been worth well over the four pounds' minimum. This novel has nothing whatsoever to do with either the maintenance or the creation of a peasant militia. Instead it is a last attempt by the emperors to maintain the theme armies on their traditional lines as a force recruited from the provincial 'gentry', serving for pay, but largely supported out of their own estates. By the mid-tenth century, however, the moment for this had passed. The élite of the Byzantine army now consisted of the tagmata and the imperial guard troops, and the imperial government became increasingly willing to commute the themes' military obligation for a money payment. During the eleventh century the theme armies, the descendants of the late Roman field armies, withered away to virtual extinction. The last signs of their existence occur in late eleventh- and early twelfth-century monastic charters where among the standard list of fiscal liabilities from which recipients are to be relieved occurs as a matter of form immunity from *strateia* – the obligation to serve in the theme army.[23]

Byzantine Defensive Strategy, *c.*750–*c.*950

The various reforms in the second half of the eighth century began a chain of developments which by the mid-tenth century had fundamentally transformed the military structure that the

Byzantines had inherited from the late Roman past. At their heart lay the establishment of a new élite force, the *tagmata*, which slowly came to displace the themes from their role as the empire's mobile field army. Over the same period the themes themselves changed. By the time Leo VI was writing at the beginning of the tenth century the word 'theme' no longer primarily meant an army, but almost always referred to the territory where that army was based. The themes had taken on a new role as a second-line territorial force, responsible not only for local defence but for local administration too.

Fundamental to this development was the adoption of a new defensive strategy in Asia Minor, in which the themes played a key role. The first clear evidence of the strategy in operation comes from Theophanes' account of the reign of Leo IV. Byzantium had benefited from the political instability in the Islamic world surrounding the fall of the Ummayad caliphate in the mid-eighth century, but by the 770s the growing threat posed by their Abbāsid successors was becoming obvious. In 778 Leo had sent Byzantine armies raiding into Syria, and a counter-attack was expected. In preparation, Theophanes tells us,

> the emperor arranged with his strategoi that they should not meet the Arabs in the field, but secure the fortresses and bring in men to guard them. He also sent officers to each fortress, who were to take about three thousand picked men to dog the Arabs' heels so that their raiding party could not disperse. Even before this they were to burn whatever fodder was to be found for the Arabs' horses. After the Arabs had been in Dorylaion for fifteen days [clearly therefore they had captured this major fortress, modern Eskişehir, lying in the territory of the Opsikion theme in north-western Asia Minor] they ran out of supplies and their animals were starving; there were heavy losses amongst them. They then retreated and besieged Amorion for one day, but when they realised it was strong and well-garrisoned, they withdrew without accomplishing anything.[24]

Tactics such as these formed the basis for the Byzantine defence of Asia Minor during the ninth and tenth centuries, by which time they had reached a high degree of sophistication and efficiency. How they should be operated is the subject of one of the most remarkable documents to survive from the Byzantine world. This is a treatise entitled 'On Skirmishing Warfare', or 'De velitatione bellica', as it is often called in the secondary literature, being the Latin title under which it was first published in 1819. It was written on the orders of the emperor Nikephoros Phokas (963–9), and although it was not completed in its present form until after his death, it was based on notes made in the 950s or 960s, probably by Nikephoros Phokas himself.

'On Skirmishing Warfare' allows for the possibility that the strategos may wish to block the frontier passes into Anatolia, but considers it safer and more effective to allow Arab armies free entrance on to the plateau. Once in Anatolia, however, the Arabs will find themselves harrassed by shadowing Byzantine forces, making it difficult to disperse to raid. Meanwhile the civilian population has been evacuated and the fodder burnt. Isolated groups of raiders will be cut off and destroyed, while the camp of the main force will be watched for any opportunity of a surprise attack by night. Lacking soft targets the Arabs may be tempted to try well-defended fortresses, but short of victuals for men and horses they will eventually have to retreat back through the passes where they now have to face Byzantine forces set to ambush a tired enemy.[25]

In large part this strategy should probably be seen as a practical reaction in the face of superior force. The Byzantines could not prevent Arab raiding, and not daring to risk direct confrontation on a battlefield more often than essential, they adapted their strategy accordingly. Nonetheless, as the author of 'On Skirmishing Warfare' knew, and as Leo IV probably knew too, it is a strategy that makes a great deal of sense in the light of regional geography. In the centre of Asia Minor lies the Anatolian plateau, surrounded by mountains which separate it from the coastlands to north, west and south, and from Armenia and Syria to the east and south-east. The axis of the eastern mountain ranges, running east to west or north-east to south-west, is such that whereas access to the Armenian highlands is relatively straightforward via certain well-defined routes, access to Syria is blocked by the line of the Taurus and Anti-Taurus mountains over which armies can only cross by a limited number of practicable passes. The best known of these is the Cilician Gates leading from Cilicia on to the plateau, but as can be seen on Map III there are a number of other options. The difficulties vary in each case, but all present a serious military problem for an army trying to force its way through in the face of a prepared enemy controlling the heights either side of the road. As noted above, the author of 'On Skirmishing Warfare' did consider the possibility of holding a pass in the face of an Arab army trying to enter Anatolia, but experience had taught the Byzantines that they had most chance of success if they waited until a tired enemy, burdened with prisoners and booty was returning home. Patience was rewarded several times over the centuries, as a number of Arab armies met with spectacular disasters in these mountains, but the decision to wait inevitably meant that Byzantine resistance would amount to a defence-in-depth, where most Byzantine–Arab warfare would be waged on Byzantine soil.

The damage to Byzantine territory that inevitably resulted was a price that Constantinopolitan governments were quite willing to pay. The military priorities for any emperor were his personal security in Constantinople, and the need to forestall coup attempts by avoiding rival centres of military power. Given the ideology of imperial victory inherited from the late Roman past, it was also very helpful to the stability of a regime to demonstrate success in battle; but it was more important to avoid a conspicuous disaster which would advertise God's anger with his sinful servant. By comparison Arab ravaging of distant provinces brought few political costs, and it would have appeared a small price to pay for keeping the enemy at arm's length.

A further Constantinopolitan priority was to defend the warmer and more fertile coastal plains of western and north-western Asia Minor, rather than the bleak and distant expanses of the Anatolian plateau. To this end the major fortresses in Asia Minor, with a few partial exceptions such as the ancient military base of Kaisareia in Cappadocia, are not sited so as to contest Arab attacks on eastern or central Anatolia, but ring the northern and western margins of the plateau. Through the eighth, ninth and tenth centuries, Arab raids were harrassed by relatively small mobile forces over most of Anatolia, and it was only if they approached the next range of mountains, threatening to push through to the coastal plains beyond that they would be likely to face direct confrontation with a Byzantine field army. Most major battles, such as Leo III's victory at Akroïnos in 740, or Theophilos' defeat in 838 were fought on the western margins of the plateau, at a point where the emperor and his advisors felt they had no choice but to stand and fight.

Given that the goal of this strategy was to protect Constantinople and the coastlands, and to a lesser extent to prevent Arab conquest and occupation of the central plateau, its application from the eighth century onwards can be regarded as a Byzantine success of immense importance. The Arabs occupied Melitene (modern Eski Malatya) in eastern Anatolia, and Kālīkalā (Byzantine Theodosioupolis, modern Erzerum) on the approaches to Armenia, but otherwise their advance was halted. Contrary to what might have been feared at the beginning of the eighth century, the settlement of Cilicia did not mark the beginning of an inexorable Arab encroachment on the remaining Byzantine territories. Fewer and fewer Arab raids from the east reached the western coastlands. The rise of Arab sea power in the central Mediterranean, and above all the Arab occupation of Crete in the 820s, meant that districts actually on the coastline were still open to attack, but for the rest of western Asia Minor lying inland from the shore, the Arab threat was effectively over. The 860s in this respect mark the end of an era.

If Constantinople and successive imperial regimes were winners by this strategy, the inhabitants of Anatolia were losers, paying a horrible price in human and economic terms. Compared with the verdant coastal plains, with their Mediterranean climate of warm winters, the expanses of Anatolia, hot and dry in summer, bitterly cold and buried beneath heavy snow for several months in winter, could appear to Mediterranean city dwellers, including the inhabitants of Constantinople, as bleak and undesirable.[26] Yet although olive trees will not bear fruit on the plateau, otherwise as any modern traveller can see, much of it is a perfectly productive agricultural region. Given the lack of documents, and even more so the backward state of medieval Anatolian archaeology, the settlement history of the plateau is obscure. In the Roman and late Roman periods much of it seems to have been settled farming country. Not as rich as the coastlands, but still supporting potential taxpayers. Some were still there in the tenth century. The instructions in 'On Skirmishing Warfare' to evacuate villagers in advance of Arab raids, and the assumption that the same villages would be the main enemy target imply as much. But the author also seems to assume that the villagers' main wealth was in animals, and when contemporary Arab sources rejoice over a successful raid what they list, apart from human prisoners, are thousands of cattle and sheep. Over the Near East as a whole, in modern times as much as medieval, the standard reaction of peasant farmers to chronic insecurity has been a drift to pastoralism. It is very little to go on, but it does seem that this was the case here.[27]

Perhaps more telling evidence for the costs of Byzantine strategy comes from Cappadocia in central Anatolia, which has attracted the attention of art historians because of its remarkable rock-cut painted churches. A nearby volcano has in the geological past covered the region with a layer of soft volcanic rock, which has been eroded over millenia into an extraordinary sculpted landscape. These cones of rock have in turn been excavated to make cave-dwellings, storehouses, stables and churches. Because this cave architecture does not need to be kept in repair like ordinary buildings, and cannot be demolished to provide a supply of new building materials, the area provides remarkable evidence for human occupation over many centuries. Interest has not surprisingly focused on the painted churches rather than on the more basic questions of settlement history, but enough is known for an obvious hiatus between the seventh and late ninth centuries to stand out. The presence of a substantial population in the Roman period is obvious enough, and the churches which mostly date to between the late ninth century and the arrival of the Turks late in the eleventh century show activity in the Byzantine period, particularly in the late tenth and eleventh century. For the period between the record is a striking blank, clear testimony to the impact of annual Arab raids.[28]

Looking at the consequences of this dour defensive battle for the empire as a whole, rather than simply for Anatolia, two features stand out. The first is that for over two centuries the empire was effectively deprived of a major part of its resources. The Byzantine state was always bound by facts of geography to be the lesser neighbour of the vast Islamic caliphate, but as

Muslim geographers noted, it was not only smaller but qualitatively poorer.[29] Whereas the economic structures which had fuelled prosperity in the late Roman Near East had been preserved in the Islamic world, in Byzantium they had to a greater or lesser extent withered away. A fundamental cause of this must have been the inability of the Byzantines to achieve territorial security outside Constantinople and its immediate hinterland.

The second is that between the eighth and the tenth century the Byzantines had gone on to the defensive and had reshaped their military, administrative and political organisation accordingly. When, from the second half of the ninth century onwards, new opportunities arose for the empire to go on to the offensive, the Byzantine army reshaped to the demands of defence was no longer organised, trained or equipped for the task. If Byzantine regimes wanted to take up these opportunities, then a new and very different army would be required, with all the social and political upheaval that would inevitably entail.

The Size of the Byzantine Army

So far in this chapter I have avoided numbers. Almost all the documentary evidence has been lost and Byzantine chroniclers, like their contemporary Islamic and Western counterparts, use numbers principally as a rhetorical tool. One can make nothing from their hundreds of thousands save that on a particular occasion there was a large army, or more accurately the chronicler wishes to give the impression that there was a large army. Nonetheless it is not a subject that can be avoided entirely. To give numbers forces me to make an unambiguous statement of my conception of the Byzantine world. A state which can deploy and control 100,000 troops or more is obviously a totally different institution from one whose military resources are to be counted in hundreds or a few thousands.

One has to start with the late Roman army. John Lydos, a civil servant in the Praetorian Prefecture of the East, working in Constantinople in the mid-sixth century, claimed that under the late third-century emperor Diocletian (under whom the

empire still included western Europe) the Roman army numbered 389,704 men, with a further 45,562 men in the navy,
making a total of 435,266.[30] He does not say where he got this
information from, but had he so wished such figures probably
did exist in the prefecture's archives which in the sixth century
were still preserved in Constantinople. Agathias, a mid-sixth-
century lawyer, again living in Constantinople and not quot-
ing his sources, says that the empire's armies were no longer
sufficient to the requirements of the state.

> Whereas there should have been a total effective force of
> 645,000 men, the number had dropped . . . to barely 150,000.
> Some of these moreover were stationed in Italy, others in Africa,
> others in Spain, others in Lazika [the western Caucasus],
> and others still in Alexandria and Egyptian Thebes. There
> were also a few near the eastern frontier with Persia. . .[31]

A further source of information in the *Notitia Dignitatum*, a
list, divided up into provinces, of the ranks and offices – both
military and civilian – of the whole empire, east and west, drawn
up in the early fifth century. For the eastern half of the Roman
empire, which concerns us, the *Notitia* provides a fairly coherent
list of the military units deployed in each province. On the
basis of prior calculations as to the size of various units in the
late Roman army, A. H. M. Jones then went on the calculate a
figure of about 352,000 for the total establishement of the army
in the eastern empire at the beginning of the fifth century,
which he regarded as conservative. This figure is made up of
104,000 in the eastern empire's field army, and a further 248,000
principally in various units called *limitanei* deplolyed on the
frontiers. The *limitanei* still existed in the mid-sixth century but
their duties were confined to local defence and internal security,
and, according to Procopios, Justinian no longer regarded them
as soldiers. If so then the 104,000 strong field army of the east
derived from the *Notitia Dignitatum*, and the 150,000 which
Agathias claims were deployed throughout Justinian's empire
would be broadly equivalent figures.[32]

If these calculations from the *Notitia Dignitatum* are taken as
having any sort of validity then it can also be argued that the
late Roman field forces deployed in the Balkans, in the east

and around Constantinople at the end of the sixth century numbered very approximately 100,000 men. These units were the ancestors of the themes in Asia Minor, and it is obviously tempting to transfer the figure of 100,000 to the seventh-century themes.[33] But on various grounds these inferences are unpersuasive.

First of all, the early seventh century was a period of enormous upheaval; apart from Herakleios' great eastern campaign of 627–8, the Roman field armies had a miserable record of defeat and disaster. Out of this mess we have no idea how many troops the Byzantines managed to reassemble in Asia Minor. Perhaps 100,000, but the likelihood is very many fewer.

Secondly, although Jones's figures have been widely accepted and repeated, they are almost certainly far too high. Some figures preserved on papyri for the payment of troops based in Egypt in the late third century have been convincingly reinterpreted to show units in the late Roman army were much smaller than Jones's calculations require. Legions, which he estimated to have been 1000 strong or more at this date, may instead have been 600 or less, while other units, which he estimated at a minimum of 500 men, are revealed in this Egyptian evidence as sometimes less than 200 strong. A conservative estimate might therefore reduce Jones's figures by a third.[34]

Since any figure is perhaps no more than a guess, these calculations may now seem rather fruitless, but they do at least help to give a sense of proportion. The late Roman army was comparatively large, powerful and well-organised. If the operational field army for the whole eastern empire in the sixth century numbered anywhere between 60,000 and 100,000, then it follows that in ancient and early medieval terms such numbers constitute a very large force indeed.

For the size of the eight- to tenth-century Byzantine army we have three pieces of evidence: the figures given by Arab geographers; the figures for the Cretan expeditions of 911 and 949 in the documents preserved in Constantine Porphyrogenitos' *De Ceremoniis*; and the figures given for Byzantine armies in three tenth-century military treatises: 'On Skirmishing Warfare', already discussed, and two others concerned with offensive warfare, conventionally known by their modern editors' Latin titles as the *De re militari* and the *Praecepta militaria*.

Of these, the Arab geographers are alone in giving a total figure for the Byzantine army and a theme-by-theme breakdown. The geographers with whom we are concerned all wrote in the ninth and tenth centuries. The oldest work is that of Ibn Khurradādhbih, an official in the central administration of Abbāsid Iraq, whose *Kitāb al-Masālik wa'-Mamālik* ('The Book of Itineraries and Kingdoms') seems to have been originally written in 846 and then later revised in 885. For the revision he added material from a book on the Byzantines written by a certain Muhammad b. Abī Muslim al-Djarmi, who had been a prisoner in Byzantine hands until his release in 845/6. Amongst other details which Ibn Khurradādhbih gives from al-Djarmi's work is a total figure of 120,000 for the size of the Byzantine army, and a list of the eastern themes plus Thrace and Macedonia in Europe. For each theme Ibn Khurradādhbih includes a note of the number of fortresses and major cities, but he does not mention the size of each theme army. Much the same material from al-Djarmi was then repeated by two other geographers, Ibn al-Fakīh, writing in 902–3, and Kudāma b. al-Dja'far al-Kātib – a bureaucrat from the same background as Ibn Khurradādhbih – writing around the years 928–32, but they both add figures for the size of each theme army:[35]

Theme	Ibn al-Fakīh	Kudāma b. al-Dja'far
Thrace	5,000	5,000
Macedonia	5,000	–
Paphlagonia	5,000	10,000
Optimaton	4,000	4,000
Opsikion	6,000	6,000
Thrakesion	10,000	6,000
Anatolikon	15,000	15,000
Seleukeia	–	5,000
Cappadocia	4,000	4,000
Charsianon	4,000	4,000
Boukellarion	8,000	8,000
Armeniakon	9,000	4,000
Chaldia	10,000	4,000
Total	**85,000**	**75,000**

The *De Ceremoniis*, Constantine Porphyrogenitos' treatise on the ceremonies of the imperial court, and its extraordinary appendices in which are preserved a number of contemporary documents from the otherwise vanished archives of the imperial administration in Constantinople, was mentioned in Chapter 1. The documents associated with the two Cretan expeditions of 911 and 949 consist in each case of lists drawn up of the troops assigned to the expedition, and of subsequent attempts by the authorities in Constantinople to determine who had actually gone and hence who should be paid what.[36] Leaving aside the large numbers of sailors and oarsmen required on both occasions – in 911 they amounted to about 34,000 – the troops sent from the theme armies and the tagmata on these expeditions was as follows:

911

Tagmata	1,037
Theme of the Thrakesion	1,000
Armenians from the theme of Sebasteia	1,000
Armenians from Platanion (in the Anatolikon)	500
Armenians from Priene (in the Thrakesion)	500
Total	**4,037**

In addition the 911 list records a number of soldiers, as opposed to sailors or rowers, in the naval units:

Imperial Fleet	– soldiers in warships	4,200
	– Russians	700
Kibyrrhaiotai	– soldiers in warships	1,190
Samos	– soldiers in warships	700
Aegean Sea	– soldiers in warships	490
Hellas	– soldiers in warships	700
Mardaïtes		5,087
Total		**13,067**
Grand Total		**17,014**

(The origins of the Mardaïtes are obscure, being variously identified as Syrian inhabitants of the mountains north of Antioch, Armenians, or, much less likely, Maronites from the mountains of Lebanon. In any case a substantial number were resettled in the empire in 686/7. Later they appear, as here, as an autonomous community based in Greece and southern Asia Minor providing large contingents of marines for service with the naval themes.)[37]

949

Tagmata	– Scholai in west	869
	– Exkoubitores	700
	– Hikanatoi	456
	– Armenians from eastern tagmata	1,000
Slavs in the Opsikion		120
Theme of the Thrakesion		950
Armenians in the Thrakesion		600
Theme of the Charpezikion (see Map XIV)		705
Total		**5,400**

The figures for the military strength of the imperial fleet and the naval themes in 949 are not directly comparable to those for 911 because the 949 documents for the most part only give the numbers of ships rather than detailing the soldiers deployed with them. However, the 949 lists do include the following:

Imperial fleet	– Russians	629
	– Toulmatzoi (Dalmatians)	368
	– prisoners	700
Mardaïtes		3,000
Total		4,697
Grand total		**10,097**

The third piece of evidence for the size of Byzantine armies is the figures given in 'On Skirmishing Warfare', the *Praecepta militaria*, and the *De re militari* – all products of the second half of the tenth century, and intended to give practical and realistic advice to future Byzantine generals.

'On Skirmishing Warfare' was a retrospective work on the type of mobile defensive warfare waged by the Byzantines on the eastern frontier between the eighth and the mid-tenth centuries. Infantry play an important role in the tactics discussed, but the author never describes them in detail or gives a number to the soldiers involved. However, he does describe a force of less than 3000 cavalry as a 'large army'; which can later be contrasted with the small force available if the strategos has only the troops of a single theme. The enemy the author has in mind is a large Arab raiding army of about 6000 horsemen, plus a body of infantry. Their number is unspecified, but the fact that the author assumes that if the cavalry has gone away to raid leaving the foot-soldiers in the camp, unprotected but for a small force of horsemen, then the Byzantine strategos with his army of just under 3000 cavalry should have no difficulties in defeating them, rather implies that their numbers were small and their military contribution limited. The same seems to be true on the Byzantine side; the infantry can make a useful supporting contribution in battle, but they are only expected to hold their own in face of the Arab cavalry under the special circumstances where they are occupying the sides of a mountain pass looking down on the enemy. The largest Byzantine army the author mentions is one with a force of from 5000 to 6000 cavalry. For most of the treatise the author advises the Byzantine commander to carry out the type of harrassing operations which are the work's main subject, but if he should be the commander of the 'whole army', with 5000 or 6000 'warlike horsemen', then harrassing is set aside. The general should 'draw them up in formation directly facing the enemy' and prepare for battle.[38]

Both the *Praecepta militaria* and the *De re militari* are concerned with offensive operations by large armies, and both reflect the rather different strategy and tactics which the Byzantines were to employ from about the mid-tenth century onwards (see Chapter 9). In particular they envisage armies with more heavy cavalry and a much larger and more powerful force of infantry than considered by the author of 'On Skirmishing Warfare'. The *Praecepta Militaria*, which only survives in part, deals with the problems facing an army invading Arab territory beyond the Taurus mountains in northern Syria; the *De re militari* is concerned with operations against the Bulgars in the Balkan mountains, and envisages the army as commanded by the emperor himself. Otherwise their outlook is very similar, and they both describe an army of either 12,000 or 16,000 infantry with between 6000 and 9000 cavalry. The *Praecepta militaria* in fact talks of between 6000 and 7500 cavalry, while the *De re militari* has in mind a force of 8200 cavalry. The author of *De re militari* does consider cases where the cavalry force is either slightly larger or slightly smaller than this figure, but he is clearly not thinking about many thousands more or less. Significantly fewer than 6000 cavalry and the author judges that the emperor 'must not set out on campaign'. In practice the largest army either of these works can imagine is not more than 25,000 men.[39]

Most recent historians who have discussed this issue base their arguments on the Arab figures, which by various means are presented as both internally coherent and consistent with the figures in the Byzantine sources. A few peculiarities and omissions, such as Ibn al-Fakīh's failure to mention the theme of Seleukeia or the huge figure of 10,000 which he gives for the mountainous theme of Chaldia in eastern Anatolia, have first to be emended on the basis that these are simply errors in the manuscript tradition. The discrepancy between the overall figure given by Ibn Khurradādhbih of 120,000 and the sub-totals of 75,000 and 85,000 to be obtained from the lists of Ibn al-Fakīh and Kudāma b. al-Dja'far can be accounted for on the basis that the latter have omitted not only the tagmata, but all the western themes apart from Thrace and Macedonia. If figures are assigned to these units roughly consistent with those given by Ibn al-Fakīh and Kudāma for the eastern themes, it is possible to find space for an extra 45,000 or 55,000 to add up to Ibn Khurradādhbih's total. Finally the apparent discrepancy between these figures and the much smaller numbers to be obtained from the Byzantine sources is explained on the grounds that the Byzantine figures are with a few exceptions for the cavalry alone. On the basis that the sixth-century historian Procopios says that Belisarios' expeditionary force to Africa in 533 consisted of 5000 cavalry and 10,000 infantry it has been suggested that 1:2 was the normal ratio of cavalry to infantry in Byzantine armies. Rather more persuasively, roughly the same ratio has been deduced from the figures given by the *Praecepta militaria* and the *De re militari*, but on the grounds that these were more mobile offensive armies, an average ratio has instead been suggested for the army as a whole of 1:4. When these calculations are applied to the Arab figures a coherent and consistent picture can then be made to emerge of a Byzantine army in the mid-ninth century numbering either about 40,000 cavalry and 60,000 infantry on a ratio of 1:2, or 24,000 cavalry and 96,000 infantry on a ratio of 1:4.[40]

If this argument is accepted then it follows that the Byzantine state in the ninth and tenth century was a very well organised and powerful institution with extraordinarily large military resources. It implies that the Byzantine empire which ruled little more than western and central Asia Minor, Greece and a few coastal areas elsewhere in the Balkans, had an army of approximately the same size as the late Roman empire in the sixth century. This would be rather peculiar given the evidence for the comparative poverty of Byzantine society, but it could be explained on the grounds that Byzantium was a highly militarised state that had devoted the greater part of its resources to the maintenance of huge armed forces. An army of this size would also place Byzantium in a totally different category from the contemporary states of western Europe. The kingdom of England in the tenth and eleventh centuries is generally regarded as a sophisticated and wealthy state, able to tap the resources and services of its subjects, but at the most optimistic level its total paper military strength did not far exceed 14,000 warriors, and no English army approached that number on campaign. Smaller still were the numbers of men available to the Ottonian rulers of tenth-century Germany. Otto I may have been able to gather a force approaching 10,000 to invade France in 946, but at the decisive battle of the Lech, where Otto defeated the Magyars in 955, the German army appears to have numbered less than 4000. Given that no one has argued that Byzantine military strength matched that of the Islamic world, it also follows that Arab military resources were greater still; which in turn would point to a fundamental divide across early medieval Europe and the Near East between the highly organised and militarised east made up of Byzantium and the Islamic world, both able to mobilise tens of thousands of troops, and a backward west, unable to achieve anything approaching the same result. The greater capabilities of the east could perhaps be explained as a consequence of the survival in Byzantium and the Islamic world of late Roman and Persian administrative and fiscal techniques – above all of the land tax – which allowed both societies to transcend the limitations still binding the west; there, it might be argued, obligations based on personal ties and only a very primitive administrative system was the rule. Such a conclusion might appear odd in the light of the unremarkable record of Byzantine armies against western opponents in southern Italy during the ninth and tenth centuries, and the lack of respect shown by Otto I of Germany and his advisors for Byzantine military capabilities during the 960s, but these objections could be surmounted. Perhaps the superior fighting qualities of the Ottonian heavy cavalry outweighed any disadvantage in numbers, or given that for Byzantium Italy was a backwater compared with the eastern front, perhaps the empire's resources were deployed with better effect elsewhere.[41]

However, this faith in the Arab evidence mistakes the nature of Arab geography. The tradition of geographical writing in Arabic had grown up in the ninth century as part of the process whereby Islamic culture – well-established by this date – created a coherent image of its place in the physical world. In some ways it can be seen as a deliberate creation of an alternative image to that of the classical Roman geographers and historians, replacing their view of the world divided between the civilised empire and the barbarians, with one of a world divided between Muslims and non-believers. The Byzantine empire – *Rūm* – was of some interest as the Muslims' ancient enemy, mentioned in the Koran, from whom they had conquered Syria, Palestine and Egypt, but it would never become more than marginal to the geographers' world view. Byzantium might deserve more space than other non-Muslim states, but it was very little compared to the true focus of their attention, the lands of Islam. Overall the impression is of slight interest, easily satisfied.[42]

Arab geographers did include some eyewitness material, but Arab geography remained essentially a literary genre, repeating and rearranging material found in other literary sources. The information on Byzantium is a classic instance of this process. Once it had become part of the tradition it was repeated with comparatively minor variations in all subsequent geographies through to the thirteenth century. In no case is there any question of a serious attempt to find accurate and up-to-date information. Once established in the tradition it could be repeated without question.

Repetition is no guarantee of the original value of the evidence. The Arab geographical tradition is an eclectic mixture of legend and fantasy with relatively reliable fact. Stories such as that of the Seven Sleepers of Ephesos,[43] whose Byzantine attendants had to clip their nails and hair as they slumbered for centuries, are included along with the list of Byzantine theme names which is broadly correct. Sometimes it is obvious which is fact and which is fiction, but in the case of the figures for the size of Byzantine armies it is far less certain. They could be correct, but equally they could be guesses, included to make a rhetorical point about the huge numbers of infidel soldiers.

Any piece of unsupported evidence in the Arab geographers therefore needs to be treated with care, but more so in this case because of the sheer unlikelihood of how the figures were obtained. It is usually believed they derive from the work of al-Djarmi, who had been a prisoner-of-war in Constantinople; yet it is very difficult to imagine how a Muslim prisoner-of-war could have had access to documents recording the strength of the Byzantine army. Even if one supposes that al-Djarmi learnt these figures from conversations with Byzantine officials it is difficult to imagine why they should have wished to tell him these things – unless of course it was all wildly exaggerated.

Seen without this dubious Arab evidence, the comparatively reliable Byzantine material from the military handbooks and the *De ceremoniis* is clear evidence for very much smaller Byzantine forces. The attempts to show that this material is consistent with a total force of 120,000 men on the basis of hypothetical cavalry/infantry ratios is wholly unconvincing. Considering the military handbooks first, the *Praecepta militaria* and the *De re militari* both presume that the maximum conceivable force to be led by the emperor himself on a major offensive expedition is no more than 25,000 men – from 6000 to 9000 cavalry and from 12,000 to 16,000 infantry. Even this, however, is clearly too many. In the first place these handbooks are describing an ideal expeditionary force; real expeditions, such as the 917 invasion of Bulgaria for which the Empress Zoe had assembled 'the whole army of the east' together with the tagmata, were no doubt significantly smaller.[44] Secondly both these are late tenth-century texts reflecting the greater numbers of infantry found to be necessary when the Byzantines embarked on offensive operations in the Balkans and the Fertile Crescent. Before this infantry forces played a much less important role. As a result, although the *Praecepta militaria* and the *De re militari* remain important pieces of evidence, the figures in 'On Skirmishing Warfare' are probably a more realistic guide to the size of armies available to the Byzantines in the eighth, ninth and tenth centuries. These, as we have seen, suggest that 3000 cavalry is a large force drawn from several themes, and that from 5000 to 6000 is the cavalry strength of the 'whole army', by which the author probably means the whole army of the east. Since it is clear from a wide range of Byzantine sources that the army of the east formed the largest part of the Byzantine army, a reasonable guess for the cavalry forces of the empire as a whole, tagmata and western themes included, is perhaps somewhere just over 10,000. For the numbers of infantry it is difficult even to guess: 20,000 perhaps? Most may well have been raised on an *ad hoc* basis for each campaign, but whatever was the case, there is no evidence to suggest the existence of the huge standing forces of infantry the figure of 120,000 men demands.

This order of magnitude is confirmed by the uniquely valuable documents from the *De ceremoniis* recording the troops sent on the Cretan expeditions of 911 and 949. Both these expeditions were major military undertakings. The loss of Crete and the failure to retake it had been an important factor in the end of the second phase of iconoclasm. To succeed in the reconquest of Crete would be a triumphant sign of God's favour; a further defeat would risk serious political consequences. On both occasions the regime which sent the army to Crete was somewhat insecure, looking for a dramatic victory to pay political dividends. Leo VI had barely survived an assassination attempt in 903 and a coup in 905. From 906 onwards he was involved in a divisive battle with the patriarch Nicholas Mystikos over the legitimacy of his fourth marriage and hence of his only son and heir. He also needed a victory to offset the humiliating memory of the Arab sack of Thessalonica in 904.[45] Similarly in 949, Constantine VII had recently seized power in a coup against his father- and brothers-in-law, and still faced threats to restore them to power. Recent military successes on the eastern frontier were more associated with members of the Phokas family who had won them, than the emperor in Constantinople. Constantine needed a success that court propaganda could portray as proof of God's favour to him and his regime.[46] Both expeditions needed to succeed. Hence the forces assembled represent the largest and best equipped expeditions the emperors could muster. Because these are naval expeditions they are perhaps not directly comparable with the figures for land expeditions from the military handbooks, but they do confirm the impression that Byzantine armies should be numbered in hundreds or thousands, and not tens of thousands. It is striking that the tagmata number no more than 1037 in 911 and 3025 in 949 when 1000 were Armenians from the east. Similarly one of the oldest and largest themes, the Thrakesion, only numbers 1000 in 911 and 950 in 949. Clearly 17,000 in 911 and 10,000 in 949 represents for the Byzantine empire very large forces indeed. The figure of 120,000 is out of all proportion with the rest of the evidence.

This conclusion has interesting implications. First of all it suggests that the military resources of the Byzantine empire were broadly comparable to those of other early medieval European states. Perhaps they were a little larger, but not on a different scale. This in turn leads to the conclusion that the preservation of late Roman administrative and fiscal techniques did not enable the Byzantines to tap and deploy the resources of their empire in a way fundamentally more effective than their western European contemporaries. Perhaps it did offer some advantages, but this conclusion strongly implies that the real importance of the late Roman inheritance was not economic or military, but political. The survival of the land tax, collected in the provinces and dispensed as salaries to a hierarchy of civilian and military functionaries at the imperial court, focused political life on the emperor and Constantinople in a way that would have been impossible in the contemporary west. As such Byzantium may not have been wealthier or more powerful than other European states, but it was more centralised and more united, and this was a vital factor in its survival.

8 The Byzantine Empire and its Non-Muslim Neighbours, *c.*600–*c.*950

THE LATE Roman empire had not simply been a Greek state, but rather a multi-ethnic Near Eastern empire. Forced on to the defensive in a desperate battle to survive, its Byzantine successor was very much more of an inward-looking institution preoccupied with preserving its orthodox purity. Yet Byzantium could not ignore the other non-Muslim peoples of the Near East. Transcaucasia and the Balkans both represented sources of military manpower to offset the huge resources of the caliphate, and if Byzantium were to hope to break out of its narrow limits as merely the empire of Constantinople then these were both areas that had to be brought within the Byzantine political and cultural orbit. Equally important was the Byzantine relationship with the steppe world which was the only Near Eastern society with a military potential that might approach that of the caliphate. Nomad allies had played a vital role in Herakleios' victories of the late 620s, and as long as the Arabs posed any threat to Constantinople it had to be an essential part of Byzantine diplomacy to keep good relations with whoever dominated the steppes north of the Caucasus.

The seventh to tenth centuries were a period of revolutionary changes among the empire's non-Muslim neighbours, and a sense of these changes is essential if events inside the Byzantine world are to be understood. For the making of orthodox Byzantium these developments are particularly crucial. Orthodox introspection was shaped between the seventh and ninth centuries by the empire's exclusion from the wider Christian world in the Transcaucasus and in Italy; and in the tenth century the political and cultural foundations of the orthodox empire were to be saved from its enemies by Rus warriors – themselves a product of the revolution which had transformed the steppe world over the previous century and a half.

Transcaucasia

Transcaucasia is the area south of the Caucasus mountains and north of the Mesopotamian plain, formed for the most part by the mountains which link Anatolia to Iran.

The indigenous population in the early middle ages can be roughly divided into three main ethnic groups speaking distinct and unrelated languages: the Armenians, the Caucasians and the Persians. The Armenians dominated the central and western Transcaucasus and were the largest and most important non-Muslim people. The Caucasians lived to the north of this and included a bewildering number of tribes speaking apparently related but for the most part mutually unintelligible languages. The two most important Caucasian peoples were the Georgians (themselves made up of separate Abasgian, Laz and Iberian peoples) who inhabited the area between the Black Sea and the upper Kur valley around Tiflis; and the Albanians, the product of an ancient confederation of eastern Caucasian tribes, who lived towards the Caspian Sea in the lower Kur valley and the adjacent hills to the west. Already by the seventh century they were heavily influenced by Armenian culture and over the course of the following four centuries the Albanians were gradually absorbed by their Christian and Muslim neighbours.[1] The third group were the Persian peoples most numerous in the south-east of the Transcaucasus south of the Kur and Araxes rivers. This is historic Azerbaidjan. The modern Republic of Azerbaidjan lies north of the Kur and Araxes in what would have been territory of the Caucasian Albanians. Its present Turkish inhabitants only arrived in the eleventh century, and whenever Azerbaidjan appears in this chapter the reference is to Persian Azerbaidjan. Among the Persian peoples of this region were the Kurds. There is very little evidence for their early history before the tenth century, but they evidently did not appear from nothing. Azerbaidjan was the scene of frequent anti-caliphal and anti-Arab revolts during the eighth and ninth centuries, and Byzantine sources talk of 'Persian' warriors seeking refuge in the 830s from the caliph's armies by taking service under the Byzantine emperor Theophilos. Not all Persians are Kurds, but given the warlike nature of Kurdish tribal society which for centuries to come was to export warriors all over

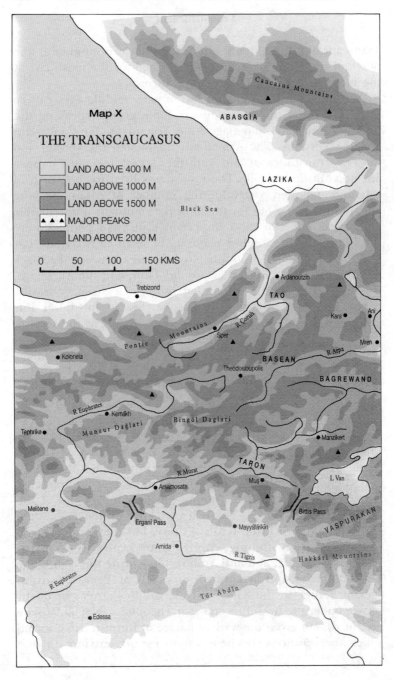

Map X

THE TRANSCAUCASUS

LAND ABOVE 400 M
LAND ABOVE 1000 M
LAND ABOVE 1500 M
▲ ▲ ▲ MAJOR PEAKS
LAND ABOVE 2000 M

0   50   100   150 KMS

Caucasus Mountains

ABASGIA

LAZIKA

Black Sea

Trebizond

Ardanoutzin

TAO

Kars

Ani

Pontic   Mountains   Sper   R Çoruh

Koloneia

BASEAN

R Arpa

Mren

Theodosioupolis

BAGREWAND

R Euphrates   Kemakh

Bingöl Daglari

Tephrike

Munzur Daglari

Manzikert

TARON

R Murat

Mus

L Van

Arsamosata

Melitene

Ergani Pass

Bitlis Pass

VASPURAKAN

Mayyafarikin

Amida

Hakkâri Mountains

R Tigris

R Euphrates

Tûr Abdîn

Edessa

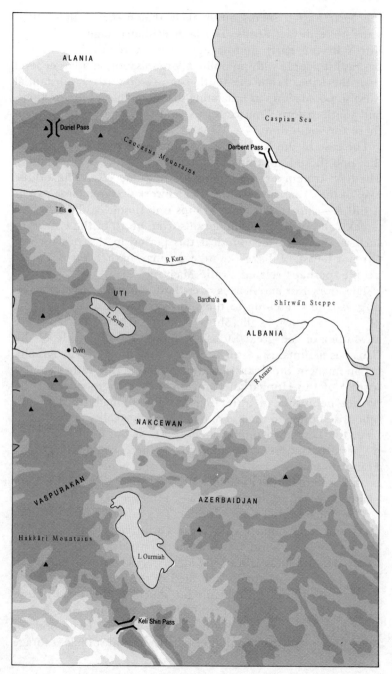

ALANIA

Caspian Sea

Dariel Pass

Caucasus Mountains

Derbent Pass

Tiflis

R Kura

UTI

Bardha'a

Shīrwān Steppe

L Sevan

ALBANIA

Dwin

R Araxes

NAKCEWAN

VASPURAKAN

AZERBAIDJAN

Hakkâri Mountains

L Ourmiah

Keli Shin Pass

the Near East it seems quite likely that many of these 'Persians' were in fact Kurds. The later evidence suggests that the Kurds in the early middle ages were a relatively primitive pastoralist people with no political organisation at a larger level than the tribe. From the tenth century onwards a substantial Kurdish population was inhabiting the mountains of the southern and south-eastern Transcaucasus, and they had probably been there for some time.[2]

The case of the Kurds is important as it serves to emphasise that one should not think of homogenous blocs of population, whether Armenians, Georgians, or any one else. The ethnic map of the Transcaucasus was a patchwork – as to a large extent it still is – and to the main groups one should add Arabs and Greeks, and pockets of immigrants from north of the Caucasus, such as the Sewordi, found at this period in the province of Uti north-east of Lake Sevan, who may have been a Turkic people, perhaps related to the Magyars.[3]

The lower Kur and Araxes rivers have created a large expanse of grassland stretching to the shores of the Caspian Sea, part of which is known as the Shīrwān steppe. These grasslands are an outlier of the great Eurasian steppe the other side of the Caucasus mountains. As such they are something of a geographical anomaly in the Transcaucasus, playing a role rather similar to that of the Hungarian plain on the northern edge of the Balkan peninsula in attracting pastoral nomads to a region otherwise hostile to their economy. A much smaller coastal plain faces the Black Sea immediately south of the Caucasus range in western Georgia, but apart from these two lowlands the Transcaucasus is a land of mountains and plateaux, where the peaks rise to between 3000 and 5000 metres, and the high plains between are often well over 1500 metres.

The climate reflects the altitude. This is a land of short summers and long bitterly cold winters with very heavy snowfall. During the First World War Russian troops advancing near Kars, where the plateau reaches 1800 metres, walked through Turkish trenches whose occupants had died of the cold.[4] Travel in the Transcaucasus can be difficult for much of the year. Before May the higher passes are still blocked by snow, and before June pre-tarmac roads were too muddy for any large body of men, who in any case would not be able to find sufficient forage for their horses. Large parts of these mountains form natural refuges, isolated from the outside world, and formidably difficult of access. Even today there are extensive upland areas which are over ten hours on horseback from the nearest road passable in a four-wheel drive vehicle.

Yet the Transcaucasus as a whole is far from being an isolated backwater. It is a region of great strategic importance; its peoples played a vital role in the affairs of all the major Near Eastern states; and at the same time the logic of its internal politics created a constant demand for outsiders to intervene.

Its strategic importance flows in large part from its position at a crossroads between the great powers of the Near East. To the north are the steppes, to the east Iran, to the south the Fertile Crescent, to the west Anatolia, with Constantinople and the western coastlands beyond. In the early middle ages the Transcaucasus was a battleground on one axis between Constantinople and first Persia and then later the Arabs, and on the other axis between the Persians and their Arab successors and the steppe powers of the lands to the north.

The interest of the outside world has not often, however, been in Transcaucasia as a whole, but has focused on certain key areas, the importance of which derives from the nature of the route system. Despite all the difficulties, Transcaucasia as a region is not inaccessible. The mountain ranges are aligned roughly on an east to west, or rather a south-east to west axis, and the main lines of the route system follow this grain of the landscape. Consequently access from Anatolia or from Persia is relatively easy, and in turn Transcaucasia forms a good starting point for an invasion of either plateau. By contrast although an enemy in Transcaucasia can threaten the steppe world beyond the Caucasus and the heartlands of Iraq and Syria to the south, both involve north–south travel against the grain of the landscape, and in practice the lines of communication are limited to certain key passes. The most important in the early middle ages were the Derbent pass, otherwise known as the Caspian Gates or the *Bāb al-Abwāb*, the 'Gate of Gates', at the eastern end of the Caucasus, which links the Kur and Araxes lowlands to the Volga steppes; the Dariel pass, otherwise known as the *Bāb al-Lān*, the 'Gate of the Alans', which crosses the central Caucasus north of Tiflis in the upper Kur basin; and on the southern side of the Transcaucasus, the Bitlis pass and the Ergani pass both of which link Armenia to the plains of Syria and Mesopotamia. Of these the importance of the Bitlis pass perhaps deserves underlining. Between the Ergani pass, over 200 kilometres to the west, and the Keli Shin pass across the Zagros mountains south of lake Ourmiah, a further 375 kilometres to the east, the Bitlis pass is the only major practicable route into the Armenian mountains, and it is the only pass providing a direct link between Mesopotamia and central Armenia. Control of the Bitlis pass has therefore always been a central strategic factor in the history of the region, long before the period covered in this book through to the twentieth century. All these passes can in theory be avoided by secondary routes. In the cases of the Bitlis it is for example possible to cross the Hakkâri mountains to the south-east of Lake Van, but is a journey only to be undertaken in good weather, not with a large army, and not in a hurry. The fundamental fact is that throughout Transcaucasia a limited number of passes provide the key to the region's strategic importance, and for the most part it has been on these areas that outside interest has focused.

The role played by Transcaucasians in the affairs of the Near East is also in many ways a product of geography. Much of the land is poor, rocky and infertile, and taken with the short growing season provided by the harsh climate, it belies the panegyrics of fertility given by medieval Armenian authors.[5] Typical of many such mountainous regions, the Transcaucasus has traditionally produced more people than it can easily feed, let alone make wealthy, and for centuries Armenians, Georgians and Kurds have left the mountains to make their fortune in the outside world as merchants, stone masons, monks and above all soldiers. The Persian shahs and later the caliphs and other Islamic rulers attracted many to the south and east, but the role played by Transcaucasian emigrants was largest in the Byzantine world. The example of the 'Persians' serving Theophilos in the ninth century has already been mentioned; Georgian monasteries first appear in Constantinople and on Mount Olympos in north-western Asia Minor in the second half of the ninth century, and from then on Georgians played an increasingly important part in the empire;[6] but the most prominent group of Transcaucasian immigrants in Byzantium were certainly the

Armenians. Four emperors – Leo V (813–20), Basil I (867–86), Romanos I (920–44) and John Tzimiskes (969–76) – seem to have been Armenian, as well as the empress Theodora, Theophilos' wife and the restorer of orthodoxy in 843. To these could be added a long list of soldiers whose Armenian names stand out in the chronicles and on lead seals: Arsabir, Artabasdos, Bardanes, Bardas, Symbatios are obvious and frequent examples. Even if only some of those named were actually Armenian the popularity of the names is significant in itself. Throughout the seventh to eleventh centuries a remarkably high percentage of theme strategoi and senior officers in the tagmata were apparently of Armenian origin.[7]

The third link tying the Transcaucasus to the rest of the Near East was the demand for outside involvement from within the Transcaucasus itself. One factor behind this was the need for protection. Rome was appealed to against the Persians, Byzantium against the Arabs, and first Persia and then the caliphate for protection against the steppe world to the north. However a more fundamental, and perhaps paradoxical, incentive lay in the structures of Transcaucasian politics which were themselves a product of the region's geography.

Transcaucasia may be relatively poor but it is not completely lacking in resources. A characteristic of the landscape over most of the region is the high basins of alluvial soil, the most fertile drawing on the volcanic deposits left by numerous extinct volcanoes. The largest are those of the Araxes and Kur valleys, but important too in a regional context are those around Lake Sevan in the east and Lake Van in south central Armenia (where in both cases the lakes moderate the extremes of the climate), and the plains of Taron, Melitene, and Basean in the west. A look at any reasonably detailed map of the region can show many more.

Each of these plains, isolated to a greater or lesser extent from its neighbour, had the potential to support local political power, which in practice was often autonomous. The consequent fragmentation of politics and society was to a large extent common to all the peoples of the Transcaucasus, but to take the example of the Armenians, as the most numerous and powerful of the Transcaucasian peoples at this period, the pattern of political fragmentation took the form of a network of

hereditary family lordships called *naxarars*. Larger political units
did exist. Up to the fifth century there had been an Armenian
monarchy to which the individual naxarar houses had owed
loyalty, and there was always a tendency for a hierarchy to develop
among the naxarars by which less powerful families recognised
the authority of the greater naxarars who were described as
išxan, 'princes'. However, these were essentially temporary arrangements reflecting the current balance of forces; the basic
political unit remained the individual naxarar house.[8]

The naxarar structure was not unchanging, but it proved im-
mensely durable. It long predated the seventh century, and
would last at least until the Mongol invasions of the thirteenth
century; aspects of it would still be present in Transcaucasian
society in the nineteenth century. The values of the naxarar
houses – aristocratic, warlike, independent, proud of their sworn
loyalty to a lord but always willing to betray an outsider for
the greater good of the family – dominated Armenian society.
Even the Armenian church was shaped by the same forces. Not
only monasteries, but also bishoprics were in effect naxarar
institutions, named after the naxarar cantons they served, and
filled by bishops recruited from the same naxarar families.[9]

The power of any particular naxarar depended upon control
of the resources of a fertile alluvial basin, and the existence of
a mountain refuge to retire to in time of crisis. (Such a district
is often referred to as a 'canton' in the modern secondary literature, to distinguish it from a 'province' of several such cantons
whose naxarars might obey a leading naxarar or išxan.) During
the early middle ages there seem to have been just over a
hundred naxarar houses in Armenia, of whom perhaps fifty
were of some importance, and five or six – the Artsruni, the
Bagratuni, the Rštuni, the Mamikoneans, the Kamsarakan, and
possibly the princes of Siwnik – were at various periods convincing
candidates to establish some form of wider hegemony over
Armenia.[10]

This system created an inherent demand for outside involvement. Naxarar houses trying to protect their autonomy from
threatening neighbours would look to outside powers for support.
Submission to a distant ruler in Constantinople or Baghdad
could appear preferable to domination by a local Armenian
rival. More important, however, the demand for intervention

also came from the larger naxarar houses trying to consolidate their power. The five or six leading naxarar families owed their position in part to their control over the largest plains and most secure mountain refuges, but also to their ability to draw on outside forces. This aspect of Transcaucasian politics has frequently been overlooked. Most general histories of Armenia tend to portray Armenian history as a struggle between the centralising forces of successive royal and princely dynasties against the centrifugal forces of the naxarar houses. The intervention of outsiders is usually regretted as undermining the natural tendency towards national unity. Yet in fact the fiercely independent naxarar houses had no tendency as such toward national unity, rather they were engaged in a constant competition for land and regional dominance. The chances of lasting success, however, were always undermined by the facts of geography, and by the natural tendency of a too successful naxarar house to provoke temporarily united opposition from its rivals. The natural state of Armenian political life was not one of unity, but of fragmentation. In practice the only means of imposing lasting central authority was by drawing on resources outside the naxarar world. Far from undermining developments toward national unity, outside intervention was the only force capable of achieving any unity in this environment.

Much the same point could be made for the Georgian kingdoms and for Caucasian Albania. If the evidence were available it would probably prove to be true for the Kurds as well. In each of these societies there was an inherent political incentive for the indigenous nobility to encourage the intervention of outside powers, and to make themselves part of the political worlds of their more powerful neighbours. The balance between a fragmented and hostile terrain, which made foreign conquest difficult and preserved the autonomy and particularism of an aristocratic warrior society, and the various factors, internal and external, which encouraged outside intervention is one of the keys to understanding Transcaucasian history, and it forms the essential context for Byzantine involvement in the region during the early middle ages.

The oldest outside influence in Transcaucasia was that of Persia. Azerbaidjan had a Persian population and was a traditional centre of the Zoroastrian religion. From the mid-sixth century BC through to the late fourth century BC most of the Transcaucasus had been part of the Persian empire, and from the first to the fifth centuries AD the independent kingdom of Armenia was ruled by the Arsacid dynasty, a junior branch of the then Persian royal house. The kingdom of Iberia – which corresponds to Kartli, the eastern half of later Georgia – also had a Persian ruling dynasty up to the sixth century AD. Armenian, Georgian and Albanian aristocratic culture was heavily influenced by Persian values. Many of the terms for Armenian nobility, for example, including that of *naxarar* itself, are Persian loan-words. Zoroastrian beliefs were widespread, far more in fact than the later Christian tradition of history writing in the Transcaucasus is prepared to admit. Persian political and cultural influence had decreased by the seventh century but remained deeply rooted.[11] One of the most obvious features of the important seventh-century history conventionally attributed to Sebeos is that the focus of Armenian interests is more on Ctesiphon and the Persian world than on events in Constantinople, and it is striking to note the list of leading Armenian naxarars who were killed or wounded fighting for the Persians at the battle of al-Kādisiyya during the Arab conquest of Iraq. Another history, Moses of Dasxuranci's *History of the Albanians*, written in the tenth century, but apparently reproducing older materials, similarly describes the heroic deeds of the *sparapet*, or 'marshal', of Albania at the same battle.[12] Even after this it is worth remembering that for many of its population, including Armenians and Georgians as well as Persians and Kurds, the Transcaucasus had much closer ties with the former Sasanian world to its south and east than with the world to the west.

From the first century AD onwards, however, Persian influence in the Transcaucasus found itself increasingly under pressure from the Roman empire advancing from the west. By the second century AD Lesser Armenia – which corresponds roughly to those parts of eastern Anatolia west of the Upper Euphrates river – had become a permanent part of Roman territory. For most of the second and third centuries the rest of independent Armenia was a Roman client kingdom, where Greek cultural values came to rival those of Persia. The culmination of this growing Roman influence came in the early fourth century when possibly in 314 (not earlier as Armenian tradition would have it) king Trdat accepted St Gregory the Illuminator as the first bishop of Armenia. The conversion of Albania, Iberia and the western Georgian kingdom of Lazika followed, probably in the 320s and 330s. The effective conversion of these peoples, and in particular of their nobility, was naturally slow and varied from area to area, but by the beginning of the fifth century Christianity had become firmly established in the Transcaucasus.[13]

For Roman interests the long-term consequences of this conversion proved somewhat ambiguous. Christianity was, as contemporaries recognised, the Roman religion; and obviously the conversion marked a decisive break with the Persian world and created important ties the Romans could exploit. However, the effect was less decisive than might have been expected. Rather than being followed up by a period of strong Roman political pressure, the secure establishment of Christianity coincided with a major setback to Roman power in the east. In 363 an imperial invasion of Persia led by the emperor Julian ended in humiliating disaster and the death of the emperor himself. To extricate the army from Iraq, Julian's immediate successor, Jovian, was forced to give way to Persian demands that the Romans abandon their allies in the Transcaucasus. In 376 the Goths crossed the Danube and two years later defeated the Roman army at the battle of Adrianople, killing the emperor Valens. Faced with crisis in the Balkans there was little chance of restoring Roman influence in Transcaucasia, and in exchange for peace in the east the Romans agreed to a partition of Armenia in 387 which left the heartlands of the Armenian kingdom together with Albania, Iberia and Lazika in Persian hands. The Armenian monarchy did not long survive; it was abolished in 428, and replaced by a Persian governor or *marzban* who had his seat in Dwin. Otherwise the Persian Transcaucasus was ruled as a collection of client kingdoms under princes loyal to the Persians, several of whom converted to Zoroastrianism.[14]

In what remained of the Roman Transcaucasus the combination of Christianity with Roman political control led to a slow but effective process of assimilation. By the seventh century Roman Armenia was no more culturally distinct than other Roman provinces in the Near East. However, after the partition of 387 these territories made up only a small proportion of the Transcaucasus, and elsewhere Christianity functioned not as a vehicle for Roman influence, but as a means of preserving the cultural and political autonomy of the local nobility. To a large extent the very identity of Armenians and Georgians was created during these years in a Christian image. In both Armenia and Georgia the establishment of Christianity involved the creation of alphabets and the subsequent development of an indigenous literature and liturgy. The achievement is remarkable, but the effect was increasingly to isolate these cultures behind a language barrier where traditions and dogma discarded by the rest of the church could be maintained.[15] Christianity became not so much a force for assimilation with the wider Christian world – which in effect of course meant the Roman world – as an ideology underpinning the social, political and cultural particularism of the Transcaucasian nobility. The account given by the sixth- or seventh-century historian, Elishe, of the failed revolt of Vardan Mamikonean in 450–1 against the Persian shah's attempts to force Zoroastrianism on the Armenian nobility, stresses not the path of personal salvation and the need to preserve the one true faith of the universal church, but the battle for their ancestral land and a traditional way of life. In Elishe's hands the rebels of 450–1 have taken on the mantle of the Jewish Maccabees who fought for their land and ancestral customs; Christianity has become the covenant of a chosen people, and Christian Armenia stands alone against the outside world.[16] Paradoxically Christianity, which outside influence had brought into the Transcaucasus, would henceforth act to mitigate the impact of outside influence in future.

Relations were further complicated by the decision of the Armenian, Georgian and Albanian churches to reject the Council of Chalcedon; a decision which was confirmed by the Council of Dwin in 505 or 506. At the time this was certainly not a move away from the orthodox consensus of the empire. The future status of Chalcedon was still in doubt, and indeed at the beginning of the sixth century the emperor himself, Anastasius, was among those who wished to reject the Council's Christology. The Georgian church was to accept Chalcedon at the beginning of the seventh century, but for the Armenian church (and the Albanian too, which in effect had no separate existence after the eighth century) the rejection had far-reaching consequences.[17] Already isolated by language, custom and its archaic traditions of ecclesiastical discipline, Elishe's sense of the Armenians as a chosen people standing alone against the world came increasingly to be reinforced by a theological underpinning.

The rejection of Chalcedon would eventually create a gulf between the Armenian and Greek churches, but one must be careful not to read this too far back in time nor to exaggerate its practical significance. Clergymen, especially monks, imbued with anti-Chalcedonian slogans, were a strong force in Armenian naxarar culture, and for many of them any temporising with the schismatic and heretic Chalcedonians who divided Christ was apostasy. Yet in practice naxarars wanting ties with Byzantium were quite prepared to compromise, and up at least to the tenth century the many thousands of Armenians who entered the service of the Byzantine emperor seem, as far as one can tell, all to have accepted the empire's Chalcedonian orthodoxy without difficulty. Even inside Armenia there was a sizeable Chalcedonian community, and a significant minority in favour of union with the Greek church. Despite its strong particularist sentiment, Christianity still created ties between the Transcaucasus and the Byzantine world which a powerful empire would have the opportunity to exploit.

There were two such periods in the early middle ages, separated by two centuries of Arab domination. The first during the sixth and seventh centuries up to the 640s was a period of remarkable Roman success. In Roman western Armenia the autonomous principalities were suppressed in favour of a conventional provincial administration; a programme of fortress building transformed the military balance with the Persians; while at the same time the Tzani, a warlike and primitive pastoral people living in the high Pontic mountains which run parallel to the Black Sea coast behind Trebizond, were, as Justinian's novel of 535 triumphantly proclaims, 'subjected to Roman domination (which is something that God has not permitted to take place up to this time and until Our Reign) ...'.[18] Meanwhile the Romans were aggressively interfering in what had since 387 been a Persian sphere of influence, exploiting as they did so ties of common Christianity. Lazika on the Black Sea coast was made a Roman client kingdom, and in the 570s Roman troops were sent to back an anti-Persian rebellion in Iberia. In the war which followed Roman raiders on occasion reached as far as Azerbaidjan and the Caspian Sea. Roman success culminated in the treaty of 591 which rewarded Maurice for his role in restoring Khusro to the Persian throne. The new frontier included Lazika and Iberia as far as but excluding Tiflis; from there it turned south to Mount Ararat, and thence south-west to the north-east corner of Lake Van. The eastern and southern shores of the lake remained Persian but the strategically vital Bitlis pass was conceded to the Romans.[19]

Given the extent of the new Roman dominance in the Transcaucasus it is not surprising that Armenian sources report some resentment from naxarars who quite rightly felt their autonomy threatened. More striking are the signs of Roman territorial power being converted into political and cultural assimilation. New heads (known as *katholikoi*) were sought for the Iberian and Armenian churches who would be willing to accept Chalcedon. This was easier in Iberia which was wholly in Roman hands, than in Armenia where an anti-Chalcedonian katholikos remained at Dwin, the traditional seat of the Armenian katholikoi, which was still in Persian territory. However, Maurice set up a rival Chalcedonian katholikos at Avan less than 50 kilometres from Dwin on the other side of the frontier. The Iberian acceptance of Chalcedon proved to be permanent, but even in Armenia the Chalcedonians appear to have enjoyed considerable support.[20] The collapse of the eastern provinces in the face of the Persians in the early seventh century restored the authority of the katholikos at Dwin over the whole Armenian church and a Council was held in 607 so that those 'who had voluntarily subjected themselves to the Greeks' could publicly recant their error. Numbers vary according to the different versions of the event, but at least five bishops, 19 abbots of major monasteries and a large number of other abbots and priests had to make a public repentence.[21]

Throughout the Near East Herakleios' extraordinary victory of 628–9 opened a perspective of lasting Roman domination. In the Transcaucasus the emperor rapidly set about establishing the new order. Dwin was still in Persian territory, but such was the extent of Roman dominance and of the Persian collapse that it no longer offered any asylum for an anti-Chalcedonian church. Despite some opposition from his own clergy, the new katholikos Ezr seems to have accepted union with the Greeks without difficulty, and in 632 this was publicly recognised at a Council held in the emperor's presence at Theodosioupolis (modern Erzerum).[22] The most detailed source to cover these years, the history attributed to Sebeos, gives a familiar picture of infighting among the Armenian naxarars as they competed for imperial office, and struggled to make Roman power serve their ends. Herakleios had first sent Mažež Gnuni, to command the imperial forces in Armenia, but in 635 he was murdered by a rival naxarar, David Saharuni, who succeeded him first as commander of the Roman forces, and was then appointed by the emperor 'išxan of Armenia' with the high court rank of *kouropalates*. David ruled for three years before being toppled by other naxarar rivals, but his lasting monument is the great church at Mren. Built during his three years as išxan, or possibly shortly before, the architecture shows Syrian influence, the sculpture Persian, while the whole is a highly distinctive achievement of Armenian culture. On the lintel of the west door appears Christ with SS. Peter and Paul. To the right of Peter is the local Armenian bishop Theophilos, and beyond him, David Saharuni himself. To the left of Paul is Narses Kamsarakan, the young heir to the powerful naxarar house of Kamsarakan, who with the Saharuni, dominated the region where Mren was built. On the lintel of the north door a relief carving shows the triumphant emperor Herakleios restoring the True Cross to Jerusalem where he is being met by the patriarch of Jerusalem, Modestos. The church and especially this remarkable group of carvings represent the short high tide of Roman hegemony in the Transcaucasus. A naxarar church in the heartland of Armenia associates two naxarar clans and their bishop with the triumphs of a Chalcedonian Roman emperor, whom they now serve. The carvings are images of a new political and cultural relationship that had hardly been established before it was swept away.[23]

The Arab conquest of Transcaucasia began in the 640s. The chronology and the exact course of events is obscure, and contradictory between the Armenian and Arab sources, but the main developments seem fairly clear. By 653 Arab pressure was enough that Theodore Rštuni, appointed prince of Armenia by the emperor, accepted generous terms from Mu'āwiya, the

Arab governor of Syria, for the submission of Armenia, Georgia and Albania. This surrender was by no means final. the Byzantines were not reconciled to their loss, and the logic of Transcaucasian politics as ever encouraged the intervention of rival outside forces. The very next year Constans II invaded Armenia with a large army and spent the winter at Dwin. But his attempt the re-establish imperial control was short-lived; following his departure for Constantinople, the remaining Byzantine forces were soon defeated by the Arabs at Nakcewan in the Araxes valley. The outbreak of the first civil war between Mu'āwiyah and Alī in 657 encouraged a further brief Byzantine return, but by 661 Arab authority had been restored. The failure of the Arab siege of Constantinople in 678, the second civil war and its unsettled aftermath in the 680s provided a third opportunity for the Byzantines and their allies in the Transcaucasus, but as before it did not outlast the political upheaval among the Arabs. By the mid-690s the Arabs were back in control, and by 706 opposition from any Armenian naxarars still tempted to contest the new order had been effectively and brutally crushed.[24]

The last area of the Transcaucasus where effective Byzantine influence could still be brought to bear was in the Georgian north-east, especially in the Çoruh valley close to Trebizond, which remained a secure Byzantine possession behind the mountain wall of the Pontic Alps, and in the west Georgian coastlands, accessible by sea and where the Byzantines kept hold of some coastal fortresses into the eighth century. Political ties between Constantinople and this part of the Transcaucasus, including shared Chalcedonian orthodoxy, were older and closer than elsewhere, but despite this as the empire's client kingdom of Lazika broke up in the seventh century so Byzantine authority evaporated. By the 690s the Abasgians, a pastoral people of the west Georgian mountains, and former subjects of the Laz kings, were wholly independent of the empire. Theophanes, in a section of the *Chronographia* apparently taken from a Life of Leo III, tells the extraordinary story of Leo's adventures in this area at the end of the 690s. Unable to overawe the Abasgians directly, the emperor Justinian II had sent Leo in an attempt to coerce them through their warlike Alan neighbours to the north-east. The operation fell apart when it became clear that there was insufficient money and troops to back up imperial posturing. The implications of Byzantine impotence are clear, and must have been obvious to contemporaries too. In the 730s the empire could do nothing to prevent an Arab invasion of western Georgia; and in 786–7 it was the Khazars not the Byzantines who acted as protectors for the newly proclaimed Abasgian kingdom, which rapidly became the dominant power over much of western Georgia. For two hundred years from the beginning of the eighth to the beginning of the tenth centuries the Byzantines were – with brief and marginal exceptions – shut out of Transcaucasia.[25]

Against the background of the overall collapse of the late Roman empire in the seventh century the loss of Transcaucasia needs little special explanation. The growing impotence of the Byzantines encouraged a rapid change of allegiance as competing noble families looked to use the new Arab power against their rivals. The Arabs left the existing fragmented structure of family politics in place, and appear to have offered very favourable terms. In Armenia, following Sasanian precedent, the naxarars were to owe cavalry service to the caliph for which they were paid an annual subsidy of 100,000 silver dirhams. Taxation was light and the level of military service seems to have been less onerous than in the past. According to Sebeos' version of the 654 treaty, Mu'āwiya promised, 'I shall not demand that the [Armenian] cavalry be sent to Syria. . . . I shall send no emirs to your fortresses, nor even a single Arab officer or cavalryman. . . . Should the Byzantines come against you, I shall dispatch as large an auxiliary force as you want.' 'Thus', Sebeos explains, 'did the satellite of anti-Christ pull [the Armenians] away from the Byzantines.'[26]

It is also worth mentioning that many Armenians, Georgians and Albanians were glad to see a new master in the Transcaucasus who shared their fear of the steppe nomads. An important factor in the close ties between the Transcaucasus and the Persian shahs had been the traditional enmity of the Persian world for these northern barbarians. The Arabs inherited not only this Persian attitude, but also their policy of defending the Caucasus passes. By contrast, the Romans tended to see the nomads as potential allies, Moses of Dasxuranci's *History of the Caucasian Albanians* preserves what seems to be a contemporary account of Herakleios' 627–8 campaign in the Transcaucasus. Mildly in favour of the victorious Christian emperor, Moses' account is violently hostile to his Turkish nomad allies: an 'ugly, insolent, broad-faced, eyelashless mob in the shape of women with flowing hair' is only a sample. Whether Christian or not the inhabitants of the eastern Transcaucasus were not pleased to see Herakleios' army, and when summoned to surrender Tiflis and Bardha'a (the latter on the edge of the Shīrwān steppe) both refused. The hatred of the nomads is not confined to one section of Moses' book, but pervades the whole work. Through to the end of the ninth century the nomad Khazars were the chief allies of the Byzantine empire. For many in the Transcaucasus, especially in the eastern lowlands, if the end of Muslim domination required the nomads to come south of the Caucasus, it was not a price worth paying.[27]

By the early eighth century the retreat of Byzantine power was such that a line drawn between Trebizond on the Black Sea and Seleukeia on the Mediterranean would have marked something close to the eastern limits of the empire. Beyond the Taurus and anti-Taurus ranges everything was in Arab hands, including the whole of what had been Roman Armenia after the treaty of 387, and almost all of what had been Roman Lesser Armenia for centuries before that. As long as the Arabs were looking forward to the imminent fall of Constantinople this frontier marked only a temporary pause, but the failure of the 718 siege and the political upheavals which preoccupied the caliphate during much of the middle decades of the eighth century led to a gradual change in strategy and outlook. On the Arab side the frontier zone began to coalesce into a fortified and settled borderland, known as the *thughūr*. The main centres of this zone were al-Massīsa (Mopsuestia), Adana, Tarsos, Maraş, al-Hadath, Malatya (Melitene), Kemākh (Kemah), and Kālīkala (Theodosioupolis, modern Erzerum). Fortification and settlement here had started before 750 under the later Ummayads, but the main developments took place in the second half of the century after the Abbāsid revolution. (Constantine V's sack of Malatya in 751 and of Kālīkala and Kemākh before the end of 754 were no more than an interlude.) The early Abbāsid caliphs, and above all Harūn al-Rashīd (786–809), colonised and fortified the area. Immigrants from as far away as Khorasan were encouraged by generous salaries and very low taxes. *Djihād* (holy war) was a religious duty and volunteers, often paid for by the state, were encouraged to come from all parts of the Islamic world. The annual raids against the Byzantines took on much of the character of a religious ritual.[28]

The reorganisation of the thughūr further isolated the Transcaucasus from effective Byzantine intervention, but more directly the heavy costs of the new fortifications and settlements, barely half of which were covered by the revenues of the frontier provinces themselves, would seem to have been one of the main reasons why the caliph al-Mansūr (754–5) took the decision to abolish the subsidies paid to the Armenian naxarars and to impose a worthwhile burden of taxation throughout the Transcaucasus. By 774 the new character of Arab rule had provoked the naxarars into a rebellion which marks a watershed in Transcaucasian politics. The bloody defeat of the rebels at the battle of Bagrewand in April 775, and the ruthless suppression of opposition in the years that followed, destroyed for good the power of several of the leading naxarar houses of earlier Armenian history. Those of the Mamikoneans, the Gnuni and the Kamsarakan who survived the slaughter did so either as the dependents of other houses, or as exiles in Byzantium. In the 780s the nobility of Iberia were similarly crushed, again with those who survived taking refuge either in Byzantium or with the western Georgian princes of Abasgia.[29]

To reinforce the new order the Abbāsids encouraged an influx of Arabs into the Transcaucasus. Previously the Khazar threat had brought about the establishment of large permanent garrisons at Bardha'a and other Albanian cities, and at Tiflis, but otherwise apart from the western fortresses facing Byzantium, the only permanent Arab settlement was at Dwin in the Araxes valley. From the late eighth century, however, nearly all the major towns had an Arab population which dominated a substantial part of the fertile lowlands of the Transcaucasus. By the mid-ninth century Christian Albania had effectively been absorbed into the Arab world, Iberia was dominated by an expanding emirate of Tiflis, the plains around Lake Van were divided between a series of small emirates, and by the end of the century the Armenians would have lost the Araxes plains around Naxcewan to another autonomous emirate.[30]

In the event, however, rather than promoting greater caliphal authority and political stability, the new Arab settlers brought a further fragmentation of Transcaucasian politics, and a new agenda of disputes and rivalries to fuel more revolts and feuds. The caliphs could either send yet more Muslim armies to enforce their authority, or more commonly turn again to the Armenian naxarars. As a result, in the long term the major beneficiaries of the upheavals of the later eighth century were not the Arab settlers but two families of Armenian naxarars, the Artsruni and the Bagratuni.

By the early ninth century, the Artsruni who had previously only been a middle-ranking naxarar house, had driven their rivals out of the mountains of Vaspurakan and established themselves as the dominant power in south-western Armenia. Unlike the Artsruni, the Bagratuni had been a leading naxarar house before the revolt of 774–5. They survived the aftermath of the battle of Bagrewand only by withdrawing to their mountain refuges near the source of the Araxes, but within a remarkably short period, through skilful politics, the use of their extensive family ties, and their control of the gold and silver mines in the upper Çoruh valley south of Trebizond, the Bagratuni had managed to recover their authority. By the early ninth century they had established themselves as the dominant Armenian clan in those areas outside the Artsruni sphere of influence. In 806 the Bagratuni, Ašot Msaker, who had bought the former estates of the Kamsarakan family on the Arpa river around Mren, was appointed prince of Armenia by the caliph. Shortly afterwards the caliph recognised the rightful possession by another branch of the Bagratuni of the lands of Tao (or Tayk in Armenian) on the borders of eastern Georgia, whence they would gradually establish themselves as princes of Iberia. By 813 the Bagratuni had also added to their possessions the former Mamikonean lands of Taron, which lie along the Euphrates valley, due west of Lake Van.[31]

In both cases the key to their power was their relationship with the caliph and his appointed governors. The Artsruni had flirted with rebellion in 774–5, but they had changed sides quickly enough to win the caliph's favour. With Arab support they had a free hand to drive their rivals from Vaspurakan. Several leading members of the Bagratuni had tried in vain to keep the family out of the 774–5 rebellion, but their successors learnt from this mistake and Bagratuni fortunes in the ninth-century were based on conspicuous loyalty to the caliphs in the face of Arab rebels, and at least up to the 860s, any approaches from Byzantium. In 838, for example, the forces of both the Bagratuni and the Artsruni followed the caliph al-Mu'tasim on the invasion of Byzantium which culminated in the sack of Amorion.[32]

The great test for the leaders of both houses came in 852–3 after a long period in which they had enjoyed considerable autonomy. Following the death of Harūn al-Rashīd in 809, his successors had been preoccupied by a bitter civil war which lasted until 819, but even when central authority was restored the end of any immediate threat from the Khazars after about 800 made the Transcaucasus something of a backwater in terms of the caliphate as a whole. Seen from the caliph's court in Iraq the most important event of these years in the Transcaucasus was the Khurramite revolt of Babek in Azerbaidjan, which lasted from 819 to 837. The Khurramites were an anti-Arab Persian sect, influenced by Shīʿite doctrines, but with their roots in a pre-Islamic Persian religious movement.[33] The strong support they enjoyed in Azerbaidjan reflected local resentment provoked by the growing influx of Arabs into the eastern Transcaucasus. Provided that the Bagratuni and the Artsruni helped (or at least did not hinder) the caliph against his enemies, which at various moments included not only the Khurramites and the Byzantines, but also local Arab emirs and the Arab governors of Armenia and Azerbaidjan, and provided they paid their taxes without too much difficulty and delay, they were allowed to pursue their interests in Armenia undisturbed.

However, in 849 the current leaders of both families became involved in a dispute over taxation with the Arab governor of Armenia, Abu Saʿīd. The affair escalated. In 850 the Artsruni and Bagratuni allied to defeat a local Arab emir who had been charged with collecting taxes in Vaspurakan. In response the caliph al-Mutawakkil sent a new governor, Abu Saʿīd's son, Yūsuf, to extract the taxes and restore his authority. Yūsuf began well, pillaging Vaspurakan and Taron, taking hostages and accepting payments and submissions; but his actions – in particular it seems his arrest of the prince of Armenia, Bagarat

Bagratuni, whom he deported to Iraq – eventually succeeded in uniting the Armenian naxarars and Arab settlers against him. During the winter of 850–1 Yūsuf was surprised in his winter quarters in the Bagratuni town of Muş (which lies in the plain of Taron) and murdered. Al-Mutawakkil's response was far beyond anything the Armenians might have expected. It happened that in 851 the caliph had available a powerful army of largely Turkish slave-soldiers, whom it suited current politics to keep occupied. On the news of Yūsuf's murder, this army under its formidable commander, Bughā the elder, was sent to the Transcaucasus. In a series of devastating campaigns Bughā crushed virtually all resistance, and by 855 very few local leaders of any importance – Armenian or Arab – were not either serving in Bughā's army, imprisoned at Samarra (the new Abbāsid capital in Iraq), hiding in the mountains, or dead.[34]

Despite the completeness of Bughā's victory, there was no question of al-Mutawakkil imposing direct rule on the Trans-caucasus, and in due course a compromise had to be reached which restored much of the earlier balance of power. The Artsruni preserved their hegemony in Vaspurakan largely intact, but the real winners from this episode were the Bagratuni who, in a manner typical of naxarar politics, had rapidly ingratiated themselves with the new outside force. Over the next few years Smbat Bagratuni and his son Ašot had the satisfaction of watching Bughā crush their rivals, including the emir of Tiflis whose destruction opened the way for the Bagratuni of Tao to expand their domination of eastern Georgia and the upper Kur valley. Smbat did not live to enjoy the rewards of his political dexterity. He died in Samarra, according to the Armenian sources, under pressure to convert to Islam. It was therefore his son, Ašot (usually known as Ašot I or Ašot the Great by modern historians), who in 862 was appointed prince of princes by the caliph with authority over the whole of Armenia, including the Arab emirates.[35]

Ašot's title, *išxan išxanac'* ('prince of princes'), may have been held by his uncle, Bagarat, before him, but it was certainly a recent development, and it may even have been coined for Ašot. Ašot's unprecedented authority, however, owed less to the title than to his skill at exploiting the opportunities that opened up after Bughā's departure from Armenia. In 861 al-

Mutawakkil was assassinated and the Abbāsid caliphate entered a political crisis from which it was never fully to recover. Against this background of declining Abbāsid power, Ašot built up Bagratuni hegemony over Armenia, eastern Georgia and what was left of Christian Albania. Finally in 884 the caliph al-Mu'tamid sent Ašot a crown and recognised him as king of Armenia.[36]

As prince of princes and later as king. Ašot continued to follow a policy of conspicuous loyalty to whoever was the legitimate Abbāsid authority in Samarra or Baghdad. Indeed a factor behind the Abbāsid authorities' recognition of Ašot's royal title was their preference for a Christian ruler of proven loyalty against both Arab rebels and the Byzantines, over the possibility of an autonomous Muslim warlord who might turn his troops on Iraq. Yet the Byzantines, as much as Ašot himself, were also a beneficiary of the decline of Abbāsid power, and his reign coincided with a growing Byzantine advance in the east (see Chapter 9). It was no longer possible simply to ignore the emperor in Constantinople.

As it had survived longest in the north-west of the Transcaucasus, so the earliest signs of reviving Byzantine influence were in the same area. Shortly after the younger branch of the Bagratuni had established themselves as princes of Iberia in 813, they seem to have adopted the Chalcedonian orthodoxy of their Iberian subjects, and they took the title of *kouropalates* from the emperor Leo V (813–20). In the 830s another branch of the Bagratuni who held the district of Sper (modern İspir in the upper Çoruh valley close to the Byzantine frontier, accepted the titles of *patrikios* and *anthypatos*. As with that of kouropalates held by their cousins, the titles brought a salary, and certainly placed their holders in a Byzantine sphere of influence. But as yet there was little real power to back it up. The empire could not save the Bagratuni kouropalates, Ašot I, from being driven out of Iberia and killed by the emir of Tiflis in about 828. Similarly, the only clear feature of a Byzantine intervention in Abasgia in the later 830s or early 840s mentioned in the chronicle known as Theophanes Continuatus is that it failed.[37]

The decisive Byzantine victory over the raiding army of the emir of Melitene in 863 marks the beginning of a new phase of Byzantine success in the east. But the balance of power altered very slowly, and from an Armenian or even a Georgian perspective the empire's armies were still a long way away. It was not until 878 that the Byzantines captured Tephrike, the headquarters of the Paulicians (a warlike Armenian sect, who had acted as anti-Byzantine allies of the Arabs), and not until the beginning of the tenth century did they push their armies further up the upper Euphrates valley in a serious attempt to take Theodosioupolis (modern Erzerum). The main thrust of Byzantine operations in the last third of the ninth century was south-east into the Anti-Taurus, not east into the Transcaucasus.

In the 860s and again in the 870s Ašot encouraged negotiations with the Byzantine patriarch of Constantinople, Photios, over the possibility of church union, but this came to nothing.[38] The emperor Basil I (867–86) recognised Ašot's pre-eminence in Armenia – although with the title of 'prince of princes' rather than 'king' or the equivalent – and after Ašot's death in 890, his son and successor Smbat I maintained similarly good relations with Basil's heir, the emperor Leo VI (886–912).[39] To call this a 'pro-Byzantine policy', however, is an exaggeration. In the detailed contemporary account of these years given by the head of the Armenian church, John the katholikos, the empire plays a distant and marginal role. When Smbat was trying to justify his treaty of 893 with the emperor Leo VI to Muhammad b. Abu'l-Sādj, the Muslim governor of Armenia and Azerbaidjan, John quotes him as follows: 'I thought that I might obtain with ease those items that you yourself and the caliph needed from the land of the Greeks, and present you with noteworthy garments, ornaments and vessels for your own use. Likewise I wished to clear the way for merchants of your faith, so that they might have access to their land, and enrich your treasury with the riches of the Greeks.'[40] A report in the *De Administrando Imperio* suggests that some Byzantine officials would have agreed he was telling the truth. Smbat's cousin, Grigor, the Bagratuni prince of Taron, was another recipient of Byzantine titles and rewards, but as the report's author sourly notes, 'while in word he pretended to esteem the friendship of the emperor, in fact he acted at the pleasure of the chief prince of the Saracens'.[41] The Byzantines were no longer shut out of the Transcaucasus, but although their influence was growing, it remained a distant and secondary factor until the tenth century.

Ašot's kingdom was not, of course, the reflection of any innate tendency toward Armenian unity, but simply a successful exploitation of the aftermath of Bughā's campaign which had done so much to crush his Armenian and Arab rivals. As soon as the effects had worn off Bagratuni hegemony inevitably provoked a bitter naxarar reaction. By good luck and political skill this was delayed until the reign of Smbat I, who in the first decade of the tenth century ineptly provoked a conflict with Yūsuf, Muhammad's brother and successor as governor of Armenia and Azerbaidjan. What followed has often been presented as a national struggle of Christian Armenians against Muslim Arabs, but the contemporary accounts of John the katholikos and Thomas Artsruni are quite clear that what was really happening was an Armenian naxarar civil war between the Bagratuni and those who had lost by their rise. Smbat's chief opponent was Gagik Artsruni, who successfully exploited Yūsuf to break the Bagratuni and in 908 to gain for himself the title of king. By 913 Smbat had been so deserted by his supporters that he had little choice but to surrender to Yūsuf, who in the following year put him to death.[42] Yet Yūsuf did not merely repeat for the Artsruni what Bughā had done for the Bagratuni half a century before. Unlike Bughā, Yūsuf had dynastic interests of his own in Transcaucasus and in the long term this made him too difficult an ally. Nor could Gagik repeat Ašot's alliance with the caliphate, which was now impotently preoccupied with its own problems in Iraq. For the Artsruni, for Smbat's son, Ašot II, for the Armenian church, for the Iberian Bagratuni and for the Abasgians – all alarmed as to where Yūsuf would turn next – and for most of the smaller naxarars, the best hope for the future seemed Byzantine military intervention. In an extraordinary letter to the child emperor Constantine VII Porphyrogenitos, John the katholikos promised that if the Byzantines intervened, the Armenians 'would rush to join the universal flock of your reasonable sheep congregated in the meadow and pursue their lives under the aegis of Roman supremacy, just like the people of Italy and all of Asia'.[43] It would be a long time before anything remotely resembling this came to pass, and John himself would find it politic not to go to Constantinople in case people should accuse him of seeking communion with the Chalcedonians, but the army which

Constantine's mother, the regent Zoe, sent to Armenia in 915 to restore Ašot II to his throne marks the beginning of a new era in Byzantine relations with the Transcaucasus. For the rest of the century growing Byzantine power would be the dominant political force in the region, and for the Byzantines there opened up the opportunities, the problems, and the hopes of reshaping the Near East which they had last seen at the beginning of the seventh century.

The Khazars

The Khazar qaganate was the heir to the western section of the Gök Türk empire, the huge steppe superpower whose sixth-century conquests had taken the Turks from the borders of China to the western edges of the Ukrainian steppes. The structure of the Gök Türk empire was that of a huge confederation headed by a *qaghan* from the ruling Ašina clan of the Turks. The cult of Tengri the Sky-God was closely associated with the Ašina who were regarded as a charismatic clan, who alone could provide a qaghan with the necessary heavenly good-fortune. As a later Turkish inscription puts it: 'Because heaven mandated it, because I, myself, possessed heavenly good-fortune, I became qaghan.' The Turks recognised the rulers of China and Tibet as having an equivalent heavenly mandate – indeed some of these political ideas had their roots in Chinese imperial ideology – but otherwise as long as his charismatic good-fortune lasted the qaghan was regarded as rightfully the all-powerful ruler of the Eurasian world. All opponents were mere rebels against heaven.[44]

Beneath the ruling qaghanal clan were the 'inner tribes', who had joined the confederation when it began in 552. Beneath them were the 'outer tribes', who had usually been forced into the confederation at a later date. Beneath them were tribute-paying vassals, often sedentary agriculturalists and traders; and beneath them slaves. From the beginning the Turkish empire had a strongly dual structure. At its inception the empire had been divided into a senior eastern and a junior western qaghanate; the former based in the ancestral lands of Mongolia and ruled by the supreme qaghan, the latter in Central Asia, ruled by the slightly lesser *yabghu qaghan*. The western qaghanate in turn was divided into two groupings (a left and a right) of five tribes each, known together as the *on ok*, the 'ten arrows'. Of these the left division was called the *Dulo*; the right the *Nou-shi-pi*.

The name 'Türk' means 'strong one', and is typical of a fairly common type of tribal name among steppe nomads, implying strength or fierceness. The term first appears as the name of the small tribe headed by the Ašina clan who seized power from their Juan-Juan overlords in 552 and founded the Gök Türk empire. Because of the subsequent fame of these Turks, the name has also been used for an important ethnic group among the Eurasian peoples who are conventionally known in the modern literature as Turkic, or more loosely as Turks, and who amongst other things in common speak a group of closely related languages, now known as Turkic, of which modern Turkish is one. The Ašina Turks were part of this ethnic group, but the confederation of the Gök Türk empire had no ethnic unity as such. To call it a Turkish empire does not imply that it was an empire of the Turkic peoples, or of the ethnic Turks. The confederation formed in 552 had no ethnic unity, but as the Türk qaghans expanded their control over the steppe, so other peoples came to call themselves 'Turks' as a mark of their political subordination to the qaghan. Throughout the early middle ages on the Eurasian steppes, the term 'Turk' may or may not imply membership of the ethnic group of Turkic peoples, but it does always mean at least some awareness and acceptance of the traditions and ideology of the Gök Türk empire, and a share, however distant, in the political and cultural inheritance of that state.

The qaghan's power over this disparate collection of nomad tribes depended upon his military supremacy, which in turn required military success to produce the rewards to guarantee loyalty. Inevitably the Gök Türk empire was an aggressive expanding state. By 559 the armies of the western qaghanate had reached the Volga steppes, driving the Avars (the remnants of the former Juan-Juan empire) to find refuge on the Hungarian plain. By 568 the Turks were negotiating with the Roman emperor with a view to a joint assault on Persia. But secure hegemony over this vast area lasted less than two decades. In 582 civil war broke out not only between but inside the two qaghanates. After 603 the western qaghanate stabilised under the yabghu qaghan, T'ung, who in 627 sent two of his subordinates with a powerful army that played a vital role in Herakleios' victory over the Persians. But on his death in 630 the western qaghanate broke up in further civil war. A remnant survived under changing leadership in Central Asia up to 766, but in the steppe lands of the North Caucasus, the Volga and the Ukraine, the former subjects of a now crumbling centre were left to fight for the Gök Türk inheritance.[45]

The events of the period 630–70 in the steppes north and east of the Black sea are extremely obscure, but it seems certain that both the Bulgars and the Khazars were tribal confederations that had been created as a means for the Turkish qaghan to control the western steppes after their conquest in the second half of the sixth century. Soon after 630 both appear led by rival qaghans: the Bulgars (to be discussed further in the penultimate section of this chapter) under a scion of the Dulo clan – the leading clan of the left division of the western qaghanate's *on ok*; the Khazars apparently under one of the Ašina clan, who apart from being the traditional charismatic ruling clan of the Turkish qaghanate, seem also to have been associated with the Nou-shi-pi, the right division of the *on ok*. The conflict may have been fuelled by tensions between the Dulo and the Nou-shi-pi which were already a factor in the civil war inside the western qaghanate, but what was at stake was hegemony over the western steppes. By 670 the Khazars, who seem to have been more closely connected with the inner tribes around the former yabghu qaghan, had broken the Bulgar confederation. Some Bulgars remained on the Pontic steppe to the north-east of the Black Sea as direct subjects of the Khazars; another group retreated north along the Volga river, where first as autonomous vassals of the Khazars, and later as an independent state, they survived until the Mongol conquests of the thirteenth century; others fled to the west, some even reaching Italy, but the most important of the western Bulgars settled on the Danube where they established a Bulgar qaghanate that lasted until the tenth century.[46]

With this background it is not surprising that the Khazar

qaghanate was a nomad state on the Gök Türk model. Indeed in many Arab and Byzantine sources the terms 'Khazar' and 'Turk' are used interchangeably. The best evidence for the internal structure of the Khazar qaghanate comes from the works of Islamic geographers writing in the ninth and especially the tenth centuries. Apart from the usual problems of cultural bias and misunderstandings within a literary tradition where information was distorted as it was passed from author to author, there is also the difficulty that the geographers give a static image of the Khazar state, whereas there is every likelihood that it had undergone considerable change since its formation in the seventh century. Most obviously the Khazars had converted to Judaism in the eighth and ninth centuries, very likely with consequences for how the state was organised, but with the evidence available much of this is bound to be obscure. Yet with this caveat the broad structure is clear enough.

The Khazar state was a confederation of nomad tribes and tribute-paying vassals under the supreme authority of the qaghan. In the Gök Türk empire the qaghan had been a charismatic leader who embodied the heavenly good-fortune granted by Tengri the Sky-God, yet at the same time he was also an active military and political leader. Among the Khazars, however, at some date before the ninth century, the cult role of the qaghan had developed so far that he had become solely a sort of talisman whose presence assured the good-fortune of the state. If the Khazars suffered defeat or famine, the qaghan might be killed as having lost his good-fortune, but otherwise he would play no part in active government. All real power was in the hands of the qaghan's deputy who appears in earlier sources as the *Išad,* and in the later as the *beg.* (The reason for the change is unknown.)[47]

At the centre of the Khazar state was the Khazar tribal union, an amalgamation of various steppe peoples of differing ethnic origins, but with Turkish leadership and it seems a Turkic language. The name 'Khazar' was probably coined by the western Türk qaghans as part of their restructuring of the western steppes after the Turkish conquests of the sixth century. What it might mean is another mystery. (The most convincing hypothesis connects it with a Turkic verb with the implication of 'wandering' or 'travelling'; a rival view suggests it refers to an especially

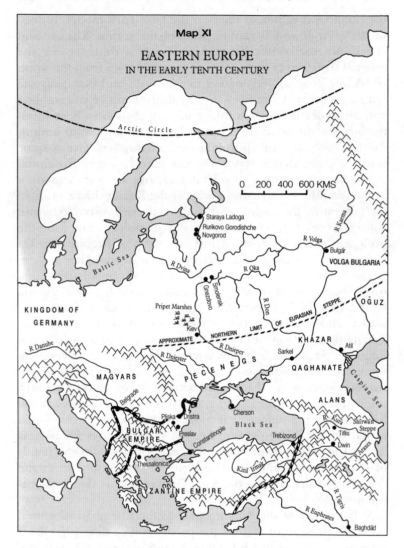

Map XI

EASTERN EUROPE
IN THE EARLY TENTH CENTURY

ferocious type of dog.)[48] Outside the Khazar tribal union, but subject to the qaghan in varying degrees were a number of tribute-paying vassals. The account of Ibn Fadlān, a tenth-century Arabic writer and traveller, implies at least 25 subject peoples whose rulers each sent a daughter to the qaghan's harem.[49] Among these were the two groups of Bulgars who had remained in the east, the Huns and Alans in the North Caucasus, the Burtas (a semi-nomadic people, living south of the Volga Bulgars and north of the inner lands of the Khazars), and a number of other Slav and Caucasian tribes. The extent of the qaghan's authority varied over the centuries, but at its maximum it covered a vast area of the western Eurasian steppe, from very approximately the Dnieper in the west to the Ural river in the east, from the Caucasus mountains in the south to the middle Volga in the north.[50]

This powerful state, drawing on the formidable military resources of the steppe world, was the only credible rival to the caliphate in the Near East during the seventh and eighth centuries. Even before Herakleios the Romans had been concerned to keep the Turkish nomads as allies against Persia; but the experience of the empire's narrow escape from conquest by the Persians at the beginning of the seventh century – in large part thanks to Herakleios' Turkish allies – made good relations with the qaghanate one of the principal aims of Byzantine diplomacy from the seventh century onwards. If the Khazars never looked likely to march on Iraq, they at least had the potential to keep the Arabs too busy defending their northern front to concentrate on the diffiicult task of capturing Constantinople. There were moments at which relations broke down, due most often to disputes over the Crimea where Byzantine and Khazar interests clashed, but these were exceptional. In the late seventh century the qaghan's sister married the emperor-in-exile, Justinian II, and reigned as empress from his recovery of power in 705 to his assassination in 711.[51] A contemporary source – the *Parastaseis Syntomoi Chronikai* – mentions an otherwise unknown Gliavanos the Khazar enthroned beside the emperor and honoured in the imperial city. In 732 Leo III married his eldest son, the future emperor Constantine V, to one of the qaghan's daughters. Their son, the emperor Leo IV (775–80) was therefore half Khazar. The qaghan's daughter is also credited with the introduction to the imperial court of a Khazar-style robe called a *tzitzakion* (from the Turkish *Çiçek*, 'flower'), which possibly argues a wider receptiveness to Khazar fashions.[52] There is some evidence, notably that for the patriarch Photios' father, Sergios, and the monk, painter and diplomat, Lazaros the Khazar, to suggest that a number of Khazars came to Byzantium, adopted Byzantine culture and became an accepted part of the empire's ruling élite.[53] In return although the Khazar state did not convert to Christianity, there was a sizeable Christian population in Khazaria, and there may even have been a number of bishoprics established under an archbishop at Doros in the Crimea.[54]

Arab–Khazar warfare began even before the Khazars had defeated the rival Bulgar qaghanate. In the 640s and 650s the Arabs tried unsuccessfully to conquer the North Caucasus steppes. The first Muslim civil war encouraged the Khazars to strike back, and in 661–2 and again in 663–4 they ravaged Caucasian Albania, until bought off by a treaty which may temporarily have made the kingdom of Albania one of the qaghan's vassals. Further large-scale Khazar raids followed in 684 and 689. There then seems to have been a lull in major operations until the early eighth century, when at the same time that pressure was increasing on Constantinople, Arab and Armenian sources again record heavy fighting on both sides of the Caucasus. Arab attacks deep into Khazar territory were matched by Khazar raids into Armenia, Albania and Azerbaidjan. On one occasion in 730 the Khazars defeated an Arab army in Azerbaidjan and then raided as far south as northern Mesopotamia near Mosul.[55]

Up to 737 neither side seems to have been able to achieve a decisive advantage, but in that year Marwān ibn Muhammed (who would later become the last caliph of the Ummayad dynasty, and who had just crushed opposition to Arab rule in Iberia and ravaged western Georgia), inflicted a shattering defeat upon the Khazars. Marwān managed to launch a surprise invasion which reached Khazaria before their army was mobilised. The qaghan was forced to flee north into the territory of the Burtas. Marwān followed, and when he had defeated a Khazar army hastily gathered to rescue the qaghan, the latter had no choice but to come to terms. By these the qaghan agreed to become a Muslim and a subject of the caliph.[56]

It remains an open question whether the Arabs would have had the resources to maintain their new-won authority in the steppe lands north of the Caucasus. Within a few years the Ummayad dynasty had fallen and the Khazars, like the Byzantines, could take advantage of a period of Arab weakness. Nothing more is heard of a Muslim qaghan or of subjection to the caliph. In 762 and again in 764 large Khazar armies ravaged Arab territories south of the Caucasus; on the second occasion sacking Tiflis. In 784 a large army of Arabs and Armenian naxarars spent the summer guarding the Caspian Gates from a threatened Khazar attack. In the event the enemy seems not to have materialised, but the army suffered serious losses from disease.[57] By this date Khazar authority was strong enough on the Black Sea Coast of the Caucasus that in 786–7 a new kingdom of Abasgia was proclaimed under Khazar protection, independent of the Byzantines and, more significantly, of the Arabs too. However, the end of the eighth century marked the end of any significant Arab–Khazar warfare. The last major Khazar raid occurred in 799; after which both sides seem to have been preoccupied elsewhere.[58]

Khazar actions from the 760s to the end of the century belie any suggestion that the qaghanate was in decline from 737 onwards. The response to the events of 737 inside Khazaria had presumably been to strangle the defeated qaghan who had so obviously lost the mandate of heaven, and replace him with another member of the charismatic Ašina clan. Although there is no evidence it is tempting to wonder whether the development of a double rulership in the Khazar state, with real power held by an išad or beg, was initially a response to this crisis.[59] Also open to speculation are the causes of the Khazar conversion to Judaism. This seems to have occurred in two phases, one of which is dated by the tenth-century geographer, Mas'ūdī, to the reign of the caliph Harūn al-Rashīd (786–809). If Mas'ūdī's date refers to the second phase, then the initial adoption of Judaism would have occurred by the end of the eighth century, and again it is tempting to wonder whether this can be linked to the aftermath of the defeat of 737.[60] The evidence is too slight for any certainty, but the first half of the eighth century does at least provide a context in which Judaism would be a natural choice for a Near Eastern great power. At that date no one but those in a state already shackled with Christianity would choose a religion so obviously productive of defeat. Islam was a religion of victory, but it can be argued that at this date it was still much closer to its Jewish roots than to the modern idea of Islam which became established from the second half of the eighth century onwards. The religion of the Arabs was in theory the religion of Abraham. It would not be surprising if the Khazars had adopted that religion, but unlike the Arabs, followed it to its logical conclusion by becoming Jews.

If the Khazar state was still powerful in the second half of the eighth century, by the ninth century there are clear signs of decline. The Khazars had increasing difficulty dealing with their enemies and vassals, and they made no attempt to take advantage of Arab difficulties to annexe territory south of the Caucasus. Ironically Khazar problems seem to have had their roots in success, and seem to be a typical case of a cycle of development common to many Eurasian steppe powers. As already discussed in Chapter 2, the nomadic economy is not self-sufficient; nomads always need the agricultural and craft products of the sedentary world. One of the primary functions of any nomad state is to provide these goods by plunder, tribute, and commerce. The Khazar state was a highly successful provider: partly through its tribute-paying vassals, partly through its military operations, and increasingly through the profits of trade, which above all meant the fur trade. In the wealthy Muslim world high-quality fur was an expensive mark of status for which there was a large demand. The best fur available came from the bitterly cold forests and tundra of northern Russia and Siberia. A vast commercial network brought the fur from the frozen north, via markets in the lands of the Volga Bulgars, down the Volga and on across the Caspian to northern Persia and thence all over the Islamic Near East. Coin finds show that this route was in operation as early as the fifth century, but its heyday began in the late eighth century when either directly or indirectly virtually the whole of this network was under Khazar control. The Khazar capital at Atil near the mouth of the Volga, which had probably begun as a winter camping ground, became a crucial entrepôt. Finds of Muslim silver coins throughout the Volga region are evidence of the huge profits of this trade from which the Khazar state became rich. In the ninth and tenth centuries the Arab geographers describe a state which has become essentially a commercial empire, its armies composed of hired mercenaries, moving further and further away from the steppe nomad background that was the true basis of its power.[61]

At the same time as the qaghanate was evolving from its militaristic nomad background toward a wealthier, more sedentary and less aggressive society, the Khazars were facing two new threats: one from the Viking Rus to the north (which will be discussed in the next section of this chapter); and one – beginning earlier, and initially more serious – from the new steppe nomad confederations advancing from the east, the Pečenegs and the Oğuz.

The threat from the steppes was ultimately a result of the break-up of the remnants of the Türk qaghanate in the mid-eighth century, and the struggle for supremacy in Mongolia and Central Asia which followed. Forced west by the rising power of the Uighurs, the Oğuz invaded Turkestan in the late eighth or early ninth century. Some sections of the Pečeneg confederation which ruled Turkestan joined the Oğuz, but the rest were driven out to the north-west into the steppes above the Caspian Sea where they posed a new threat to the Khazar qaghanate's eastern borders.[62]

The essential evidence for the upheavals which transformed the western steppes in the ninth century comes from a collection of diplomatic reports preserved in Constantine Porphyrogenitos' *De Administrando Imperio*. These include an account of Pečeneg history from a Pečeneg source; and also two accounts given by the Magyars or Hungarians (whom the text significantly calls *Tourkoi*, 'Turks') of how the Pečeneg advance forced them to move west, and finally to retreat over the Carpathian mountains into the great Hungarian plain, where their descendants live to this day. All these accounts appear to be Byzantine records of oral information given by the Pečenegs and Magyars respectively. Naturally they are partial, certainly obscure and contradictory, and probably tendentious too, but they provide the only fairly coherent narrative of these events that has survived. Without them we would know almost nothing about a steppe revolution that transformed the world of Byzantium's northern neighbours. They therefore deserve careful analysis.[63]

Read together the two accounts describe how 'in the beginning' the Pečenegs lived between the Volga and the Ural rivers,
from where they were ejected by an allied Khazar–Oğuz attack. The Pečenegs then 'fled and wandered around, searching
for a place to settle', until they came to 'Lebedia' where the
Magyars then lived, whom they drove west to a new home in
'Atelkouzou'.[64] Seemingly at this stage – the text does not make
quite clear when this occurred in relation to other events –
the Magyars were joined by a body of Khazar rebels, the *Kabaroi*,
who from then on formed an important section of the Magyar
confederation.[65] Later, during the reign of Leo VI (886–912),
when the Magyars were involved as Byzantine allies in a war
against the Bulgars, the Pečenegs joined in on the Bulgar side
to attack the Magyars, driving the latter off the Ukrainian steppes
and into modern Hungary.[66]

Neither Lebedia nor Atelkouzou can be identified from other
sources. However, in order to make sense of the events during
Leo VI's reign Atelkouzou must be north of Bulgaria adjacent
to the Lower Danube and east of the Carpathians. Similarly
Lebedia must be somewhere on the steppes west of the area
between the Volga and Ural rivers from which the Pečenegs
had just been expelled. Broadly speaking therefore, Lebedia
was the steppe lands east of the Dnieper, perhaps extending
to the Volga, and Atelkouzou was those to the west of the Dnieper
stretching as far as the Danube.

Dating these events is more difficult. The *De Administrando
Imperio's* 'in the beginning' can be qualified by the evidence of
a Uighur diplomatic document of the second half of the eighth
century preserved in Tibetan which proves the Pečenegs at that
date to have been in Turkestan.[67] Unfortunately no eastern
source gives any useful clue as to when the Pečenegs might
have been driven out, beyond the broad implication of somewhere in the late eighth or early ninth century.

The second phase of the Pečeneg advance, which forced the
Magyars out of Atelkouzou and into Hungary, and which the
De Administrando Imperio places in the reign of Leo VI, can be
securely dated to 894–6 by other Byzantine and western references to the same event.[68] The date of the first phase is more
contentious.

One that commonly appears in the literature and that can

be rejected at once is 889. This comes from the Chronicle of Regino of Prüm who describes under the entry for that year how the Hungarians were driven out of their territory in 'Scythia' among the marshes of the Don by their neighbours the Pečenegs. Searching for somewhere to settle the Hungarians came first to Pannonia (that is the great Hungarian plain), and then later began to raid Carantania (Austria), Moravia and Bulgaria. After 889 Regino does not mention them again until 901, apart from a short entry under the year 894 which refers not to events in that year but to someone's future fate at the hands of the Hungarians.[69] Regino's Chronicle was not compiled on a year by year basis but instead written in one piece in about 908. At other points in his Chronicle Regino makes a number of serious chronological mistakes – misdating, for example, Charles the Bald's defeat by the Bretons from 851 to 860 – and it seems quite obvious here that he has misplaced the events of 894–6 to an entry under 889. Wondering why he should have chosen 889 is likely to be no more significant than pondering his other mistakes, and the date can be dropped from the discussion.[70]

In any case a date in either the 880s or 890s – both of which are often suggested – seems to give too short a period to fit in the events which must be placed between the two Pečeneg advances. The *De Administrando Imperio* tells us that the Magyars had been attacked by the Pečenegs 'on many occasions'. Since the first attack was when they were driven out of Lebedia, and the last was when they were forced out of Atelkouzou, there must be enough time in between for these 'many occasions'. There also has to be long enough for the Magyars to be reorganised under the leadership of their first prince, Arpad, and for the Kabaroi to be assimilated into the new nomad state.[71]

More important, such a late date also creates difficulties with those sources which place the Magyars near the Danube and the Pečenegs west of the Volga long before the 880s. One of these is the curious story from the Logothete's chronicle of a colony of prisoners-of-war captured by the Bulgars in Macedonia in 813 and settled on the northern border of Bulgaria near the Danube. In the later 830s they made contact with the emperor Theophilos and a naval expedition was sent out to bring them home. Before they reached the ships the escaping prisoners-of-war had first to fend off a pursuing Bulgar force, and then – somewhere north of the Danube – fight three engagements with a people called at various points in the text, *Oungroi*, *Tourkoi* and *Ounnoi*, whom the Bulgarians had called to their aid. These look very like the Hungarians, whom the *De Administrando Imperio* calls 'Turks'.[72] Both the Logothete and Theophanes Continuatus (who places the Pečenegs west of the Volga at this same period)[73] are tenth-century sources, and they could be rejected as anachronistic and mistaken; but this would be difficult for the Annals of St Bertin, which records a raid by the 'Ungri' on Germany in 862. At this point the text of the Annals is a near contemporary document written by Hincmar, archbishop of Rheims, who died in 882.[74]

The evidence to solve this problem comes again from the *De Administrando Imperio*. First of all, however, it is important to remember the point made in Chapter 1 that this is not a homogenous work, composed all at one period. Instead it is a 'scrapbook', put into its final form by the emperor Constantine VII Porphyrogenitos in the mid-tenth century, but filled with materials composed in earlier periods. This is most obvious in the case of the Georgian and Armenian chapters (cc. 43–6) where the documents copied are basically concerned with events in the late ninth and early tenth century, and were composed very shortly afterwards. Later they received some rather haphazard revision, and a few comments were added which do something to bring them up to date, but the early tenth-century core of these chapters has remained untouched. This even extends to a comment passed on Constantine Lips (who had been sent out as an imperial agent to Taron at the end of the ninth century) that he was 'now *anthypatos*, *patrikios*, and great hetaireiarch' – 'now' in this case must be at the time the document was written in the early tenth century, because he had ceased to be hetaireiarch before the end of July 913 and he was killed in battle on 20 August 917.[75]

The same applies to the chapters on the Magyars and Pečenegs. They are early tenth-century documents which had received no more than cursory revisions and additions by the time they were copied into Constantine's book in the mid-tenth century. As a result when they talk of the 'present day', unless there are the fairly obvious signs of deliberate revision, what it means is not *c*.950, but instead *c*.900–10.

At the beginning of chapter 37 the *De Administrando Imperio* says that the Pečenegs were attacked by the Khazar–Oǧuz alliance 'fifty years ago', Given that these documents report information derived from the oral tradition of the groups concerned, it is almost certainly a mistake to the take the phrase 'fifty years ago' too exactly. The work of anthropologists on the nature of oral tradition, already referred to in Chapter 4, would suggest a much looser sense of 'two or three generations ago', rather than an absolutely exact number of years. We should therefore be thinking in terms of a period between forty-five and seventy-five years, hence somewhere between about 825 and 865.

Looking at other evidence for the ninth century it becomes clear that within this period the 830s stand out as years of upheaval on the steppes. The first clue of something peculiar happening is the memorial inscription of a Bulgar general who had been sent by the qaghan of the Danube Bulgars, Omurtag (814/15–c.831), with an army into the Ukraine, but who drowned in the river Dnieper.[76] In 839 a Rus embassy to Constantinople could not return northwards because of the danger from hostile barbarians.[77] About the same time took place the curious episode of the building of Sarkel, a Khazar fortress on the Don.

According to Byzantine accounts a Khazar embassy arrived in Constantinople asking the Byzantines to build the city of Sarkel for them. The then emperor, Theophilos, agreed and sent Petronas Kamateros with a fleet to the Crimea and thence to the Don river. According to the *De Administrando Imperio*, 'since the place had no stones suitable for the building of the city, he made some ovens and baked bricks in them and with these he carried out the building of the city . . .'. On his return Petronas advised the emperor to reorganise the Crimea into a military theme under a strategos. Theophilos took his advice, and Petronas was appointed to the new command, known as the theme of the Klimata.[78]

One can take this story at face value – in which case it implies that the Khazars were in some trouble, and had appealed to their old ally for help, and the Byzantines had loyally responded. But this may be too simple. In the first place it is difficult to see why the Khazars should have needed the Byzantines to build Sarkel. There were a number of walled cities in Khazaria, and the Arab geographers who mention them give no indication that the Khazars needed to import outside builders. Of course Sarkel may have been an exception, but in that case a second difficulty arises. Ukrainian archaeologists think they have identified Sarkel, and the site is a very convincing candidate: a large fortress, of the right date and in the right place on the Don. But there is nothing Byzantine about this site. Instead it is a fortified settlement everything about which is, to quote the excavator, 'characteristic of the entire culture of the Don region in the eighth and ninth centuries'.[79]

In view of these discrepancies it may be closer to the truth to read the accounts of the Byzantine building of Sarkel as a cover-story for an expedition that went wrong. There is no doubt that in 838–9 the Byzantines did set up the theme of the Klimata.[80] Also at about this time there took place the failed expedition to Abasgia which was one of the first steps in the Byzantine return to Transcaucasian politics. Both Abasgia and the Crimea were areas where Byzantine and Khazar interests overlapped; but for at least a century both had been effectively part of the Khazar sphere of influence. Against that background Byzantine actions in both areas at the end of the 830s stand out as blatant attempts to take advantage of Khazar problems. In this context a likely explanation of the Sarkel episode is that the Byzantines, possibly on the invitation of a local commander, tried to seize this important fortress, but then found it necessary to beat a diplomatic retreat. Later when the Khazars had partially recovered from the crisis of the late 830s and good relations between Constantinople and Atil were restored, a story was manufactured – convenient for both sides – of a request for friendly help.

If this seems a far-fetched interpretation, it is worth comparing it with the story recorded in the *De Administrando Imperio* about the Iberian city of Ardanoutzin in the mountains of Tao. In the 920s Ašot Kiskasis, the Bagratuni lord of this strategic fortress, well beyond the existing frontier, so detested his son-in-law Gurgen that he made a secret promise to the emperor Romanos Lekapenos (920–44) to hand over the city. A small Byzantine force hurried to Ardanoutzin, and an imperial flag was set up on the fortress. At this point the other Iberian Bagratuni learnt what had happened, and wrote to the emperor telling him that if this force were not withdrawn at once they would go over to the Arabs. Romanos promptly disowned the Byzantine commander, explaining that he had been acting without orders, and the force retreated in some embarrassment.[81] What happened here is no more bizarre than what is being suggested for Sarkel.

Whatever actually happened at Sarkel the events do show that the Khazars were facing serious difficulties during the later 830s which prevented them from making an active response to Byzantine interference in Abasgia and the Crimea. That these were difficult years for the Khazars has long been recognised, but the link has not often been made with the Pečeneg invasion described in the *De Administrando Imperio*. In part this is because the *De Administrando Imperio*'s account of Pečeneg attacks and the Magyar move from Lebedia into Atelkouzou has usually been understood to refer to events at the end of the ninth century; while apart from Theophanes Continuatus, no near contemporary Byzantine or Arab source explicitly places the Pečenegs west of the Volga so early. But another reason is that it has long been believed there were more likely candidates to blame for the Khazars' difficulties.

One of these is the Viking Rus. There is some evidence for Rus raiders in the Black Sea region in the first half of the ninth century, but there is nothing to suggest this was anything more than the usual small-scale raiding for slaves and booty which Vikings and nomads turned to when more peaceful types of trade failed to produce a profit. Such violence was a feature of normal life and presented no threat to the qaghanate. In any case the Rus seem to have been clients of the Khazars at this date, and since the Annals of St Bertin state that the Rus envoys to Constantinople could not return home to the north in 839 because of the danger of savage barbarian peoples, it would appear to follow that the danger came from someone other than them.[82]

The second candidate – and still the most widely accepted – is the Magyars or Hungarians. For over a century historians have been aware that although the Hungarian language bears traces of strong Turkic influences, it is without any doubt one of the Finno-Ugric group of languages. Speakers of Finno-Ugric languages – who include the modern Finns – were originally peoples of the Russian forest zone, north of the Ukrainian and

Volga steppes. The particular structure and vocabulary of the Hungarian language associates the 'Proto-Hungarians' with the modern population of the lands around the confluence of the Kama and Volga rivers, west of the Ural mountains. Scholars of Hungarian linguistics have also noticed in the Turkic elements of Hungarian links with the Turkic spoken by the peoples of Bashkiria, the area to the south-east of the Kama–Volga confluence and north of the Caspian Sea. On the basic of this linguistic evidence it has been suggested that over the course of the eighth century a Finno-Ugric-speaking group of 'Proto-Hungarians' living as sedentary hunters and farmers in the forests of the Kama–Volga region, gradually moved south-east on to the steppes north of the Caspian Sea. As they did so they acquired the skills of steppe nomads and certain elements of Turkic steppe culture. There they came in contact with the Pečenegs who were being forced west by the Oğuz. In face of Pečeneg pressure, the 'Proto-Hungarians' moved west in the 830s into 'Lebedia', where their arrival caused a crisis for the Khazar state.[83]

This hypothesis for the origins of the Magyars seems a great deal to base on uncorroborated linguistic evidence, especially when the De Administrando Imperio preserves a rather different version of early Magyar history as told by the Magyars themselves. Despite the fact that by the time the De Administrando Imperio report was compiled the Magyars lived in the Hungarian plain far from any effective Khazar pressure, the Magyars continued to see their past in terms of being traditional Khazar allies and clients. The text shows they shared many aspects of Khazar culture and ideology, including the distinctive Turkic institution of double rulers, one of whom plays a solely talismanic role. The first Magyar leader to be named, Lebedias, is given a 'noble Khazar bride' by the qaghan; and the first 'prince' of the Magyars is appointed by the qaghan and made prince, 'according to the custom of the Khazars ... by lifting him upon a shield'. Most important of all they called themselves 'Turks', which has no ethnic implications but which in this context is a very loaded term.[84] The Khazar qaghanate was the heir to the Gök Türk qaghanate, and the Khazars were themselves known as Turks. For the Magyars to feel themselves to be Turks places them unambiguously in the political and cultural orbit of the Khazar qaghanate. As the *De Administrando Imperio* shows, even in the Hungarian plain they continued to define themselves in relation to the Khazars by still calling themselves Turks. Unlike the Danube Bulgars, no Magyar ruler ever aspired to a title higher than that of one of the qaghan's subordinates. Even in the eleventh century, after the destruction of the Khazar qaghanate, the king of Hungary called himself king of the 'Western Turks': a title that implies not only the recognition of an Eastern Turkey, but in terms of Gök Türk political ideology which regarded the eastern half of the qaghanate as the senior branch, also carries the idea of the superiority of a lord of the 'Eastern Turks', whether or not he actually existed.[85] The only suggestion that the *De Administrando Imperio* makes that the Magyars might have recognised a separate non-Turkish past, turns out to be illusory. The text mentions that in Lebedia, 'they were not called Turks at the time, but had the name *Sabartoi Asphaloi*, for some reason or another'. The *Sabartoi Asphaloi*, meaning the 'Undefeated Sabirs', had been a nomad confederation in the sixth century, defeated by the Avars and later assimilated into the Khazar tribal confederation. We have in effect come round in a circle to the Khazars again.[86]

The picture of the Magyars that emerges from the *De Administrando Imperio* is therefore one of an autonomous part of the Khazar confederation. The existence of such ties does not mean that the relationship was always peaceful. Nomad confederations by their nature were unstable institutions requiring the ruling tribe repeatedly to enforce control by displays of military power. The Khazar confederation is likely to have been no exception, and the revolt of the Kabaroi, who the *De Administrando Imperio* tells us went off to become a part of the Magyar confederation as they moved to Atelkouzou on the Lower Danube, looks a typical example. Yet such disturbances were a normal part of steppe politics and the fact remains that according to the evidence of the *De Administrando Imperio* the Magyars were not wild newcomers threatening the security of the qaghanate, but a generally reliable and loyal part of the Khazar establishment.

Why they spoke a Finno-Ugric language of the forest peoples rather than a Turkic or Iranian language of the steppes is an interesting but ultimately unanswerable question. There are two obvious possibilities. One is that perhaps groups of Finno-Ugric Proto-Hungarians did move on to the steppes where they acquired the skills of steppe nomads. The incentive would have been to share in the political and military dominance exercised by their nomad neighbours.[87] The other is that a Turkic nomad minority ruling over greater numbers of Finno-Ugric-speaking sedentary tribute-payers and slaves was gradually converted to speaking a Finno-Ugric language. Especially if a substantial number of the women were Finno-Ugric-speaking captives from raids on the northern forests, it would take only a few generations before most of the population had learnt Finno-Ugric rather than Turkic from their mother. The same thing happened to the Mongol tribes in the thirteenth- and fourteenth-century Near East, and to the Danube Bulgars between the seventh and tenth centuries. Without other evidence one can only guess, but the fact that all but two of the seven Magyar tribal names (not including the Kabaroi) have Turkic rather than Finno-Ugric roots, and the fact that the Magyar ruling élite so long regarded themselves as Turks, even when the Khazar qaghanate had ceased to exist, perhaps makes the second a more likely possibility.[88]

If the Magyars are recognised as being Khazar clients by the 830s, this leaves only the Pečenegs to play the role of disruptive newcomers – a conclusion which tallies with the evidence of both the De Administrando Imperio and Theophanes Continuatus. The initial Khazar response to the Pečeneg threat was clearly a disaster. The anti-Pečeneg alliance with the Oğuz misfired in that within a short time the defeated Pečenegs had crossed the Volga and driven the Magyars to Atelkouzou, leaving the Khazar confederation split in two by the Pečenegs in Lebedia, and facing two unruly nomad confederations – the Pečenegs and the Oğuz – either side of the Khazar heartland on the lower Volga. However, the Khazars did recover. The De Administrando Imperio shows that they managed to keep ties with the Magyars, and the fact that a tenth-century Persian text called the Hudūd al-Alām refers to the Pečenegs as the 'Khazarian Pečenegs' suggests that the Khazars tried hard to integrate the newcomers into the Khazar political system.[89] But the attempt failed. As the De Administrando Imperio again shows, the institutions of Pečeneg society, while typical of Turkic nomad groups on the Eurasian steppes, bear no traces of Khazar influence. Unlike the Khazars and Magyars, where nomadic élites ruled what was essentially a sedentary agricultural and commercial economy, the Pečenegs and the Oğuz seem to have been still fully nomadic. As a result both groups were poorer than their new neighbours, less centralised, less controllable – and more formidable on the battlefield.[90] By the second half of the ninth century the Khazars were no longer in control of the Ukrainian steppes.

During the 840s and 850s none of these events demanded an immediate response from the Byzantines, but on 18 June 860 a large fleet of Viking Rus raiders appeared in front of Constantinople. The emperor Michael III and the main field army was away on the eastern frontier, leaving the Rus to ravage the unprotected suburbs on both shores of the Bosphoros. The Byzantines were completely taken by surprise, and a mood of apocalyptic panic gripped the city. In Hagia Sophia the patriarch Photios preached two sermons which have survived urging the population to repent of their sins and so avert God's wrath; and to beg for the intercession of the Mother of God, the holiest of the city's protective relics, the Virgin's robe, was processed round the walls by a huge crowd chanting the litany and pleading for deliverance. Thanks, it appeared, to this last measure the city was saved. The Rus broke camp and sailed away, taking with them an enormous booty, and leaving behind, according to Photios' second sermon, a ghastly record of brutality, murder and vandalism; and a badly frightened population.[91]

The immediate Byzantine response was to send an embassy to their old allies the Khazars, but the very fact of the attack proved that the alliance was no longer the key to security in the north.[92] The Rus raid of 860 marks the beginning of a Byzantine search for a new ally north of the Black Sea.

One option was in effect the continuation of past policy but with the alliance focused on the Khazars' clients, the Magyars, rather than on their masters in Atil. In its favour was the fact that the Magyars were well placed to attack the Bulgars south of the Danube, as well as those of the Rus who lived on the Dnieper around Kiev; against it was the fact that the Magyars were frightened of the Pečenegs, and in 860 at least they had not stopped a Rus attack. In 894–6 the Byzantines did use the

Magyars as an ally against the Bulgars, but after some immediate success the result was to provoke a Pečeneg intervention which removed the Magyars from the Ukraine for good.

The obvious alternative was to build up a new relationship with the Pečenegs themselves, and this was to be the corner-stone of Byzantine steppe policy for much of the tenth century. The advantages of the Pečeneg alliance are set out in the first ten chapters of the *De Administrando Imperio*. The Bulgars, the Magyars and the Rus were frightened of them: 'So long as the emperor of the Romans is at peace with the Pečenegs, neither Rus nor Turks can come upon the Roman dominions by force of arms, nor can they extract from the Romans large and inflated sums in money and goods as the price of peace, for they fear the strength of this nation which the emperor can turn against them while they are campaigning against the Romans.... To the Bulgars also the emperor of the Romans will appear more formidable, and can impose on them the need for tranquillity, if he is at peace with the Pečenegs....'[93] More specifically against a repeat of the 860 attack, the *De Administrando Imperio* states, 'Nor can the Rus come at this city of the Romans, either for war or trade, unless they are at peace with the Pečenegs'.[94] The problem with the Pečenegs from a Byzantine perspective was that it was very difficult to build reliable ties with this decentralised nomad state. The Pečenegs wanted nothing from the Byzantines save a constant supply of luxury goods. They did not need Byzantine military support or political approbation; they showed no interest in conversion to Christianity. Hence the alliance depended on the payment of large subsidies, brought at regular intervals by Byzantine envoys.[95] The Pečenegs had learnt to demand a high price for their services, and if they failed to fulfil – as was the case on several occasions in the tenth century – there was little the Byzantines could do in response. An attempt to persuade the Magyars to attack the Pečenegs had met with a straight refusal.[96] In theory they might be threatened with an Oğuz attack, but before the eleventh century this was not a very credible threat. The Pečenegs were thus an indispensable but rather unsatisfactory ally.

Another possible ally were the Alans, an Iranian people settled in the north Caucasus. For most of the seventh and eighth centuries they seem to have been clients of the Khazar qaghans, but with the decline of Khazar power in the ninth century the king of the Alans became an important independent ruler able, according to one Arab geographer, to draw on the services of 30,000 horsemen. At the beginning of the eighth century the Byzantines had hoped to use the Alans against their Abasgian neighbours to the south-west, but the collapse of Byzantine power in the Transcaucasus that followed shortly afterwards seems to have ended diplomatic contacts until the late ninth century. At about this time they appear in a Khazarian Hebrew document as part of an otherwise unattested coalition organised by the Byzantines against their former Khazar allies. Certainly in the years immediately following 914 the king of the Alans and his entourage were open to Byzantine influence, and accepted conversion to Christianity. An archbishop was appointed for Alania, but a supportive letter from the patriarch Nicholas Mystikos written shortly afterwards reveals that the new hierarch found his task hard. Nicholas' letters and the Arab geographers are in agreement that only the Alan élite converted while most of their subjects remained pagans. In 932 the king abjured his new faith and kicked out the Byzantine clergy. Christianity was later re-established, but Alania never became a secure part of the orthodox world. The Alans were too remote from Byzantium to be reliable as either Christians or allies. As the *De Administrando Imperio* notes they could be used to threaten the Khazars, and in the eleventh century at least Alans are known to have served the emperor as soldiers, but the king of the Alans and the emperor had few real interests or enemies in common. The Alans could not replace the Khazars or rival the Pečenegs as a focus of Byzantine diplomacy.[97]

It is against this background of the decline of Khazar power, and the search for new allies north of the Black Sea, that Byzantine relations developed with the Rus – with far-reaching consequences for both parties.

The Rus

The century after 850 – the age of Khazar decline and the Byzantine search for a new order in the lands north of the

Black Sea – was also the era when the Russian state was created, a development whose long-term significance compares with that of the rise of Islam or the discovery of America. Typically of such crucial events in the early middle ages, the evidence is slight and controversial, and the secondary literature vast and misleading.

Among the things which can be known about this period are certain permanent facts of Russian geography. The land between the Black Sea and the Arctic Ocean, bounded by the Ural mountains to the east and the Carpathians, the Pripet marshes and the Baltic to the west, can be approximately divided into three parallel belts: the steppes, the forest zone and the tundra. The 'wooded steppe' forms the intermediate zone between the steppe proper and the forests of central Russia; the pine forests of the 'taiga' fill the equivalent place between the forest zone and the bare tundra to the north. Looked at on a map, the wooded steppe begins just south of Kiev, and the taiga by Novgorod. For a farmer Russia is an unprofitable landscape. The harsh climate of short hot summers and long cold winters (getting colder and longer as one moves east), provides a short growing season – about half that of western Europe; while the pattern of rainfall ensures that water supplies are only adequate where the soil is worst. The best soils in Russia, those of the belt of black earth (*chernozem*), beginning south of Kiev, receive low rainfall and suffer frequent drought. Before the sixteenth century they were also the lands of the steppe nomads.

The major economic activities of early medieval Russia were pastoral nomadism on the southern steppes, and hunting and fur-trapping in the forests. Agriculture was vital for subsistence, but later Russian experience suggests that no one was a farmer save by default.

For the inhabitants of the forest zone the fur trade was an unrivalled opportunity to make a profit from the environment, but the trade was only possible because of another feature of Russian geography – the river system. Huge distances and long winters meant that, save for short journeys, land communications played a very small role in forest Russia until the development of the railway. Their place was filled by the main Russian rivers which flow over hundreds of miles north–south.

Joined by tributaries from east and west they form a network of navigable waterways that with a few short portages link the Baltic to the Black Sea and the Caspian, and hence the fur-producing forests and tundra to the wealthy markets of the Islamic world.

For the history of the early middle ages the main rivers to be aware of are the Volga, the Don and the Dnieper. Each flowing from the heart of forest Russia, they can all be reached by short portages from the rivers which flow west into the Baltic. The Don and the Dnieper both flow into the Black Sea; the Volga flowed through the lands of the Volga Bulgars, past the Khazar capital of Atil into the Caspian.

Before the ninth century the Russian forests were inhabited by a variety of primitive Finno-Ugrian and Slav peoples, living in scattered settlements, the more organised having a clear identity as individual tribes. The forest peoples traded fur with the steppe nomads to the south; the more accessible to nomad power paid tribute and were raided for slaves, who in turn passed down the trade routes to the south – many to end as eunuchs in Baghdad. (To attempt to define what constituted trade, tribute or booty is not a very useful exercise, save perhaps as a reminder that this was not a polite commercial world.) In so far as it was within reach, and worth the effort to exploit, this world fell within the orbit of the Khazar qaghanate.

In the century following 850 the Russian forest zone underwent a political, social and economic revolution. By 950 there was a Russian state, whose armies in 965 sacked Atil and so effectively destroyed the Khazar qaghanate; and there were towns – the greatest amongst them Kiev on the Dnieper and Novgorod in the north – whose inhabitants included merchants and crafts-men, warriors, farmers and slaves. There is no doubt that this process is associated with the appearance of the 'Rus', but until quite recently there has been a reluctance in Russia to recognise that the Rus were Vikings from Scandinavia.

The earliest Russian account, the chronicle known as the *Povest' vremennych let* ('The tale of bygone years') or sometimes as the 'Russian Primary Chronicle', which tells of the Viking Rurik being invited from Scandinavia, only dates in its surviving form from the early twelfth century, but it does include two treaties with the Byzantines, one dated to 911, the other to

945, which are clearly copies of original documents. Both contain lists of envoys 'of the Rus nation' followed by a series of unequivocally Scandinavian names. For example, in the 911 treaty: 'Karl, Ingjald, Farulf, Vermund, Hrollaf, Gunnar, Harold . . .' and so on. This can be confirmed from a variety of other contemporary sources. The west Frankish Annals of St Bertin, which in this context are an independent and reliable witness, record under the entry for 839 that the emperor Theophilos had sent with a Byzantine embassy to the court of the Frankish emperor, Louis the Pious, 'some men . . . called Rhos', with the request that they might be given a safe conduct back to their own land. Louis was suspicious that they might be spies and on investigation found that 'they belonged to the tribe of the Swedes'. Ibn Fadlān, who accompanied the ambassador sent by the caliph in 921–2 to the Volga Bulgars, met there a company of Rus traders. The funeral he describes in detail of the Rus chief, burnt with a slave-girl in a ship-burial, is a plain parallel of Viking practice elsewhere. The Italian historian Liudprand of Cremona reports his step-father's eyewitness account of the Rus attack on Constantinople in 941: 'There is a certain northern people, whom the Greeks call *Rousios* from the colour of their skins, whom we from the position of their country call "northmen". . . .' A few years later a Byzantine envoy travelled down the Dnieper with the Rus. His report, preserved in the *De administrando imperio*, draws a distinction between the Rus and the Slavs, and gives the names in both languages for the rapids on the Dnieper. Those in the Rus language are Scandinavian. Finally the presence of Scandinavians in ninth and tenth-century Russia has been confirmed by excavations at Gnezdovo, near Smolensk on the Dnieper, at Staraya Ladoga and Ryurikovo Gorodischche, north and south of Novgorod respectively.[98]

The evidence from archaeology at the same time makes another point. Material that can be identified as Scandinavian is confined to the lower levels of these sites. In the ninth and early tenth century there was an identifiable Viking community, distinct from their Slav neighbours. Long before the end of the tenth century these Vikings had been assimilated into a Slav Russian culture. The same point can be made from the evidence of names and of language. Up to the mid-tenth century the rulers of Kiev had Scandinavian names such as Igor and Olga, but in 945 the new young prince of Kiev bore the wholly Slav name of Svyatoslav. Similarly, if in the 940s the Byzantine envoy on the Dnieper meant by the Rus language a type of Scandinavian, by the early eleventh century, any reference to the Russian language would without any doubt be to Slavic. The point is important because it suggests a role for the Rus, not as part of a process of mass Scandinavian migration and settlement in the east, but as a relatively small group whose activities acted as a catalyst for fundamental changes among the peoples of the forest zone.

In some ways this accords with the version of early Russian history given in the *Povest'*, which tells with some contradictions of how the Chuds, the Slavs, the Krivichians and the Ves' invited the Rus from Scandinavia to rule over them. They chose three brothers, who migrated with their kinsfolk. The eldest of them was Rurik, who set himself up in Novgorod, and from whom the later ruling princess of the Russian state were descended. Kiev itself was occupied by two brothers, Askold and Dir, who were not kinsmen of Rurik but had been given permission by him to go south. They were later killed by Rurik's kinsman and successor, Oleg, who established himself at Kiev which was from then on the capital of the new Rus state.[99]

However, this cannot be taken at face value. The *Povest'* is a Slavic text compiled in about 1115 at the Cave monastery in Kiev, an important centre of the twelfth-century church, and one closely connected with the princes of Kiev. The compiler certainly had access to written sources, which include the account of SS. Boris and Gleb, the treaties with Byzantium of 911 and 945, and the Chronicle of George the Monk, which gives the *Povest'* its overall framework of world history and chronology. But for much of his material – especially for his coverage of the century from 850 – the compiler was dependent on the flexible and distorting medium of oral tradition.[100]

By 1115 some of this tradition was almost certainly written down, but the fact that references to events 'in the present day' only appear in the entries after 1044 suggests that this had happened only a generation or two before the *Povest'* was compiled. The ability of oral tradition to reshape its account of the past to serve current needs has already been touched upon in the section on 'The Islamic Conquests' in Chapter 4. Anthropologists have suggested that under settled and stable conditions two generations is about the limit of an accurate account of the past. In this context the two centuries between the mid-ninth and the mid-eleventh century is obviously a very long time indeed, and quite long enough for the basic structure of the story, let alone the details, to have been transformed out of recognition.

With this in mind it is significant to note that the *Povest'* bears traces of the compiler's attempts to mesh together a number of contradictory traditions, and there are several loose ends. (These discrepancies are good evidence that the compiler of the surviving text did have access to written sources. An oral telling of these stories would have been much more effective at binding the various traditions together into a coherent whole.) An obvious example is Rurik's two brothers, who appear at the beginning of the story never to be mentioned again.[101] Anthropologists have recorded hundreds of ethnic origin stories where the people descend from a number of brothers – the number reflecting the current divisions of the group. The classic example often quoted is that of the Gonja of northern Ghana whose chiefs claimed descent from seven brothers, reflecting the seven divisions of the Gonja state. This was the version recorded at the end of the nineteenth century, but by 1956–7 when the anthropologist Jack Goody recorded these stories again, two of the Gonja divisions had disappeared – one annexed by their neighbours, and one abolished by the British – and now the Gonja tradition knew only five brothers. The other two had disappeared with the divisions their existence had once explained.[102] Rurik's vanished brothers stand out in the *Povest'* as the ghosts of a story that once explained a different political structure from the centralised state of eleventh- and twelfth-century Kiev.

The same conclusion can be drawn from the story of Askold and Dir. By the twelfth century Kiev had long been the undisputed capital of the Rus state; its princes owed the legitimacy of their political power to their descent from Rurik, and ultimately to the origin myth of Rurik's invitation to become ruler of Russia. One would have expected that a story of the first appearance of the Rus at Kiev would have linked these aspects together so that it could serve as, in effect, a validating charter of the Kievan princes' authority. But instead the *Povest'* explicitly tells us that Askold and Dir were not Rurik's kinsmen; they were merely *boyars* ('nobles') whom Rurik had given permission to go south. Even when one of Rurik's kinsmen does later come to claim Kiev the story continues to be vague and rather suspicious. Oleg is said to be one of Rurik's kin, but the relationship is never defined. He appears in the *Povest'* as a fantastic figure who sails round Constantinople on wheeled boats in a siege that never happened, and returns home in ships with brocade sails. At Kiev he kills Askold and Dir on the grounds that they were 'not of princely stock', conveniently producing at this moment Rurik's son, Igor, as a justification for his action.[103] (Igor, whose existence can be confirmed by Byzantine sources, died in 945 with a wife and young son; eighty-five years after his supposed father is said to have been invited to rule Russia.) From this point on in the *Povest'* all attention is focused on Kiev, and Novgorod and the north fades into the background.

The story of Askold and Dir in the *Povest'* is an anomaly, and was clearly once an entirely separate origin legend which justified a different political order in Kiev than rule by the Rurikid princes. The detail that they were Rurik's boyars, and the tale of Oleg, are an attempt to link Askold and Dir to the north Russian Rurik legend. Why the *Povest'* presents the link in this form can only be speculated. Presumably Askold and Dir were too well known as characters in stories current about Kiev's past for them to be ignored, and perhaps it served the purposes of eleventh-century politics to have a story which made Askold and Dir (and hence any supposed descendants) subordinates to, rather than kinsmen of, the Rurikid princes.

None of this can serve as the basis for a judgement on whether Rurik, Askold and Dir or Oleg ever existed, let alone whether they behaved as the *Povest'* describes. To attempt to uncover 'real' historical events in these stories is akin to the British fantasy of uncovering the 'real' king Arthur – and as meaningless. The important point is that at the earliest level the *Povest'* contains stories that were not originally focused on Kiev, and thus the text stands as evidence of a fundamental retelling of tradition to place the city on the Dnieper at the centre of Rus politics – where it had not always been.

There is other, independent evidence to confirm this hypothesis. According to the *Povest'* Kiev was already a city when Askold and Dir arrived there in the mid-ninth century. It had been founded by three brothers many centuries before. Until recently it was believed that this story was supported by archaeological evidence, but new excavations at Kiev and reassessment of the work of earlier archaeologists has shown that before the late ninth century, Kiev, in effect, did not exist. The signs of settlement are limited to a few primitive huts, indistinguishable from other scattered settlements in the surrounding countryside. It was only in the tenth century that Kiev was transformed into a substantial settlement. Before that it was not a centre of any sort, Rus or otherwise.[104]

The same point can also be deduced from the Arab geographers, who are unanimous in their belief that the main artery of Rus trade was not the Dnieper, but the Volga – 'the river of the Rus' – and that the land of the Rus was somewhere in the vicinity of the Volga Bulgars. Only a mid-tenth century tradition represented by al-Istakhrī and Ibn Hawkal seems to be aware even of the existence of Kiev.[105]

The Rus appear in the Arab geographers principally as warriors and traders, for whom farming the poor soils of forest Russia was of little importance. They trade with the Bulgars and Khazars, and raid the Slavs whom they send to the slave markets of the east. From time to time the Rus had sailed down the Volga into the Caspian – ravaging the coastlands of northern Persia on perhaps three occasions in the early tenth century, and in 943–4 capturing Bardha'a in Transcaucasian Albania where they stayed for nearly a year.[106] Ibn Fadlān, who actually saw them on the Volga in 921, gives a vivid impression of these extraordinary Viking traders, making fortunes in silver dirhems on this wild commercial frontier. His account is an exotic mixture of strange beliefs, sex, money and violence – bizarrely removed from the domestic order of tenth-century Islamic Baghdad.[107]

Traditionally this Arab material has been discounted in favour of the pre-eminence of the Dnieper route past Kiev to Byzantium, in large part because of the two tenth-century treaties between Byzantium and the Kievan Rus preserved in the *Povest'*.[108] Amongst other things these deal with Rus traders coming to Constantinople. The treaties certainly prove the trade existed, but there is nothing to suggest either that it was very important or of long standing. The Byzantine envoy who went to Kiev in the 940s highlights the drawbacks of the Dnieper as a major trade route. Going down the river the Rus boats had to be unloaded at each of the six sets of rapids, and then, all the while exposed to Pečeneg attack, vessels and cargo had to be hauled up to 6 miles round the obstacle.[109] How the Rus came back is not explained. It should therefore not be surprising that excavations at Kiev, Smolensk, and elsewhere have revealed very little evidence for any commerce with the Byzantine world. The absence of Byzantine coins could perhaps be explained away as the reflection of a Byzantine reluctance to allow the export of imperial coinage; but if the trade was in some other commodity then it has left virtually no trace. The widespread belief in the Dnieper route to Constantinople as one of the great commercial arteries of the early medieval world is no more than an unsubstantiated article of faith.[110]

The contrast with the evidence that has survived to support the Arab account of the Volga route is striking. Islamic pottery – less important for the pottery itself than for what it suggests in the way of other goods from the Islamic world that once went with it – is quite a common find at sites along the Volga, and some has been discovered in Scandinavia itself. But more conclusive is the evidence of the coin finds. Substantial numbers of silver dirhems minted in Persia have been found in hoards along the Volga route – apparently deposited there from the early ninth century onwards; and by the mid-ninth century at the latest these coins were reaching Scandinavia. Towards the end of the century huge new silver deposits were found in Afghanistan, and from about 893 these were minted into dirhems by the Sāmānid emirs of Transoxania. Within twenty years very large quantities of this silver had entered the Volga trading system, where it is found in hoards all along the river and into Scandinavia. Most of the huge numbers of silver coins carried by the Rus traders described by Ibn Fadlān in 920–1 were presumably Sāmānid coins.[111]

With this material one can say with confidence that the Volga, not the Dnieper, was the primary artery of Rus trade; and that it was the vast profits of the fur trade through Atil and on to the Islamic world, and not commerce with Byzantium, that brought the Viking Rus into this region in the first place. It is much more difficult to decide what sort of role the Rus played on the Volga. Were they simply traders? Or did they create a Rus state on the Volga route – possibly somewhere near Novgorod, or possibly on the Oka river which flows into the Volga south-east of Moscow – which predated Kiev, and which the *Povest'* has cut out of the story?

The crucial evidence again comes from the Arab geographers, amongst whom one can identify at least four separate traditions concerning the Rus. The oldest of these, that preserved by Ibn Khurradādhbih, who seems to have written the first version of his *Kitāb al-Masālik wa'l-Mamālik* in 846, makes no mention of any Rus prince or king, but only talks of the Rus as a tribe of fur-traders who travel from the most distant parts to the Mediterranean and via the Caspian as far as Baghdad.[112] The second tradition, first recorded by Ibn Rusta, who was writing between 903 and 913, but copying older materials, tells of the Rus living 'in a peninsula surrounded by marshes . . . three days across'. It is unclear quite where he has in mind, but it is certainly not Kiev and it could be either of the possibilities for a Rus centre on the Volga route. Ibn Rusta then adds, 'Their prince has the title of qaghan of the Rus'.[113]

This last sentence is an extraordinary piece of information. As discussed in the previous section of this chapter on the Khazars, the title of 'qaghan' in Turkic ideology implied a heavenly mandate endowing its charismatic holder with claims to power over the whole steppe world. The two heirs to the sixth-century Gök Türk qaghanate in the west were the Khazars and the Danube Bulgars. No other nomad power on the western steppes made any pretensions to this title. If Ibn Rusta's information is correct, then various conclusions follow. First the title must have been granted by the Khazar qaghan. For the Rus prince to call himself 'qaghan' without Khazar approval would have been pointlessly provocative; and there are parallels among the Gök Türks of the leader of a subordinate section of the Türk confederation being granted the title of *baz qaghan* ('vassal qaghan'). Second, if the Rus prince was granted such a title, ahead of the Bulgars, the Burtas, and the Magyars, then it also implies that the Volga Rus were of such importance in the ninth century as to deserve a pre-eminent place among the Khazar qaghan's clients.[114]

Other evidence has also survived which appears to confirm these conclusions. A third tradition among the Arab geographers is represented by Ibn Fadlān's eyewitness account of his 920–1 journey to the land of the Volga Bulgars. Ibn Fadlān does not call the Rus ruler a qaghan, instead simply referring to him as the 'king of the Rus', but his description of the king notes several aspects of how he was treated by his followers which are direct parallels of the protocol surrounding other Turkic rulers including the Khazar qaghan. The king, for example, like the qaghan, is solely a sacred talismanic ruler, who never touches the ground, and for whom real power is wielded by a deputy.[115]

Later Kievan Rus tradition also associates Rus rulers with the title 'qaghan'. In the eleventh century, Hilarion, the metropolitan of Russia, calls the princes of Kiev, Vladimir (978–1015) and Yaroslav ((1019–54), both by the title of qaghan. A little later, a grafitto on the walls of the cathedral of Hagia Sophia in Kiev gives the same title to Yaroslav's son, Svyatoslav II (1073–6).[116]

Finally there is the entry for the year 839 in the Annals of St Bertin. The relevant sentence reads: 'He [Theophilos] sent with them some men, whom they – that is his people – called *Rhos*, whose king, named *chacanus*, had sent them to him, so they said, for the sake of friendship.'[117]

As already mentioned, Louis was suspicious of these *Rhos*, or Rus, and on investigation they turned out to be Swedes. *Chacanus* is obviously the title 'qaghan', and it is usual to see in this passage confirmation of Ibn Rusta's and Hilarion's independent evidence that the Rus ruler was indeed called by the remarkable title of qaghan. However, all the entry really says is that the Rus were ruled by the qaghan, who had sent them to the Byzantine emperor. Forgetting for a moment the other mentions of a Rus qaghan, the easiest way to understand the passage is that Rus were subjects of the Khazar qaghan who had sent them out of friendship to visit the emperor in Constantinople. The assumption that the qaghan in this entry must be a Rus qaghan seems totally unwarranted.

Without the St Bertin evidence, the rest of the case for a Rus qaghan begins to look rather weak. The examples of Kievan rulers in the eleventh century being called 'qaghan' post-date the Rus sack of Atil in 965. The title of qaghan, with its claims to lordship over the steppe world, is likely to be no more than ideological booty from the 965 victory. Having destroyed the Khazar qaghanate, their conquerors might well have felt entitled to the title. The Arab evidence too is open to question. Ibn Rusta was not an eyewitness, but a collector of older written materials and it seems quite possible that the reference is no more than a mistake on the same lines as misreading the Annals of St Bertin to create a qaghan of the Rus where only the qaghan of the Khazars was intended. Perhaps the point cannot be proved, but since not even the Magyar ruler was called 'qaghan', it seems far-fetched that the ruler of the Rus was really given this title. To put this in the context of Viking experience elsewhere, just as a source which declared that the ruler of the Vikings in England, Ireland or France was called 'emperor' would be dismissed as an incredible mistake, so a Rus 'qaghan' seems unbelievable in the east.[118]

Yet the evidence of Ibn Rusta is still important. Taken with Ibn Fadlān's description of the Rus king on the Volga in 920–1 treated in the same manner as the Khazar qaghan, and with the Annals of St Bertin's story of Rus being sent by the qaghan to the Byzantine emperor, at the very least it implies that the Volga Rus were clients of the Khazar qaghan. This seems to be confirmed by the fourth strand of the Arab geographical tradition on the Rus, that preserved by Mas'ūdī, who died shortly after 956. Mas'ūdī says that 'the Rus and the Slavs . . . serve as the mercenaries and slaves of the qaghan'. A sector of the Khazar capital of Atil was inhabited by the Rus who had their own judge whom they shared with the Slavs and other pagans. Mas'ūdī also describes how shortly after 912 a large Rus fleet was given permission by the qaghan to go raiding in the Caspian on condition that he received a half share of the booty. On their return the Rus were attacked and defeated by the qaghan's irate Muslim subjects. The qaghan had not been able to prevent this Muslim attack, but according to Mas'ūdī he had warned the Rus that it was coming.[119]

A picture therefore emerges of the Rus on the Volga route as autonomous clients of the qaghan, still close to their Viking roots, but increasingly influenced by the Turkic culture of the Khazars. An early twelfth-century geographer, al-Marwazī, who for the most part of his description of the Rus draws on the same sources as Ibn Rusta, adds the detail that at one stage the Rus converted to Islam. There is no means of knowing whether this is true or not, but made rich by the profits of trade with the Islamic world, the future of the Rus at the beginning of the tenth century must have seemed linked to the east and to Islam – not to the south, to Byzantium and to Christianity.[120]

Against this background the rise of Kiev from a few rural huts in 850 to the undisputed centre of a powerful Rus state in just over a century stands out as an extraordinary development. The explanation seems to lie in the Byzantine search during the century after 860 for a new ally north of the Black Sea; and, paradoxically, in the lack of advantages which Kiev offered to its rulers. After 860 the Byzantines were willing to give recognition and a monopoly of access to the empire to any Rus leader who could prevent a repetition of the 860 attack, and who could ensure a reliable supply of Rus mercenaries and traders bringing furs and other forest products. The Volga Rus were too distant, too influenced by Turkic culture, and too closely involved in the vastly profitable Volga trade route to fulfil this role. The rulers of Kiev, however, had every incentive and no alternative to making the most of their links with Byzantium.

Far away from the riches of the Volga route and too close to the steppes for safety, the Rus at Kiev had from the first needed to be well-organised. The Byzantine envoy whose account of the Kievan Rus in the mid-tenth century survives as chapter nine of the *De Administrando Imperio*, describes how the Rus chiefs dispersed from Kiev at the beginning of November in order to spend the winter months at the expense of their tribute-paying Slav subjects. Every spring they would gather in Kiev, and on boats provided by the Slavs, and with slaves, furs, wax and honey collected as tribute they would sail to the south and Byzantium. Only if united and well-organised could they hope either to maintain control over the neighbouring Slav tribes, or to avoid destruction at the hands of the Pečenegs. Even basic survival on the Dnieper demanded the creation of a primitive state.

This primitive political organisation was the base from which the rulers of Kiev persuaded the Byzantines to grant them a monopoly of access, and a recognition of their status as princes of Rus. This in turn gave the princes of Kiev an enhanced authority from which they were able to create real political and military power.

Not surprisingly, the chronology of this rise to dominance is controversial. A crucial change took place after the Rus attack on Constantinople in 860, but there had been earlier contacts. Ibn Khurradādhbih, referring to a period before 846, knew of Rus merchants who had been to Byzantium;[121] and it seems that there were Rus raiders operating in the Black Sea in the first half of the ninth century, and perhaps even earlier. The evidence for this comes from two controversial Saint's Lives. The first of these, the Life of St Stephen of Sougdaia, mentions a certain Baivallir, who led a large Rus army from Novgorod to ravage the Crimea in about 790. Unfortunately the Life, which contains a number of serious inconsistencies – including the fact that Novgorod did not exist in 790 – is only preserved in full in a fifteenth-century Russian version where the original Greek Life has been reworked to serve the current interests of the metropolitan of Novgorod. There is nothing impossible about a raid at this date, but equally the story may simply be a fiction concocted to serve the metropolitan's desire for an early Novgorodian hero whose deeds would pre-date the activities of Rurik, Oleg and Igor described in the *Povest'*. More reliable is the Life of St George of Amastris among whose posthumous miracles is the repulse of a Rus raid against his shrine in the city of Amastris on the south coast of the Black Sea. St George died between 802 and 811, and the earliest manuscript dates to the tenth century. The Life has few contemporary details, and it has been suggested either that the whole Life was written after 860 – when the shock of the Rus attack on Constantinople would have encouraged the author to attribute a topical anti-Rus miracle to the Saint – or that the Rus episode is a post-860 insertion, added to the text when it was copied in the tenth century for the same reasons. However, a strong case has been made that the Life is the work of Ignatios the Deacon, the iconoclast cleric who died in 847 (for whom see Chapter 6 above); the Rus episode is of one piece with the rest of the text; and that the omission of the usual anti-iconoclast rhetoric makes it very unlikely it was composed after the restoration of icons in 843. The argument therefore currently favours those who wish to accept the reality of this raid, which would then have occurred somewhere between 802–11 and 843.[122]

A further scrap of evidence points to the existence of Vikings who had settled in Constantinople in the late eighth and early ninth centuries. Two men with the name 'Inger' are mentioned in Byzantine sources for the first half of the ninth century. One was metropolitan of Nicaea in about 825, the second was related to a prominent family of the early ninth century – the Martinakioi. He was also the father of the empress Eudokia – herself mistress of the emperor Michael III (842–67), and wife of his successor, Basil I (867–86). The name, which is certainly not Greek, appears to be the equivalent of the Scandinavian 'Igor', which implies that long before 860 at least two Vikings had come from the north and been accepted into the Byzantine hierarchy.[123]

Yet none of these early contacts seems to have had a great impact on either the Byzantines or the Viking Rus; and it is quite clear both from the patriarch Photios' sermons made at the time of the Rus attack in 860, and from the new awareness and fear of the Rus which marks Byzantine sources from that date onwards, that the attack on Constantinople was a profound shock which made the Byzantines aware of what they perceived as a new people from the north.[124]

As already discussed, the major consequence for the Byzantines of the 860 attack was the realisation of the emptiness of Khazar power, and of the need for new allies in the north. To begin with Kiev played no part in these calculations. In 860 Kiev hardly existed, and hence the story in the *Povest'* of Askold and Dir leading the 860 attack from Kiev must be fiction. The raid is more likely to have come from the wealthier and more powerful Volga Rus, whose comparable long-range expeditions into the Caspian are described in the Arab sources, and who could easily have entered the Black Sea via the river Don.

Early Byzantine approaches to the Rus during the 860s and 870s can be assumed, on the same grounds that Kiev barely existed at this date, to have been aimed at the Volga Rus. Theophanes Continuatus mentions the presence of Rus envoys in Constantinople shortly after 860, where they were baptised by the patriarch Photios. A few years later, in 867, Photios sent a letter to the eastern patriarchs which declares, in a section of general good news, that the Rus had been baptised and had accepted a bishop.[125] Later the same year the emperor Michael III was murdered in a coup led by his successor, Basil I. Photios was also deposed in the change of regime and his predecessor, Ignatios, brought back to the patriarchal throne. In the biography of Basil I commissioned by his grandson, Constantine Porphyrogenitos, in the mid-tenth century, there is no mention of Photios' approaches to the Rus, but instead their conversion is credited to the emperor Basil, and we are told that Ignatios sent an archbishop to the Rus who convinced the prince and the elders of his entourage to convert by a timely miracle. These stories and Photios' letter were composed within a context of current Byzantine ecclesiastical politics, and any information they give about the Rus as such is only incidental; but they are evidence of the new axis of Byzantine diplomacy in operation.[126]

The political rise of Kiev probably starts at the beginning of the tenth century when there is archaeological evidence for rapid growth on the site of the city.[127] An important document which may support this is the 911 treaty between the Byzantines and Rus preserved in a Slavonic version in the *Povest'*. The text stands out as something copied from a written source rather than passed on by oral tradition, and the clauses covering such topics as shipwreck, settlement procedures in case of disputes between Byzantine subjects and Rus, arrangements for the return of prisoners and such like look genuine. The mention of Rus mercenaries in the emperor's service can also be confirmed by the documents of the 911 Cretan expedition which list 700 Rus serving in the imperial fleet. However, there are problems. The *Povest'* places the treaty in the context of the deeds of Oleg – the fabulous conqueror of Kiev who sailed round Constantinople in boats on wheels – which does not inspire confidence; and the main body of the text does not actually mention Kiev. Hence the possibility remains that this treaty was originally made with another group of non-Kievan Rus, and was only later added to the Kievan historical tradition. With so many other examples of tampering in the *Povest'* it is well to keep an open mind.[128]

Whether or not the 911 treaty marks a genuine early stage,

the key developments took place in the 940s. In 941 prince Igor of Kiev led a major expedition to Constantinople. Like the 860 expedition it was a surprise attack, timed – presumably deliberately – to appear when the main Byzantine forces were away on the eastern front. In the event the Rus were defeated with heavy losses, but the point had been made. The prince of Kiev was a powerful ruler, able like the Rus on the Volga to launch major fleets against the empire, and a prince with whom the Byzantines could come to terms with benefits to both parties. The Byzantines were encouraged to hurry by the threat of a new Kievan attack in 944, and in the following year a treaty was agreed.[129]

Like the treaty of 911, that of 945 is preserved in a Slavonic version in the *Povest'* , but compared with the earlier text it is longer, more specific, and without any doubt at all refers to Kiev and its princes. As such it is a vital and reliable source for early Russian history. The role of the prince of Kiev stands out in the treaty. No Rus were to be allowed entry to Constantinople unless provided with a certificate by the prince of Kiev – an incentive, by the way, for the development of a Kievan chancellery. If the Byzantines wanted Rus to serve in the imperial forces, they were to apply to the prince of Kiev who would provide them. In return the Byzantines promised the prince military assistance should he need it.[130]

Just as the Volga Rus had assimilated Turkic political ideology, so the Kievan Rus were clearly moving toward an assimilation of Byzantine political and religious culture. But the process was brought to a temporary halt when shortly after agreeing to the treaty with Byzantium, Igor was killed by his Slav tributaries. Control of Kiev passed to his wife Olga, acting as regent for their young son, Svyatoslav. The Cretan expedition of 949 deployed nearly 600 Rus, who were presumably provided under the terms of the 945 treaty; but it was not until 957 that Olga was sufficiently secure to resume her husband's Byzantine policy. In that year Olga, accompanied by her nephew, and 15 other relations, 22 representatives of the princes of the Rus, 44 merchants, 18 handmaidens, two interpreters and a priest, went to Constantinople.

Exactly what happened next is unclear, and sorting out the permutations has provoked a lively debate. Leaving aside the inherently unreliable *Povest'* there are three crucial pieces of evidence: a near contemporary account of Constantine VII's reign which the late eleventh-century historian, John Skylitzes, copied into his own work; a chronicle written between 966 and 968 by Adalbert of St Maximin, the future archbishop of Magdeburg, who in 961 was appointed 'bishop for the Rus people' and sent to Kiev; and a description of Olga's reception in Constantinople in September 957, preserved in the *De Ceremoniis*. Skylitzes says that Olga was baptised in Constantinople, and places the event in Constantine's reign (he died in November 959). Adalbert states that 'envoys from Helena [Olga's baptismal name], queen of the Rus, who was baptised in Constantinople in the reign of Romanos of Constantinople [Romanos II, 10 November 959–15 March 963], came to the king [Otto I] and falsely, as it later became clear, asked for a bishop and priests to be ordained for that people'. The first bishop to be ordained died before he could set out, and so Adalbert was sent instead. But by the time he reached Kiev in 961 or 962, the mission was no longer welcome, and Adalbert had to struggle back to Germany, losing several of his companions on the way. The *De Ceremoniis* account gives a secure date and a detailed description of an apparently friendly reception in which Olga was treated as one of the imperial family, and given the highest female rank below the empress of *Zoste Patrikia*, 'Girdled Lady'. It does not mention the baptism, but possibly the event was ignored as irrelevant to the chapter's principal concern which was to describe the reception of various foreign envoys of whom Olga's Rus were only one example.[131]

Obolensky offers the elegant solution that the 957 negotiations broke down at the last moment. Olga returned to Kiev and asked for a bishop from the Germans – a move calculated to alarm the Byzantines. Romanos II succeeded as sole emperor on 10 November 959 and shortly afterwards sent envoys to Olga offering baptism, and presumably asking for the military help which turns up in 961, when a Rus contingent took part in the invasion of Crete. Olga came to Constantinople a second time, probably in 960, where she was baptised and a treaty agreed.

The drawbacks with this interpretation are that it contradicts Skylitzes' account, and that the warm reception of Olga into the heart of the imperial family, as described by the *De Ceremoniis*, would make most sense if she had been baptised with the empress Helena standing as her godmother – hence the baptismal name. It is also possible to read Adalbert's account as implying that Olga was already baptised when the envoys came to Germany in 959. Adalbert's reference to Romanos as the emperor at the time of Olga's baptism could easily be a mistake, influenced by the fact that Romanos was the emperor during the period when Adalbert was actually in Kiev. An alternative to Obolensky is therefore the suggestion that Olga was baptised in Constantinople in 957, but opened negotiations with the Germans in 959 with the aim either of extracting further concessions from the Byzantines or of giving herself more room for manoeuvre. Adalbert's mission collapsed either because she got the terms she wanted from the new emperor, Romanos, or for internal reasons; it is quite conceivable that influential figures in Kiev other than Olga saw the German clergy as dangerous rivals, and preferred the relationship with Byzantium, which brought mutual benefits but as yet no Greek interlopers.

In either case Olga's acceptance into the imperial family, and into the heights of the Byzantine hierarchy, was an extraordinary achievement for a Kievan state less than a century old, and underlines the importance of Byzantine–Kievan ties for both parties. Yet it was still close to a further thirty years before the official conversion of the Rus state. One explanation of this perhaps rather surprising delay has already been suggested, a desire to keep potentially influential clergy out of Kiev. The strength of pagan sentiment is another likely factor. But it was also the result of accidental circumstances, and there is no evidence to support the frequently made assertion of an 'anti-Byzantine' party.

Olga's son, the pagan Svyatoslav, was preoccupied with using the new power and unity of the Kievan state finally to destroy Kiev's eastern rivals on the Volga. After he came of age in the early 960s Svyatoslav launched a series of expeditions to impose his authority on the peoples of the Volga and Oka rivers, many of whom were tributaries of the Khazar qaghan. This culminated in a joint attack on Atil in alliance with the Oğuz nomads from the east. The sack of Atil destroyed the Khazar qaghanate, and as such was a crucial event, marking the end of one of the great powers of the early medieval Near East. In 737 the Khazars had survived a similar disaster at the hands of the Arabs, but then they had been a real steppe-nomad power. The Khazars of the tenth century were a largely sedentary and urban society, using the revenues of trade as much as tribute to pay a heterogeneous mercenary army; with Atil in ruins the qaghanate fell apart. For the Rus its fall was a remarkable achievement, but since their military skills were unequal to those of the nomads on the open steppe, Svyatoslav was in no position to replace Khazar domination of the southern steppes with his own. Indeed the assault on Atil had presumably been something in the nature of a amphibious raid, taking advantage of the city's position on a river to avoid any threat from the qaghan's nomad allies. Former Khazar tributaries in the forest zone now paid their tribute to Kiev, but the steppes themselves – bar possibly an isolated Rus outpost at Sarkel – were inherited by the Oğuz and the Pečenegs.[132]

Seen from Constantinople the destruction of the Khazar qaghanate was a momentous event, but it did not involve the diplomatic revolution that it would have entailed a century earlier. Byzantium had already transferred its interest to the qaghanate's Rus destroyers. Despite the fact that Svyatoslav was a pagan, links between Kiev and Constantinople remained strong. Rus soldiers continued to serve in imperial armies, and in 967 Svyatoslav agreed at the request of the emperor Nikephoros Phokas (962–9) to fulfil one of the traditional roles of the empire's allies in the north by leading an army into Bulgaria.[133] Disentangling what happened next from the inevitably biased and confused Russian and Greek sources is both complicated and uncertain. In August 967 Svyatoslav crossed the Danube and invaded Bulgaria. The Bulgars were defeated and Svyatoslav spent the winter at Little Preslav (Pereyaslavets) in the Dobrudja. In the following year came the news that the Pečenegs were besieging Kiev, and Svyatoslav hurried back to save his mother and sons; but this first visit to the deep south seems to have given him new ideas. Bulgaria was evidently a much better place to base a Rus state than the poor cold north; in the words the *Povest'* ascribes to Svyatoslav, 'I do not care to remain in Kiev, but should prefer to live in Pereyaslavets on the Danube, since that is the centre of my realm, where all riches are concentrated . . . '.[134] By the summer of 969 Svyatoslav was back in Bulgaria, conquering the entire country.

This was obviously not in Byzantine interests, but Svyatoslav himself may not at first have seen it in this anti-Byzantine light. According to two Greek accounts Svyatoslav was persuaded to return to Bulgaria by Nikephoros Phokas' ambassador of 967, a certain Kalokyros, a *patrikios* and son of one of the leading citizens of Cherson, who had designs on the imperial throne.[135] Bearing in mind that at this time in the 960s and early 970s Nikephoros Phokas was widely detested as a tyrannical usurper, and after his murder in December 969, his successor John Tzimiskes (969–76) had no better claim to the throne, Svyatoslav may well have thought that backing an alternative candidate was a sensible way to establish himself in Bulgaria with imperial approval. The Byzantine historian, Leo the Deacon, gives to Svyatoslav the provocative response to John's envoys, 'Let [the Romans] withdraw from Europe, which does not rightly belong to them, and retire to Asia; otherwise there will be no peace between the Rus and the Romans'.[136] But it is difficult to regard this as anything other than a literary cliché. Hostile barbarian leaders are always boastfully overconfident in Byzantine stories, especially when, as Leo knew, Svyatoslav was heading for disaster. In the event John Tzimiskes managed to achieve a firm grip on power in Constantinople, before turning the imperial armies on Svyatoslav's Rus. After three bloody defeats Svyatoslav was cornered in Dristra on the Danube, where following a three-month siege he was forced to come to terms. In exchange for food and a safe-conduct back to the north, he undertook to leave Bulgaria and never again attack the empire or its possessions.[137]

The war itself did not alter the importance of Byzantine–Kievan ties. If Svyatoslav had been successful in moving the centre of the Rus state to the Danube then the Byzantines would no doubt have seen him as a dangerous regional rival and chronic hostilities would have been the result. But the 971 treaty restored the status quo. Svyatoslav promised, as Igor had in 945, to provide the emperor with troops when required, and in return the emperor confirmed Rus trading privileges in Constantinople together with the provision that no Rus merchant could trade save with the permission of the prince of Kiev. This might have been the moment for Svyatoslav to convert his state to Christianity, but in the event he was dead within a year in circumstances which underline the weaknesses of the Rus position in Kiev on the Dnieper river, and hence their need for good relations with Byzantium.

Svyatoslav set out by boat up the Dnieper in the autumn of 971. As part of the agreement for the Rus to leave Bulgaria, the Byzantine emperor had agreed to send ambassadors to the Pečenegs asking them to give the Rus free passage, but when Svyatoslav's party reached the first rapids where it was necessary to disembark and travel round by land they found the way blocked by hostile nomads. Rather than risk trying to force a way through, Svyatoslav returned to the mouth of the river, presumably to give Byzantine diplomacy more time to work. After a miserable and hungry winter Svyatoslav may well have felt forced by the complaints of his warriors to try again as soon as possible. But the attempt failed; as Syatoslav's men tried to carry their boats round the rapids, the Pečenegs attacked. Svyatoslav was killed. According to the *Povest'*, 'The nomads took his head, and made a cup out of his skull, overlaying it with gold, and they drank from it'.[138]

The rest of the 970s passed in a bitter succession struggle among Svyatoslav's sons, which was not resolved until Vladimir seized sole control of Kiev in 980. Even then it would be a further eight years before Vladimir and his people were officially converted to the Byzantine religion. But when it did finally take place the conversion was the logical culmination to a diplomatic revolution that in less than a century had transformed an unimportant community of Viking and Slav raiders and merchants into Byzantium's key ally in the north.

The Balkans

The events of the first half of the seventh century created an unprecedented power vacuum in the Balkans which would shape the history of the region through to the last quarter of the tenth century, and would have fundamental consequences for the future development of the Balkans through to the present day.

After 610 the Avar qaghanate had looked set to establish its domination over the peninsula, but the humiliating failure of the qaghan's forces to capture Constantinople in 626 struck a blow from which Avar power never wholly recovered. To the north of the Hungarian plain the Avars' Slav tributaries rebelled under the leadership of a Frankish merchant named Samo who set up a powerful but apparently short-lived kingdom centred in what is now the Czech Republic.[139] Within the Avar confederation itself several of the 'outer' nomad groups seem to have thrown off the qaghan's authority. Somewhere around 630 Koubratos, leader of the Onogur Bulgars, broke from the Avar confederation and concluded a treaty with the emperor Herakleios. Others may well have followed. The decline in Avar power seems to have been cumulative over the century. About forty or fifty years later another Bulgar called Kouber, who had been given the leadership of a 'tribe' in the Avar confederation made up of the descendants of Roman prisoners-of-war captured in the years between 610 and 626, also rebelled against the qaghan. Kouber was himself proclaimed qaghan by his half-Roman tribe, and seems to have settled in the region of Thessalonica, where he tried to seize the city by an unsuccessful coup. There were no doubt other groups too, and like Kouber's little qaghanate, equally ephemeral.[140]

The Croats and Serbs have also been seen by some historians as rebels who broke away from the Avars to set up their own states in the 620s with the blessing of the emperor Herakleios. But the only evidence is an anachronistic story preserved in the *De Administrando Imperio* which seems to have been invented in the late ninth or early tenth century to give historical precedent to current Byzantine policies. It is really no more than an origin myth and can hardly be taken seriously.[141]

Any detailed account of these years is impossible to create from the sources that have survived, but the main point is clear enough. After 626 what power the Avars continued to wield was increasingly limited to the Hungarian plain and its immediate hinterland. In so far as the qaghans still played an international role, their interests were focused on the potentially dangerous Frankish world to their west, while their disintegrating former empire in the Balkans was left to its own devices.

If a steppe power was not to dominate the Balkans from the north, then past experience would have led contemporaries to expect that the Romans would control the peninsula from the

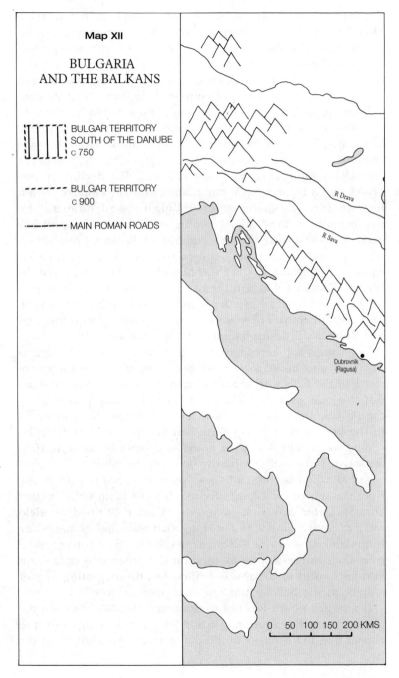

Map XII

BULGARIA
AND THE BALKANS

BULGAR TERRITORY
SOUTH OF THE DANUBE
c 750

BULGAR TERRITORY
c 900

MAIN ROMAN ROADS

R Drava

R Sava

Dubrovnik
(Ragusa)

0   50 100 150 200 KMS

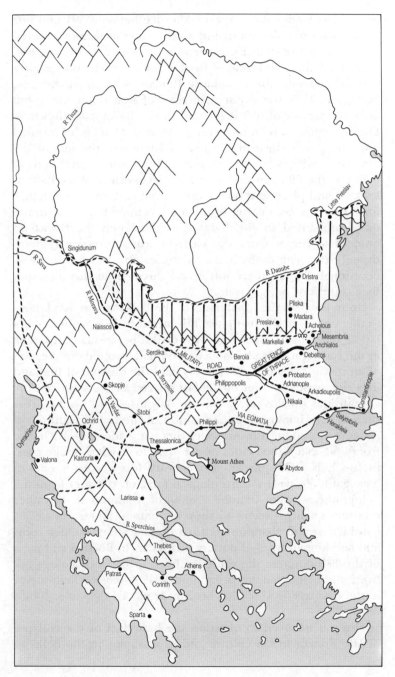

Little Preslav
R Tisza
Singidunum
R Sava
R Danube
Dristra
R Morava
Pliska
Naissos
Madara
Preslav
Achelous
Markellai
Mesembria
Serdika
MILITARY ROAD
Beroia
GREAT FENCE OF THRACE
Anchialos
Debeltos
Skopje
Philippopolis
Probaton
Adrianople
Arkadioupolis
Constantinople
R Strymon
R Vardar
Stobi
Nikaia
Dyrrachion
Ochrid
Philippi
VIA EGNATIA
Selymbria
Thessalonica
Herakleia
Valona
Kastoria
Mount Athos
Abydos
Larissa
R Sperchios
Thebes
Athens
Patras
Corinth
Sparta

south-east. Under the emperor Maurice between 591 and 602 the Romans had done much in a short time to restore imperial authority in the Balkans. Maurice's assassination in 602, and even more the withdrawal of Roman forces by Herakleios after 610 to deal with the crumbling Roman position in the east, had opened the way for sixteen years of Avar domination; but after the victory of 629 it seemed in the Balkans as elsewhere that the empire was on the verge of a new golden age of restored imperial power. Instead the rise of Islam and the loss of the eastern provinces left the empire fighting for survival, and as before in the fifth and sixth centuries the demands of the Balkans took second place to those of the crucial eastern front. Henceforth until the last quarter of the tenth century Byzantine armies only intervened in the Balkans either when there was no immediate threat from the east, or when insecure regimes thought they could obtain easy victories on this front, or, very occasionally, when there was a real threat from this direction that could not be ignored.

Up to the 680s the inhabitants of the Balkans were left largely to themselves. In the first place this meant the Romanised population speaking Latin in the west of the peninsula and Greek in the east. Traditionally Romanisation had involved the creation of an urban culture and economy, and the division of the land into city territories. But by the last quarter of the sixth century city life was on the retreat in the Balkans, and in some areas such as the Haimos mountains south of the Lower Danube, in Albania and along the Adriatic, there is evidence for a move from long-established cities in the plain to smaller 'refuge sites' in the hills.[142] In the seventh century this process seems to have gathered pace. Archaeological work on city sites from the Peloponnese to the Danube – some of it admittedly of rather doubtful quality – seems to show a common pattern of decay, contraction and abandonment. As in Asia Minor copper coins and late Roman types of pottery disappear. In Boeotia and parts of the Peloponnese the evidence from urban archaeology has been supplemented by programmes of extensive field-survey in the countryside which has broadly produced the same gloomy result.[143]

There is no need to question the basic fact of the collapse of late Roman urban culture and its economy in the Balkans, but the picture of total disaster does need some refinement. In the first place the archaeological evidence needs to be discounted against the failure of most archaeologists until quite recently to be interested in low grade medieval remains, and against the continuing inability to recognise early medieval pottery. This is especially a problem for those carrying out field surveys. Results have sometimes seemed to show a virtual disappearance of any population at all in parts of Greece during the seventh century, but a sceptic could reasonably point out that without some sort of diagnostic pottery to reveal early Byzantine period settlement sites whatever population there was would be invisible to a survey team crossing the countryside identifying and dating settlements by the scatter of pottery fragments human occupation leaves behind.

Some cities certainly did survive in the Balkans. The best documented case is that of Thessalonica whose activity in the seventh century is revealed by a collection of miracles performed by St Demetrios, whose wonder-working shrine lay in the city. This text, usually known as the *Miracles of St Demetrios*, is made up of two separate collections of stories. The first was composed by John, the archbishop of Thessalonica, probably shortly after 610; the second is the anonymous work of a citizen of Thessalonica, possibly a clergyman, writing about seventy years later. Together they are an extremely valuable source for the seventh-century Balkans, and without them there would be very little to say. The *Miracles* deserve detailed study, but in a sentence they show a community still aware of its corporate identity as the citizens of Thessalonica, and able to survive and defend itself from its enemies.[144]

The *Miracles* are a unique survival, but the kind of continuity they describe among the Romanised population of the Balkans was almost certainly not. Apart from Thessalonica another 17 cities are known because their bishops attended the Councils of 680–1 or 692 in Constantinople. Most of these were from Thrace, but the bishop of Stobi in northern Macedonia came in 680–1, and the bishop of Dyrrachion on the Adriatic coast of Albania came in 692.[145] The small total and the large areas not represented at either Council is striking proof of the collapse of Byzantine authority in the Balkans, but it is not evidence that only these sees still existed. Serdika, for example, seems to have survived. In the sixth century Serdika (modern Sofia) had been an important fortress and staging post on the main road across the Balkans to the middle Danube. In 618 there were refugees from Serdika in Thessalonica at the time of the Avar siege. After this there is no mention of the site for nearly two hundred years but in 809 Theophanes states that Serdika was captured by the Bulgars and there was still a Christian population to flee south and take refuge again in Thessalonica. The survival throughout this period of the sixth-century church of Sveta Sofiya, which lies outside the city walls, is another important piece of evidence. Clearly despite the silence of the sources Serdika did have a continuous history.[146] At Philippopolis (modern Plovdiv), which lies 130 kilometres to the south-east, the fact that the walls were in good repair in 784, and that it too had a Christian population to evacuate in the early ninth century, suggests that this city had also been continuously occupied.[147] Another example is Patras in the north-west of the Peloponnese. In about 807, inspired by a vision of their patron saint, St Andrew the Apostle, the citizens of Patras had sallied out to rout a besieging force of Slavs before the strategos and his troops from Corinth had arrived. This episode (recorded in the *De Administrando Imperio*) combined with the existence of a city cult of St Andrew suggests that Patras had been occupied continuously since the sixth century despite the silence of the sources.[148] The *De Administrando Imperio* also records that in Dalmatia and Albania, several 'Roman' cities survived either on their ancient sites, or more frequently by moving to hill-tops and islands. Many of the details in the *De Administrando Imperio* are of course unreliable, but the general picture is confirmed by archaeology – especially by the material from the Komani–Kruja group of cemeteries in northern Albania, the product of an isolated, poor, but Romanised and Christian culture. In any case the most important feature of the *De Administrando Imperio*'s account is the fact that in the ninth and tenth century there still were communities in the western Balkans who consciously thought of themselves as 'Roman'.[149]

Clearly the late Roman economy had collapsed here as almost everywhere else in the Byzantine world and urban life was at a very low ebb. Wherever archaeological evidence is available – for example, from Corinth and Athens, or from northern

Albania – it points to small settlements and a poor level of material culture. Yet the fact remains that the descendants of the Romanised Christian population still existed in the seventh and eighth centuries as a consciously separate group. They have been paid little attention by historians but it is hard to believe they did not play a major role in the shaping of the early medieval Balkans.

Also present in the seventh and eighth centuries were the ancestors of the modern Albanians. They are not mentioned in the written sources until the eleventh century, but like the Kurds in the Transcaucasus, the Albanians did not appear from nothing, and the presence of these indigenous transhumant nomads exploiting the high pastures of the western Balkans should not be forgotten.[150]

However, the major beneficiaries of the seventh-century power vacuum were neither the 'Romans' nor wild men from the hills, but two comparative newcomers – the Slavs and the Bulgars. The primitive social and political culture of the Slavs at this period has already been described. Under other circumstances they would have been subject to the same processes of Romanisation that had been working on the inhabitants of the peninsula since the Roman conquest. Indeed this is what did happen in the south. Leaving aside the vexed question of how many Slavs were involved, it is quite clear that those who did settle in areas such as the Peloponnese, Attica or the hinterland of Thessalonica where Byzantine authority soon reasserted itself, were gradually absorbed into a Greek-speaking and Christian world where they were indistinguishable from other 'Romans'. But elsewhere the collapse of Roman power in the seventh century opened the way for the greater part of the Balkans to be turned into the Slav land it is today.[151]

The *Miracles of St Demetrios* provide the best evidence for this process at work. In the first collection dating from the early seventh century the Slavs appear as clients of the Avar qaghans; by the time of the second collection in the last quarter of the century there were a number of small independent Slav tribes settled in the hinterland of Thessalonica. From the perspective of the author of the *Miracles* several of these seem to have been clients of the emperor in Constantinople. For example, one of the tribes near Thessalonica was the Rhunchinai whose king Perboundos dressed as a 'Roman', spoke Greek and was regarded in some way as an imperial subject. Similar and equally obscure ties linked to Constantinople the Drougoubitai who lived in the plain around modern Prilep, 150 kilometres north-west of Thessalonica. But the reality, clear enough in the miracle stories, is of effectively independent Slav groups whose leaders might wish to acknowledge Byzantine overlordship as a means to enhance their own status, and who might be bribed, or defeated by a special expedition sent from Constantinople, but who under normal circumstances were well beyond effective imperial control. The further from Constantinople or Thessalonica the weaker Byzantine influence inevitably was, and the picture over the peninsula as a whole is one of extreme political fragmentation where small tribal groups were able to lead an independent existence that would never have been possible had it not been for the collapse of Avar and Roman power.[152]

The other major beneficiaries were the Bulgars. These were a confederation of several groups of steppe nomads, whose ancestors had been present in the Ukrainian steppe for several centuries as members of successive nomad states. Among them were a group who had been part of the Gök Türk confederation in the late sixth and early seventh centuries, but had been defeated in the power struggle with the Khazars that had followed the break up of the Gök Türk empire in 630. Other Bulgar groups were previously a part of the Avar confederation who had thrown off the qaghan's rule in the period after 626. Two examples have already been mentioned: Koubratos, the leader of the Onogur Bulgars, and Kouber, the Bulgar who founded an ephemeral qaghanate near Thessalonica.

Following their defeat by the Khazars, the Bulgar confederation on the Ukrainian steppe had broken apart. According to Theophanes, one section remained as tributaries of the Khazar qaghanate; a second moved north-east to form the core of the future Volga Bulgar state; two others travelled west to the Hungarian plain and to Italy, where they became subjects of the Avars and the Byzantine governor in Ravenna respectively; and finally, what seems to have been the main section, under the leadership of Asparuch crossed the Danube in the late 670s and settled in the Dobrudja. This area of steppe grasslands south of the Danube delta was in theory imperial territory, and in 680 or 681 Constantine IV led a substantial Byzantine army and fleet to expel them. The expedition failed and suffered a bloody defeat as it tried to pull out. Constantine could not have afforded to deploy key elements of the main Byzantine field army in the Balkans for long, and in the following year he came to terms with Asparuch, recognised his control of the Dobrudja and an adjacent territory between the Danube and the Haimos mountains, and agreed to pay the Bulgars an annual tribute.[153]

Much of the history of the Bulgar state will always remain unknown for lack of evidence. For the most part we are dependent on Byzantine sources inadequate to explain the Byzantine world let alone a neighbour they seem to have known little about, and regarded with a mixture of fear, hostility and contempt. However, some independent evidence does exist. In the first place there is a slowly growing corpus of archaeological material; there is a list of Bulgarian rulers which possibly goes back to a late eighth-century original; and most important, there are the so-called Proto-Bulgar inscriptions. Of these about 70 longer than a few words are known. With the exception of a few written in Turkic runes and a few in Turkic but written in Greek script, the rest are in Greek. They date from the early eighth century through to the tenth, although very few post-date the conversion to Christianity in 864/5. They include formal accounts of the deeds of the qaghans, victory proclamations, peace treaties, building inscriptions, inventories and funerary inscriptions. A series were carved on the cliffs at Madara, a site intimately linked with the charismatic good-fortune of the Bulgar qaghans; otherwise they are cut on stones and buildings, some on portable objects and they include a number of seals.[154]

From this material it is possible to see that the Bulgar qaghanate was a steppe nomad state on the Turkic model familiar from the Gök Türks and the Khazars. The Bulgars seem to have spoken a Turkic language, and terms and titles in the Proto-Bulgar inscriptions can be paralleled in those from the Orkhon valley in Central Asia. The title of qaghan with its claims to universal rule and its association with Tengri the Almighty Sky-God was directly inherited from the Gök Türk qaghans. The ruling clan of the Bulgar state on the Danube claimed to be descendants of the Dulo – the leading clan of the left division of the qaghanate of the western Gök Türk. The Bulgar state was structured with the typical nomadic division between inner and outer clans, beneath whom were tributary peoples – in this case mostly Slav tribes – who had no part in the state save as its subjects. Like other nomad states the Bulgar qaghanate had at Pliska a permanent winter camping-ground which gradually developed into a settled capital. Although by the ninth century Pliska included a core of substantial stone buildings, and numerous wooden structures of a type known as 'sunken huts', usually associated with Slav settlements in the Balkans, the key feature of the site is the 21 kilometre outer line of earthworks. They are revetted with stone and enclose an area of 2300 hectares. The existence of this vast enclosed area places the site outside the tradition of Roman cities in the Balkans and links it to the great nomad camps of the Eurasian steppes.[155]

Yet at the same time the Bulgars and their state bear the marks of the strong influence of late Roman and Byzantine culture, and it is clear that Byzantines and Bulgars had much more in common than the hostile anti-barbarian accounts of writers such as Theophanes would suggest. Long before Asparuch led the Bulgars to the Dobrudja the ancestors of his confederation had generations of contact with the Roman world. The Kutrigurs and Utigurs – both Bulgar peoples – had been allies and enemies of the Romans since the fifth century. Numerous Bulgars had served in the imperial army, and it is striking to see that when the Bulgar confederation on the Ukrainian steppe broke up in the face of the Khazars, among those groups of Bulgars who did not follow Asparuch were some who went to serve with the imperial army in Italy. Koubratos, the leader of the Onogur Bulgars, who has already been mentioned for his revolt against the Avar qaghan in 630, became a Christian, a Roman ally, and was rewarded with the court rank of *patrikios*. Kouber, the Bulgar leader of the half-Roman tribe who settled near Thessalonica, also had links with the imperial government in Constantinople. He had asked the emperor's permission to settle in the Balkans, and although the *Miracles* describe the episode in terms of an attempted coup against the city, the fact remains that one of Kouber's associates, a Bulgar called Mauros, was made *strategos* of Thessalonica.[156] Asparuch's treaty of 681 and his acceptance of an annual subsidy was a recognition that the Bulgars were only there by permission of the emperor, and the subsidy marked as much their status as the emperor's clients – recipients of his generosity – as it did the military success which had forced the Byzantines to come to terms. In 695 Constantine's son, Justinian II, was deposed, and with his tongue cut and his nose slit he was exiled to Cherson. When he was restored in 705 it was with the military support of Asparuch's successor, the Bulgar qaghan Tervel, whom Justinian clearly regarded as an imperial client. Tervel was brought to the palace, invested with an imperial *chlamys* (a long cloak which formed part of court costume), and proclaimed *kaisaros* – 'caesar', a rank in the imperial hierarchy second only to the emperor. Tervel apparently sat side by side enthroned with Justinian, who ordered that the court should make obeisance to them jointly. Despite a Byzantine attack on the Bulgars very shortly afterwards, and Justinian II's assassination in 711, relations remained sufficiently close for the qaghan to harass the Arab armies besieging Constantinople in 717.[157]

There is no evidence that Tervel was ever formally baptised, but equally there is no sign that the Bulgars positively rejected the Byzantine religion. At the least Tervel must have been able to compromise with Christianity to take part in the palace ceremonies of 705–6, and one of his lead seals bears the inscription, 'Mother of God, aid the Caesar Tervel'.[158] At Pliska itself there was a large basilical church, put up at some date in the fifth, sixth or seventh centuries, probably (but not certainly) before the Bulgars came there. It is not known whether it was used as a church, but it did remain in use throughout the early middle ages and a number of graves and inscriptions associated with it show that whether Christian or not it was seen as a sacred site.[159] The Bulgar state had been established in what had been – as a militarised frontier province – one of the most securely Romanised areas of the Balkans at the beginning of the seventh century. As a result an important section of the qaghans' subjects would have been Christian, and it therefore seems probable that the Bulgars, like other Turkic nomad states, adopted a tolerant syncretist approach to rival deities. The aid of both Tengri and the Mother of God was presumably better than that of only one.

The Proto-Bulgar inscriptions provide further evidence of the

Bulgars' receptiveness to late Roman culture. The fact that with very few exceptions they were written in Greek rather than in Turkic runes is a major point in itself, but it is reinforced by the content of the inscriptions which includes Bulgar officials with late Roman/Byzantine titles, late Roman/Byzantine terminology, and dating by the Byzantine system of fifteen-year indiction cycles.[160] While inscriptions on stone had been common in the late Roman world, they had largely disappeared in the Byzantine empire after the early seventh century. Hence there was very little in the way of contemporary Byzantine epigraphy for the Bulgars to have copied. In view of the rather limited literary qualities of the Proto-Bulgar inscriptions – described by some scholars as 'provincial' – it seems quite probable that like the influence of Christianity they reflect not so much a direct copying of Constantinople as the continuing part played by the former Roman population in the new Bulgar state.

Turkic tradition brought the new state a nomad ruling élite with the military skills of steppe warriors, and an ideology of a centralised state that could be independent of the emperor in Constantinople. Roman tradition brought skills in building, writing, and one may reasonably guess record keeping and organisation, that were potentially of immense value. As important, the Roman tradition provided an ideology and an idea of the state that could include the qaghan's non-Bulgar subjects. How the balance between the Turkic and Roman inheritance operated in practice is unknown. However, it is clear that both parts of the Bulgar heritage were vital for the new state's survival.

'Survival' is the right word here because although the power vacuum in the Balkans allowed the Bulgars to establish themselves south of the Danube, the Byzantines were not happy with the existence of a Bulgar state on what was regarded as imperial territory and made repeated attempts at its destruction. These came in periods when there was a lull in hostilities on the eastern frontier. After Constantine IV's initial expedition in 680–1, Justinian II campaigned against the Bulgars in 687–9, and again in 709, but the major attempt came in the mid-eighth-century breathing space provided by the fall of the Ummayads. Constantine V turned the eastern armies on the Bulgars in a concerted attempt to destroy the qaghanate.[161] In the event he came very close, winning a number of major victories which created a legend of the emperor as a triumphant military leader, but he failed to destroy the Bulgars – and the failure is testimony to the resilience, fighting skills and ideological coherence of the Bulgar state.

The key strategic factor in these wars was the positioning of the Bulgar heartlands and the capital at Pliska north of the protective barrier of the Haimos mountains. For a Byzantine general leading an army against the Bulgars the Haimos presented a major obstacle and a series of choices. In the first place while the north face of the range slopes gently down to the Danube plain, the south facing the Byzantines dropped steeply into the plain of Thrace making the range far more difficult to cross from the south than the north. At the same time the altitude of the Haimos increases as one goes west. A Byzantine general therefore could either choose to follow the comparatively level coast-road which goes round the mountains by the shore of the Black Sea where the Bulgars would probably expect them and be prepared, or attempt the inherently dangerous manoeuvre of crossing one of the Haimos passes in the hope of catching the Bulgars by surprise, and possibly also of fighting on ground where the Bulgars' skills as nomad cavalry would be less effective. Over the centuries of Byzantine–Bulgar warfare the Byzantines tried both the coastal route and most of the Haimos passes. They had some successes and a number of spectacular disasters by both routes. Overall it is clear that the defensive advantage which the mountains gave to a state on the Danube was vital to Bulgar survival – and never more so than during Constantine V's onslaught from 759 to 775.

Over the last quarter of the eighth century the increasing threat in the east from the new Abbāsid caliphate generally preoccupied Constantine's successors, but when possible Irene and Constantine VI sent armies into the Balkans. The principal targets of these campaigns were the small Slav tribal units – known in the Byzantine sources as the *Sklaviniai* – which had grown up in the seventh century. It seems likely that the main attraction was not so much booty or tribute but the propaganda value of easy military victories which could be celebrated in Constantinople. Indeed Irene's expedition of May 784 when, according to Theophanes, she and her son 'went forth . . . carrying tools and musical instruments' to rebuild the city of Beroia and rename it Irenopolis seems to have been more like a triumphal procession from the start and hardly deserves to be called a campaign.[162]

The northern Sklaviniai in the vicinity of the Haimos had long been clients of the Bulgar qaghans. Hence Byzantine operations were for the most part concentrated on the areas around Thessalonica, in Thessaly and even as far south as Attica and the Peloponnese which were all well outside any Bulgar sphere of interest. But in the later 780s and in the 790s – probably tempted by memories of Constantine V's victories – the Byzantines began to extend their operations into eastern Thrace where the Bulgars felt threatened, and there were a series of touchy confrontations and sharp engagements.[163] In 797 Constantine VI was blinded by his mother Irene, and she in turn was toppled in a coup led by Nikephoros in 802. The new regime was as insecure as its predecessors and like them its achievements would be measured against the military triumphs of Constantine V. Under Nikephoros hostilities continued to escalate until in 811 they culminated in another full-scale attempt to destroy the Bulgar state, now ruled by the qaghan Krum.

Nikephoros' campaign began successfully. With an army that included all those that could be transferred from the eastern front, the emperor marched to Markellai, a fort south of the Haimos range at the eastern end. Here, according to Theophanes (whose account should be treated with caution: see the section on hagiography in Chapter 1), Krum sent envoys to offer peace, but they were rejected. The Byzantine army then crossed the Haimos and pressed on to Pliska, which was sacked and plundered. However, if Nikephoros expected the Bulgar qaghanate to collapse then he was badly mistaken. As the Byzantine army retreated over the Haimos range to Thrace it was ambushed and in the ensuing battle utterly defeated. Among the long list of the slaughtered Byzantine dignitaries was the emperor himself. Again, according to Theophanes, he suffered the same fate that would later befall Svyatoslav, the Rus ruler of Kiev. Krum had the emperor's head cut off and hung on a pole for a number of days; later it was turned into a silver-coated cup from which the qaghan made the chiefs of his Slav tributaries drink.[164]

Krum followed up this extraordinary victory by a series of

campaigns in the following year into Thrace and Macedonia. The Byzantine position in the Balkans crumbled. While Debeltos actually fell to a siege, many other Byzantine fortresses, including Anchialos, Beroia, Nikaia, Probaton, Philipopolis and Philippi, were simply abandoned by their fleeing inhabitants. In the autumn Krum offered generous terms. The frontier would be returned to where it had been before the phase of Byzantine expansion at the expense of the Slavs in the late eighth century; the qaghan would receive an annual payment of clothing and dyed skins worth the comparatively small sum of 100 pounds of gold; fugitives were to be returned to each side; and accredited merchants were to be free to trade in both lands. The proposal, which would have involved the return of all the territory that had fallen to the Bulgars since the war began, is clear evidence that the Bulgars had no expansionist plans at Byzantine expense. But for Krum, as for his successor Symeon at the beginning of the tenth century, the problem was to persuade the Byzantines to accept any agreement however generous. The Bulgar victory and Nikephoros' death had thrown the empire into political turmoil. No emperor who suffered repeated defeats at the hands of the Bulgars could expect to establish a secure regime; but equally the shaky regimes which resulted from Krum's successes could not have survived the political humiliation of agreeing to the qaghan's terms – whatever they might be. A total Bulgar victory was in practice unattainable because of Constantinople's impregnable triple walls; while limited victories, however wide-ranging and successful, would bring the Bulgars no nearer the achievement of a stable peace. Bulgar armies ravaged Thrace and Macedonia capturing cities as far as the sea of Marmara; in October 812 Mesembria – the only remaining Byzantine fortress on the Black Sea coast – fell to the Bulgars; and in 813 Krum's armies took Adrianople. At the same time the Bulgars threatened to attack the imperial city itself and plundered its suburbs. Byzantine counter-attacks all failed, as did a bungled assassination attempt. Krum died in April 814, but the problem of how to extract a peace from the empire remained for his successors.[165]

In the event the impasse seems to have been broken by a minor Byzantine victory. The emperor Leo V led a Byzantine raid to Mesembria in 816 which managed to ambush and defeat a Bulgar army. Having celebrated this 'triumph' in Constantinople to achieve the maximum political effect, Leo was finally in a position to negotiate. The new qaghan Omurtag agreed to terms that were essentially the same as those offered by Krum in 812 and in effect restored the frontier to what it had been in the mid-eighth century. The peace was to last for thirty years, and it was probably in the aftermath of this agreement that to protect themselves from future Byzantine aggression the Bulgars built the line of earthworks known as the Erkesiya, or the Great Fence, which runs 130 kilometres from the Maritsa valley at Konstanteia north-east to the Black Sea.[166]

A Byzantine lexicon compiled about 1000, known as the *Souda*, contains a story which credits Krum also with the destruction of the Avar qaghanate. This is at best an exaggeration. Well-informed contemporary western sources state that the Avars fell to the Franks. The qaghanate had survived since the seventh century on the Hungarian plain, but by the second half of the eighth century it was no longer a formidable nomad power. Excavations of Avar cemeteries have revealed an élite whose material culture was little different from their sedentary Germanic and Slav subjects. Like the Khazar qaghanate in its last century, the eighth-century Avar state seems to have lost much of its aggressive nomad militarism just when it was faced with a dangerous new threat. Frankish pressure culminated in 796 when Charlemagne's armies sacked the Avar Ring – a winter camping-ground and capital akin to Pliska. The huge plunder of gold and silver amazed contemporaries and made this arguably the greatest of Charlemagne's victories. Again like the Khazar qaghanate after the sack of Atil – but notably unlike Krum's Bulgars after the fall of Pliska – the sack of the Ring led rapidly to the break-up of the Avar state.[167]

It has been suggested that sections of the Avar confederation who thought of themselves as Bulgars may have moved east to join their cousins on the Lower Danube, bringing new military manpower and increasing the Turkic nomad component in the Bulgar state; it has also been claimed that Krum himself was one of the Avar Bulgars, but there is no evidence for either hypothesis.

Even if the Avars were not conquered by the Bulgars, Krum's successors were certainly beneficiaries of the disappearance of

the qaghanate. At the same time as his victories over the Byzantines provided temporary security in the south-east, the collapse
of the Avar qaghanate opened the way for expansion in the
west. The process remains rather obscure. To the north-west
of the Bulgar heartlands on the Lower Danube the Avar's former
Slav tributaries either fell under the control of their Frankish
conquerors, or – as in the case of Croatia and the powerful
Moravian kingdom – managed to establish themselves as
effectively independent states. The Bulgars took over Belgrade,
and during the 820s tried to terrorise the Slavs along the Drava
into submission; they may also have imposed tribute on the
peoples of Transylvania, but in general it seems that Bulgar
expansion in this direction was limited, and went no further
than the River Tisza.[168] To the west Bulgar advances were also
blocked by the development of a Slav state; in this case Serbia
which appears in the ninth century in the mountains west of
the Morava river. The *De Administrando Imperio* may be guilty
of Serbo-Byzantine wishful thinking when it tells of the Bulgars
being defeated in two attempts to conquer Serbia in the mid-
ninth century; but an independent Serbia is real enough, and
any Serb submission to the Bulgar qaghan went no further than
the payment of tribute.[169] Instead the main field of expansion
was to the south-west where the Byzantine defeat had given
the Bulgars a free hand to annexe the still-surviving Sklaviniai.
By the 860s at the latest Bulgar territory included the whole of
eastern Thrace and the greater part of Macedonia, stretching
as far west as the area around Ohrid and Lake Prespa, with a
corridor to the Adriatic Sea near Valona; and as far south as
the Rhodope and the edges of the plain around the city of
Thessalonica. The Bulgar qaghanate had become the dominant
power in the Balkans.[170]

Yet despite these advances the Bulgar position was still fundamentally insecure. The geography of the Balkans imposed a
fragmented pattern on the expanded Bulgar state. Outside the
core area around Pliska the Bulgar lands were essentially a
patchwork of isolated valleys and small plains, accessible by
difficult routes often impassable in winter, and hemmed in by
high mountains where the qaghan's writ was unlikely to run.
The population was similarly divided between Turkic Bulgars,
Greek-speaking 'Romans', and a kalaidoscope of mostly Slav

tribes. The qaghanate had been created and defended by a ruling élite of Turkic Bulgars whose nomad military skills came from the steppes. However, the grasslands necessary to support their nomad culture did not exist in the Balkans, and over the long run they were bound to be assimilated by the sedentary world around them. The break-up of the Avar qaghanate had perhaps brought an influx of new Turkic nomads, but in time they would be subject to the same erosion of their nomadic culture, and even with their aid the Bulgars had not been able to take over the one significant area of steppe grasslands in eastern Europe – the Hungarian plain. At the same time as the Bulgars were losing the traditions and skills that had brought them a military advantage they were facing new and dangerous threats. To the south-east there was still Byzantium. Since 811 a combination of internal difficulties and warfare in the east had prevented any major outbreak of hostilities, but that situation was obviously not permanent. The Byzantines continued to regard the whole of the qaghanate's lands as properly imperial territory and in due course the Bulgars could expect another attempt at their destruction. To the north-east the upheaval of the 830s on the Ukrainian steppes had brought the Magyars to the Bulgar borders. In the first place they were dangerous simply as steppe nomads who might follow the same route that had once brought the Bulgars themselves to the Balkans; but secondly as Khazar clients and hence as natural allies of the Byzantines they opened the dangerous possibility of an attack on two fronts that would not be answered by the traditional Bulgar strategy of a defence based on the Haimos mountains.

It is against this background that one should see the conversion of the Bulgars. Christianity was attractive as the religion of the great powers of ninth-century Europe. To be pagan placed any people in an exposed position as an acceptable target for aggression; conversion on the other hand opened up possibilities of alliances and diplomatic ties which might off-set the threat of Byzantine attack. There is evidence that the Bulgars had also had contacts with the Muslim world – either directly or via the Volga Bulgars who converted to Islam at about this time.[171] However, this was not a viable alternative. The Danube qaghanate was too far from any Islamic power for this to offer a political advantage; and in any case a large proportion of the qaghan's subjects were already Christian.

It has already been suggested that the Bulgars took a tolerant and syncretist approach to religion similar to that of other Turkic steppe peoples, but most historians would set against this the stories of violent persecution carried out by the qaghans in the first third of the ninth century, and the martyrdom of Enravotas, a son of the qaghan Omurtag who was put to death by his brother, the qaghan Malamir (831–6).[172] However, the evidence needs to be treated with caution. The story of Enravotas is only known from Theophylact of Ohrid's *Martyrion*, written in the late eleventh or early twelfth century. Even if Theophylact was using an older Slavic source it seems quite likely that Enravotas' martyrdom was a late ninth- or tenth-century story manufactured after the Bulgar conversion to Christianity to give the ruling house a family saint. Otherwise all the stories of violent persecution come from Byzantine sources and date from the period after 811 when Bulgar success in the Balkans was encouraging an alarming number of the emperor's subjects to defect to the enemy. The Proto-Bulgar inscriptions name several of the qaghan's commanders who are clearly Byzantines; Theophanes mentions a siege engineer with a court title who joined Krum, and most significantly he also reveals that the citizens of Debeltos together with their bishop went over to the Bulgars. Since the qaghan would seem to have had nothing to gain from persecution, and there is no other evidence to suggest that the Bulgars ever pursued a hostile anti-Christian policy, the stories are perhaps most convincingly seen as Byzantine anti-Bulgar propaganda. Presumably they were intended to harden the resistance of Byzantine cities in the Balkans to Bulgar attack, and deter Byzantine officials from seeking rewards in the qaghan's service.[173]

The immediate circumstances of the conversion were a complicated political crisis which developed during the 860s to involve not only the Byzantines and Bulgars, but the Germans, the Moravians and the papacy. In the early 860s growing German and Bulgar alarm at the new power of the Slav state of Moravia seems to have encouraged the East Frankish king, Louis the German, and the Bulgar qaghan, Boris, to plan a joint attack on the Moravians with the understanding that the Bulgars would convert to Christianity and accept missionaries from Germany. Either as cause or effect of this alliance – the chronology is uncertain – the Moravian prince Rstislav sent an embassy to Constantinople in 862 to ask for Byzantine missionaries who would replace the German priests operating in Moravia under the aegis of the see of Salzburg. The Byzantines were only too pleased to see the Moravians turn to them for help. The prospect of the Bulgar qaghanate becoming a Frankish client was extremely worrying, and the Moravian request offered the chance of reciprocal interference in what was regarded as a Frankish sphere of influence which might persuade Louis to back off.[174]

More positively for the Byzantines, on 3 September 863 in a battle whose consequences will be explored in Chapter 9 the emperor's uncle, Petronas, inflicted a decisive defeat on a major Arab raiding army in Anatolia. With the Arab threat temporarily neutralised the main units of the Byzantine field army could be transferred to the Balkans, and in 864 they were launched on an invasion of Bulgaria. Both Byzantine and Frankish accounts agree that Boris was not in an immediate position to resist. The main Bulgar army was deployed in the north against Moravia, and its effectiveness was reduced by famine in the qaghan's lands. He rapidly came to terms, agreeing to his own baptism as the emperor's godson and to Byzantine priests being allowed access to carry out the conversion of his people.[175]

This was a remarkable Byzantine triumph, but over the next two years it was almost lost. The dominant figures at the imperial court since 858 had been the young emperor Michael III's uncle, the caesar Bardas, and the latter's protégé, the patriarch Photios. In 865 the qaghan Boris was baptised, taking the new baptismal name of Michael after his imperial godfather, and then left to deal with a rebellion of those of his subjects who were terrified at losing the protection of the Sky-God Tengri. In 866 the caesar Bardas and his imperial nephew set out to expel the Arabs from Crete. Success where Michael's iconoclast father and grandfather had failed would have been a further political triumph, but in the event the expedition got no further than the west coast of Asia Minor. In April 866, while still in camp before embarking, Bardas was assassinated by Michael's companion and confidant, Basil, who was presumably acting with at least the emperor's tacit consent. With the immediate threat of Byzantine invasion removed Boris rapidly set about trying to achieve better terms for his conversion.[176]

His options were increased by the bad-tempered schism that by 866 divided Constantinople from the church of Rome. Photios' election as patriarch in 858 had been entirely uncanonical. Not only had he been a layman rushed through the clerical orders to priesthood to make him eligible – contrary to all ecclesiastical law – but he took the place of an illegally deposed predecessor, the patriarch Ignatios. Up until 863 Photios' position had been backed – or at least tolerated – by Pope Nicholas I, who was looking to be rewarded by the return to his jurisdiction of the ecclesiastical provinces of Illyricum (in this sense the whole of the western Balkans including Thessalonica), Sicily and Calabria which had been annexed to the Constantinopolitan patriarchate in the eighth century. When Nicholas saw that Photios had no intention of paying for his support, he changed tactics, denounced Photios as a usurper, and in November 866 excommunicated him – a move that was promptly reciprocated.[177]

For the next four years Boris brilliantly manoeuvred between Rome, Constantinople and the Germans to extract the maximum advantage. Within months of Bardas' murder Boris had sent embassies to Louis the German and and the pope asking for missionaries, and had expelled the Greek clergy. In 867 the Germans arrived, but they in turn were soon ejected by the papal team who managed to gain the qaghan's support. Their success, however, was short-lived. While Boris was inviting missionaries from the west to Bulgaria, Basil – the murderer of April 866 – was establishing himself as the dominant figure at the imperial court. Finally, in September 867, he seized the throne itself. Michael III was murdered on 21 September, and Basil was promptly proclaimed emperor – the emperor Basil I. Within days the old regime was cleared out. Photios was deposed on 25 September, and Ignatios restored to the patriarchal throne.[178]

The end of Boris' manoeuvring was always most likely to be a *rapprochement* with Constantinople. Germany was too far away, the papacy could offer no military help, while shared religion might deter Byzantine aggression. In any case the bulk of the qaghan's Christian subjects were Greek-speaking and already had ties with the Byzantine church. But what the evidence shows

Boris wanted was a church that, although subordinate to the patriarch of Constantinople or the pope in Rome, would nonetheless be autonomous. Anything less would hardly be acceptable to the dignity of the qaghanate.[179] Before 867 neither Photios nor Pope Nicholas was willing to make this concession, but the new regime in Constantinople wanted to come to terms, and the autonomy of the Bulgar church was a small price to pay to prevent Boris joining the western church. The decisive moment came at the Oecumenical Council of 869–70 which had been called by Basil I and Ignatios to settle Photios' schism with Rome. The Council was held in Constantinople in the presence of three papal legates. They were there to approve the resumption of communion between the two churches, and seem to have been taken wholly by surprise when the Byzantines and Bulgars stage-managed the appearance of a Bulgar delegation who asked the Council to decide whether they owed obedience to Rome or Constantinople. Packed with Byzantine bishops the answer was inevitable, and the papal legates could do nothing save protest.[180] Papal dissatisfaction rumbled on through the 870s, but with a growing Arab threat in southern Italy that made Byzantine military support a priority, the subordination of the Bulgar church to Constantinople was a *fait accompli*.

Boris thus gained an autonomous church under an archbishop of Bulgaria. The reality of this autonomy was reinforced in the later ninth century by the adoption of a Slav liturgy. This came about as a consequence of the Byzantine mission that Michael III had sent to Moravia in 863. Its leaders had been two Slav-speaking brothers from Thessalonica, Constantine (often known by his religious name of Cyril) and Methodios. Constantine had devised an alphabet for the Slav language, later known as 'Glagolitic', and a literary form of the language – Old Church Slavonic – into which he translated the liturgy of St John Chrysostom, some of the essential daily offices, the Psalter and the New Testament. On this basis the brothers set up a native Moravian church using Slavonic rather than the two established liturgical languages of Latin and Greek. Constantine died in 869 in Rome were the brothers had gone to receive papal approval for their Slavonic liturgy, but pope Hadrian could do little to protect Methodios once he had returned to Moravia. In 870 the mission's patron, Rstislav, was overthrown by his nephew, Zwentibald, operating with German help. Methodios was arrested, tried by a German synod in Regensburg and imprisoned in Swabia. He was released in 873 and returned to Moravia, but Zwentibald was no longer very interested in a Byzantine alliance nor in a Moravian Slavonic church. Methodios died in April 885, and by the end of the year Zwentibald had expelled his disciples.

Boris accepted these refugees with enthusiasm and sent them to establish a Slavonic church in the newly conquered Sklaviniai around Ohrid in Macedonia. The mission was a great success; by the end of the ninth century the Bulgar church had widely adopted the Slavonic liturgy, and for the future, Bulgar culture and identity was to be closely tied to Old Church Slavonic.[181] It is worth noting, however, that this development was apparently accidental. Boris accepted the Slavonic liturgy because it was not Greek, it already existed, and had been approved by Rome and Constantinople. The choice of Slavonic does not necessarily imply that the Bulgars had been so Slavicised by the 860s that it was no longer a Turkic culture. There is not enough evidence to prove the point either way, but it seems probable that Slavicisation of the Bulgar élite was more a gradual consequence of the adoption of the Slavonic liturgy than a cause.

Boris retired to a monastery in 889, leaving the throne to his eldest son, Vladimir. Rumour in distant Lorraine had it that Vladimir inaugurated a pagan revival that forced Boris to come out of retirement in 893, overthrow Vladimir whom he blinded, and replace him with his younger brother, Symeon. Since there is no corroboration for this story it is much more likely that Vladimir died of natural causes. One would otherwise have expected at least an allusion in Byzantine sources to the events that brought his brother to power.[182]

Symeon was arguably the most successful of the Bulgar qaghans. He surmounted a series of crises to achieve recognition of Bulgaria as an empire on an equal footing with the Roman, and to inaugurate forty years of peace between Byzantium and the Bulgars. Yet this achievement has often been overlooked. As usual the problem is one of inadequate sources. There may once have been Bulgar histories written like the Proto-Bulgar inscriptions in Greek. But the destruction of the Bulgar state in the eleventh century, and the shift from a

Bulgarian church and laity literate in Greek to one literate in Old Church Slavonic left no one with an interest in preserving such texts. Hence, barring a few inscriptions and some slight information from western authors, we are dependent on the Byzantine materials. These consist in the first place of the various versions of the Logothete's Chronicle. Preoccupied with Byzantine court politics, the chronicler detests the Bulgars and presents Symeon as a rabid barbarian. His account is obviously unreliable but nonetheless provides the essential narrative on which all the modern secondary accounts are based. More important, but also more subtle in their misinformation, are the letters of the patriarch Nicholas Mystikos. As mentioned in Chapter 1, these are not an archival collection, but instead a carefully doctored selection of materials designed to show Nicholas in the best light as a stylist, as a man of piety and principle, and as a brilliant diplomat who manipulated the uncouth barbarian Symeon. As such they form in effect the documentary justification for the official line taken by the emperor Romanos Lekapenos and his regime in the later 920s – which is independently known thanks to the survival of a speech delivered at the imperial court on the peace with Bulgaria in 927.[183] What relationship Nicholas' collected letters bear to what he originally wrote, what has been omitted and what rewritten, is now impossible to say, but the convenient correlation between the surviving letters and the speech – which represents what was politically correct a few years after Nicholas' death in 925 – makes it almost inconceivable that this is really what the patriarch thought and wrote under very different political circumstances ten years earlier. As so often when working with Byzantine sources, one has to keep an open mind, and be alert to where one may be being misled.

Symeon's first crisis grew from a minor Bulgar campaign in Macedonia in 894, said to have been provoked by a trade dispute, but probably undertaken more with a view to establishing the military credentials of the new regime. In the event the Bulgars inflicted a stinging defeat on a Byzantine force that included sections of the emperor's bodyguard. The humiliation was made worse and turned into a major political issue that demanded a response when some Khazars serving in the regiment were sent back to Constantinople mutilated with their noses slit. Since the main Byzantine forces were deployed in the east, the emperor Leo VI (886–912) turned to the Magyars, as the traditional Byzantine allies on the western steppes, to punish the Bulgars. In 895 a fleet was sent to the Danube to ferry the nomad cavalry across, and those land forces available in the west were sent to Thrace to keep Bulgar attention fixed on their southern frontier. Symeon was caught entirely off-guard. The Magyars ravaged Bulgaria and defeated the qaghan's armies three times before withdrawing to the north. Meanwhile imperial envoys had established a truce with the Arabs in the east, allowing the major units of the Byzantine field army to be transferred to the western front in preparation for a full-scale invasion of the weakened qaghanate. But yet again the Bulgars proved to be resilient opponents. Symeon countered the Magyar threat by appealing to the Pečenegs who drove the Magyars from the Ukrainian steppe to take refuge on the Hungarian plain. With the Magyars otherwise occupied Symeon was able to concentrate on the Byzantine army invading from the south, and in 896 at Bulgarophygon near Adrianople the Bulgars won an important victory. The treaty which followed confirmed Bulgar domination of the Balkans, and to emphasise this the Byzantines agreed to make an annual payment to the qaghan which Symeon no doubt presented as tribute. Yet the fact that Symeon was willing to restore 30 forts that his troops had captured in the general area of Albania suggests that Bulgarophygon had not left the Byzantines helpless, and that he too was keen to make peace. The three-year war had been a Bulgar victory, but at a price in ravaged territory which emphasised how exposed Bulgaria still was to Byzantine aggression.[184]

The remaining years of Leo VI's reign were from a Bulgar point of view a period of peaceful consolidation. The capital was transferred from Pliska to Great Preslav, about 60 kilometres to the south-west but still to the north of the Haimos mountains. Major building work continued there for several decades, including a lavishly decorated palace, and a number of churches, one of which, the Round Church, seems to have taken its plan from that of the Prophet Elijah in Constantinople, put up in the Great Palace by the emperor Basil I in the 870s.[185] In 904 Thessalonica was sacked by an Arab fleet after a three-day siege. As they withdrew the Bulgars may temporarily have occupied the city, but they did not stay, and a boundary stone found 22 kilometres north of Thessalonica bearing the date 904 seems to mark the qaghanate's souther frontier.[186]

In 912 Leo died, leaving a young son – Constantine VII Porphyrogenitos – who was not yet seven. Leo was succeeded as emperor by his brother, Alexander, who followed a familiar pattern of new regimes on both sides of the frontier and provoked a war with the Bulgars. But in just over a year Alexander was also dead, leaving political chaos as a hastily arranged regency council led by the patriarch Nicholas Mystikos tried to deal with a Bulgar army that by August 913 was besieging Constantinople. Exactly what happened next is a mystery, but it is certain that negotiations took place at which the regents agreed to some major concession, and that following that Nicholas himself went outside the walls to meet Symeon and carry out some form of coronation. In the event whatever was granted proved to be a liability both for Nicholas and his co-regents, and for later Byzantine diplomacy. As a result any explicit reference to the 'coronation' was weeded from Nicholas' letter collection, and the official line proclaimed in the speech on the 927 peace with Bulgaria, and repeated in the Logothete's Chronicle, was that the coronation had been a deliberate sham, performed by a canny patriarch to get rid of a dangerous barbarian at a moment of Byzantine weakness.[187]

There seem to be four possibilities of what the coronation actually implied at the time. One would be that Symeon was merely being adopted as the emperor's spiritual son. A second would be that he was being brought within the Byzantine hierarchy with the same rank of 'caesar' that the qaghan Tervel had been granted by the emperor Justinian II in the early eighth century. A third would be a variation on this. It seems from one of Nicholas' later letters that the young Constantine was to be betrothed to one of Symeon's daughters. Perhaps therefore Symeon was being crowned as the official imperial father-in-law – the *basileopater*: a potentially key position in court politics. Yet none of these seems important or shocking enough to demand the silence in Nicolas' letters and the later historical tradition. They would only bring Symeon any new authority if he were to come to Constantinople and operate within the world of Byzantine palace politics. Rumour known to the Italian Liudprand of Cremona in the mid-tenth century had it that Symeon had been educated in Constantinople as a boy, but he never entered the city as qaghan and there is nothing to suggest that he ever considered it. The fourth possibility, and much the most likely, is that Symeon was actually in 913 being crowned emperor of the Bulgars.[188]

The title – which Symeon did use[189] – would have been the natural culmination of Bulgar policy since the 860s, and indeed in some ways since their arrival in the Balkans in the seventh century. As Christian rulers the title of 'qaghan' had lost much of its charismatic content, while that of 'emperor' would assimilate the rank and pretensions of the qaghanal title to the Christian Byzantine hierarchy. The coronation did not break any fundamental concept of Byzantine political thinking. The *basileos*, or 'emperor' of the Romans stood at the pinnacle of legitimate secular authority, but the title was not unique. Within the imperial court in Constantinople there were often several emperors at once arranged in a collegiate hierarchy. During the last years of Leo VI's life, for example, Leo himself, his younger brother Alexander, and his young son Constantine were all emperors; and thoughout the early middle ages it is common for Byzantine coins to show a row of figures each bearing the imperial insignia. Even outside Constantinople the title was not unique. From the late third century to the fifth century there had been eastern and western Roman emperors; and from 812 the Byzantines recognised the existence of a Carolingian emperor in the west.[190]

Symeon's success was tarnished by the fact that his title had not been granted by an established adult male emperor but by a politically insecure regency council. Early in 914 Nicholas and his colleagues were toppled in a coup led by Constantine's mother, Zoe, who almost immediately tried to overturn the 913 agreement. Symeon responded by raiding Thrace where the Armenian commander of Adrianople handed the city over to the Bulgars, and Zoe was forced to come to terms. An embassy, headed by the Keeper of the Imperial Inkstand – always a key figure at the imperial court – went to Symeon with 'many gifts'. The 913 treaty was confirmed, and in return the Bulgars handed back Adrianople.[191]

In spite of this successful defence of Bulgar interests which
was followed by two-years peace, Symeon's underlying problem
remained. The new regime was jut as shaky as its predecessor.
Zoe – known as *Karbonopsina*, 'with the coal-black eyes' – had
been Leo VI's mistress until she gave birth to his only son,
Constantine. The scandal of the subsequent marriage – Leo's
fourth – had split the church into two factions, one led by
Nicholas, the other by a rival patriarch, Euthymios, appointed
by Leo VI in 907. With this background Zoe badly needed the
legitimacy that victory over the Bulgars could give. A truce was
patched up in the east, envoys were sent to the pagan Pečenegs,
and in 917 a totally unprovoked and savage assault was launched
on Christian Bulgaria. God, however, clearly disapproved. A
fleet sent to the Danube failed to ferry the Pečenegs across
the river, and the main field armies of the east marching up
the Black Sea coast suffered at Achelous the most catastrophic
Byzantine defeat since the emperor Nikephoros' Bulgar campaign of just over a century before.[192]

Like Krum after 811, Symeon faced a fundamental dilemma.
His armies could not force their way through the triple land-
walls of Constantinople; while inside the city there was no authoritative government with whom he could negotiate. Zoe's regime
staggered on until the beginning of 919 when it was finally
toppled in a coup headed by her old enemy, Nicholas Mystikos.
The patriarch's authority was equally fragile, and from the end
of March onwards the real power in the palace was the *droungarios*
of the fleet, Romanos Lekapenos. (The same who had failed
to bring the Pečenegs across the Danube in 917.) On 27 April
919 – to the horror of his main rival, the domestic of the scholai,
Leo Phokas – Romanos married his daughter, Helena, to the
young emperor Constantine thus making himself *basileopater*.
Leo Phokas' strength lay in the tagma regiments based outside
the city, but once he had lost control of the palace and the
emperor his support soon crumbled. Within a few months, Leo
had been arrested and blinded. For the rest of 919 and 920
Romanos rode out a series of counter-plots and reinforced his
hold on power, until on 17 December 920 Romanos was crowned
emperor in his own right. Constantine Porphyrogenitos survived but only as a silent and junior partner.[193]

During this period military operations continued at a low

level. Nicholas' letters point to 'talks about talks', and the *De Administrando Imperio* suggests that Symeon was preoccupied during 919 and 920 with preventing a Byzantine attempt to install an anti-Bulgar ruler in Serbia. After Romanos' coronation the tempo increased. Romanos himself seems to have believed that the restoration of church unity achieved by the so-called 'Tomos of Union' in July 920 would gain God's favour and produce military victory. But the following years proved him wrong. Byzantine forces in Thrace suffered a series of bloody defeats and Symeon's armies ravaged up to the walls of Constantinople burning several famous suburban palaces and churches. During these years Symeon seems to have made contact with the Muslim rulers of North Africa and Tarsos in an attempt to find an ally who would provide his forces with naval support. By 923 or 924, however (the date is controversial and cannot be decided on the basis of the evidence available), both parties were wiling to negotiate and a summit meeting was arranged. Neither side trusted the other, and to avoid any threat of an ambush the two leaders met on a specially constructed jetty built in the Golden Horn at Kosmidion, about 1 kilometre beyond the walls of Constantinople which Symeon could reach by land and to which Romanos could sail in a warship.[194]

What was said on the jetty is completely unknown. The account given in the Logothete's Chronicle which has sometimes been quoted as if it were a verbatim text is nothing but official Byzantine wishful thinking composed after the event. The only clue comes at the end of the Logothete's account: 'They say that two eagles flew overhead while the emperors were meeting and cried out and copulated and that they immediately separated from each other and one went towards the city while the other flew towards Thrace.' The Logothete, writing in the 960s, then goes on to interpret this as a bad omen, but that sounds very much like hindsight. The portent of two eagles is just the sort of rhetorical image one would expect to find in a court panegyric and its obvious implication – underlined by the fact that the Logothete calls Symeon 'emperor' – is that a peace was agreed and that Romanos recognised Symeon's imperial title and his equal status to the emperor in Constantinople.[195]

This extraordinary triumph of Bulgar arms and diplomacy

was limited in Symeon's lifetime by Romanos' failure to ratify the treaty. Three surviving letters from Romanos to Symeon show the Byzantines willing to pay an annual tribute, but making difficulties over territory and over the form of Symeon's imperial title. Symeon seems to have called himself 'emperor of the Bulgars and Romans'. 'Emperor of the Bulgars' was no problem. The Byzantines recognised the Carolingians and their Ottonian successors in the west as 'emperors of the Franks', but since 812 imperial protocol had explicitly reserved the formula, 'emperor of the Romans', for the emperor in Constantinople. In none of these letters is there any indication that Symeon implied by this title a claim to the imperial city or to any other of Romanos' territories. It seems much more likely that for Symeon it represented an explicit recognition of his rightful authority over his 'Roman' subjects inside the Bulgar state, and also of the legitimacy of his rule over lands that up to the seventh century had been part of the Roman empire. For Romanos the delay was worthwhile, partly because the title embodied a real issue of imperial primacy, but also because Symeon was now an old man, he had four sons, and his death could be expected to inaugurate a period of dissension and military weakness in Bulgaria.[196]

Symeon died on 27 May 927. But otherwise Byzantine hopes were not fulfilled. Symeon's eldest son by his second marriage, Peter, successfully established himself, intimidated his Slav enemies to the west and launched a raid into Byzantine territory. Romanos, now increasingly preoccupied with the eastern front, had no wish to restart a major Bulgar war and rapidly made peace. Peter was to marry Romanos' granddaughter, Maria; he was to receive an annual tribute – which the Byzantines chose to describe as a maintenance payment for Maria; Bulgar control of the Sklavinai of Macedonia was recognised; and an exchange of prisoners was agreed. The Bulgar ruler was recognised as an emperor, and Symeon's previous (but undated) establishment of the Bulgarian church under its own patriarch was also recognised. In return Peter agreed to the title of 'emperor of the Bulgars', and recognised Romanos' imperial primacy by referring to him as his 'spiritual father'.[197]

The years which followed the peace of 927 through to 965 can be seen as the golden age of the Bulgar state. Boris, Symeon and Peter had successfully led the Bulgars through the transition from a steppe nomad to a sedentary state which the Avars and Khazars before them had failed to survive. Some evidence for Bulgar culture at this period comes from Kastoria (now in northern Greece but then in Bulgar territory) where three small churches date to the late ninth or early tenth century, and one more was probably built at the beginning of the eleventh century before the Byzantine conquest. The Kastoria churches imply a wealthy, settled and Christian world. If the traditional date for the Slavonic treatise of Kosmas the Priest in the second half of the tenth century were secure, then this picture might be extended with confidence to the rest of the Bulgar lands. Kosmas' treatise against the Bogomils is best known as one of the key sources for these heretical Balkan dualists, who believed the visible material world was a creation of the devil, but the treatise also gives a vivid picture of contemporary Bulgaria. It describes a wealthy, book-owning, monastery-founding Bulgar élite behaving just as their Byzantine equivalents across the frontier. Unfortunately Kosmas' dates are controversial. The tenth-century is possible, but the case for the early thirteenth century is equally strong. Kosmas' description of Bulgaria, however, is no evidence either way. It would fit the thirteenth century, but it could also describe the new Bulgar empire during the tenth-century peace.[198]

Yet fundamental strategic problems remained. The Bulgar state was still ringed by aggressive neighbours who were all potential enemies. Beyond the Danube were the Pečenegs and Magyars, and further to the north-east was the growing power of the Rus; to the west and north-west were the Serbs and Croats – the latter in particular had inflicted a sharp defeat on a Bulgar army in Symeon's last years.[199] To the south and south-east was Byzantium which, despite the current peace, nearly three centuries of experience had proved to be a dangerous and unreliable neighbour.

Byzantine sources mention Magyar raids reaching the empire in 934, 943, 958 and 961, and evidently these must have passed through Bulgar territory on their way; in 944 the *Povest'* records a Pečeneg raid across the Danube; and there were probably other unrecorded incursions.[200] Yet none of these need have bean very serious. The Magyar invasion of Bulgaria in

895 had no apparent effect on Symeon's ability to defeat a major Byzantine field army in the following year. Perhaps more alarming for the Bulgars was the rebuilding of the traditional alliance between the Magyars and Byzantium broken when they had been driven from the Ukrainian steppes on to the Hungarian plain by the Pečenegs after 895. Magyar rulers were baptised in Constantinople in about 948 and 952, and on the second occasion a Byzantine monk was sent back to become bishop of *Tourkia* – Hungary – where 'he converted many to the faith'. Like the similar alliance with the Moravians in the same area in the 860s, these ties opened the possibility of co-ordinated attacks from north and south against the Bulgars. Not surprisingly Peter sent envoys to the German king Otto I in 965 – again echoing the diplomatic manoeuvres of a hundred years before.[201]

However, the crisis which finally overwhelmed the Bulgar state did not come from either of its steppe nomad neighbours. In 965 or 966 Bulgar ambassadors arrived at the court of the emperor Nikephoros Phokas (963–9) to collect the annual tribute. Perhaps this was no more than the usual annual tribute-collecting mission, but it may also have been an attempt to take advantage of Byzantine preoccupations elsewhere. In any case it proved to be a disastrous *casus belli*. Nikephoros fresh from victories in the east, refused to make any payment; and after a military demonstration on the Bulgar frontier in Thrace, turned to his northern ally, Svyatoslav, the ruler of the Kievan Rus, to intimidate the Bulgars.[202] In August 967 Svyatoslav crossed the Danube and (see the previous section of this chapter: The Rus) captured the Bulgar capital of Preslav, where he spent the winter. In 968 he returned to Kiev to fend off a Pečeneg attack. There is no reason to believe that this had been encouraged by the Byzantines, but it certainly suited imperial policy that Svyatoslav did not stay too long in the Balkans.

Peter was now keen to make peace with the Byzantines on Nikephoros' terms, and Luidprand of Cremona, acting as Otto I's ambassador to Constantinople, witnessed the friendly treatment of the Bulgar envoys during June and July 968 which betokened the current good relations between Byzantium and the Bulgars. As a guarantee, Peter's two sons, Boris and Romanos, were sent to Constantinople; and a marriage was planned be-

tween two Bulgar princesses and the late Constantine Porphyrogenitos' two grandsons, Basil and Constantine – then ten and
eight years old respectively. Nikephoros Phokas had thus achieved
security on his western front, allowing him to deploy all his
resources in the east.[203] But this situation lasted only a few
months. At the beginning of 969 the emperor Peter died, and
later in the year Svyatoslav returned. Within a few months the
Bulgar state had collapsed, and Nikephoros was faced with the
real possibility of a Rus state in the Balkans. At the same time
Svyatoslav was said to be backing Nikephoros' former ambassador, the patrikios Kalokyros, in an attempt on the imperial
throne.[204]

Nikephoros could do little at once since the main Byzantine
field forces were actively engaged in the east. Then on 11
December 969 he was murdered in a palace coup by a rival
general, John Tzimiskes, who promptly seized the throne.
Meanwhile Svyatoslav seems to have consolidated his position
in Bulgaria. Late in 969 or early in 970 his forces crossed the
Haimos mountains, and captured Philippopolis (modern Plovdiv),
the key Bulgar fortress in eastern Thrace. By-passing well-defended Byzantine Adrianople (modern Edirne), the Rus then
passed on along the main road to Constantinople. Whether
this was simply a typical Viking Rus raid for booty, or was indeed a deliberate attempt to install Kalokyros in Constantinople
is impossible to say. In the event the new emperor's brother-
in-law, Bardas Skleros, gathered a scratch army and finally
stopped the Rus advance at Arkadioupolis (modern Lüle Burgaz)
less than 80 kilometres from the imperial city.[205]

Svyatoslav retreated north of the Haimos, but the Byzantines
were prevented from following up their victory by continuing
resistance from the surviving members of the Phokas family to
the accession of Nikephoros' murderer. It was not until the
spring of 971 that John Tzimiskes was able to send a fleet to
the Danube, and himself lead the major units of the eastern
field army against Svyatoslav.[206]

The campaign which followed ended in a complete Byzantine victory. The Rus do not seem to have been numerous
enough to face the emperor's forces in open battle, and hence
the fighting centred on two hard-fought sieges. The first was
of the Bulgar capital, Great Preslav, which fell on 13 April; the

second was of Dristra (also known as Dorostolon, modern Silistra) on the Danube, where in July 971 Svyatoslav was forced to surrender on terms. For the Bulgar royal family the events were a disaster. Peter's sons, Boris and Romanos, seem to have been sent back to Bulgaria as soon as news of their father's death had reached Constantinople, but they were soon captured by Svyatoslav, and stayed as Rus prisoners in Preslav until the city fell to the Byzantines in April 971. Initially John Tzimiskes seems to have recognised Boris as emperor of the Bulgars, but after the fall of Dristra he had clearly changed his mind. John's triumphant return to Constantinople was carefully stage-managed to produce the maximum political capital for a regime whose power had begun in murder. Met by the patriarch, and a crowd of ecclesiastical and lay dignitaries at the Golden Gate at the southern end of the land walls, John rode in procession on a white horse, behind a triumphal wagon which bore a captured icon of the Virgin and the Bulgar imperial regalia. Behind the emperor rode the Bulgar emperor Boris. When they had ridden the $2\frac{1}{2}$ kilometres through the city to the Forum of Constantine the procession halted, and against a background of chanting hymns of thanksgiving to the Mother of God and to Christ, and in full view of the assembled citizens of Constantinople, Boris was symbolically divested of his regalia as emperor of the Bulgars. The procession then moved on to Hagia Sophia, where the Bulgarian crown was given to God, and Boris was 'raised up' to the rank of *magistros*.[207]

This was not the end of the Bulgar empire. John Tzimiskes, like Nikephoros Phokas before him, was more interested in the east, and there is no evidence of a co-ordinated campaign to establish imperial control in the Balkans. The Byzantines appear to have taken over the existing Bulgar fortifications on the Lower Danube and established military governors at Dristra and in the Dobrudja. There was also a Byzantine *strategos* at Preslav – now renamed Ioannoupolis after the emperor John. The large number of lead seals found on the site certainly points to administrative activity, but the fact that the post was filled as a joint command with the existing theme of Thrace suggests a rather *ad hoc* arrangement. Otherwise the rest of Bulgaria was apparently left to its own devices, and in the far west surviving elements of the Bulgar élite were able to regroup.[208]

Their leaders were the four sons of a certain Count Nicholas – David, Moses, Aaron and Samuel – known together as the *Kometopouloi*, 'the sons of the count'. (Nicholas is said to have been an Armenian, which if true would serve to emphasise the ethnic diversity of the Bulgar élite.) David and Moses were killed in 976, Aaron died in 987 or 988 by which date Samuel was well established as the *de facto* ruler of the Bulgars. The titular emperor, however, seems to have been Romanos, the second of Peter's two sons. On John Tzimiskes' death in 976 it seems that Boris and his brother Romanos had escaped from Constantinople where they had been for the last five years. At the Bulgar frontier Boris was accidentally killed by a guard who failed to recognise him. Romanos survived and according to Yahya ibn Saʿīd, the Christian Arabic historian who reports the most likely version of events, he was crowned emperor, presumably by the patriarch of Bulgaria (now re-established in the west). In 991 Romanos was captured by the Byzantines and taken to Constantinople. Only on his death in captivity in 997 did Samuel finally become the next emperor of the Bulgars.[209]

Yet even if the Bulgar state had survived, the events of 967–71 marked a fundamental break in Bulgar history, and opened a new phase in Byzantine involvement in the Balkans. Once John Tzimiskes had taken the decision to stage a public humiliation of Boris and a symbolic ending of the Bulgar empire, his successors would find it almost impossible to go back to a Bulgar–Byzantine relationship based on the near equality of two empires. Once Romanos and then Samuel had been proclaimed emperor, the Byzantines were almost bound by the implications of John's ceremonies to enforce imperial sovereignty over them. With very little room for compromise this dilemma opened the way for nearly forty years of increasingly bitter warfare.

There is another aspect of the events of 967–71 that is worth stressing. The collapse of Bulgar resistance in 969 does not necessarily indicate any particular fault or prior weakness in the Bulgar state, over and above those inherent in all early medieval societies. As with Ostrogothic Italy in the sixth century, the late Roman east in the seventh century, Visigothic Spain in the eighth century, or Anglo-Saxon England in the eleventh century, historians have traditionally been quick to read into their final conquest a picture of a state ripe for disaster. It has been a theme of this section that the Bulgars had dangerous neighbours; and all early medieval states characterised as they were by small ruling élites were liable to political collapse in the face of invasion. An obvious example is the fall of Anglo-Saxon England after the battle of Hastings. The Bulgars in 967–71 were hampered by Peter's death and the usual problems of a succession that deprived them of effective leadership, and they were facing in the Viking Rus a formidable enemy which it is useful to remember they were not alone among ninth- and tenth-century states in finding very difficult to resist. What made their position worse, however, was the role of Byzantium. The Bulgar state had prospered in the Balkans as long as the empire was preoccupied elsewhere. As the strategic balance altered in the east from the later ninth century onwards so – as in the 590s – the Byzantines were gaining the freedom to choose where to deploy their military resources. Even without the incentive of Svyatoslav's invasion Byzantium's militaristic rulers would always have been likely sooner or later to think of Bulgaria as a traditional enemy and an ancient part of the empire due for reconquest. Under such circumstances the outlook for the Bulgar state was not good.

The Western Provinces

In 600 substantial areas of the western Mediterranean were still ruled from Constantinople. These included a large area of North Africa (equivalent to roughly half of what is now modern Tunisia), a small strip of southern Spain centred on Cartagena and the islands of Corsica, Sardinia and Sicily. On the Italian mainland about one third of the peninsula was imperial territory under the authority of the governor (described, as was the governor of Africa, as the *exarch*) whose capital was at Ravenna. The exarchate included the lands around the mouth of the River Po, part of the coastline to the north and a block of territory to the south which linked Ravenna to the other main imperial enclave around Rome where the former imperial capital was effectively administered by the pope. In the north-west a strip of the Ligurian coast centred on Genoa, and in the south an enclave around Naples and much of what is now known as Calabria and Apulia were also imperial territory. The rest of the peninsula was ruled by the Lombards who, since their arrival in 568, had created a powerful kingdom in the north with its capital at Pavia, and an autonomous duchy of Benevento which dominated much of the south.

None of these territories was of prime importance for Constantinople. Even in the sixth century the west had been secondary to the demands of the eastern frontier, and often tertiary behind the Balkan peninsula which could demand attention if only because of its closeness to the imperial capital on the Bosphorus. In 600 the military situation in the west was already fragile and the disasters which overwhelmed the empire in the east during the decades which followed inevitably prevented any effective intervention. In Spain the Byzantines were expelled in 624 when the Visigoths conquered Cartagena. In Italy Lombard expansion continued broken only by temporary truces. Most of the remaining territory north of the Po was lost in the first half of the century leaving little more than the islands in the coastal lagoon at the head of the Adriatic where Venice would develop, first as a refuge from the Lombards, and then from the first half of the eighth century as an autonomous Byzantine duchy. Liguria was conquered in about 643; and in the south the Lombards seized Salerno from the duchy of Naples and overran Apulia. Corsica was also lost to the Lombards, and although Sardinia survived as an autonomous Byzantine duchy whose church apparently recognised the authority of Constantinople rather than Rome (presumably to avoid exploitation at the hands of Roman aristocrats acting as agents of the pope) imperial rule was otherwise entirely nominal. In Africa, open to Arab attack from the east after the loss of Egypt in 642, the end came with the fall of Carthage in 698.

Yet even with little more than Sicily and a shrinking portion of the Italian mainland there were still important ties linking Constantinople to what survived of its western provinces. In the first place there was a shared sense of a 'Roman' identity. On the provincial side this could involve looking to Constantinople for leadership and defence, and for the rewards and status of imperial titles and salaries. In Constantinople this evoked

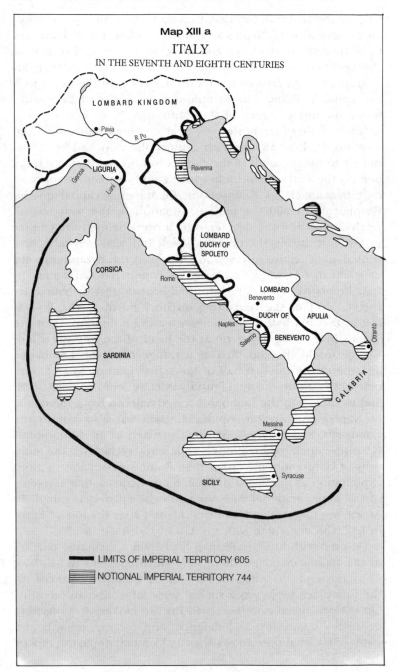

Map XIII a

ITALY

IN THE SEVENTH AND EIGHTH CENTURIES

LOMBARD KINGDOM

Pavia

R Po

Genoa

LIGURIA

Luni

Ravenna

LOMBARD
DUCHY OF
SPOLETO

CORSICA

Rome

LOMBARD

Benevento

DUCHY OF

Naples

APULIA

Salerno

BENEVENTO

Otranto

SARDINIA

CALABRIA

Messina

SICILY

Syracuse

▬▬▬ LIMITS OF IMPERIAL TERRITORY 605

≣≣≣ NOTIONAL IMPERIAL TERRITORY 744

Map XIII b

ITALY
c 980

LIMITS OF IMPERIAL TERRITORY

A LONGOBARDIA

B CALABRIA

TERRITORIES OF FĀTIMID CALIPH

PRINCIPALITY OF CAPUA-BENEVENTO

PRINCIPALITY OF SALERNO

ITALIAN TERRITORIES OF THE GERMAN EMPEROR OTTO II

PAPAL PATRIMONY

a surprisingly durable sense that these were territories that the emperor had a right and a duty to rule. In mainland Italy this sense was further reinforced by the existence of the city of Rome and its bishop, the pope. Even when Constantinople did not accept in full papal claims to ecclesiastical primacy throughout the empire, the pope was still accorded a primacy of honour among the five patriarchates of Rome, Constantinople, Alexandria, Antioch and Jerusalem. In the late Roman church councils on whose decisions Constantinopolitan orthodoxy was based the popes had played a key part, and for successive emperors struggling to rebuild a relationship with God that would bring victory to the Christian forces, tradition and intellectual coherence demanded that any new doctrinal decision received papal assent. Finally the eastern emperors were encouraged to look west by the prospects of wealth to be exploited. In Italy, as war-torn as Asia Minor, this was only to be obtained at the expense of bitter local protest, but the surprisingly abundant seventh-century gold and copper coinage found on Sicily suggests that here at least imperial hopes were not unrealistic.[210]

At the same time powerful forces were also pulling Constantinople and the west apart. Most obviously there was a cultural division between the Greek-speaking east and the predominantly Latin west that was accentuated in the seventh and eight centuries as the Byzantine state struggling for survival was cut down to an inward-looking Greek core. Sicily was again something of an exception as a predominantly Greek-speaking island, but outside Calabria mainland Italy was very largely Latin, and before 698 Byzantine Africa had been a Latin culture too. The division was made worse in the seventh and eighth centuries by imperial attempts to create a new religious order. Both monotheletism and iconoclasm were responses to eastern problems – respectively the need to come to terms with the Monophysites and to halt the Arab advance – which meant little to westerners who felt their orthodox identity threatened by these impious novelties whose subtleties were often lost in a language they did not understand. Greek-speaking Sicily and Calabria were more amenable to imperial control, but neither doctrine was accepted in Rome which became a temporary refuge for dissenters from the east. The schism over monotheletism lasted less than fifty years and in the midst of it the monothelete emperor, Constans II (641–68), attended mass with the pope in St Peter's without difficulty, but iconoclasm lasted the greater part of the eighth century and much of the first half of the ninth, and during that period the emperors in Constantinople were repeatedly denounced as wicked persecutors. Leo III (717–41) widened the gulf by confiscating papal properties in Sicily, southern Italy and Illyricum (the western Balkans), and transferring the ecclesiastical provinces of Illyricum and Sicily from the authority of the papacy to that of the patriarch in Constantinople.[211]

These divisions could probably have been bridged but would have demanded an active Constantinopolitan involvement in the west and increasingly over the seventh and eighth centuries this the east failed to give. With imperial forces committed to defending Asia Minor from the Arabs, the Italians and Africans were largely left to defend themselves. Even when Constans II came to the west in 663 as the last emperor to visit Rome the military results of his expedition were meagre, and other campaigns led by the exarchs had no greater success. Expectation had been that Constans II had come to drive out the Lombards – repeating the sixth-century reconquista of Italy from the Ostrogoths – but in the event he failed even to take Benevento, and what struck the near contemporary compiler of this section of the collection of papal biographies known as the *Liber Pontificalis* was not a military event at all, but the emperor's plunder of Rome for its bronze decorations (including the metal tiles of the Pantheon) and the dreadful taxes he imposed on all his western territories.[212] Imperial authority and its most practical manifestation, taxation, was only acceptable if in return the empire provided security. In Africa Arab conquest came before any move towards autonomy could make much progress, but in Italy the tax revolt of 727 when 'scorning the exarch's arrangement, they all elected their own dukes, and in this way tried to achieve freedom for the Pope and themselves', was a decisive event from which imperial authority outside Sicily and the south never recovered.[213]

After 727 Byzantine Italy north of Calabria was essentially independent, and if one hesitates to use that term it is only because the popes, who were the effective leaders of non-Lombard Italy, had as yet nothing to put in the emperor's place, and the increasing pressure from a succession of hostile and successful Lombard kings made the need for outside protection ever greater. A crucial point was reached in 751 when the Lombard king Aistulf finally conquered Ravenna, and in the following years began seriously to threaten Rome. Byzantine help was out of the question. Aside from the fact that Constantine V was a wicked iconoclast, the emperor himself had no more realistic policy of recovering Ravenna than to persuade the pope to intervene with Aistulf on his behalf. The only option if Rome was not to be conquered by the Lombards was to look elsewhere, and in 753 – brushing aside a last minute Byzantine diplomatic attempt to hold him back – Pope Stephen II crossed the Alps to meet the Frankish king, Pepin III.[214]

The Franks were the dominant military power in eighth-century western Europe, and their alliance with the papacy amounted to a diplomatic and political revolution. Pepin invaded Italy twice in 754 or 755 and again in 756, the same year that Aistulf died. The Lombards were defeated and Ravenna and the lands of the former exarchate transferred to papal rule. Internal problems within the Frankish kingdom allowed the Lombards to recover, but in 773 in the face of a new Lombard threat to Rome, Pepin's son and successor, Charlemagne, was persuaded by Pope Hadrian I to come his aid. In 774 Pavia was conquered and the Lombard kingdom brought to an end as Charlemagne crowned himself king of Italy. The final step was taken on Christmas Day 800 when Pope Leo III crowned Charlemagne emperor of the Romans.[215]

The event did not apparently cause the horror in Constantinople that historians have sometimes suggested. Theophanes, writing here as a contemporary, shows no particular alarm at Charlemagne's coronation, and Einhard (the contemporary Frankish biographer of Charlemagne) was probably right in thinking that the principal Byzantine fear came from an initial assumption that anyone who was crowned must be a rebel and intend to march on Constantinople. Even so Charlemagne's imperial coronation stands as a symbolic event of great significance, marking a crucial stage in the division of Byzantium and the west, and the final replacement of an axis between Old Rome and New Rome, with one between the papacy and northern Europe.[216]

Irene, the empress at the time of the coronation in 800, was deposed in 802 and her successor, Nikephoros I, refused to recognise Charlemagne's title. The refusal was almost certainly not on grounds of principle but a display of the new regime's toughness in contrast with Irene's 'feminine weakness', and was intended for internal consumption. By 812 Frankish pressure on what remained of Byzantine territory in Italy, and Nikephoros' disastrous death at the hands of the Bulgars in the previous year, had persuaded Michael I (811–13) to come to terms. At the Frankish court at Aachen Byzantine ambassadors acclaimed Charlemagne as *basileos*. Specifically the western emperor was not conceded the title of 'emperor of the Romans' which was henceforth reserved in Byzantine protocol for the emperor in Constantinople, and to underline the point was introduced into the inscription on imperial coins.[217]

During the first half of the ninth century, while Byzantium struggled to cope with the aftermath of the Bulgar triumph of 811 and a series of Arab victories in Asia Minor, the situation in what was left of imperial territory in the west decayed still further. Sicily had been attacked by the Arabs in the seventh and eighth centuries, but compared with other areas of the empire it had remained relatively secure. In 826, Ziyādat-Allāh, the Aghlabid emir of North Africa, sent an army to invade Sicily – apparently encouraged by a certain Euphemios, a local Byzantine naval commander who hoped to install himself as ruler of Sicily with Arab help. Euphemios soon disappears from view, and by 859, despite the repeated dispatch of reinforcements from Constantinople, more than half the island was under Arab control. Meanwhile on the mainland territory under imperial control had been reduced to no more than parts of Calabria and the area around Otranto at the tip of the heel. The duchy of Naples was entirely autonomous, refused Byzantine requests for naval support, and changed its rulers without any reference to Constantinople. It had even removed any reference to the emperor from its coins. Venice, far to the north at the head of the Adriatic, was a more compliant autonomous duchy, willing to send fleets to help Byzantine forces in south Italian waters, but it was already by the mid-ninth century developing into a thriving commercial city state that was not the empire's to command.[218]

All attempts to halt the Arab conquest of Sicily proved vain.

Syracuse, which Constans II had temporarily used as an imperial capital in the 660s, fell in 878, and the last significant stronghold, Taormina, fell in 902.[219] But by the end of the century Byzantine authority on the mainland had undergone a surprising revival. A sense that these were Byzantine provinces had survived in Constantinople and during the ninth century the political situation developed to favour imperial intervention.

During the early decades of the ninth century the dominant power in the south was the Lombard duchy of Benevento, which had avoided conquest in the 780s by accepting what proved to be a nominal Frankish overlordship. However, the greatly expanded duchy of the early ninth century proved unable to maintain its political unity. In 839 the duchy was split by a bitter civil war between Benevento and Salerno that led to a permanent division. Shortly afterwards the counts of Capua broke from Salerno and by 860 they were established as the rulers of a third Lombard state. The duchy of Naples also began to fragment with Amalfi and Gaeta each pursuing its own political path. This fragmentation – reminiscent of the politics of Armenia and the Transcaucasus – naturally favoured outside intervention.[220]

Arab raiders are mentioned in the area as early as 812, but they were first brought into south Italian politics by the dukes of Naples trying to protect themselves from Lombard aggression in about 836. They were soon being employed by all the south Italian states, serving as mercenaries but also acting in their own interests and in those of the Aghlabid rulers of Sicily and North Africa. In 838 Arabs from North Africa sacked Brindisi. In 840 and 841 they plundered Taranto and Bari – both former Byzantine ports now under Lombard rule. In 846 an Arab fleet sailed up the Tiber and sacked the suburbs of Rome, including the basilica of St Peter's. The same year another Arab force reoccupied Taranto and established an autonomous emirate, dedicated to raiding and to commerce – particularly in slaves. The next year, 847, yet another Arab contingent did the same at Bari.[221]

During the 850s Arab raiders operated profitably throughout the south. The local princes were usually safe in their own cities, but they lacked the strength to defend the countryside and in any case they were themselves employing Arab mercenaries to ravage their neighbours' lands. A major effort to defeat the Arabs was eventually undertaken by Louis II who as king of Italy from 844, and western emperor from 850, had an obligation as titular king of the Lombards to defend the south. (It would also have served his political purposes to reward the north Italian nobility with the profits of a southern war.) Unfortunately for Louis the Arabs proved far tougher enemies than he had expected. The emperor campaigned against Bari in 852, 867, 869, and possibly in 847 and 866 as well, but he only took the city in 871.[222] At this moment of rather belated triumph the Beneventans began to suspect him of preparing to subdue them. They moved first and took the emperor prisoner. He was released after a month, but only with the promise that he would never return to Benevento again. Louis' imperial dignity was fundamentally impaired by this episode – which is widely reported in Byzantine and western sources; so much so that he had to be recrowned by Pope Hadrian at Rome in the next year. His death with no son to succeed him in 875 marks the end of Carolingian intervention in the south.[223]

Since 812 Constantinople had continued to send occasional embassies to the Carolingians and to the papacy. The embassy of 839 which incidentally brought 'some men called Rhos' to the court of the emperor Louis the Pious has already been mentioned; three years later in 842 another embassy, this time to Louis' son the emperor Lothar I, arranged for the betrothal of Lothar's son, Louis II (the future emperor and king of Italy), to the daughter of the Byzantine emperor, Theophilos.[224] In the event the marriage did not take place. During the 860s the struggle over the Christian future of a converted Bulgaria had shown again how useful it was to be able to apply pressure in Italy to persuade the papacy to defer to Byzantine interests. In the later 860s a Byzantine fleet was sent to relieve Ragusa (Dubrovnik) from an Arab attack, and it may have been shortly afterwards that a naval theme of Dalmatia was established with its capital at Ragusa giving the Byzantines a new naval presence in the Adriatic.[225] In 868 while Louis II was preparing for his fourth attempt on Bari some Byzantine naval support was arranged – whether at Louis' request or at Byzantine suggestion is not clear – and at the same time Constantine, the son of the emperor Basil I (867–86) was betrothed to Louis' daughter, Ermengarde. As in 842 the marriage never occurred and the joint operation in 869 was a fiasco ending in mutual recrimination. The *De Administrando Imperio* and Theophanes Continuatus claim that a Byzantine army and the emperor's Slav tributaries played a major part in the capture of Bari in 871, but since no other Italian source is aware of their presence this story looks like later invention.[226]

It was only after Louis' death that the Byzantines finally stepped in to play a major role in southern Italy. On Christmas Day 876 Gregory, the Byzantine governor of Otranto, occupied Bari at the invitation of its Lombard citizens, afraid of an Arab attack. In 877 Byzantine envoys approached all the south Italian states to set up an alliance against the Arabs. In the same year Pope John VIII sent a letter to Gregory asking for naval protection for Rome – a request which in effect conceded that the subordination of the new Bulgar church to Constantinople was a *fait accompli*. In 880, two years after the shocking loss of Syracuse, an army made up of troops from the western themes put an end to the emirate of Taranto. Shortly afterwards troops from the eastern themes of Cappadocia and Charsianon arrived and during 885–6 northern Calabria was conquered. In 891 the establishment of a new order in the south was formalised by the creation of a theme, roughly covering the area of Apulia, and pointedly – for the Lombard states – named Longobardia.[227]

Byzantine power in the south had been restored to a level it had not reached since the early eighth century. It brought Constantinople the benefits of a more compliant papacy – which in any case was increasingly trying to follow an independent path from Louis II's successors as kings of Italy, and therefore was often open to Byzantine approaches. The south Italian rulers were keen to be given Byzantine titles, emulated Byzantine culture, and were intermittently willing to recognise Byzantine overlordship. For the first time for more than a century the coinage of Naples bore the emperor's name. More dramatically, it was also introduced on the coins struck in Lombard Salerno and Benevento.[228]

One should not misunderstand the nature of the Byzantine position. Neither Longobardia nor Calabria (which was actually administered under what was left of the theme of Sicily) were themes exactly comparable to those in Asia Minor. Much of what was theoretically theme territory was often outside the strategos' control. Imperial authority depended on diplomatic skills, client management, the playing off of rivals, and frequently the payment of large tributes to the Arab rulers of Sicily and North Africa, only occasionally backed by the use of force. Even in 885–6 the emperor Leo VI describes Nikephoros Phokas the elder, the strategos of Charsianon temporarily commanding in southern Italy, as treating the Lombards with great care. Byzantine troops were forbidden to loot or take slaves, and Lombard cities that recognised imperial authority were granted tax exemptions. This was less an example of the general's wisdom and humanity than a reflection of the fact that Byzantine control of the south was dependant on the acquiescence of the local élites.[229] But the empire had returned to Italy, and should a future emperor transfer attention from the eastern frontier to the west, there was clearly the scope for further advances into former imperial territory.

9. The Age of Reconquest, 863–976

The Byzantine Offensive in the East

IN THE SUMMER of 860 Umar, the emir of Melitene (known to Arabs and modern Turks as Malatya) and his ally Karbeas, the leader of the Paulician sect who controlled the territory around Tephrike on the Upper Euphrates, raided deep into Byzantine Anatolia. He returned with over 12,000 head of livestock. The attacks were followed up by raids from Tarsos and from the Syrian frontier districts which netted over 15,000 horses, cattle, donkeys and sheep, as well as an unknown number of prisoners. Finally a seaborne raid from the Syrian ports sacked the important Byzantine naval base at Attaleia (modern Antalya) on the south coast of Asia Minor. 860 was exceptionally dreadful for the inhabitants of Byzantine Anatolia, but the raiding forces which struck the plateau in that year are representative of all that had gone wrong for the Byzantine empire on its eastern borders since the seventh century.[1]

The emirates of Melitene, Tarsos, and the less powerful Kālī-kalā (modern Erzerum, Byzantine Theodosioupolis), had their whole purpose in raiding the infidel Byzantines. Melitene was most dangerous of all since its presence on the western side of the Anti-Taurus mountains gave the Arabs a secure base on the plateau and effectively turned the natural defences of Anatolia so they no longer protected the Byzantines. The balance of warfare was not all one way, but the existence of these emirates kept the Byzantines on the defensive, and their annual ravagings kept Asia Minor poor.

The Paulicians were a warlike Armenian sect whose beliefs, while still a matter of some controversy, seem to have involved the dualist notion of a cosmic struggle between a good God and an evil demiurge who had created the material world. In the 840s the Paulicians had established themselves on the Upper Euphrates. Apart from the considerable military threat they posed to the Byzantine population of Anatolia, they are arguably most significant as an extreme example of the consequences of the loss of the Armenian and Transcaucasian world to the Arabs.

What had once been a secure area of Roman hegemony was now beyond Byzantine influence. Arab cities like Melitene or Kālīkalā were small islands of Arab power surrounded by the mountainous world of western Armenia; yet it was the Byzantines who were on the defensive, and the mountains and their people were generally reliable clients of the caliph's governors.

In 863 Umar struck again with the full raiding army of Melitene. Riding across Anatolia his forces swung north to seize the port city of Amisos (modern Samsun) on the Black Sea coast before turning south to head back across the plateau to Melitene. But he was intercepted. An army commanded by the emperor Michael III's brother-in-law, Petronas (and possibly by the emperor himself), consisting of the combined forces of the four tagmata and the armies of nine themes and two *kleisourai* (frontier districts), trapped Umar near the Halys river northeast of Ankara. The emir was killed and his army all but annihilated. A few weeks later, Alī b. Yahya, from an Arab family long-settled in Armenia, a veteran of many successful raids into Anatolia and the man who had commanded the forces of Tarsos in 860, was also surprised by a Byzantine raiding force, this time operating far from its bases in Upper Mesopotamia. He too was killed. In the same year the Paulician leader, Karbeas, died – it seems from natural causes, but it would still have appeared to the Byzantines as the just judgement of a wrathful God.[2]

In retrospect Petronas' victory stands out as a turning point which marks the beginning of more than a century's Byzantine advance in the east. The battle was the first decisive victory over one of the raiding emirates, and it was one from which Melitene never recovered. With the major central bastion of Arab power on Byzantium's eastern borders fatally weakened the empire had the opportunity to transform its strategic position and to deal with its enemies one by one. Even at the time contemporaries saw it as a major event. In Constantinople the victors processed in triumph through the city to the hippodrome where the heads of the defeated were displayed and the stage-managed crowd chanted acclamations praising God and the emperor. In Baghdad and Samarra the shocking news led to riots and an enthusiastic clamour to volunteer for *djihād* against the infidel.[3]

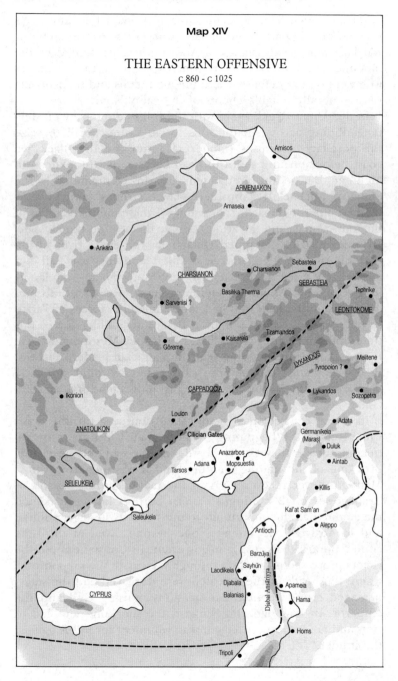

Map XIV

THE EASTERN OFFENSIVE
c 860 - c 1025

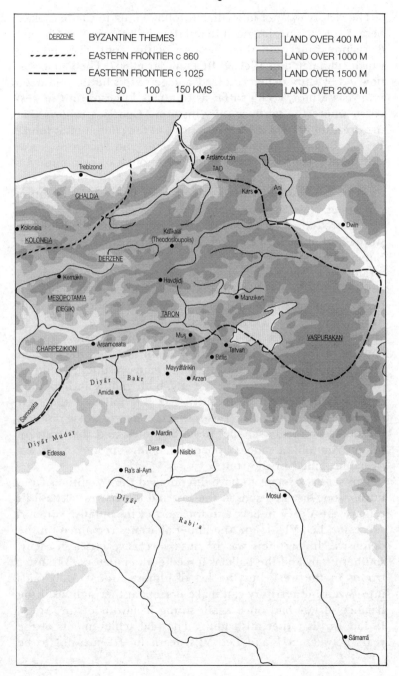

BYZANTINE THEMES

DERZENE   BYZANTINE THEMES

EASTERN FRONTIER c 860

EASTERN FRONTIER c 1025

0   50   100   150 KMS

LAND OVER 400 M

LAND OVER 1000 M

LAND OVER 1500 M

LAND OVER 2000 M

Trebizond

• Ardanoutzin

TAO

CHALDIA

Kars •   • Ani

• Koloneia

• Dwin

KOLONEIA

Kalikala
(Theodosioupolis) •

DERZENE

• Kemakh

• Havdjidj

MESOPOTAMIA
(DEGIK)

• Manzikert

TARON

Muş •

VASPURAKAN

CHARPEZIKION   • Arsamosata

Tatvan •

Bitlis •

Mayyafarikin •

Diyār   Bakr   • Arzen

Samosata   • Amida

Diyār Mudar

• Mardin

Dara •   • Nisibis

• Edessa

• Ra's al-Ayn

Diyār   • Mosul

Rabi'a

• Sāmarrā

The victory was not immediately followed up, in the first place because of the pressing need to interfere in Bulgaria (see Chapter 8, section four) and then because of the political infighting which culminated in Michael III's murder in 867. The Paulicians, now led by Chrysocheir, took advantage of this lull to raid deep into Asia Minor, going so far as to attack Ephesos on the west coast, where the tenth-century historian Genesios reports that the dreadful heretic stabled his horses in the church of St John.[4] By 871 Basil I – Michael III's murderer and successor – was sufficiently secure in power and free enough of commitments in the west to begin an offensive in the east but its results and those of subsequent Byzantine efforts over the next half-century can appear less than dramatic. Basil himself was lucky not to be captured when he made his first attempt to take the Paulician stronghold of Tephrike in 871. In 872 Chrysocheir was trapped, rather like the emir of Melitene in 863, when returning from a raid, defeated and killed, but it was to be a further six years before Tephrike fell.[5] During this period Byzantine armies led by the emperor in person or by senior strategoi raided into Arab territory to sack Arsamosata and Sozopetra in 873,[6] to attack Germanikeia (Maraş), Adata and the territory of the emirate of Tarsos on the Cilician plain in 878, and the Cilician plain again in 879, but no dramatic gains resulted. Melitene survived two attempts to take the city, both ending in Byzantine defeats.[7] The second of these in 882 was followed the next year by an attempt to take Tarsos which ended in worse disaster; the domestic of the scholai, Kesta Stypiotes, and the strategoi of the Anatolikon and Cappadocia being among the heavy casualties killed in the rout.[8]

This set-back seems to have discouraged the Byzantines from further long-distance raids in the east and for the rest of Basil I's reign to his death in 886, and for most of his putative son and successor, Leo VI's reign, the imperial armies remained on the defensive. In part this was because successive crises in Sicily, southern Italy and the Balkans forced both emperors to transfer troops to the west, but the list of almost annual Arab raids into Byzantine territory can make it seem at first sight as if the balance of war had once again swung in favour of the Arabs. In fact this is rather misleading. The real achievements of the years between 871 and Leo VI's death in 912 are not to be found in the occasional long-distance raid to sack an Arab city – however successful and however much imperial propaganda might celebrate such a triumph – but in the steady transformation of the frontier zone so that by 912 the Arabs had been pinned back behind the Taurus and Anti-Taurus, while at the same time the Armenian clans who dominated the mountains had been turned from clients of the Arabs into clients of the emperor.

There were two complementary aspects to this development. One was the Byzantine conquest of former Paulician territory and of such fortresses as Loulon (which lies in the northern approaches to the Cilician Gates) that had given the Arabs a permanent base north of the mountain ranges. These gains which vastly improved Byzantine security on the eastern frontier may appear less dramatic than the failure to take Melitene or Tarsos, but in the long run they were of great importance.[9] Such local successes also had the far-reaching effect of convincing the nobility of western Armenia that the Byzantine emperor rather than the caliph or his governors was the most likely source of immediate reward and future regional power. In 872 – the same year that Chrysocheir was killed – K'urdik (or Koutikios as the Byzantines called him) the Armenian lord of the hill country which lay between the Anti-Taurus and Melitene, voluntarily submitted to Basil I and became an imperial client.[10] K'urdik, previously a loyal ally of the emir of Melitene, appears to have been one of the Mamikonean clan, but he was only the most prominent of a number of Armenian defectors, and their example was followed by others. After 886 Manuel, another Mamikonean, whose lordship of Degik lay in the mountains north of Melitene and south-east of Tephrike came over to Leo VI with his four sons. At about the same time Ašot 'the long armed', possibly one of the Bagratuni of Taron, came to Constantinople and entered the emperor's service.[11] With him was a certain Melias whose admittedly remarkable career can serve as an illustration of what this transfer of allegiance meant in practice on the eastern frontier.

Melias, as he was known to the Byzantines, or Mleh, to use the Armenian form – the name comes from the Arabic malīh, 'beautiful' or 'fine', and is a reminder of the strongly Arab-influenced cultural milieu from which these Armenian nobles came – was a member of one of the lesser naxarar clans, possibly the Varažnuni whose lands lay in the mountains north of the plain of Taron. He first appears as Ašot's vassal and he fought with him in the Byzantine army that was defeated by the Bulgars at Bulgarophygon in 896. After his patron's death in the battle Mleh returned to the eastern frontier where operating as an imperial client in close co-operation with the neighbouring strategoi he began to carve out an autonomous lordship in the same hill country to the west of Melitene where a generation earlier K'urdik had been based. In 905 Mleh and several Armenian nobles were expelled from their lands as part of a political struggle between the emperor Leo VI and Andronikos Doukas and his supporters. By 908 all had been recalled and Mleh was back in the same hill country where shortly afterwards his authority received imperial confirmation when Leo VI appointed him *kleisourarch* (the commander of a frontier district of lesser status than a theme) of Lykandos. His expanding territories are explicitly mentioned in Arab sources as a growing threat to Melitene, but a violent Arab counter-attack in 909 failed to do more than dislodge the Armenians from their more outlying positions.[12] By Leo VI's death in 912 Mleh's activities, which can be paralleled by those of other Armenians in the mountains north and north-east of Melitene, had transformed the strategic position in the east. As the Byzantines increasingly opened up Armenia and the Transcaucasus to imperial influence so the outposts of Arab power became correspondingly insecure. It was arguably only a matter of time before Melitene, Kālīkalā and the Arab cities around Lake Van would be forced to come to terms. Beyond that if the mountains north of the Fertile Crescent were in hostile Byzantine hands then Syria and northern Mesopotamia would become a borderland and even their rule by the Arabs would be at risk.

The expedition of 915 sent by Zoe's regency government to support the Bagratuni Ašot II against the emir Yūsuf of Azerbaidjan has already been highlighted as evidence of the new Byzantine forward policy in the east but it was not in fact to be followed up for more than a decade. In 917 Zoe's regime arranged a truce with the caliph in Baghdad and transferred much of the strength of the eastern armies – including Mleh's troops from Lykandos which had recently been promoted to the rank of a theme – to the west ready for an assault on Bulgaria. The result was the disaster at Achelous in August 917 and a war which kept the Byzantines preoccupied with their western frontier for most of the next ten years.

The peace of 927 allowed the emperor Romanos Lekapenos to give his domestic of the scholai, John Kourkuas, a free rein in the east. Kourkuas launched a dramatic long-distance raid against Dwin in 928. The former capital of the Arab governors of Armenia, which was still the seat of a Muslim emir, just managed to survive the domestic's assault, but the campaign was a potent demonstration of the new reach of the emperor's armies. The same message was broadcast later in 928 when Kourkuas' armies reached Lake Van and the Bitlis pass, nearly 500 kilometres from the nearest imperial territory.[13] But the most important development of this period was the blockade of Melitene. Two attempts in 927 and 928 to take the city by storm failed, as did an attempt by Mleh to infiltrate Melitene disguising his men as Armenian masons. After this the Byzantines concentrated on the indirect strategy of using their dominance of the hills around Melitene's fertile plain to force the city into submission. From a ring of small fortresses the Byzantines and their Armenian allies ravaged the city's hinterland. By 931 the citizens who had watched their agricultural base go up in flames had no choice but to ask for terms. An embassy to Romanos led by the grandson of the Umar who had been emir in 863 promised to pay tribute and 'Thenceforth', as the Logothete's chronicle gleefully reports, 'they campaigned with the Romans against their fellow Agarenes [the Byzantine term for Muslim Arabs], and came into [Constantinople] with the Romans in the triumphs, leading Agarene prisoners; which was a remarkable and extraordinary sign of the misfortune of the godless Agarenes'. This alliance, however, lasted less than a year and in November Mleh who had occupied part of Melitene was forced out by the arrival of Muslim forces sent by the caliph under the command of Saʿīd b. Hamdān to save the city. In fact Saʿīd could do little to help and once his army had returned to Mosul the Byzantines began once again systematically to destroy Melitene's plain. The citizens held out until 19 May 934 when famine forced them to surrender. This time John Kourkuas offered only a stark choice between conversion to Christianity or expulsion from the city.[14]

The fall of Melitene was a profound shock to the other Muslim cities of the frontier zone where there was anxious speculation as to what the next Byzantine target would be.[15] The emirate of Tarsos was in some ways an obvious enemy. Throughout the 920s its armies of local troops and visiting volunteers wishing to pass a season fighting for the faith had raided far into Anatolia, and as recently as 931 raiders from Tarsos had burnt the fortress at Amorion; but in fact it suited Byzantine purposes to leave Cilicia in peace. Afraid of provoking a counterattack the Tarsiotes halted all offensive operations, and although they are not specifically mentioned in the reports of the truce agreed between Romanos Lekapenos and their overlord the Ikhshīdid ruler of Egypt in 937 the fact that there was quiet on the Taurus front of the next six years makes it likely this peace had been part of the terms.[16]

Instead the conquest of Melitene opened the way for further penetration into the Armenian highlands. By 940 Byzantine forces had occupied Arsamosata, a fortress second only in importance to Melitene itself on this stretch of the frontier, and had established control of the Munzur dağ and the Bingöl dağ, whence they could apply pressure north against Kālīkalā and south-east against the emirates in the plains around Lake Van.[17]

Up to 929 the Muslims of the frontier zone could still hope for some help from the Abbāsid government in Baghdad, but after 932 the only active military assistance came from the Hamdānid ruler of Mesopotamia, al-Hasan b. Abd Allāh b. Hamdān – almost always known by his honorific title of *Nasir al-Dawla*, 'Defender of the State' – or more exactly from his younger brother, Alī, famous as *Sayf al-Dawla*, 'Sword of the State', whom Nasir al-Dawla put in charge of the Diyār Bakr (the northern sector of the Djazīra with its capital at Amida, modern Diyarbakır) in 934. Sayf al-Dawla's early efforts to halt the Byzantine advance were no more promising than those of his uncle, Saʿīd b. Hamdān, who had just failed to save Melitene. The city of Amida kept out a Byzantine raiding force in 936 but wholly by its own efforts with no help from the Hamdānids. In 938 Sayf al-Dawla himself led a raid into the lands around Melitene, and some Arab sources describe a crushing victory over the domestic John Kourkuas; but since better informed Arab accounts show the Byzantine offensive pressing on regardless during these years, the story is evidently spurious and the expedition served little purpose.[18]

More interesting and important are the events of 940. Leaving Mayyafārikīn (Roman Martyropolis, modern Turkish Silvan) in the spring Sayf al-Dawla led an army up the Bitlis pass (the key route which links the Djazīra to central Armenia) to the shores of Lake Van. The Arab sources are confused and contradictory as to what happened next. One version is that Sayf al-Dawla ordered a number of Armenian rulers to appear before him at Tatvan at the eastern end of the lake. Amongst the list of those who submitted it is not surprising to find the Arab emirs of the plains around Lake Van, but also listed are Ašot, prince of Taron, Gagik, the king of Vaspurakan, and the prince of princes, whom commentators have assumed to be the Bagratuni, Abas (929–53). Having received their submission and occupied several strategic fortresses, including the vital castle at Bitlis, which he took over from the Arab emir of Hilat, Sayf al-Dawla pressed on to ravage the Byzantine territory around Kālīkalā before returning safely to the Diyār Bakr. A second version tells a similar story but in reverse. Sayf al-Dawla marched up the Bitlis pass and then on to the area around Kālīkalā, destroying the new Byzantine fortress at Hafdjidj in the Bingöl dağ, before returning to the Diyār Bakr. The same year he made a second journey to Lake Van where he was approached by 'the king of Armenia and Georgia' – and again it is presumed that the Bagratuni Abas is meant – who ceded various fortresses, and made submission. Following this other Armenian princes submitted. Sayf al-Dawla then ravaged part of the plain of Taron before heading north again to raid Byzantine territory west of Kālīkalā and finally returning to the Diyār Bakr.[19]

There are various obvious problems with these accounts. The second version with its story of two ascents into the Armenian mountains and two campaigns in the direction of Kālīkalā suggests that the author himself had conflicting accounts which he reconciled by turning one original campaign into two. The inference that Abas Bagratuni submitted to Sayf al-Dawla may simply be a modern misunderstanding. Gagik Artsruni, the king of Vaspurakan, regarded himself as prince of princes, and as a ruler whose territories lay to the south of Lake Van he seems a more likely candidate than Abas whose power was centred far to the north-east. But details aside, the core of the story sounds reasonable enough. The Armenians had traditionally used rival outside forces to gain their own ends, and if Sayf al-Dawla could demonstrate that he had the military strength to stop the Byzantine advance east – and that surely was the point of the campaign towards Kālīkalā and the claimed destruction of Havdjidj – then they were prepared to make the equally traditional signs of submission to someone who (wholly theoretically) was a representative of the caliph in Baghdad. If the Chalcedonian Bagratuni of Iberia were unwilling, as Constantine Porphyrogenitos tells us, to support the Byzantine blockade of Kālīkalā because they would rather it were in the hands of an impotent Muslim emir than a powerful Christian emperor, then how much more ambiguously must the non-Chalcedonian princes of central and southern Armenia have watched the steady Byzantine advance to the east?[20] There was therefore an opportunity for Sayf al-Dawla to rebuild a system of pro-Arab clients who would contest Byzantine dominance of the mountains; indeed the ineffectiveness of the attempts to save Melitene showed that without such an alliance the Arab position was doomed. But what is really significant about Sayf al-Dawla's Armenian campaign is that it had no apparent consequences and was never followed up. In the next year Sayf al-Dawla followed his brother to Iraq in an attempt to stop the take-over by the Persian Buyīds, and when that had failed he mounted an equally unsuccessful attempt to conquer Syria from the Egyptian Ikhshīdids. It was only when all other opportunities had been exhausted that in 945 Sayf al-Dawla returned to the frontiers with Byzantium and over the next few years began to construct a new territorial base centred on Mayyafārikīn in the Diyār Bakr and Aleppo in northern Syria. From the later 940s through to the early 960s Sayf al-Dawla was the Byzantines' leading opponent in the east, but he never made any further attempt to build alliances in Armenia and in effect gave up any attempt to contest the empire's control of the mountains. By so doing he allowed the Byzantines an uncontested strategic advantage which none of his other successes could seriously disturb.

With the Hamdānids for the most part occupied elsewhere the Byzantines spent the 940s consolidating their control of the highlands and for short periods raiding freely in northern Syria and the Djazīra. In 941 John Kourkuas was held back by the news of the Rus attack on Constantinople, but for the next three years he led his forces over the Anti-Taurus (presumably using the Ergani pass from Melitene) and ravaged at will. Arzen, Mayyafārikīn, Dara, Ra's al-Ayn and Amida were sacked and columns of prisoners and booty taken back to the north.[21] The prize John Kourkuas and Romanos Lekapenos wanted was the *Mandylion* of Edessa. This was an icon, almost certainly painted in the sixth century, which was believed to be a piece of cloth on which Christ had wiped his face miraculously imprinting an image of his features. As an icon 'not painted by human hands', the Mandylion had played a crucial part in the arguments over the status of icons in the eighth and ninth centuries, and its location at Edessa, at that stage far beyond the reach of Byzantine arms, had ensured its preservation from destruction by the iconoclasts. To orthodox Byzantium of the tenth century the Mandylion was one of the most famous and hence most potent miracle-working icons, and its capture would bring enormous benefits to any imperial regime that could secure the credit. Edessa was attacked in both 942 and 943 and its hinterland subjected to the same treatment that had brought Melitene to its knees. Eventually the emir of Edessa was persuaded to negotiate. John Kourkuas agreed to leave the city in peace, and the emir promised to take no part in hostile operations against the Byzantines, and most important to hand over the Mandylion. On 15 August 944 the icon reached Constantinople where a triumphant entry was staged, intended to make public demonstration of God's favour to Romanos' regime and His continued protection of a city still shaken by the Rus attack of 941.[22]

In the event Romanos' rule lasted for barely four more months. On 16 December his two sons and co-emperors, Stephen and Constantine, deposed their father and exiled him to the island of Prote (one of the Princes' Islands in the sea of Marmara) where he was tonsured as a monk. Just over a month later, on 27 January 945 they in turn fell to a coup which sent the brothers into exile and brought to the throne Leo VI's son, Constantine VII Porphyrogenitos, who though crowned emperor as a two-year old in 908 only now came to power.[23] This palace revolution brought with it an important change of personnel on the eastern front. As a close supporter of Romanos Lekapenos, John Kourkuas had been dismissed in December 944. Constantine in turn dismissed his immediate replacement, an ally of the two Lekapenos brothers, and appointed Bardas Phokas as domestic of the scholai.[24]

The years 946 and 947 appear to mark a lull in operations as the new regime established itself, but in 948 long-distance raids resumed when an army commanded by Bardas Phokas' second son, Leo, sacked Adata (Arab Hadath), a crucial stronghold just south of one of the main passes which led from Mleh's former territory of Lykandos into northern Syria.[25] For the emperor and his closest associates in Constantinople the critical undertaking of 949 was the attempt to recapture Crete. To succeed where successive attempts since the initial Arab conquest of the island in the 820s had failed would have provided Constantine's regime with the vital legitimacy of military victory; but unfortunately the invasion followed what had become almost an established pattern and ended in disaster. (It is noteworthy that the chronicle account most sympathetic to the regime, that of Theophanes Continuatus, omits to mention the campaign entirely.)[26]

The year 949 also saw a military success which marks another significant stage both in the collapse of Arab power in Armenia and the Transcaucasus, and in the progress of the Byzantine eastern offensive. Kālīkalā, the most northerly of the raiding emirates, its territory exposed to repeated devastation, fell at last to a Byzantine assault. Its Arab population was expelled and it was eventually resettled by Greeks and Armenians.[27] The conquest was the culmination of many years persistant pressure and it brought the empire to what could have been a secure and stable frontier in the east.

Attempts in the following years by Constantinople to negotiate a peace with Sayf al-Dawla testify to a strong body of opinion which thought that this was the place to stop.[28] Their views would have been reinforced through the early 950s as Sayf al-Dawla launched a series of successful raids into Anatolia, and inflicted a run of bloody defeats on the new domestic of the scholai. Bardas Phokas was already in his mid-sixties when he took over command. A Byzantine source prepared to praise the exploits of his sons, Nikephoros and Leo, could only say of the father, 'Whenever he had been appointed to a command under another, he displayed himself an excellent strategos, but from the moment command of all the armies was given over to his judgement he benefited the Roman empire little or nothing.' Whatever the political considerations involved, in strictly military terms the appointment had plainly been a mistake.[29]

On the Arab side there were also those, especially in Tarsos (which Sayf al-Dawla had brought under his authority and back into the war), who wanted to negotiate and rightly feared that continued warfare could only lead to a Muslim disaster. But on neither side did the peacemakers achieve their end. Sayf al-Dawla's political legitimacy was too closely bound up in his role as a leader of the holy war for him easily to disengage. At the same time his victories – especially that of 953 when Bardas Phokas was put to flight leaving his son, Constantine, in Sayf al-Dawla's hands, where he died afterwards in Aleppo – created a cycle of violence from which it would have been difficult to withdraw without politically damaging loss of face.[30] Yet from a Byzantine perspective if the war was to continue imperial forces clearly needed to take much better advantage of the position of strategic dominance gained over the last half-century. They needed new tactics, new armies, new leadership and new strategic goals.

None of these appeared overnight, but in the mid-950s the changes to achieve them gradually came to fruition. New armies and tactics had been developing since at least the 930s. From the beginning of the tenth century considerable thought had been given to the proper constitution of armies and the tactics they should employ. This had led to an unprecedented output of military manuals, generically known as *taktika*. As a work that looks back, recording traditional Byzantine tactics of mobile defence in depth before they disappeared and were forgotten, 'On Skirmishing Warfare' stands apart. The other taktika, namely the *Sylloge Tacticorum*, the *Praecepta militaria*, the *De re militari* and the *Taktika* of Nikephoros Ouranos, were all concerned with the tactics to be employed in the offensive warfare of the future. All four stress the crucial role of close co-operation between strong infantry forces and heavy cavalry.[31]

In the 930s John Kourkuas had ground down the resistance

of Melitene with mobile raiders, but by the 940s he was operating in the Djazīra and it is likely to have been there – almost
certainly copying his Arab enemies – that Byzantine offensive
tactics evolved. The basic idea was that substantial forces of
infantry, who were to include a combination of heavily and
lightly equipped spearmen, as well as archers and slingers, should
form up in a square which would be able to resist the assaults
of enemy cavalry and provide a safe haven in which the Byzantine
cavalry could regroup. The earliest witnesses to these tactics
are the short text known as the *Syntaxis Armatorum Quadrata* of
perhaps the 930s or 940s, and the *Sylloge Tacticorum* of about
950, but the impression given is of an over complicated rather
theoretical approach unlike the *Praecepta* of the mid-960s which
is clearly based on practical battlefield experience.[32]

The idea of an infantry square may appear fairly simple, but
as the *Praecepta* shows – itself intended to be a practical document cutting out unnecessary complications – it required large
forces (12,000 on paper) of well-trained infantry under experienced officers to carry it out. Also necessary were equally experienced forces of heavy cavalry, capable of performing the
complicated battlefield manoeuvres required to move in and
out of a square, and with the equipment, expertise and nerve
to mount frontal assaults on an enemy square.[33] If the tactics
were developed in the 940s it comes as no surprise that it was
not until the second half of the 950s that the Byzantines were
in a position to put them fully into practice. Behind this process
was firstly the growing size and importance of the tagmata,
and secondly the raising of large new infantry units.

By the mid-950s the tagmata had long ceased to be a central
field force of a few regiments based in Constantinople but had
expanded and spread into the themes. The 1000 Armenians
from the 'eastern tagmata' who were sent on the Cretan expedition of 949 are a case in point.[34] The change is reflected in
the organisation of the newly conquered regions on the eastern
frontier. The old themes were not expanded in size nor were
new themes on the old model set up, but small themes (known
in the Byzantine sources as 'Armenian themes') were established
each consisting of little more than a city or fortress and its
surrounding plain, with the strategos acting as a garrison
commander. Such an arrangement offered no more than a set

of fixed defensive strongpoints; and both the mobile back-up in case of an enemy attack and the offensive strength for a Byzantine advance were provided by tagmatic armies whose commanders, with the title of *doux*, are recorded from the 960s onwards. By 976 37 small 'Armenian themes' are recorded, while the expanded eastern tagmata were under the command of the *doukes* of Chaldia, Mesopotamia, and Antioch, who in turn were under the command of the domestic of the scholai.[35]

The old themes continued to exist and to provide cavalry forces for imperial armies into the eleventh century. In 958 the troops of the Thrakesion, the Boukellarion and the Opsikion defeated a Magyar invasion of Thrace; and during the 960s legislation was issued to increase the minimum amount of land which a theme cavalryman must keep, specifically, as the text states, in order to cover the increased costs of heavy cavalry equipment. However, at the same time the obligation to serve in the theme armies was increasingly being commuted for a cash payment. For the future Byzantine armies would increasingly depend on the tagmata for their cavalry forces and the themes as military units would slowly disappear.[36]

The new infantry forces were recruited outside the older military organisation. Divided into thousand-strong units of mixed heavy and light infantry and archers known as *taxiarchiai* they were recruited from all over the empire but included large numbers of Armenians. The chronology of these units is not clear. The term *taxiarchia* appears for the first time in this sense in the *Praecepta* of the mid-960s by which time they were no longer a novelty.[37]

The changes were progressive and had certainly not all taken effect by the second half of the 950s, but by that date they were well under way, and gave Byzantine commanders the means for the first time to wage offensive war in the east on an equal or better footing than their Islamic enemies.

New leadership came in 955 when Bardas Phokas, by now in his mid-seventies, was finally replaced as domestic of the scholai by his eldest son, Nikephoros Phokas. Even his family admitted that Bardas' expertise was in the mobile tactics of defensive warfare against Arab raiders.[38] His departure brought a new generation whose outlook had not been shaped by the careful caution of an empire on the defensive. New strategic goals followed shortly afterwards, and a key step was taken in 957 when Adata – already captured and abandoned in a long-distance raid as recently as 948 – was permanently occupied. The Byzantine empire had decisively embarked on a new strategy of conquest beyond the Taurus and Anti-Taurus.[39]

Progress between 957 and 976 was remarkably rapid – and this was in spite of the distractions of three changes of regime in Constantinople, two coups, a rebellion, the successful conquest of Crete in 961, the disastrous attempt to do the same in Sicily in 964,[40] the Bulgarian crisis of 967, and the Rus war of 970–1. In 958 Samosata on the Euphrates was captured; in 962 the conquest of Cilicia was begun, while the fall of Anazarbos, Germanikeia (Maraş) and Duluk (near modern Gaziantep) left the Byzantines in undisputed control of the western passes across the Anti-Taurus. In the same year, Nikephoros Phokas – who stayed as domestic of the scholai in the east for Constantine Porphyrogenitos' son and successor, Romanos II (959–63) – sacked Aleppo, Sayf al-Dawla's Syrian capital. Much of the following year was taken up with Nikephoros' seizure of power after Romanos' early death, but in December the new emperor returned to Cilicia. Adana fell in 964 and in 965 the whole emirate collapsed; Tarsos surrendering on 16 August 965. The departure of its citizens as displaced refugees marked the end of Arab Cilicia. In the same year Cyprus was annexed. In 966 Nikephoros raided at will over much of the Djazīra where Dara and Nisibis were abandoned on the news of his approach. The emperor then turned his armies on Syria where it is reported that as the price to avoid destruction Hierapolis (Manbidj) was forced to hand over the *Keramidion* – the Holy Tile imprinted with the face of Christ, miraculously transferred by contact with the Mandylion. In February 967 Sayf al-Dawla died, a sick and defeated man. In the same year the Armenian principality of Taron was annexed to the empire. In 968 Nikephoros Phokas massacred, captured and burnt in a swathe from Mayyafārikīn to the Syrian coast, where Djabala and Laodicea were occupied. The great fortress city of Antioch, now isolated and blockaded by Byzantine garrisons left behind to wreck its hinterland from fortresses in the surrounding hills, held out for another year, but it too fell on 28 October 969, the same year that Sayf al-Dawla's effective heirs in Aleppo were forced to agree a humiliating treaty that made them the empire's tribute-paying clients.[41]

Less than a month later Nikephoros Phokas was murdered in a palace coup, but under his successor, John Tzimiskes, the offensive went on. In 972–3 John was poised in the region of Nisibis and Dara, contemplating, it is reported, a march on Baghdad. Instead in 975 he led his forces south into Syria, the Lebanon and northern Palestine. Ba'albek in the Beka'a valley was captured, and the new ruler of Damascus, a recently arrived Turk called Alptakīn, agreed to pay tribute. This dramatic raid may have been intended to test the possibility of occupying Palestine, but its more immediate target was the cities of the Mediterranean coast and the fortresses which would ensure control of its mountainous hinterland. Although Tripoli held out, Beirūt was captured and the Byzantines took over the fortresses of Sayhūn and Barzūya in the mountains of the Djabal Ansāriyya which run parallel to the Mediterranean south of Antioch.[42]

John Tzimiskes achieved no more. He returned to Constantinople where he died on 11 January 976. The empire's eastern limits at his death ran from the Syrian coast within 30 kilometres of Tripoli to the Euphrates in northern Syria; from there along the southern edge of the Anti-Taurus to the head-waters of the Murat su within striking distance of Lake Van, and thence north via the head-waters of the Araxes to meet the Black Sea at the mouth of the Çoruh river. The lands from which the Arabs and their allies had launched annual raids during three centuries to ravage Asia Minor were all under imperial rule. Tarsos, Melitene, Kalīkalā and Tephrike were each the seat of a Byzantine strategos; Hamdānid Aleppo survived as a Byzantine protectorate; the ruler of Damascus paid tribute and on all sides Muslim and Armenian rulers waited nervously for the next advance. The contrast with 860 could scarcely be more dramatic or more complete.

The Decline of the Abbāsid Caliphate

After a glowing description of the former wealth and splendour of Arab Cilicia and its chief city, Tarsos, the tenth-century geographer, Ibn Hawkal, notes gloomily: 'But the inhabitants have perished and their wealth is departed so that it is as if all this had never been; their mark on the land has been wiped out as if no one had ever lived in these places.' Many of his contemporaries, he tells us in the next chapter, thought the cause of these disasters lay in the power and wealth of the infidel Byzantine empire, but they were wrong: 'In reality its position is precarious, its power insignificant, its revenues small, its population poor and wealth rare, its finances are in a bad state and resources minimal.' The Mahgreb – the area of North Africa ruled by the Fātimids before their conquest of Egypt in 969 – had more potential than the empire. Byzantine victories were due, he believed, solely to the disunity of Islam, its lack of order and the endless revolts, rebellions and civil wars which pitted Muslims against Muslims, and 'left the field open to the Byzantines and allowed them to seize that which was previously closed to them, and to have ambitions that until recently would have been unthinkable'.[43]

Ibn Hawkal was not an entirely neutral observer. A traveller, trader and scholar from Nisibis he had watched the frontier zone collapse to the Byzantines. Before 967 he had written in praise of the Hamdānids but he had been disillusioned by their failure to protect Syria and the Djazīra from Christian aggression, and by the time of the third revision of his great work, *Kitāb al-Sūrat* al-Ard ('The Description of the Earth'), in about 988, he was at least sympathetic to the Shī'ite Fātimids who had established themselves as rival caliphs to the Abbāsids in Baghdad. Therefore Ibn Hawkal's criticism of the current disunity of Islam and his comparison between the Mahgreb and Byzantium is of a piece with his expressed wish that the Fātimid caliph might soon reign in all the lands of Islam. Yet the fact remains that his judgement is essentially correct. Byzantium was not as poor and impotent as he claimed – important factors in the Byzantine advance had been the military skills honed in the long battle to protect Asia Minor from annual Arab raids during the seventh to ninth centuries; the military reforms which by the second half of the tenth century had created a field army capable of long-distance offensive operations in the Fertile Crescent; and the ability to harness the Armenian and Transcaucasian world in support of imperial war aims – but his point that the empire's successes were primarily due to Muslim disunity can be demonstrated by the chronology.

Throughout the seventh, eighth and ninth centuries the ebb and flow of Byzantine military success had followed the gravitational pull of events in the Islamic world. In the 860s new Byzantine successes coincided with a prolonged crisis at the heart of the Abbāsid caliphate. In the later 890s some order was re-established and with it easy Byzantine gains stopped. After 928 the caliphate spiralled into a new and deeper crisis from which it never recovered. During the years from the 930s to the 970s the Byzantines were faced by no more than local or at best regional opposition and they took advantage accordingly. Only in the later 970s did a new generation of more powerful Muslim states establish themselves.

The causes of the caliphate's collapse were largely political and structural, and were arguably inherent in the Islamic empire from its creation in the seventh century. The Ummayad dynasty had fallen in the mid-eighth century because of its inability to halt the fighting among its Arab tribal subjects who provided the early caliphate with its military strength. The later Ummayads and still more their Abbāsid successors endeavoured to escape this fate by investing in warriors imported as slaves who would be loyal to the caliph. Such slave-soldiers (*ghilmān,* singular *ghulām*), mostly Turks from Central Asia, provided the crack troops of the Abbāsid heyday during the late eighth and early ninth century, but there were fundamental difficulties.

For the most part fanatically loyal to the individual caliph who had bought them, trained them, and in many cases made them rich, the ghilmān were nonetheless resented foreigners, isolated in a land which despised them as barbarians. One caliph might look after their interests; his successor, with ghilmān of his own to reward or looking to find support from Arab groups in Baghdad, might abandon them to their enemies. The consequences of an unsympathetic caliph were too dangerous for these slave-soldiers to follow a path of disinterested neutrality. The crisis of the 860s was brought on by a savage struggle between the Turkish ghilmān and their Arab rivals, and among rival ghulām units, to ensure a caliph who would protect their interests. By the end of the 920s the Abbāsid system was no longer capable of producing a caliph with the power to rule an empire.

At the same time as central authority in Iraq was breaking down the provinces were increasingly developing an independent political life of their own. Originally the small Muslim élites who had conquered these regions had been tied to the caliph's authority because only support from the centre could ensure their domination of a hostile non-Muslim majority. By the ninth and tenth centuries this was no longer the case. Muslims were now the large majority throughout the caliphate, and provincial leaders could base their power on reliable local support. Hence there was little incentive to serve the interests of a distant regime preoccupied with extracting revenues to pay for an army of alien slaves. From Persia to North Africa local dynasties were establishing themselves who, even when originally appointed as Abbāsid governors and continuing to pay lip-service to Abbāsid authority, pursued a wholly independent path.

In the tenth century the division between centre and province was in many cases exacerbated by religious differences which had their roots in the earliest history of the caliphate, but which now came to have political consequences dividing the Muslim world. Part of the opposition to the Ummayads in the seventh and eighth centuries had believed that the caliph as *Imām* or 'supreme teacher' to the Muslim community should be a descendant of the family of the Prophet. Unlike the Ummayads, the Abbāsids could claim to be among the Prophet's kin on the basis of descent from his paternal uncle, Abbās. Although widely accepted, a minority rejected this claim as fraudulent, and sought the true Imām among the descendants of Alī, the Prophet's nephew. Down to 765 there was tolerably broad agreement among the Shī'ites (from *Shī'at'Alī*, 'the party of Alī') as to the hereditary descent of the Imāmate among Alī's heirs, but in that year the group split between those who came to accept the Imāmate of Dja'far al-Sādik's younger son, Mūsa, and those who recognised Dja'far's elder son, Ismā'il (whence the group's name of *Ismā'īlī*) as Imām. The former (known as Twelver Shī'ites) traced the Imāmate down to an eleventh Imām who died without heir in 874, after which it was held that the twelfth Imām existed in hiding and would one day appear messiah-like to establish a reign of justice, and usher in the end of the world. The latter, the Ismā'īlī, by the tenth century had further divided between those who recognised Ubayd Allah, the Fātimid ruler of the Maghreb, as Imam, and the Karmatī, who rejected the Fātimids as imposters.

At the beginning of the tenth century the Abbāsid caliphs remained the accepted religious leaders of most of the Islamic world, but that position was under growing threat. Shī'ite propagandists from the various sects were operating in most provinces, and in some areas had attracted a considerable following. The greatest danger came from the two sects who had managed to turn this support into aggressive political power. In 909 the Fātimids had toppled the autonomous but pro-Abbāsid Aghlabids in North Africa and were planning to march east on Baghdad. Two early attempts to take Egypt in 913–15 and 919–21 failed, but the danger remained to preoccupy the Ihshīdid rulers of Egypt, and rather more distantly to threaten Baghdad. Much closer to home were the Karmatī whose centre was at Bahrayn on the Gulf, but who were also influential among the Syrian tribes. They had already besieged Damascus, defeated a caliphal army and plundered pilgrim caravans in the first decade of the century, but from 923 to a truce in 939 they waged a devastating war in southern Iraq which at times had the Abbāsid regime struggling for survival. Between 927 and 929 Baghdad was effectively besieged, and in 930 the Karmatī sacked Mecca taking away the Black Stone of the Ka'ba as a trophy. Inevitably the Abbāsid caliphate was far more concerned to deal with these threats than any distant danger from infidel Byzantium.

Exacerbating Abbāsid difficulties – and in part stemming from them – was the relative economic decline of Iraq and the consequent shift in the balance of power within the Islamic world in favour of Egypt. The wealth of Iraq, based on a sophisticated system of irrigation agriculture, had underpinned early Abbāsid power; but from the mid-ninth century the system began to decay. A disastrous blow was the revolt of the Zandj, the slaves, mostly black Africans, who worked the reclaimed marshlands of southern Iraq. The revolt which lasted from 869 until its final brutal suppression in 883 diverted large Abbāsid armies from deployment elsewhere and, compounded by the effects of the Karmatī wars during the first half of the tenth century, did lasting damage to the Iraqi economy. Economic decline

and the growing inability of central authority to extract sufficient revenues from its subjects contributed to a spiral of financial
crisis. By the 930s the caliphate, unable to pay its armies, was
in effect bankrupt.

Under these circumstances it was essential to keep control
of Egypt and to tap its resources, but here as elsewhere the
later ninth- and tenth-century Abbāsids proved unable to overcome the forces of provincial separatism. Ahmad b. Tūlūn, a
Turkish ghulām, who had once arrived in Iraq as one of a
present of slaves sent to the caliph al-Maʿmūn, was appointed
governor of Egypt in 868, and in theory remained a loyal servant of the Abbāsids, making payments to the central government in Baghdad. In practice Ibn Tūlūn and his successors
pursued their own interests and spent most of Egypt's resources
building a powerful army of black and Turkish ghilmān with a
view to dominating Syria and Palestine. In 905 the Abbāsids
managed to topple Ibn Tūlūn's grandsons, but more direct
Abbāsid rule proved just as ineffective in using Egypt to buttress the caliph's power in Iraq. In 935 one in a succession of
short-lived Turkish ghulām governors, Muhammad b. Tughdj
(a native of Farghāna in Central Asia) managed to establish
himself at the same time as the caliphate's ability to exercise
any effective authority was rapidly coming to an end. In 936
he was granted the title of *Ikhshīd*, once that of the kings of
Farghana, and it is as the Ikhshīdids that he and his dynasty
are generally known. His descendants and the black eunuch
Kāfūr who from 946 to his death in 968 was the dominant
figure in the regime, ruled Egypt nominally as loyal servants
of the Abbāsid caliph, but in practice they pursued the same
independent path as the Tūlūnids before them. Egypt had
slipped irrevocably from Iraqi control.

As the old order was breaking apart, a new order was coming into being. One pillar of the new order was an independent Egypt which under various guises would henceforth play
the part of great power in the Near East for the rest of the
middle ages; the other was the rise of a powerful Persian state
in the form of the Būyid confederation. This new force in Near
Eastern politics had its basis in the military skills of the predominantly Shīʿite Daylami mountaineers of northern Persia which enabled Alī b. Būga and his brothers (whence Būyid,

or sometimes Buwayhid) to establish themselves as rulers of western and central Persia and eventually Iraq – although Iraq was always something of an ungovernable annexe to the main centres of Būyid power in Persia. The Fātimids finally achieved the conquest of Egypt in 969; the Būyid Ahmad b. Būga (Alī's younger brother, usually known by his honorific title Mu'izz al-Dawla, 'Glorifier of the State') had conquered Iraq in 945, but it was not until the later 970s that either regime was securely established. Hence from the end of the 920s when Abbāsid military power dissolved, to the establishment of secure Fātimid and Būyid authority in the later 970s, the Byzantines had an opportunity for expansion in the Near East without precedent since the creation of the Islamic empire in the seventh century.

During this period Byzantium faced no major power on its eastern and south-eastern front. The emirate of Tarsos had been politically linked with Egypt since the ninth century when Palestine, Syria and Cilicia had submitted to Ibn Tūlūn, and Egyptian support had been a factor in the strength of Tarsiote raids into Asia Minor; but their Ikhshīdid successors in the tenth century were preoccupied with the Fātimid threat and in so far as they concerned themselves with Tarsos it was to avoid provoking a Byzantine alliance with their Shī'ite enemies.

The only opponent capable of making serious counter-attacks against the Byzantines was the Hamdānids, but it is worth emphasising how very limited their power was. The Hamdānids were not an alien dynasty of ghulām governors who had established a *de facto* independence, but a branch of the Banu Taghlib tribe who had built up a local dominance over their tribal rivals in the ninth century by means of a close and usually loyal relationship with the Abbāsid caliphs in Baghdad. When Abbāsid power began to crumble they had tried to shore it up by interventions in Iraq, but outclassed by the superior forces of the Būyids they had no choice but to carve out independent principalities in Syria and the Djazīra – the emirates of Aleppo and Mosul respectively. Their failure to defeat the Būyids was indicative of a recurrent inability to match the military power of their neighbours. If they relied on the local Arab tribal forces which had brought them to power in the first place it made them more politically acceptable to their subjects but such armies were no match either for Byzantine troops or for the armies of Turkish ghilmān, Daylamis and Kurds that the Būyids and Ikhshīdids could put in the field. If they invested in armies of ghilmān it aroused bitter local resentment, and in any event they were constrained by the lack of resources to pay for them – a lack made steadily worse by devastating Byzantine raids.

The lack of resources was not offset by any union between Aleppo and Mosul. The Hamdānids did not prefigure the powerful Zengid state of the twelfth century in the same area. Unlike under Zengid rule, the two emirates never co-operated. In the 930s and early 940s, before Sayf al-Dawla had come to Aleppo, he had supported his brother Nasir al-Dawla's ambitions in Iraq, but after 942 he played no further part, and Nasir al-Dawla never contributed anything to the war with the Byzantines.

Sayf al-Dawla only came to the Byzantine frontier for want of other options. Driven out of Iraq, and unable to seize southern Syria from the Ikhshīdids, Sayf al-Dawla was able to establish himself in Aleppo, Mayyafārikīn and Tarsos because the Ikhshīdids were happy to see someone else with the responsibility of waging Holy War against the infidel. Even in this region Hamdānid control was never complete. Sayf al-Dawla's eloquent court poets hide a reality in which important parts of northern Syria and the western Djazīra – notably Edessa – refused to recognise his authority. Much of Sayf al-Dawla's time, even at the height of Byzantine operations, was taken up with campaigns against local resistance. His posthumous reputation is that of a great war-leader against the Byzantines, but in many respects Sayf al-Dawla was a paper tiger, short of money, short of soldiers and with little real base in the territories he controlled. By the time of his death in 967 the emirate of Aleppo was defeated and bankrupt; its survival into the eleventh century depended entirely on its status as a Byzantine protectorate.

In view of this situation beyond the frontier the success of the Byzantine offensive comes as little surprise. What is more curious is why it took so long to begin the conquest of northern Syria, why progress was so slow, why the Byzantines made such difficulties out of dealing with Sayf al-Dawla, and why there was not more enthusiasm for reconquering the lost provinces of the late Roman empire.

The Costs of Success: Byzantium, 863–976

States which have become accustomed to the profits of expansion and conquest run into difficulties when expansion halts or is even reversed, and annual influxes of booty are replaced by the unprofitable demands of frontier defence. A good ninth-century example is the Carolingian empire where the drying up of the inflows of plunder that had paid for the magnificence of Charlemagne's court exacerbated his successors' political problems.[44]

Tenth-century Byzantium is the reverse case. The empire had managed to survive the crises of the seventh century by adapting to a dour struggle for survival – a battle of defence with few glorious victories, little booty and no new lands to conquer. The key to survival had been the effective exploitation of late Roman institutions and political traditions, above all the imperial court at Constantinople on which all political life was focused, and which acted as the sole significant fount of wealth and status. The resources of the empire were tapped through taxation and dispersed in *rogai* (salaries) to a political élite who could find little else to attract their ambition in a poor and war-ravaged Asia Minor.

Constantinople's role was reinforced by a particularly Byzantine development of late Roman Christian culture. Byzantium was above all the land of orthodoxy, 'correct belief', which ensured God's favour to His chosen people, and which was defined in the imperial city. Orthodoxy, rather than any sense of Roman-ness, was what held the empire together and ensured that the population of its territories looked to Constantinople as a focus of its identity.

This political and cultural system was remarkably successful. The military experience of the seventh to mid-ninth century was – with temporary exceptions – one of dogged if somewhat ineffective defence punctuated by spectacular disasters. Yet the empire never looked like falling apart from within and never faced any serious threats of secession in its Asia Minor and south Balkan heartlands. (The case of Italy and Sicily being exceptional for the very reason that their local élites were to a large degree outside the orbit of the Constantinopolitan court.) The only danger the empire faced was conquest from without.

From the later ninth century onwards, by which time any
real threat of conquest had disappeared, the political and cultural structure which had preserved Byzantium through its Dark
Age began to face new difficulties, paradoxically, brought on
by success. Firstly, the advances in the east and the new security these obtained for the rest of Asia Minor created alternative sources of wealth and status that could counter-balance
the authority of Constantinople. The experience of successful
warfare on the eastern front created new solidarities and a new
sense of identity among the militarised population of the borderlands. Constantinople could increasingly appear as a distant parasite, associated with intrusive tax collectors and civil
officials resented as carpet-bagging outsiders. Secondly, the
conquest after 957 of wide areas of the northern Fertile Crescent not only further threatened Constantinople's role as sole
source of wealth, but possibly more significant threatened the
ideological coherence of the empire. Muslims were the least
of the problem. Many had left to find new homes in lands that
were still under Islamic rule, others had been resettled by the
Byzantines as prisoners-of-war in Asia Minor.[45] Those that remained were inevitably excluded from any significant role in
the new order. The difficulty lay with the large Christian populations. Armenians and Syrians had their own strong cultural
traditions and a sense of identity bound up in their languages,
churches and literature. For the Monophysite majorities in both
areas the Constantinopolitan church was at best deeply mistaken,
at worst heretical. Even the Melkites – the Chalcedonian largely
Arabic-speaking Christians of the Islamic world who shared Constantinople's definition of orthodoxy – felt themselves to have
little in common with a Greek church with which they had
lost contact centuries before. It is striking, for example, to see
that as late as 966 the Melkite patriarch of Antioch, Christopher,
was a loyal supporter of Sayf al-Dawla against the emir's enemies in the city who wanted to come to terms with the
Byzantines.[46] None of these differences was in theory insurmountable. Greek, Armenian and Syrian Christianity had shared roots
in late Roman culture, and indeed the late Roman empire was
an example of how cultural differences could be submerged in
a widely shared sense of belonging to a Christian Roman empire. However, in practice concessions on either side were difficult

to make given the fog of mutually incomprehensible languages and the way ecclesiastical arrangements, ceremonies and details of theology were so closely bound up with group identity. For the Constantinopolitan élite the identity at stake was that of the orthodox empire, and the fear existed that an alliance between disaffected soldiers in the eastern armies and the non-orthodox peoples of the east would endanger the unity of the empire and the relationship with God that had so far preserved the state from destruction.

The earliest signs of important change are the appearance of a group of eastern military families who would come to dominate Byzantine politics in the tenth century: the Phokades, the Maleïnoi, the Argyroi, the Skleroi, the Kourkuai and the Doukai – to name only the leading representatives of a wider phenomenon. These families were the principal local beneficiaries as the balance of warfare swung in favour of the Byzantines, both in terms of the tangible benefits of annual inflows of booty and estates newly secure from enemy raids, and the more intangible but equally important advantages of the growing confidence and sense of identity among the inhabitants of the frontier zone. All had substantial eastern estates, an extensive network of kin, clients and dependants among the eastern themes, and close links with the world beyond the frontier, especially that of the Armenian naxarars with whom the Byzantines were becoming increasingly involved. (The Phokades, the Skleroi and the Kourkuai seem to have been originally Armenian families, but the others too had close if undefined ties.)[47]

The new world these families occupied can be illustrated by looking at Cappadocia, the heartland of the related Phokas and Maleïnos clans. A prosperous agricultural region in the late Roman period, the paucity of evidence for the seventh to mid-ninth centuries reveals the familiar pattern of decline and poverty. However, from the second half of the ninth century onwards, and increasing in numbers dramatically from the beginning of the tenth century, churches, chapels, monasteries and hermit's cells were cut into the soft volcanic tufa. A number include lavish fresco cycles, the best reflecting the latest and no doubt most expensive Constantinopolitan taste.[48]

By the early tenth century at the latest – coinciding with the speeding up of the Cappadocian church boom – the military families had between them gained an effective monopoly over the key commands on the eastern frontier. The major frontier themes of the Anatolikon, the Charsianon, Cappadocia, Seleukeia and Chaldia were increasingly held by no one but the Phokades, the Maleïnoi, the Argyroi, the Kourkuai, the Doukai and their close relations. Even the post of domestic of the scholai who in practice acted as commander-in-chief on the eastern frontier was difficult to fill outside this group. When a member of these families rebelled or fell out of favour either they or their heirs were soon reappointed. Andronikos Doukas fled the empire in 907 to die an apostate exile in Baghdad, but his son Constantine was back in the empire by the next year and was soon strategos of the Charsianon – taking over from Eustathios Argyros who himself had been strategos between two periods of exile, during the second of which he died in Melitene. His sons' careers carried on regardless.[49] (The destruction of the Doukas family after the failed coup of 913 was an unparalleled event that seems to have shocked contemporaries and is perhaps best interpreted as the panicked reaction of a frightened and insecure regency regime in its first few months.)[50]

Yet the military families' ability to convert their growing domination of the frontier world into power at the centre was slow in coming. To begin with their appearance hardly wrought great changes in the patterns of Byzantine politics, and one must be careful not to exaggerate the distinctiveness of these families when they first appear. Their early use of surnames (which are very rare in Byzantine sources before the mid-ninth century) certainly shows a conscious pride in *eugeneia*, 'noble birth', and an awareness of being part of a family group that could include several branches and whose virtues were passed on from generation to generation; but the eastern military families were not alone in the use of such surnames. Some of the earliest examples come from civil families based in Constantinople.[51]

Similarly their actions and careers during the ninth and early tenth century follow fairly traditional paths. Those of the Skleroi, for example, seem at this date to fit into a long-established pattern of Armenian and other foreigners coming to Constantinople, serving in the imperial army and winning the rewards of high court rank and rich salaries. Originally perhaps from western Armenia, by the early ninth century some Skleroi had entered Byzantine service while others were clients of the emir of Melitene. The earliest reference is to a Leo Skleros who in 811 seems to have been removed from a post in Constantinople and sent to be strategos of the Peloponnese. Another Skleros may have been active in the east in the mid-century when he was asked by the patriarch Photios to carry a letter to one of the eastern metropolitans; but the next Skleros to appear brings us back to Constantinople and the west. In 894 Niketas Skleros, holding the high court rank of patrikios, was sent by Leo VI to negotiate with the Magyars their attack on Bulgaria. This Skleros may also have been a former commander of the imperial fleet.[52]

The Phokades too followed a traditional path to success. Either the descendants of a converted Arab from Tarsos or, much more likely, of an Armenian family from Iberia, in either case by the mid-ninth century the Phokas family were established in Cappadocia on the Byzantine eastern frontier, where in the 870s they attracted the notice of Basil I. Their military skills, political loyalty and imperial favour brought them high office and court titles. The first named Phokas is Nikephoros (usually called 'the elder' to distinguish him from his grandson, the emperor of the same name). His father who in 872 had been a *tourmarches* – a divisional officer – of one of the eastern themes, later commanded the themes of Cherson, the Aegean Sea and finally the senior eastern theme of the Anatolikon. Nikephoros became one of the emperor's *oikeioi*, his close companions or familiars. He moved to Constantinople where Basil gave him a palace and the post of protostrator that involved responsibility for the imperial stables and the duty of accompanying the emperor on horseback. Later Nikephoros was appointed strategos of the Charsianon – one of the front-line themes in the east – before in 885 he was sent to take command of all Byzantine forces in Italy. Recalled on Basil's death in 886 by Leo VI who shared his father's affection for Nikephoros, he was appointed domestic of the scholai, a post he probably held until his death in 896.[53] Like the careers of the ninth-century Skleroi, those of the early Phokades can be paralleled by several earlier examples. Nikephoros' career echoes that of the future Leo III attracting the attention of Justinian II in the late seventh century; and indeed of his own patron, Basil, who had himself been an oikeios of Michael III. Both families in fact are good

examples of the way the imperial court could operate, attracting ambitious provincials to the centre and tying them to the
service of the empire.[54]

The wider pattern of politics between the 860s and the 920s
also follows for the most part traditional lines. The sources for
this period are contradictory and wildly biased so that no 'auth-
orised' narrative account is possible. Modern historians have
constructed several rival versions depending on whether they
give primacy to one source or another, and if one is willing to
recognise that all these sources are in different ways deliberately misleading the possibilities become almost endless. However, taken as a whole what they do give – whether their stories
are true or not – is a picture of a political world focused on
Constantinople and the court, where power elsewhere in the
form of wide estates, or a clientele in the army, has very limited bearing on politics at the centre. Basil I's rise to power
entirely on the basis of the emperor's favour is a case in point.
His grandiose Armenian ancestry is a later fiction to disguise
an utterly obscure background. But once crowned and in control of Constantinople the opposition of several strategoi could
be simply brushed aside.[55] Similarly Leo VI spent his entire
reign in Constantinople. Outside the imperial city Byzantine
armies suffered a number of humiliating disasters, but the
political dangers Leo faced were all inside the court. If he could
keep control there – which he did, despite some alarms such
as an assassination attempt in 903 – Leo was secure. In 905,
for example, Andronikos, head of the great Doukas family and
a successful domestic of the scholai, rebelled (or possibly was
tricked into rebellion) Once it became clear that Constantinople was secure the threat to Leo's rule vanished. Andronikos
sat for several months with his kinsmen and dependants in the
virtually impregnable fortress of Kabala (10 kilometres west of
Ikonion, modern Konya) before fleeing to Baghdad.[56]

The rise of Romanos Lekapenos is another good illustration.
The Lekapenoi, or rather the Abastaktoi, 'the unbearable', as
Romanos' ancestors called themselves, were an Armenian family who like the Skleroi and the Phokades had managed to win
imperial favour. In this case Romanos' father had saved Basil I's
life when on campaign against the Paulicians in 872. Yet
despite the eastern military background provincial support

played no discernable part in Romanos' rise to the throne. In Leo VI's later years he had lived in Constantinople and served for a period as strategos of the naval theme of Samos. Possibly in 912, the year of Leo's death, he was appointed droungarios of the fleet. In the critical years after the disastrous Byzantine defeat by the Bulgars at Achelous in 917 Romanos used the fleet as a base to seize control of the imperial palace and the fourteen-year old emperor, Constantine Porphyrogenitos. His crucial supporters were palace officials fearful that Leo Phokas, the elder Nikephoros' son and domestic of the scholai, would seize power for himself. Leo had the backing of the eastern armies, a loyal family and a widespread network of clients in the east, but once Romanos was in control of Constantinople and the palace his position crumbled away. There was no civil war and in August 919 the now blinded Leo was paraded in mockery through the streets of the imperial capital.[57]

By the 920s the eastern families were still somewhat removed from power at the centre. But the threat was there, and they were crucially placed to take full advantage of each new gain in the east.

The year 934 marks an important new stage in the relationship between the eastern military families and central government. The emperor Romanos Lekapenos was already concerned by reports reaching Constantinople describing wealthy landowners – which in effect inevitably meant office-holders, whether civil, military or ecclesiastical – buying up the lands of peasants and smaller landowners hit first by a famine in 927–8, and most recently by an exceptionally long and bitter winter. In May 934 Melitene finally fell. Its conquest had already brought substantial profits in booty to the eastern armies, and in future it would allow them to exploit more effectively lands that were already Byzantine but had hitherto been exposed to what remained of Melitene's military potential. The same beneficiaries – and above all the kin and clients of John Kourkuas, the domestic of the scholai who had captured the city – were now poised to take over Melitene's fertile plain. In response to these developments which threatened to enrich the emperor's subjects in ways that were not under his control, Romanos took two steps which were to set a pattern for his successors.[58]

Firstly he annexed the plain of Melitene as a *kouratoreia*, a separately administered body of imperial estates. Such estates had been extensive in the late Roman period but they had shrunk to a small remnant after the seventh century, presumably as large-scale ownership of land in war-ravaged Asia Minor became less attractive. From the beginning of the ninth century onwards their extent gradually increased, as first Michael I and then Romanos himself brought estates they had held before they became emperor into imperial hands; but the acquisition of Melitene significantly altered their scale and political significance.[59] It gave the emperor a more direct presence on the eastern frontier, and by keeping the major share of the gains from the new conquest in imperial hands it offered a promising means of harnessing the eastern advance and the families who were leading it to central control.

In September of the same year Romanos issued a new law, or 'novel', aimed at preventing the 'more powerful' as the text calls them from buying up peasant land. Building on earlier legislation, the novel strictly enforces a peasant's obligation to offer any land intended for sale, lease or share-cropping to other members of the village community (beginning with his kin and moving by degree to those who were only his neighbours and fellow villagers). Any powerful outsider who had acquired land in a village taking unjust advantage of the recent crisis brought about by the famine and harsh winter was simply to be ejected with no compensation; if they had paid a just price for the property they were also to be ejected but with the repayment of the purchase price either by the original owners, their kinsmen or other members of the village community. If landownership by the powerful in the village pre-dated the famine and they were not accused of acting oppressively (in which case they would be ejected with or without compensation depending on the circumstances) they could remain but they were strictly forbidden from acquiring more village land. In future any powerful person who broke the law was to be ejected with no compensation.[60]

On the face of it the legislation is concerned to protect the village community. Central government valued these self-governing communities largely for their duty of joint-liability for their members' taxes. However – aside from the possibility of undue influence and corruption – it is not obvious that this duty could not have been equally well fulfilled in a village where a wealthy outside landowner owned much of the land. Indeed in many villages it was clearly common for one family or group of families from within the village to prosper and buy out their neighbours so creating a comparable situation to the one the novel is supposedly designed to prevent. Romanos explicitly if unrealistically condemns this and threatens to reduce such newly wealthy villagers to their original state, but in fact it was a process beyond imperial control and the lack of any clearly defined sanction against them in the novel makes it plain that the preservation of an ideal village community was not the emperor's chief concern.[61] Increasingly peaceful and secure, Asia Minor was becoming more prosperous and with it the village communities were changing, usually in the direction of greater distinctions of wealth between rich and poor within the community. Imperial novels could not halt this process and if this had been the principal purpose of Romanos' legislation its impact would have been very limited. Instead the main target of the novel was the powerful, and the preservation of village communities in their current form was merely a pretext. Romanos issued the legislation and it was followed up by his successors for the rest of the century because it gave central government a new means of curbing the increasing dominance of the countryside by aristocratic families – including but not exclusively the military families of the eastern frontier.

A further development which had the effect of lessening the power of the strategoi inside their themes and hence the influence of the military families who held these posts was the gradual creation for the first time since the eighth century of a separate civil administration in the themes under officials known as theme judges. The early stages of this process are not well documented or dated, nor can they be directly associated with Romanos but it was certainly under way during his lifetime. At the beginning of the tenth century the strategoi were still responsible for both the civil and military administration of their themes. The two most senior civil officials were the *protonotarios* and the *chartoularios* who reported to the offices in Constantinople of the *sakellion* and *stratiotikon* respectively. Part of their role was expressly understood to be to keep central government informed of the activities of their strategoi but even so they remained under the strategos' authority. Theme judges are attested but solely as judicial officials lower in the hierarchy than the protonotarios and chartoularios and, like them, subordinate to the strategos. During the early decades of the tenth century there are signs that the civil administration of the themes was gaining more independent authority, and (where mentioned) the leading civil official appears to be the theme judge. In 911 when the strategos of Hellas and his military staff were deployed in an unsuccessful expedition against Crete the theme judge appears in contemporary documents preserved in the *De Ceremoniis* as the acting civil authority in the theme. Documents from the archives of Mount Athos dating to the 920s show the judge of the theme of Thessalonica holding the same court rank as the strategos and apparently sharing responsibility for administrative decisions. Although one has to be cautious in applying later conditions to the tenth century, judges in the eleventh century certainly tended to be civil officials in Constantinople whose careers would typically include two or three short spells of provincial administration in different themes, and who were more likely to reflect the interests of central government than those of the local military families.[62]

In so far as such limited sources as the various versions of the Logothete's chronicle enable us to tell, Romanos Lekapenos seems to have maintained his authority well during the twenty-four years of his reign. For all but eighteen months of this period John Kourkuas was domestic of the scholai, and there is no evidence that he was anything other than a loyal servant of the emperor. However, there are traces of tensions. Preserved in Theophanes Continuatus is the summary of a lost history of Kourkuas' deeds in eight books written by a certain Manuel, protospatharios and judge, who acclaims John Kourkuas as a new Trajan or Belisarios. Manuel was probably writing in the late 950s or early 960s, but if these comparisons (especially that with the soldier emperor Trajan) were current twenty years earlier, at the height of Kourkuas' career, supporters of the Lekapenoi would have had reason to be suspicious. Bearing in mind how the Kourkuas family and their wider circle of kinsmen, clients and dependants had had every opportunity to establish themselves as the leaders of the frontier world during John's period of office it is not surprising that as soon as they seized power Stephen and Constantine Lekapenos sacked Kourkuas in December 944. In both the *Story of the Image of Edessa*, written by a supporter of Constantine Porphyrogenitos, and in the comparatively pro-Lekapenos account preserved in the Logothete's Chronicle, John Kourkuas is entirely written out of his finest hour – the forced surrender by the emir of Edessa of the sacred Mandylion and its triumphant entry on 16 August 944 into the imperial city. Clearly even if the Lekapenoi and Constantine Porphyrogenitos might fight amongst themselves to be associated with this triumph, there was no question of any credit going to the powerful eastern general who had actually won the victory.[63]

Although the Logothete does not tell us any more about John Kourkuas' replacement than that he was 'the patrikios Pantherios, a relative of the emperor Romanos', he can probably be identified. It is almost certain that he would have been a member of one of the eastern military families. After twenty-two years of leadership by the Kourkuas family, and with the other military families filling the rest of the commands on the eastern frontier, no one else would have had the necessary experience. Most of the leading families can be ruled out on various grounds, but there is a gap in our knowledge of the Skleros family at exactly this period. Pantherios was not a common Byzantine name, and the Skleroi are the only eastern family who are known to have used it. This combined with the fact that patrikios Pantherios Skleros is known from a lead seal now in the Hermitage Museum at St Petersburg argues in favour of a recent suggestion that the new domestic was a Skleros.[64]

Pantherios Skleros – supposing the identification to be correct – lasted just over a month. Stephen and Constantine Lekapenos deposed their now elderly father, Romanos, on 16 December 944, but on 27 January 945 the Lekapenoi brothers were arrested at dinner by Constantine Porphyrogenitos who (aged forty) took power for the first time. Both the December and the January coups involved several members of the eastern frontier families, including the Phokades and the Argyroi, and two Armenian families, the Kourtikioi and the Tornikioi (the latter being kinsman of the princes of Taron); but they remained classic palace plots in the traditional Byzantine style.

They turned on whispered conversations in dark corners leading to suddent arrests and a new regime before most Constantinopolitans, let alone outsiders, knew what was happening. The opinions of the armies on the frontier still counted for nothing.[65]

On one level the politics of Constantine Porphyrogenitos' reign from 945 to 959 and that of his son, Romanos II Porphyrogenitos, from 959 to 963 continue the pattern of the previous two decades. New gains were annexed as imperial *kouratoreiai*, and the land legislation was used as a means of disciplining the aristocracy in the provinces. Constantine Porphyrogenitos' novel on the soldiers, already discussed in Chapter 7 for its legislation in defence of the traditional organisation of the themes, was also deliberately framed to stop the eastern generals building up their own private armies. Within their themes the strategoi's authority continued to be circumscribed by the growing independence of the civil administration under the theme judge. The treaties 'On Skirmishing Warfare', composed in the 960s and 970s but reflecting conditions in the previous decade seen from the perspective of the military families, complains bitterly about the authority which theme judges had come to exercise at the expense of the strategos.[66]

Constantine and Romanos can also be seen carefully keeping what political control they could over the military families. The Argyroi were given no post in the east but were sent to take command in southern Italy and the Balkans, presumably with the intention of splitting them from their natural eastern allies.[67] The command of the 949 expedition to Crete, which held out the prospect of a triumphant boost to the reputation of the new regime, was kept from all the military families – despite its reliance on eastern troops to do the fighting – and entrusted to Constantine Gongylios, a eunuch of the imperial bedchamber.[68] Another eunuch served on the eastern frontier. Romanos Lekapenos' illegitimate son Basil, who had been castrated as a child, was made patrikios by the emperor Constantine and given the highest eunuch office of *parakoimomenos* (Keeper of the Imperial Bedchamber). In 958 he was sent to share the command of the army that took Samosata, and he was granted a triumphal procession in the hippodrome on his return.[69] In

the newly conquered territories of the east the influence of
the military families was bound to be strongest and the possibilities of inserting an effective local commander whose primary loyalties were to a distant emperor in Constantinople
correspondingly weak. However, the organisation of newly conquered territories into small 'Armenian themes' each under a
separate strategos did at least create a body of new officers
who reported directly to the emperor rather than a series of
posts subordinate to the existing strategoi. Finally, and perhaps most significantly, during the first half of the 950s – despite what looks rather like deliberate obstruction from the
domestic of the scholai – Constantine tried hard to negotiate
peace with Sayf al-Dawla and a halt to further advance.

Yet in other ways this was a period of decisive change. Apart
from Constantine himself the major beneficiaries of the down-
fall of the Lekapenoi were the Phokas family. Since the humiliating failure to Leo Phokas' attempt to seize power in 919
the Phokades had been out in the political wilderness. In 941
Leo's brother Bardas was temporarily recalled to take command
of troops hastily gathered to oppose the Rus attack on Constantinople at a time when John Kourkuas was still hurrying
back from the east, and this softening of their exclusion may
explain the presence of Bardas Phokas and his sons, Nikephoros
and Leo, in the imperial palace in December 944. But Constantine's rise to power brought about a revolution in their
prospects. Bardas was raised to the rank of magistros and appointed domestic of the scholai, his eldest son, Nikephoros,
was made strategos of the Anatolikon, Leo became strategos
of the Phokas-heartland of Cappadocia, and his third son,
Constantine, received the southernmost frontier theme of
Seleukeia. Other themes would have gone to Bardas' close kinsmen, the Maleïnoi.[70]

During the first half of the 950s the Phokades achieved a
position of strength but only one comparable to that held by
the Kourkuai for most of Romanos' reign. However, after
Nikephoros Phokas had succeeded his father as domestic of
the scholai in 955, and with the beginning of the era of Byzantine conquests beyond the Taurus and Anti-Taurus in 957, the
Phokas clan was able to play a new role in Byzantine politics.
The public demonstration of this was the series of public

triumphs which were celebrated in Constantinople from 956 onwards. Particularly under Constantine Porphyrogenitos an effort was made by the emperor to merge the achievements of the Phokas family in the triumph of the regime. The focus for the 956 triumph was not, as on later occasions, a victorious general's parade in the hippodrome but the ritual trampling underfoot by the emperor of Sayf al-Dawla's cousin, Abu'l-Ashāʿir, elsewhere in the city. Nonetheless the real role of the Phokades and their allies who had actually captured the prisoner must have been fairly obvious. The message would have been made even plainer by Leo Phokas' triumph of 960, when unlike 956 they paraded through the hippodrome with a great procession of booty and captives; and by those of Nikephoros Phokas in 961 after the conquest of Crete, and in April 963 after the sack of Aleppo. The latter triumph would have been arranged beforehand, but it actually took place just after Romanos II's death when Nikephoros was looking to reinforce his political position. Booty from the Cretan triumph two years before was brought out again to remind onlookers that he had succeeded where all previous attempts for more than a century had failed. Also included was part of St John the Baptist's cloak which had been found in Aleppo. Nikephoros was evidently determined that unlike John Kourkuas and the Mandylion in 944 the credit for this relic should not be hijacked by anyone else.[71]

The practical demonstration of this new power came when Nikephoros was proclaimed emperor in Kaisareia in Cappadocia by the eastern armies on 2 July 963, less than three months after his triumph in Constantinople. The situation was in several ways comparable to that of 919 when his great-uncle Leo had tried to seize power. The imperial capital was in the hands of a regency for Romanos II's two young sons (Basil II aged about five and Constantine VIII aged two or three) led by an able eunuch Joseph Bringas, who had been the dominant figure at court through Romanos' reign. The role played by Romanos Lekapenos in 919 looked set for Marianos Argyros commander-in-chief of the western armies, who had been offered the throne by Bringas and who now occupied the city with his troops. The empress Theophano and Basil (the former parakoimomenos) were opposed to Marianos and Joseph, but so had been the empress Zoe to Romanos Lekapenos. Yet in spite of this the opposition dissolved when Nikephoros reached Constantinople. A large proportion of the citizens made clear their active support for the victorious general, the eunuch Basil brought his retainers on to the streets, and Nikephoros entred the city and was crowned emperor on 16 August. It would be too much to say that an old order of Byzantine politics had been swept aside, but Nikephoros certainly represented a new balance of power in the empire, and his rise to the throne was a direct consequence of the military gains of the previous century.[72]

In some respects Nikephoros Phokas was a conventional Byzantine ruler in the pattern set by his immediate predecessors. The Italian Liudprand of Cremona's hostile but very observant account of his embassy to Constantinople in 968 shows the emperor playing a similar ceremonial role to that played by the palace-bound Constantine Porphyrogenitos, and in this respect it may be significant that Constantine's *De Ceremoniis* – his treaties on court ceremony – was revised and added to during Nikephoros' reign.[73] Nikephoros' treatment of the eastern aristocracy outside the Phokas clan also continued many aspects of his predecessors' policies. Newly conquered land in the east did go to the Phokas family, and to their allies such as the eunuch Basil whom Nikephoros restored to the position of parakoimomenos; but a great deal, including a large part of the fertile plain of Tarsos (conquered in 965) went into new imperial kouratoreia. The land legislation was maintained and despite the harsh criticism of theme judges in the treatise 'On Skirmishing Warfare', which was written on Nikephoros' orders at exactly this period, there is no sign of their removal or of any limitation of their powers.[74]

Yet 'On Skirmishing Warfare', is important evidence for a new mood in Byzantine politics. The treatise is written from the perspective of the eastern military families and shows a deep suspicion of Constantinople and its works which was soon reciprocated by the capital and its citizens. Skylitzes' source and the Arab geographer Ibn Hawkal both report that Nikephoros' regime was intensely unpopular, and their evidence is confirmed by Nikephoros' decision to build a high defensive wall round part of the imperial palace. The area was chosen to include the palace harbour of the Boukoleon lying to the south-east of the hippodrome and most of the more important buildings put up by Basil I and Constantine Porphyrogenitos, but it left out the area to the north stretching along the east side of the hippodrome as far as Hagia Sophia which had traditionally played a large role in imperial ceremonies. Nikephoros had in effect provided himself with a heavily fortified citadel with separate access to the outside world from where he could safely defy the citizens of Constantinople. Clearly the support he had enjoyed in the city in 963 had not lasted long and Nikephoros did not feel secure in his capital.[75]

The interests of those who were neither members nor clients of the Phokas clan, nor beneficiaries of the profits of successful war in the east, were bound up in the maintenance of the existing political system focused on Constantinople, and their growing objections to Nikephoros' rule centred on two issues: the emperor's devotion to his army and to continued advance in the east, and his religious policies.[76]

On the first Nikephoros was accused by his critics of showing favouritism to his soldiers, and of bankrupting the empire to pay for his wars. As well as being blamed for new and heavy taxes, and increased military obligations on all levels of society, the emperor was criticised for introducing a light-weight version of the nomisma known as the *tetarteron*, in which, it was alleged, all government payments were to be made, while all receipts were to be collected only in the old full-weight nomisma. Even his admirers accused the emperor's brother, Leo Phokas, of fraudulent speculation in the city's grain market.[77]

Whether the story of grain speculation is correct or not matters little. It serves as a further illustration of how bad relations between the emperor and his capital had become. Of the rest, much appears to have a basis in truth. The attitudes expressed in 'On Skirmishing Warfare' would lead one to expect a regime tolerant of the excesses of the military. The costs of an army capable of waging offensive war in the east were no doubt great; Nikephoros' own novels testify to an attempt to increase the obligation for military service; and the tetarteron is a fact, although the explanation as to its purpose is monetary nonsense (such a policy would simply have led to the rapid disappearance of the old full-weight nomisma), it presumably was intended to raise revenue.[78]

However, looking at the evidence of coin finds, new build-

ings, pottery, and what archaeological materials are available
from Byzantine towns – in other words the same items used to
show the collapse of the late Roman economy during the seventh century and the subsequent poverty of the Byzantine world
– tenth-century Byzantium was enjoying marked economic
growth, and it would be reasonable to imagine that it could
well have afforded the costs of war.[79] What was at stake was
clearly not the bankruptcy of the empire but a political equation that money spent on warfare – which in effect meant patronage for the military families, their dependents and allies – was
not available to be dispensed at court in the traditional manner.
The accusation that title holders no longer received their salaries
should perhaps not be taken seriously but it is further expression
of a perception among the old order that the rewards were
going elsewhere. Liudprand of Cremona records the sharp
reaction of officials of the new regime to his kind memories of
Constantine Porphyrogenitos: 'Constantine was a soft man who
spent all his time in the palace . . . but the emperor Nikephoros
is *tachycheir* – which means dedicated to matters of war – and
abhores the palace like the plague.' The threat to the traditional political establishment could not have been put more
plainly.[80]

The second issue on which Nikephoros was attacked by his
critics was his religious policies. The donations of previous
emperors to churches and charitable foundations were to be
stopped and a law was promulgated forbidding such grants in
future. On the pretext that bishops were keeping for the use
of the clergy money intended for the poor, the emperor presided
over a synod – packed, his enemies alleged, with corrupt and
time-serving bishops – which enacted that in future all episcopal
appointments had to be approved by the emperor. Worst of
all the emperor made the appalling demand that any soldier
who fell in battle should be honoured as equal to the martyrs.[81]

As with the criticism of his favouritism for the military and
his heavy expenditure on war, these accusations certainly have
a basis in truth. Nikephoros did issue a novel in 964 which
deplores the insatiable greed of monasteries and forbids new
foundations. Above all no one is to give land and property to
monasteries, charitable foundations, metropolitans or bishoprics
– they have too much already.[82] The attempt to control episcopal

appointments is not otherwise attested but sounds likely enough, and while the martyrdom story may be no more than abusive rumour it does fit a theme in Byzantine writing on the special status of soldiers fighting the infidel running from Leo VI's *Taktika* at the beginning of the tenth century through to 'On Skirmishing Warfare'.[83] Yet Nikephoros could not be accused of being either impious or anti-monastic. This was the same man who had brought relics of St John the Baptist and the holy keramidion back from the east, who maintained a strict personal devotion to the cult of his hermit uncle, St Michael Maleïnos, and had himself intended to become a monk. He was a generous benefactor to the Great Lavra, the ascetic monastery founded by his spiritual father, St Athanasios, on Mount Athos, and in the 964 novel he explicitly encourages his subjects to found and support hermitages and ascetic retreats (*lavrai*). The real issue was not the emperor's piety but a belief among the traditional ecclesiastical establishment that it was being discriminated against in favour of practitioners of the newly fashionable ascetic monasticism who were popular among the eastern military families. As with the issue of military expenditure what caused resentment and fear was the perceived threat to the old order at the hands of a new force in Byzantine politics.[84]

A final aspect of Nikephoros' regime that is not covered in the surviving accusations of his critics but that was equally threatening to the existing order was his relations with the eastern Christians. Nikephoros was personally orthodox and his links outside the empire were with the Chalcedonian Iberians – had anything else been the case his enemies would certainly have pointed it out; however, an offensive policy in the east required good relations with the Monophysites and to that end Nikephoros was willing to overlook doctrinal impurity. In about 965, following successful negotiations, the emperor issued a document promising Mar John Sarigita, the patriarch of the Syrian Monophysites (known as Jacobites), that if he and his people were to repopulate the district of Melitene they would be guaranteed freedom from persecution by the Chalcedonians. Mar John accepted and to the horror of the local Chalcedonians there followed a rapid spread of new Monophysite monasteries and bishoprics in the region. Nikephoros himself, if the Monophysite historians can be relied upon, seems to have hoped to persuade the Jacobites to accept union with the Chalcedonians. In 969 the emperor brought Mar John and four of his bishops to Constantinople to spend the summer at a series of meetings presided over by the orthodox patriarch Polyeuktos. By the end of the summer – according to the Jacobite accounts – nothing had been achieved and Nikephoros was reduced to threatening them with prison and exile. Perhaps Nikephoros could not personally be tarred with accusations of heresy, but it must have been obvious to the Constantinopolitan clergy who watched these proceedings that the eastern conquests to which the emperor was so committed were likely to endanger the empire's orthodox purity with who knew what consequences in divine disfavour.[85]

By 969 there were many in Constantinople who wished to be rid of their warrior emperor, but secure in his newly fortified palace and backed by a devoted and well-rewarded army he was in an almost impregnable position. In the event his enemies were saved by a split among the military families. John Tzimiskes was Nikephoros Phokas' nephew through his mother who was the emperor's sister, but his closer ties were with the Kourkuai – his father being the son of John Kourkuas' brother, Theophilos – and the Skleroi, to whom he was linked via his wife, Maria. In 963 he had apparently been chief among those encouraging Nikephoros to march on Constantinople and he had been rewarded by appointment as domestic of the scholai. After 965, however, he must have been forced out of office because soon afterwards the domestic's role was filled by a loyal dependent of the Phokas family, the eunuch Peter. By 969 John Tzimiskes was plotting to murder the emperor.[86]

Two other soldiers dissatisfied with the Phokas regime were Michael Bourtzes and Isaac Brachamios. They had been left in charge of one of the garrisons blockading Antioch in 969. Anti-Phokas sources tell a story of how Michael and Isaac persuaded a traitor inside Antioch to put one of the main towers on the city's upper defences into their hands. Seizing the opportunity they occupied the tower, and heroically held it against great odds for three days and nights until the eunuch Peter arrived with the main Byzantine forces. Yahya b. Saʿīd, a Christian Arab who later came to live in Antioch and who was quite sympathetic to the Phokades, tells a less dramatic story in which Michael and Isaac share the credit with others. However, it is clear that they played an important part in the capture of Antioch and were conspicuously ill-rewarded, while it was Nikephoros' kinsman, Eustathios Maleïnos, who was appointed the first strategos of Antioch.[87]

Finally the plotters had the support of the empress Theophano, mother of the two young emperors, Basil and Constantine, who had married Nikephoros in September 963, and of the eunuch Basil, who like John Tzimiskes seems to have fallen out of favour with the Phokas regime. Theophano's actions were widely explained by the rumour that she had become Tzimiskes' mistress. While this may be true Theophano and Basil were also the last remaining members of the old establishment who were in any position to influence events.

On the night of 10/11 December John Tzimiskes, Michael Bourtzes, Isaac Brachamios and a small group of their supporters, presumably with the help of the empress Theophano, climbed into Nikephoros' Boukoleon palace from the side facing the sea. They headed for the imperial bedchamber but to their horror they found it empty. Panic that the plot had been betrayed was only stilled by a palace eunuch who revealed that the emperor was sleeping on the floor of a small room set aside for his meditations wrapped in the bearskin which had once protected St Michael Maleïnos. The emperor was slaughtered at once and John Tzimiskes presented as his successor to a startled palace.[88]

Despite being a murderer, the new emperor is treated quite favourably by the sources who were hostile to Nikephoros. In part this is because John successfully defeated the Rus and expelled them from the Balkans in 970–1. Since their first appearance before the city in 860 the Rus had had pride of place as the citizens' most feared enemy and any emperor who defeated them could expect to be received with enthusiasm.[89] Much more important, however, was the simple fact that he was not Nikephoros and his coup represented an unexpected reprieve from Phokas rule. Yet in fact John Tzimiskes' regime equally amounted to rule by the military families. The Phokas clan and their allies were expelled from office and their leaders sent into exile. Two serious attempts to topple John in 970 and 971 both failed, and after the second the late emperor's brother Leo, together with his eldest son, Nikephoros, were blinded. But in their place the new regime promoted the Skleroi, the Kourkuai, and other families – some even related to the Phokades – who could be bought over by high titles and senior commands. Neither the empress Theophano (whom it was convenient to saddle with the responsibility for Nikephoros' murder) nor the eunuch Basil gained much from the change of emperor. Nor did the traditional ecclesiastical establishment. The patriarch Polyeuktos had apparently demanded from John Tzimiskes as the price of his coronation firstly that Theophano and two of the lesser conspirators be sent into exile (thus fixing something of a fig leaf over the church's acquiescence in the murder of an emperor) and secondly that the synodal decision allowing the emperor to approve all appointments to bishoprics be revoked. If this is true it was a meaningless concession since the following years showed the emperor had effective control of the appointment and removal of patriarchs – as in the expulsion of Polyeuktos' successor Basil I in 973 and his replacement by Anthony I Stoudios – let alone mere bishops.[90] It is also striking that no chronicler makes any mention of John overturning Nikephoros' legislation on monastic properties. The novel which eventually did so is attributed in the body of the text to Basil II and dated to April 988. The only grounds to reattribute this to John is a later note in the margin of one of the manuscripts.[91] Against this are documents surviving on Mount Athos which show that John Tzimiskes shared all his predecessor's prejudices in favour of hermits and ascetic monks of the Athos type, and that he was desperate to win the forgiveness of St Athanasios of the Great Lavra. Under these circumstances it is difficult to believe that he would have revoked Nikephoros' great novel which was so much in their favour.[92] In effect therefore for the traditional élite outside the military families – of which the official church hierarchy was part – the coup did little more than replace one military regime with another.

Again just as his predecessor, John's main aim was to achieve conquests in the east. Leo the Deacon talks of Baghdad, and John himself names Jerusalem and Cairo.[93] But a reconquest of the former Roman empire in the Near East demanded a large army, which in turn entailed high costs, heavy taxes, and generous rewards to the soldiers and their commanders to ensure their enthusiastic loyalty. It also required a prolific source of new recruits, which in effect meant that as before the emperor would have to establish good relations with the Armenian world, and he could not afford to be too fussy about Chalcedonian orthodoxy. The appeal would have instead to be concentrated on the idea of a common Christianity shared by Arabs, Armenians, Syrians and Greeks; and the implications of that were of a Roman empire whose political ties went far beyond an identity based on Constantinopolitan orthodoxy.

Very shortly after he had seized the throne in December 969 John released the Jacobite patriarch and his bishops and sent them back to Melitene rejoicing. At the same time he appointed the Armenian Mleh – presumably a close kinsman of the Mleh who had been strategos of Lykandos and an ally of his great-uncle John Kourkuas – as domestic of the scholai. In 974 an exchange of embassies between the emperor and the Bagratuni king Ašot III led to Ašot promising to provide John with substantial military assistance. The following year John sent to Ašot a letter triumphantly describing the course of his third eastern campaign which had seen the submission of Damascus as another client state of the empire, and Byzantine forces operating in Palestine.[94]

The text only survives in the work of a twelfth-century Armenian historian, Matthew of Edessa, and there must inevitably be doubts as to whether it is genuine. However there are several points in its favour. It stands apart from the rest of Matthew's text both in terms of style and vocabulary. It is also marked out by its command of the details of Syrian politics and geography as they relate to the events of 975 and of the organisation of the Byzantine army. Finally it is similar in style and content to other imperial victory dispatches, such as those of Herakleios preserved by Theophanes and the *Chronikon Paschale*, or those of Basil I which were used in Book Five of Theophanes Continuatus.

Unfortunately modern discussion of this text has been almost entirely concerned with whether or not the letter is an accurate account of the campaign. This misses the point. It is a work of propaganda, and as such it was designed to receive maximum publicity among the Armenian naxarars with a view to cementing the military alliance with Ašot III and encouraging a wider Armenian involvement in the imperial war effort. It is intended to persuade them that if all Christian warriors were to work together, the Islamic Near East would be at their feet. Exaggeration in such a context is only to be expected.

Taken together with the chapter in 'On Skirmishing Warfare' which urges the special status due to soldiers defending the Christian empire from its enemies, John Tzimiskes' letter of 975 gives some idea of the eastern military families' political vision of the future. It shows them looking for an expansive militarised empire, in which all Christians throughout the Near East would identify themselves as rightful subjects of the Roman emperor. It was a vision with which to re-establish the Roman superpower destroyed by the rise of Islam; it was also a vision profoundly threatening to the orthodox empire centred on Constantinople that had survived the superpower's fall.[95]

John Tzimiskes did not live to bring it about. He returned to Constantinople from the east in the autumn of 975, and by 10 January 976 he was dead. Perhaps one should not believe the hostile story that the eunuch Basil had poisoned the emperor, but he like many others in the imperial city must have been grateful that the second soldier emperor lasted fewer years even than the first.[96]

10. The Reign of Basil II, 976–1025

The Byzantine World in 976

AS SEEN from the perspective of the eighteen-year old Basil II
and that of his closest advisors the world in 976 was one which
had changed radically over the previous century. When Basil's
namesake, his great great grandfather, Basil I, seized the throne
in 867 the empire's eastern borders had not reached the Taurus and Anti-Taurus ranges; Armenia had effectively been an
Arab sphere of influence, and the long-standing alliance with
the Khazar qaghanate had been one of the fixed points of
imperial policy. In the Balkans the empire had faced the powerful Bulgar state. Crete and Cyprus had been in Arab hands,
and Sicily had rapidly been going the same way. On the south
Italian mainland the imperial presence had amounted to little
more than the outposts of Otranto and Reggio. At John
Tzimiskes' death in January 976 the empire stretched to Syria
and the Djazīra. The former raiding emirates of Melitene, Kālīkalā and Tarsos were the seats of Byzantine strategoi; Aleppo
was a Byzantine protectorate and the ruler of Damascus recognised himself to be the emperor's subject. Western Armenia
was imperial territory to within a day's ride of Lake Van; further east most of the greater Armenian naxarars were effectively the emperor's clients. To the north of the Caucasus the
Khazar qaghanate had disappeared. The empire's allies in the
northern world were now the nomad Pečenegs who dominated
the Ukrainian steppe, and the Rus – although this was somewhat in abeyance as a consequence of the war of 970–1 and
the political chaos in Kiev which followed. The Bulgar qaghanate
no longer existed, and its territories had been annexed to the
empire. Crete and Cyprus were both imperial themes, and although the last outpost on Sicily had fallen as recently as 965
the position on the mainland had been transformed.

Inside the empire the court operated much as in the ninth
century, but the central control of Byzantine society that it

represented was under threat. The principal challenge was from the eastern military families. They still wanted the status and salaries which court titles and imperial office brought, but they were much less biddable than their ancestors had been before victory turned the eastern frontier into a land of opportunity. Great estates in the east, a network of kinsmen, clients and dependants who formed the core of the empire's most effective armies, and close links with the Armenian, Arab and Kurdish warlords on the other side of the frontier that depended on personal ties rather than any institutional arrangement made them uneasy subjects. Worse for Basil II the experience of the last thirteen years had persuaded many of the easterners that their generals were the natural rulers of the empire. (It is striking in this context to see how often Arab sources confuse the domestic of the scholai with the emperor – in the east the former was likely to be a much more potent and immediate figure.)

The threat to central control also lay in the growing wealth of Asia Minor now steadily reviving with the return of peace and security. Most of what one may call the non-eastern élite – the civil officials, ecclesiastics, and also soldiers who were not part of the eastern networks of kinship and dependency – were still tied to Constantinople by the traditional bonds of salary and status, but in a wealthier empire opportunities for investment in land and commerce were inevitably creating a society less dependant on its curial paymasters and thus potentially less loyal to the imperial government. However, in practice what ensured their support for Basil II was their experience of two successive eastern generals on the imperial throne. The story, recorded by the eleventh-century historian Skylitzes but repeating a near-contemporary source, of Nikephoros Phokas complacently allowing his Armenian troops to cause trouble in Constantinople while savagely punishing Constantinopolitans who rioted in protest, sums up much of what they hated: favouritism to alien soldiers whose adherence to non-orthodox heresies rendered them by definition non-Roman in preference to the orthodox inhabitants of the city which embodied the Roman empire.[1] They would endure much not to have another arrogant general lording over the city from the new imperial citadel of the Boukoleon – or worse still hardly visiting the capital while he showered his favours on the army in the east.

Behind the eastern military families was a large army, fresh from John Tzimiskes' last triumphant campaign, and very different in organisation and outlook from that of the ninth century. The themes were still there but only on the eastern frontier where they were controlled by the military families, and in some areas of the Balkans, such as Thrace and Macedonia, was military service still performed in person. For the most part it had been commuted into cash payments which went towards paying for the expanded cavalry tagmata and the large forces of infantry (many of whom were Armenian) required to wage offensive warfare in the east.

This confident, numerous, multi-ethnic and heterodox force was in marked contrast to the cautious defensive army of the ninth century. It was also a world apart from Constantinople. The primary loyalty of the soldiers was to their generals; and they were suspicious of the capital as money-grabbing, anti-military and in the eyes of many, heretical.

The power of the eastern families exercised through their dominance of the army was partially offset by the central government's continued control of taxation, and hence of the revenues necessary to pay the army. In theory this control had been strengthened by the creation of a civilian administration in themes under the judge, although in practice one wonders how independent such a figure could be in the eastern heartlands of the military families. Similarly, the expansion of the imperial estates and the legislation available against landowners who bought up peasant lands was only really of use from a position of strength. In the case of the estates, for example, their administrators in 976 were presumably favoured clients of the families who had supported John Tzimiskes and to regard them as a buttress for imperial authority in the east would be rather disingenuous. The Byzantine system still benefited a ruler who held Constantinople, but never before had there been such a potential threat to his authority.

One real advantage that Basil II could look to was the bitter feud which now split the military families into two hostile camps. John Tzimiskes' murder of Nikephoros Phokas and the blindings and exiles that had been necessary to establish his authority had created a permanent divide, and among the Phokades a keen desire for revenge. With even moderate political skills

Basil could expect that any opposition to his rule would not be united.

The Great Civil Wars, 976–89

John Tzimiskes died in January 976 leaving no son. The senior member of the group of related families on which John's regime had been based was Bardas Skleros. At the time Bardas was commander-in-chief of the eastern tagmata – hence in effect second-in-command to the emperor himself – and he clearly expected to succeed John as co-emperor with the young Basil II and Constantine VIII, and holder of effective power. In the event the eunuch Basil (who again held the post of *parakoimomenos*) was determined to keep the general out. Whether he was acting in pursuit of his own ambition or in what he saw to be the interests of his imperial nephews is impossible to say, but all the sources seem to be agreed that for the time being decision making was in the eunuch's hands.[2]

Under these circumstances war was inevitable. When the spring came Bardas Skleros, who was based in the region of Melitene, was acclaimed emperor. The *parakoimomenos* had tried in the months since Tzimiskes' death to limit the resources at Skleros' disposal by demoting him to be doux of Mesopotamia, but he still enjoyed powerful backing. Many Armenians (both those already serving in imperial forces, and independent princes from outside the empire) supported Skleros' campaign; as did Arab leaders (again including those from outside the empire such as the emir of Amida and the late Sayf al-Dawla's nephew, Abū Taghlib, the emir of Mosul, as well as Christian Arabs settled in imperial territory).[3] He was strongly opposed in Constantinople, where there was little wish to see another soldier emperor from the east; and by the western armies, which since 963, when Marianos Argyros had tried in vain to keep Nikephoros Phokas out of the imperial city, had been steadily hostile to the eastern military. But Skleros' greatest handicap was the split within the eastern armies brought about by the 969 murder. During 976, 977, 978 and 979 support for Skleros among the eastern military fluctuated in response to the course of the war. An important aim of many if not most soldiers in the east was to make sure they were not irretrievably committed to the losing side, but there was an influential core of kinsmen, clients and dependents of the Phokas clan for whom Bardas Skleros had inherited the guilt for Nikephoros' murder. Their support for the regime in Constantinople might be at best luke-warm, and their real loyalty to Leo Phokas' second son, Bardas, still in exile on the Aegean island of Chios, but at least the parakoimomenos did not face the united opposition which had swept Nikephoros Phokas to power in 963.

In the summer of 976 Bardas Skleros' forces managed at the second attempt to break out from the plain of Melitene westwards into the theme of Lykandos where in the region of modern Elbistan they defeated an army commanded by the eunuch Peter (a long-standing Phokas client) and Eustathios Maleïnos, one of a family closely related to the Phokades. The victory caused a rush of support to the Skleros side. The strategic fortress of Tzamandos declared for Skleros giving him command of the routes into Cappadocia; Michael Bourtzes, one of the conspirators of 969, joined Skleros bringing with him control of Antioch of which he was doux; and the Armenian Michael Kourtikios came over with Attaleia and the fleet of the Kibyrrhaiotai.[4]

Following this alarming news the parakoimomenos sent the eunuch Leo and the patrikios John with full authority to take charge of the war in Asia Minor. This appointment is a classic instance of the sources failing to give enough information. Leo was imperial protovestiarios, the second highest ranking court eunuch after the parakoimomenos. It is easy to see that he was chosen as someone to steady the situation and encourage the field commanders to an effective prosecution of the war but without giving dangerous power to a political rival. Hence he must presumably have been a reliable member of the Constantinopolitan establishment who could be trusted not to plot with the eastern generals. But who was the patrikios John? Possibly an experienced soldier sent to act as Leo's advisor. But from where, and who were his kinsmen? It is tantalising not to know to whom the parakoimomenos was willing to turn at this critical moment.[5]

Initially Leo and John managed to achieve some success. In the autumn of 977 with the remains of the eunuch Peter's army that had gathered at Kotyaion (modern Kütahya) they seem to have pushed south-east along the road to Ikonion. Following the traditional tactics of Byzantine defensive warfare, Skleros had detached a shadowing force under Michael Bourtzes and Romanos Taronites to harrass their progress. The appearance of the Arabs from Aleppo bringing the protectorate's annual tribute to Constantinople provoked an unplanned fight in which Michael and Romanos were bloodily defeated. The anti-Armenian spirit of the Constantinopolitan side is well illustrated by the aftermath when all the Armenian prisoners were slaughtered 'for being the first to join the rebellion'.[6]

To stem the flow of desertions which followed this set-back, Skleros had little choice but to risk a pitched battle. The armies met at a site, probably slightly further east along the route to Ikonion, called Rageai, and Skleros' forces were triumphant. Among the heavy casualties on the defeated side were the patrikios John and the eunuch Peter. The protovestiarios Leo was captured, and Skleros made a point of punishing those who had deserted his army with blinding – a punishment for treason against the emperor.[7]

Skleros was now in control of most of Asia Minor and could at last begin his march on the imperial capital. The position of the parakoimomenos was plainly desperate, and under these circumstances he brought Bardas Phokas from Chios to Constantinople and offered him command of the armies. Phokas accepted, and as magistros and domestic of the scholai he left for Cappadocia to raise troops. What the new commander offered was first of all the means to obtain the active co-operation of the Phokas faction among the eastern military. Indeed it is reasonable to wonder whether a factor in Skleros' success up to this point had not been a reluctance among the Phokades and their allies to prosecute actively a war in defence of the eunuch Basil. The possibility of using the Skleros threat to force the release of Bardas Phokas must have been in many people's minds from the moment Skleros had been acclaimed emperor. Secondly the Phokas link in turn offered a means of bringing the Georgians of Iberia and their ruler, David of Tao, into the war.[8]

The Iberian intervention is an important illustration of how the personal ties of the military families with their eastern neighbours were paramount over any idea of a treaty with the empire as such. The Chalcedonian Iberians were already contending with the Armenian clans prominent among Skleros' backers for control of the region between Theodosioupolis (former Kālīkalā) and Lake Van, but it was not until Bardas Phokas whom they regarded as a kinsman and friend was released from Chios that they were prepared to enter the war. A crucial source for the intervention is the Life of John and Euthymios, co-founders with Tornikios (or Tornik') of the Iviron monastery on Mount Athos. All three were Iberian nobles who had abandoned the world for an ascetic life on the holy mountain: John and his son Euthymios arriving in the 960s. Tornikios following in the first half of the 970s. The Life tells how faced with disaster the young emperors and their mother, the empress Theophano, appealed to Tornikios to come out of the monastery and lead an army against Skleros. Tornikios was with much reluctance persuaded, and eventually set out via Constantinople to Tao where David gave him an army of 12,000 Iberians to defeat the 'tyrant'. (The figure of 12,000 means no more than a large number.)[9]

The basic story is correct and can be confirmed from other sources, but evidently by the 1040s when the Life was written it had long become politic to portray Tornikios and David acting out of sympathy for the plight of the emperors, and to omit any mention of Bardas Phokas at all. In fact the Iberians had long had close ties with the Phokades. The Phokas family either was Iberian or more certainly had Iberian kinsmen. Nikephoros Phokas had ceded the district of Upper Tao to David as a reward for his participation in the campaign against Tarsos. Bardas Phokas and David had been friends since the former's period as doux of Chaldia and Koloneia (which borders Tao to the west) in 968–9. Of the Iberian monks on Mount Athos, Euthymios had for a period been brought up at Nikephoros' court – where he would presumably have known Bardas – and when his father John came to Constantinople, the emperor welcomed him and allowed Euthymios to go with his father and become a monk. Tornikios had been given the high-ranking title of patrikios by Nikephoros. He too would almost certainly have known Bardas Phokas when the latter was doux of Chaldia and Koloneia, and it is quite probable that Tornikios and Bardas had fought together on the emperor's eastern campaigns in the 960s. Finally, all three monks were closely associated with Nikephoros' spiritual father, St Athanasios of the Great Lavra. Contrary to the picture in the Life, the fact that the Iberians made no move to join the war until 978–9 makes it plain that they only did so in support of their Phokas allies.[10]

Even then David and Tornikios drove a hard bargain. David had to be paid a high price in territorial concessions and the title and annual salary of a *kouropalates*. Tornikios took back to Mount Athos a long list of precious objects and more than 1200 pounds of gold which was later invested in vast Macedonian estates.[11]

The Georgian sources, including the Life, not surprisingly give the credit for Skleros' defeat to David or Tornikios, but the one Greek account to mention them also admits that their role was crucial. Neither of Phokas' first two encounters with Skleros' forces was successful. He was defeated at the battle of Pankaleia near Amorion on 19 June 978, and again in the theme of Charsianon at Basilika Therma (a site 100 kilometres north of modern Kayseri) in the autumn. Even so it was clearly an achievement to keep his forces in the field until Iberian help could arrive. Finally on 24 March 979 at a second battle in Charsianon at Sarvenisni (probably near modern Kirşehir) Phokas and the Iberians won a decisive victory. Skleros managed to escape the disaster and fled to his Arab allies.[12] Unfortunately he reached the northern Djazīra just in time to watch his Hamdānid supporter, Abū Taghlib, driven out by the forces of the Būyid ruler of Iraq, Adud al-Dawla. Skleros and his companions were taken to Baghdad where they were kept for the next seven years.[13]

Phokas' victory settled nothing. The struggle for power in the empire continued, but now as a political cold war in which the Phokades prepared to seize the throne by force, and the regime in Constantinople endeavoured to undermine their influence. Much of this would have remained hidden but for a remarkable text preserved in an eleventh-century Iraqi chronicle. This is the report of a Būyid ambassador, Abd Allah b. Shahrām, made to Adud al-Dawla on his return from Constantinople in 982, and it provides a fascinating insight into tenth-century Byzantine internal politics at a crucial juncture. Ibn Shahrām was in Constantinople for several months including the winter of 981–2. The parakoimomenos is still the leading figure at court, but the emperor Basil II is shown as an independent force with his own loyal supporters. Even if his room for manoeuvre was limited by his opponents, Basil as emperor was still an essential part of most political decisions. (Basil's younger brother Constantine VIII is not even mentioned which confirms the impression given by all the other sources of a junior emperor kept out of active politics.) The emperor's main enemies were the Phokas family who since the recall of 978 now dominated the eastern army and were a strong presence at court. In addition to Bardas Phokas and his blinded but still active father, the *kouropalates* Leo, many of the strategoi whom Ibn Shahrām saw in Constantinople during the winter would evidently have been their political allies if not kinsmen. Bardas Phokas distrusted the young emperor – as he candidly told the Būyid ambassador. Basil in turn distrusted him and apparently had good information that Bardas was already plotting rebellion.[14]

Most interesting is the information Ibn Shahrām gives about the parakoimomenos. Although publicly close, the emperor and the parakoimomenos no longer trusted each other. Ibn Shahrām implies that the parakoimomenos was moving toward the Phokas camp. Quite why is not explained, but an obvious factor is the presence of the Constantinopolitan civil official Nikephoros Ouranos, Keeper of the Imperial Inkstand for Basil II and in regular close contact with the emperor. The parakoimomenos regarded Nikephoros Ouranos as a dangerous rival for Basil's favour; and the emperor in turn was evidently using Nikephoros as a means of escaping the parakoimomenos' influence.

The issue which had brought Ibn Shahrām to Constantinople and which brings these differences to light was that of a proposed peace treaty. Adud al-Dawla wanted in effect to sell his prisoner Bardas Skleros to Constantinople in exchange for the transfer of the Aleppo protectorate to the Būyids, plus various frontier concessions. At stake for Adud al-Dawla was the means to take over Syria and from there march against the Fātimids in Egypt. Basil II wanted peace, enabling him to cut down on the size of the eastern armies and thus undermine the Phokades; and he wanted Skleros back in Byzantine custody, partly in order to remove the threat of a new Skleros bid for the throne, and partly again in order to lessen his dependence on the Phokades who were needed to counter the Skleros danger. To achieve these ends he was willing to pay the high price of giving up Aleppo.

Naturally the Phokades and more interestingly the parakoimomenos were opposed to any peace. However, taking advantage of a serious illness which temporarily removed the parakoimomenos from negotiations, Basil II acting through Nikephoros Ouranos came to an arrangement with Ibn Shahrām which in essence conceded the Būyid's terms. The parakoimomenos recovered to face a *fait accompli* and Ibn Shahrām set off to Baghdad in triumphant mood. The only cloud he saw on the horizon was that the parakoimomenos had manoeuvred Nikephoros Ouranos into accompanying him to make the agreement with Adud al-Dawla, thus giving himself the opportunity to re-establish his dominance at court.[15]

In fact, however, the treaty was overtaken by events. By the time Ibn Shahrām and Nikephoros Ouranos reached Baghdad Adud al-Dawla was already seriously ill, and he died on 26 March 983. His son Samsām al-Dawla took over in Baghdad but Būyid power in the Djazīra soon began to disintegrate. Taking advantage of Būyid decline, Bakdjūr (a former Hamdānid ghulām, now ruling in Homs) and the Banū Khilāb bedouin backed by Fātimid forces marched on Aleppo. Only two years earlier the city's ruler Abū'l-Ma'ālī (Sayf al-Dawla's son, also known by the honorific title, Sa'ad al-Dawla, which he had been granted by the Būyids) had had to be forced by Bardas Phokas to pay tribute to Byzantium, but he now appealed to the emperor for help. If the Fātimids took over in Aleppo there would be nothing to exchange, so Basil II had no choice but to send Bardas Phokas and a large army to the rescue. The domestic reached Aleppo towards the end of September 983 and pursued Bakdjūr and his retreating allies to Homs. Bakdjūr abandoned the city and Homs was given over to a savage Byzantine sack.[16]

Both Samsām al-Dawla and Basil II were still interested in the treaty but it would have to wait until the Būyids had sufficiently recovered their authority in Syria and the Djazīra to take advantage of its terms. Meanwhile Samsām al-Dawla preferred to keep Bardas Skleros in reserve.

In 985 Fātimid forces seized the Byzantine outpost of Balanias on the Syrian coast (modern Bāniyās, about 50 kilometres south of Latikiya) and Abu'l-Ma'ālī again refused tribute. In response Leo Melissenos (a political ally of the Phokades) was appointed doux of Antioch and sent to recover Balanias, while Bardas Phokas invaded the territories of Aleppo. The campaign was conducted in a rather curious manner. Instead of a direct assault on Aleppo such as had been successful in 983, Phokas first of all sacked the town of Killis (60 kilometres north of Aleppo and just north of the modern Turkish border), after which he withdrew into Byzantine territory and then marched south along the Orontes valley before finally beginning a siege of Apameia (100 kilometres south-west of Aleppo). Perhaps taking advantage of the Byzantine forces' concentration elsewhere, Abu'l-Ma'ālī now sent Hamdānid troops to sack the famous Melkite monastery of Kal'at Sam'an in the limestone hills between Aleppo and Antioch. When the news reached Constantinople of the destruction of the holy shrine of St Simon Stylites and the massacre of the monks, Basil II sent orders to Phokas to stop the siege of Apameia.[17]

While this peculiar campaign was developing, the emperor took the dramatic step of dismissing the parakoimomenos. He was stripped of his property and kept under house arrest where he died a few months later. When the news reached Syria Leo Melissenos at once abandoned the siege of Balanias. But in fact he had acted too soon. There was no revolt and Basil II was still for the time being securely in charge. Leo was ordered to go back to Balanias and capture the fortress or else pay personally the whole costs of the campaign. As soon as Balanias had fallen Leo was removed from his command, and Bardas Phokas was demoted from domestic of the scholai to being doux of Antioch and *stratelates* of the east.[18]

The sources do not give us enough information to see exactly what was happening. Was Bardas Phokas' campaign of 985 a carefully considered strategy to force Aleppo into submission – if so one could see it as successful since in 986 Abu'l-Ma'ālī did come to terms and the tribute was resumed – or was it that he was waiting for the signal to rebel but Basil II moved first and dismissed his co-conspirator the parakoimomenos? In that case Leo Melissenos would have been acting according to a prearranged plan and was embarrassingly caught out. A number of hypotheses are possible but the one clear fact is that in 985 political tensions at court and in the armies were running high.

In 986 without consulting Bardas Phokas or the other current eastern commanders Basil II invaded Bulgaria. Since John Tzimiskes' death in 976 the Bulgars had re-established their empire under it seems the titular rule of Romanos, and the *de facto* leadership of Samuel and his surviving brothers. Taking advantage of the war with Skleros they had expanded from the area around Prespa and Ohrid to control all the western areas of the former Bulgar state. Between 976 and 980 their influence had reached the extent that the Byzantine strategos of Hellas based at Larissa in Thessaly had acknowledge Bulgar authority. After 980 the strategos explained away this extraordinary concession as a subtle means of keeping the Bulgars at bay, but it presumably indicates that there had been a widespread collapse of the Byzantine position in the Balkans.[19] By 986 only the eastern section of John Tzimiskes' conquest of Bulgaria seems to have remained in Byzantine hands.

Such a rapid reversal of the triumph of 971 reflected badly on Basil II's regime and on his own status as an emperor for whom God would bring victory. The poet, retired soldier and monk, John Geometres, writing it seems in Constantinople in 985 could foretell disasters to come in Bulgaria and hoped for Nikephoros Phokas to come back and save the empire. A victory over the Bulgars was badly needed and if Basil II were to take the field himself – the first emperor of his family to do so since Basil I in 878 – it would do something to answer such criticisms as those implicit in John Geometres' poems, and to break his enemies' monopoly of the virtues appropriate for the role of warrior emperor.[20]

Unfortunately the campaign only led to disaster. On the night of 16–17 August, as Basil retreated from an unsuccessful siege of Serdika (modern Sofia), his army was ambushed, routed and slaughtered, with the emperor himself lucky to reach Constantinople alive.[21]

Basil II's defeat must have seemed an indication of divine judgement to the Phokades; in Baghdad it persuaded Samsām al-Dawla that the time had come to free Bardas Skleros. The Būyid ruler's position had declined even further over the last three years, and the most profitable use of his captive seemed now to send him back to Byzantium with the intention that he should seize the throne and then gratefully make concessions to Baghdad. Once the terms had been set out in a treaty and agreed to, Bardas Skleros – recognised by the Būyids as emperor – was released to make good his claim. He arrived at Melitene in January 987 and at once set about gathering support. As before, Armenian and Arab troops were prominent.[22]

The news of Skleros' return left the humiliated emperor little choice but to re-appoint Bardas Phokas as domestic of the scholai, and hope that the Phokades' hatred of those who had overthrown Nikephoros in 969 would convince them that Skleros was their greater enemy. In fact Phokas opened negotiations, apparently proposing that they should rule as co-emperors, himself in Constantinople and the west, Skleros in the east. At their second meeting however Phokas arrested him, and until 989 Skleros remained a prisoner at the fortress of Tyropoion in the theme of Lykandos. Finally, on 15 August or 14 September 987 – the sources disagree on this as on much else – at the house of Eustathios Maleïnos in the theme of Charsianon where his supporters had gathered, Bardas Phokas was acclaimed emperor and the long-expected war began.[23]

Unlike 976–8 there was no preliminary battle for Asia Minor. With very little overt opposition Bardas Phokas was accepted as emperor. He had the backing of most of the eastern military families, the large majority of the eastern armies – including some of those who had joined Skleros earlier in the year – and the Iberians. Like Nikephoros Phokas in 963 he could march directly on Constantinople, but once there he faced his major problem. Unlike his uncle's coup, Bardas Phokas did not have any active support inside the city. The parakoimomenos who had brought his men on to the streets in 963 to back Nikephoros Phokas, was no longer there – deposed by Basil II two years before – and the emperor seems to have been careful to ensure that there existed no influential fifth column to let the enemy in. Bardas Phokas' strategy therefore seems to have depended on a combination of military display to convince Basil and the city that his position was hopeless, and a blockade to cut off food supplies and thus undermine the emperor's support. To serve the first goal Kalokyros Delphinas – a former katepan of Italy, probably of Iberian origin – led an advance guard to

Chrysopolis (modern Üsküdar) on the Asian shore within sight of the imperial palace; while to achieve the second Bardas Phokas began the siege of Abydos, the key fortress that commanded the southern end of the Dardanelles near modern Çanakkale.[24]

Under these desperate circumstances Basil began to look for allies. Later Arab sources mention a seven-year truce agreed between the emperor and the Fātimids in 987–8 – although it is arguable that the emperor involved was not Basil II but Bardas Phokas who would apparently have had more to gain by an agreement that covered his southern flank.[25] This was also the moment that Basil decided to overturn Nikephoros Phokas' legislation against the acquisition of land by monasteries, churches or charitable institutions. The new novel's description of its predecessor as one 'whose issuance was unjust and insolent not only to the churches and charitable institutions but to God himself, [and] has been the cause and source of the present evils and of the general upheaval and disturbance . . .' obviously suits the position in April 988 rather better than that of an alternative date in John Tzimiskes' reign.[26] Basil was in part bidding to ensure the support of the city's traditional ecclesiastical establishment by explicitly associating himself with their interests against the ascetic monasticism patronised by the Phokades, but it should also be read as a genuine appeal to regain divine favour. Basil II would have been quite unnatural in a Byzantine context not to have been searching for whatever had offended God, and brought His anger on the emperor's head. No doubt the Constantinopolitan clergy were keen to point out that Nikephoros' murder, John Tzimiskes' short reign (and possibly murder too), and the civil wars had all followed this wicked novel. In such a crisis a repeal was well worth trying.

Yet to survive Basil still needed troops and for these he turned to Vladimir, the prince of Kiev. In exchange for the hand of the emperor's sister, Anna, Vladimir promised that he would be baptised, and that he would send a substantial force of Rus warriors to Basil's aid.[27]

For both the Rus and the Byzantines this was an event of great significance. For both parties it was the culmination of a process beginning in the ninth century which had seen the gradual replacement of the Khazars by the Rus as the empire's chief allies in the north. For the Rus it confirmed Kievan dominance; and in the buildings, ceremonies and literature of the new religion it gave Vladimir and his successors the means to display and articulate that dominance. The *Povest*'s mythical picture of Kievan hegemony in terms of providential inevitability was only possible in a Christian context.

For the Byzantines the price had been high. Anna was a *porphyrogennetes*, 'born in the purple': a legitimate princess born when her father Romanos, himself a *porphyrogennetos*, was the reigning emperor. In the 950s her grandfather, Constantine Porphyrogenitos, had written:

> For if any nation of these infidel and dishonourable tribes of the north shall ever demand a marriage alliance with the emperor of the Romans . . . this monstrous demand of theirs you shall rebut with these words, saying: 'Concerning this matter also a dread and authentic charge and ordinance of the great and holy Constantine is engraved upon the sacred table of the universal church of the Christians, Hagia Sophia, that never shall an emperor of the Romans ally himself in marriage with a nation of customs differing from and alien to those of the Roman order, especially with one who is infidel and unbaptised, unless it be with the Franks alone. . . .'[28]

Even the Franks could be refused. In 968 Liudprand of Cremona had been told, 'It is an unheard of thing that a porphyrogennetes daughter of a porphyrogennetos emperor should marry a foreigner'; and his attempt to bring up Peter of Bulgaria's marriage to the emperor Christopher Lekapenos' daughter had been dismissed with the reply: 'But Christopher was not a porphyrogennetos.' When Otto II did finally marry a Byzantine princess in 972, it had been Theophano, John Tzimiskes' niece, who had not been born in the purple.[29]

Both inside and outside Constantinople the fact that Anna was being sent to marry a prince of the Rus made the concession worse. The citizens of Constantinople had feared and hated the Rus since 860. If the alliance miscarried the city might well change sides to the eastern military who had been consistently hostile to these barbarians. The contemporary historian Leo the Deacon, a sympathiser of the Phokades and a critic of Basil II, consistently portrays the Rus as dangerous and savage barbarians whom it is the duty of the emperor to crush.[30]

But Basil II had little choice. With Bardas Phokas threatening his throne he needed military help, and with the revenues of Asia Minor denied to him, his sister was his most exchangeable asset. In the event Rus assistance enabled him to break the Phokades and thereafter impose his authority on the empire. The chronology of the negotiations, of Vladimir's baptism, of the Rus arrival and the military operations that followed are all controversial. The Byzantine, Armenian and Arab sources are brief and contradictory, and the *Povest'* is typically little more than subsequent myth-making. In particular there has been a problem with the Rus capture of Cherson in 989. Was this a move to force a reluctant Basil II to fulfil the treaty terms; or an operation against a rebel stronghold carried out by the emperor's allies?[31] However, the main points are clear. With Rus help Basil II was able first to launch a surprise attack that destroyed Kalokyros Delphinas' forces at Chrysopolis (988 or in the first quarter of 989); and then on 13 April 989 at Abydos – which was still resolutely holding out – Basil's army inflicted a crushing defeat on the Phokas forces in which Bardas himself was killed.[32]

Some resistance continued for the rest of the year. Bardas Skleros was released by his captors from Tyropoion, and was joined by some of the survivors from Phokas' defeat, including Bardas' son, Nikephoros (known as 'wry-neck') and other members of the clan. For the most part they seem to have been holding out for an amnesty, to avoid the fate of Kalokyros Delphinas who had been impaled at Chrysopolis, or that of the captives of the battle of Abydos who had been publicly humiliated in a triumphal procession through the streets of Constantinople. Fairly generous terms were eventually agreed and Bardas Skleros submitted to Basil II on 11 October 989. For the first time for a generation an emperor in Constantinople, not of the military families, was the unquestioned master of the state.[33]

The Triumph of Constantinople, 990–1025

The most enduring image of Basil II has been that given by Michael Psellos in the *Chronographia* of the emperor as a dour and terrible warrior, scornful of learning and literature, who spent the greater part of his life on campaign with his army.[34] Michael Psellos (1018–post-1081?) was an eleventh-century Constantinopolitan civil grandee *par excellence*, a writer, a scholar and a philosopher. His letters and writings, including the *Chronographia*, show a world seen from the perspective of the imperial city, where the empire outside often appears in a manner reminiscent of the well-known cartoon, 'The New Yorker's View of the World'. Basil II, by Michael Psellos' own account, was the antithesis of all that he represented. Yet Basil's victory over Bardas Phokas had halted the tenth-century slide away from an empire centred on Constantinople toward an empire of the eastern armies that would look to a future of Near Eastern hegemony. The defeat of Phokas and his supporters fixed Byzantium as a Greek-speaking, orthodox empire securely focused on Constantinople. Men such as Michael Psellos and the circle of Constantinople-educated theme judges, ecclesiastics, soldiers and civil officials who feature in his letters were the beneficiaries.

In 990 the thirty-two year old Basil II was in an extraordinarily strong position. The defeat of Bardas Skleros in 979 had left the young emperor dependent on the Phokas clan and their allies who had come to his rescue; the victory of 989 had been won by the emperor alone, using his own forces and his own allies. The Rus intervention had been crucial, not only because it had turned the war decisively in Basil's favour, but also because it had left the emperor without any obligation to a military leader inside the empire whose power could rival his own. After 989 the Rus stayed on as a special *tagma* who accompanied the emperor on campaign. (Some of these Rus were also it seems employed as palace guards, responsible for the emperor's personal security. As such they were the origin of the Varangian guard, initially a Rus regiment but later recruited from other peoples, including after 1066 the English.) Well-paid for their service new recruits were easily obtained from the north, and Basil's Rus warriors became a distinctive feature of the imperial army in the eyes of the Arab and Armenian historians who mention them.[35] Their role in Byzantine politics can be compared to that of the imported Turkish *ghilmān* under the earlier Abbāsid caliphs. Both gave independent military strength to the central government, allowing the emperor and caliph respectively to free themselves from dependence on ambitious generals in the provinces. Basil II's Rus warriors were a logical extension of the development of the tagmata discussed in Chapter 6 – a means of keeping military power in the emperor's hands. Already under Nikephoros Phokas and John Tzimiskes Armenian and Iberian troops had made up a significant proportion of the imperial armies; in the future Turks, Franks, Pečenegs, Germans, Alans, Abasgians, English and others would be used to fight the empire's wars. Under Basil II and his immediate successors native-born Byzantines were still the basis of the empire's military strength, but a trend was clearly evident toward the twelfth-century situation when Benjamin, a Jewish traveller from Tudela in north-eastern Spain, could say of the empire: 'They hire from amongst all nations warriors called *loazim* [barbarians] to fight with the . . . Turks; for the natives are not warlike, but are as women who have no strength to fight.'[36]

From this position of strength Basil II moved first to break the power of the military families who had so nearly overthrown him. Aside from the Phokades who with one exception were savagely punished and dispossessed in the immediate aftermath of 989, the aim was not to destroy these families – indeed that was hardly feasible since they were still needed as experienced soldiers, commanders and administrators – but to limit their independence from central government authority.

To this end Basil avoided where possible having members of the leading military families in key positions. Michael Psellos snidely says that Basil, 'surrounded himself with a body of picked men, who were not outstanding in intelligence, nor remarkable in their family, nor very much educated in letters, and to these he entrusted imperial missives, and confided secret matters'. One of these Psellos later names as John the Orphanotrophos (a leading political figure during the 1030s and early 1040s). 'A eunuch of mean and contemptible status . . . whom the emperor Basil used very familiarly, and to whom he confided

secret matters, although', Psellos admits, 'without raising him
to any distinguished office . . .'. Senior military commands seem
to have gone to new families – 'new' in the sense that they
had not previously held high office – such as the Dalassenoi,
the Komnenoi or the Xiphiai. Unlike his brother Constantine
VIII when he ruled alone from 1025 to 1028 after Basil II's
death, or Constantine's son-in-law and successor, Romanos III
Argyros (1028–34), Basil did not apparently make much use of
court eunuchs to hold senior provincial commands.[37] However,
the same principle of using loyal creatures of central government
rather than potentially unreliable members of the military families
is evident in the career of Nikephoros Ouranos whom Basil
used as domestic of the scholai in the west (996–9) and later
as doux of Antioch (999–c. 1006).

Nikephoros first appears in Ibn Shahrām's account of the
981–2 embassy holding the archetypal bureaucratic office of
Keeper of the Imperial Inkstand, and he is identified as Basil II's
key ally inside the court. Significantly Ibn Shahrām does not
see him as a balance to the Phokades, but as a rival and comparable figure to the eunuch Basil, the parakoimomenos. His
well-educated letters (which by the way do something to refute
Michael Psellos' aspersions quoted above) reinforce the
impression of Nikephoros as a cultured Constantinopolitan,
civilian and courtier.[38] In 982 he went to Baghdad where the
skills of a diplomat not a soldier were required, and at this
stage there is no reason to imagine that he had had any military experience. But in 996 Basil II needed a politically reliable commander for the field army in the Balkans. In the
previous twelve months Bulgar armies, ravaging the countryside around Thessalonica, had captured one doux and killed
another. Desertion to the Bulgars was rife among the senior
commanders in the Balkans. The possibility of losing
Thessalonica through its commander changing sides was to be
avoided at all costs. Nikephoros Ouranos was a man of proven
political loyalty in even more difficult circumstances, and what
he did not know about commanding armies could presumably
be remedied by a professional advisor. In the event the appointment was a great success. Nikephoros was credited with
defeating the Bulgar emperor, Samuel, at the battle of Sperchios
in Thessaly, and in December 999 he was sent to take over as

doux of Antioch, where again he was to succeed (or at least could be described as succeeding) where the military men had failed.[39]

However, the military families were still inevitably prominent. As another means of control Basil II regularly employed members of the eastern families in the Balkans, where they were far from their traditional heartlands; and similarly, after the fall of the Bulgar empire in 1018, transferred members of the Bulgar nobility to the east. A conspicuous example is Bardas Skleros himself who was given estates near Didymoteichon in Thrace and was expected to serve on the Bulgar campaign of 991. When Skleros did not turn up Basil must have expected the worst, and he was only given permission to remain behind when the emperor saw for himself that Skleros was not plotting but genuinely too ill to travel. (He died a month later.)[40]

Otherwise Basil II used most of his predecessors' methods – but to greater effect and on a larger scale. Substantial areas of the east had been brought into imperial hands from the 930s onwards, mostly in the form of imperial estates (*kouratoreiai*). Some of this land was used for political rewards and bribes. The son of the last emperor of Bulgaria, for example, was given estates in Charsianon, and Senekerim–John Artsruni ceded his kingdom of Vaspurakan in exchange for lands in Sebasteia and Cappadocia which could well have been confiscated from the Phokas family.[41] However these were exceptions, and through conquest and confiscation much more came in than was given away. Victory in the civil wars had certainly given Basil more scope for political confiscations than his predecessors had enjoyed, but the major novelty of his reign concerns the so-called 'fiscal lands'. It was already well-established practice for the *genikon* to confiscate land whose owners ceased to pay the due tax. After an initial period of *sympatheia* (tax relief) which could last up to thirty years, the land was declared *klasma* and consfiscated. The *genikon* then tried to sell the land as quickly as possible, if necessary at a very low price and with up to fifteen years tax relief to encourage purchasers. From Basil's reign onwards, however, klasmatic land was increasingly kept in the hands of the *genikon* and farmed by tenants who would henceforth pay rent to the state. To meet the workload the *oikeiakon*, which had previously been a subordinate department of the *genikon*, grew to become a sekreton in its own right. This procedure was only practicable and profitable because the empire was becoming wealthier and more secure; there was a growing demand for land and rents were rising. But clearly it also suited Basil's political purposes that such land should be kept out of private hands.[42]

In 995 the emperor saw the military families on their home ground for the first time. The highlight was evidently the meeting with the magistros Eustathios Maleïnos who welcomed the emperor, now returning through Cappadocia to Constantinople, on to his estates, and from his own resources lavishly provided whatever Basil and his army might require. The brief account in Skylitzes' *Synopsis historiōn* is tantalising. It had been on one of Eustathios Maleïnos' estates that Bardas Phokas had been proclaimed emperor in 987. Eustathios had been one of Phokas' closest suporters, and a close ally of the emperor Nikephoros Phokas before that. Was this simply the hospitality that a powerful and rich man owed an emperor? Or perhaps, more likely, was this a display of strength to remind Basil that Eustathios and his kind could not be ignored? It seems hard to believe that this was an innocent gesture. If this was the case Basil rose to the challenge. The emperor took Eustathios Maleïnos back with him to Constantinople where he was kept in comfortable imprisonment for the rest of his life, and on his death all his estates were confiscated.[43]

Explicitly referring to his recent travels, Basil issued in January 996 a draconian novel to prevent the *dynatoi* from taking over the lands of village communities. The forty-year prescription beyond which village land could not be recovered was abolished; there was to be no compensation for any improvements carried out while the 'powerful' interloper had been in possession; nor any repayment of the purchase price. No unwritten evidence from the *dynatos* was to be permitted, and where an imperial chrysobull was presented all those issued between Basil's accession (which might mean either 963 or 976) and the fall of the parakoimomenos in 985 were automatically invalid unless they had been re-submitted to the emperor and confirmed by a note in his own hand. In other cases boundary clauses in chrysobulls would only be recognised if they could be confirmed from the records of the genikon or 'from other evidence'. A few years later Basil went further and ordered that in those cases where a dynatos did legitimately own property in a village community – and this seems chiefly to have affected monasteries and bishops – the property was to be regarded an integral part of the community and the dynatos was to be held liable for any non-payment of taxes.[44]

As with his predecessors' legislation the 996 novel makes little economic or fiscal sense, but its political purposes are clear and they are underlined in later versions of the text which specifically name the Phokades, the Maleïnoi and the Moselai as examples of the powerful whose abuses were to be connected.[45] The provisions governing chrysobulls are particularly interesting. In effect Basil was declaring that any claim to property would depend on documents issued by the central government which in turn would be the only judge of whether or not they were valid. Political opponents could rely upon their chrysobulls being rejected as fraudulent.[46]

The purpose of these policies was to maintain the traditional structure of a political élite tied to Constantinople by the bonds of salaries and service. The measures must have created a great deal of resentment, especially in Cappadocia where the immigration of the Artsruni princes – alien, non-orthodox Armenians – finally provoked rebellion in 1022. The only important member of the Phokas family to escape the disaster of 989, Nikephoros 'wry-neck' Phokas, led the revolt. Despite apparently quite widespread support, when Nikephoros was assassinated the whole rebellion collapsed. This non-event is a good indication of the success of Basil's restoration of Constantinople power.[47]

Such a conservative policy required Basil II to halt the eastern offensive. The power and independence of the eastern military families had been a consequence of success in the east, and the reverse also followed: eastern conquests would only have been possible with their enthusiastic cooperation. Even so, as the fighting over Aleppo in 980s at a time when Basil was trying to make peace with the Būyids had shown, disengagement was not easy. In 992 the Fātimid armies led by the Turkish ghulām Mangūtakīn began a sustained offensive in northern Syria with the goal of conquering the Byzantine protectorate of Aleppo. Only the year before the doux of Antioch, Michael Bourtzes, had successfully sent troops to aid its Hamdānid emir, Abu'l-Ma'ālī (alias Sa'ad al-Dawla), against the attack of a local rival. The preservation of an independent Aleppo was supposedly one of the key-stones of Byzantine policy, and at this stage there was no indication that a Fāṭimid victory would not be followed by an actively prosecuted *djihād* against the infidel empire in which all the gains of the previous half-century might be lost. Yet even after Michael Bourtzes had suffered two crushing defeats (in 992 and 994), the territory of Antioch had been ravaged and Fāṭimid raiders had reached as far as Maraṣ, it still took the desperate messages of Lu'lu' (a Hamdānid ghulām who since December 992 had been the effective ruler of Aleppo for Abu'l-Ma'ālī's young son, Abu'l-Faḍāil Sa'īd al-Dawla) for the emperor to be convinced that Aleppo was on the point of falling, and that when it did Antioch would inevitably follow. At this very late stage – in February or March 995 – Basil finally acted, and according to the Arab sources at once set out to the east from the Balkans where he was campaigning against the Bulgars. Basil covered the nearly 1400 kilometres in sixteen or seventeen days, and arrived at Aleppo totally unexpected. Mangūtakīn had considerably larger and obviously well-rested forces, but the story goes that having no suspicion that relief was on its way he had ordered the cavalry horses to be sent out to pasture on the spring grass in the plains around Aleppo. Faced by the emperor's army – even one that was badly travel weary and reduced to those who had been able to keep up – Mangūtakīn did not dare risk battle without his vital shock troops. Setting fire to the camp they had built during the thirteen-month siege and destroying as much of the stores and equipment as possible he retreated to Damascus. This was an extraordinary triumph but it seems to be symptomatic of Basil's eastern policy that no Byzantine source even mentions it. He stayed on long enough to make a brief attempt to capture Tripoli, which would have reinforced the Byzantine position on the Mediterranean coast, before returning to Constantinople – via Eustathios Maleïnos in Cappadocia. A further Fāṭimid offensive was only halted by the death of the caliph al-Azīz in August 996.[48]

In 997 Basil ignored an attempt by Mangūtakīn to come over to the Byzantines bringing control of Damascus, but another Byzantine disaster, this time the defeat and death of the doux of Antioch, Damianos Dalassenos, in 998, did bring Basil back to Syria in September 999. Again he took the opportunity to stabilise the situation, made another half-hearted attempt on Tripoli before leaving to winter in Cilicia, preparatory to a campaign in Armenia the following year.[49]

In 1001 Basil II agreed to a ten-year truce with the new Fātimid caliph al-Hākim, and this formed the basis for Byzantine policy in the east during the rest of Basil's reign. It was renewed in 1011 and 1023. In 1009 al-Hākim had ordered the destruction of the church of the Holy Sepulchre in Jerusalem. For Nikephoros Phokas or John Tzimiskes this would have been an ideal *casus belli*. A war to avenge the sacrilegious destruction of the shrine would have been popular among all eastern Christians, while in Palestine bitter anti-Fātimid feeling, especially among the powerful bedouin tribes, would have welcomed the emperor's intervention. But Basil did nothing. Even the Fātimid occupation of Aleppo in 1017 produced no more than a temporary closing of the frontier. Basil seems to have decided that no vital interest was at stake, and the form could be preserved if its new ruler Azīz al-Dawla were treated as an independent emir of Aleppo rather than a Fātimid governor. In fact Azīz al-Dawla soon began to behave as if this were true, and towards the end of 1020 al-Hākim was rumoured to be planning an expedition to bring his governor to order. Azīz al-Dawla is reported to have appealed to Basil II for help, and the emperor seems to have set out for Syria. On 14 February 1021 al-Hākim mysteriously disappeared and Azīz al-Dawla sent messages to Basil who had now reached Cilicia that his help was no longer wanted and that if he pressed on he would be treated as an enemy. Basil does not seem to have been offended and led his armies into Armenia, which strongly suggests that even if the story has been correctly reported by the Arab sources Basil's real purpose had always been to achieve strategic surprise in Armenia. In 1022 Azīz al-Dawla was murdered and the Fātimids re-established control. Basil was so little concerned by this development that when the Banū Kilābī bedouin – with whom the Byzantines had good relations – captured Aleppo in 1024 and persuaded Constantine Dalassenos, the doux of Antioch, to help them with siege engineers to drive the Fātimid garrison out of the citadel, the emperor was furious and ordered that the Byzantine forces should pull out at once.

All attempts to involve him in the bedouin uprising that shook Fātimid power in Syria and Palestine during 1024–5 were wholly in vain.[50]

In the Djazīra too, Basil made little effort to exploit the vacuum left by the retreat of Būyid power after 983. By 1000 the region was divided between the leaders of the bedouin Banū Ukayl at Mosul, the Kurdish Marwānids in the Diyār Bakr – although not in Amida itself which was under the control of a local sheikh – and the Banū Numayr in the Dīyar Mudar around Edessa. Bādh, the founder of Marwānid fortunes, had supported Bardas Skleros in 987 and Basil was keen to enforce direct allegiance to the empire rather than local ties with military families. Before Basil could act Bādh was killed outside Mosul in 990, but in 992–3 Byzantine forces ravaged the Marwānid territories around Lake Van until they agreed to recognise the emperor's sovereignty and pay tribute in exchange for ten-year truce. Bādh's successor had been his nephew, al-Hasan b. Marwān, who was assassinated in 997; he was succeeded by his brother, Mumahhid al-Dawla, who in turn submitted to Basil and was given the title magistros and the office of doux of the east. Mumahhid al-Dawla was murdered in 1011, and leadership of the Marwānids passed to the third brother, Nasr al-Dawla. The available evidence suggests that Nasr al-Dawla followed a more independent line, but if so Basil II was not sufficiently interested to intervene. The Banū Numayr were treated as no more than an occasional nuisance, to be dealt with by local forces at Antioch almost as a matter of frontier policing. The political fragmentation of the Djazīra had created the ideal conditions for a Byzantine conquest. Edessa, Amida, Mayyāfārikīn and Mosul were all targets that Nikephoros Phokas or John Tzimiskes might have attacked, but Basil was not to be moved.[51]

Compared with his reluctance to advance further in Syria or the Djazīra, Basil II's actions in Armenia and the Transcaucasus seem at first sight to be a dramatic continuation of his predecessor's offensives. In 990 David of Tao was pressured into making the emperor the heir to his lands which made up a huge swathe of territory from the Çoruh valley in the north to the edge of Lake Van. When David died in 1000 Basil marched the same year into Tao to put the agreement into effect. In about 1019 David-Senekerim Artsruni, heir to the kingdom of

Vaspurakan promised to cede his inheritance to the emperor, and in 1021 or 1022 his father Senekerim-John exchanged Vaspurakan for lands in Cappadocia, and the former kingdom became a Byzantine province under a *katepano*. The emperor had gained the eastern and southern shores of Lake Van and a huge mountainous territory stretching south and east of the lake over the modern Turkish borders into what is now Iran. There are no strictly contemporary figures but a twelfth-century source gives 72 fortresses, 3040 villages and 10 cities. In January 1022 the Armenian katholikos, Peter, handed over to Basil who was wintering with his army in Trebizond, a document from John-Smbat, the Bagratuni king of Ani, pledging that on his death his kingdom should pass into the hands of the emperor. By 1025 the great majority of central and western Armenia was under Byzantine rule, and the territory of the kingdom of Ani on the middle Araxes was due to follow. The empire's frontier in the Transcaucasus had returned virtually to where it had been in 600.[52]

Modern Armenian historians and Byzantinists have been tempted to see these events in terms of aggressive Byzantine expansion at Armenian expense, but in fact contemporary and near-contemporary Armenian sources suggest a rather different approach is necessary. In the first place Basil II receives relatively favourable treatment in all these sources. Even those such as the twelfth-century Matthew of Edessa who in general are bitterly anti-Chalcedonian and anti-Byzantine in other contexts can praise Basil.[53] Others – especially those from Vaspurakan itself – can be even more enthusiastic. The second continuator of Thomas Artsruni's history can talk of Senekerim-John turning 'to the emperor of the Greeks as a son to his father', and of how 'the Greeks filled with divine love had compassion for the appeal of their children and summoned them from their various provinces. They gave them gifts, appointed them at the royal court, gave them great cities in exchange for their cities, impregnable fortresses and provinces. . .'. The continuator was writing in the twelfth century but presumably he reflects an older interpretation.[54] It is also striking that there is so little evidence of any opposition to the Byzantine 'annexations', or in the case of exchange of territory, of much reluctance to move. There is as much in fact to show positive enthusiasm for both processes. Obviously one could argue that these sources are distorted by their association with princes and kings who could have been trying to present an acceptable face to what had really been ruthless Byzantine pressure; but given that the mountainous areas concerned could have resisted unwanted Byzantine advances for years if the naxarars had so wished this is not convincing.

As in earlier periods of the history of Armenia and the Transcaucasus it seems essential to see this process not only in terms of the policies and interests of the outside power, but also in terms of how the local nobility made use of outsiders to serve their own ends. For all Transcaucasians the predominant feature of this period is the collapse of any effective great power rival to Byzantium in the region. Armenian and Georgian politics remained fragmented by geography and kinship and in need of outside resources to support the power of local rulers. Politics was at one level a constant attempt to involve outsiders in one's own cause and to overturn the alliances of one's rivals. But with the collapse of the caliphate as a great power, these schemes had to be pursued in relation to Byzantium. The empire could certainly be a threat, but it was above all a great jam-pot to be exploited. One can see these years as an Armenian and Georgian conquest of Byzantium just as much as a Byzantine conquest of the Transcaucasus.

Byzantium was not a passive partner to these schemes. Basil II wanted military support although, with the halting of the eastern offensive, on a lesser scale than his predecessors. As important Basil wanted political security. Above all he did not want powerful states in the Transcaucasus whose ties were to the military families on the eastern frontiers rather than to the emperor. In 978 Basil had been forced to reappoint Bardas Phokas as domestic of the scholai in order to bring David of Tao into the war against Skleros, and between 987 and 989 David's support for Phokas's own rebellion had almost lost Basil his throne. The most defensive policy in the east could not ignore the region, and Basil was therefore inevitably sucked in.

Basil's attack on David of Tao in 990 was the consequence of the events of 978 and 987–9; an emperor who had barely survived fourteen years of hot and cold civil war could hardly have left the ruler of this powerful principality to meddle at will in Byzantine politics. David had no son, and his intended heir was seemingly his cousin, Bagrat III, the Bagratuni king of Abasgia and son of Gurgen Bagratuni, the king of Iberia. Many of David's subjects already served the empire, and there were advantages to being ruled by a distant emperor rather than Bagrat. But above all they were keen to benefit from Byzantine wealth and clearly had no intention of shutting themselves out of the opportunities the empire represented. On Basil's side the annexation of Tao was neither the simple desire to expand imperial territory, nor a determination to keep what might anachronistically be described as the 'Georgian nation' divided. Basil gave titles and subsidies to Bagrat III and Gurgen, carefully respected what territories had belonged to David and what were rightfully lands of the king of Iberia, and also it seems granted some of what had been David's possessions to Gurgen. In 1008 he made no difficulties when Gurgen died and Bagrat became king of a united Georgian kingdom of Abasgia and Iberia. Conflict did break out when Bagrat III was succeeded as king of Georgia by his son George I in 1014. From the unsatisfactory evidence available it seems that what was at stake were conflicting claims over land that had been David's but had been held since 1001–2 by Gurgen and Bagrat. Basil II was now heavily engaged in Bulgaria, and did not come east to attack George until 1021–2, when two campaigns inflicted serious damage on Georgia. The emperor's aims seem to have been fulfilled when George submitted, and the important point is that the victory was not used to achieve any further territorial advance.

In the case of Vaspurakan the motives on the Armenian side seem to have been fear of the growing threat from the Kurdish emirs in Azerbaidjan combined with the prospect of what seemed a better future in Cappadocia.[55] In the case of Ani John-Smbat seems to have wanted to involve the Byzantines in supporting his position against rivals from within his own family. In neither case is there any good evidence to suggest that they were forced into ceding their lands against their will. What Basil II hoped to gain is unclear. Evidently not a strategic base for future advances. Control of Vaspurakan would have been useful for a conquest of the Djazīra but as already stated Basil never made any move in that direction, and in any case the one city –

Bitlis – that because of its control of the vital Bitlis pass linking Armenia and the Djazīra would have been essential to such a conquest remained in the hands of an independent Muslim emir. Hence the most likely incentive for Basil's actions would appear to have been an extension of the motives that had brought him into Tao: a desire to keep political control and prevent Armenian military support going to potential rebels and rivals. The involvement of Georgians and Armenians, among them David-Senekerim of Vaspurakan, in the abortive revolt of Nikephoros 'wry-neck' Phokas in 1022 showed that the threat was still there. Basil II showed no more sign of wishing to conquer Armenia than Syria or the Djazīra, but in this case the Armenians were inviting him in, and Basil had little choice but to accept if he wanted to avoid others taking the imperial place. Byzantine expansion, virtually in spite of the emperor, shows that there was the basis for fruitful co-operation in a Christian empire to reconquer the Near East, but Basil's aims in the east were not conquests but stability, and a potential turning point in Near Eastern history was passed by.

Free for the first time since the seventh century of an unavoidable preoccupation with the eastern front, Basil II turned the empire's armies to the conquest of the Balkans. The restored Bulgar empire with its centre at Ohrid in the modern Republic of Macedonia had by 990 reversed most of John Tzimiskes' conquests, and was now pressing on into previously secure Byzantine territory. A number of imperial strategoi and officials had gone over to the Bulgars and the loss of all the empire's Balkan themes seemed quite possible.[56] Even without this prospect Basil needed to offset the memory of his 986 disaster in Bulgaria with a success that would match John Tzimiskes' victories; and a Balkan war also offered the means to keep the eastern military employed far from their political homes.

Unfortunately, how Basil II's conquest of Bulgaria was achieved is very obscure. The only Byzantine chronicle to have survived for the years 990–1025 is that copied into John Skylitzes' *Synopsis historīon* and even by the meagre standards of Byzantine history-writing it leaves much to be desired. For the east this is not so important because Skylitzes' evidence can be supplemented with material from much better historians including Yahya b. Saʿīd and Stephen of Taron. What they have to say sometimes touches on the Balkans, but it is not central to their concerns and it is usually impossible to judge whether they are repeating reliable information or ill-informed gossip. We are therefore effectively dependent on Skylitzes' account.

Skylitzes' coverage of the Bulgar wars is not without value. One of the surviving manuscripts contains a number of brief interpolations and corrections on Balkan history added by Michael, an early twelfth-century bishop of Devol (a see whose exact site is not known but lying somewhere in the district south of Ohrid). Since Michael was writing so close to what had been the Bulgar capital it is reasonable to suppose that his information is fairly reliable.[57] It also seems that many of the individual pieces of information recorded in Skylitzes' account can be trusted. Where one can cross-check with documents from Mount Athos or the inscriptions from lead seals the details are usually correct. For example Skylitzes mentions that a certain John Chaldos was released in 1018 after twenty-two years' captivity in Bulgar hands. It therefore follows that he was captured in 996 and Michael of Devol adds the detail that he was doux of Thessalonica. This is confirmed by a document dated to Spetember 995 and surviving at the Iviron monastery on Mount Athos which bears the autograph signature 'John Chaldos, the doux', and names him in the text as doux of Thessalonica.[58] But beyond this type of information Skylitzes' account is confused and contradictory, it leaves great gaps in the narrative and at some points it is evident nonsense.

One of the major problems is the battle usually known as Kleidion, a pass somewhere north of Thessalonica, where according to Skylitzes the Bulgars suffered a decisive defeat in July 1014. The Bulgar emperor Samuel managed to escape but many of his army were killed and more were taken prisoner. Basil had 15,000 Bulgar captives blinded, leaving a single one-eyed man for every hundred to lead them back to their emperor. When Samuel saw this ghastly sight he fell senseless to the ground, and died two days later. On this episode stands Basil's later reputation as 'Basil the Bulgar-slayer' (a description which does not appear until the late twelfth century). After this defeat the Bulgars were crushed into submission with great savagery, and the Bulgar state utterly destroyed.[59]

Almost all modern accounts repeat this story, but in fact

Skylitzes' confusions preserve enough information to show that this account must be wrong. In the first place Kleidion was not a decisive battle. It was part of a two-prong Byzantine attack, of which the other force under Theophylact Botaneiates was heavily defeated. Skylitzes gives this a passing mention but its significance is proved by the fact that rather than press on after his 'decisive victory' Basil could only retreat to the base he had started from.[60] The blinding of the 15,000 is a fantasy. Had Basil committed this atrocity he would effectively have disabled the Bulgar state: 15,000 men is a huge force for the early middle ages, yet Skylitzes' own account shows that the war continued during 1015 and 1016 without any very significant Byzantine success. Far from dropping dead of shock Samuel died – as likely of old age as anything else – while his forces were continuing to resist very effectively. What seems to have happened is that after his death in October 1014 there was a crisis of leadership when first Samuel's son and successor, Gabriel Radomir, was murdered by his cousin, John-Vladislav in 1015; and then John-Vladislav himself was killed besieging the fortress of Dyrrachion in 1018. Under these circumstances resistance did finally crumble, but arguably only when the Bulgar nobility felt that rule by Basil II was the best option still available.[61]

Even then Basil had to offer a reasonably generous peace. The Bulgar leaders were offered lands in the east, and the existing system of taxation in kind was maintained rather than impose payment in gold coin as elsewhere in the empire. Ohrid ceased to be the seat of the patriarch of Bulgaria, but it did continue as a very privileged autonomous archbishopric keeping control over all its existing suffragan sees.[62]

To a large degree Bulgar domination of the Balkans had been made possible by Byzantine preoccupation with the east, and although a well-organised and relatively powerful regional state, the Bulgar qaghanate had often looked fragile when its dangerous Byzantine neighbour had been free to attack. Basil II's halting of the eastern offensive allowed him from 991 onwards to wage war in the west. Svyatoslav of Kiev and John Tzimiskes had each conquered Bulgaria in a single campaigning season, yet Basil II – if Skylitzes is to be believed – took over a quarter of a century of nearly annual campaigns.

There is a case that Skylitzes is exaggerating and that warfare was by no means continuous. Skylitzes' account of heavy fighting in the 990s seems to be confirmed by references to Bulgar raids in contemporary documents from Mount Athos, and his story of Nikephoros Ouranos' victory over Samuel at the battle of Sperchios in 997 which prevented a Bulgar invasion of Greece is supported by Yahya b. Sa'īd, the Christian Arab historian writing at Antioch in the earlier eleventh century. Yahya goes on to say that after the truce with the Fātimids (probably therefore 1001 or 1002) Basil fought the Bulgars for four years until he won a 'complete victory'; which, if believed – although of course without knowing on what Yahya based this statement there is no means of making a critical judgement – might suggest some form of Bulgar submission in 1006 or 1007, and peace until the war re-opened in 1014.[63] But even cutting Basil's Bulgar campaigns down to their minimum, they are much less impressive than those of Nikephoros Phokas and John Tzimiskes. What this perhaps indicates is the military cost of Basil's political victories over the eastern military families. Purged of the politically unreliable they were a much less formidable force.

Basil II's conquest of Bulgaria marks a fundamental westward shift in the political interests of the Byzantine empire. Developments in Italy reflect the same trend. When Basil was four years old in 962 the German king Otto I had been crowned emperor by the pope in Rome, reviving memories of Carolingian claims, and threatening the apparently fragile Byzantine domination of the south. In fact the impact of the German emperors in the region proved to be slight. Byzantine defences held up during a war with Otto I in 968–70, and most of the empire's south Italian clients remained loyal. John Tzimiskes was willing to buy off this new power by marrying his niece, Theophano, to Otto's son, Otto II in 972, and recognising their imperial title. This proved only temporarily successful. After his father's death Otto II took advantage of the obvious Byzantine instability during the early year's of Basil II's reign to invade the south with a large German army. The pretext for this invasion had been a campaign against the Arabs, whose chronic raiding remained a serious problem in the south, and in the event the Byzantines had little to do but watch as the Arabs destroyed Otto II's army at Stilo in Calabria on 13 July 982. The western emperor barely managed to escape alive, his prestige irretrievably damaged. Again Byzantine defences had held up well and it is evidence of the success of Byzantine administration that among those rewarded by the *katepano* (the title of the governor of the Italian provinces after about 969) for their loyalty during 981–2 were several *Latin* bishops.[64]

After 982 there was a slow consolidation and extension of Byzantine control, marked by the occupation of several cities and fortresses in northern Apulia, where it seems that the great Lombard shrine to St Michael the Archangel, Monte Gargano, now fell under Byzantine rule. The long-running revolt of Meles from 1009 to 1018 shows that as before the area was short of Byzantine troops, but it was finally brought to an end by the katepano Basil Boioannes who came to Italy with a force of Rus warriors who crushed Meles' imported Norman allies at the battle of Cannae. The new katepano continued the process of consolidation (succesfully fending off another German intervention in 1022) so that by 1025 Byzantine rule in the south was much more of a territorial reality, where the imperial administration operated in manner far closer to other regions of the empire than ever before. Consolidation was also reflected in what amounts to a Byzantinisation of southern culture, visible in art, architecture and the increasing use of Greek in formerly Latin areas. The south was becoming a part of the Byzantine world rather than simply an area of Byzantine military hegemony.[65]

In 1025, ignoring an opportunity to exploit the current difficulties of the Fātimid regime in Syria, Basil II sent the eunuch Orestes with an army from the western themes to co-operate with Basil Boioannes in an invasion of Sicily. The emperor was to follow with a full expeditionary force. In the event Basil died aged 67 on 15 December 1025. The invasion went ahead but Orestes was defeated.[66]

Basil's final plans had miscarried, but the decision to ignore the east and intervene in Sicily is indicative of what he had achieved. His victory in the civil wars of the 970s and 980s, and the destruction of the military aristocracy which followed, marks a turning point in Byzantine history. Thanks to Basil II Byzantium would remain an empire dominated from Constantinople that had turned its back on the Near East. The future would be with orthodox Byzantium not with the Near Eastern empire of the late Roman world revived.

Notes

1. SOURCES FOR EARLY MEDIEVAL BYZANTIUM

1. N. Oikonomides, 'The Lead Blanks Used for Byzantine Seals', in *Studies in Byzantine Sigillography*, I, ed. N. Oikonomides (Washington, D.C., 1987), pp. 97–103.

2. John Lydus, *De Magistratibus*, in *Ioannes Lydus on Powers*, ed. A. C. Bandy (Philadelphia, Penn., 1983), pp. 160–3.

3. Ninth-century deed of sale (897): *Actes de Lavra*, I, ed. P. Lemerle, A. Guillou and N. Svoronos (Archives de l'Athos V, Paris, 1970), pp. 85–91.

4. For example, G. Duby, *La société aux xi' et xii' siècles dans la région mâconnaise*, 2nd edn (Paris, 1971); P. Toubert, *Les structures du Latium médiéval*, 2 vols (Rome, 1973).

5. *DAI*, cc. 9, 46, 52, pp. 56–63, 214–23, 256–7.

6. *De Cer.*, pp. 651–60, 664–78, 696–9.

7. See S. D. Goitein, *A Mediterranean Society*, 5 vols (Berkeley, Cal., 1967–88), I, pp. 1–28.

8. J. Darrouzès, *Épistoliers byzantins du x' siècle* (Archives de l'orient Chrétien VI, Paris, 1960), pp. 217–48.

9. Photius, *Epistulae et Amphilochia*, ed. B. Laourdas and L. G. Westerink, 6 vols (Leipzig, 1983–8), pope: nrs 288, 290; III, pp. 114–20, 123-38, qaghan of Bulgaria: nrs 1, 271, 287; I, pp. 1–39; II, pp. 220–1; III, p. 113–14; prince of princes of Armenia: nrs 284, 298; III, pp. 1–97, 167–74; katholikos of Armenia: nr. 285; III, pp. 97–112; eastern patriarchs: nrs 2, 289; I, pp. 39–53; III, pp. 120–3; Nicholas I, patriarch of Constantinople, *Letters*, ed. R. J. H. Jenkins and L. G. Westerink (CFHB VI, Washington, D.C., 1973), Bulgaria: nrs 3–31; pp. 16–215; al-Muktadir: nrs 1, 102; pp. 2–13, 372–83; emir of Crete: nr. 2; pp. 12–17; Abasgia: nrs 46, 51; pp. 264–7, 278–81; Italian rulers: nrs 82, 145; pp. 338–43, 458–61; pope: nrs 32, 53, 56, 77; pp. 214–45, 286–93, 298–9, 330–3.

10. Photius, *Bibliotheca*, ed. R. Henry, 8 vols (Paris, 1959–77), I, p. 99; W. T. Treadgold, *The Byzantine Revival 780–842* (Stanford, Cal., 1988), pp. 376–8.

11. Georgius Monarchus, *Chronicon*, ed. C. de Boor, rev. P. Wirth, 2 vols (Stuttgart, 1978); date: P. Lemerle, 'Thomas le Slave', *TM*, I, 259, n. 13.

12. The Logothete's Chronicle has not been edited as such, and is only available in print from manuscripts which included the Chronicle as part of a later compilation or as a continuation of George the Monk. References will be to the text published as Georgius Monarchus, *Vitae imperatorum recentiorum*, in Theophanes Continuatus, ed. I. Bekker (CSHB, Bonn, 1838), pp. 763–924, and occasionally to that known as Leo Grammaticus, *Chronographia*, ed. Bekker (CSHB, Bonn, 1842).

13. One manuscript of Pseudo-Symeon *magistros* is published as Symeon Magistrus, *Chronographia*, in Theophanes Continuatus, ed. Bekker, pp. 603–760; the anti-Photian pamphlet: *ibid.*, pp. 668–71.

14. Theo. Cont., pp. 426–9.

15. Theo. Cont., pp. 436–81, 753–60 (Pseudo-Symeon *magistros*); A. Markopoulos, 'Le témoinage du Vaticanus Gr. 163 pour la période entre 945–963', *Symmeikta*, III (1979), 83–119.

16. See J. Forsyth, 'The Byzantine–Arab Chronicle (938–1034) of Yahyā b. Saʿīd al-Antākī', 2 vols (University of Michigan Ph.D. thesis, 1977).

17. Theo. Cont., pp. 436–69; Skylitzes, pp. 233–47.

18. Peter the Monk, 'Vita S. Ioannicii', ed. J. Van den Gheyn, *AASS*, Novembris ii.l (Brussels, 1894), p. 427; C. Mango, 'The Two Lives of St Ioannikios and the Bulgarians', *HUS*, vii (1983), 393–404.

19. Theo., p. 490.

20. See C. Mango, 'The Life of St Andrew the Fool Reconsidered', *Rivista di studi Bizantini e Slavi*, ii (1982), 297–313; cf. L. Rydén: The Date of the Life of Andreas Salos', *DOP*, xxxii (1978), 129–55, and 'The *Life* of St. Basil the Younger and the Date of the *Life* of St. Andreas Salos', *HUS*, vii (1983), 568–86.

21. Theodorus Studitae, *Epistulae*, ed. G. Fatouros, 2 vols (CFHB xxxi, Berlin, 1992), nr 420; i, pp. 400*–01*; ii, pp. 588–9.

22. J. W. Hayes, *Excavations at Saraçhane in Istanbul*, ii (Princeton, N.J., 1992).

2. THE STRATEGIC GEOGRAPHY OF THE NEAR EAST

1. Via Egnatia: see N. G. L. Hammond, *A History of Macedonia*, 3 vols (Oxford, 1972–88), i, pp. 19–58; the military highway: J. K. Jirecek, *Die Heerstraße von Belgrad nach Constantinopel und die Balkanpässe: Eine historisch-geographische Studie* (Prague, 1877).

2. R. Byron, *The Road to Oxiana* (London, 1937), p. 228.

3. F. Burnaby, *A Ride to Khiva* (London, 1877), pp. 134–5.

4. A. M. Khazanov, *Nomads and the Outside World*, tr. J. Crookenden (Cambridge, 1984), pp. 28–33; Byron, *The Road to Oxiana*, p. 228.

5. P. Burnham, 'Spatial Mobility and Political Centralization in Pastoral Societies', in *Pastoral Production and Society [Production pastorale et société]* (Cambridge, 1979), pp. 349–60.

6. Khazanov, *Nomads and the Outside World*, pp. 3, 70, 81, 161–2, 164, 222–32.

7. D. Morgan, *The Mongols* (Oxford, 1986), pp. 86–8; D. Sinor, 'Horse and Pasture in Inner Asian History', *Oriens extremus*, xix (1972), 171–83; R. P. Lindner, 'Nomadism, Horses and Huns', *Past and Present*, xcii (1981), 3–5, 14–18. It is worth noting that 20,000 is still a considerable military potential and therefore Lindner's conclusion (p. 19) that, '[the Huns'] chiefs soon fielded armies which resembled the sedentary forces of Rome' is misleading.

8. Leo of Synada, *Correspondence*, ed. M. P. Vinson (CFHB xxiii, Washington, D.C., 1985), pp. 68–9, 127; L. Robert, *A travers l'Asie Mineure* (Rome, 1980), pp. 155, 276, 286, 348.

9. See D. Morgan, *Medieval Persia, 1040–1797* (London, 1988), pp. 6, 25; R. P. Lindner, *Nomads and Ottomans in Medieval Anatolia* (Bloomington, Ind., 1983).

10. J. M. Wagstaff, *The Evolution of Middle Eastern Landscapes* (London, 1985), pp. 17–20, 139–41, 148–51; R. M. Adams, *Land behind Baghdad* (Chicago, Ill., 1965).

11. P. Crone, *Meccan Trade and the Rise of Islam* (Oxford, 1987); cf. W. Montgomery Watt, 'Makka 1: The Pre-Islamic and Early Islamic Periods', in *EI/2*, vi, pp. 144–5.

12. For the idea of a variety of options to be exploited see W. Lancaster, *The Rwala Bedouin Revisited* (Cambridge, 1981).

13. R. W. Bulliet, *The Camel and the Wheel* (New York, 1975); cf. M. McDonald, 'Near Eastern Nomads and the Evolution of Bedouin Life', in *Archaeology and the Rise of Islam*, ed. J. Johns (Antiquity special number i, June 1995).

14. Bedouin raiding is currently a controversial issue. For the approach

taken here see B. Isaac, *The Limits of Empire* (Oxford, 1990), pp. 68–74; and the chapter bibliography.

15. D. F. Graf, 'Zenobia and the Arabs', in *The Eastern Frontier of the Roman Empire*, ed. D. H. French and C. S. Lightfoot, 2 vols (BAR, Int. Ser. DLIII, Oxford, 1989), I, pp. 143–67; Isaac, *Limits of Empire* pp. 220–8; F. Millar, *The Roman Near East, 31 BC–AD 337* (Cambridge, Mass., 1993), pp. 319–336; cf. I. Shahid, *Rome and the Arabs* (Washington, D.C., 1984), pp. 38–41, 149–53.

16. M. Hendy, *Studies in the Byzantine Monetary Economy, c. 300–1450* (Cambridge, 1985), pp. 613–18.

3. THE ROMAN WORLD IN 600

1. M. Hendy, *Studies in the Byzantine Monetary Economy, c. 300–1450* (Cambridge, 1985), pp. 613–18.

2. A. H. M. Jones, *The Later Roman Empire*, 2 vols (Oxford, 1964; repr. 1986), I, pp. 607–86; M. Whitby, *The Emperor Maurice and his Historian* (Oxford, 1988), pp. 138–83, 250–304; Maurikios, *Strategicon*, ed. G. T. Dennis, tr. E. Gamillscheg (CFHB XVII, 1981); tr. G. T. Dennis, *Maurice's Strategikon* (Philadelphia, Penn., 1984).

3. John of Ephesus, *Historiae Ecclesiasticae pars tertia*, ed. and Latin tr. E. W. Brooks (CSCO CVI, Scriptores Syri LV, Louvain, 1936); English tr. R. Payne-Smith, *The Ecclesiastical History of John of Ephesus* (Oxford, 1860); John of Ephesus, 'Lives of the Eastern Saints', ed. and tr. E. W. Brooks, PO, XVII–XIX (1923–5); Severus b. al-Muqaffa, 'History of the Patriarchs of the Coptic Church of Alexandria', ed. and tr. B. Evetts, PO, I, V, X (1904–15); Michael le Syrien, *Chronique*, 3 vols, ed. and tr. J.-B. Chabot (Paris, 1899–1905).

4. 'Histoire de Saint Maurice, empereur des Romains', ed. and tr. L. Leroy and F. Nau, PO, V (1910), pp. 773–8.

5. Whitby, *The Emperor Maurice*, pp. 213–15; P. Allen, *Evagrius Scholasticus the Church Historian* (Louvain, 1981), pp. 21–2, 27, 42; J. Moorhead, 'The Monophysite Response to the Arab Invasions', *Byz*, LI (1981), 579–9.

6. L. S. B. McCoull, *Dioscorus of Aphrodito: His Work and His World* (Berkeley, Cal., 1988), pp. 1–2, 5–15, 63–6, 72–6, 147–59.

7. N. Garsoïan, 'Le rôle de l'hiérarchie Chrétienne dans les rapports diplomatiques entre Byzance et les Sassanides', *REArm*, X (1973–4), 119–38; A. Guillaumont, 'Justinien et l'église de Perse', *DOP*, XXIII–XXIV (1969–70), 41–66; S. Brock, 'Christians in the Sasanid Empire: a Case of Divided Loyalties', in *Religion and National Identity*, ed. S. Mews (Studies in Church History XVIII, Oxford, 1982), pp. 1–19.

8. Maurikios *Strategicon*, pp. 262, 474; tr. Dennis, pp. 77, 159; *Chronikon Paschale*, pp. 167–8, and n. 454.

9. Theophylact Simocatta, *Historia*, ed. C. de Boor, rev. P. Wirth (Stuttgart, 1972), IV.13.24, p. 177; tr. M. Whitby and M. Whitby, *The History of Theophylact Simocatta* (Oxford, 1986), p. 123; Sebeos, tr. Macler, pp. 15, 27; tr. Bedrosian, pp. 20, 41; see also the map in the endpapers of H. Hübschmann, *Die altarmenischen Ortsnamen* (repr. Amsterdam, 1969).

10. Roman diplomacy among the Lombards and Gepids: Procopius, *Wars*, VIII.18–19, 25; pp. 234–50, 316–20.

11. Slavs: Maurikios, *Strategikon*, pp. 370–86; tr. Dennis, pp. 120–6; Procopius, *Wars*, VII.14, 21–30, pp. 268–72; V. Popović, 'La descente des Koutrigours, des Slaves et des Avares vers la mer Égée: le témoinage de l'archéologie', *Comptes rendus de l'Academie des inscriptions* (1978), 596–648.

12. John of Ephesus, *Historiae Ecclesiasticae*, VI.25; tr. Payne-Smith, pp. 432–3.

13. Maurikios, *Strategicon*, pp. 370–86; tr. Dennis, pp. 120–6.

14. Whitby, *The Emperor Maurice*, pp. 176–84.

15. *Ibid.*, pp. 218, 251–3; R. C. Blockley, *The History of Menander the Guardsman* (Liverpool, 1985), pp. 110–27, 146–7, 170–9.

16. S. T. Parker, *Romans and Saracens: A History of the Arabian Frontier* (American Schools of Oriental Research, Dissertation series VI, Winona Lake, Ind., 1986), pp. 149–59; future work may call into question the picture of such a pronounced Diocletianic build-up and later moth-balling but on the evidence currently available this seems still the most likely interpretation: see D. Kennedy, 'The Roman Frontier in Arabia (Jordanian Sector)', *Journal of Roman Archeology*, V (1992), 473-89.

17. John of Ephesus, *Historiae Ecclesiasticae* III.40–1, 54; IV.39–43; VI.3–4, tr. Payne-Smith, pp. 236–42, 296–8, 304, 370–9, 413–15.

18. M. Sartre, *Trois études sur l'Arabie romaine et byzantine* (Collection Latomus CLXXVIII, Brussels, 1978), pp. 192–3; post-583 Byzantine clients: A. Guillaume, *The Life of Muhammad: A Translation of Ibn Ishaq's Sīrat Rasūl Allāh* (Oxford, 1978), pp. 532–3; al-Tabarī, I, pp. 2347, 2394; raid into Iraq: Theophylact Simocatta, VIII.1.1–2, p. 283; tr. Whitby and Whitby, p. 209.

19. P. Crone, *Meccan Trade and the Rise of Islam* (Oxford, 1987), pp. 46–50.

20. M. Kaplan, *Les hommes et la terre à Byzance* (Paris, 1992), pp. 5–87.

21. E. Patlagean, *Pauvreté économique et pauvreté sociale à Byzance 4ᵉ – 7ᵉ siècles* (Paris, 1977), pp. 73–112; H. W. Catling and D. Smyth, 'An Early Christian Osteotheke at Knossos', *Annual of the British School at Athens*, LXXI (1976), 25–39.

22. Theophylact Simocatta, VI.1.1–2, pp. 220–1; tr. Whitby and Whitby, p. 158.

23. Cf. A. M. Watson, *Agricultural Innovation in the Early Islamic World: the Diffusion of Crops and Farming Techniques, 700–1100* (Cambridge, 1983).

24. Kaplan, *Les hommes et la terre*, pp. 135–83.

25. For example, Léontios de Neapolis, *La vie de Syméon le fou et vie de Jean de Chypre*, ed. A.-J. Festugière and L. Rydén (Paris, 1974), p. 95; *The Life of St. Nicholas of Sion*, ed. and tr. I. Ševčenko and N. P. Ševčenko (Brookline, Mass., 1984), pp. 82–4; Procopius, Wars, III.16.10; II, pp. 144–6; J. Durliat, 'Taxes sur l'entrée des marchandises dans la cité de *Carales*–Cagliari à l'époque byzantine (582–602), *DOP*, XXXVI (1982), 1–14.

26. *Le Synekdèmos d'Hiéroklès*, ed. E. Honigmann (Brussels, 1939), pp. 12–48; Jones, *The Later Roman Empire*, I, pp. 712–18.

27. *PLRE*, II, pp. 612–15.

28. R. W. Bulliet, *The Camel and the Wheel* (New York, 1975), pp. 216–36; C. Mango, *Le développement urbain de Constantinople (IVᵉ–VIIᵉ)* (TM, monographies II, Paris, 1985), p. 32.

29. G. Dagron, 'Les villes dans l'Illyricum protobyzantin', in *Villes et peuplement dans l'Illyricum protobyzantin* (Rome, 1984), pp. 1–19; A. Poulter, 'The Use and Abuse of Urbanism in the Danubian Provinces During the Later Roman Empire', in *The City in Late Antiquity*, ed. J. Rich (London, 1992), pp. 99–135; M. Whittow, 'Ruling the Late Roman and Early Byzantine City: A Continuous History', *Past and Present*, CXXIX (1990), 13–20.

30. C. Mango, *Byzantium: The Empire of New Rome* (London, 1980), p. 40.

31. C. Morrisson, 'Monnaie et prix à Byzance du Vᵉ au VIIᵉ siècle', in *Hommes et richesses dans l'empire byzantin*, 2 vols (Paris, 1989–91), I, pp. 239–60.

32. Whittow, 'Ruling the Late Roman and Early Byzantine City', 20, n. 37.

33. S. Tortorella, 'La ceramica fine da mensa Africana dal IV al VII secolo

D.C.', in *Società romana e impero tardantico*, III, ed. A. Giardana (Rome, 1986) pp. 211–25; and distribution maps in J. W. Hayes, *Late Roman Pottery* (London, 1972), pp. 462–4.

34. C. Panella, 'Le anfore tardoantiche: centri di produzione e mercati preferenziali' in *Società romana e impero tardantico*, III, pp. 251–84; D. P. S. Peacock and D. F. Williams, *Amphorae and the Roman Economy* (London, 1986).

35. Whittow, 'Ruling the Late Roman and Early Byzantine City', 13–16.

36. G. Tchalenko, *Villages antiques de la Syrie du nord*, 3 vols (Paris, 1953–8); H. Kennedy, 'The Last Century of Byzantine Syria: A Reinterpretation', *Byzantinische Forschungen* X (1985), 141–83.

37. E. Cruickshank Dodd, *Byzantine Silver Stamps* (Washington, D.C., 1961), pp. 1–35, 178–94.

38. *West-Syrian Chronicles*, pp. 133–4.

39. M. C. Mundell Mango, *Silver From Early Byzantium* (Baltimore, Md, 1986), pp. 3–15.

40. J.-P. Sodini, *et al.*, *Déhès (Syrie du nord) campagnes I–II (1976–1978)* (Paris, 1981), pp. 267–87, 294–301.

41. Procopius, *Wars*, II.23.1; tr. Dewing I, p. 464.

42. G. Tate, *Les campagnes de la Syrie du nord du iiᵉ au viiᵉ siècle*, I (1992), pp. 243–56.

43. P. Mayerson, 'The Ancient Agricultural Regime of Nessana and Central Negev', *Excavations at Nessana*, ed. H. D. Colt, I (London, 1962), pp. 211–63.

44. J. Johns, 'Islamic Settlement in Ard al-Kerak', *Studies in the History and Archaeology of Jordan*, IV (1993), 363–8; A. McQuitty and R. Falkner, 'The Faris Project: Preliminary Report on the 1989, 1990 and 1991 Seasons', *Levant*, XXV (1993), 37–61.

45. A. R. Bridbury, 'The Black Death', *Economic History Review*, 2nd ser., XXVI (1973), 590–1.

4. THE FALL OF THE OLD ORDER

1. J. Prebble, *Glencoe* (London, 1966), p. 168.

2. Maurikios, *Strategikon*, ed. G. T. Dennis, tr. E. Gamillscheg, (CFHB XVII, 1981), pp. 376–8; tr. G. T. Dennis, *Maurice's Strategikon* (Philadelphia, Penn., 1984), pp. 122–3.

3. Theophylact Simocatta, *Historia*, ed. C. de Boor, rev, P. Wirth (Stuttgart, 1972), VIII.13.3–6, VIII.15.8, pp. 309, 314; tr. Whitby and Whitby, *The History of Theophylact Simocatta* (Oxford, 1986), pp. 230–1, 235; *PLRE*, III, pp. 1293–4.

4. For the chronology (based on the conclusions of B. Flusin and J. D. Howard-Johnston) see the chapter bibliography.

5. Sebeos, tr. Macler, pp. 56–7; tr. Bedrosian, p. 82.

6. Sebeos, tr. Macler, pp. 30–31, 34–5, 36–7, 53–4; tr. Bedrosian, pp. 44–5, 51–2, 54–5, 79–80.

7. Sebeos, tr. Macler, p. 62; tr. Bedrosian, p. 89.

8. Theo., p. 292.

9. *Chronikon Paschale*, pp. 696–7; tr. Whitby and Whitby, pp. 145–6.

10. Antiochus Strategius, *La prise de Jérusalem par les Perses en 614*, ed. and tr. G. Garitte (CSCO CCIII, Louvain, 1960); reaction in Constantinople: *Chronikon Paschale*, pp. 704–5; tr. Whitby and Whitby, pp. 156–7.

11. Sebeos, tr. Macler, pp. 79–80; tr. Bedrosian, pp. 101–2.

12. Nik., p. 62.

13. *Oxyrhynchus Papyri*, LI, ed. J. R. Rea (London, 1984), nr 3637, pp. 101–4; *ibid.*, LV, ed. Rea (London, 1988), nr 3797, pp. 75–8; *ibid.*, LVIII, ed. Rea (London, 1991), nr 3959–60, pp. 116–26.

14. *Chronikon Paschale*, pp. 712–13; tr. Whitby and Whitby, p. 165

15. Lemerle, *Les plus anciens recueils*, I, pp. 184–9; II, pp. 94–103.

16. *Chronikon Paschale*, pp. 716–26; tr. Whitby and Whitby, pp. 169–81.

17. C. Mango, 'Deux études sur Byzance et la Perse Sassanide', *TM*, IX (1985), 105–13.

18. E. Cruickshank Dodd, *Byzantine Silver Stamps* (Washington, D.C., 1961), p. 178; S. S. Alexander, 'Heraclius, Byzantine Imperial Ideology, and the David Plates', *Speculum*, LII (1977), 217–37.

19. *West-Syrian Chronicles*, pp. 16, 18, 138–40; Theo., pp. 328–9; A. Palmer, 'Une chronique syriaque contemporaine de la conquête arabe: essai d'interprétation théologique et politique', in *La Syrie de Byzance à l'Islam*, ed. P. Canivet and J.-P. Rey Coquais (Damascus, 1992), pp. 31–46.

20. See J. Goody and I. Watt, 'The Consequences of Literacy', in *Literacy in Traditional Societies*, ed. J. Goody (Cambridge, 1968), pp. 31–4; D. P. Henige, *The Chronology of Oral Tradition: Quest for a Chimera* (Oxford, 1974); J. C. Miller, 'Listening for the African Past' in *The African Past Speaks*, ed. J. C. Miller (Folkstone, 1980), pp. 1–59; J. Vansina, *Oral Tradition as History* (London, 1985), pp. 13–32.

21. J. Johns *et al.*, 'The Faris Project: Preliminary Report upon the 1986 and 1988 Seasons', *Levant*, XXI (1989), 63–95; A. McQuitty and R. Falkner, 'The Faris Project: Preliminary Report on the 1989, 1990 and 1991 Seasons', *Levant*, XXV (1993), 37–61.

22. P. Crone, *Meccan Trade and the Rise of Islam* (Oxford, 1981), pp. 203–30; Crone *Slaves on Horses* (Cambridge, 1980), pp. 3–17; S. Leder, 'The Literary Use of the *Khabar*: A Basic Form of Historical Writing', in *The Byzantine and Early Islamic Near East I: Problems in the Literary Source Material*, ed. A. Cameron and L. I. Conrad (Princeton, N.J., 1992), pp. 277–315; L. I. Conrad, 'The Conquest of Arwād: a Source-Critical Study in the Historiography of the Early Medieval Near East', in *ibid.*, pp. 317–401.

23. *West-Syrian Chronicles*, pp. xxviii–xxxii, 1–44; Conrad, 'The Conquest of Arwād: a Source-Critical Study', pp. 322–48, 399–401.

24. Cf. F. Donner, *The Early Islamic Conquests* (Princeton, N. J., 1981) pp. 111–55; R. -J. Lilie, *Die byzantinische Reaktion auf die Ausbreitung der Araber* (Munich, 1976), pp. 40–68.

25. A. Guillaume, *The Life of Muhammad: A Translation of Ibn Ishaq's Sīrat Rasūl Allāh* (Oxford, 1978), pp. 532, 534; al-Tabarī, I, p. 2347; *West-Syrian Chronicles*, p. 145; Theo., p. 335.

26. G. Dagron and V. Déroche, 'Juifs et Chrétiens dans l'Orient chrétien du vii⁵ siècle, *TM*, XI (1991), 17–28; P. Crone and M. Cook, *Hagarism: The Making of the Islamic World* (Cambridge, Mass., 1977), pp. 3–9.

27. A. Walmsley, 'Pella/Fihl after the Islamic Conquest (A.D. 635–c. 900): A Convergence of Literary and Archaeological Evidence', *Mediterranean Archaeology*, I (1988) 143–53; H. Kennedy, 'The Impact of Muslim Rule on the Pattern of Rural Settlement in Syria', in *La Syrie de Byzance à l'Islam*, pp. 291–7.

28. C. Morrison, 'Byzance au vii⁵ siècle: le témoinage de la numismatique', in *Byzantium: Tribute to Andreas Stratos*, 2 vols (Athens, 1986), I, pp. 149–63.

29. J. W. Hayes, *Late Roman Pottery* (London, 1972), pp. 323, 345, 368, 424; Hayes, *Excavations at Saraçhane*, II, pp. 3–4, 8, 12–15, 61.

30. C. Mango, *Byzantine Architecture* (London, 1986), pp. 89–107.

31. Mango, *Le développement urbain de Constantinople*, pp. 51–62, for the aqueduct of Hadrian rather than Valens: *ibid.*, p. 20; M. F. Hendy, 'The Coins', in R. M. Harrison, *Excavations at Saraçhane in Istanbul* (Princeton, N. J., 1986) I, pp. 278–372.

5. HOW THE ROMAN EMPIRE SURVIVED

1. *La vie merveilleuse de saint Pierre d'Atroa (†837)*, ed. and tr. V. Laurent (Brussels, 1956), p. 149.

2. *West-Syrian Chronicles*, p. 178, and n. 445; al-Tabarī, I, pp. 2872–85.

3. J. H. Pryor, *Geography, Technology and War* (Cambridge, 1988), pp. 12–24.

4. *Codex Theodosianus*, XV.1.51; tr. C. Pharr, *The Theodosian Code* (New York, 1952), p. 429; Theo., p. 96.

5. C. Mango, *Le développement urbain de Constantinople (ive–viie)*, (TM, monographies II, Paris, 1985), pp. 46–9, 56 n. 30; Niketas Paphlagon, 'Vita Ignatii', *PG*, CV, col. 517.

6. Herakleios' wall: *Chronikon Paschale*, p. 726; tr. Whitby and Whitby, p. 181; sea walls: Mango, *Le développement urbain de Constantinople*, p. 25, n. 12.

7. C. Wickham, 'The Other Transition: From the Ancient World to Feudalism', *Past and Present*, CIII (1984), 3–36.

8. J. F. Haldon, *Byzantium in the Seventh Century* Cambridge, 1990), pp. 173–207; F. Dölger, *Beiträge zur Geschichte der byzantinischen Finanzverwaltung besonders des 10. und 11. Jahrhunderts* (Byzantinisches Archiv IX, Munich, 1927).

9. Haldon, *Byzantium in the Seventh Century*, pp. 147–50; Haldon, 'Military Service, Military Lands, and the Status of Soldiers: Current Problems and Interpretations', *DOP*, XLVII (1993), 11–14; M. Hendy, *Studies in the Byzantine Monetary Economy, c.300–1450* (Cambridge, 1985), pp. 294–9; Dölger, *Beiträge zur Geschichte der byzantinischen Finanzverwaltung*, pp. 54–9; some tax continued to be paid in kind in the tenth century: Constantine Porphyrogenitus, *Three Treatises on Imperial Expeditions*, ed. J. F. Haldon, (CFHB XXVIII, Vienna, 1990), pp. 88 (ll, 101–4), 168.

10. Theo., pp. 412, 446; Nik., p. 160.

11. P. Spufford, *Money and its Use in Medieval Europe* (Cambridge, 1988), pp. 19–21.

12. J. Ebersolt, *Le Grand Palais de Constantinople* (Paris, 1910); C. Mango, *The Brazen House: A Study of the Vestibule of the Imperial Palace of Constantinople* (Copenhagen, 1959).

13. J. B. Bury, *The Imperial Administrative System in the Ninth Century* (British Academy Supplementary Papers I, London, 1911), pp. 7–36; Oikonomidès, *Les listes*, pp. 281–301.

14. *Ibid.*, pp. 297–8; J. F. Haldon, *Byzantine Praetorians* (Poikilia Byzantina III, Bonn, 1984), pp. 138–9, 155–6 and n. 238; *Chronikon Paschale*, pp. 625–7; tr. Whitby and Whitby, pp. 123–5; I. Hay, *The Royal Company of Archers 1676–1951* (Edinburgh, 1951), pp. 166–7, 200–1.

15. Oikonomidès, *Les listes*, pp. 81–235.

16. P. Magdalino, 'Byzantine Snobbery', in *The Byzantine Aristocracy, IX to XIII Centuries*, ed. M. Angold (BAR Int. Ser. CCI, Oxford, 1984), pp. 58–78; Magdalino, 'Honour among Rhomaioi: the Framework of Social Values in the World of Digenes Akrites and Kekaumenos', *BMGS*, XIII (1989), 183–218; J. Pitt-Rivers, 'Honour and Social Status', in *Honour and Shame. The Values of Mediterranean Society*, ed. J. G. Peristiany (London, 1966), pp. 21–77.

17. Hendy, *Studies in the Byzantine Monetary Economy*, pp. 157–60, 178–95;

Chronikon Paschale, p. 706; tr. Whitby and Whitby, p. 158; *Ecloga*, ed. L. Burgmann (Frankfurt am Main, 1983), XVI.4, p. 224; Theo., p. 449; Theo. Cont., p. 173; Ibn Khordādhbeh, *Kitāb al-Masālik wa'l-Mamālik*, ed. M. J. de Goeje (Bibliotheca Geographorum Arabicorum VI, Leiden, 1889), p. 84; *De Cer.*, pp. 692–4, 696–7.

18. Liudprandus Cremonensis, *Opera*, 3rd edn, ed. J. Bekker (MGH SRG, Hannover, 1915), pp. 157–8.

19. P. Lemerle, '*Roga* et rente d'état aux xᵉ-xiᵉ siècles', *REB*, XXV (1967), 77–100.

20. For example, a rich merchant in the early seventh century turns to his patron, a eunuch of the imperial bedchamber, to track down a fraudster: G. Dagron and V. Déroche, 'Juifs et chrétiens dans l'orient du viiᵉ siècle', *TM*, XI (1991), 215–19, 237–8; eighth-century imperial complaints about the corruption of judges and their favouritism towards the rich: *Ecloga*, prooimion, pp. 164–6; the brother-in-law of the emperor Theophilos (829–42) acting as if above the law: Theo. Cont., pp. 93–4; the late tenth-century Keeper of the Imperial Inkstand asking a provincial judge not to choose his estates for billeting troops: *Epistoliers byzantins du xᵉ siècle*, ed. J. Darrouzès (Paris, 1960), pp. 241–2; eleventh-century advice that assumes that most judges take bribes, a powerful man will protect his clients from the tax collector: Cecaumenus, *Strategicon*, ed. B. Wassiliewsky and V. Jernstedt (St Petersburg, 1896), pp. 6, 40–42; eleventh-century case of peasants being driven from their land by the violent attacks of a protospatharios in alliance with a provincial judge: *JGR* IV, pp. 88, 177.

21. Theo., 344, 349, 351; Haldon, *Byzantine Praetorians*, p. 188 and n. 415.

22. *Synaxarium ecclesiae Constantinopolitanae*, ed. H. Delehaye (Brussels, 1902), pp. 721–3.

23. G. Ostrogorsky, *History of the Byzantine State*, 2nd edn, tr. J. Hussey (Oxford, 1968), pp. 95–8, 133–7; D. M. Górecki, 'The Slavic Theory in Russian Pre-Revolutionary Historiography of the Byzantine Farmer Community', *Byz*, LVI (1986), 77–107.

24. W. Ashburner, 'The Farmer's Law', *Journal of Hellenic Studies*, XXX (1910), 85–108; XXXII (1912), 68–95.

25. P. Lemerle, *The Agrarian History of Byzantium* (Galway, 1979), pp. 28–48; G. Ostrogorsky, 'Agrarian Conditions in the Byzantine Empire in the Middle Ages', *Cambridge Economic History*, 2nd edn (Cambridge, 1966), pp. 205–34.

26. M. Kaplan, *Les hommes et la terre à Byzance du viᵉ an xiᵉ siècle* (Paris, 1992), pp. 383–8; N. Svoronos, 'Notes sur l'origine et la date du Code Rural', *TM* VIII (1981), 487–500; cf. L. Burgmann, 'Ist der Nomos Georgikos vorjustinianisch?', *Rechtshistorisches Journal*, I (1982), 36–9.

27. *Vie de Théodore de Sykeon*, ed. A.-J. Festugière, 2 vols (Subsidia hagiographica XLVIII, Brussels, 1970), I, pp. 24–8, 38–9, 46, 55–6, 59–60, 113, 119–20; Kaplan, *Les hommes et la terre*, pp. 180–81.

28. Hendy, *Studies in the Byzantine Monetary Economy*, pp. 619–26, 634–45; W. T. Treadgold, 'The Military Lands and the Imperial Estates in the Middle Byzantine Empire', *HUS*, VII (1983), 619–31; Ostrogorsky, *History of the Byzantine State*, pp. 97–8.

29. J. F. Haldon, *Recruitment and Conscription in the Byzantine Army c. 550–c. 950* (Österreichische Akademie der Wissenschaften, phil.-hist. Klasse CCCLVII, Vienna, 1979), pp. 17–19, 41–81; R.-J. Lilie, 'Die zweihundertjährige Reform. Zu den Anfängen der Themenorganisation im 7. und 8. Jahrhundert', *Byzantinoslavica*, XLV (1984), 190–201.

30. Theo., pp. 300, 303.

31. *Ecloga*, XVI.1–2, pp. 220–4.

32. Haldon, 'Military Service, Military Lands, and the Status of Soldiers', 14–18; A. Dunn, 'The *Kommerkiarios*, the *Apotheke*, the *Dromos*, the *Vardarios*, and *The West*', *BMGS*, XVII (1993), 3–15.

33. J. D. Howard-Johnston, 'Thema', in *Maistor, Classical, Byzantine and Renaissance Studies for Robert Browning*, ed. A. Moffatt (Canberra, 1984), pp. 189–97; cf. J. Koder, 'Zur Bedeutungsentwicklung des byzantinischen Terminus *Thema*, *JÖB*, XL (1990), 155–65.

34. Haldon, *Byzantium in the Seventh Century*, pp. 208–20; R.-J. Lilie, '*Thrakien* und *Thrakesion*. Zur byzantinischen Provinzorganisation am Ende des 7. Jahrhunderts', *JÖB*, XXVI (1977), 7–47.

35. Haldon, *Byzantium in the Seventh Century*, pp. 194–207; Lilie, 'Die zweihundertjährige Reform', 31–6.

36. Theo., pp. 355, 361, 363.

37. *De Cer.*, p. 663, l. 3; cf. *Notitia dignitatum*, ed. O. Seeck (Berlin, 1876), p. 25 (ll, 27, 32), 124 (l. 215).

38. C. Foss, *Byzantine and Turkish Sardis* (Cambridge, Mass., 1976), pp. 57–9; a full plan and description of this fortress has yet to be published.

39. T. S. Brown, *Gentlemen and Officers: Imperial Administration and Aristocratic Power in Byzantine Italy A.D. 554–800* (British School at Rome, 1984), pp. 82–108, 144–63.

40. J. F. Hendy and M. Byrne, 'A Possible Solution to the Problem of Greek Fire', *BZ*, LXX (1977), 91–9.

41. Theo., p. 354, 396.

42. *DAI*, pp. 68–70; V. Christides, *The Conquest of Crete by the Arabs (ca. 824: A Turning Point in the Struggle between Byzantium and Islam* (Athens, 1984), pp. 63–6.

43. Theo., p. 397.

44. Procopius, *Wars*, VIII.23.29–38, tr. Dewing, v, pp. 296–302; M. Whitby, *The Emperor Maurice and his Historian* (Oxford, 1988) pp. 70, 78, 155, 161, 180; *Chronikon Paschale*, pp. 723–5; tr. Whitby and Whitby, pp. 177–9; Nik., pp. 58–60.

45. H. Ahrweiler, *Byzance et la mer* (Paris, 1966), pp. 19–26; Lemerle, *Les plus anciens recueils*, II, pp. 154–7.

46. Theo., pp. 344, 345–6, 352–3.

47. B. Rankov, 'Rowing Olympias: A Matter of Skill', in *The Trireme Project. Operational Experience 1987–90. Lessons Learnt*, ed. T. Shaw (Oxbow Monograph XXXI, Oxford, 1993), pp. 50–57: Thucydides quoted on p. 57.

48. C. Mango, *Byzantium: The Empire of the New Rome* (London, 1980), pp. 29–31.

49. C. Mango, 'Constantinople, ville sainte', *Critique*, XLVIII (1992), 625–33.

50. E. Fenster, *Laudes Constantinopolitanae* (Miscellanea Byzantina Monacensia IX, Munich, 1968), pp. 97–131; S. Yerasimos, 'Apocalypses constantinopolitaines', *Critique*, XLVIII (1992), 609–24; G. Dagron, *Constantinople imaginaire* (Paris, 1984), pp. 315–30.

51. L. Rydén, 'The Andreas Salos Apocalypse, Greek Text, Translation and Commentary', *DOP*, XXVIII (1974), text: 201–14; translation: 215–25; date: C. Mango, 'The Life of St. Andrew the Fool Reconsidered', *Rivista di Studi Bizantini e Slavi*, II (1982) 297–313.

52. Numbers of clergy: J. Konidaris, 'Die Novellen des Kaisers Herakleios', *Fontes Minores* V, ed. D. Simon (Frankfurt, 1982), pp. 62–72; ecclesiastical theatre: e.g. *De Cer.*, ed. Vogt. I, pp. 3–28.

53. 'Vie de saint Luc le stylite (879–979)', ed. F. Vanderstuyf, *PO*, XI (1915), 215–16, 239–41.

54. Skylitzes, pp. 255, 280; P. Meyer, *Die Haupturkunden für die Geschichte der Athos-Klöster* (Leipzig, 1894), p. 103.

55. 'Vita S. Theophanis confesoris', ed. B. Latysev, *Mémoires de l'Academie de Russie*, 8th series, XIII (1918), pp. 2–5.

56. A. H. M. Jones, *The Later Roman Empire* (Oxford, 1964) II, pp. 874–9, 894–929; G. Dagron, 'Le christianisme dans la ville byzantine', *DOP*, XXXI (1977), 19–23.

57. Agnellus, 'Liber pontificalis ecclesiae Ravennatis', *MGH SRLI* (Hannover, 1878), pp. 265–391; 'Gesta episcoporum Neapolitanorum', *ibid.*, pp. 398–436.

58. Lemerle, *Les plus anciens recueils*, II, pp. 73–6, 171–4; R. Cormack, *Writing in Gold* (London, 1985), pp. 50–94.

59. 'Life of George of Amastris', ed. V. Vasilievskij, *Russko-vizantiiskiia izledovaniia* (St. Petersburg, 1893), pp. 26, 37–41, 43–6, 60, Athos; *Actes du Prôtaton*, ed. D. Papachryssanthou (Archives de l'Athos VII, Paris, 1975), p. 201, ll. 3, 10; *Actes d'Iviron* I, ed. J. Lefort, N. Oikonomidès and D. Papachryssanthou (Archives de l'Athos XIV, Paris, 1985), p. 128, l. 69; D. Papachryssanthou, 'Histoire d'un évêché byzantin: Hiérissos en Chalcidique', *TM*, VIII (1981), 381–2; Latros: *Acta et diplomata graeca medii aevi sacra et profana*, ed. F. Miklosich and J. Müller, 6 vols (Vienna, 1860–90), IV, p. 312; Leo, metropolitan of Synada, *Correspondence*, ed. and tr. M. P. Vinson (CFHB XXIII, Washington, D. C., 1985), pp. 32, 50.

60. Foss, *Ephesus after Antiquity*, pp. 112–15, 125–8, 135.

61. Cormack, *Writing in Gold*, p. 84 (fig. 24), 154 (fig. 53); C. Jolivert-Lévy, *Les églises byzantines de Cappadoce* (Paris, 1991), pls 3 (fig. 3), 4–5, 8 (fig. 1), 40 (figs 1–2); 'Vita S. Lazari', ed. H. Delehaye, *AASS*, Novembris III, col. 571; 'De aedificatione templi S. Sophiae', ed. T. Preger, *Scriptores originum Constantinopolitanae*, 2 vols (Leipzig, 1901–7), I, p. 86.

62. *Notitiae episcopatuum ecclesiae Constantinopolitanae*, ed. J. Darrouzès (Paris, 1981).

63. For example Photius, *Epistolae*, nrs 281, 292; II, pp. 233–61; III, pp. 153–9; Nicholas I, *Letters*, nrs 123, 157, 177, 182; pp. 414–16, 478, 506, 512.

64. J. Darrouzès, *Recherches sur les ΟΦΦΙΚΙΑ de l'église byzantine* (Paris, 1970), pp. 28–32, 46–8; J. Hajjar, *Le synode permanent dans l'église byzantine des origines au xi⁵ siècle* (Rome, 1962).

65. G. Ostrogorsky, 'Byzantine Cities in the Early Middle Ages', *DOP*, XIII (1959), 45–66.

6. THE SHOCK OF DEFEAT

1. M. Gluckman, *Custom and Conflict in Africa* (Oxford, 1956), pp. 81–6; E. E. Evans-Pritchard, *Witchcraft, Oracles and Magic among the Azande* (Oxford, 1937).

2. C. Mango, 'Diabolus Byzantinus', *DOP*, XLVI (1992), 215–23; C. Stewart, *Demons and the Devil: Moral Imagination in Modern Greek Culture* (Princeton, N.J., 1991), pp. 137–61.

3. For example, 'Adversus Constantinum Caballinum', *PG*, XCV, col. 333A; *The Homilies of Photius, Patriarch of Constantinople*, tr. C. Mango (Cambridge, Mass., 1958), pp. 106–10.

4. *Chronikon Paschale*, pp. 705–6; tr. Whitby and Whitby, pp. 158, 167–8.

5. *Chronikon Paschale*, pp. 727–8; tr. Whitby and Whitby, pp. 182–3; Georgio

di Pisidia, *Poemi I. Panegirici epici,* ed. A. Pertusi (Ettal, 1959), pp. 133–6, 225–30.

6. Theo., pp. 328–30; *West-Syrian Chronicles,* pp. 140–1, 148; Mansi, XI, cols 564–8.

7. Theo., pp. 330; Mansi, X, cols. 991–8.

8. S. Brock, 'An Early Syriac Life of Maximus the Confessor', *AB,* XCI (1973), cc. 23–4, 318–19.

9. Theo., pp. 330–2, 341–52.

10. Theo., pp. 353–6, 359–62; Nik., pp. 84–6, 90–2; *Liber pontificalis,* I, pp. 350–5, 359–60, 372–3; tr. Davis I, pp. 74–8, 84; Mansi, XI, cols 196–204, 930–6; P. J. Alexander, *The Byzantine Apocalyptic Tradition* (Berkeley, Calif., and London, 1985), pp. 48–9; *Die Apokalypse des Ps.-Methodios,* ed. A. Lolos (Beiträge zur klassischen Philologie LXXXIII, Meisenheim am Glan, 1976), pp. 123–8.

11. Theo., pp. 365–70, 377, 382–4, 386–7, 390–1; Nik., pp. 93–4, 98, 104–6, 114–16, 120–2; *West-Syrian Chronicles,* p. 80; al-Tabarī, II, pp. 1185, 1191, 1197–8, 1200, 1236, 1305–6; Lilie, *Die byzantinische Reaktion auf die Ausbreitung der Araber* (Munich, 1976), pp. 112–22.

12. Rydén, 'The Andreas Salos Apocalypse. Greek Text, Translation and Commentary', *DOP,* XXVIII (1974), 202, 216; C. Mango, 'The Life of St. Andrew the Fool Reconsidered', *Rivista di Studi Bizantini e Slavi,* II (1982), 305–8, 310–13.

13. Theo., pp. 405–6; E. W. Brooks, 'The Arabs in Asia Minor (641–750) From Arabic sources', *Journal of Hellenic Studies,* XVIII (1898) 198.

14. Georgio di Pisidia *Poemi I, Panegirici epici,* ed A. Pertusi (Ettal, 1960), pp. 79, 193; Theo., p. 298; Theodore Syncellus, ed. L. Sternbach, *Analecta Avarica* (Cracow, 1900), p. 304.

15. *Vita Willibaldi,* ed. O. Holder-Egger (MGH Scriptores XV.1, Leipzig, 1887), p. 101.

16. Theo., p. 406.

17. Mansi, XIII, cols 100–5, 108–28.

18. C. Mango, 'The Beginnings of Iconoclasm in Byzantium and the Near East': I am very grateful to Professor Mango for allowing me to see a copy of this paper in advance of publication.

19. P. Grierson, *Byzantine Coins* (London, 1982), pp. 97–8, pl. 17, nos 296–8; R. Cormack, *Writing in Gold* (London, 1985), pp. 96–101.

20. S. Blair, 'What is the Date of the Dome of the Rock?', in *Bayt al-maqdis: 'Abd al-Malik's Jerusalem,* ed. J. Raby and J. Johns (Oxford Studies in Islamic Art IX, Oxford 1992), pp. 81–5; J. Walker, *A Catalogue of the Muhammadan Coins in the British Museum,* 2 vols (London, 1941–56), I, pls I–XXII; II, pls I–X, XII–XIII; Grierson, *Byzantine Coins,* pp. 144–9, pl. 34; Grierson, 'The Monetary Reforms of 'Abd al-Malik: Their Metrological Basis and their Financial Repercussions', *Journal of the Economic and Social History of the Orient,* III (1960), 241–64; K. A. C. Creswell, *Early Muslim Architecture,* 2nd edn (Oxford, 1969), I.1, pp. 65–123, 217–322.

21. Mango, 'The Beginnings of Iconoclasm'; V. Déroche, 'La polémique anti-judaïque au vi^{e}et au viie siècle. Un mémento inédit, les *Képhalaia'*, *TM,* XI (1991), 290–3.

22. Theo., pp. 411, 424, 427, 430, 433; Nik., pp. 130, 138–40, 148–52; Lilie, *Die byzantinische Reaktion,* pp. 148–69.

23. M. McCormick, *Eternal Victory: Triumphal Rulership in Late Antiquity, Byzantium and the Early Medieval West* (Cambridge, 1986), pp. 134–7; 'Vita S. Stephani iunioris', *PG,* C, col. 1172.

24. *Ecloga,* pp. 1–12, 160–2; B. Meyer-Plath and A. M. Schneider, *Die*

Landmauer von Konstantinopel II (Denkmäler antiker Architektur VIII, Berlin, 1943), pp. 5, 133 nr 36; V. Peschlow, *Die Irenenkirche in Istanbul* (Tübingen, 1977), pp. 212–13; S. Gero, *Byzantine Iconoclasm During the Reign of Constantine V* (CSCO CCCLXXXIV, Louvain, 1977), pp. 53–66; R. Cormack, 'The Arts During the Age of Iconoclasm', in *Iconoclasm*, ed. A. Bryer and J. Herrin (Birmingham, 1977), pp. 35–44.

25. Theo., pp. 451–2; Mansi, XIII, 209.

26. J. F. Haldon, *Byzantine Praetorians* (Poikilia Byzantina III, Bonn, 1984), pp. 231–5.

27. R. Reidinger, *Die Präesenz- und Subscriptionslisten des VI oekumensichen Konzils (680/81)* (Bayerische Akademie der Wissenschaften, phil.-hist. Klasse, Abhandlungen, neue Folge LXXXV, Munich, 1979); Mansi, XIII, col. 232.

28. Theo., pp. 436–8; Nik., pp. 154–8; 'Vita S. Stephani iunioris', cols 1137, 1175–7.

29. C. Zuckerman, 'The Reign of Constantine V in the Miracles of St. Theodore the Recruit', *REB*, XLVI (1988), 191–210; 'Gesta episcoporum Neapolitanorum', pp. 422–3.

30. Theo., pp. 461–2.

31. Theo., pp. 413–21; Nik., pp. 132–8; P. Speck, *Artabasdos, der rechtgläubige Vorkämpfer der göttlichen Lehren* (Poikilia Byzantina II, Bonn, 1981), pp. 146–51.

32. Gero, *Byzantine Iconoclasm During the Reign of Constantine V*, pp. 121–9.

33. Theo., pp. 437–42; Nik., pp. 156–60.

34. P. Brown, 'A Dark Age Crisis: Aspects of the Iconoclastic Controversy', *English Historical Review*, LXXXVIII (1973), 1–34 [= P. Brown, *Society and the Holy in Late Antiquity* (London, 1982), pp. 251–301]; M.-F. Rouan, 'Une lecture "iconoclaste" de la vie d'Étienne le jeune', *TM*, VIII (1981), 415–36.

35. C. Mango, 'St. Anthusa of Mantineon and the Family of Constantine V', *AB*, C (1982), 401–9.

36. J. Herrin, *The Formation of Christendom* (Oxford, 1987), pp. 417–24.

37. Theo., p. 454.

38. J. Herrin, 'Women and Faith in Icons in Early Christianity', in *Culture, Ideology and Politics*, ed. R. Samuel and G. Stedman Jones (London, 1982), pp. 56–83.

39. Theo., pp. 463–75.

40. Theo., pp. 476–80.

41. Theo., p. 491.

42. Theo., pp. 496, 501; *Scriptor incertus*, p. 349.

43. P. Alexander, 'The Iconoclastic Council of St. Sophia (815) and Its Definition (*Horos*)', *DOP*, VII (1953), 35–66.

44. P. Lemerle, 'Thomas le Slave', *TM*, I (1965), 255–97.

45. J. H. Pryor, *Geography, Technology, and War* (Cambridge, 1988), pp. 102–7.

46. F. Dvornik, *La Vie de Saint Grégoire le Décapolite et les Slaves macédoniens au ix⁰ siècle* (Travaux publiés par l'Institut d'études Slaves V, Paris, 1926), pp. 53–4.

47. Theo. Cont., pp. 76–7, 79–82.

48. Theo. Cont., p. 88; *De Cer.*, p. 645; Grierson, *Byzantine Coins*, pp. 177–8, pl. 42, nr 766; for the date cf. W. Treadgold, 'The Problem of the Marriage of the Emperor Theophilus', *Greek, Roman and Byzantine Studies*, XVI (1975), 329–5.

49. Mc Cormick, *Eternal Victory*, pp. 146–52; for the dates cf. W. Treadgold, 'The Chronological Accuracy of the *Chronicle* of Symeon Logothete for the years 813–45', *DOP*, XXXIII (1979), 172, 178.

50. Grierson, *Byzantine Coins*, pp. 182–3, pl. 45, nr 810.

51 Theo, Cont., pp. 98, 139–48; GM cont., pp. 739, 798, 806, 809; *De Cer.*, pp. 582, 586–7; S. Eyice, 'Quatre édifices inédits ou mal connus', *Cahiers archéologiques*, x (1959), 245–50.

52. Theo. Cont., pp. 125–31; Genesios, pp. 44–9; GM cont., p. 805; Michel le Syrien, III, pp. 95–9; *Chron. 1234*, II, pp. 23–4; al-Tabarī, III, pp. 1236–56; Vasiliev, *Byzance et les Arabes I. La dynastie d'Amorium (820–861)*, French edn, H. Grégoire and M. Canard (Brussels, 1935), pp. 275, 333–5; there have been several attempts to reconstruct the events of 838: J. B. Bury, 'Mutasim's March through Cappadocia in A.D. 838', *Journal of Hellenic Studies*, XXIX (1909), 120–9; Vasiliev, *Byzance et les Arabes*, I, pp. 144–77; W. T. Treadgold, *The Byzantine Revival, 780–842* (Stanford, Cal., 1988), pp. 297–305; archaeological work at Amorion is only at a very early stage, but see R. M. Harrison, 'Amorium 1987. A Preliminary Survey', *Anatolian Studies*, 175–9; 'Amorium 1990, The Third Preliminary Report', *ibid.* XLI (1991), 215–17; 'Amorium Excavations, 1991', *ibid.* XLII (1992), 207–22; 'Excavations at Amorium: 1992 Interim Report', *ibid.* XLIII (1993), 147–62.

53. J. Gouillard, 'Le Synodikon de l'Orthodoxie', *TM*, II (1967), 119–29.

54. GM cont., pp. 809–10; Leo Gram., pp. 227–8.

55. Euodios Monachos, *Hoi Sarantaduo Martyres tou Amoriou*, ed. S. Euthymiades (Hagiologikē Bibliothekē II, Nea Smyrna, 1989), pp. 18–30: a near-contemporary account of the 42 martyrs of Amorion stressing the link between iconoclasm and defeat.

56. C. Mango, 'When was Michael III Born?', *DOP*, XXI (1967), 253–8.

57. Theodorus Stouditae, *Epistolae*: the second volume provides a German summary.

58. J. Darrouzès, *Recherches sur les ΟΦΦΙΚΙΑ de l'église byzantine* (Paris, 1970), pp. 314–18.

59. The letters are due to appear shortly in a new edition by C. Mango (CFHB, Washington, D.C.) and I am very grateful to Professor Mango for access to draft texts of the letters. See C. Mango, 'Observations on the Correspondance of Ignatius, Metropolitan of Nicaea (First Half of the Ninth Century)', *Texte und Untersuchungen zur Geschichte der altchristlichen Literatur*, CXXV (1981), 403–10; lives: 'Ignatii diaconi Vita Tarasii archiep. CP', ed. I. Heikel, *Acta Societas Scientiarum Fennicae*, XVII (1891), 395–423; *Nicephori archiep. CP. opuscula historica*, ed. C. de Boor (Leipzig, 1880), pp. 139–217; authorship of iambic poem on Thomas the Slav: *Suidae Lexicon*, ed. A. Adler, 5 vols (Leipzig, 1928–38), II, pp. 607–8; iconoclast epigrams: Theo. Cont., p. 143; P. Speck, 'Die ikonklastischen Jamben an der Chalce', *Hellēnika*, XXVII (1974), 376–80.

60. *The Life of Michael the Synkellos*, ed. and tr. M. B. Cunningham (BBTT I, Belfast, 1991), pp. 44, 48, 82–4; C. Mango, 'Documentary Evidence on the Apse Mosaics of St. Sophia', *BZ*, XLVII (1954), 396–7.

61. Pseudo-Sym., pp. 628–30; Theo. Cont., pp. 90–2, 103–4; 'Vita Theodorae imperatricis', ed. W. Regel, *Analecta Byzantino-russica* (St Petersburg, 1891), pp. 1–19.

62. *The Synodikon Vetus* ed. J. Duffy and J. Parker (CFHB XV, Washington, D.C., 1979), p. 196; C. Mango, 'The Liquidation of Iconoclasm and the Patriarch Photius', in *Iconoclasm*, ed. Bryer and Herrin, pp. 133–40.

63. Genesios, pp. 17–18, 50, 55, 59; Leo Gram., pp. 228–9; *Synaxarium ecclesiae Constantinopolitanae*, p. 244; P. Karlin-Hayter, 'Études sur deux histoires du règne de Michel III', *Byz*, XLI (1971), 455. The identification of the eunuch and patrikios Theoktistos whose martyrdom and feastday are mentioned in the *Synaxarium* with the eunuch Theoktistos who restored icons

has been hindered by the mistaken belief, perpetuated by the *Oxford Dictionary of Byzantium*, III, p. 2056, that Theoktistos held the rank of magistros.
The magistros Theoktistos mentioned at Theo., pp. 492, 500 is another man.
  64. Pseudo Sym., pp. 643–5; Genesios, p. 53; Theo. Cont., p. 116; 'Vita
Methodii', *PG*, C, cols 1252–3.
  65. Nik., p. 48; Theo., p. 351.
  66. H. Kennedy, 'The Melkite Church from the Islamic Conquest to the
Crusades: Continuity and Adaptation in the Byzantine Legacy', *17th International Byzantine Congress, Major Papers* (New York, 1986), pp. 325–43.
  67. For example, *Annales Bertiniani*, ed. G. Waitz (MGH Scriptores rerum
Germanicarum, Hannover, 1883), pp. 19, 28, 98, 105; tr. J. L. Nelson, *The
Annals of St-Bertin* (Manchester, 1991), pp. 44, 54, 154, 162.

7. THE BYZANTINE RESPONSE: ON TO THE DEFENSIVE

  1. H. Kennedy, 'Arab Settlement on the Byzantine Frontier in the Eighth
and Ninth Centuries', *Yayla*, II (1979), 22–4; J. F. Haldon and H. Kennedy,
'The Arab–Byzantine Frontier in the Eighth and Ninth Centuries: Military
Organisation and Society in the Borderlands', *ZRVI*, XIX (1980), pp. 82–4,
106–9.
  2. H. Ahrweiler, *Byzance et la mer* (Paris, 1966), pp. 30–3, 81–3; Theo.,
pp. 405, 410.
  3. J. P. Haldon, *Byzantine Praetorians* (Poikilia Byzantina III, Bonn, 1984),
pp. 164–82, 191–227.
  4. Procopius, *Anekdota*, ed. and tr. H. B. Dewing (Cambridge, Mass., 1935),
XXIV.15–23, pp. 284–6.
  5. Haldon, *Byzantine Praetorians*, pp. 228–35, 297–318.
  6. Theo., pp. 461–2.
  7. F. Halkin, *Euphémie de Chalcédoine. Légendes byzantines* (Subsidia
hagiographica XLI, Brussels, 1965), pp. 97–8.
  8. Haldon, *Byzantine Praetorians*, pp. 236–45.
  9. *ibid.*, pp. 245–52.
  10. Leo. Gram., p. 215; Theo. Cont., pp. 110–12; al-Tabarī, III, pp. 1234–
5; 'Acta 42 martyrum Amoriensium', ed. V. Vassilievskij and P. Nikitin, *Mémoires
de l'Académie Imperiale des sciences de St.-Petersbourg*, 8th series, hist.-phil., class,
VII.2 (1905), p. 27.
  11. Oikonomidès, *Les listes*, pp. 209 (ll. 19–21), 327–8; *De Cer.*, pp. 478,
576, 660; Theo. Cont., p. 358.
  12. M. N. Adler, *The Itinerary of Benjamin of Tudela* (London, 1907), p. 13.
  13. Theo., p. 449.
  14. Leo VI, 'Tactica', *PG*, CVI, col. 680.
  15. J. F. Haldon, *Byzantium in the Seventh Century* (Cambridge, 1990), pp.
196–207, 215, 230; F. Winkelmann, *Byzantinische Rang- und Ämterstruktur im
8. und 9. Jahrhundert* (Berlin, 1985), pp. 118–38, 142–3; Oikomomidès, *Les
listes*, pp. 51 (ll. 25–6), 53 (l. 3), 294, 343–4, 348–9; specifically on the survival of the Praetorian Prefect, see *De Cer.*, ed. Vogt, I, p. 56; Mansi, XVI, cols
18, 309; and the discussion in Haldon, *Byzantium in the Seventh Century*, pp.
201–2 and n. 110.
  16. Leo VI, 'Tactica', cols 976–7; 'Skirmishing Warfare', pp. 214–16; G.
Dagron, 'Byzance et la modèle Islamique au xᵉ siècle à propos des *Constitutions tactiques* de l'empereur Léon VI', *Comptes rendus de l'Academie des inscriptions* (1983), pp. 219–42.

17. 'Skirmishing Warfare', p. 164; *De re militari*, pp. 276, 310; Leo VI 'Tactica', col. 700.

18. *De Cer.*, p. 669.

19. Theo., p. 486.

20. 'Vie et office de saint Euthyme le jeune', ed. L. Petit, *Revue de l'orient chrétien*, VIII (1903), 172–3; 'Vie de saint Luc le stylite', pp. 200–1; *The Life of St. Nikon*, ed. D. F. Sullivan (Brookline, Mass., 1987), p. 222.

21. For example, *Épistoliers byzantins*, ed. Darrouzès, pp. 130–1.

22. *JGR*, I, pp. 222–6.

23. For example, *Actes de Lavra* I, p. 218, l. 37.

24. Theo., p. 452.

25. 'Skirmishing Warfare', pp. 154–214, 226–32.

26. Leo, metropolitan of Synada, *Correspondence*, pp. 68–70; L. Robert, 'Les kordakia de Nicée, le combustible de Synnada et les poissons-scies. Sur des lettres d'un métropolite de Phrygie du xᵉ siècle. Philologie et réalités', *Journal des Savants* (1961), 115–66.

27. 'Skirmishing Warfare', pp. 152, 164, 170, 174, 184–6, 212; al-Tabarī, III, pp. 1357, 1449, 2103; Vasiliev, *Byzance et les Arabes*, II.2, pp. 148.

28. N. Thierry, 'Monuments de Cappadoce de l'antiquité romaine au moyen âge byzantin' in *Le aree omogenee della Civiltà Rupestre nell'ambito dell'Impero Byzantino: la Cappadocia*, ed. C. D. Fonseca (Università degli studi di Lecce, Saggi e Ricerche VI, Galatina, 1981), pp. 39–73; A. J. Wharton, *Art of Empire* (London, 1988), pp. 13–37.

29. Ibn Hauqal, *Configuration de la terre (Kitab Surat Al-Ard)*, tr. J. H. Kramers and G. Wiet (Paris, 1965), p. 192; al-Muqaddasi, *Ahsan at-taqāsīm fī ma'rifat al-aqālīm*, in. A. Miquel (Damascus, 1963), p. 140; *Hudūd al-Ālam*, tr. V. Minorsky (E. J. W. Gibb Memorial Series V, Cambridge, 1970), p. 157; cf. A. Miquel, *La géographie humaine du monde musulman jusqu'au milieu du IIᵉ siècle*, 4 vols (Paris, 1967–88), II, pp. 447, 472–4.

30. John Lydus, *De mensibus*, ed. R. Wuensch (Leipzig, 1898), I.27, p. 13.

31. Agathias, *The Histories*, ed. R. Keydell (CFHB II, Berlin, 1967), V.13.7–8, p. 180.

32. A. H. M. Jones, *The Later Roman Empire* (Oxford, 1964), I, pp. 680–3; II, pp. 1449–50.

33. Haldon, *Byzantium in the Seventh Century*, pp. 251–3.

34. R. Duncan-Jones, *Structure and Scale in the Roman Economy* (Cambridge, 1990), pp. 114, 117.

35. Ibn Khordādhbeh, pp. 77–80, 196–9; E. W. Brooks, 'Arabic Lists of the Byzantine Themes', *Journal of Hellenic Studies*, XXI (1901), 67–77; Miquel, *La géographie humaine du monde musulman*, II, pp. 391–9.

36. *De Cer.*, pp. 651–60, 664–9.

37. Theo., pp. 361, 363–5, 397; *DAI*, c. 21, ll. 3–9, c. 22, ll. 9–26, c. 50, ll. 169–221, pp. 84, 92–4, 240–2; *EI/2*, II, pp. 456–8; H. M. Bartikian, 'Hē lysē tou ainigmatos tōn Mardaitōn', in *Byzantium: Tribute to A. N. Stratos* (Athens, 1986), pp. 17–39.

38. 'Skirmishing Warfare', pp. 192–4, 200–4, 214.

39. *De re militari*, pp. 246–54, 268, 274; *Praecepta Militaria*, pp. 1–2, 7, 9, 12–17.

40. J. D. Howard-Johnston, 'Studies in the Organization of the Byzantine Army in the Tenth and Eleventh Centuries' (University of Oxford D.Phil. thesis, 1971), pp. 134–40; W. T. Treadgold, *The Byzantine State Finances in the Eighth and Ninth Centuries* (Eastern European Monographs CXXI, New York, 1982), pp. 15–19, 29–31, 116–17; Treadgold, *The Byzantine Revival, 780–842*

(Stanford, Cal., 1988), pp. 352–3; M. Hendy, *Studies in the Byzantine Monetary Economy c. 300–1450* (Cambridge, 1985) p. 182.

41. England: the figure is calculated on the basis of a total English hideage of *c.* 70,000 hides, and a military obligation of one man to five hides: H. C. Darby, *Domesday England* (Cambridge, 1977), p. 336; R. P. Abels, *Lordship and Military Obligation in Anglo-Saxon England* (London, 1988), pp. 97–131, 186; Ottonian Germany: K. J. Leyser, 'The Battle at the Lech, 955. A Study in Tenth-century Warfare', *History*, I (1965), 16–17 and nn. 67, 69. The English figure is particularly significant since over the course of the tenth century most rulers in north-western Europe came to rely on heavily armoured and highly expensive cavalry to form the core of their armies. England did not follow this development until after 1066. Pre-tenth century armies, such as those of Charlemagne, relying on lighter cavalry and infantry are likely to have been larger than those of the tenth century onwards, but the English evidence suggests not so much larger that their numbers could have approached the figures given by the Arab sources for Byzantium. See J. France, 'The Military History of the Carolingian Period', *Revue Belge d'Histoire Militaire*, XXVI (1985), 81–99. I am very grateful to Dr France for sending me a copy of this important paper.

42. Miquel, *La géographie humaine du monde musulman*, I, pp. 35–68, 153–89; II, pp. 381–3, 449–51.

43. Ibn Khordādhbeh, pp. 78–9.

44. GM cont., p. 880.

45. *Vita Euthymii Patriarchae CP.*, ed. P. Karlin-Hayter (Brussels, 1970), pp. 67–97; GM cont., pp. 860–70; that this expedition was aimed at Crete is confirmed by Theo. Cont., p. 474.

46. Theo. Cont., pp. 436–7, 445–6; Skylitzes, pp. 234–9, 245–6.

8. THE BYZANTINE EMPIRE AND ITS NON-MUSLIM NEIGHBOURS, *c.* 600–*c.* 950

1. R. H. Hewsen, 'Ethno-History and the Armenian Influence upon the Caucasian Albanians', in *Classical Armenian Culture*, ed. T. J. Samuelian (Armenian Texts and Studies IV, Philadelphia, Pa., 1982), pp. 27–40.

2. Leo, Gram., p. 215; Theo. Cont., pp. 110–12; al-Tabarī, III, p. 1381; 'Vaticanus Gr. 163', 99, l. 9; *EI/2*, V, pp. 63–4, 438–53; V. Minorsky, *Studies in Caucasian History* (Cambridge, 1953), pp. 112–13; W. Barthold, *An Historical Geography of Iran*, tr. S. Soucek (Princeton, N.J., 1984), pp. 214–29; M. van Bruinessen, *Agha, Shaikh and State* (London, 1992), pp. 50–132.

3. Laurent/Canard, pp. 69–70, n. 121.

4. F. Braudel, *The Mediterranean and the Mediterranean World in the Age of Philip II*, tr. S. Reynolds, 2 vols (London, 1972–3), p. 28, n. 6.

5. For example, *The History of Lazar P'arpec'i*, tr. R. W. Thomson (Atlanta, Ga., 1991), pp. 42–4; Moses Khorenats'i, *History of the Armenians*, tr. R. W. Thomson (Harvard Armenian Texts and Studies IV, Cambridge, Mass., 1978), pp. 331–2.

6. P. Peeters, 'Saint Hilarion d'Ibérie', *AB*, XXXII (1913), 253–5, 264; *Actes d'Iviron*, I, pp. 13–24; P. Lemerle, *Cinq études sur le xiᵉ siècle byzantin* (Paris, 1977), pp. 158–61.

7. P. Charanis, *The Armenians in the Byzantine Empire* (Lisbon, no date); A. Kazhdan, 'The Armenians in the Byzantine Ruling Class Predominantly in the Ninth Through Twelfth Centuries', in *Medieval Armenian Culture*, ed. T. J. Samuelian and M. E. Stone (Armenian Texts and Studies vi, Chico, Cal., 1983), pp. 440–52.

8. N. Adontz, *Armenian in the Period of Justinian*, tr. N. G. Garsoïan (Lisbon, 1970), pp. 183–251, 289–371; Laurent/Canard, pp. 96–108.

9. Adontz, *Armenian in the Period of Justinian*, pp. 253–88.

10. Laurent/Canard, pp. 121–53; *The Epic Histories Attributed to P'awstos Buzand*, tr. and comm., N. G. Garsoïan (Cambridge, Mass., 1989), pp. 350, 362–3, 382, 385–6, 402, 408–9.

11. *The Epic Histories*, pp. 51–5; J. R. Russell, *Zoroastrianism in Armenia* (Cambridge, Mass., 1987); D. M. Lang, 'Iran, Armenia and Georgia', in *Cambridge History of Iran*, 7 vols (Cambridge, 1968–), III.1, pp. 505–36.

12. Sebeos, tr. Macler, pp. 98–9; tr. Bedrosian, pp. 126–8; *The History of the Caucasian Albanians by Movsēs Dasxuranci*, tr. C. J. F. Dowsett (London, 1961), pp. 110–13.

13. R. W. Thomson, 'Mission, Conversion and Christianisation: The Armenian Example', *HUS*, XII/XIII (1988/9), 27–45; C. Toumanoff, *Studies in Christian Caucasian History* (Georgetown, Va., 1963), pp. 78, 83, 366–77, 421–2.

14. Ammianus Marcellinus, *Rerum Gestarum Libri*, ed. J. C. Rolfe, 3 vols (Cambridge, Mass., 1935–9), XXV.7.9, p. 532; *ibid.*, tr. W. Hamilton, (Harmondsworth, 1986), p. 304; *The Epic Histories*, pp. 233–4, 334; Adontz, *Armenia in the Period of Justinian*, pp. 8–24, 165–82.

15. V. Inglisian, 'Die armenische Literatur', in *Handbuch der Orientalistik*, I.7, ed. G. Deeters (Leiden, 1963), pp. 156–250; Laurent/Canard, pp. 177–8; Thomson, 'Mission, Conversion and Christianisation', pp. 44–5.

16. Elishē, *History of Vardan and the Armenian War*, tr. R. W. Thomson (Cambridge, Mass., 1982), pp. 9–18, 24–5, 27.

17. Rejection of Chalcedon and the Council of Dwin: *Narratio de rebus Armeniae*, ed. and comm. G. Garitte (CSCO CXXXII, subsidia IV, Louvain, 1967), pp. 31–6, 108–75; Georgia: Ukhtanes of Sebasteia, *History of Armenia*, tr. Z. Arzoumanian, 2 vols (Fort Lauderdale, Fla., 1985–8), II, pp. 118–24.

18. Adontz, *Armenia in the Period of Justinian*, pp. 75–164; J. D. Howard-Johnston, 'Procopius, Roman Defences North of the Taurus and the New Fortress of Citharizon', in *The Eastern Frontier of the Roman Empire*, ed. D. H. French and C. S. Lightfoot, 2 parts (BAR Int. Ser. DLIII, Oxford, 1989), pp. 203–29; *Corpus Iuris Civilis*, ed. T. Mommsen *et al.*, 3 vols (Berlin, 1928–9), III, p. 1, ll. 10–12.

19. M. Whitby, *The Emperor Maurice and his Historian* (Oxford, 1988), pp. 216–18, 252–3, 262–8, 273, 304; Sebeos, tr. Macler, pp. 15, 27; tr. Bedrosian, pp. 20, 41; H. Hübschmann, *Die alttermenischen Ortsnamen* (Strasbourg, 1904), pp. 228–32, and map in endpapers.

20. Sebeos, tr. Macler, pp. 30–7, 53–4; tr. Bedrosian, pp. 44–57, 79–80; *Narratio de rebus Armeniae*, pp. 39–41, 225–54; Yovhannēs Drasxanakertc' i, *History of Armenia*, tr. and comm. K. H. Maksoudian (Atlanta, Ga., 1987), pp. 95–7; Ukhtanes of Sebasteia, pp. 77–8, 122.

21. *Narratio de rebus Armeniae*, pp. 42, 254–77; Yovhannēs Drasxanakertc'i, p. 96; Ukhtanes of Sebasteia, pp. 79–86.

22. *Narratio de rebus Armeniae*, pp. 42–5, 278–337; Sebeos, tr. Macler, p. 91–2; tr. Bedrosian, p. 117; Yovhannēs Drasxanakertc'i, pp. 99–100; Toumanoff, *Studies in Christian Caucasian History*, pp. 476–7.

23. Sebeos, tr. Macler, pp. 92–4; tr. Bedrosian, pp. 117–21; M. Thierry and N. Thierry, 'La cathédrale de Mrèn et sa décoration', *Cahiers archéologiques*, XXI (1971), 43–77.

24. Sebeos, tr. Macler, pp. 100–1, 109–10, 132–5, 138–9, 142–3, 145–8; tr. Bedrosian, pp. 128–30, 141–4, 158–62, 166–8, 171–3, 175–82; Theo., pp.

344–5, 363, 372; *History of Lewond*, tr. and comm. Z. Arzoumanian (Philadelphia, Pa., 1982), pp. 50–67; al-Tabarī, I, pp. 2674–5, 2806–7, 2871; al-Balādhuri, *Kitāb Futūh al-Buldān*, tr. P. K. Hitti, *The Origins of the Islamic State*, 2 vols (Beirut, 1966), I, pp. 305–22.

25. B. Martin-Hisard, 'La domination byzantine sur le littoral oriental du Pont Euxin (milieu du viiᵉ–viiiᵉ siècles)', *Byzantino-Bulgarica*, VII (1981), 141–54; Martin-Hisard 'Les Arabes en Géorgie occidentale au viiiᵉ siècle: étude sur l'idéologie politique Géorgienne', *Bedi Kartlisa*, XL (1982), 105–38; Laurent/Canard, pp. 68 (n. 110), 127–8; *EI/2*, I, pp. 100; Theo., pp. 370, 391–4.

26. Sebeos, tr. Macler, pp. 132–3; tr. Bedrosian, pp. 158–9; *History of Lewond*, p. 114; Laurent/Canard, pp. 201, 209.

27. *The History of the Caucasian Albanians*, pp. 77–88, 94–5, 98–102, 104, 106; Laurent/Canard, p. 211.

28. J. F. Haldon and H. Kennedy, 'The Arab–Byzantine Frontier in the Eighth and Ninth Centuries: Military Organisation and Society in the Borderlands', *ZRVI*, XIX (1980), 107–15; Theo., p. 427; Nik., p. 142.

29. *History of Lewond*, pp. 113, 129–39; Laurent/Canard, pp. 202–5.

30. Laurent/Canard, pp. 197–8, 213–14; K. Hitchins, 'The Caucasian Albanians and the Arab Caliphate', *Bedi Kartlisa*, XLII (1984), 234–45; A. Ter-Ghewondyan, *The Arab Emirates in Bagratid Armenia*, tr. N. G. Garsoïan (Lisbon, 1976), pp. 33–44, 51–66.

31. Laurent/Canard, pp. 123–45; C. Toumanoff, 'The Bagratids of Iberia from the Eighth to the Eleventh Century', *Le Muséon*, LXXIV (1961), 5–29, 254–5, 273–4.

32. *History of Lewond*, pp. 132–3; Genesios, p. 47, l. 24; Theo. Cont., p. 127, l. 2.

33. Laurent/Canard, pp. 133–4, 357–81.

34. Yovhannēs Drasxanakertc'i, pp. 118–24; Thomas Artsruni, *History of the House of Artsrunik'*, tr. R. W. Thomson (Detroit, Mich., 1985), pp. 178–264; Laurent/Canard, pp. 147–52.

35. Yovhannēs Drasxanakertc'i, p. 124; Thomas Artsruni, pp. 238, 255.

36. Yovhannēs Drasxanakertc'i, pp. 125, 127–8; a less enthusiastic Artsruni perspective: Thomas Artsruni, pp. 270, 282–3, 285, 293; Laurent/Canard, pp. 311–24.

37. Toumanoff, 'The Bagratids of Iberia', 12–13; J. Muyldermans, *La domination Arabe en Arménie* (Louvain, 1927), p. 113; Stephen of Taron I, p. 171–2; Theo. Cont., pp. 137, 203; G. L. Huxley, 'Theoktistos, Abasgia and Two Eclipses', *Byzantinoslavica*, L (1989), 9–10; Laurent/Canard, pp. 54, 67, 233–4, 248–52, 319.

38. Photius, *Epistulae*, nr 2 (ll. 38–47), 284, 298; I, p. 41; III, pp. 4–112, 167–74; J. Darrouzès, 'Deux lettres inédites de Photius aux Arméniens', *REB*, XXIX (1971), 137–81; Laurent/Canard, pp. 344–56.

39. *De Cer.*, p. 686.

40. Yovhannēs Drasxanakertc'i, p. 138.

41. *DAI*, c. 43, ll. 9–11, p. 188.

42. Yovhannēs Drasxanakertc'i, pp. 155–8, 160–77; Thomas Artsruni, pp. 345–8.

43. Yovhannēs Drasxanakertc'i, p. 197.

44. P. B. Golden, *Khazar Studies*, 2 vols (Budapest, 1980), I, pp. 37–42; Golden, 'Imperial Ideology and the Sources of Political Unity Among the Pre-Činggisid Nomads of Western Eurasia', *Archivum Eurasiae Medii Aevi*, II (1982), 42–9.

45. P. B. Golden, 'The Peoples of the South Russian Steppes', in *The Cambridge History of Early Inner Asia*, ed. D. Sinor (Cambridge, 1990), pp. 305–13; Golden, 'Imperial Ideology and the Sources of Political Unity', 40–1, 50–4.

46. Theo., p. 358; Golden, *Khazar Studies*, I, pp. 49–60.

47. Golden, 'Imperial Ideology and the Sources of Political Unity', pp. 58–60; Golden, *Khazar Studies*, I, pp. 97–106.

48. *Ibid.*, I, pp. 123–33.

49. M. Canard, 'La relation du voyage d'Ibn Fadlān chez les Bulgares de la Volga', *Annales de l'Institut d'Études Orientales de l'Université d'Alger*, XVI (1958), 138.

50. Golden, *Khazar Studies*, pp. 86–97.

51. Theo., pp. 372–3.

52. *Ibid.*, pp. 409–10; *Constantinople in the Eighth Century: The Parastaseis Syntomoi Chronikai*, ed. and tr. A. Cameron and J. Herrin (Leiden, 1984), pp. 98, 212; *De Cer.*, ed. Vogt, I, pp. 17, 78–80, 82, 84, 131–2, 175–6; II, p. 21; *De Cer.*, p. 440; Golden, *Khazar Studies*, pp. 175–6.

53. C. Mango, 'Documentary Evidence for the Apse Mosaics of St. Sophia', *BZ*, XLVII (1954), 396–7; J. Gouillard, 'Le Photius de pseudo-Syméon Magistros', *Revue historique du sud-est européen*, IX (1971), 397–404.

54. *Notitiae episcopatuum ecclesiae Constantinopolitanae*, pp. 31, 241–2; P. Peeters, 'Les Khazars dans la Passion de S. Abo de Tiflis', *AB*, LII (1934), 25.

55. Golden, *Khazar Studies*, I, pp. 59–63.

56. Al-Balādhuri, pp. 325–6; Golden, *Khazar Studies*, I, pp. 63–4.

57. *History of Lewond*, pp. 125–6, 144.

58. Golden, *Khazar Studies*, I, pp. 65–7; Laurent/Canard, p. 68, n. 110; Martin-Hisard, 'La domination byzantine sur le littoral oriental du Pont Euxin', 153–4.

59. Mas'ūdī, *Les prairies d'or*, tr. B. de Meynard and P. de Courteille, rev. C. Pellat, 4 vols (Paris, 1962–89), I, p. 163; Golden, *Khazar Studies*, I, pp. 100–2.

60. Mas'ūdī, *Les prairies d'or*, I, p. 161; P. B. Golden, 'Khazaria and Judaism', *Archivum Eurasiae Medii Aevi*, III (1983), 127–56; N. Golb and O. Pritsak, *Khazarian Hebrew Documents of the Tenth Century* (Ithaca, N.Y., 1982), pp. 26–9.

61. Golden, *Khazar Studies*, I, pp. 102–3, 107–11; J. Martin, *Treasure of the Land of Darkness* (Cambridge, 1986), pp. 5–14; T. S. Noonan, 'Why Dirhams First Reached Russia: The Role of Arab–Khazar Relations in the Development of the Earliest Islamic Trade with Eastern Europe', *Archivum Eurasiae Medii Aevi*, IV (1984), 151–282; Noonan, 'Ninth-century Dirhem Hoards From European Russia: A Preliminary Analysis', in *Viking Age Coinage in the Northern Lands*, ed. M. A. S. Blackburn and D. M. Metcalf (BAR Int. Ser. CXXII, Oxford, 1981), pp. 47–118.

62. P. B. Golden, 'The Migrations of the Oğuz', *Archivum Ottomanicum*, IV (1972), 50–9.

63. *DAI*, cc. 37–40, pp. 166–79.

64. *Ibid.*, c. 37, ll. 1–14; c. 38, ll. 3–4, 24–31; c. 40, ll. 23–5, pp. 166, 170–2, 176.

65. *Ibid.*, c. 39, ll. 2–14; c. 40, ll. 3–4, 6–7, p. 174.

66. *Ibid.*, c. 38, ll. 55–60; c. 40, ll. 7–27, pp. 174–6.

67. J. Bacot, 'Reconnaisance en haute Asie septentrionale par cinq envoyés ouigours au viiie siècle', *Journal Asiatique*, CCLIV (1956), 147.

68. GM cont., pp. 853–5; Leo VI, *Tactica*, col. 956; *Annales Fuldenses*, ed. G. H. Pertz, rev. F. Kurze (MGH Scriptores rerum Germanicarum, Hannover,

1891), pp. 125–6, 129–30; tr. T. Reuter, *The Annals of Fulda* (Manchester, 1992), pp. 129, 131, 135–6.

69. Regino Prumiensis, *Chronicon* (MGH SRG, Hannover, 1890), pp. 132–3, 143, 148.

70. G. Györffy, 'Sur la question de l'établissement des Petchénègues en Europe', *Acta Orientalia Academia Scientiarum Hungaricae*, xxv (1972), 284–6; J. M. H. Smith, *Province and Empire: Brittany and the Carolingians* (Cambridge, 1992), p. 133.

71. *DAI*, c. 3, l. 3; c. 38, ll. 31–56; c. 39, ll. 7–10, pp. 50, 172–4.

72. GM cont., pp. 818–19.

73. Theo. Cont., p. 122.

74. *Annales Bertiniani*, p. 60; tr. Nelson, p. 102.

75. *DAI*, c. 43, ll. 42–4, p. 190; Theo. Cont., pp. 371, 384, 386, 389; GM cont., pp. 866, 877–8, 881–2; cf. S. Runciman, in *DAI*, ii, *Commentary*, ed. R. J. H. Jenkins (London, 1962), pp. 162–3.

76. V. Beševliev, *Die protobulgarischen Inschriften* (Berlin, 1963), nr 58, p. 281.

77. *Annales Bertiniani*, pp. 19–20; tr. Nelson p. 44.

78. Theo. Cont., pp. 122–3; *DAI*, c. 42, ll. 20–55, pp. 182–4.

79. Golden, *Khazar Studies*, i, pp. 67–8; Ibn Rusta, *Kitāb al-A'lāk al-Nafīsa*, tr. G. Wiet, *Les atours précieux* (Cairo, 1955), p. 160; Mas'ūdī, *Les prairies d'or*, i, pp. 161, 165; S. A. Pletneva, *Ot kočevii k gorodam* (Moscow, 1965), pp. 34, 43–5.

80. Oikonomidès, *Les listes*, p. 49, l. 19; for the date (838–9, not *c.* 833, cf., *ibid.*, p. 353), see W. Treadgold, 'Three Byzantine Provinces and the First Byzantine Contacts with Rus', *HUS*, xii/xiii (1988/9), 134–5.

81. *DAI*, c. 46, ll. 56–165, pp. 216–22.

82. Cf. A. A. Vasiliev, *The Goths in the Crimea* (Cambridge, Mass., 1936), pp. 108–12; Treadgold, 'Three Byzantine Provinces', pp. 135–44.

83. Golden, *Khazar Studies*, i, pp. 69–77; Golden, 'The Peoples of the Russian Forest Belt', in *Cambridge History of Early Inner Asia*, pp. 242–8; Obolensky, *The Byzantine Commonwealth: Eastern Europe, 500–1453* (London, 1971), pp. 231–2.

84. *DAI*, c. 38, ll. 13–19, 31–55; c. 40, 47–68.

85. Golden 'Imperial Ideology and Sources of Political Unity', pp. 61–2; T. Halasi-Kun, 'Some Thoughts on Hungaro-Turkic Affinity', *Archivum Eurasiae Medii Aevi*, vi (1986–8), 31–9; G. Györffy, 'Système des residences d'hiver et d'été chez les nomades et les chefs hongrois au xe siècle', *ibid*, i (1975), 54–9.

86. Golden, *Khazar Studies*, i, pp. 34–6.

87. See Lindner, 'What was a Nomadic Tribe?', 698–700; W. Irons, 'Nomadism as a Political Adaptation: The Case of the Yomut Turkmen', *American Ethnologist*, i (1974), 635–58.

88. Halasi-Kun, 'Some thoughts on Hungaro-Turkic Affinity', pp. 32, 37–8.

89. *Hudūd al-Ālam*, tr. V. Minorsky, p. 160.

90. *DAI*, c. 37, ll. 2–33, p. 166; *Sharaf al-Zamān Tāhir: Marvazī on China, the Turks and India*, tr. V. Minorsky (London, 1942), pp. 32–3; Golden, 'Imperial Ideology and the Sources of Political Unity', 63–6; A. M. Khazanov, *Nomads and the Outside World* tr. J. Crookenden (Cambridge, 1984), pp. 178–9.

91. *The Homilies of Photius, Patriarch of Constantinople*, tr. C. Mango (Cambridge, Mass., 1958), pp. 74–110.

92. 'Life of Constantine the Philosopher', tr. M. Kantor, *Medieval Slavic*

Lives of Saints and Princes (Ann Arbor, Mich., 1983), pp. 43–63.

93. *DAI*, c. 4, ll. 3–8; c. 5, ll. 3–5, pp. 50–2.

94. *Ibid.*, c. 2, ll. 16–18, p. 50.

95. *Ibid.*, c. 7, p. 54.

96. *Ibid.*, c. 8, ll. 23–33, p. 56.

97. Mas'ūdī, *Les prairies d'or*, ɪ, p. 173; Golb and Pritsak, *Khazarian Hebrew Documents*, pp. 115, 136; Theo., p. 391; Nicholas I, *Letters*, nrs 23 (ll. 66–70), 51–2, 118, 133; pp. 160, 278–86, 406–8, 432–4; Ibn Rusta, p. 167; *DAI*, cc. 10–11, pp. 62–4; Golden, *Khazar Studies*, ɪ, pp. 93–7.

98. *PVL*, pp. 65–6; *Annales Bertiniani*, pp. 19–20, tr. Nelson, p. 44; Canard, 'La relation du voyage d'Ibn Fadlān', 116, 122–34; Liudprandus Cremonensis, pp. 137–8; *DAI*, c. 9, pp. 56–62; H. Clarke and B. Ambrosiani, *Towns in the Viking Age* (Leicester, 1991), pp. 115–24.

99. *PVL*, pp. 59–61.

100. G. Podsalsky, *Christentum und theologische Literatur in der Kiever Rus' (988–1237)* (Munich, 1982), pp. 202–15.

101. *PVL*, pp. 59, 233–4, n. 20.

102. Goody, Watt, 'The Consequences of Literary', p. 33.

103. *PVL*, pp. 60–1, 64–5.

104. *Ibid.*, p. 60; J. Callmer, 'The Archaeology of Kiev to the End of the Earliest Urban Phase', *HUS*, xɪ (1987), 323–64.

105. Ibn Hauqal, ɪ, pp. 12–13, 15; ɪɪ, pp. 378, 382–3, 387–8; Miquel, *Le géographie humaine du monde musulman*, ɪɪ, pp. 332–5; *Hudūd al-Ālam*, pp. 432–8.

106. Mas'ūdī, *Les prairies d'or*, ɪ, pp. 166–7; Ibn Miskawayh, *Tadjārib al-umam*, ed. and tr. H. F. Amedroz and D. S. Margoliouth, *The Eclipse of the Abbasid Caliphate*, 7 vols (Oxford, 1920–21), v, pp. 67–74; *History of the Caucasian Albanians*, p. 224; Golden, *Khazar Studies*, ɪ, p. 80.

107. Canard, 'La relation du voyage d'Ibn Fadlān', 116–35.

108. *PVL*, pp. 64–8, 73–7.

109. *DAI*, c. 9, ll. 30–71, pp. 58–60.

110. T. S. Noonan, 'The Monetary History of Kiev in the Pre-Mongol Period', *HUS*, xɪ (1987), 397–9.

111. T. S. Noonan, 'Why Dirhams First Reached Russia: The Role of Arab–Khazar Relations in the Development of the Earliest Islamic Trade with Eastern Europe', *Archivum Eurasiae Medii Aevi*, ɪv (1984), 151–282; Noonan, 'When and How Dirhams First Reached Russia: A Numismatic Critique of the Pirenne Theory', *Cahiers du Monde Russe et Soviétique*, xxɪ (1980), 401–69; Noonan, 'Monetary Circulation in Early Medieval Rus': A Study of Volga Bulgar Dirham Finds', *Russian History/Histoire russe*, vɪɪ (1980), 294–311; Noonan 'Ninth-century Dirham Hoards from European Russia: A Preliminary Analysis', in *Viking Age Coinage in the Northern Lands*, ed. Blackburn and Metcalf, pp. 47–118.

112. Ibn Khordādbeh, pp. 115–16.

113. Ibn Rusta, p. 163.

114. P. B. Golden, 'The Question of the Rus Qağanate', *Archivum Eurasiae Medii Aevi*, ɪɪ (1982), 77–97.

115. Canard, 'La relation du voyage d'Ibn Fadlān', 134–5.

116. S. Franklin, *Sermons and Rhetoric of Kievan Rus'* (Cambridge, Mass., 1991), pp. 3, 17–18, 26; S. A. Vysockij, *Drevnerusskiie nadpisi Sofii Kievskoi, xi–xiv. v.* (Kiev. 1966), pp. 42, 49–52.

117. *Annales Bertiniani*, pp. 19–20, tr. Nelson, p. 44.

118. Cf. Golden, 'The Question of the Rus Qağanate', 88–9; J.-P. Arrignon,

'Remarques sur le titre de kagan attribué aux princes russes d'après les sources occidentales et russes des ixe–xie s.', *ZRVI*, XXIII (1984), 67–71.

119. Mas'ūdī, *Les prairies d'or*, I, pp. 162–7.

120. *Sharaf al-Zamān Tāhir*, tr. Minorsky, pp. 23, 36, 118–19.

121. Ibn Khordādbeh, p. 115.

122. C.f. O. Pritsak, 'At the Dawn of Christianity in Rus': East meets West', *HUS*, XII/XIII (1988/9), 87–113; Treagold, 'Three Byzantine Provinces', 132–44.

123. C. Mango, 'Eudocia Ingerina, the Normans and the Macedonian Dynasty', *ZRVI*, XIV/XV (1973), 17–27.

124. *Homilies of Photius*, tr. Mango, p. 96.

125. Theo. Cont., p. 196; Photius, *Epistulae* nr 2, ll. 293–302; I, p. 50.

126. Theo. Cont., pp. 342–3.

127. Callmer, 'Archaeology of Kiev', 331–2, 339.

128. *PVL*, pp. 65–8; *De Cer.*, p. 654.

129. GM cont., pp. 914–16; *PVL*, pp. 71–2; Liudprandus Cremonensis, *Opera*, 3rd edn, ed. J. Bekkers (MGH SRG, Hannover 1915), pp. 137–9.

130. *PVL*, pp. 73–7.

131. *Ibid.*, pp. 78, 82; P. Hollingsworth, *The Hagiography of Kievan Rus'* (Cambridge, Mass., 1992), p. 171; *De Cer.*, pp. 594–8, 664; Skylitzes, p. 240; Regino Prumiensis, p. 170; J. Featherstone, 'Ol'ga's Visit to Constantinople', *HUS*, XIV (1990), 293–312; D. Obolensky, 'Ol'ga's Conversion: The Evidence Reconsidered', *HUS*, XII/XIII (1988/9), 145–58.

132. *PVL*, p. 84; Ibn Miskawayh, V, p. 233; Ibn Hauqal, I, p. 15; II, pp. 382–4; Golden, *Khazar Studies*, I, pp. 82–3.

133. *PVL*, pp. 84–5; Leo Diaconus, p. 63; Skylitzes, p. 277; Theo. Cont., pp. 476, 481; Liudprandus Cremonensis, p. 190.

134. *PVL*, p. 86.

135. Leo Diaconus, pp. 77, 79; Skylitzes, pp. 277, 288.

136. Leo Diaconus, p. 105.

137. *Ibid.*, pp. 107–8, 132–9, 156; Skylitzes, pp. 289, 297, 309–10; *PVL*, pp. 87–90.

138. Leo Diaconus, p. 157; Skylitzes, p. 310; *PVL*, p. 90.

139. *The Fourth Book of the Chronicle of Fredegar*, ed. and tr. J. M. Wallace-Hadrill (London, 1960), pp. 39–40, 56–8.

140. Nik., p. 70; *PLRE*, III, p. 763; Lemerle, *Les plus anciens recueils* I, pp. 222–34; ii, pp. 137–53.

141. *DAI*, c. 31, ll. 8–34, 58–60; c. 32, ll. 7–16, 146–8; c. 33, ll. 8–10; c. 34, ll. 5–6; c. 35, ll. 6–9; pp. 146–52, 160–4.

142. A. G. Poulter, 'Town and County in Moesia Inferior', in *Ancient Bulgaria*, ed. A. G. Poulter, 2 vols (Nottingham, 1983), pp. 97–9; Poulter, 'Urbanism in the Danube Provinces', in *The City in Late Antiquity*, ed. J. Rich (London, 1992), pp. 98–135; V. Popovič, 'Byzantins, slaves et autochtones dans les provinces de Prévalitane et Nouvelle Épire', in *Villes et peuplement dans l'Illyricum protobyzantin*, pp. 198–201; B. Bavant, 'La ville dans le nord d'Illyricum (Pannonie, Mésie I, Dacie et Dardanie)', in *ibid.*, pp. 245–88.

143. A. Bon. *Le Péloponnèse byzantin jusqu'en 1204* (Paris, 1951), pp. 49–55; A. Frantz, *Late Antiquity A.D. 267–700* (The Athenian Agora XXIV, Princeton, N.J., 1988), pp. 117–20; R. L. Scranton, *Medieval Architecture in the Central area of Corinth* (Corinth XVI, Cambridge, Mass., 1957), pp. 27–33; K. M. Edwards, *Coins 1896–1929* (Corinth VI, Cambridge, Mass., 1933); J. Bintliff, 'The Development of Settlement in South-west Boeotia', in *La Béotie antique* (Colloques internationaux du CNRS, Paris, 1985), pp. 49–70; T. H. van Andel, C. N.

Runels and K. O. Pope, 'Five thousand Years of Land Use and Abuse in the Southern Argolid, Greece', *Hesperia*, LV (1986), 103–28.

144. Whittow, 'Ruling the Late Roman and Early Byzantine City', 23–4; J. D. Howard-Johnston, 'Urban Continuity in the Balkans in the Early Middle Ages', in *Ancient Bulgaria*, II, pp. 245–6.

145. Mansi, XI, cols 611–18, 626–30, 639–54, 987–1006. Excavations at Stobi appear to show that, if not completely abandoned, the site was only occupied on a very small scale after the later sixth century, see J. R. Wiseman, 'The City in Macedonia Secunda', in *Villes et peuplement dans l'Illyricum protobyzantin*, pp. 306–13; however, the bishop of Stobi named in 680–1 cannot simply have been the titular incumbent of a defunct see resident in Constantinople since in that case one would expect to find a long list of such names, as occurs in the fourteenth and fifteenth centuries with sees lost to the Turks.

146. Howard-Johnston, 'Urban Continuity in the Balkans', pp. 247–8; Theo., p. 485.

147. Howard-Johnston, 'Urban Continuity in the Balkans', p. 248; Theo., pp. 457, 496.

148. Howard-Johnston, 'Urban Continuity in the Balkans', p. 247; *DAI*, c. 49, pp. 228–32.

149. *DAI*, c. 29, ll. 217–84, 287–9; c. 30, ll. 120–33, pp. 134–8, 146; Popovič, 'Byzantins, slaves et autochtones', 214–28.

150. *Ibid.*, 228–32.

151. J. Herrin, 'Aspects of the Process of Hellenization in the Early Middle Ages', *Annual of the British School of Archaeology at Athens*, LXVIII (1973), 113–26.

152. Lemerle, *Les plus anciens recueils*, I, pp. 134, 175, 179, 209–11; II, pp. 46–9, 88–93, 111–16.

153. Theo., pp. 356–9; Nik., pp. 86–90, 196.

154. S. Runciman, 'The Bulgarian Princes' List', in *Ancient Bulgaria*, II, pp. 232–41; Beševliev, *Die protobulgarischen Inschriften*.

155. Golden, 'Imperial Ideology and the Sources of Political Unity', 57–9; *Pliska-Preslav*, I, ed. Z. Vužarova (Sofia, 1979), pp. 44–176; R. Rashev, 'Pliska – the First Capital of Bulgaria', in *Ancient Bulgaria*, II, pp. 255–69.

156. Lemerle, *Les plus anciens recueils*, I, p. 230, l. 10; G. Zacos and A. Veglery, *Byzantine Lead Seals*, I (Basel, 1972), nr 934, pp. 635–6.

157. Theo., pp. 374–6, 382, 400–1; Nik., pp. 102–4, 114, 126–8; *West-Syrian Chronicles*, pp. 80, 215–16; Paulus Diaconus, 'Historia Langobardorum', ed. L. Bethman and G. Waitz, *MGH SRLI*, p. 181; *Constantinople in the Early Eighth Century*, ed. Cameron and Herrin, p. 98.

158. Zacos and Veglery, *Byzantine Lead Seals*, I, nr 2672, p. 1441.

159. Mango, *Byzantine Architecture*, pp. 172–3.

160. For example, Beševliev, *Die protobulgarischen Inschriften*, nrs 47, 56, pp. 220–1, 260.

161. Theo., pp. 364, 376, 429, 431–3, 436, 446–8; Nik., pp. 104, 144, 148–52, 156.

162. Theo., pp. 456–7.

163. *Ibid.*, pp. 464, 467–8, 470.

164. *Ibid.*; pp. 490–2; I. Dujčev, 'La chronique byzantine de l'an 811', *TM* I (1965), 205–54.

165. Theo., pp. 495–503; *Scriptor incertus*, ed. F. Iadevaia (Messina, 1987), pp. 50–8; Beševliev, *Die protobulgarischen Inschriften*, nrs 2–3, 16–31, 47, pp. 125–6, 177–86, 220–1.

166. Theo., Cont., pp. 24–5; Genesios, p. 10; Beševliev, *Die protobulgarischen*

Inschriften, nr 41, pp. 220–9; P. Soustal, *Thrakien* (TIB VI, Vienna, 1991), pp. 261–2; W. Treadgold, 'The Bulgars' Treaty with the Byzantines in 816', *Rivista di Studi Bizantini e Slavi*, IV/V (1985), 213–20; cf. J. B. Bury, 'The Bulgarian Treaty of A.D. 814 and the Great Fence of Thrace', *English Historical Review*, XXV (1910), 276–87.

167. W. Pohl, *Die Awaren* (Munich, 1988), pp. 288–323; *Suidae Lexicon*, ed. A. Adler, 5 vols (Leipzig, 1928–38), I, pp. 483–4; *Annales regni Francorum*, ed. G. H. Pertz, rev. F. Kurze (MGH SRG, Hannover, 1895), pp. 82–4, 87–8, 97–8; Eginhard, *Vie de Charlemagne*, ed. L. Halphen (Paris, 1938), p. 38; tr. L. Thorpe, *Two Lives of Charlemagne* (Harmondsworth, 1969), p. 67.

168. *Annales regni Francorum*, pp. 149, 165–6, 173–4; *Annales Fuldenses*, pp. 25–6 (these entries are not in Reuter's translation), 35; tr. Reuter, p. 24; Beševliev, *Die protobulgarischen Inschriften*, nr 59, pp. 285–7; Theophylact of Ohrid, 'Vita Clementi', ed. N. L. Tunitskij, *Monumenta ad SS. Cyrilli et Methodii successorum vitas resque gestas pertinentia* (Sergiev Posad, 1918), p. 114; John VIII, *Epistolae* (MGH Epistolae VII, Hannover, 1974), p. 60, ll. 25–6.

169. *DAI*, c. 31, ll. 58–67; c. 32, ll. 38–49; pp. 150, 154.

170. Beševliev, *Die protobulgarischen Inschriften*, nrs 13–15, 46, pp. 156–76, 215–19; Theo. Cont., p. 165; Leo Gram., pp. 232, 235; Theophylact of Ohrid, 'Vita Clementi', pp. 116–18; D. Obolensky, *Six Byzantine Portraits* (Oxford, 1988), pp. 21–4.

171. Nicholas I, *Epistolae* (MGH Epistolae VI, Hannover, 1974), p. 599; Ibn Rusta, pp. 158–9.

172. *Synaxarium ecclesiae Constantinopolitanae*, cols 414–16; Theophylactus Achridensis, 'Martyrium SS. Quindecim illustrum martyrum', *PG*, CXXVI, cols 193–7.

173. Beševliev, *Die protobulgarischen Inschriften*, nrs 41, 47, pp. 220–9; Theo., pp. 485, 495.

174. *Annales Fuldenses*, pp. 56, 62; tr. Reuter, pp. 49, 51; *Annales Bertiniani*, p. 72; tr. Nelson, p. 118; Nicholas I, *Epistolae*, p. 293; 'Life of Constantine the Philosopher', p. 66; 'Life of Methodius', tr. Kantor, *Medieval Slavic Lives of Saints and Princes*, pp. 111–12.

175. *Annales Bertiniani*, p. 85; tr. Nelson, p. 136; GM cont., p. 824; cf. Theo. Cont., pp. 162–5: determined not to give credit to Michael III and the caesar Bardas.

176. *Annales Bertiniani*, p. 85; tr. Nelson, p. 137; GM cont., pp. 829–30; Theo. Cont., pp. 164, 204–6, 235–8.

177. Nicholas I, *Epistolae*, pp. 438–9, 533–40; Mansi, XVI, cols 128, 136, 198; *Liber Pontificalis*, II, pp. 178–9.

178. *Annales Fuldenses*, p. 65; tr. Reuter, p. 56; *Annales Bertiniani*, pp. 85–6; tr. Nelson, pp. 137–8; *Liber Pontificalis*, II, pp. 164–5; Photius, *Epistolae*, I, pp. 41–2; Theo. Cont., pp. 210, 242–3; GM cont., pp. 836–7, 841.

179. Nicholas I, *Epistolae*, p. 592.

180. *Liber Pontificalis*, II, pp. 182–4.

181. Obolensky, *Six Byzantine Portraits*, pp. 8–33.

182. Regino Prumiensis, pp. 95–6; cf. Theophylactus Achridensis, 'Martyrium SS. Quindecim illustrum martyrum', col. 213.

183. R. J. H. Jenkins, 'The Peace with Bulgaria (927) Celebrated by Theodore Daphnopates', in *Polychronion. Festschrift F. Dölger* (Heidelberg, 1966), pp. 287–303.

184. GM cont., pp. 853–5.

185. Mango, *Byzantine Architecture*, pp. 173–4.

186. GM cont., p. 863; G. Kolias, *Léon Choirosphactès, magistre, proconsul et*

patrice (Athens, 1939), pp. 46–7, 113; Beševliev, *Die protobulgarischen Inschriften*, nr 46, pp. 215–19.

187. Jenkins, 'The Peace with Bulgaria', pp. 291, 295; GM cont., p. 877–8.

188. Nicholas I, *Letters*, nr 16, ll. 73–7; p. 108; Lindprandus Cremonensis, p. 87; cf. P. Karlin-Hayter, 'The Homily on the Peace with Bulgaria of 927 and the "Coronation" of 913', *JÖB*, XVII (1968), 32–8.

189. Beševliev, *Die protobulgarischen Inschriften*, nrs 69, 88, 90, pp. 299–301, 329–30, 331–2; Theodore Daphnopates, *Correspondance*, ed. and tr. J. Darrouzès and L. G. Westerink (Paris, 1978), p. 73, ll. 59–60, 69.

190. *Annales regni Francorum*, p. 136.

191. GM cont., pp. 879–80; Nicholas I, *Letters*, nr 8, pp. 44–52.

192. GM cont., pp. 880–2; Nicholas I, *Letters*, nr 9, pp. 52–68.

193. GM cont., pp. 882–90.

194. Nicholas I, *Letters*, nrs 11–29, pp. 72–202; *DAI*, c. 32, ll. 99–126, p. 158; GM cont., pp. 892–9; Nicholas I, *Miscellaneous Writings*, ed. and tr. L. G. Westerink (CFHB XX, Washington, D.C., 1981), pp. 58–68; Skylitzes, pp. 264–5; Mas'ūdī, *Les prairies d'or*, I, pp. 164–5.

195. GM cont., pp. 899–902.

196. Theodore Daphnopates, *Correspondance*, pp. 57–85.

197. GM cont., pp. 904–7; *De Cer.*, p. 690; *DAI*, c. 13, ll. 147–75, pp. 72–4.

198. A. W. Epstein, 'Middle Byzantine Churches of Kastoria', *The Art Bulletin*, LXII (1980), 190–207; Cosmas le prêtre, *Le traité contre les Bogomiles*, tr. H.-C. Puech and A. Vaillant (Paris, 1945), pp. 71, 86, 95–6, 100, 112, 116, 118–23; M. Dando, 'Peut on avancer de 240 ans la date de composition du traité de Cosmas le Prêtre contre les Bogomiles?', *Cahiers d'études Cathares*, 2nd ser., C (1983), 3–25; *ibid.*, CI (1984), 3–21.

199. *DAI*, c. 32, ll. 126–8, p. 158.

200. GM cont., pp. 913, 917; Theo. Cont., pp. 462, 480; *PVL*, pp. 72–3; Liudprandus Cremonensis, p. 199.

201. Skylitzes, p. 239; *DAI*, c. 40, ll. 63–5, p. 178; *Relacia Ibrāhīma ibn Ja'kūba z podrózy do Krajów slowiańskich w przekazie al-Bekrīegó*, tr. T. Kowalski (Monumenta Poloniae Historica, n.s. I, Cracow, 1946), p. 148.

202. Leo Diaconus, pp. 61–3.

203. Liudprandus Cremonensis, pp. 185–6; Leo Diaconus, p. 79; Skylitzes, p. 255.

204. Leo Diaconus, pp. 78–9.

205. Leo Diaconus, pp. 89, 103–8; Skylitzes, pp. 279, 287–9.

206. Leo Diaconus, pp. 128–9; Skylitzes, p. 294.

207. Leo Diaconus, pp. 136, 138, 159; Skylitzes, pp. 297, 310–11.

208. N. Oikonomidès, *Les listes*, p. 265, l. 9; p. 267, l. 34; p. 269, ll. 9, 16, 361, 363; I. Jordanov, 'La stratégie de Preslav aux xe–xie siècles selon les données de la sigillographie', in *Studies in Byzantine Sigillography*, I, ed. N. Oikonomides (Washington, D.C., 1987), pp. 89–96; I. Jordanov and V. Tăpkova-Zaimova, 'Quelques nouvelles données sur l'administration byzantine au Bas-Danube (fin du xe–xie s.)', in *Géographie historique du monde méditerranéen*, ed. H. Ahrweiler (Paris, 1988), pp. 119–21.

209. Stephen of Taron II, pp. 124–5; Yahyā ibn Sa'īd al-Antākī, 'Histoire', ed. and tr. I. Kratchkovsky and A. Vasiliev, *PO*, XXIII.2 (1932), pp. 418–9, 431, 446; cf. Skylitzes, pp. 255–6, 328–30, 346.

210. Brown, *Gentlemen and Officers*, pp. 144–59, 175–8, 180; Grierson, *Byzantine Coins*, pp. 129–38.

211. Brown, *Gentlemen and Officers*, pp. 158–63, 178–80; *Liber Pontificalis*, I, pp. 332, 336–8, 341, 343–4, 392, 404, 409, 415–16; tr. Davis, I, pp. 67–72, 92;

II, pp. 11–12, 15, 19–20; Paulus Diaconus, 'Historia Langobardorum', *MGH SRLI*, pp. 181–2; Theo., pp. 404, 410.

212. *Liber Pontificalis*, pp. 343–4; tr. Davis, I, p. 72; Paulus Diaconus, 'Historia Langobardorum', pp. 146–50.

213. *Liber Pontificalis*, I, pp. 403–4; tr. Davis, II, pp. 10–11.

214. *Ibid.*, I, pp. 442, 444–6; tr. Davis, II, pp. 56, 58–61.

215. *Ibid.*, I, pp. 452–4, 493, 495–9; II, p. 7; tr. Davis, II, pp. 71–3, 133, 135–42, 190–1.

216. Theo., p. 475; Eginhard, *Vie de Charlemagne*, pp. 48–50; tr. Thorpe, p. 71.

217. P. Grierson, 'The Carolingian Empire in the Eyes of Byzantium', *Settimane di studio del Centro italiano di Studi sull'alto Medioevo*, XXVII (1981), pp. 908–12.

218. Vasiliev, *Byzance et les arabes*, I, pp. 344–5, 356–69; Theo. Cont., pp. 81–3; A. Sambon, *Recueil des monnaies médiévales du Sud d'Italie avant la domination normande* (Paris, 1919), p. 74; B. M. Kreutz, *Before the Normans* (Philadelphia, Pa, 1991), pp. 15–17, 72–3; D. Nicol, *Byzantium and Venice* (Cambridge, 1988), pp. 20–34.

219. Vasiliev, *Byzance et les arabes*, II.2, pp. 133–7.

220. Kreutz, *Before the Normans*, pp. 20–5, 69, 71.

221. *Annales Bertiniani*, p. 34; tr. Nelson, p. 63; *Liber Pontificalis*, II, pp. 99–101; G. Musca, *L'emirato di Bari, 847–71*, 2nd edn (Bari, 1967), pp. 17–18, 20, 22, 25–8, 36; Kreutz, *Before the Normans*, pp. 24–35.

222. Ioannis Diaconus, 'Gesta episcoporum Neapolitanorum', ed. G. Waitz, *MGH SRLI*, p. 433; Erchempertus, 'Historia Langobardorum Beneventanorum', ed. G. Waitz, *MGH SRLI*, pp. 242, 247; *Annales Bertiniani*, pp. 81, 98–9, 105–6; tr. Nelson, pp. 130, 154, 162; *Chronicon Salernitanum*, ed. V. Westerbergh (Stockholm, 1956), pp. 116, 118, 121; Kreutz, *Before the Normans*, pp. 32, 37–45, 171, n. 18.

223. *Annales Bertiniani*, p. 118; tr. Nelson, pp. 175–6; Erchempertus, 'Historia Langobardorum Beneventanorum', *MGH SRLI*, pp. 247–8; *Chronicon Salernitanum*, pp. 121–2; *DAI*, c. 29, ll. 115–69, pp. 128–32; Theo. Cont., pp. 293–6; Kreutz, *Before the Normans*, pp. 45–7.

224. *Annales Bertiniani*, pp. 19, 28, 43; tr. Nelson, pp. 44, 54, 78; Grierson, 'The Carolingian Empire in the Eyes of Byzantium', p. 903.

225. *DAI* c. 29, ll. 94–101, pp. 126–8; Theo. Cont., pp. 289–90; J. Ferluga, *L'amministrazione bizantina in Dalmazia* (Venice, 1978), pp. 164–89; *Catalogue of Byzantine Seals at Dumbarton Oaks and in the Fogg Museum of Art*, I, ed. J. Nesbitt and N. Oikonomides (Washington, D.C., 1991), pp. 46–8.

226. *Annales Bertiniani*, pp. 105–6; tr. Nelson, p. 162 (Hincmar mistakenly thinks that Louis' daughter was to marry the emperor Basil himself, rather than Basil's son, Constantine: cf. Anastasius Bibliothecarius, *Epistolae* (MGH Epistolae VII, Hannover, 1928), p. 410); *Chronicon Salernitanum*, pp. 104, 107; *DAI*, c. 29, ll. 103–12, p. 128; Theo. Cont., p. 293.

227. Erchempertus, 'Historia Langobardorum Beneventanorum', *MGH SRLI*, p. 249; V. von Falkenhausen, *Untersuchungen über die byzantinische Herrschaft in Süditalien vom 9. bis ins 11. Jahrhundert* (Wiesbaden, 1967), pp. 18–19, n. 128, pp. 21–5; John VIII, *Epistolae*, pp. 45–6; GM cont., pp. 845, 852; Theo. Cont., pp. 305–6, 312–13; Skylitzes, pp. 262–3.

228. Kreutz, *Before the Normans*, pp. 62–6, 72, 74, 102; H. Taviani-Carozzi, *La principauté Lombarde de Salerne*, 2 vols (Rome, 1991), I, pp. 183–7, 221–6; Sambon, *Recueil des monnaies médiévales du sud d'Italie*, p. 77.

229. Leo VI, *Tactica*, col. 896.

9. THE AGE OF RECONQUEST, 863–976

1. al-Tabarī, III, p. 1449.
2. Theo. Cont., pp. 179–83; Genesios, pp. 67–9; GM cont., p. 825; al-Tabarī, III, p. 1509; G. Huxley, 'The Emperor Michael III and the Battle of Bishop's Meadow (A.D. 863)', GRBS, XVI (1975), 443–50.
3. De Cer., ed. Vogt, II, p. 136; McCormick, Eternal Victory, pp. 150–2; al-Tabarī, III, p. 1510.
4. Genesios, p. 86.
5. GM cont., p. 841; Theo. Cont., pp. 267, 272–6; Genesios, p. 85; al-Tabarī, III, p. 1865; P. Lemerle, 'L'histoire des Pauliciens d'Asie mineure d'après les sources grecques', TM, V (1973), 103–8.
6. Theo. Cont., p. 268; al-Tabarī, III, p. 1880; Lemerle, 'L'histoire des Pauliciens', 108: although Theo. Cont. and al-Tabarī agree that Basil attacked Samosata (Arabic Sumaysāt) on the Euphrates south of the Anti-Taurus, the target was the less famous Arsamosata (Arabic Shimshāt), about 125 kilometres east of Melitene on the Murat Su. The campaign, as described by Theo. Cont., is deliberately intended to repeat and surpass Theophilos' campaign of 837 which Byzantine sources also wrongly credit with taking Samosata (GM cont., p. 798). In fact Theophilos took Arsamosata, as recorded by the Syriac sources (Michel le Syrien, III, p. 89; Chron. 1234, II, p. 15), and confirmed by geographical logic. It follows that Arsamosata was the target in 873 too.
7. al-Tabarī, III, pp. 1930–1, 2026; GM cont., p. 844; Theo. Cont., pp. 278–80, 283–6; Genesios, p. 82; Lemerle, 'L'histoire des Pauliciens', 104–8.
8. al-Tabarī, III, p. 2103; Theo. Cont., pp. 286–8; GM cont., p. 847.
9. al-Tabarī, III, pp. 1886, 1915; Theo. Cont., pp. 267, 277–9; DAI, c. 50, ll. 167–8, p. 240; F. Hild and M. Restle, Kappadokien (TIB II, Vienna, 1981), pp. 139, 209, 223, 237, 257–8.
10. Theo. Cont., pp. 268, 358; J. Markwart, Südarmenien und die Tigrisquellen (Vienna, 1930), pp. 294–5.
11. DAI, c. 50, ll. 111–26, p. 238; Constantine Porphyrogenitos, De Thematibus, ed. A. Pertusi (Studi e testi CLX, Vatican, 1952), pp. 73, 75; G. Dedeyan, 'Mleh le grand, stratège de Lykandos', REArm, XV (1981), 75–8.
12. De Thematibus, pp. 75–6; DAI, c. 50, ll. 133–66, pp. 238–40; GM cont., p. 881; Ibn Khordādhbeh, p. 194; al-Tabarī, pp. 2286–7; Dedeyan, 'Mleh le grand', 78–102.
13. Vasiliev, Byzance et les arabes, II.2, pp. 149–51; Stephen of Taron, II, pp. 24–5; DAI, c. 45, ll. 55–8, p. 208.
14. Vasiliev, Byzance et les arabes, II.2, pp. 149, 151–4; GM cont., pp. 907–8.
15. Vasiliev, Byzance et les arabes, II.2, pp. 62–3.
16. Ibid., II.2, pp. 147, 149–50, 152–3; Byzantine–Egyptian truce: ibid., pp. 172–3, 203–13, 223.
17. Ibid., II.2, pp. 122, 153–4 (Samosata = Arsamosata); DAI, c. 45, ll. 160–71; c. 50, ll. 126–32, 167–8; pp. 212–14, 238–40; E. Honigmann, Die Ostgrenze des Byzantinischen Reiches von 363 bis 1071 (Brussels, 1935), pp. 79–80, 194–5; J. D. Howard-Johnston, 'Byzantine Anzitene', in Armies and Frontiers in Roman and Byzantine Anatolia, ed. S. Mitchell (BAR Int. Ser. CLVI, Oxford, 1983), pp. 240, 270, n. 51.
18. Vasiliev, Byzance et les arabes, II.2, pp. 121–2, 239–40.
19. Ibid., II.2, pp. 115, 122–3, 357.
20. DAI, c. 45, ll. 90–2, 170–1, pp. 208–10, 214.
21. GM cont., p. 915; Yahyā b. Saʿīd, PO, XVIII.5 (1924), pp. 730, 733; Vasiliev, Byzance et les arabes, II.2, pp. 156, 174, 223.

22. Constantine Porphyrogenitos, 'Narratio de Imagine Edessena', *PG*, CXIII, cols 423–54; Yahyā b. Saʿīd, *PO*, XVIII.5 (1924), pp. 730–32; GM cont., pp. 918–19; Vasiliev, *Byzance et les arabes*, II.2, pp. 156–7, 174; A. Cameron, 'The History of the Image of Edessa: The Telling of a Story', *HUS*, VII (1983), 80–94.

23. Theo. Cont., pp. 436–7; GM cont., p. 921; Skylitzes, pp. 234–7.

24. Theo. Cont., p. 426, 445–6; Skylitzes, p. 238; GM cont., pp. 916–17, 921: the first piece of evidence for this sequence of events is the figure of twenty-two years and seven months given for Kourkuas' period of office (Theo. Cont., p. 426), which if Leo Argyros was domestic of the scholai for two months between April and June 922 (*DAI*, c. 50, ll. 150–2, p. 240; J.-F. Vannier, *Families byzantines: Les Argyroi (ixe–xiie siècles)*, Paris, 1975, p. 26) would give December 944 as the date of Kourkuas' dismissal; the second is the statement in Skylitzes (p. 327) that Bardas Phokas was made domestic as a reward for his loyalty to Constantine in 945. The order of events in this section of the Logothete's Chronicle is so confused that GM cont., pp. 916–17, only proves that he was replaced by the Lekapenoi brothers, rather than giving any relative date.

25. Yahyā b. Saʿīd, *PO*, XVIII.5 (1924), p. 767; Skylitzes, p. 245.

26. *De Cer.*, pp. 664–78; Skylitzes, pp. 245–6; Leo Diaconus, pp. 6–7.

27. Yahyā b. Saʿīd, *PO*, XVIII.5 (1924), p. 768; Theo. Cont., p. 428; Stephen of Taron, II, p. 38.

28. 'Vita S. Pauli Iunioris', ed. H. Delehaye, *AB*, XI (1892), p. 74; Skylitzes, p. 241–2; Vasiliev, *Byzance et les arabes*, II.2, pp. 116–17, 127, 196, 268, 320–2, 328–31, 334–7; R. J. Bikhazi, 'The Hamdanid Dynasty of Mesopotamia and North Syria 254–404/868–1014', 3 vols (University of Michigan Ph.D. thesis, 1981), pp. 710–16.

29. Skylitzes, pp. 240–1.

30. *Ibid.*, pp. 241–2; Yahyā b. Saʿīd, *PO*, XVIII.5 (1924), p. 771; Vasiliev, *Byzance et les arabes*, II.2, pp. 126–7, 175, 181–2, 196, 243, 327, 361–2.

31. E. McGeer, 'Infantry Versus Cavalry: The Byzantine Response', *REB*, XLVI (1988), 135–45.

32. E. McGeer, 'The *Syntaxis Armatorum Quadrata*: A Tenth-century Tactical Blueprint', *REB*, L (1992), 219–29; *Sylloge tacticorum, quae olim 'Inedita Leonis tactica' dicebatur*, ed. A. Dain (Paris, 1938), pp. 65–93; *Praecepta Militaria*, pp. 2–4, 6–9; McGeer, 'Infantry Versus Cavalry', 136–8.

33. *Praecepta Militaria*, pp. 2–3.

34. *De Cer.*, p. 666.

35. N. Oikomonidès, 'L'organisation de la frontière orientale de Byzance aux xe–xie siècles et le taktikon de l'Escorial', *Actes du XIVe Congrés International des études byzantines* (Bucharest, 1974), I, pp. 285–302 [= Oikomonidès, *Documents et études sur les institutions de Byzance (viie–xve s.* (London, 1974), nr XXIV]; Oikomonidès, *Les listes*, pp. 263, 267–9, 344–6, 354–63; 'Skirmishing Warfare', pp. 150 (ll. 4–5), 152 (l. 11); G. Zacos, *Byzantine Lead Seals*, II (Berne, 1984), nrs 503–4, 1016, pp. 265, 446.

36. Theo. Cont., pp. 462–3; *JGR*, I, pp. 255–6.

37. *Praecepta Militaria*, p. 3; Oikonomidès, *Les listes*, pp. 333–6.

38. Theo. Cont., p. 459; 'Skirmishing Warfare', p. 148.

39. Yahyā b. Saʿīd, *PO*, XVIII.5 (1924), p. 774.

40. Skylitzes, p. 267; Leo Diaconus, pp. 65–7.

41. Theo. Cont., p. 461; Skylitzes, pp. 249–50, 252–3, 267–73; Leo Diaconus, pp. 17–18, 35–6, 51–3, 55–61, 70–4, 81; 'Vaticanus Gr. 163', 99–100; Vasiliev, *Byzance et les arabes*, II.2, pp. 175, 183; Yahyā b. Saʿīd, *PO*, XVIII.5 (1924), pp. 775, 784, 787, 793–4, 796, 805, 807, 815–16, 823, 825–6; Stephen of Taron,

II, pp. 38, 43–4; 'The Chronicle of Matthew of Edessa', tr A. E. Dostourian (Rutgers University Ph.D. thesis 1972), p. 6.

42. Skylitzes, pp. 287, 311; Leo Diaconus, pp. 160–2, 165–6, 168; Yahyā b. Sa'īd, *PO*, XXIII (1932), pp. 353–4, 368–9; 'The Chronicle of Matthew of Edessa', pp. 18–30; Stephen of Taron, II, p. 48; M. Canard, 'Les sources arabes de l'histoire byzantine aux confins des xe et xie siècles', *REB*, XIX (1961), pp. 293–5; T. Bianquis, *Damas et la Syrie sous la domination Fatimide (359–468/969–1076)*, 2 vols (Damascus, 1986–9), I, pp. 93–9.

43. Ibn Hauqal, I, pp. 182, 195.

44. T. Reuter, 'The end of Carolingian Military Expansion', in *Charlemagne's Heir*, ed. P. Godman and R. Collins (Oxford, 1990), pp. 391–405.

45. *De Cer.*, pp. 694–6; Vasiliev, *Byzance et les arabes*, II.2, p. 154; Yahyā b. Sa'īd, *PO*, XXIII (1932), pp. 794, 796–7, 805, 815–16, 826.

46. 'La Vie du patriarche melkite d'Antioche Christophore (†967) par le protospathaire Ibrahīm b. Yuhanna. Document inédit du xe siècle', ed. and tr. H. Zayat, *Proche-orient chrétien*, II (1952), 19, 25–7, 31, 333, 337–9, 343.

47. J.-C. Cheynet, *Pouvoir et contestations à Byzance (963–1210)* (Paris, 1990), pp. 213–27.

48. Epstein, *Art of Empire*, pp. 13–37; idem, *Tokalı kilise: Tenth-century Metropolitan Art in Byzantine Cappadocia* (Washington, D.C., 1986), pp. 33–51.

49. D. I. Polemis, *The Doukai* (London, 1968), pp. 16–25; Vannier, *Familles byzantines: les Argyroi*, pp. 22–9.

50. GM cont., pp. 876–7.

51. E. Patlagean, 'Les débuts d'une aristocratie byzantine et le témoinage de l'historiographie: système des noms et liens de parenté aux ixe–xe siècles', in *Byzantine Aristocracy*, ed. Angold, pp. 23–43.

52. W. Seibt, *Die Skleroi* (Vienna, 1976), pp. 19–28.

53. J.-C. Cheynet, 'Les Phocas', in G. Dagron and H. Mihăescu, *Le traité sur la guérilla de l'empereur Nicéphore Phocas* (Paris, 1986), pp. 289–96.

54. Theo., p. 391; GM cont., pp. 819–21, 827.

55. Theo. Cont., pp. 212–13, 240–1.

56. *Vita Euthymii Patriarchae CP.*, ed. P. Karlin-Hayter (Brussels, 1970), pp. 67–71; Theo. Cont., p. 372; Polemis, *The Doukai*, pp. 17–20.

57. GM cont., pp. 841, 870, 882–90.

58. *JGR*, I, pp. 207, 210; GM cont., pp. 908–9.

59. *Ibid.*, p. 908; M. Kaplan, 'Maisons impériales et fondations pieuses: réorganisation de la fortune impériale et assistance publique de la fin du viiie à la fin du xe siècle', *Byz*, LXI (1991), 340–64.

60. *JGR*, I, pp. 208–13.

61. *Ibid.*, I, p. 211.

62. H. Ahrweiler, 'Recherches sur l'administration de l'empire byzantin aux ixe–xie siècles', *Bulletin de correspondence hellénique*, LXXXIV (1960), 68–70; *De Cer.*, p. 657; *Acts de Lavra*, I, p. 102 (to be dated 922: *Actes d'Iviron*, I, pp. 106–7); *Actes d'Iviron*, I, p. 108; *Actes du Prôtaton*, pp. 191 (l. 14), 198, 201 (l. 3).

63. Theo. Cont., pp. 426–9; GM cont., pp. 918–19; Constantine Porphyrogenitos, 'Narratio de Imagine Edessena', cols 444–5, 448–9, 452–3.

64. GM cont., p. 917; Cheynet, *Pouvoir et contestations à Byzance*, p. 269 n. 52; cf. Seibt, *Die Skleroi*, pp. 27–8, 85.

65. Theo. Cont., pp. 436–7.

66. *Ibid.*, pp. 443–4; 'Skirmishing Warfare', p. 216.

67. Theo. Cont., pp. 453–4, 462–3, 480.

68. Skylitzes, pp. 245–6.

69. Theo. Cont., pp. 461–2, 466.

70. GM cont., pp. 915, 921; Skylitzes, p. 238; 'Skirmishing Warfare', p. 148; Theo. Cont., p. 479.

71. McCormick, *Eternal Victory*, pp. 159–68.

72. Skylitzes, pp. 256–60; Leo Diaconus, pp. 38–48; 'Vaticanus Gr. 163', p. 100.

73. Lindprandus Cremonensis, pp. 180–2, 185; *De Cer.*, pp. 433–40.

74. *JGR*, I, pp. 253–5; Skylitzes, pp. 311–12; F. Hild and H. Hellenkemper, *Kilikien und Isaurien* (TIB V, Vienna, 1990), p. 59; Zacos, *Byzantine Lead Seals*, II, nos 108, 729, pp. 94, 344–5.

75. Skylitzes, pp. 271, 275; Ibn Hauqal, I, p. 194; Leo Diaconus, p. 64.

76. Skylitzes, pp. 273–5.

77. Leo Diaconus, p. 64.

78. *JGR*, I, pp. 255–6; Hendy, *Studies in the Byzantine Monetary Economy*, p. 507; Hendy, 'Light Weight Solidi, Tetartera, and The Book of the Prefect', *BZ*, LXV (1972), 63–73.

79. C. Morrisson, 'Monnaie et finances dans l'empire byzantin x^e–xive siècle', in *Hommes et richesses*, II, pp. 298–304; A. Harvey, *Economic Expansion in the Byzantine Empire, 900–1200* (Cambridge, 1989), pp. 56–65, 86–90, 135, 148–9, 160–2, 190–2, 207–26.

80. Skylitzes, p. 274; Lindprandus Cremonensis, pp. 205–6.

81. Skylitzes, pp. 274–5.

82. *JGR*, I, pp. 249–52: tr. in P. Charanis, 'The Monastic Properties and the State in the Byzantine Empire', *DOP*, IV (1948), 53–118.

83. Dagron, and Mihăescu, *Le traité sur la guérilla de l'empereur Nicéphore Phocas*, pp. 259–74, 284–87.

84. R. Morris, 'The Two Faces of Nikephoros Phokas', *BMGS*, XII (1988), 100–10.

85. J. S. Assemani, *Bibliotheca orientalis Clementino-Vaticana*, 2 vols (Rome, 1719–21), II, p. 133; G. Dagron, 'Minorités ethniques et religieuses dans l'orient byzantin à la fin du xe et au xie siècle: l'immigration Syrienne', *TM*, VI (1976), 177–87.

86. Cheynet, *Pouvoir et contestations à Byzance*, pp. 270, 327; Cheynet, 'Les Phocas', pp. 306–7, 313, n. 80; Oikonomidès, *Les listes*, p. 334.

87. Skylitzes, pp. 271–3; Yahyā b. Sa'īd, *PO* XVIII.5 (1924), pp. 816–17, 822–3, 825; J.-C. Cheynet and J.-F. Vannier, *Études prosopographiques* (Paris, 1986), p. 19, n. 16.

88. Skylitzes, pp. 279–80; Leo Diaconus, pp. 84–9.

89. C. Mango, 'A note on the Ros-Dromitai', *Hellenika*, IV (1953), 460; J. Shepard, 'Some Problems of Russo-Byzantine Relations, c. 850–c. 1050', *Slavonic and East European Review*, LIII (1974), 12–14; G. Dagron, *Constantinople imaginaire* (Paris, 1984), pp. 146, 329, n. 57.

90. Skylitzes, pp. 285–6, 311; Yahyā b. Sa'īd, *PO*, XVIII.5 (1924), pp. 832–3.

91. *JGR*, I, p. 259; N. Svoronos, *La Synopsis Major des Basiliques et ses appendices* (Paris, 1964), p. 22, n. 3; cf. P. Lemerle, *The Agrarian History of Byzantium* (Galway, 1979), pp. 110–12.

92. *Actes de Prôtaton*, pp. 97–9, 209–15; *Vitae duae antiquae Sancti Athanasii Athonitae*, ed. J. Noret (Corpus Christianorum, series Graeca IX, Turnhout, 1982), pp. 54–6, 168–9; Morris, 'The Two Faces of Nikephoros Phokas', pp. 113–14.

93. Leo Diaconus, p. 162; 'The Chronicle of Matthew of Edessa', pp. 26, 29.

94. 'The Chronicle of Matthew of Edessa', pp. 16–20, 22–32; Yahyā b. Sa'īd, *PO*, XXIII.2 (1932), p. 353; N. Thierry, 'Un portrait de Jean Tzimiskès en Cappadoce', *TM*, IX (1985), 477–84.

95. 'Skirmishing Warfare', pp. 214–16.
96. Skylitzes, pp. 311–13.

10. THE REIGN OF BASIL II, 976–1025

1. Skylitzes, pp. 275–6.
2. *Ibid.*, p. 314; Yahyā b. Sa'īd, *PO*, XXIII.2 (1932), p. 372; Michael Psellos, *Chronographia*, ed. E. Renauld, 2 vols (Paris, 1926–8), I, p. 3.
3. Skylitzes, pp. 314, 316; Stephen of Taron ii, pp. 56–7; Yahyā b. Sa'īd, *PO* XXIII.2 (1932), pp. 372, 377–8.
4. Skylitzes, pp. 317–20, 322; Leo Diaconus, p. 170; Yahyā b. Sa'īd, *PO*, XXIII.2 (1932), pp. 372–4.
5. Skylitzes, p. 320.
6. *Ibid.*, pp. 320–1.
7. *Ibid.*, pp. 321–2.
8. *Ibid.*, pp. 324, 326; Stephen of Taron II, pp. 59–60; Yahyā b. Sa'īd, *PO*, XXIII.2 (1932), p. 374.
9. B. Martin-Hisard, '*La Vie de Jean et Euthyme* et le statut du monastère des Ibères sur l'Athos', *REB*, XLIX (1991), 89–91.
10. *Ibid.*, 87–8, 95; *Actes d'Iviron*, I, pp. 4, 9, 21; Cheynet, *Pouvoir et contestations à Byzance*, pp. 324, 330–1.
11. Martin-Hisard, '*La Vie de Jean et Euthyme*', 93–7; *Actes d'Iviron* I, pp. 23–4; Stephen of Taron II, pp. 59–60.
12. Skylitzes, pp. 324–7; Yahyā b. Sa'īd, *PO*, XXIII.2 (1932), pp. 375, 399; Stephen of Taron II, p. 61; M. Tarchnišvili, 'Le soulèvement de Bardas Skléros', *Bedi Kartlisa*, XVII/XVIII (1964), 96.
13. Yahyā b. Sa'īd, *PO*, XXIII.2 (1932), pp. 396–8, 400–1; Stephen of Taron II, pp. 62–6.
14. H. M. Amedroz, 'An Embassy from Baghdad to the Emperor Basil II', *Journal of the Royal Asiatic Society* (1914), 915–42.
15. Skylitzes, p. 327; M. Canard, 'Deux documents arabes sur Bardas Skleros', *Studi Bizantini e Neoellenici*, V (1939), 55–69.
16. Yahyā b. Sa'īd, *PO* XXIII.2 (1932), pp. 412–13; Bianquis, *Damas et la Syrie*, I, pp. 143–5.
17. Yahyā b. Sa'īd, *PO*, XXIII.2 (1932), pp. 415–16.
18. *Ibid.*, XXIII.2 (1932), p. 417; Michael Psellos I, pp. 12–13; Psellos mistakenly dates the parakoimomenos' fall to after 989.
19. Cecaumenus, *Strategicon*, p. 65.
20. Ioannes Geometres, *PG*, CVI, cols 920, 934; A. Leroy-Molinghen, 'Les fils de Pierre de Bulgarie et les Cométopoules', *Byz*, XLII (1972), 410–11; Skylitzes, p. 283.
21. *Ibid.*, pp. 330–1; Yahyā b. Sa'īd, *PO*, XXIII.2 (1932), pp. 418–19; Stephen of Taron II, pp. 126–7.
22. Yahyā b. Sa'īd, *PO* XXIII.2 (1932), pp. 419–21; Skylitzes, pp. 332–4; Stephen of Taron II, pp. 127–8.
23. Yahyā b. Sa'īd, *PO*, XXIII.2 (1932), pp. 421–3; Skylitzes, pp. 332, 335–6; Stephen of Taron ii, p. 129.
24. Skylitzes, p. 336; Yahyā b. Sa'īd, *PO*, XXIII.2 (1932), p. 423; Stephen of Taron II, pp. 129–30.
25. F. Dölger, *Regesten der Kaiserurkunden des oströmischen Reiches von 565–1453*, 3 vols (Munich, 1924–32), nr. 770, pp. 98–9; J. Forsyth, 'The Byzantine–Arab Chronicle (938–1034) of Yahyā b. Sa'īd al-Antāki', 2 vols (University

of Michigan Ph.D thesis, 1977), II, pp. 434–5.

26. *JGR*, I, p. 259.

27. Skylitzes, p. 336; Yahyā b. Saʿīd, *PO*, XXIII.2 (1932), p. 423; Stephen of Taron, II, pp. 164–5.

28. *DAI*, c. 13, ll. 106–16, p. 70.

29. Liudprandus Cremonensis, p. 184; *Die Urkunden Otto II* (MGH Diplomata Regum et Imperatorum Germaniae II.1, Hannover, 1888), p. 29, l. 28.

30. A. Poppe, 'How the Conversion of Rus' Was Understood in the Eleventh Century', *HUS*, XI (1987), 287–9.

31. Poppe, 'The Political Background to the Baptism of the Rus'. Byzantine–Russian Relations between 986–89', *DOP*, XXX (1976), 211; D. Obolensky, 'Cherson and the Conversion of Rus': An Anti-revisionist View', *BMGS*, XIII (1989), 244–56.

32. Skylitzes, pp. 336–8; Yahyā b. Saʿīd, *PO*, XXIII.2 (1932), pp. 424–6; Michael Psellos I, pp. 9–11.

33. Skylitzes, pp. 338–9; Yahyā b. Saʿīd, *PO*, XXIII.2 (1932), pp. 426–7; Michael Psellos I, pp. 14–18.

34. *Ibid.*, pp. 18–24.

35. Stephen of Taron II, p. 164; Yahyā b. Saʿīd, *PO*, XXIII.2 (1932), p. 458; Aristakès de Lastivert, *Récit des malheurs de la nation arménienne* (Brussels, 1973), p. 4; Skylitzes, pp. 355, 389, 394; N. Oikonomidès, 'L'évolution de l'organisation administrative de l'empire byzantine au xiᵉ siècle (1025–1118)', *TM*, VI (1976), 144.

36. M. N. Adler, *The Itinerary of Benjamin of Tudela* (London, 1907), p. 13.

37. Michael Psellos, I, pp. 19, 44–5; Cheynet, *Pouvoir et contestations à Byzance*, pp. 307–12, 333–6.

38. Darrouzès, *Épistoliers byzantins du xᵉ siècle*, pp. 217–48.

39. Skylitzes, pp. 341–2, 345, 364; Yahyā b. Saʿīd, *PO*, XXIII.2 (1932), pp. 446–7, 460, 466–7; W. Felix, *Byzanz und die islamische Welt im früheren 11. Jahrhundert* (Vienna, 1981), pp. 51–2, nn. 28–9.

40. Cheynet, *Pouvoir et contestations à Byzance*, pp. 308–9, 335–6; *Actes d'Iviron*, I, pp. 152–4; Yahyā b. Saʿīd, *PO*, XXIII.2 (1932), pp. 430–1; Aristakès de Lastivert, p. 7.

41. Skylitzes, pp. 354–5, 413.

42. Michael Psellos I, p. 19; N. Oikonomidès, 'Das Verfalland im 10.–11. Jahrhundert: Verkauf und Besteuerung', *Fontes Minores* VII (Frankfurt, 1986), pp. 161–8; Oikonomidès, 'Terres du fisc et revenu de la terre aux xᵉ–xiᵉ siècles', in *Hommes et richesses dans l'empire byzantin*, II, pp. 321–37; Oikonomidès, 'L'évolution de l'organisation administrative de l'empire byzantine au xiᵉ siècle', 135–41.

43. Skylitzes, p. 340.

44. *JGR*, I, pp. 262–72; Skylitzes, p. 347.

45. *JGR*, I, p. 264, n. 24; N. Svoronos, 'Remarques sur la tradition du texte de la novelle de Basile II concernant les puissants', *ZRVI*, VIII.2 (1964), 428–314.

46. *JGR*, I, p. 267; Michael Psellos I, pp. 12–13.

47. Skylitzes, pp. 366–7; Aristakès de Lastivert, p. 19; Forsyth, 'The Byzantine–Arab Chronicle of Yahyā b. Saʿīd', p. 565.

48. Yahyā b. Saʿīd, *PO*, XXIII.3 (1932) pp. 438–44, 447, 449–50; Stephen of Taron ii, pp. 146–7; Bianquis, *Damas et la Syrie*, I, pp. 192–209.

49. Yahyā b. Saʿīd, *PO*, XXIII.3 (1932), pp. 451–2, 455–60; Stephen of Taron II, pp. 149–50, 160; Bianquis, *Damas et la Syrie*, I, pp. 226, 236–43.

50. Bianquis, *Damas et la Syrie*, I, pp. 250, 291, 294, 298, 307, 318–24; II, pp. 398–9, 453–4.

51. Yahyā b. Saʿīd, *PO*, XXIII.3 (1932), pp. 421, 460; Stephen of Taron ii, pp. 151–2, 162; H. F. Amedroz, 'The Marwānid Dynasty at Mayyāfāriqīn in the Tenth and Eleventh Centuries A.D.', *Journal of the Royal Asiatic Society* (1903), 124, 127, 131–2; Forsyth, 'The Byzantine–Arab Chronicle of Yahya b. Saʿīd', pp. 467, 473, 478–512, 554–5.

52. Yahyā b. Saʿīd, *PO*, XXIII.3 (1932), pp. 429–30; 460; Stephen of Taron II, pp. 162–7; Aristakès de Lastivert, pp. 2–8, 11–25; 'The Chronicle of Matthew of Edessa', pp. 46–8, 55–60; Cecaumenus, p. 96; Marquart, *Südarmenien und die Tigrisquellen*, pp. 465–6; Forsyth, 'The Byzantine–Arab Chronicle of Yahyā b. Saʿīd', pp. 465–76, 557–76.

53. 'The Chronicle of Matthew of Edessa', pp. 51–2, 58, 64–5; Aristakès de Lastivert, pp. 25–6.

54. Thomas Artsruni, p. 370; J.-P. Mahé, 'Basile II et Byzance vus par Grigor Narekacʿi', *TM*, XI (1991), 555–73.

55. Stephen of Taron II, pp. 156–7, 168–9; W. Felix, *Byzanz und die islamische Welt im früheren 11. Jahrhundert* (Vienna, 1981), pp. 137–9.

56. Skylitzes, pp. 343, 363.

57. *Ibid.*, pp. xxvi, xxix–xxxv.

58. *Ibid.*, pp. 347, 357; *Actes d'Iviron*, I, pp. 153–4.

59. Skylitzes, pp. 348–9.

60. *Ibid.*, pp. 350–1.

61. *Ibid.*, pp. 352–60.

62. *Ibid.*, pp. 360–5, 413; H. Gelzer, 'Ungedruckte und wenig bekannte Bistümerverzeichnisse der orientalischen Kirche', *BZ*, II (1893), 40–66.

63. *Actes d'Iviron*, I, p.170, ll. 18–20; Actes de Lavra, I, p. 117, l. 11; Yahyā b. Saʿīd, *PO*, XXIII.2 (1932), pp. 446, 461.

64. Liudprandus Cremonensis, pp. 182, 184, 189, 194, 206–7; *Die Urkunden Konrad I. Heinrich I. und Otto I* (MGH Diplomatum regum et imperatorum Germaniae I, Hannover, 1879–84), nr 235, ll. 25–31, p. 325; Thietmar Merseburgensis, *Chronicon*, ed. R. Holtzmann (MGH SRG, Berlin, 1935), pp. 122–7; von Falkenhausen, *Untersuchungen über die byzantinische Herrschaft in Süditalien*, pp. 155–6, 168–9; Kreutz, *Before the Normans*, pp. 102–6, 122–3.

65. von Falkenhausen, *Untersuchungen über die byzantinische Herrschaft in Süditalien*, pp. 51–8; Wharton, *Art of Empire*, pp. 127–56.

66. Skylitzes, p. 368.

Bibliography

INTRODUCTORY NOTE

This bibliography is not complete. Any attempt would be out of place here, and would duplicate the useful bibliographies in the *Oxford Dictionary of Byzantium*, ed. A. Kazhdan, 3 vols (Oxford, 1991). It is biased toward books and articles in English, and excludes items in Russian, Bulgarian and Serbo-Croat. Much has been left out; partly through pressure of space, but also to make it possible to highlight publications I have found particularly important, interesting or enjoyable. Texts in the original language are referred to in the notes, but only appear in the bibliography where accompanied by a translation or especially helpful notes. All the unpublished Ph.D. theses listed are available from University Microfilms International. Apart from a general section, the bibliography is divided according to the book's chapters, and serves in part as a supplement to the notes.

GENERAL

C. Mango, *Byzantium: The Empire of New Rome* (London, 1980) is essential reading, together with papers I–IV in Mango's collected papers, published as *Byzantium and Its Image* (London, 1984). G. Ostrogorsky, *History of the Byzantine State*, tr. J. Hussey, 2nd edn (Oxford, 1968) is dated but still helpful for a basic narrative. J. Herrin, *The Formation of Christendom* (Oxford, 1987) is readable and well informed on Byzantium, but also valuable in placing changes in Byzantine politics and culture in the context of relations with the west. For Byzantium in a Balkan, Russian and steppe context, see D. Obolensky, *The Byzantine Commonwealth: Eastern Europe, 500–1453* (London, 1971). G. Constable and A. Kazhdan, *People and Power in Byzantium: An Introduction to Modern Byzantine Studies* (Washington, D.C., 1982) is interesting but not a place to start.

Two general studies on agrarian history which deal with the whole period from the seventh to the eleventh century are P. Lemerle, *The Agrarian History of Byzantium from the Origins to the Twelfth Century* (Galway, 1979) – a revised English translation of his seminal study first published as 'Esquisse pour une histoire agraire de Byzance: les sources et les problèmes', *Revue historique*, CCXIX (1958), 33–74, 254–84; *ibid.*, CCXX (1958), 43–94 – and M. Kaplan, *Les hommes et la terre à Byzance du vi^e au xie siècle* (Paris, 1992). Lemerle is still valuable, but as far as the written materials are concerned, the latter is now the standard guide.

The *Tabula Imperii Byzantini*, I – (Vienna, 1976–) is a regional site-by-site survey of the empire that has become an essential reference work. The introduction to each volume provides a useful summary of regional history. They are based for the most part on written sources plus site visits; they do not represent the badly needed archaeological survey of the empire, but they are a very useful compendium of current knowledge. Volumes to 1993: J. Koder and F. Hild, *Hellas und Thessalia*, I (1976); F. Hild and M. Restle, *Kappadokien (Kappadokia, Charsianon, Sebasteia und Lykandos)*, II (1981); P. Soustal, *Nikopolis und Kephallēnia*, III (1981); K. Belke, *Galatien und Lykaonien*, IV (1984);

F. Hild and H. Hellenkemper, *Kilikien und Isaurien*, V (1990); P. Soustal, *Thrakien (Thrakē, Rodopē und Haimimontos)*, VI (1991); K. Belke and N. Mersich, *Phrygien und Pisidien*, VII (1990). On individual topics one should usually begin with the *Oxford Dictionary of Byzantium*. Most people, places and issues related (even vaguely) to the Islamic world are covered in the *Encyclopaedia of Islam*, New Edition (Leiden, 1960–). In 1994 it had reached vol. VII (Mif–Naz) and progress is reasonably rapid. Note also the *Supplement* volumes (Leiden, 1980–), and the valuable separate indices which enable the main volumes to be used more effectively. Some of the earlier entries are now rather dated and should be used with caution, but as a whole this is a major tool for anyone interested in the medieval Near East.

CHAPTER 1. SOURCES FOR EARLY MEDIEVAL BYZANTIUM

The volumes of the *Archives de l'Athos*, III– (Paris, 1964–) are a major resource. (Vol. I, *Actes de Lavra*, ed. G. Rouillard and P. Collomp, has been superseded by a new edition in vols V, VII, X and XI; vol. II, *Actes de Kutlumus*, ed. P. Lemerle, was reissued as vol. II.2 with important revisions in 1988.) The texts are edited with a full French summary and important commentary. Each volume has an extended introduction. Few texts have been translated, but one exception is found in R. Morris, 'Dispute Settlement in the Byzantine Provinces in the Tenth century', in *The Settlement of Disputes in Early Medieval Europe*, ed. W. Davies and P. Fouracre (Cambridge, 1986), pp. 125–47.

A large and growing number of inscribed lead seals have been published. The more important publications are: V. Laurent, *Corpus des sceaux de l'empire byzantin*; II, *L'administration centrale* (Paris, 1981); V.1–3: *L'église* (Paris, 1963–72); Laurent, *Les sceaux byzantins du Médailler Vatican* (Vatican City, 1962); Laurent, *La Collection Orghidan* (Paris, 1952); G. Zacos and A. Veglery, *Byzantine Lead Seals* (Basel, 1972); G. Zacos, *Byzantine Lead Seals*, II (Berne, 1984); W. Seibt, *Die byzantinischen Bleisiegel in Österreich*, I (1978–); N. Oikonomides, *A Collection of Dated Byzantine Lead Seals* (Washington, D.C., 1986); *Catalogue of the Byzantine Seals at Dumbarton Oaks and in the Fogg Museum of Art*, I, *Italy, North of the Balkans, North of the Black Sea*, ed. J. Nesbitt and N. Oikonomides (Washington, D.C., 1991). Each of these volumes includes helpful commentary. In addition see the *Studies in Byzantine Sigillography*, ed. N. Oikonomides, I– (1987–).

Still valuable as more extensive text-by-text guides to Byzantine literature than the *Oxford Dictionary of Byzantium* are H.-G. Beck, *Kirche und Theologische Literatur im byzantinischen Reich* (Handbuch der Altertumswissenschaft XII.2.1, Munich, 1959); Gy. Moravcsik, *Byzantinoturcica*, 2nd edn, I (Berlin, 1958); and H. Hunger, *Die hochsprachliche profane Literatur der Byzantiner*, 2 vols (Handbuch der Altertumswissenschaft XII.5.1–2, Munich, 1978).

The various forms and genres of Byzantine literature are introduced in Mango, *Byzantium*, with which it is useful to read I. Ševčenko, 'Levels of Style in Byzantine literature', *Jahrbuch der Österreichischen Byzantinistik*, XXXI (1981), 289–312. For the state of Byzantine literature in the early seventh century see the papers by M. Whitby, and A. Cameron, in *The Byzantine and Early Islamic Near East, I: Problems in the Literary Source Material*, ed. A. Cameron and L. I. Conrad (Princeton, N.J., 1992), pp. 25–105. On Byzantine literary culture see P. Lemerle, *Byzantine Humanism*, tr. H. Lindsay and A. Moffatt

(Canberra, 1986). R. Scott, 'The Classical Tradition in Byzantine Historiography', and M. Mullett, 'The Classical Tradition in the Byzantine Letter', in *Byzantium and the Classical Tradition*, ed. M. Mullett and R. Scott (University of Birmingham 13th Spring Symposium of Byzantine Studies 1979, Birmingham, 1981) are both valuable. Mullett is the author of a number of interesting and important papers including 'Writing in Early Mediaeval Byzantium', in *The Uses of Literacy in Early Medieval Europe*, ed. R. McKitterick (Cambridge, 1990), pp. 156–85; and 'The Language of Diplomacy', in *Byzantine Diplomacy*, ed. J. Shepard and S. Franklin (Aldershot, 1992), pp. 203–16, on diplomatic letters.

On specific Byzantine chronicles and histories, see: C. Mango, 'Who Wrote the Chronicle of Theophanes?', *ZRVI*, XVIII (1978), 9–17 [= Mango, *Byzantium and Its Image*, nr XI]; Mango, 'The *Breviarium* of the Patriarch Nicephorus', in *Byzantium: Tribute to Andreas N. Stratos*, 2 vols (Athens, 1986), II, pp. 539–52; R. J. H. Jenkins, 'The Classical Background of the Scriptores Post Theophanem', *DOP*, VIII (1954), 13–30; A. Markopoulos, 'Sur les deux versions de la Chronographie de Symeon Logothete', *BZ*, LXXVI (1983), 279–84; W. Treadgold, 'The Chronological Accuracy of the *Chronicle* of Symeon Logothete for the Years 813–845', *DOP*, XXXIII (1979), 159–97.

On hagiography, after that given by Mango, *Byzantium*, F. Halkin, 'L'hagiographie byzantine au service de l'histoire', *Thirteenth International Congress of Byzantine Studies, Oxford, 1966. Main Papers* XI (Oxford, 1966), pp. 1–10, is a good introduction. H. Delehaye's works are still important; see especially his *Les saints stylites* (Brussels, 1923), and *Cinq leçons sur la méthode hagiographique* (Brussels, 1934). Otherwise there is a useful collection of papers in *The Byzantine Saint*, ed. S. Hackel (University of Birmingham 14th Spring Symposium of Byzantine Studies 1980, Studies supplementary to Sobornost v, London, 1981). E. Malamut, *Sur la route des saints byzantins* (Paris, 1993) uses saints' lives to explore the culture, society and human geogrpahy of the Byzantine world.

Most specific texts in translation will be referred to under the relevant chapter but three frequently mentioned texts that make essential reading are: *The Chronicle of Theophanes*, tr. H. Turtledove (Philadelphia, Pa., 1982) – a translation and commentary on the full text by C. Mango and R. Scott is due to appear shortly; Nikephoros, patriarch of Constantinople, *Short History*, ed. and tr. C. Mango (CFHB XIII, Washington, D.C., 1990), with brief but very interesting commentary; and Constantine Porphyrogenitus, *De Administrando Imperio*, ed. Gy. Moravcsik, tr. R. J. H. Jenkins (CFHB I, Washington, D.C., 1967). Constantine Porphyrogenitus, *De Administrando Imperio II. Commentary*, ed. R. J. H. Jenkins (London, 1962) is still useful but badly needs a replacement. Some entertaining steps toward the necessary reassessment of Constantine and his works are taken by I. Ševčenko, 'Re-reading Constantine Porphyrogenitus', in *Byzantine Diplomacy*, ed. Shepard and Franklin, pp. 167–95.

For Byzantine archaeology, in addition to Foss's works listed under chapter four below, see also C. Foss and D. Winfield, *Byzantine Fortifications: An Introduction* (Pretoria, 1986). Important work linking field work to the documents of Mount Athos has been carried out in eastern Macedonia by J. Lefort – see under chapter nine below. The excavations at Amorion and survey work on medieval castles in Anatolia is reported each year in the British Institute of Archaeology at Ankara's journal, *Anatolian Studies*. Work in Greece is reported in the *Archaeological Report* published as an annual supplement to the *Journal of Hellenic Studies*.

For art and architecture see R. Cormack, *Writing in Gold* (London, 1985); C. Mango, *Byzantine Architecture* (London, 1979); R. Krautheimer, *Early Christian and Byzantine Architecture*, 4th edn (Pelican History of Art, Harmondsworth, 1986); L. Rodley, *Byzantine Art and Architecture: An Introduction* (Cambridge, 1994).

For basic information on coinage see P. Grierson, *Byzantine Coins* (London, 1982). Interesting material for the whole period can be mined from M. Hendy, *Studies in the Byzantine Monetary Economy, c. 350–1450* (Cambridge, 1985).

CHAPTER 2. THE STRATEGIC GEOGRAPHY OF THE NEAR EAST

For the Balkans, Obolensky, *The Byzantine Commonwealth* is very helpful and clear; N. G. L. Hammond, *A History of Macedonia*, I (Oxford, 1972) provides useful information on the Via Egnatia that remains relevant for the middle ages. J. Cvijič, *La Péninsule Balkanique* (Paris, 1918) is a classic work of descriptive geography that can be extremely useful to the medieval historian, as can the volumes of the *Geographical Handbook Series* (Naval Intelligence Division, London): *Greece*, 3 vols (1944–5); *Jugoslavia*, 3 vols (1944–5); *Albania* (1945).

For the steppes, Obolensky's book is again a good introduction. On the nomad world, see A. M. Khazanov, *Nomads and the Outside World*, tr. J. Crookenden (Cambridge, 1984); D. Sinor, 'Horse and Pasture in Inner Asian History', *Oriens extremus*, XIX (1972), 171–83; plus R. Tapper, 'Anthropologists, Historians, and Tribespeople on Tribe and State Formation in the Middle East', in *Tribes and State Formation in the Middle East*, ed. P. S. Khoury and J. Kostiner (London, 1991), pp. 48–73, which serves to caution historians too keen to apply anthropological models.

For the Near East in general, see J. M. Wagstaff, *The Evolution of the Middle Eastern Landscapes* (London, 1985); and X. de Planhol, *Les fondements géographiques de l'histoire de l'Islam* (Paris, 1968). On Iran and Iraq, P. Christensen, *The Decline of Iranshahr* (Copenhagen, 1993) is important.

For Anatolia in particular, the *Geographical Handbook Series: Turkey* 2 vols (London, 1942–3) is a useful source of basic geographical information about terrain, routes and climate. Also a good introduction, and one of the few on this list likely to make you laugh, is J. D. Howard-Johnston and N. Ryan, *The Scholar and the Gypsy* (London, 1992) – an account of travelling in Turkey in pursuit of Byzantine landscapes.

Specifically on the vexed question of relations between the bedouin and the settled population of the Fertile Crescent, for work which stresses co-operation and co-existence see: L. E. Sweet, 'Camel Raiding of North Arabian Bedouin: A Mechanism of Ecological Adaptation', *American Anthropologist*, LXVII (1965), 1132–50; D. F. Graf, 'Rome and the Saracens: Reassessing the Nomadic Menace', in *L'Arabie préislamique et son environnement historique et culturel*, ed. T. Fahd (Leiden, 1989), pp. 341–400; E. B. Banning, 'Peasants, Pastoralists, and *Pax Romana*: Mutualism in the Highlands of Jordan', *Bulletin of the American Schools of Oriental Research*, CCLXI (1986), 25–50; Banning, '*De Bello Paceque*: A Reply to Parker', *ibid.*, CCLXV (1987), 52–4. Not everyone is convinced: S. T. Parker, *Romans and Saracens: A History of the Arabian Frontier* (Winnona Lake, Ind., 1986); Parker, 'Peasants, Pastoralists, and *Pax Romana*: A Different View', *Bulletin of the American Schools of Oriental Research*, CCLXV (1987), 35–51. W. Lancaster, *The Rwala Bedouin Revisited* (Cambridge, 1981)

BIBLIOGRAPHY

is a classic study of a bedouin tribe which helps to put the problem in perspective. Also relevant is R. W. Bulliet, *The Camel and Wheel* (Cambridge, Mass., 1975) who arguably overstates his case, but the book is certainly highly readable.

For the strategic implications of the Mediterranean Sea, J. H. Pryor, *Geography, Technology and War* (Cambridge, 1988) is lively and important.

CHAPTER 3. THE ROMAN WORLD IN 600

A. H. M. Jones, *The Later Roman Empire*, 3 vols (Oxford, 1964) should be the first place to explore any late Roman topic. Essentially a work of reference, this study opened up the late Roman world to a generation of historians. It is strongest on the empire's civil and military administration. For late Roman culture in a broader sense, see P. Brown, *The World of Late Antiquity* (London, 1971) – readable and full of ideas; A. Cameron's helpful survey, *The Mediterranean World in Late Antiquity, A.D. 395–600* (London, 1993); G. Fowden, *Empire to Commonwealth: Consequences of Monotheism in Late Antiquity* (Princeton, N.J., 1993) – a wide-ranging interpretative essay; and G. W. Bowersock's brief but inspiring lectures, *Hellenism in Late Antiquity* (Cambridge, 1990).

Specifically on late Roman Christianity, the works of S. Brock, several of which are collected in S. Brock, *Syriac Perspectives on Late Antiquity* (London, 1984), and *Studies in Syriac Christianity* (Aldershot, 1992), are essential. Those of P. Brown are equally important, but their focus either on the period before the sixth century or on the west, makes them less relevant here. However, P. Brown, *Society and the Holy in Late Antiquity* (Berkeley, Cal., 1982), is a useful collection of important papers. A different view of the significance of doctrinal differences which sees them heading toward crisis at the end of the sixth century, is found in S. A. Harvey, *Asceticism and Society in Crisis* (Berkeley, Cal., 1990). For the Chalcedonians, P. Allen, *Evagrius Scholasticus the Church Historian* (Louvain, 1981) is useful. For the church in late Roman cities, see G. Dagron, 'Le christianisme dans la ville byzantine', *DOP*, XXXI (1977), 1–25; Dagron, 'Two Documents Concerning Mid-Sixth Century Mopsuestia', in *Charanis Studies: Essays in Honor of Peter Charanis*, ed. A. E Laiou (New Brunswick, N.J., 1980), pp. 18–30. S. Mitchell, *Anatolia: Land, Men and Gods in Asia Minor*, 2 vols (Oxford, 1993), II, pp. 109–50, contains an important analysis of the church in the Anatolian countryside.

Unlike many historians I do not see a growing social and economic crisis at the end of the sixth century that provides the context for the loss of the eastern provinces to the Arabs. Some of the arguments are explored in M. Whittow, 'Ruling the Late Roman and Early Byzantine City: A Continuous History', *Past and Present*, CXXIX (1990), 3–29. For counter-arguments, see H. Kennedy, 'The Last Century of Byzantine Syria: A Reinterpretation', *Byzantinische Forschungen*, X (1985), 141–83; and Cameron, *The Mediterranean World in Late Antiquity, A.D. 395–600*, pp. 152–96. In general on this theme there is some important material in *Hommes et richesses dans l'empire byzantin*, I (Paris, 1989); J.-P. Sodini, 'La contribution de l'archéologie à la connaissance du monde byzantin (ive–viie siècles)', *DOP*, XLVII (1993), 139–84; and G. Tate, *Les campagnes de la Syrie du nord du iie au viie siècle*, I (Paris, 1992). The latter revises in several major respects the conclusions of G. Tchalenko's still-important classic work, *Villages antiques de la Syrie du nord*, 3 vols (Paris, 1953–8) – not to be missed if only for the wonderful photographs of northern Syria. E. Patlagean,

Pauvreté économique et pauvreté sociale à Byzance, 4ᵉ–7ᵉ siècles (Paris, 1977) remains interesting. Also important is C. Roueché, *Aphrodisias in Late Antiquity* (Journal of Roman Studies Monographs v, 1989), whose publication and analysis of the inscriptions from this city in western Turkey is a model that should be widely followed.

The political and strategic outlook in 600 is analysed in M. Whitby, *The Emperor Maurice and His Historian* (Oxford, 1988) – a very important study to be read with *The History of Theophylact Simocatta*, tr. M. Whitby and M. Whitby (Oxford, 1986), and *Maurice's Strategikon*, tr. G. T. Dennis (Philadelphia, 1984).

Relations with the Arabs and the desert frontier have recently produced a large and lively literature. Especially helpful are M. Sartre, *Trois études sur l'Arabie romaine et byzantine* (Collection Latomus 178, Brussels, 1978), and B. Isaac, *The Limits of Empire* (Oxford, 1990). The works of I. Shahīd raise important issues. Up to 1994, two volumes of his trilogy on Byzantium and the Arabs before the rise of Islam had appeared: *Byzantium and the Arabs in the Fourth Century* (Washington, D.C., 1984); and *Byzantium and the Arabs in the Fifth Century* (Washington, D.C., 1989). *Byzantium and the Arabs in the Sixth Century*, I (Washington, D.C.) is due to appear shortly.

CHAPTER 4. THE FALL OF THE OLD ORDER

The chronology for this chapter rests on the work of J. D. Howard-Johnston, 'Heraclius' Persian Campaigns and the Revival of the East Roman Empire, 622–30', *War in History* (forthcoming); and B. Flusin, *Saint Anastase le Perse et l'histoire de la Palestine au début du viiᵉ siècle*, 2 vols (Paris, 1992) which together replace the older literature.

Most of the essential texts are available in translation with commentary. Particularly recommended are: *Chronicon Paschale, 284–628 AD*, tr. M. Whitby and M. Whitby (Translated Texts for Historians VII, Liverpool, 1989); *The Seventh Century in the West-Syrian Chronicles*, introduced translated and annotated, A. Palmer, S. Brock and R. Hoyland (Translated Texts for Historians XV, Liverpool, 1993). The late seventh-century history attributed to bishop Sebeos (whether or not the attribution is correct matters little since Sebeos is otherwise unknown) is available in two translations: Sebeos, *Histoire de Héraclius*, tr. F. Macler (Paris, 1904); *Sebēos' History*, tr. R. Bedrosian (Sources of the Armenian Tradition, New York, 1985). Some of George of Pisidia's poems are available with an Italian translation and commentary, Giorgio di Pisidia, *Poemi I, Panegirici epici*, ed. A. Pertusi (Ettal, 1960); an English translation and commentary by Mary Whitby is in preparation and will appear in the series Translated Texts for Historians published by Liverpool University Press. The *Acta* of St Anastasios the Persian and other associated texts are edited and translated with an important commentary in Flusin's *Saint Anastase le Perse* noted above, and provide remarkable contemporary evidence for the Persian occupation of Palestine and Christian reaction.

A major work of reference for the seventh century up to 641 is *The Prosopography of the Later Roman Empire*, III.a–b, ed. J. R. Martindale (Cambridge, 1992). The *PLRE* is an extremely useful tool, but note that it only covers secular élites, and omits the clergy, minor officials, local notables and other lesser mortals.

For the rise of Islam, basic guidance can be found in R. S. Humphreys, *Islamic History: A Framework for Inquiry*, rev. edn. (London, 1991). For Muhammad, the Koran and the sources for the Prophet's lifetime see the short and essential M. Cook, *Muhammad* (Oxford, 1983). A fairly conservative line is followed in H. Kennedy, *The Prophet and the Age of the Caliphates: The Islamic Near East from the Sixth to the Eleventh Century* (London, 1986); and F. Donner, *The Early Islamic Conquests* (Princeton, N.J., 1981). The detailed narrative in W. E. Kaegi, *Byzantium and the Early Islamic Conquests* (Cambridge, 1992), is the result of turning a blind eye to the problems posed by the sources. However, there is a growing body of dissenting literature which includes, P. Crone and M. Cook, *Hagarism: The Making of the Islamic World* (Cambridge, 1977); P. Crone, *Meccan Trade and the Rise of Islam* (Oxford, 1987); P. Crone and M. Hinds, *God's Caliph* (Cambridge, 1986); J. Koren and Y. D. Nevo, 'Methodological Approaches to Islamic Studies', *Der Islam*, LXVIII (1991), 87–107; F. E. Peters, 'The Quest of the Historical Muhammad', *International Journal of Middle Eastern Studies*, XXIII (1991), 291–315; S. Ledar, 'The Literary Use of the *Khabar*', in *The Byzantine and Early Islamic Near East*, I, pp. 277–315; L. Conrad, 'The Conquest of Arwād: A Source-Critical Study in the Historiography of the Early Medieval Near East', in *ibid.*, pp. 317–401. Attempts to revise the early history of Islam have been met with considerable hostility from Muslims and non-Muslims. Do not be put off by the dismissively critical reviews some of this work has received.

For the economic consequences of the seventh century see C. Foss's seminal works: 'The Persians in Asia Minor and the End of Antiquity', *English Historical Review*, XC (1975), 721–47; 'Archaeology and the "Twenty Cities" of Byzantine Asia', *American Journal of Archaeology*, LXXXI (1977), 469–86; *Byzantine and Turkish Sardis* (Cambridge, Mass., 1976); *Ephesus After Antiquity: A Late Antique, Byzantine and Turkish City* (Cambridge, 1979). But note the cautionary comments of J. Russell, 'Transformations in Early Byzantine Urban Life: The Contribution and Limitations of Archaeological Evidence', *The 17th International Byzantine Congress: Major Papers* (New Rochelle, N.Y., 1986), pp. 137–54.

The numismatic evidence is clearly set out in C. Morrison, 'Byzance au viie siécle: le témoinage de la numismatique', in *Byzantium. Tribute to Adreas Stratos*, 2 vols (Athens, 1986), I, pp. 149–63.

For pottery as evidence for economic change some of the most interesting work has come from J. Hayes in Constantinople and Cyprus, and P. Arthur in Italy: e.g. Hayes, *Excavations at Saraçhane in Istanbul*, II (Princeton, N.J., 1992); Hayes, 'Problèmes de la céramique des viie–ixe siècles à Salamine et à Chypre', in *Salamine de Chypre. Histoire et archéologie. État des recherches* (Paris, 1980), pp. 375–80; Arthur, 'Aspects of the Byzantine Economy: An Evaluation of Amphora Evidence from Italy', in *Recherches sur les céramiques byzantines*, ed. V. Déroche and J.-M. Spieser (Paris, 1989), pp. 79–93.

For Constantinople see C. Mango, *Le développement urbain de Constantinople (ive–viie siècles* (Paris, 1985), with Hayes noted above on the pottery from Saraçhane, and M. Hendy's catalogue of the coins from the same site in R. M. Harrison, *Excavations at Saraçhane in Istanbul*, I (Princeton, N.J., 1986), pp. 278–373.

A very important text for its picture of Anatolia c. 600 is the Life of Theodore of Sykeon. The greater part is available in English as one of the *Three Byzantine Saints*, tr. E. Dawes and N. H. Baynes ((London, 1948); the full text with French translation and commentary is found in *Vie de Théodore de Sykeôn*, ed. A.-J. Festugière, 2 vols (Brussels, 1970). Mitchell, *Anatolia: Land Men and Gods in Asia Minor*, II, pp. 122–50, discusses the life in detail.

For Syria and Palestine, see P. Pentz, *The Invisible Conquest: The Ontogenesis of Sixth and Seventh Century Syria* (Copenhagen, 1992), and the papers in *La*

Syrie de Byzance à l'Islam, viie–viiie siècles, ed. P. Canivet and J.-P. Rey-Coquais (Actes du Colloque international Lyon – Maison de l'Orient Méditerranéen, Paris – Institut du Monde Arabe, 11–15 Septembre 1990, Damascus, 1992).

CHAPTER 5. HOW THE ROMAN EMPIRE SURVIVED

On Constantinople itself we are waiting for C. Mango's book on the city to appear. Meanwhile there is much of importance in his already mentioned *Le développement urbain de Constantinople*, and in the articles collected as *Studies on Constantinople* (London, 1993). Used with caution the works of Janin are helpful: *Constantinople byzantine*, 2nd edn (Paris, 1964); *Le géographie ecclésiastique de l'empire byzantin. Le siége de Constantinople et le patriarcat oecuménique I. Les églises et monastères*, 2nd edn (Paris, 1969). After the *Oxford Dictionary of Byzantium*, they are usually the first place to look. For the mental picture the Byzantines had of their city, see G. Dagron, *Constantinople imaginaire* (Paris, 1984). One of the major sources Dagron discusses has been published with an English translation and commentary: *Constantinople in the Early Eighth Century: The Parastaseis Syntomoi Chronikai*, ed. A. Cameron and J. Herrin (Leiden, 1984) – well worth reading for the bizarre impression it gives of Byzantium and Byzantines at the beginning of the eighth century.

For the walls, as well as Foss and Winfield, *Byzantine Fortifications*, see F. Krischen and T. von Lüpke, *Die Landmauer von Konstantinopel*, I (Berlin, 1938); B. Meyer-Platn and A. M. Schneider, *ibid.*, II (Berlin, 1943).

Studies of the Great Palace reflect the preconceptions of nineteenth- and twentieth-century culture as much as they do early medieval Byzantium. For the palace seen through the eyes of the Parisian École des beaux arts, see J. Ebersolt, *Le grand Palais de Constantinople* (Paris, 1910). Closer to the middle ages is C. Mango. *The Brazen House: A Study of the Vestibule of the Imperial Palace of Constantinople* (Copenhagen, 1959).

For court ceremonies, processions, etc., see M. McCormick, 'Analyzing Imperial Ceremonies', *Jahrbuch der Österreichischen Byzantinistik*, XXXV (1985), 1–20; A. Cameron, 'The Construction of Court Ritual: The Byzantine Book of Ceremonies', in *Rituals of Royalty: Power and Ceremonial in Traditional Societies*, ed. D. Cannadine and S. Price (Cambridge, 1987), pp. 106–36; for military triumphs see M. McCormick, *Eternal Victory Triumphal Rulership in Late Antiquity* (Cambridge, 1986).

The first 83 chapters of Book One of the *De Ceremoniis* are translated into French, plus commentary: Constantin VII Porphyrogénète, *Le livre des cérémonies*, ed. and tr. A. Vogt, 4 vols (Paris, 1935–40).

On court ranks and titles, and civil and military offices, the key texts are the orders of precedence known as *taktika* and the treatise on the arrangement of court banquets composed by Philotheos. An edition of all these, French translation and essential commentary, are to be found in N. Oikonomidès *Les listes de préséance byzantines des ixe et xe siècles* (Paris, 1972). An older edition of Philotheos, without translation but with still useful English commentary, is that of J. B. Bury, *The Imperial Administrative System in the Ninth Century* (British Academy Supplementary Papers I, London 1911). Important work on these texts and on this topic as a whole is found in two studies by F. Winkelmann: *Byzantinische Rang- und Ämterstruktur im 8. und 9. Jahrdhundert* (Berlin, 1985), and *Quellenstudien zur herrschenden Klasse von Byzanz im 8. und 9. Jahrhundert* (Berlin, 1987). Equally important is the brilliant study by P. Lemerle, '*Roga* et rente d'état aux xe–xie siècles', *REB*, XXV (1967), 77–100.

J. F. Haldon, *Byzantium in the Seventh Century* (Cambridge, 1990), argues for fundamental change taking place in most aspects of Byzantine culture during the seventh century. The book is particularly valuable for its analysis of changes in the empire's civil and military organisation, where he builds on recent German work, especially that of Winkelmann.

Haldon's study is also a sound introduction to Byzantine taxation on which there is a large, but scattered, literature; see Lemerle, *The Agrarian History of Byzantium*; Kaplan, *Les hommes et la terre à Byzance*; Hendy, *Studies in the Byzantine Monetary Economy*; N. Oikonomidès, 'De l'impôt de distribution à l'impôt de quotite à propos du premier cadastre byzantin (7e–9e siècle)', *ZRVI*, XXVI (1987), 9–19; J. F. Haldon, '*Synônê*: Reconsidering a Problematic Term of Middle Byzantine Fiscal Administration', *BMGS*, XVIII (1994), 116–53; and F. Dölger, *Beiträge zur Geschichte der byzantinischen Finanzverwaltung besonders des 10. und 11. Jahrhunderts* (Byzantinisches Archiv IX, Munich, 1927). The latter is an edition with detailed commentary of a probably tenth-century text usually known as the Fiscal Treatise. G. Ostrogorsky gives a German translation and further commentary in 'Die ländliche Steuergemeinde des byzantinischen Reiches im X. Jahrhundert', *Vierteljahrschrift für Sozial- und Wirtschaftgeschichte*, XX (1927), 1–108. There is an English translation in C. M. Brand, 'Two Byzantine Treatises on Taxation', *Traditio*, XXV (1969), 36–50.

On the army and the origins of the themes, the essential studies are R.-J. Lilie, 'Die zweihundertjährige Reform. Zu den Anfängen der Themenorganisation im 7. und 8. Jahrhundert', *Byzantinoslavica*, XLV (1984), 27–29, 190–201; W. E. Kaegi, 'Some Reconsiderations on the Themes (7th to 9th Centuries', *Jöb*, XVI (1967), 39–53; and J. F. Haldon, 'Military Service, Military Lands, and the Status of Soldiers: Current Problems and Interpretations', *DOP*, XLVII (1993), 1–67: the latter is an extremely useful survey and discussion of the literature.

The Farmer's Law is translated into English: W. Asburner, 'The Farmer's Law', *Journal of Hellenic Studies*, XXXII (1912), 68–95. Kaplan *Les hommes et la terre à Byzance*, provides a full discussion. For the *Ekloga* see the edition with introduction and German translation, *Ecloga: Das Gesetzbuch Leons III. und Konstantinos V*, ed. L. Burgmann (Forschungen zur byzantinischen Rechtsgeschichte X, Frankfurt am Main, 1983); there is an English translation, E. H. Freshfield, *A Manual of Roman Law: The Ecloga* (Cambridge, 1926).

The subject of the *kommerkiarioi* and their relationship with the army and commerce has produced lively argument – rather glossed over in the *Oxford Dictionary of Byzantium*, s.v. 'kommerkiarios'. For an overview with full bibliography see Haldon, 'Military Service, Military Service, Military Lands, and the Status of Soldiers', 14–18. The key studies are N. Oikonomides, 'Silk Trade and Production in Byzantium from the Sixth to the Ninth Century: The Seals of the Kommerkiarioi', *DOP*, XL (1986), 33–53; Hendy, *Studies in the Byzantine Monetary Economy*, pp. 626–62; A. Dunn, 'The *Kommerkiarios*, the Apotheke, the Dromos, the Vardarios, and The West', *BMGS*, XVII (1993), 3–24.

On the Byzantine navy see H. Ahrweiler, *Byzance et la mer* (Paris, 1966); R. H. Dolley, 'The Warships of the Later Roman Empire', *Journal of Hellenic Studies*, XXXVIII (1948), 47–53. The texts deserve reassessment but the most fruitful line of research in future is likely to lie with marine archaeology. See F. van Doorninck, 'Byzantium, Mistress of the Sea: 330–641', in *A History of Seafaring Based on Underwater Archaeology*, ed. G. F. Bass (London, 1972), pp. 134–57; G. F. Bass and F. H. van Doornick, *Yassı Ada*, I (College Station, 1982).

The church as a social institution has been little studied for seventh- to eleven th-century Byzantium although relevant material appears in many publications. A general introduction is provided by J. Hussey, *The Orthodox Church in the Byzantine Empire* (Oxford 1986). For the secular church operating in the provinces see D. Papachryssanthou, 'Histoire d'un évêché byzantin: Hiérissos en Chalcidique', *TM*, VIII (1981), 373–96. Monasticism is better covered, especially by R. Morris, *Monks and Laymen in Byzantium 843–1118* (Cambridge, 1995).

CHAPTER 6.   THE SHOCK OF DEFEAT

Prophecies of the empire's future which shed light on contemporary expectations are introduced and discussed in P. J. Alexander, *The Byzantine Apocalyptic Tradition*, ed. D. deF. Abrahamse (Berkeley, Calif., 1985). The apocalypse of St Andrew the Fool, dated by Mango to the early eighth century – 'The Life of St. Andrew the Fool Reconsidered', *Rivista di Studi Bizantini e Slavi*, II (1982), 297–313 – is translated in L. Rydén, 'The Andreas Salos Apocalypse. Greek Text, Translation and Commentary', *DOP*, XXVIII (1974). The original Syriac text of the apocalypse of Pseudo-Methodios is translated and discussed by S. Brock in *West-Syrian Chronicles*, pp. 222–53.

A good introduction to iconoclasm is Cormack, *Writing in Gold*. Several useful papers appear in *Iconoclasm*, ed. A. Bryer and J. Herrin (University of Birmingham 9th Spring Symposium of Byzantine Studies 1975, Birmingham, 1977). Both Gero's studies – *Byzantine Iconoclasm During the Reign of Leo III* (Louvain, 1973), and *Byzantine Iconoclasm During the Reign of Constantine V* (Louvain, 1977) – helpfully tackle source problems and clarify the difficulties. P. Brown, 'A Dark Age Crisis: Aspects of the Iconoclastic Controversy', *English Historical Review*, LXXXVIII (1973), 1–34, puts iconoclasm in a wider context as part of a struggle for control over the sources of power in Byzantium. Also of particular interest among a vast bibliography are H. Belting, *Likeness and Presence: A History of the Image Before the Era of Art*, tr. E. Jephcott (Chicago, Ill., 1994); P. J. Alexander, *The Patriarch Nicephorus of Constantinople* (Oxford, 1958); A. Grabar, *L'iconoclasme byzantin*, 2nd edn (Paris, 1984); and J. Moorhead, 'Iconoclasm, the Cross and the Imperial Image', *Byz*, LV (1985), 165–79.

There are useful collections of texts in D. J. Sahas, *Icon and Logos: Sources in Eighth-century Iconoclasm* (Toronto, 1986); and C. Mango, *The Art of the Byzantine Empire 312–1453* (Englewood Cliffs, N.J., 1972). Some of the less than incisive anti-iconoclast writings of the patriarch Nikephoros are translated in Nicéphore, *Discours contre les iconoclastes*, tr. M.-J. Mondzain-Baudinet (Paris, 1989). See also *The Life of Michael the Synkellos*, ed. and tr. M. B. Cunningham (BBTT I, Belfast, 1991), and *La vie merveilleuse de saint Pierre d'Atroa († 837)*, ed. and tr. V. Laurent (Brussels, 1956).

The political history of the period is inevitably coloured by anti-iconoclast propaganda and for the ninth century by later chroniclers' political biases. Important attempts to disentangle this mess are P. Lemerle, 'Thomas le Slave', *TM*, I (1965), 255–97; and the papers of P. Karlin-Hayter; 'Études sur les deux histoires du règne de Michel III', *Byz*, XLI (1971), 452–96; 'Michael III and Money', *Byzantinoslavica*, LI (1989), 1–80.

A different view of iconoclasm and of the Byzantine world in general based on a strong faith in the veracity of early medieval sources, is found in W. Treadgold. *The Byzantine Revival, 780–842* (Stanford, Cal., 1988).

CHAPTER 7. THE BYZANTINE RESPONSE: ON TO THE DEFENSIVE

The best discussion of Arab–Byzantine warfare in the seventh and eighth century is in R.-J. Lilie, *Die byzantinische Reaktion auf die Ausbreitung der Araber* (Munich, 1976). For the ninth century, see A. A. Vasiliev, *Byzance et les Arabes I, La dynastie d'Amorium (820–867)*, French edn, H. Grégoire and M. Canard (Brussels, 1935), with an important appendix of translated Arabic texts. Texts for the seventh and eighth centuries are translated into English in E. W. Brooks's papers: 'The Arabs in Asia Minor (641–750) from Arabic Sources', *Journal of Hellenic Studies*, XVIII (1898), 182–208; 'Byzantines and Arabs in the Time of the Early Abbasids', *English Historical Review*, XV, (1900), 728–47, XVI (1901), 84–92; 'The Campaign of 716–718 from Arabic Sources', *Journal of Hellenic Studies*, XIX (1899), 19–33. There is also now the tremendous achievement of the English translation of al-Tabarī: *The History of al-Tabarī*, ed. I. Abbas *et al.*, 38 vols (SUNY Series in Near Eastern Studies, Albany, N.Y., 1985–).

One of the key Byzantine texts, 'On Skirmishing Warfare' is edited and translated into English as one of the *Three Byzantine Military Treatises*, ed. G. T. Dennis (CFHB XXV, Washington, D.C., 1985). *Le traité sur la guérilla de l'empereur Nicéphore Phocas*, ed. G. Dagron and H. Mihâescu (Paris, 1986) is a slightly preferable edition with French translation and extremely important extended commentary.

The borderlands are discussed in J. F. Haldon and H. Kennedy, 'The Arab–Byzantine Frontier in the Eighth and Ninth Centuries: Military Organisation and Society in the Borderlands', *ZRVI*, XIX (1980), 79–116.

On the organisation of the Byzantine army, J. F. Haldon's studies are essential: *Recruitment and Conscription in the Byzantine Army c. 550–c 950* (Österreichische Akademie der Wissenschaften, phil.-hist. Klasse CCCLVII, Vienna, 1979); *Byzantine Praetorians* (Poikila Byzantina III, Bonn, 1984); 'Military Service, Military Lands, and the Status of Soldiers', *DOP*, XLVII (1993). See also the appendices to the *De Ceremoniis* which deal with the conduct of imperial expeditions, edited by Haldon under the the the title, Constantine Porphyrogenitus, *Three Treatises on Imperial Expeditions* (CFHB XXVIII, Vienna, 1990).

For the Arab geographers, on the Byzantine themes in particular see E. W. Brooks, 'Arabic Lists of the Byzantine Themes', *Journal of Hellenic Studies*, XXI (1901), 67–77, in general see the monumental study of A. Miguel, *La géographie humaine du monde musulman jusqu'au milieu du 11ᵉ siècle*, 4 vols (Paris, 1967–88) – vol. II, pp. 381–481, deals with the geographers' perception of Byzantium.

J. D. Howard-Johnston, 'Studies in the Organization of the Byzantine Army in the Tenth and Eleventh Centuries' (University of Oxford D.Phil. thesis, 1971), is currently only available in the Bodleian Library, Oxford, and the Dumbarton Oaks Research Library, Washington, D.C., but is due to be published in Oxford by Oxbow Publications.

CHAPTER 8. THE BYZANTINE EMPIRE AND ITS NON-MUSLIM NEIGHBOURS, *c.* 600–*c.* 900

Transcaucasia

A growing number of sources are available in translation, opening up what had been a very specialist area to wider interest: Bishop Ukhtanes of Sebasteia, *History of Armenia*, II, tr. Z. Arzoumanian (Fort Lauderdale, Flo., 1985); *His-*

tory of Lewond, The Eminent Vardapet of the Armenians, tr. Z. Arzoumanian (Philadelphia, Pa., 1982); J. Muyldermans, *La domination Arabe en Arménie* (Louvain, 1927); *The History of the Caucasian Albanians by Movsēs Dasxuranci*, tr. C. J. F. Dowsett (London, 1961); Thomas Artsruni, *History of the House of Artsrunik'*, tr. and commentary R. W. Thomson (Detroit, Mica., 1985); Yovhannēs Drasxanakertc' i, *History of Armenia*, tr. and commentary K. H. Maksoudian (Atlanta, Ga, 1987); Étienne Açogh'ig de Daron, *Histoire universelle*, tr. E. Dulaurier (Paris, 1883); Étienne Asolik de Tarôn, *Histoire universelle*, tr. F. Macler (Paris, 1917).

Place names vary according to language and political context: the best guides are H. Hübschmann, *Die altarmenischen Ortsnamen* (Indogermanische Forschungen XVI, Strasbourg, 1904; repr. Amsterdam, 1969) – there is a useful map in the back – and the appendices of *The Epic Histories Attributed to P'awstos Buzand*, tr. and commentary N. Garsoïan (Cambridge, Mass., 1989), which form an important guide to people and places relevant for periods well beyond the scope of the *Epic histories*.

Important secondary literature includes J. Laurent, *L'Arménie entre Byzance et l'Islam depuis la conquête arabe jusqu'en 886*, revised M. Canard (Lisbon, 1980) – this has completely replaced Laurent's original work published in 1919; R. Grousset, *Histoire d'Arménie* (Paris, 1947); A. Ter-Ghewondyan, *The Arab Emirates in Bagratid Armenia*, tr. N. G. Garsoïan (Lisbon, 1976); N. Adontz, *Armenia in the Period of Justinian*, tr. N. G. Garsoïan (Lisbon, 1970); C. Toumanoff, *Manuel de généalogie et de chronologie pour l'histoire de la Caucasie chrétienne* (Rome, 1976).

On Armenians and Georgians in Byzantium see: P. Charanis, *The Armenians in the Byzantine Empire* (Lisbon, no date); B. Martin-Hisard, 'Du Taok'lardzheti à l'Athos: moines Géorgiens et réalités sociopolitiques (ixe–xie siècles)', *Bedi Kartlisa*, XLI (1983), 34–46.

Sites in eastern Turkey are covered in T. A. Sinclair's monumental *Eastern Turkey: An Architectural and Archaeological Survey*, 4 vols (London, 1987–90). The volumes of the *Documents of Armenian Architecture*, ed. A. Manoukian and A. Manoukian, I– (Milan, 1967–) are valuable especially for their photographs of landscape as well as buildings. The church at Mren is discussed in M. Thierry, N. Thierry, 'La cathédrale de Mrèn et sa décoration', *Cahiers archéologiques*, XXI (1971), 43–77. For the Georgian churches and their inscriptions see W. Djobadze, *Early Medieval Georgian Monasteries in Tao, Klarjet'i, and Savšet'i* (Forschungen zur Kunstgeschichte und christlichen Archäologie XVII, Stuttgart, 1992).

The Khazars

In general on the steppe world, see P. B. Golden, *An Introduction to the History of the Turkic Peoples* (Wiesbaden, 1992), and from a Byzantine perspective, Obolensky, *The Byzantine Commonwealth*. On the Khazars, Golden, *Khazar Studies*, 2 vols (Budapest, 1980) is essential, See also D. M. Dunlop, *The History of the Jewish Khazars* (Princeton, N.J., 1954); Golden, 'Khazaria and Judaism', *Archivum Eurasiae Medii Aevi*, III (1983), 127–56; Golden, 'Nomads and their Sedentary Neighbours in Pre-Činggisid Eurasia', *ibid.*, VII (1987–91), 41–81.

On the political ideology of the Turkic states and the role of the qaghan see Golden, 'Imperial Ideology and the Sources of Political Unity among the Pre-Činggisid Nomads of Western Eurasia', *Archivum Eurasiae Medii Aevi*, II (1982), 37–76.

For the steppe crisis of the ninth century, what happened and when, see Golden, 'The Migrations of the Oğuz', *Archivum Ottomanicum*, IV (1972), 45–84; G. Györffy, 'Sur la question de l'établissement des Petchénèques en Europe', *Acta Orientalia Academia Scientiarum Hungaricae*, XXV (1972), 283–92. On the tenth century, see F. E. Wozniak, 'Byzantium, the Pechenegs and the Rus': the Limitations of a Great Power's Influence on its Clients in the Tenth-century Eurasian Steppe', *Archivum Eurasiae Medii Aevi*, IV (1984), 299–316. *The Cambridge History of Early Inner Asia*, ed. D. Sinor (Cambridge, 1990) with some exceptions, that include the useful articles by Golden, is disappointing, and sometimes spectacularly misleading.

Most of the texts are translated and discussed in the secondary literature, but see also N. Golt and O. Pritsak, *Khazarian Hebrew Documents of the Tenth Century* (Ithaca, N.Y., 1982), as well as those listed under the Rus section below.

T. S. Noonan's articles on coinage and trade are essential: 'Why Dirhams First Reached Russia: The Role of Arab–Khazar Relations in the Development of the Earliest Islamic Trade with Eastern Europe', *Archivum Eurasiae Medii Aevi*, IV (1964), 151–282. Noonan, 'Byzantium and the Khazars: A Special Relationship?', in *Byzantine Diplomacy*, ed. Shepard and Franklin, pp. 109–32, argues that Byzantine–Khazar relations were of much less importance than I have suggested here.

The Rus

The Laurentian text of the *Povest' vremennych let* is translated as *The Russian Primary Chronicle*, tr. and commentary S. H. Cross and D. P. Sherbowitz-Wetzor (Cambridge, Mass., 1953). The Slavonic sources for early Rus' history are gradually being translated as part of the *Harvard Library of Early Ukrainian Literature. English Translations*, including so far, *Sermons and Rhetoric of Kievan Rus'* tr. S. Franklin (Cambridge, Mass., 1991), and *Hagiography of Kievan Rus'*, tr. P. Hollingsworth (Cambridge, Mass., 1992).

On the Kievo-centric view of these sources see S. Franklin, 'Borrowed Time: Perceptions of the Past in Twelfth-century Rus', in *The Perception of the Past in Twelfth-century Europe*, ed. P. Magdalino ((London, 1992), pp. 157–71.

Photios' sermons on the Rus attack of 860 are translated and discussed in *The Homilies of Photius, Patriarch of Constantinople*, tr. and commentary, C. Mango (Cambridge, Mass., 1958).

The Arabic and Persian geographers mention the Rus as part of their wider coverage of the northern world. Some texts are translated in the secondary literature, but one should also be aware of the following; Mas'ūdī, *Les prairies d'or*, tr. B. de Meynard and P. de Courteille, rev. C. Pellat, 4 vols (Paris, 1962–89); Ibn Fadlān's important account is available in French translation in M. Canard, 'La relation du voyage d'Ibn Fadlān chez les Bulgares de la Volga', *Annales de l'Institut d'Études Orientales de l'Université d'Alger*, XVI (1958), 41–146, and in English in J. E. McKeithen, 'The Risālah of Ibn Fadlān: An Annotated Translation with Introduction', (Indiana University Ph.D. thesis 1979); *Hudūd al-'Ālam*, 2nd edn, tr. V. Minorsky (Cambridge, 1970) – with valuable commentary; *Sharaf al-Zamān Tāhir Marwazī on China, the Turks and India*, tr. V. Minorsky (London, 1942).

There is a vast but not very helpful secondary literature on early Russian history. Exceptions include, Obolensky, *Byzantine Commonwealth*; P. Sawyer, *Kings and Vikings* (London, 1982), c. 8 – an excellent introduction which also helps to place the activities of the Vikings in Russia in a wider European context; J. Shepard, 'Some Problems of Russo-Byzantine Relations *c.* 860–*c.* 1050', *Slavonic and East European Review*, LII (1974), 10–33; L. Müller, *Die Taufe Russlands: Die Frühgeschichte des russischer Christentums bis zum Jahre 988* (Munich, 1988); the papers in *Varangian Problems*, ed. K. R. Schmidt (Scando-Slavica Supplementum I, Copenhagen, 1970); P. B. Golden, 'The Question of the Rus Qağanate', *Archivum Eurasiae Medii Aevi*, II (1982), 77–97; T. S. Noonan, 'When Did the Rūs/Rus' Merchants First Visit Khazaria and Baghdad?', *ibid.*, VII (1987–91), 213–17. The fur trade, one of the key factors in early Russian history, is explored in J. Martin, *Treasure of the Land of Darkness* (Cambridge, 1986). Also note the papers in the important Proceedings of the International Congress Commemorating the Millennium of Christianity in Rus'–Ukraine, published as *HUS*, XII/XIII (1988/9). Those by D. Obolensky, A. Carile, O. Pritsak and W. Treadgold are likely to be most useful. The latter two argue the case for a much earlier important Rus presence in the Black Sea region than I can detect.

The data and place of the baptism of Olga has given rise to an informative debate. See D. Obolensky, 'Russia and Byzantium in the Tenth Century', *Greek Orthodox Theological Review*, XXVIII (1983), 157–71; Obolensky, 'The Bapstims of Princess Olga of Kiev: The Problem of the Sources', in *Philadelphie et autres études* (Byzantina Sorbonensia IV, Paris, 1984); Obolensky, 'Ol'ga's Conversion: The Evidence Reconsidered', *HUS*, XII/XIII (1988/9), 145–58; J. Featherstone, 'Ol'ga's Visit to Constantinople', *HUS*, XIV (1990), 293–312.

J. Callmer, 'The Archaeology of Kiev to the End of the Earliest Urban Phase', *HUS*, XI (1987), 323–64, is an important reassessment of the evidence which clears away the fiction of Kiev as a major city in the mid-ninth century. Also useful is *The Archaeology of Novgorod, Russia*, ed. M. A. Brisbane, tr. K. Judelson (Society for Medieval Archaeology Monograph Series XIII, Lincoln, 1992).

The Balkans

For general surveys of Balkan history see Obolensky, *Byzantine Commonwealth*, and J. V. A. Fine, *The Early Medieval Balkans* (Michn, 1991).

For the seventh century the essential text is the Miracles of St Demetrios, which has been edited with French summaries and a full and authoritative commentary: P. Lemerle, *Les plus anciens recueils des miracles de saint Démétrius*, 2 vols (Paris, 1979–81). R. Cormack, *Writing in Gold*, c. 2, serves as an English introduction. The Chronicle of Monemvasia seems to me of very little importance; however, see P. Charanis, 'The Chronicle of Monemvasia', *DOP*, V (1950), 139–66.

The decline of Roman culture in the Balkans and the nature of Slav settlement are discussed in the important collection of papers published as *Villes et peuplement dans l'Illyricum protobyzantin* (Rome, 1984). Particularly interesting perhaps are those of G. Dagron on cities, and V. Popovič on sub-Roman culture in Albania, but as a whole this is a lively collection which includes several papers in English. Another important collection in *Ancient Bulgaria*, ed. A. Poulter, 2 vols (Nottingham, 1983). Especially the editor's paper on refuge sites in the Haimos range and that of J. D. Howard-Johnston on relations between the Roman and Slav population and the fate of cities during the sixth to eighth centuries are well worth finding. Both P. Lemerle, 'Invasions et migrations dans les Balkans depuis la fin de l'époque romaine jusqu'au viiie siècle', *Revue historique*, CCXI (1954), 265–308, and A. Bon, *Le Péloponnèse byzantin jusqu'en 1204* (Paris, 1951) remain useful.

For the Avars see W. Pohl, *Die Awaren. Ein Steppenvolk in Mitteleuropa, 567–822 n. Chr.* (Munich, 1988). The lack of an equivalent English-language work is a large gap in the literature.

Specifically on the Bulgar qaghanate the standard surveys are V. Beševliev, *Die protobulgarischen Periode der bulgarischen Geschichte* (Amsterdam, 1981); R. Browning, *Byzantium and Bulgaria* (London, 1975); and S. Runciman, *A History of the First Bulgarian Empire* (London, 1930). Given the importance of the Bulgar state in the early middle ages there is clearly room for a major new study.

Since most of the evidence comes from hostile Byzantine sources, the protobulgar inscriptions are of immense interest, and deserve to be much better known. The standard edition with commentary is V. Beševliev, *Die protobulgarischen Inschriften* (Berlin, 1963). The Bulgar–Byzantine treaty of possibly 816 is translated into English in J. B. Bury's still valuable discussion, 'The Bulgarian Treaty of A. D. 814, and the Great Fence of Thrace', *English Historical Review*, XXV (1910), 276–87. For the date see W. Treadgold, 'The Bulgars' Treaty with the Byzantines in 816', *Rivista di Studi Bizantini e Slavi*, IV/V (1985), 213–20.

Among the Byzantine sources, up to 813 Theophanes is the most important source, but see also the account of Nikephoros disastrous invasion of 811 in I. Dujčev, 'La Chronique byzantine de l'an 811', *TM*, I (1965), 205–54.

For the mission of Cyril and Methodios to Moravia, and their posthumous impact on Bulgaria, the Slavic lives are translated in *Medieval Slavic Lives of Saints and Saints and Princes*, tr. M. Kantor (Ann Arbor, Mich., 1983). There is also a useful collection of translated texts in *Kiril and Methodius: Founders of Slavonic Writing*, ed. I. Duichev, tr. S. Nikolov (East European Monographs CLXXII, Boulder, Col., 1985). This area of Balkan history has produced a large and fairly lively literature. See especially I Ševčenko, 'Three Paradoxes of the Cyrillo-Methodian Mission', *Slavic Review*, XXIII (1964), 220–36; F. Dvornik, *Byzantine Missions Among the Slavs* (New Brunswick, N.J., 1970); J.-M, Sansterre, 'Les missionaires latins, grecs et orientaux en Bulgarie dans la seconde moitié du ixe siècle', *Byz*, LII (1982), 375–88; and D. Obolensky, *Six Byzantine Portraits* (Oxford, 1988) which contains relevant studies of Clement of Ohrid and Theophylact of Ohrid.

For Symeon's reign Nicholas I's *Letters* are essential, as is the material in the *De Administrando Imperio*. The emperor Romanos I Lekapenos' letters are available in Théodore Daphnopatès, *Correspondance*, ed. J. Darrouzès and L. G. Westerink (Paris,, 1978). See also for its translated text R. J. H. Jenkins, 'The Peace with Bulgaria (927) Celebrated by Theodore Daphnopates', in *Polychronion. Festschrift F. Dölger* (Heidelberg, 1966), pp. 287–303; the commentary should be treated with caution. The secondary literature for tenth-century Bulgaria tends to be rather disappointing, but there are useful items, for example, I. Božilov, 'L'idéologie politique du tsar Symeon: Pax Symeonica', *Byzantino-Bulgarica*, VIII (1986), 73–88; and J. V. A. Fine, 'A Fresh Look at Bulgaria Under Tsar Peter I (927–69)', *Byzantine Studies/Études byzantines*, V (1978), 88–95 – the latter countering the widespread view of Bulgaria after 927 as a war-weary state wracked by social upheaval and Magyar raids. A. W. Epstein, 'Middle Byzantine Churches of Kastoria', *The Art Bulletin*, LVII (1980), 190–207, is also important for its picture of a thriving church-building community under Bulgar rule. Cosmas le prêtre, *Le traité contre les Bogomiles*, tr. H.-C. Puech and A. Vaillant (Paris, 1945), is a fundamental text for the history of Balkan dualism which also gives considerable incidental information on contemporary Bulgar culture. The translation includes a valuable introduction, but against Puech and Vaillant's widely accepted case for a late tenth-century date see M. Dando, 'Peut on avancer de 240 ans la date de composition du traité de Cosmas le Prêtre contre les Bogomiles?', *Cahiers d'études Cathares*, 2nd ser., C (1983), 3–25; *ibid.*, CI (1984), 3–21, who argues persuasively for the early thirteenth. D. Obolensky, *The Bogomils* (Cambridge, 1948) remains important.

The Western Provinces

For the gradual divorce of Italy and the papacy from Byzantium and the emperor the key text is the *Liber Pontificalis*, translated for the seventh and eighth centuries as *The Book of the Pontiffs (Liber Pontificalis)*, tr. R. Davis (Translated Texts for Historians V, Liverpool, 1989), and *The Lives of the Eighth Century Popes (Liber Pontificalis)*, tr. R. Davis (Translated Texts for Historians XIII, 1992). The best commentaries are Herrin, *The Formation of Christendom*; T. Brown, *Gentlemen and Officers*; T. F. X. Noble, *The Republic of St Peter: The Birth of the Papal State, 680–825* (Philadelphia, Pa., 1984); together with Davis' own to his translation of the eighth-century papal lives.

For the loss of Sicily see J. Johns, *Early Medieval Sicily: Continuity and Change from the Vandals to Frederick II, 450–1250* (forthcoming in this same series); and A. A. Vasiliev, *Byzance et les Arabes I. La dynastie d'Amorium (820–867)*, French edn, H. Grégoire and M. Canard (Brussels, 1985), which apart from a fully referenced narrative, also contains an important collection of Arabic texts in French translation. G. Musca, *L'emirato di Bari 847–871*, 2nd edn (Bari, 1967) is a valuable study of the Muslims in southern Italy, and of the Lombard, Frankish and Byzantine response.

The return of Byzantium to the south is best approached via B. Kreutz, *Before the Normans* (Philadelphia, Pa., 1991), an excellent survey focused on the Lombards which helps to put Byzantine actions in context. Chapter five in Epstein, *Art of Empire* can also serve as an introduction. For a detailed narrative and analysis see J. Gay, *L'Italie méridionale et l'empire byzantin* (Paris, 1904). Gay's monumental work is a classic of French historical scholarship which still retains its value. Since Gay southern Italy has continued to inspire some astute historical studies, including V. von Falkenhausen, *Untersuchungen über die byzantinische Herrschaft in Süditalien von 9. bis ins 11. Jahrhundert* (Wiesbaden, 1967) – also available in a partially revised Italian translation as *La dominazione bizantina nell'Italia meridionale dal IX all'XI secolo* (Bari, 1978): in either version the best guide to Byzantium in the south; *I Bizantini in Italia*, ed. G. Cavallo *et al.* (Milan, 1982); J.-M. Martin, *La Pouille du vi^e au xiie siècle* (Collection de l'École française de Rome clxxix, Rome, 1993) – a monumental but very readable study, among whose merits is that of placing Apulia in context as both a Byzantine province and a part of western Europe; von Falkenhausen, 'A Provincial Aristocracy: The Byzantine Provinces in Southern Italy (9th–11th Century)', in *Byzantine Aristocracy*, ed. Angold, pp. 211–35; J. Shepard, 'Aspects of Byzantine Attitudes and Policy towards the West in the Tenth and Eleventh Centuries', in *Byzantium and the West c. 850–c. 1200*, ed. J. D. Howard-Johnston (Proceedings of the 18th Spring Symposium of Byzantine Studies, Amsterdam, 1988), pp. 67–94 – an important paper, the first half of which emphasises the frailty of Byzantine administration in southern Italy and the generally marginal place of the West in tenth-century imperial thinking.

A. Guillou, 'Production and Profits in the Byzantine Province of Italy (Tenth to Eleventh Centuries)', *DOP*, xxviii (1974), 91–109, is interesting and well worth reading, but its conclusions of great wealth from silk are hard to accept. Of more importance as evidence with which to explore the world of the Byzantine south is the archaeological work, especially of J.-M. Martin and G. Noyé. See, for example, Martin and Noyé, 'Les villes de l'Italie byzantine (ixᵉ–xiᵉ siècle)', in *Hommes et richesses*, ii, pp. 27–62; Martin and Noyé, 'Guerre, fortification et habitats and Italie méridionale du vᵉ au xᵉ siècle', *Castrum* iii (1988), 225–36; Noyé, 'La Calabre et la frontière, viᵉ–xᵉ siècles', *Castrum*, iv (1992), 227–308 – each of these has a full bibliography. Also interesting is the section on Italy in A. J. Wharton, *Art of Empire: Painting and Architecture of the Byzantine Periphery* (University Park, Pa., 1988).

Specifically on the tensions between Byzantine and the West provoked by the growing power of the Ottonians in the tenth century Liudprand of Cremona is an important and readable source. An English translation, *The Works of Liudprand of Cremona*, tr. F. A. Wright (London, 1930), has been reissued as part of Everyman's Library (London, 1992). A better translation with text and commentary of the 'Embassy of Constantinople' is published as Liudprand of Cremona, *Relatio de legatione Constantinopolitana*, ed. B. Scott (Bristol, 1993). For discussion see K. Leyser 'The Tenth-century in Byzantine Western Relationships', in *The Relations between East and West in the Middle Ages*, ed. D. Baker (Edinburgh, 1973), pp. 29–63; Leyser 'Ends and Means in Liudprand of Cremona', in *Byzantium and the West c. 850–c. 1200*, ed. Howard-Johnston, pp. 119–43; C. M. F. Schummer, 'Liudprand of Cremona – a Diplomat?' in *Byzantine Diplomacy*, ed. Shepard and Franklin, pp. 197–201. Byzantine–Ottonian relations are also the subject of K. Leyser, 'Theophanu Divina Gratia Imperatrix Augusta: Western and Eastern Emperorship in the Later Tenth Century', in Leyser, *Communications and Power in Medieval Europe: the Carolingian and Ottonian Centuries*, ed. T. Reuter (London, 1994), pp. 143–64.

CHAPTER 9. THE AGE OF RECONQUEST, 863–976

The essential guide is A. A. Vasiliev, *Byzance et les Arabes ii. La dynastie Macédonienne (867–959)*. 1: *Les relations politiques de Byzance et des Arabes à l'époque de la dynastie Macédonienne (première période 867–959)*, French edn. M. Canard (Brussels, 1968); 2: *Extraits des sources Arabes*, French edn, H. Grégoire and M. Canard (Brussels, 1960). In some respects it is looking a little dated, but overall it is clear, well-documented, and the collection of translated Arabic source material is extremely useful. Comparatively few Arabic texts are available in English translation. *The History of al-Tabarī*, ed. Abbas *et al.* stops in 915, and Ibn Miskawayh, *Tadiārib al-umam*, ed. and tr. H. F. Amedroz and D. S. Margoliouth, *The Eclipse of the Abbasid Caliphate*, 7 vols (Oxford, 1920–1), vols 1–3 text, vols 4–6 translation, is rarely very interested in the Byzantines. With some important exceptions most of the relevant material in Ibn Miskawayh is shared with other sources, principally Ibn al-Athīr, who gives a fuller version.

On the Paulicians and the reign of Basil I the chronology and conclusions of *Byzance et les Arabes* have been overturned by P. Lemerle, 'L'histoire des Pauliciens d'Asie Mineure d'aprés les sources grecques', *TM*, v (1973), 1–144. See also the important collection of texts for the history of the Paulicians in Ch. Astruc *et al.*, 'Les sources grecques pour l'histoire des Pauliciens d'Asie Mineure', *TM*, iv (1970), 1–227. I find the argument of N. G. Garsoïan, *The Paulician Heresy* (The Hague, 1970), that the Paulicians were not dualists, unconvincing.

For the eastern frontier and Armenian borderlands after the Paulicians the *DAI*, cc. 43–6, 50, is fundamental evidence. For an examination of all the sources for Mleh's career, including the *DAI*, see G. Dédéyan, 'Mleh le grand, stratège de Lykandos', *REArm*, XV (1981), 73–102.

The 'Story of the Image of Edessa', attributed to Constantine Porphyrogenitos, is translated in I. Wilson, *The Turin Shroud* (Harmondsworth, 1978), pp. 313–31 – the conclusions of the book as a whole are wrong; see A. Cameron, 'The History of the Image of Edessa: The Telling of a Story', *HUS*, VII (1983), 80–94.

For Byzantine relations with the Hamdānids, and for guidance to events after 959 see M. Canard, *Histoire de la dynastie des H'amdanides de Jazīra et de Syrie* (Algiers, 1951)l; and R. J. Bikhazi, 'The Hamdanid Dynasty of Mesopotamia and North Syria 254–404/868–1014' (University of Michigan Ph.D. thesis, 1981) who revises Canard's conclusions in several important respects. E. Honigmann, *Die Ostgrenze des byzantinischen Reiches von 363–1071* (Brussels, 1935) also covers the period after 959.

One of the key sources for these years, particularly for Byzantine relations with Aleppo, is the Arabic history of Yaḥyā b. Saʿīd which as far as the year AD 1013 is edited with a French translation in *PO*, XVIII. 5 (1924), 705–833; and XXIII. 3 (1932), 349–520. J. Forsyth, 'The Byzantine–Arab Chronicle (938–1034) of Yaḥyā b. Saʿīd al-Antākī', 2 vols (University of Michigan Ph.D. thesis, 1977) is not only the essential discussion of the text but also an important analysis of tenth-century history.

The treaty which turned Aleppo into a Byzantine client is translated and discussed in W. Farag, *The Truce of Safar A. H. 359 December–January 969–70* (Birmingham, 1977).

On John Tzimiskes' eastern campaigns see M. Canard, 'La Date des expéditions Mésopotamiennes de Jean Tzimiscès', *Mélanges Henri Gregoire*, 4 vols (Brussels, 1949–53) [= *Annuaire de l'institut de philologie et d'histoire orientales et slaves* IX (1949)–XII (1952)] II, pp. 99–108; P. E. Walker, 'The "Crusade" of John Tzimiskes in the Light of New Arabic Evidence', *Byz*, XLVII (1977), 301–27. The letter to Ašot is translated in *The Chronicle of Matthew of Edessa*, tr. A. E. Dostourian (Rutgers University Ph.D. thesis, 1972) – now published as A. E. Dostourian, *Armenia and the Crusades, 10th to 12th Centuries: The Chronicle of Matthew of Edessa* (Lanham, Md. 1993).

The best introduction to developments in the Islamic world is Kennedy, *The Prophet and the Age of the Caliphate*. For the role of the Turks see C. Bosworth, 'Barbarian Incursions: The Coming of the Turks into the Islamic World', in *Islamic Civilisation 950–1150*, ed. D. S. Richards (Oxford, 1973), pp. 1–16; P. Crone, *Slaves on Horses* (Cambridge, 1980); and the article 'Ghulām' in *EI/2*. On the Hamdānids see Canard and Bikhazi above. On the Fātimid intervention in Syria see T. Bianquis, *Damas et la Syrie sous la domination Fatimide*, 2 vols (Paris, 1986–9).

On Byzantine relations with the Christian populations of the newly-conquered eastern territories, G. Dagron, 'Minorités ethniques et religieuses dans l'orient byzantin à la fin du Xᵉ et au XIᵉ siécle: l'immigration Syrienne', *TM*, VI (1976), 177–87, is particularly helpful.

For military and administrative reorganisation as essential text is the Escorial Taktikon edited by N. Oikonomidès, whose commentary in *Les listes de preséance* is of prime importance, and is also a good starting point. A fuller discussion is found in H. Ahrweiler, 'Recherches sur l'administration de l'empire byzantin aux ixᵉ–xi siècles', *Bulletin de correspondance hellénique*, LXXXIV (1960), 1–111, which still remains the standard work. Specially on the eastern frontier is Oikonomidès, 'L'organisation de la frontière orientale de Byzance aux xe–xi^esiècles et le taktikon de l'Escorial', *Actes du XIVe Congrès International des études byzantines* (Bucharest, 1974), pp. 285–302; the same paper is also found in Oikonomidés' collected papers: *Documents et études sur les institutions de Byzance (viie–xve)* (London, 1974), nr xxiv. On the tagmata there is a useful survey in H.-J. Kühn, *Die byzantinische Armee im 10. und 11. Jahrhundert: Studien zur Organisation der Tagmata* (Vienna, 1991).

For comparison with the tactics described in 'On Skirmishing Warfare' see E. McGeer, 'The *Syntaxis armatorum quadrata*: A Tenth-century Tactical Blueprint', *REB*, ι. (1992), 219–29; the 'De re militari', translated as 'Campaign Organisation and Tactics' in *Three Byzantine Military Treatises*, ed. and tr. G. T. Dennis, pp. 246–35; and J.-A. de Foucault, 'Douze chapitres inédits de la *tactique* de Nicéphore Ouranos', *TM* v (1973), 281–311. The important treatise attributed to Nikephoros II Phokas and commonly known by its Latin title as the *Praecepta militaria* is due to appear in the near future in a new edition by E. McGeer, McGeer is also the author of a useful analysis of one aspect of the tactical innovations of the tenth century: 'Infantry Versus Cavalry: The Byzantine Response', *REB*, xi.vi (1988), 135–45. Both the commentary in *Le traité sur la guérilla de l'empereur Nicéphore Phocas*, ed. Dagron, Mihǎescu, and Dagron, 'Byzance et le modèle islamique au xe à propos des *Constitutions Tactiques* de l'empereur Léon VI', *Academie des Inscriptions et Belles-Lettes. Comptes rendus* (1983), 219–43, are important and lively analyses of the changing Byzantine response to the Arabs.

Among the studies on Byzantine internal politics in this period the edition with English translation and commentary of the *Vita Euthymii Patriarchae CP.*, ed. and tr. P. Karlin-Hayter (Brussels, 1970); R. Morris, 'The Two Faces of Nikephoros Phokas', *BMGS*, xii (1988), 83–115; and Morris, 'Succession and Usurpation: Politics and Rhetoric in the Late Tenth Century', in *New Constantines: The Rhythm of Imperial Renewal in Byzantium, 4th–13th Centuries* (Society for the Promotion of Byzantine Studies, Publication ii, Aldershot, 1994), pp. 199–214, stand out.

The land legislation is covered in Lemerle, *Agrarian History of Byzantium*; Kaplan, *Les hommes et la terre à Byzance*; A. Harvey, *Economic Expansion in the Byzantine Empire, 900–1200* (Cambridge, 1989); and R. Morris, 'The Powerful and the Poor in Tenth-century Byzantium', *Past and Present*, ιxxiii (1976), 3–27 – the latter is especially clear and useful.

Although the military families and their new role in tenth-century politics is touched upon in almost every work on the period, only recently has a general analysis of the phenomenon appeared. J.-C. Cheynet, *Pouvoir et contestations à Byzance (963–1210)* (Paris, 1990) can be highly recommended, but as the title indicates it does not cover either the ninth or tenth century. *The Byzantine Aristocracy, IX–XIII Centuries*, ed. M. Angold (BAR, Int. Ser. ccxxi, Oxford, 1984) is an excellent collection of papers, among which E. Patlagean on names, P. Magdalino on the aristocratic 'house' in its various senses, and R. Morris on monasteries may be especially helpful.

Studies on specific families include: J.-C, Cheynet, 'Les Phocas', in *Le traité sur la guérilla de l'empereur Nicéphore Phocas*, ed. Dagron and Mihǎescu, pp. 289–315; D. I. Polemis, *The Doukai* (London, 1969); J.-F. Vannier, *Familles byzantines: Les Argyroi (ixe–xiie siècles)* (Paris, 1975); W. Seibt, *Die Skleroi* (Vienna, 1976); J.-C. Cheynet and J.-F, Vannier, *Études prosopographiques* (Paris, 1986) – on the Bourtzes, Brachamios and Dalassenos families.

Studies of specific regions are less common, with the exception of Cappadocia where the painted rock-cut churches have long attracted attention. The greater part of the huge bibliography is concerned with fairly narrow art-historical issues, but the paintings and churches have also been used to explore the Byzantine world in a more general sense. For example see Wharton, *Art of Empire* – the best starting point; A. W. Epstein, *Tokalı kilise: Tenth-century Metropolitan Art in Byzantine Cappadocia* (Washington, D.C., 1986); N. Thierry, 'Les enseignements historiques de l'Archéologie cappadocienne', *TM*, VIII (1981), 501–19; Thierry, *Haut Moyen Âge en Cappadoce*. *Les églises de le région de Çavuşin*, I (Paris, 1983); Thierry, 'Un portrait de Jean Tzimiskès en Cappadoce', *TM*, IX (1985), 477–84; L. Rodley, The Pigeon House Church, Çavuşin', *Jahrbuch der Österreichischen Byzantinistik*, XXXIII (1983), 301–39; and Rodley, *Cave Monasteries of Byzantine Cappadocia* (Cambridge, 1985). There is also a useful collection of papers which together amount to a regional study of Byzantine Cappadocia: *Le aree omogenee della Civiltà Rupestre nell'ambito dell'Impero Bizantino: la Cappadocia*, ed. C. D. Fonseca (Atti del Quinto Convegno Internazionale di Studio sulla Civiltà Rupestre Mediovale nel Mezzogiorno d'Italia, Galatina, 1981): particularly important are the papers by Dedeyan on Armenians in Cappadocia, and by Kaplan on great estates.

Note also the important discussion of tenth-century Hellas (central Greece) by C. L. Connor, who has linked the evidence of the wall-paintings in the crypt of Hosios Loukas to that provided by the saint's life: C. L. Connor, *Art and Miracles in Medieval Byzantium* (Princeton, N.J., 1991); *The Life and Miracles of St Luke*, ed. and tr. C. L. and W. R. Connor (Brookline, Mass., 1994).

The growing prosperity of tenth-century Byzantium is obvious enough, almost wherever you look, but the lack of archaeological research leaves its nature and causes obscure. Kaplan, *Les hommes et la terre à Byzance*, and Harvey, *Economic Expansion in the Byzantine Empire, 900–1200*, are both important, but largely limited to the written materials, and perhaps unduly gloomy about the strengths of the Byzantine rural economy. On cities see Foss' studies of Ephesos and Sardis listed under chapter four above, together with M. Angold, 'The Shaping of the Medieval Byzantine *City*', *Byzantinische Forschungen*, X (1985), 1–37. There is also a valuable collection of papers published as *Hommes et richesses dans l'empire byzantin II, viiie–xve siècle*, ed. V. Kravari, J. Lefort and C. Morrison (Paris, 1991). The papers by Lefort are particularly interesting. Combining the documentary material from Mount Athos with field work in south-eastern Macedonia, Lefort has been able to give a comparatively detailed picture of rural development through the middle ages. Another useful study by Lefort on the same theme is 'Radolibos: population et paysage', *TM*, IX (1985), 195–234; his current work in north-western Turkey (Bithynia) promises to be of similar interest. Nautical archaeology also holds out the prospect of important new evidence. See the preliminary reports on the Serçe Liman wreck: G. F. Bass and F. H. van Doorninck, Jr, 'An 11th century Shipwreck at Serçe Liman, Turkey', *International Journal of Nautical Archaeology and Underwater Exploration*, VII (1978), 119–32; Bass, 'Glass Treasure from the Aegean', *National Geographic*, CLIII/6 (June 1978), 768–93; Bass, 'A Medieval Islamic Merchant Venture', *Archaeological News*, VII/2–3 (1979), 84–94.

CHAPTER 10: THE REIGN OF BASIL II, 976–1025

There is still no general study of Byzantium under Basil II to replace G. Schlumberger, *L'épopée byzantine à la fin du xe siècle*, 3 vols (Paris, 1896–1905) – well worth examining not least as an example of the high quality of publishing a hundred years ago. Some of the issues such a study would need to examine are explored in Cheynet, *Pouvoirs et contestations* – now the best discussion of the revolts – and in the works on individual families listed under chapter nine above. A brief view of Basil's reign and its legacy forms the introduction to M. Angold, *The Byzantine Empire, 1025–1204* (London, 1984).

A crucial text for the light it sheds on court politics under Basil II is Ibn Shahrām's report, translated in H. M. Amedroz, 'An Embassy from Baghdad to the Emperor Basil II', *Journal of the Royal Asiatic Society* (1914), 915–42, and in H. F. Amedroz and D. S. Margoliouth, *The Eclipse of the Abbasid Caliphate*, VI, pp. 22–35. For a later eleventh-century perspective on Basil's reign see Michael Psellus, *Fourteen Byzantine Rulers*, tr. E. R. A. Sewter (Harmondsworth, 1966), or Michel Psellos, *Chronographie*, ed. and tr. E. Renauld, 2 vols (Paris, 1926–8).

For the Georgian intervention, B. Martin-Hisard, 'La *Vie de Jean et Euthyme* et le status du monastère des Ibères sur l'Athos', *REB*, XLIX (1991) – which includes a translation of one of the main Georgian sources – is essential, as is the introduction to *Actes d'Iviron* I.

For developments in the east much of the material for chapter nine is relevant here too. See Canard, *Historie de la dynastie des H'amdanides de Jazīra et de Syrie*; and Bikhazi, 'The Hamdanid Dynasty of Mesopotamia and North Syria 254–404/868–1014'. The Arabic history of Yahyā b. Sa'īd only grows in importance with Basil's reign, and Forsyth's discussion of the text, 'The Byzantine–Arab Chronicle (938–1034) of Yahyā b. Sa'īd al-Antākī', continues to be essential reading. Bianquis, *Damas et la Syrie sous la domination Fatimide* remains helpful, and can be supplemented after 1000 by W. Felix, *Byzanz und die islamische Welt im früheren 11. Jahrhundert* (Vienna, 1981) – a useful survey which ties together events in Syria and the Djazīra with those in Armenia and the Transcaucasus.

For Armenia a key issue is the attitude to Basil II shown by Armenian authors. As well as Stephen of Taron II and Thomas Artsruni (listed in the Transcaucasus section of chapter eight above), see Aristakès de Lastivert, *Récit des malheurs de la nation arménienne* Brussels, 1973); and J.-P. Mahé, 'Basile II et Byzance vus par Grigor Narekac'i', *TM*, XI (1991), 55–73. Beyond the general works on the Transcaucasus already listed, Forsyth, 'The Byzantine–Arab Chronicle' contains the most helpful discussion.

For the Rus intervention and Vladimir's conversion see W. Vodoff, *Naissance de la chrétiénité russe: La conversion du prince Vladimir de Kiev (988 et ses conséquences (xie–xiiie siècles)* (Paris, 1988); A. Poppe, 'The Political Background to the Baptisms of Rus'. Byzantine–Russian Relations Between 986–89', *DOP*, XXX (1976), 195–244– to be read with D. Obolensky, 'Cherson and the Conversion of Rus'; An Anti-revisionist View', *BMGS*, XIII (1989), 244–56; A. Poppe, 'How the Conversion of Rus' was Understood in the Eleventh Century', *HUS*, XI (1987), 287–302. The Proceedings of the International Congress Commemorating the Millennium of Christianity in Rus'–Ukraine, published as *HUS* XII/XIII (1988/89), are also interesting.

Beyond the general works listed in the Balkan section of chapter eight above, Bulgaria and the Balkans are poorly served, and the subject cries out for a new study. N. Adontz, 'Samuel l'Arménian, roi des Bulgares', in Adontz, *Études Arméno-byzantines* (Lisbon, 1965), pp. 347–407, makes some useful points.

For Italy see the works by Gay, Kreutz and von Falkenhausen listed in the section of the Western Provinces in chapter eight above. Felix, *Byzans und die islamische Welt im früheren 11. Jahrhundert* covers Byzantine–Arab relations in Sicily and southern Italy in the early eleventh century. An important source for Byzantine attitudes towards the papacy is *The Correspondence of Leo, Metro-*

politan of Synada and Syncellus, ed. and tr. M. P. Vinson (CFHB XXIII, Washington, D.C., 1985). D. M. Nicol, *Byzantium and Venice: A Study in Diplomatic and Cultural Relations* (Cambridge, 1988) gives a brief introduction to relations with Venice.

Index